MACMILLAN

100 YEARS OF AMERICAN FILM

MACMILLAN

100 YEARS OF AMERICAN FILM

Frank Beaver
Editor in Chief

MACMILLAN LIBRARY REFERENCE USA
New York

Cover Design by Judy Kahn

Macmillan Library Reference USA
1633 Broadway, 7th Floor
New York, NY 10019

Manufactured in the United States of America

Printing number
1 2 3 4 5 6 7 8 9 10

ISBN: 0-02-865380-7
LC #: 99-048482

Library of Congress Cataloging-in-Publication Data

100 years of American film : selections from the Twayne dictionary of film terms and History of American cinema and Twayne filmmakers series / Frank Beaver, editor in chief.
p. cm.
Includes bibliographical references and index.
ISBN 0-02-865380-7 (alk. paper)
1. Motion pictures—United States—Encyclopedias. I. Title: One hundred years of American film. II. Beaver, Frank Eugene.
PN1993.5.U6 A59 1999
791.43′0973′03—dc21 99-048482

This paper meets the requirements of ANSI/NISO Z39.48-1992 (Permanence of Paper).

Contents

D

E

J

K

L

M

N

O

P

R

S

Preface

100 Years of American Film is an engaging, easy-to-use and reliable reference source for film buffs, students researching American culture, and the library patron seeking information on a favorite film. While movie fans will certainly find basic information on big stars and blockbuster films in this volume, *100 Years of American Film* is also a serious reference for students and researchers. It provides historical context for movies, discusses films and their genres as they relate to American history and culture, and examines the business of filmmaking.

Grand in scope, *100 Years of American Film* is organized in an A-to-Z format. Fascinating articles explore America's greatest and most popular movies and film genres and present profiles of influential producers and directors as well as screen legends.

Features

To add visual appeal and encourage further research, the page format and appendices include the following helpful features.

- **Popular Quotations:** Great lines from favorite films.
- **"Notable & Quotable" Quotations:** Relevant, often provocative quotations about the movie business from industry insiders appear in the margin.
- **"Budgets and Box Office" Facts:** A margin feature offering fascinating facts about shoestring smashes and big-budget bombs.
- **Photographs:** Chosen to complement the text, two hundred eye-catching photographs include film stills and candid shots of stars and directors at work.
- **Film Facts:** An extensive collection of movie trivia, fascinating facts, and unknown details about the movie business.
- **Academy Award Nominees and Winners**: A list of every Academy Award nominee and winner for Best Picture, Best Director, Best Actor, and Best Actress.
- **Reference Aids**: A comprehensive index, extensive cross-references, and a glossary of film terms enhance the usefulness of the volume.

Acknowledgments

100 Years of American Film contains nearly two hundred illustrations, obtained with the patient assistance of Mary Corliss and her staff at the

Film Still Archives of the Museum of Modern Art. Editor Frank Beaver, Professor of the Program in Film and Video at the University of Michigan, also generously contributed stills from his extensive private collection.

The articles herein, selected by Frank Beaver, were commissioned for this volume and excerpted from *Scribner's History of American Cinema,* edited by Charles Harpole (vol. 3 by Richard Koszarski, and vol. 4 by Donald Crafton); Twayne's *Pump 'Em Full of Lead* by Marilyn Yaquinto; Twayne's *Dictionary of Film Terms* by Frank Beaver; and the Twayne Filmmakers Series. We would also like to acknowledge Gene Brown, *Movie Time: A Chronology of Hollywood and the Movie Industry from Its Beginnings to the Present* (Macmillan USA, 1995) and Patrick Robertson, *The Guinness Book of Movie Facts and Feats* (Guinness Publishing Ltd., 1988). Gerry Azzata, Kenneth Cassady, Constance Clyde, William Kaufman, Mark LaFlaur, Linda Leuzzi, Thomas McCarty, James Mercurio, Karen Meyers, Lisa Clyde Nielsen, Renee Skelton, and Tracey Topper also contributed material for this volume.

This book would not have been possible without the hard work and creativity of our staff. We offer our deepest thanks to all who helped create this marvelous work.

Introduction

Scholars and art historians have noted the significance of the motion picture as a major cultural phenomenon of the twentieth century. This scientifically realized form of artistic expression was still in its infancy in 1900; yet already, curious viewers were being captivated by the flickering films being shown in peep-show parlors and makeshift store theaters. Most were films less than a minute in length that depicted short action vignettes lifted from life or from the stage: boxers sparring, a cat fight, street scenes, a vaudeville performer in drag, an actor and actress kissing in medium close-up.

Throughout the century the motion picture medium would continue a progressive path that saw aesthetic refinement, ongoing technical innovation, commercial venture, and audience response interacting with powerful effect. Narrative storytelling on celluloid would discover and then continue to explore unique methods of shaping its larger-than-life tales—tales that would often be played out within a context of "movie star" mythology and within the confines of psychologically affective movie theaters. Motion pictures swelled the public imagination and even as they seemed to falter from time to time in the presence of competing entertainment industry and societal flux, somehow the medium bounced back and survived its challenges.

An overview of the motion picture in its twentieth-century time frame promises a rich compendium of material that necessarily embraces the popular culture parameters of the medium as well as the artistic genius to which it gave rise. Few would debate the ongoing mass appeal of movies. At the same time, numerous critics, historians, and film scholars have argued convincingly on behalf of cinema as representing, potentially and actually, great modern art. When asked what were the significant works of art of the twentieth century, the British art historian and former director of London's National Gallery Sir Kenneth Clark replied that many, in his estimation, would be films. Similarly, the Italian-cinema historian Peter Bondanella has argued that perhaps Italy's greatest contribution to twentieth-century art has been its motion pictures.

By tracing this happy symbiosis of entertainment (pleasure) and art (genius) in the cinema, one approaches the magnitude of the subject. By 1900 numerous film companies had been organized for the production and distribution of films in the United States: Edison, Biograph, Essanay, Vitagraph, the K.M.C.D. Syndicate, among others. In 1905 Harry Davis and John P. Harris opened the "Nickelodeon" in Pittsburgh, Pennsylvania—the first fully equipped, specially decorated motion picture theater that presented regularly scheduled film showings day and evening.

Artistically, the film narrative took a giant leap in 1903 with Edwin S. Porter's *The Great Train Robbery,* a one-reel film that set the tone for the screen western. A frontier setting, a robbery holdup, a posse chase, and a concluding shootout were all introduced in a brief ten minutes, and these elements would become standard conventions of western screen mythology. Equally significant was Porter's use of techniques that were uniquely cinematic, especially parallel development of plotting events and the pull of the story forward through *in media res* action. *The Great Train Robbery* showed that the motion picture story could move about freely through time and space, and that audiences would find this structural fragmentation exciting rather than disorienting. Porter's film was still the most popular motion picture in the United States six years after its release.

D. W. Griffith, to many the greatest American film director of the first two decades of the century, went to work for Edwin Porter at the Edison Studios in 1907. On becoming a director the next year at Biograph, Griffith would significantly improve on what he had learned in his apprenticeship with Porter. In hundreds of one-reel films made between 1908 and 1912 Griffith proved himself the master of parallel development, crosscutting, and the "last-minute rescue" technique. He explored dialectical social commentary in *A Corner in Wheat* (1909); he taught his actors to use naturalistic restraint in their pantomimed screen performances, thereby enhancing the emotional power and credibility of his films. With *Judith of Bethulia* in 1913 Griffith moved the American motion picture toward feature length. Two years later the epic Civil War/Reconstruction film *The Birth of a Nation* (1915) showed that D. W. Griffith was indeed a motion picture genius. Too, this controversial film with its heroic treatment of the Ku Klux Klan gave notice of the social and political potential within motion picture storytelling. President Woodrow Wilson on seeing *The Birth of a Nation* said Griffith's film was "like writing history with lightning." Other great epics followed: *Intolerance* (1916), *Hearts of the World* (1917), *Way Down East* (1920), and *Orphans of the Storm* (1921).

The films of D. W. Griffith introduced performers who would become American silent-screen movie stars (Lillian Gish, Mary Pickford, Mae Marsh, Constance Talmadge) who helped spur the "star system" as a sustaining element of film production during Hollywood's studio era. Lionel Barrymore's appearance in Griffith's *The New York Hat* (1912) indicated the willingness of "legitimate" actors to embrace the new medium of film. And the sensational popular success of Griffith's screen epics gave rise to more and bigger film theaters, and in large cities to the creation of ornate "movie palaces" where the moviegoing experience could match the grandeur of the films being shown.

Other important film artists emerged as contemporaries of Griffith. Producer Mack Sennett with his slapstick Keystone Kops became the "King of Comedy." Charlie Chaplin's "little tramp" character imbued screen comedy with an ingenious air of pathos, and the little tramp figure would in time become one of the world's most recognizable icons. In 1917 Buster Keaton made his first film, *The Butcher Boy,* with Fatty Arbuckle, thereafter perfecting a deadpan comic screen persona that led to the label "the great stone face." Working as a director for the Lasky Company, Cecil B. DeMille was responsible for some of the most trenchant and sophisticated domestic-drama films produced during the medium's silent years. DeMille's best films were those made with Gloria Swanson that explored, candidly, sex and marriage: *The Heart of Nora Flynn* (1916), *Old Wives for New* (1918), *Don't Change Your Husband* (1919), *Male and Female* (1919), *Why Change Your Wife?* (1920), and *The Affairs of Anatol* (1921). The adult, independent, sensuous nature of Swanson's screen characters brought to filmgoers a fresh image of the American woman. In 1923 DeMille produced and directed *The Ten Commandments,* and its huge box office success resulted in a stylistic turn to opulent screen spectacles and to DeMille's reputation as Hollywood's premier "showman" until his death in 1959.

By the early 1920s all the major Hollywood studios were in place; only RKO would develop later in 1928. These production companies (Paramount, Fox, Columbia, Warner Bros., Metro-Goldwyn-Mayer, Universal, United Artists) were efficient, compartmentalized organizations, run by front-office management and fueled by the stars they created: Mary Pickford, Douglas Fairbanks, Pola Negri, and Rudolph Valentino at Paramount; Theda Bara, Tom Mix, Janet Gaynor, and George O'Brien at Fox; Erich von Stroheim and Lon Chaney at Universal; and Mary Astor and Rin-Tin-Tin at Warner Bros. M-G-M developed such a fine collection of contract actors that its star-system logo became "More Stars Than There Are in Heaven."

When new sound technology was incorporated into *The Jazz Singer* at Warner Bros. in 1927, other studios acted quickly to adapt their shooting stages for the production of "talkies." Genre pictures sprang to new life. M-G-M turned out the first musical, *The Broadway Melody,* in 1929 and RKO followed that same year with the musical *Rio Rita.* Warner Bros. found success with hard-talking, underworld-populated gangster films—*The Lights of New York* (1928), *Little Caesar* (1930), *The Public Enemy* (1931)—and in the "backstage musicals" of Busby Berkeley. Fox found its musical singing and dancing talent in child star Shirley Temple, and initiated production of Fox Movietone News, which brought weekly news to motion picture theaters. As M-G-M moved into the sound era, the studio flourished with its glamorous stars, lavish "production values," and a prestige concept devoted to the making of films from classic literary works: *Anna Christie* (1930), *Strange Interlude* (1932), *Mutiny on the Bounty* (1935), *David Copperfield* (1935), and *The Good Earth* (1937). RKO used stop-action special effects to make *King Kong* in 1933, and the next year in *Flying Down to Rio* first displayed the extraordinary singing/dancing chemistry of Fred Astaire and Ginger Rogers. From these genre and studio films of the 1930s came the greatest of America's screen legends: James Cagney, Edward G. Robinson, Jeanette MacDonald, Nelson Eddy, Greta Garbo, Fred Astaire, Ginger Rogers, Katharine Hepburn, Spencer Tracy, Humphrey Bogart, Clark Gable, Boris Karloff, Jean Harlow, Joan Crawford, Clara Bow, Errol Flynn, Cary Grant, Gary Cooper, Bette Davis, Barbara Stanwyck, Judy Garland, Mickey Rooney, Shirley Temple, Tyrone Power, James Stewart, John Wayne, Marlene Dietrich, and Lucille Ball among them. Technicolor, introduced initially by RKO in the feature film *Becky Sharp* (1934), was yet another technological innovation that, along with sound, boosted audience attendance during the Depression-era 1930s. Color found full acceptance as an enhancing production value with the release of *Gone with the Wind* (1938) and *The Wizard of Oz* (1939).

At the height of the studio years, in its golden age of the 1930s and '40s, Hollywood displayed remarkable skill at creating motion pictures that satisfied mass audience tastes due to wise organizational management and to the success of the star system. At the same time, stylish, gifted directors of artistic integrity emerged within the studio system: John Ford, Howard Hawks, Frank Capra, Ernst Lubitsch, Charlie Chaplin, George Cukor, Billy Wilder, Orson Welles, and John Huston. These "auteur" directors, as they would eventually be labeled, made great contributions to cinematic art in films of enduring popularity—motion pictures as diverse as *Citizen Kane* (1941) and *It's a Wonderful Life* (1946); *It Happened One Night* (1935) and *Stagecoach* (1939); *Modern Times* (1936) and *The Grapes of Wrath* (1940). Industry and artistry, commerce and quality: together sustenance of Hollywood's studio-era success and of the motion picture's hold on an adoring public.

Genre film production was, and remains, another key factor in the resiliency of the American film industry. It has been observed that the appeal of genre films results from the pleasures that filmgoers derive from experiencing the repetition of familiar characters and well-understood narrative conventions and value systems. In the 1930s gangster films, musicals, westerns, screwball comedies, romance pictures, and disaster films were essential staples of genre output. The film noir psychological thrillers that emerged notably at the end of World War II represented yet another American genre that sustained itself to the end of the century. With its dark images, brooding characters, and big city locations the noir picture was as essentially American as the western and gangster film. *The Big Sleep* (1946) and *The Lady from Shanghai* (1948) were classic early examples. At century's end continuity and popularity of the noir genre could be seen in such films as *Basic Instinct* (1992), *Seven* (1995), *The Usual Suspects* (1995), and *L.A. Confidential* (1997).

It seems that the history of American cinema can be divided into two equal halves—that part that occurred up to 1950 and that which came after. When Joe Gillis (William Holden) says to onetime superstar Norma

Desmond (Gloria Swanson) in Billy Wilder's *Sunset Boulevard* (1950), "You were a big star," Desmond replies, "I *am* big; it's the pictures that got small." Her comment rang with pointed irony because motion pictures were indeed changing—moving toward greater realism, smaller budgets, a new breed of actor. Actors Studio-trained Marlon Brando starred in his first film in 1950, *The Men*, Fred Zinneman's psychological study of post–World War II paraplegics. James Dean and other popular method actors would soon follow.

Other events were affecting Hollywood in 1950: the full-fledged emergence of network television; the mass exodus of Americans away from the cities (and the neighborhood movie theater) to the suburbs; introduction of night baseball; increased travel. In the face of new lifestyles and new competition for the entertainment dollar, movie ticket sales began to plummet after 1947. To make economic matters worse, in 1948 the U.S. Supreme Court ruled that the film industry's huge studio-theater chain corporations violated antitrust laws, and it decreed that Hollywood's studios must divest themselves of their theaters by 1950. By the end of 1948 M-G-M had already reduced its payroll by nearly 50 percent; by 1950 Warner Bros. had cut its number of contract actors in half.

Within the American film industry it became clear that the studio system as it had once existed was a thing of the past. Crisis and change brought new credos: fewer, but bigger and better films, new technology to titillate (3-D, CinemaScope, stereophonic sound, more technicolor), freer use of candid dramatic material.

In the second half of the twentieth century motion picture production became a hit-or-miss proposition. The 1960s brought youth activism and a rash of counterculture films: *Easy Rider* (1969), *Alice's Restaurant* (1969), *Five Easy Pieces* (1970). These films were designed to appeal to the young and they contained large amounts of rock, folk, and country music. Thereafter more and more films would be produced for younger filmgoers. In the 1970s the reemergence of screen epics—*The Godfather* (1972) and disaster films (*The Poseidon Adventure*, 1972)—along with big-budget action films such as *Jaws* (1975), *Rocky* (1976), and *Star Wars* (1977) resulted in a blockbuster mentality that would prevail through century's end.

At the same time the "indie" film surfaced as an alternative to Hollywood's big-budget calculations. Indies were made on lower budgets, were personally tailored and character oriented. Their appeal came through their honesty, spontaneity, provocative characters, and ironic humor and insight. Early examples were *Sweet Sweetback's Baadasssss Song* (1971), *Girlfriends* (1978), and *The Return of the Secaucus Seven* (1980). The ongoing popularity of indies was evident in the 1990s in *The Brothers McMullen* (1995), *Chasing Amy* (1997), *Happiness* (1999), and *The Blair Witch Project* (1999).

As the American motion picture prepared to enter the twenty-first century, established directors were maintaining reputation with work that showed impressive versatility, moving from stylish entertainment films to works imbued with passionate social commentary. Steven Spielberg offered *Jurassic Park* (1993) along with *Schindler's List* (1993) and *Saving Private Ryan* (1998). Jonathan Demme followed his psychological thriller *The Silence of the Lambs* (1991) with *Philadelphia* (1993), a compassionate film about AIDS discrimination. Martin Scorsese returned to his familiar tough-character film interests in *GoodFellas* (1990) before making *The Age of Innocence* (1993), a screen adaptation of Edith Wharton's novel of 1870s social manners in New York City.

Also at century's end American college and university film schools were continuing to turn out eager would-be writers and directors who were anxious to "break into Hollywood" or produce the next successful indie. Interest in filmmaking careers was never higher.

Significantly, the appeal of the motion picture for audiences of all ages could still run high. The enormous successes of *The English Patient* (1996), *Titanic* (1997), and *Saving Private Ryan* (1998) offered proof that quality films could still generate broad audiences.

Indeed, at century's end the motion picture showed that it could still captivate with a visceral impact like that experienced at the very beginning of filmgoing. By 1999 digitally supplied images, combined with new electronic editing systems, moved screen fantasies such as *The Matrix* (1999) and *Star Wars, Episode 1: The Phantom Menace* (1999) toward a dynamic realism that belied their formative creation. Openly frank films such as Stanley Kubrick's *Eyes Wide Shut* (1999) and Spike Lee's *Summer of Sam* (1999) could still provoke audiences in the way that an undulating belly dancer or the fake stop-action execution of *Mary, Queen of Scots* titillated naïve viewers in the earliest years of filmmaking.

Altogether, one finds in 100 years of cinema a great record of achievement where stimulation and artistry merge in unforgettable ways. This reference compendium examines that record in all its diversity.

ACADEMY OF MOTION PICTURES

The Academy of Motion Picture Arts and Sciences was formed by Hollywood's silent-film community just as the silent film itself was about to pass from the scene. Among the announced goals of the Academy were to foster cooperation among creative leaders, cooperate on technical research, and provide a common forum for various branches and crafts. Today the Academy is best known for its annual awards ceremony, but in its initial months it was far more concerned with the threat to industrial "harmony" posed by incipient unionization.

In 1918, when the average budget for a (silent) feature film was about $60,000, top actress Mary Pickford was earning $250,000 per film.

On November 29, 1926, the major producers had finally signed the Studio Basic Agreement, which codified their relationship to organized stagehands, carpenters, electricians, painters, and musicians. Prior to this date jurisdictional quarrels among competing unions had weakened and divided the organized labor force, but when the International Alliance of Theatrical Stage Employees and Motion Picture Machine Operators was finally able to establish its jurisdiction over studio craft workers, industry leaders were forced to capitulate.

The "talent," however, was still unorganized. Honorary societies such as the Screen Writers' Guild of the Authors' League of America or the American Society of Cinematographers did not function as unions. But with the signing of the Studio Basic Agreement, unionization was in the air, and Actors' Equity, which had been trying without success to organize the studios since 1922, announced plans for a new campaign.

Enter the Academy. Within weeks of the signing of the Studio Basic Agreement, Louis B. Mayer had suggested a new industry organization to supplement the activities of the Hays Office, especially in regard to this new labor issue. By March the International Academy of Motion Picture Arts and Sciences had elected its first officers, with Douglas Fairbanks as its president.

The Academy consisted of five distinct branches: actors, directors, producers and production executives, technicians (including cinematographers), and writers. However, it soon became apparent that the producers' branch was controlling the agenda for its own benefit. It co-opted the other branches on such tricky issues as the 10 percent wage cut of 1927, a threatened blow to nonunion labor that the Academy claimed credit for rescinding.

While all this was moving forward, the Academy's committee on merit awards announced a dozen categories that would be the basis for an annual series of citations. Films released between August 1, 1927, and August 1, 1928, would be eligible—in effect, the last year of the silent cinema. Earlier awards had been given by trade papers, fan magazines, and "better films" committees, but what made the Academy's awards interesting were their final two categories. There was no citation for "Best Picture." Instead, Academy members were asked to vote on *two* production awards. The Merit Committee understood a distinction between art and commerce, and thus had established equal prizes for films that excelled in each area. The award for "outstanding motion picture production" was clearly intending to honor the craft of producing, one of the Academy's five component branches, while that for "artistic, worthy and original production" suggests aesthetic criteria.

Today, the top film nod has been consolidated into the award for Best Picture. Every March, the Academy Awards presentation is watched by millions around the world, with the awards for Best Actor, Best Actress, and Best Director, along with that for Best Picture, typically capturing most of the public's attention.

See Acting; Fairbanks, Douglas; Screen Actors Guild; Writer

ACTING

The film actor has been defined in many ways: as a nonactor, as a mannequin, as a "maker of faces." These descriptive labels result in part from the mosaic, edited nature of film construction. A film performance, like a film scene, is often "built" rather than shot. It has also been said that the screen actor is more dependent on physical characteristics than the stage actor and that physique and facial features often determine the kinds of roles a film actor plays throughout an entire career.

Because of the possibility for candid, natural acting and because the screen performance does not always demand refined theatrical skills, the film actor has often been described by theorists as an individual whose art is that of effective behaving. "Behaving" in motion-picture acting implies concessions to the piecemeal process of filmmaking. Unlike the stage actor, who enjoys the benefit of a continuous performance, the film actor must usually develop a character in bits and pieces and usually out of story-line sequence. The director guides the actors from scene to scene, often giving them on the spot the emotions and actions required in a given situation.

notable & quotable

"The most effective performances are those in which the audience identifies with the characters and the situations they face, then become the characters in their own minds."

Marlon Brando, actor, 1994

Rehearsal time is often kept to a minimum because of both the shooting process and the economics of filmmaking.

A popular theory is that the best film performance is behavioristic—one in which the actor is completely without the airs and self-sufficient qualities of the trained artist. The film actor, some critics argue, must not appear to be acting at all. This claim is based on the assumption that the motion picture is a medium committed to realism. Many directors have, in fact, favored untrained actors, as in the case of Italian neorealist films. Film actors of long standing, however, contend that the successful screen performer utilizes skills equal to those of the theatrical performer.

The degree to which an actor is allowed to reflect on characterization and to make the effort to reveal subtleties of character varies from director to director. Michelangelo Antonioni has said: "The film actor ought not to understand, he ought to be." Federico Fellini has told his film actors, "Be yourselves and don't worry. The result is always positive." Other directors (D. W. Griffith, George Cukor, Arthur Penn, Lawrence Kasdan, for example) have sought closer collaboration with the film actor in developing a character for the screen.

At least four facets of a screen actor's performance can be critically evaluated: (1) the physical dynamics of the character; (2) the inner spirit of the character; (3) the cinematic control of the character; and (4) the truth of the character. A screen performance is physically dynamic when the actor's movements, physique, facial features, and personality traits attract and hold the attention of the audience. The inner spirit of the character is the quality of the performance in revealing subtle emotions and character shadings. The truth of the character refers to the success of the actor in revealing a character who seems dramatically believable. Cinematic control of the character refers to a proper use of the medium, the ability of the actor to create a character without overplaying or underplaying. The screen performance in varying degrees demands vocal, facial, and physical restraint because of the more intimate and realistic nature of the film medium. The large size of the motion-picture screen itself creates a demand for actor restraint.

See Academy of Motion Pictures; Feature film; Screen Actors Guild; Star system; Writer

ACTUALITÉ

An *actualité* refers to a documentary-like film. Historically, *actualités* are associated with the early work of the Lumière brothers in France. Films of workers leaving a factory, a train arriving at a station, and a mother feeding her child present "actual" views of the world. Unlike the later work of Robert Flaherty (*Nanook of the North,* 1922), the Lumière films were often uninterrupted recordings of events in motion. Flaherty frequently staged or restaged scenes in creating his environmental studies. The motion-picture camera, placed at a single recording position, was the exclusive agent in the Lumière views of everyday life, omitting the expressive role of editing. These short *actualités* are viewed as the beginning of the documentary impulse in filmmaking and the recognition of the motion-picture camera's penchant for realism.

Contemporary independent filmmakers often return to the concept of the *actualité* in examining subject matter. Andy Warhol's *Sleep* (1963) and *Empire* (1964) can be described as extended *actualités.* In these films Warhol simply photographed a sleeping man in one case and the Empire State Building in another, allowing his camera to run for lengthy periods of time from a single, unvaried angle of view. These uninterrupted views of actuality in which the independent filmmaker's involvement is minimal have led to the label "minimal cinema" or "minimalist film."

See Cinema verité; Documentary; Independent filmmaker; Neorealism; Realist cinema

ADAPTATION

A screenplay that has been adapted from another source, such as a play, novel, short story, or biography, and rewritten for the screen is an adaptation. Best-selling novels are a major source for film adaptations, mainly because of the commercial appeal of an already popular book title.

Screen adaptations from novels and plays have generated a considerable amount of theoretical discussion about similarities and differences in the storytelling media. Many of the discussions of adaptations center on the differences between the visual nature of film and the novel's opportunities for expression through descriptive prose and the literary trope (metaphors and similes). To film theorists such as Siegfried Kracauer and George Bluestone, an adaptation of a book for the screen implies the need to translate literary images into visual images. The adaptation is, they say, necessarily different from the original if it is to be an effective screen story. Although film writers often include forceful dialogue in the script, many of the essential elements of characterization and plot in a film emerge through nonverbal communication: costumes, makeup, physique, and action.

The screenwriter is also usually committed to an economy of expression in adapting stories from another medium. The film story is bound by a time

constriction that traditionally has resulted in films of approximately two hours or fewer in length. What may be richness of detail in a novel can become distracting in a motion picture. The screenwriter usually aims for a swift, economical development of character and plot. Often secondary characters and subplots from a novel are used minimally in a film because they clutter and interrupt the steady development of dramatic crises that are essential to the success of a motion picture. For this same reason screenwriters in adapting a novel usually select the active parts of the plot and ignore elements that do not relate to it directly. A memorable minor character in a book may be only a background extra in a film, and an idea that an author develops poetically and metaphorically in a novel may be reduced to a passing line of dialogue or an image on the screen.

Theorists do not suggest that either the novel or the motion picture is a more desirable medium than the other. Outstanding screen adaptations can be significantly different from the parent novel and yet be equal to the novel in quality. What the film *The African Queen* (1951), based on a popular descriptive novel, lost in adaptation it gained in the unforgettable performances of Humphrey Bogart and Katharine Hepburn. In adapting *The Godfather* (1972), screenwriters Mario Puzo and Francis Ford Coppola were able to present a romantic pageant that rivaled the best that the epic screen had ever achieved despite deletions and concessions to action rather than character. Ideas taken from the novel and brought to imagistic life on the screen revealed the heart of Puzo's book, if not its full substance.

Particularly successful in adapting literary works to the screen, Ruth Prawer Jhabvala demonstrates in *The Europeans* (1979), *A Room with a View* (1985), *Howards End* (1992), and *The Remains of the Day* (1993) the degree to which an adaptation can retain richly nuanced character details and subtleties of human interaction. These films, directed by James Ivory, are stylish period pieces that focus on the manners and mores of characters defined originally in novels by Henry James (*The Europeans*), E. M. Forster (*A Room with a View, Howards End*), and Kazuo Ishiguro (*The Remains of the Day*).

See Remake; Writer

AFRICAN QUEEN, THE

The African Queen (1951) was a landmark in several illustrious movie careers: for the director, John Huston, who was nominated for Oscars in the Best Director and Best Screenplay categories (he collaborated with James Agee on the script), and for the legendary costars, Katharine Hepburn (her

"Lady, you got ten absurd ideas to my one."

Humphrey Bogart as Charlie Allnut in *The African Queen* (1951)

A

AFRICAN QUEEN, THE

remarkable performance was Oscar-nominated) and Humphrey Bogart, whose dead-on portrayal of a gritty, earthy riverboat skipper won him his sole Academy Award.

The film is set in east Africa at the beginning of World War I. Charlie Allnut (played memorably by Humphrey Bogart) is the coarse captain of a small steamer who runs supplies to villages along the river. One stopover takes him to a small village presided over by a daft missionary, the Rev. Samuel Sayer (Robert Morley), and his repressed, priggish, unmarried sister, Rose (Katharine Hepburn), both serenely devoted to their calling and oblivious to the anomaly of their stiff Edwardian bearing amid the steamy wilds of Africa, an irony that affords the earthy Allnut no little amusement and discomfort. This cultural gulf between American urban gruffness and

The repressed Rose (Katharine Hepburn) convinces the boorish Charlie Allnut (Humphrey Bogart) to use his boat to sabotage a German warship in The African Queen. *Some of the film's scenes were actually shot in Turkey.* ▶

British upper-crust fastidiousness is played up throughout the film. In an early scene, for example, the natives that Rev. Sayer has been trying to Christianize show more interest in Bogart's discarded cigar butt than in their pastor's church service.

Upon his later return to the small village, Allnut finds that the village has been overrun by the Germans and that the Rev. Sayers has died. Allnut agrees to guide Rose back to safety on his boat. On the trip downriver, tensions mount rapidly between the roustabout and the spinster, who is appalled by Allnut's lack of manners and chronic drunkenness. Huston took full advantage of the peculiar chemistry that developed between Bogart and Hepburn and played up the budding romance between their characters. One of the finest moments of the film comes when Rose and Charlie confront their gigantic differences. When she speaks of her nostalgia for the peaceful Sunday afternoon back in her beloved England, he responds bluntly that "on Sunday afternoons I was always sleeping one off." When he collapses in relief that they have not drowned or been dashed against the rocks after a particularly treacherous stretch of rapids, she observes blithely, "I never dreamed any mere physical sensation could be so stimulating." Later, when Charlie seeks his own stimulation in the form of "a drop too much" of gin, excusing himself by pointing out that "it's only human nature," Rose archly explains that "nature, Mr. Allnut, is what we are put into this world to rise above." After a hundred minutes of such repartee, interspersed with preposterously adventurous feats, director John Huston was then faced with either remaining consistent with the original book, or inventing an ending worthy of the silliness that preceded it. He opted for silliness.

Ever driven by the missionary's self-sacrificing sense of duty, Rose devises a daring plan to thwart the Germans: she urges Allnut to set out for a lake in central Africa, where they will sabotage and sink the great German ship the *Louisa*. His resistance quickly crushed by her iron determination, Allnut sets off on the journey, and the two, evolving from sworn enemies to lovers, surmount a series of adversities before losing their way and nearly succumbing to despair before their ship is providentially tossed by stormy water toward the lake where the *Louisa* sits.

Charlie improvises some homemade torpedoes, and the two doughty commandos proceed with a nighttime assault on their target, only to run afoul of a fierce storm that sinks the steamer and sends them right into the arms of their intended victims. The Germans subject Charlie and Rose to a summary trial in which they are convicted as spies and saboteurs and sentenced to death by hanging. Granted one last request, they ask to be married before the execution, and their wish is indulged in a poignant ceremony.

The high melodrama that follows is reminiscent of the Saturday afternoon serials of the 1930s. As the ropes tighten around their necks, Charlie's

"By the power vested in my by Kaiser Wilhelm II, I pronounce you man and wife. Proceed with the execution."

Peter Bull as the German captain in *The African Queen* (1951)

boat miraculously surfaces and smashes into the *Louisa*, wreaking havoc. As the Germans flee the sinking warship, Charlie and Rose swim ashore to begin their life together. Although the film's too-pat ending rankled critics, *The African Queen* remains a favorite with audiences even today.

See Bogart, Humphrey; Hepburn, Katharine; Huston, John

ALL ABOUT EVE

"Bill's 32. He looks 32. He looked it five years ago. He'll look it 20 years from now. I hate men."

Bette Davis as Margot Channing in *All About Eve* (1950)

All About Eve (1950), directed and written by Joseph L. Mankiewicz, rose above the common run of backstage melodramas to emerge as a benchmark of taste and sophistication among major Hollywood studio releases. Seldom had the treacheries and glories of show business ambition been portrayed with greater wit and pathos than in this tour de force about a young actress's predatory relationship with an aging, fading star. The film won six Oscars, including Best Picture, Supporting Actor, Director, Screenplay, Sound Recording, and Costume Design.

The film opens at the ceremony at which the Sarah Siddons Award for Distinguished Achievement will be presented. The eminent New York theater critic Addison De Witt (George Sanders) introduces himself and others attending, including Karen Richards (Celeste Holm), her husband, the playwright Lloyd Richards (Hugh Marlowe), and the Broadway actress Margo Channing (Bette Davis). Eve Harrington (Anne Baxter) is being honored as the youngest recipient ever to win the award as best actress. As she reaches out to accept the award, the shot freezes. For the remainder of the film, the events leading to the ceremony unfold in a flashback.

Eve, an adoring fan who has followed Margo Channing to Broadway to pursue her ardent theatrical ambitions, is granted the opportunity to meet Margo, her idol. Feigning tears, Eve uses her best acting abilities to elicit Margo's sympathy and concern with her hard-luck tale. The act works. Margo invites Eve into her home and gives her a job as her confidential assistant/secretary. Eve is perfectly positioned to begin scratching her way to the top.

As Eve methodically ingratiates herself with Margo's friends and associates, Margo's initial sympathy for Eve begins to cool. Margo even questions her boyfriend Bill's (Gary Merrill) attentions to Eve. Both Eve and Margo attend a glamorous party at which the young schemer, donning a mask of innocent veneration, plies various theater luminaries—Addison De Witt, his young lady friend, the breathless blonde bombshell Miss Casswell (Marilyn Monroe), a producer, Max Fabian (Gregory Ratoff), Bill Simp-

son, Margo's fiancé, a famous playwright, Lloyd Richards, and his wife, Karen—for a break as an actress. Increasingly aware of Eve's machinations, Margo administers a memorably sardonic, drunken tongue-lashing to her assembled friends. Margo's suspicions are borne out when Eve, enlisting Karen's aid, talks her way into a job as Margo's understudy.

Margo's insights into Eve's treachery are shared only by her loyal maid, Birdie (Thelma Ritter); Margo's bitter fits of temperament strike everyone else as the indulgences of megalomania. Karen, in fact, is so appalled at what she perceives as Margo's mistreatment of Eve that she arranges to get Margo to the country for a weekend and contrives to delay her return long enough to allow Eve, as Margo's understudy, to go onstage in Margo's place. Eve, meanwhile, has made sure that the town's leading critics will be in attendance, and her powerful performance launches her as a star.

Claudette Colbert was originally slated to play Margo Channing in All About Eve. *But Bette Davis won the role, and an Oscar nomination for her efforts. She is shown here (left) with Anne Baxter (center) as the scheming Eve Harrington.*
▼

After her superb performance, Eve flirts with Bill, but he rebuffs her, saying, "I'm in love with Margo. Hadn't you heard?" Eve instead turns her attentions to the critic, De Witt, who accommodatingly writes a poison pen review about Margo. Eve next goes after Karen's husband, Lloyd, convincing him that she would be perfect for the starring role in his new play, a role that Margo was originally to play.

Later, Bill proposes to Margo, who, wearied by the intrigues of the stage, accepts and retires from the theater. With Margo out of the way, the path is clear for Eve, who steals Lloyd away from Karen. But De Witt objects to her alliance with Lloyd, wanting her for himself. He threatens to expose her real, sordid background. Devastated, Eve agrees that she belongs to him. Suddenly she is the victim of her own trap, unable to escape. Still, success is hers, no matter what the cost.

The film dissolves to the present at the awards ceremony, where Eve has just received the award trophy. Eschewing the party afterward, she returns to her apartment, where she is startled by Phoebe, a starstruck fan. In an ironic ending, the film audience realizes that it won't be long before Phoebe, like Eve, will be climbing the ladder of success at any cost.

See Davis, Bette; Mankiewicz, Joseph

ALL QUIET ON THE WESTERN FRONT

All Quiet on the Western Front (1930), the antiwar epic based on Erich Maria Remarque's widely admired novelistic indictment of modern warfare, is generally regarded as Lewis Milestone's masterpiece, his most important work in terms of both subject and style. Most of the contemporary reviews were ecstatic, and the Motion Picture Academy recognized his achievement with Oscars for Best Picture and Best Direction.

The film opens on the home front at the beginning of World War I. In Dolbenberg, the hometown of Paul Baumer (Lew Ayres), the protagonist, the townsfolk prattle on about the glory of war as a local regiment parades through the streets. The scene then shifts to Paul Baumer's classroom, where the professor is ranting patriotically about the "Fatherland" and urging immediate enlistment, to the enthusiastic cheers of the students.

The scene shifts, and a heavy gate opens to reveal a huge parade ground at a military camp where Paul is undergoing basic training. Himmelstoss (John Wray), the chief trainer, enjoys himself immensely as he forces the recruits to crawl through acres of mud, screaming at them to keep their faces in it. The recruits are beginning to sense some of the ugliness of war.

At length, two officers announce from their lofty perch on horseback that this group of "Iron Youth" is ready for the front.

Through a train window the recruits receive their first view of the results of war, ruined buildings and Red Cross cars full of wounded, as shells begin to fall. Here Paul and his comrades meet the other soldiers in the company: Westhus (Richard Alexander), Detering (Harold Goodwin), and Tjaden (Slim Summerville). "Kat" Katcinsky (Louis Wollheim) is the "Papa" of the group. When the men move up to their first assignment, stringing barbed wire across a section of the front lines, Papa Kat leads his "children" in this frightening initiation to war. Kat tries to prepare them for

Lewis Milestone's adaptation of Erich Maria Remarqué's novel All Quiet on the Western Front *is considered one of the greatest war (or, more accurately, anti-war) films ever made.*

◀

the shock of shellfire, warning them to bury themselves in the lap of Mother Earth. Behm (Walter Rodgers) and several others foul their pants in a paroxysm of fear. Behm's fear proves prophetic: the most hesitant to enlist, and the last to be signed up, he is the first to die. Blinded by a shell splinter, he staggers, screaming, out of the trench and is cut down by an enemy machine gun.

This scene proves only a prelude to the first major battle, which follows before the "Iron Youth" can recover from the shock of Behm's death. First, they are quartered in a frontline dugout under heavy shellfire for three days, with only the trench rats for company. As the shelling intensifies, the camera begins to pick out individuals who are starting to crack. Franz Kemmerich (Ben Alexander) becomes the most notable example, screaming in horror in a tight close-up. When part of the ceiling collapses under a direct hit, Kemmerich runs wailing into the trenches, where he is badly wounded by shell fragments. As soon as the others have returned to the dugout after helping Kemmerich, a whistle shrills the warning of an enemy charge. The Second Company pours out of the dugout entry along the trench, taking their positions on the firing lines. The audience follows the ebb and flow of the action, charge and retreat and countercharge; great masses of men move in large groupings intercut with telling individual details.

The next scene is one of rest and relaxation and hearty eating after the action and noise of the battle. In a dressing station in a bombed-out church, Kemmerich, who has lost his leg, lies suffering, near death. As Kemmerich dies, Paul prays over him with great emotion.

After Paul tells the story of Kemmerich's death to his comrades, he gives the fallen soldier's boots to Muller (Russell Gleason). The camera then follows the soldiers in the march back to the front. There they are the focus of a charge across "no-man's-land," until a sudden explosion drops Muller's body into the frame. Next, Peter inherits the boots, and as they mount the parapet of a frontline trench, Peter slides to the bottom, a bullet hole in his temple. Paul then gets the boots.

In the following scene a heavy bombardment catches the company passing by the graveyard of the church, earlier used as a dressing station. As the troops scramble for cover, Paul is wounded for the first time, nicked in the wrist by a shrapnel splinter. He dives into a shell hole only to discover that it is an open grave. Recoiling in horror from the symbolism of death inherent in his shelter, Paul races from the graveyard, only to encounter an attack by enemy infantry. Once more he takes cover in a shell crater, as the enemy troops leap over him in their advance and retreat. He draws his knife in preparation for hand-to-hand combat, and when one French soldier lands near him while dodging German fire, Paul stabs him several times.

As night turns the scene into a near Gothic horror, Paul is trapped in another grave, this time next to a man enduring a torturous death. His groans and sobs at last force Paul to approach him, trying to ease his death as much as he can. The dead man's wide-open, death-shocked eyes are one of the film's most powerful images.

Having killed for the first time, Paul badly needs to escape the horrors of the war. Luckily, the company is given a short rest in a rear area where Paul can forget his new knowledge by drinking beer in the easy camaraderie of the canteen. Inflamed by the beer, Paul and his comrades find three young women hungry enough to trade their bodies for bread and sausage. The young German men and young French women develop feelings for one another that transcend the blind national antipathies of war.

Back at the front, Paul suffers a serious wound that sends him first to the hospital, and then back to his hometown, where, returning to the classroom, he finds the professor lecturing another group of potential Iron Men. Paul rises to tell the boys, "It is not beautiful and sweet to die for country . . . it is better not to die." The students jump up to jeer at the "coward" and drive him from the classroom. Paul soon leaves to return to the front, unable to stand the hypocrisy of the home front. He discovers the Second Company now manned by boys of only sixteen and seventeen years old. Kat tells him the sad stories of Westhus and Detering and the others, now dead or seriously wounded, but word of the Armistice is in the air. The sky is full of enemy aircraft, however, and one of the bombs kills Kat.

Despite the impending Armistice, the despondent Paul feels as if he has no future in war or in peace. On a quiet afternoon in October of 1918, Paul sits lost in his thoughts, as a soldier's harmonica plays softly in the background. Slowly he rises above the sandbags to reach for a fluttering butterfly. As Paul extends his arm, he is cut down by a bullet from a French sniper. Paul's hand, shown in close-up, relaxes in the peace of death as a superimposed image shows young recruits marching to their first action over a huge forest of grave markers.

See Milestone, Lewis; War film

ALLEN, WOODY

Woody Allen was born Allen Stewart Konigsberg in the Flatbush section of Brooklyn, New York, on December 1, 1935. Allen is best known as an award-winning filmmaker whose neurotic "little man" character constantly struggles with anxieties about the absurdities of modern life.

As a youngster, Allen was an unexceptional student who compensated by acting the class clown. At age sixteen he began sending jokes to columnists such as Walter Winchell and Ed Sullivan. At the same time he also

took the name Woody Allen because he felt it was more glamorous than his given name. The frequent one-liners he sent to columnists eventually caught the attention of press agent David O. Alber, who gave Allen his first foray into show business: ghostwriting jokes for stars like Guy Lombardo, Sammy Kaye, and Arthur Murray. While still in high school, Allen was signed by the William Morris Agency. Allen later attended college, but with little interest. In fact, the now-famous filmmaker failed a course in movie production at New York University and dropped out of film courses at City College of New York after only a week.

In 1954, at nineteen, Allen went to Hollywood as part of the NBC Writer's Development Program and worked on the *Colgate Comedy Hour*. That same year Allen wed his first wife, sixteen-year-old Harlene Rosen; the marriage lasted five years. Four years later, Allen's managers, Jack Rollins and Charles Joffe, convinced Allen to tell his own jokes. He made his debut at the Duplex in Greenwich Village in 1961.

Director Woody Allen, right, has shot most of his films on location in his hometown of New York City. ▼

The years between his first nightclub appearance and his first major film in 1969 were busy ones. He met actress-comedienne Louise Lasser in 1962 and married her in 1965. They were divorced in 1968, but Lasser and Allen remained friends, and she has appeared in several of his films.

Always a prolific writer, Allen continued to produce essays and short stories, several of which were published in the *New Yorker*. In 1966 Allen wrote his first play, *Don't Drink the Water*, which opened on Broadway and in 1969 was made into a film starring Jackie Gleason. His next play, *Play It Again, Sam*, opened in 1968 to good reviews, and began the friendship between Allen and his costar Diane Keaton, with whom he later had a long-term relationship.

Also during this time, Allen continued to appear at the Blue Angel nightclub, honing his act. Impressed with Allen, Charles Feldman asked him to rewrite the script for *What's New, Pussycat?* for $60,000. *What's New, Pussycat?* paved the way for Allen to become the relatively independent filmmaker he is today, and by 1969 he'd made his first major film—*Take the Money and Run*—which he wrote, directed, and starred in. By the early 1970s Allen was on his way to stardom with a string of films such as *Everything You Always Wanted to Know About Sex* (*but were afraid to ask)* (1972), *Sleeper* (1973), *Love and Death* (1975), and his best-loved film, *Annie Hall*, which took home four Academy Awards. Starring Allen and Diane Keaton, *Annie Hall* follows the on-again, off-again romance of the nebbish comedy writer Alvy Singer and his flaky lover, Annie. The film also ignited a fashion craze among women who imitated the baggy, masculine clothing favored by the film's female lead.

Allen's first noncomic film, *Interiors*, opened in 1978, followed by *Manhattan* in 1979. *A Midsummer Night's Sex Comedy* was released 1982, followed by *Zelig* in 1983 and *Broadway Danny Rose* in 1984. In 1985, the same year he released *The Purple Rose of Cairo*, Allen was nominated for an Academy Award for Best Director for *Broadway Danny Rose*. A prolific filmmaker, a few of Allen's many recent films include *Hannah and Her Sisters* (1986), *Husbands and Wives* (1992), *Manhattan Murder Mystery* (1993), *Bullets Over Broadway* (1994), *Mighty Aphrodite* (1995), *Everybody Says I Love You* (1996), and *Deconstructing Harry* (1997). In 1997 Allen also set off a controversy when he married Soon-Yi Previn, the adopted daughter of actress Mia Farrow (with whom Allen had a twelve-year relationship that included the adoption of two children and the birth of a natural son) and composer Andre Previn. Allen's most recent film is *Celebrity* (1998). In each of his films, Allen reprises his "little man" persona: a neurotic, self-effacing character who is bedeviled by women, frustrated by sex, and distrustful of optimism.

See Annie Hall; *Keaton, Diane; Streep, Meryl*

notable & quotable

"If my film makes one more person miserable, I feel I've done my job."

Woody Allen, writer/director

ALTMAN, ROBERT

Robert Altman was born on February 20, 1925, in Kansas City, Missouri. Altman's adolescence was strongly influenced by gambling, and Altman recalls learning a lot about losing from his father, an oft-unsuccessful gambler.

Altman attended Wentworth Military Academy in Lexington, Missouri, through junior college. In 1943, at age eighteen, he entered the army and flew fifty missions as a bombardier over the Dutch East Indies. Upon his release in 1948 he took several odd jobs.

Later Altman became fascinated with film and began writing scripts and studying international cinema. He wrote *The Bodyguard* (1948), and sold the screenplay in Hollywood. Following this success, Altman spent a year in New York City writing plays and novels. But as these endeavors did not produce any offers, Altman returned to Kansas City and began learning many aspects of documentary film. It was in Kansas City that Altman designed sets, operated cameras, began directing industrial films, and eventually produced a series of short technical films for the farm equipment company International Harvester.

notable & quotable

"Altman has to introduce an element of risk on top of the risks that all directors take."

Pauline Kael, critic, 1981

Venturing into commercial filmmaking, Altman began work on *The Delinquents* in 1955. Then, after the death of James Dean that same year, he and collaborator George W. George quickly assembled and codirected *The James Dean Story*. However, the film was not released until 1957, and the box office returns were dismal.

Altman moved to Hollywood in 1957, where he directed episodes for various television shows, including *Combat*, *The Millionaire*, *The Whirlybirds*, and others. His experience in television refined his technical abilities, and he learned to work quickly and efficiently. He also developed valuable alliances within the industry. Although his nonconformist attitude sometimes caused problems, Altman was able to take advantage of the expanding industry—there was usually a production team looking for an experienced director—and he worked steadily from 1957 to 1963.

But by 1964 Altman had had enough of all the restrictions and pressures of the television industry. He formed Lion's Gate Films, but soon dropped the venture, and thus began a long period of unemployment.

In 1966 Altman accepted an offer from Warner Brothers to direct *Countdown*, a low-budget science-fiction film about Lee Stegler's trip to the moon. Although *Countdown* endured artistic and commercial difficulties, it led to *That Cold Day in the Park* (1968). Memorable only for its emergent directorial trademarks and style, *Cold Day in the Park* did garner some recognition for Altman for his casual treatment of frigidity, incest, and prostitution, leading directly to his involvement in *M*A*S*H* (1970).

With at least seventeen directors either uninterested or unavailable, Altman accepted the opportunity to direct the war farce. He also needed to make a major film very badly after the poor performance of *Cold Day in the Park*. A rather disjointed story about a pair of renegade doctors serving in a MASH unit during the Korean conflict, *M*A*S*H* is probably Altman's funniest film. Although it initially received an "X" rating, the studio protested and was able to get the rating changed to "R." Despite its racy content, *M*A*S*H* played well to both the young and hip and more traditional audiences.

After the success of *M*A*S*H*, Altman was recognized as a major talent, and he was able to abandon the studios and set out on his own. He solidified Lion's Gate Films, Ltd., and his first production was *Brewster McCloud* (1970), his own personal favorite. The story relates the activities of young Brewster, who lives in a fallout shelter in the Houston Astrodome. Altman's next film, *McCabe and Mrs. Miller* (1971), starred Warren Beatty. In it, Altman adapted a series of traditional western events, motifs, and ideals to capture this atypical vision of Manifest Destiny. *Images* (1972), an unusual Altman project in its restraint, was a study of a character in a vacuum.

Director Robert Altman's 1970 hit M*A*S*H, *widely considered to be his funniest film, provided the basis for the long-running television series of the same name.*

Altman's choice of source material for his next three films—*The Long Goodbye* (1973), an adaptation of a Raymond Chandler novel; *Thieves Like Us* (1974), a story of gangsters during the Depression; and *California Split* (1974), a "hip" treatment of gambling— indicates that he desired projects that would appeal to larger audiences than his previous films.

Nashville (1975) marked the high point of Robert Altman's film career. His most controversial, it was also his most successful gamble. Consistent with his later films, *Nashville* examined the widespread presence of apathy and complacency in American culture. *Buffalo Bill and the Indians, or, Sitting Bull's History Lesson* (1976) had one of the most talented casts that Altman had ever assembled. However, the film did poorly, apparently because it presumed more knowledge of history than most viewers could bring to the theater.

His next series of films were all produced for Twentieth Century-Fox, including *Three Women* (1977), which had mostly negative reviews, *A Wedding* (1978), for which Altman received consistent critical support, *Quintet* (1979), *Perfect Couple* (1979), and *Health* (1980).

Popeye (1980) had to be the Altman film that best displayed his ability to create a world of fantasy. A Walt Disney film, the story revolved around Sweethaven's residents, a microcosm of conservative American society.

In 1981 Altman began working on a film entitled *Lone Star*, but the film was later canceled because United Artists felt that Altman had pushed back the starting date for shooting too far. Altman maintained that the studio was simply scared of a possible financial loss, and dropped the film without warning after he had spent half a year on preproduction development. This was the last straw for Altman. He began dissolving his interests and commitments to Lion's Gate, and soon the studio was sold in its entirety for $2.3 million. He then turned to directing one-act plays in Los Angeles and off-Broadway. He ended his sabbatical from cinema, though, to film the play *Come Back to the Five and Dime, Jimmy Dean, Jimmy Dean* (1982). His next film was also based on a play, *Streamers* (1983), followed by *Secret Honor* (1984), *Fool for Love* (1985), *Aria* (1987), *Beyond Therapy* (1987), and *Vincent & Theo* (1990).

The Player (1992), one of Altman's more popular films, was the story of a movie studio executive who receives death threats from a rejected screenwriter. Next came *Black & Blue* (1993), *Short Cuts* (1993), stories about the everyday lives of Los Angeles residents, *Prêt-à-Porter* (1994), a story of human foibles against the backdrop of the fashion world, and *Kansas City* (1996), about the Kansas City underworld of 1934.

Altman's most recent films include *The Gingerbread Man* (1998), based on a John Grisham thriller, *Cookie's Fortune* (1999), a murder mystery set in a small town in Mississippi, and *Another City, Not My Own* (1999), based on a Dominick Dunne novel.

See Kael, Pauline; M*A*S*H; *Rudolph, Alan*

AMADEUS

The winner of the Oscar for Best Picture in 1984, *Amadeus* is a brilliant drama about composer Wolfgang Amadeus Mozart and court musician Antonio Salieri. Based on a stage play by Peter Shaffer and directed by Milos Forman, the movie not only has fine acting and wonderful period costumes, but it also features the magnificent and passionate music of Mozart.

The film begins in the 1820s with an aging Antonio Salieri (F. Murray Abraham) seated in his room in an insane asylum, waiting for death to overtake him. He is confessing his sins to a young priest. His confession transports us back to a time thirty years before, when Salieri was the official court composer to Emperor Joseph II (Jeffrey Jones), the ruler of Austria.

Amadeus *won an Oscar for its detailed costumes, like the one worn by actor Tom Hulce in the title role.*

As court composer, Salieri is the most successful and famous composer in Europe. But he is soon eclipsed by twenty-six-year-old Wolfgang Amadeus Mozart (Tom Hulce), a musical genius who arrives in Vienna from Salzburg. Salieri is disgusted with the crude, boorish manners and lusty behavior of the young composer, and he wonders with amazement how such a person could compose such glorious music. He realizes that Mozart's talent must come from God, and he laments that God did not bestow such a talent on him. He feels betrayed, and complains to his confessor that God gave him a longing for music but made him mute.

Driven by jealousy, Salieri does everything he can to sabotage the young Mozart and keep him from gaining fame and fortune. But for every work that Salieri composes, Mozart surpasses it effortlessly. Yet, Salieri manages to keep the good graces of Emperor Joseph, who has little knowledge of music, and retains his position at the court.

Meanwhile, Mozart feverishly works on composing and staging various operas, including *The Marriage of Figaro*, *The Magic Flute*, and *Don Giovanni*, and he has raucous parties with the cast and crew. All the while, Mozart's young, loving wife, Costanze (Elizabeth Berridge), protects her husband, gives him moral support, and participates in some of his antics.

Though Salieri fumes with jealousy, he also recognizes and appreciates the greatness of Mozart's music. As the years pass by, he finds himself more and more astounded by the composer's musical genius. Yet, the hate grows stronger within him as well. While watching Mozart's *Don Giovanni*, a dark opera inspired by the death of Mozart's domineering father, Leopold, Salieri thinks of a way to destroy his rival.

After collapsing in a fever on the premier night of *The Magic Flute*, Mozart is brought to his home by Salieri. From his bed the next day, the composer begins work on a Requiem Mass while Costanze is away. Mozart works feverishly on the Mass, becoming increasingly ill as the work proceeds. Salieri takes this opportunity to play upon Mozart's feverish state and frighten him, while offering to help take notations for the composer as his illness grows worse. There is an implication that Salieri is poisoning Mozart, but the film never resolves that issue.

Salieri plans to steal Mozart's Requiem when it is finished and claim it as his own. But Costanze returns and tells Salieri to go away and leave her ailing husband alone. Before he is able to finish the work, Mozart dies and is buried in a pauper's grave. The film shifts back to the aged Salieri, who, having confessed his sins to the amazed young priest, is ready to meet his fate. In the end he realizes that Mozart's divinely inspired music will endure while his will fade into obscurity after his death.

In addition to winning the Academy Award for Best Picture, *Amadeus* also won Oscars for Supporting Actor, Director, Adapted Screenplay, Costume Design, Art Direction, Sound, and Makeup.

notable & quotable

"If he [Mozart] were alive today, he'd be writing for Broadway and Hollywood. He wanted to reach as many people as possible."

Twyla Tharp, choreographer for Amadeus, *1998*

"From now on you [God] and I are enemies because you choose as your instrument a boastful, lustful, smutty, infantile boy and give me for reward only the ability to recognize the incarnation."

F. Murray Abraham as Salieri in *Amadeus* (1984)

AMERICAN GRAFFITI

One of the hallmark films of the 1970s, George Lucas's *American Graffiti* was a box-office smash, and many people rank it among the top 100 films of all time. There was little fanfare when this low-budget film was released in 1973, but something in its look back to one night in a small California town touched a nerve and made moviegoers nostalgic for a time of innocence, romance, and uncharted possibilities.

Set on a summer evening in 1962, *American Graffiti* focuses on the hopes and dreams of four friends contemplating their future. After the school dance, groups of teenagers begin cruising up and down the town's

One of director George Lucas's first films, American Graffiti *recalled a more innocent, romantic time for many moviegoers.*

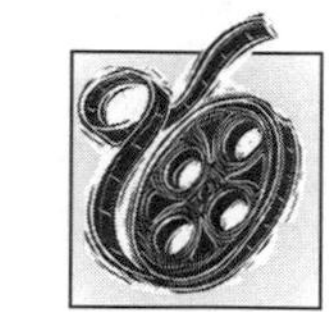

"*We just can't stay 17 forever.*"

Ron Howard as Steve Bolander in *American Graffiti* (1973)

main drag in their cars, all the while listening to rock-and-roll on the radio. They also stop at Mel's Drive-In to get hamburgers and talk.

Curt Henderson (Richard Dreyfuss) and Steve Bolander (Ron Howard) are leaving for college the next day. Out for one more night of fun, each has doubts about going to college, and their thoughts turn to the future. As they cruise around town, Steve thinks about the fact that he must leave behind his longtime girlfriend, Laurie (Cindy Williams), who is Curt's sister. Curt, the brightest boy in his class and a scholarship winner, is racked with doubts about his future. All his life he has worked toward college, but now that the moment is at hand, he wonders whether he shouldn't take some time to rethink his future. Unattached, Curt keeps seeing a beautiful blond in a white Thunderbird. Convinced that she is his destiny, he searches for her the entire night. But each time he gets near, the elusive and enchanting girl slips away.

Meanwhile, Steve is full of confidence and has many reasons why he's ready to leave town. When he suggests to Laurie that they date others while he's away, she reacts badly to the suggestion, which surprises Steve. The emotional turmoil of Steve's leaving is taking a toll on Laurie. She loves Steve very much, and has done everything possible to make their relationship a good one. But she is now caught between what she wants—for Steve to stay—and letting him pursue his dreams.

Also cruising the streets are Terry (Charles Martin Smith), a fumbling nerd, and John (Paul Le Mat), an older kid with the fastest car in town. Neither is headed for college the next day. Terry is the class bumpkin, a hopeless case whose only ambition is to be a "cool dude." He tails after older boys who have fast cars and sexy girls. John's hot rod is fast and sleek, great for attracting the attention of the girls, as well as the cops. Feeling lonely, he's on the prowl for some female company. He picks up thirteen-year-old Carol (Mackenzie Phillips), thinking she's older. But he finds himself stuck with a chattering teenager who embarrasses him just by being in the car where everyone can see them together.

John soon has more pressing concerns than Carol, however. A rival hot-rodder, Bob Falfa, challenges him to a drag race. John is tired of continually having to defend his position as the best. He's seen the wrecks of others who failed, and he doesn't want that to happen to him. Nevertheless, he accepts the challenge.

The entire group gathers at remote Paradise Road to watch the race between John and Bob. Bob's car blows a tire and crashes, leaving John the winner. Fortunately, Bob is not killed. Having watched the race and witnessed the near-fatal crash, Terry feels that he has experienced his ultimate moment. Moreover, an attractive, older girl named Debbie (Candy Clark) has accepted an offer to ride in his car.

The next morning, Steve decides to stay home with Laurie and not attend college. Curt, on the other hand, has banished all doubts and leaves, deciding that he doesn't want to remain at home and stay seventeen forever.

American Graffiti is based on director George Lucas's own experiences growing up and cruising the streets of Modesto, California. The autobiographical touch and documentary style of the film gives it an emotional focus and depth that continues to charm audiences. Moreover, Lucas's integration of classic rock-and-roll into the film captures the spirit of the time and reinforces its nostalgic feeling.

The film was nominated for five Academy Awards, including Picture, Director, Original Screenplay, Film Editing, and Supporting Actress (won by Candy Clark, who played Debbie). It established the reputation of George Lucas as one of America's finest filmmakers. The movie also helped launch the careers of a number of the young actors who starred in it, including Richard Dreyfuss, Ron Howard, Cindy Williams, Suzanne Somers, and Harrison Ford.

See Ford, Harrison; Lucas, George

AMERICAN IN PARIS, AN

The winner of six Academy Awards, including that for Best Picture, *An American in Paris* (1951) is one of the most elegant and celebrated musicals in the history of the cinema. Directed by Vincente Minnelli, the lavish production features twenty-one of the most memorable songs of George and Ira Gershwin, a scrupulous re-creation of the streets of Paris on the MGM back lot, and, most important, the incomparable dancing and choreography of Gene Kelly and Leslie Caron, whom Kelly discovered in a French ballet company.

"Brother, if you can't paint in Paris, you might as well give up and marry the boss's daughter."

Gene Kelly as Jerry Mulligan in *An American in Paris* (1951)

The movie opens by introducing Jerry Mulligan (Gene Kelly), an American ex-GI. Mulligan has remained in Paris after World War II to paint and study art. He lives on the West Bank of the Seine in a small garret above a cafe in Montmartre. Jerry's friend Adam Cook (Oscar Levant) is an aspiring American musician who hopes to become a concert pianist. The morose and mordant Adam, who plays piano in a nearby bistro, used to work as an accompanist for the successful music-hall entertainer Henri Baurel (Georges Guetary), a dapper-looking older Frenchman with graying hair.

At the bistro where Adam plays, Henri shows Adam a picture of Lise Bouvier (Leslie Caron), his nineteen-year-old fiancée, telling how he rescued Lise from the Nazis years earlier and raised her after she was orphaned. Henri explains how he grew to love her as she developed into a woman. As he describes Lise's personality, images of her appear in a series of vignettes, each with a different Gershwin tune and colorful costume, setting, and background.

Extravagant, well-choreographed dance numbers made An American in Paris *one of the most celebrated musicals in history.*

Meanwhile, Jerry struggles to sell his paintings. His fortunes turn sharply upward upon meeting Milo Roberts (Nina Foch), a wealthy American heiress who buys two of his paintings. Milo sends a chauffeured car to fetch Jerry and bring him to her hotel so she can pay him for the paintings. When he arrives, she offers him a drink and tells him a little of herself. She then invites him to attend a party at her room later that evening. Jerry leaves and is soon dancing and singing for joy because of his good fortune.

Arriving at Milo's hotel that evening, Jerry discovers that he is the only guest. When Milo makes advances, Jerry returns her money and begins to leave. But Milo apologizes and explains that she is really more interested in his painting talent. She persuades Jerry to stay, and they go out for dinner at a Montmartre club, where Milo tells Jerry about her important connections in the art world. While at the club, Jerry spots the young and beautiful Lise and learns her name. He begins flirting with her and they dance, much to the annoyance of Milo, who feels slighted. Her pride wounded, Milo leaves the club and returns to her hotel.

The next morning Jerry meets Milo at a cafe. She apologizes for the night before, and they agree to meet for lunch. Jerry then visits the shop where Lise works and asks her to go out with him. Hesitant at first, she finally agrees to meet him that night. Filled with happiness, Jerry goes to Adam's apartment and exults in song and dance.

That night, Lise and Jerry meet and walk together along the banks of the Seine. They express their love in one of the film's most romantic song-and-dance numbers. But Lise, guilt-stricken because she is promised to Henri, suddenly runs away to see Henri perform at a club. Before leaving, however, she agrees to see Jerry again. Lise arrives at the club just as Henri has finished his show. He is overjoyed about plans to tour America with her after they are married.

Meanwhile, back at his apartment, Jerry endures some teasing from Adam about having a rich patroness. Milo then arrives and takes Jerry to see a studio she has set up for him. He says he can't afford it, but she tells him he can pay her back later. He finally agrees. Soon Jerry is feverishly painting in the new studio.

Although they are in love, Jerry and Lise keep their relationship with Milo and Henri a secret from each other. While Jerry and Adam are at the cafe, Henri arrives and announces his forthcoming marriage. In an ironic twist, Jerry tells Henri about his own love for a young girl he has met, but he does not reveal her name.

While walking along the Seine again, Lise decides to tell Jerry the truth—that she is engaged to be married. Although she loves Jerry, she feels obligated to marry Henri because of all that he has done for her. Though distraught, Jerry and Lise decide not to see each other again. Depressed by his breakup with Lise, Jerry invites Milo to a gala masked ball. Coincidentally, Lise and Henri attend the same ball. The four characters contemplate their fates, and Jerry ultimately tells Milo of his love for Lise. During the evening, Jerry goes out to a balcony, where he finds Lise. The two lovers say a final good-bye and embrace.

The movie now shifts to an imaginative dream ballet, in which Jerry repeatedly sees, pursues, and loses Lise in a series of colorful vignettes. Each of the dream sequences is arranged in a style reminiscent of a famous Impressionist painter. This seventeen-minute tour de force was an unprecedented venture into balletic art in American musicals and cost $450,000 to mount (more than $2 million in 1999 dollars). At the end of the ballet, Jerry comes back to reality and finds himself alone with a red rose in his hand. Just then, he looks down the street and sees Lise giving a farewell kiss to Henri, who has discovered Lise's love for Jerry and graciously stepped aside so that Lise can be free to be with the one she loves. In the touching final scene, Lise runs to Jerry, and they embrace.

See Musical film

A

ANDERSON, LINDSAY

Lindsay Anderson was born in Bangalore, India, in 1923, where his father was stationed with the Royal Engineers. He was educated in public schools in the south of England (one, Cheltenham College, became the setting for *If. . .*) and studied classics at Oxford in 1941 while enrolled in preofficer training. He served in the 60th Rifles and the Intelligence Corps from 1943 to 1946, then returned to Oxford and graduated with an M.A. in English in 1948.

When Anderson began to write criticism for *Sequence* (formerly the magazine of the Oxford University Film School) in 1947, he—by sheer luck he often says—was given the chance to make industrial documentaries for a Yorkshire factory manager. Although he had been a great fan of movies in college, a member of the Oxford University Film Society, and had acted in several university drama productions, Anderson knew nothing about filmmaking. He learned to make films by trial and error. By the time he finished his "apprenticeship" period around 1954, he began to secure funding for his own projects. In 1955, his documentary *Thursday's Children* won the Oscar for Best Short Subject. Now that he was making films himself, Anderson's impatience with the mediocrity and prescriptive narrative style of most British films of the time was even more keen.

Although Anderson raged against his home country of England, he never considered leaving it. He recognized the power of widespread roots and maintaining a connection to something. His early documentaries explored the kind of connections he saw in John Ford's movies: affection and community expressed concretely without reference to class, family background, or biography of any sort. Ironically, his feature work began to explore the tension between isolation and community, between alienation and belonging, by portraying characters who weren't connected to anything in a meaningful way.

Every film during his first decade of fiction filmmaking features characters who don't have visible families or any kind of other connection with their environment. Frank Machin, in *This Sporting Life* (1963), tries desperately to make spiritual connections and fails; Mick Travis is socially connected to his environment in *If. . .* (1968), but hardly in a fruitful way—he in fact severs the connection at film's end by shooting down the officials and patrons of his school. The same type of estrangement is apparent in Anderson's two short films of the 1960s: the girl in *The White Bus* (1966) returns to her hometown to find nothing but a pervasive detachment and loneliness, and while the students in *The Singing Lesson* (1967) have a family of sorts in their classroom, they are dissociated in every way from the people outside the school. Michael Travis, in *O Lucky Man!* (1973), is, of course, the most bizarrely detached from his world: every connection he thinks he makes is illusory.

Besides isolation, Anderson's anarchist and antiestablishment attitudes drive each of his films. From Richard Harris's carousing violent character in *This Sporting Life* to the surreal, New Wave-influenced style in *If. . .* , Anderson was constantly trying to show that "Attitude means a style. A style means an attitude." His outrageousness continued in *Brittania Hospital* (1982), a scathing satire on the state of Britain's health services and unions. Not until his last motion picture, *The Whales of August* (1987), was he able to calm his insurgent impulses to make a film that wasn't contrary.

As individualistic as Anderson may have been, he and writer David Storey had a long-term creative partnership of sorts. Anderson directed, for the stage, every one of Storey's plays. Storey, who had similar obsessions with the tensions of sexual, psychological, and class relations, wrote the novel and the screenplay for Anderson's debut feature, *This Sporting Life*.

Director Lindsay Anderson's work often explores the tension between alienation and belonging.

▼

After Anderson's death, Storey eulogized him eloquently, saying, "He loved what he hated and hated what he loved in a seamless circle of retributory affections. He was . . . a liberating spirit."

Lindsay Anderson died in 1994 of a heart attack.

ANIMATION

Animated film is one in which individual drawings are photographed frame by frame. Usually each frame differs slightly from the one preceding it, thus giving the illusion of movement when the frames are projected in rapid succession.

J. R. Bray and Earl Hurd made the medium of animated film economically feasible by their separate development, in 1914, of what became the Bray-Hurd process. While previous animated films such as *Gertie the Dinosaur* (1914) were created by drawing each frame separately and completely, that same year Bray conceived of the background as a separate plane, animating only the necessary foreground elements. The modern use of celluloid overlays was developed by Earl Hurd. Through the use of transparent plastic "cels," various layers of action could be sandwiched and only the necessary "moving" elements, such as an arm or a mouth, were animated. When combined with Raoul Barre's introduction that same year of the peg system for registering the various overlays, all the key elements of animation technology had been established by 1915.

Of the five top-grossing films of the 1940s, four were animated: *Cinderella*, *Pinocchio*, *Fantasia*, and *Bambi*. The most popular, *Cinderella* (1949) earned $38.5 million.

While the Bray-Hurd process made rapid expansion of animated film production possible, it severely diluted the quality of the work. Truly imaginative work within the studio system awaited the arrival of Ko-Ko the Clown and Felix the Cat. Produced by Pat Sullivan and animated by Otto Mesmer, Felix was the first animated character to develop his own following. Often compared to the early Charlie Chaplin in his resourcefulness and physical grace, Felix also had a wry sense of humor. Making free use of his ubiquitous tail, which might serve as a ladder or form itself into a floating question mark, Felix was in complete command of the stylized space designed for him by his creators.

During the pre-1927 period, most animation studios remained modest affairs. A few key animators and their support teams went from one small outfit to another, with releasing arrangements changing so frequently that little could be taken for granted. Walt Disney, who drifted to Los Angeles in 1923 after failing in Kansas City, would change the face of the animated film industry again by the end of the decade. In the late 1920s Disney contracted to deliver thirty of his "Mickey Mouse" cartoons to Columbia Pictures, a contract that would provide the needed base on which Disney would build his company's innovation of sound and allow it to take advantage of Columbia's powerful studio patrons and marketing leverage. By the early thirties Mickey Mouse was a bona fide screen star. Disney took animation even further, adding color and utilizing the CinemaScope wide screen. His full-length animated films, such as *Pinocchio* (1940) and *Cinderella* (1950), enjoyed enormous popularity with the filmgoing public, as have Disney's more recent animated films, such as *Beauty and the Beast* (1991) and *Aladdin* (1992). In the 1980s animation also became popular on prime-time television, with the appearance of the long-running *The Simpsons* and non-mainstream hits such as *Beavis and Butthead* and *South Park* in the 1990s.

See Clay animation; Fantasia; Snow White and the Seven Dwarfs

ANNIE HALL

In *Annie Hall,* Alvy Singer (Woody Allen) sees much of the contemporary world as contradictory, transitory, and unreliable; he is restless, skeptical, and at times paranoid. In such a world, "love fades" or true passion and genuine human connection do not last, and as Alvy says, it is hard to get our heads around that. In this film, Allen portrays a New York Jewish comedy writer approaching middle age; he is streetwise about urban sophistication, and Annie (Diane Keaton), his flaky lover from Chippewa Falls, Wisconsin, is a creative innocent. But the relationship has broken up when the story begins, and the film is both an autopsy and a reminiscence. Unlike screwball comedies before it, the film is not concerned with how opposites eventually unite, but with why this important love did not endure. Woven into Alvy's self-conscious quest for answers is a look at the stress that contemporary culture places on romance, and a reflexive examination of the relationship of art to life.

In his opening words, Alvy, at forty, reveals his fear of aging, change, and death; yet he tells us that his depression over Annie is unusual because he had a reasonably happy childhood. Following his references to his relatively happy childhood, we see him as a depressed child who grew up during World War II—this accounts in part for his personality, "which is a little nervous."

Alvy's is also not the mainstream American family. Alvy's emasculating, shrewish mother reduces carrots to shavings as she derides Alvy for distrusting everyone, and she dismisses Alvy's early anxieties about the cosmos by screaming in frustration, "What is that your business? . . . What has the

notable & quotable

"The scene where the lobsters escape . . . we used a handheld camera to exaggerate the nervous tension and the chaos. On the take we selected, Diane and I . . . couldn't stop laughing."

Woody Allen, director/writer, 1999

Annie Hall's *Diane Keaton launched an androgynous fashion craze with her baggy pants and menswear tie and vest.* .

universe got to do with it? You're here in Brooklyn! Brooklyn is not expanding!" She and Alvy's father reveal how moral ambiguity has crept into everyday life as they argue heatedly and comically about whether cleaning women should be allowed to steal. Frank Capra, George Cukor, and Howard Hawks never gave their characters a family so colorful, so New York, so Jewish, or so confusing.

From Alvy's perspective, reemphasized as he interrupts his own recollections by making an adult appearance within the scene, days at school evoke further distrust. Incompetent cartoon teachers preside over rigid classrooms filled with dull or competitive schoolmates who soon lose their innocence, growing up to be methadone addicts and owners of a "profitable dress company." A rosy colored filmland childhood is as far from Alvy's experience as Annie's rural Wisconsin is from his Coney Island home beneath a roller coaster that shakes his tomato soup each time it passes.

Adult Alvy's interruption of his own narrative not only emphasizes its subjectivity, but reminds us that we are watching a film. Moreover, his interruption and stream of early memories are only two in a long series of disruptions to classical narrative structure that also serve to violate conventional boundaries between fiction and reality, to indicate Alvy's confusion, and to contrast pointedly with the comforting architecture of traditional screwball film. As Alvy sifts through his associations, so the audience must deal not only with the pieces into which his life has flown, but with Alvy's attempts to make sense of them.

From the onset of their relationship, Annie and Alvy are extreme opposites. Initially, Annie is a crazy, humanizing antitoxin for Alvy's seriousness, and he plays a slow-moving, cautious straight man to her disorderly, kinetic character. On the way to the tennis court where they first meet, Alvy frets about anti-Semitism. In contrast, during the tennis match the camera catches Annie's spontaneity as she happily flails away at a tennis ball.

Annie is dressed in an unconventional tramplike costume that declares her creative individuality and her independence. Her fumbling mannerisms make her a relative of Allen's natural and innocent "little men" in earlier films, and she presents an androgynous picture that may suggest that despite her apparent lack of ease, she is authentic and complete at the core.

Like other screwball couples, Annie and Alvy come from different cultures and classes. Annie's man's tie was a gift form her Grammy Hall in Chippewa Falls; Alvy observes that his Jewish Grammy was too busy getting raped by Cossacks to give him gifts. Annie does not fear death as he does, and she takes risks. She drives through town with abandon; he is too nervous to own a car. At an Easter dinner in Chippewa Falls with Annie's family, where they serve ham and talk about swap meets and boats, Alvy imagines himself a Hasidic rabbi among midwestern Wasps. A split screen emphasizes the contrarieties to show Alvy's family at a holiday meal, arguing loudly, eating furiously, and discussing sickness.

At first Alvy and Annie complement one another. She helps him to rediscover spontaneity and love, and she appreciates his humor and his experienced advice about her singing career. Alvy feels compelled, however, to distrust her innocence. While he admires her, he also eventually denies her "wholeness," her uniqueness. In attempting to change her, he divides her from herself. She becomes a "newer woman," more self-confident, more self-conscious, and more worldly, but like the absurd alternatives in earlier Allen films, neither Annie as innocent nor Annie as experienced is entirely compatible with her neurotic partner.

Like the screwball couples who disentangled their problems and nurtured their relationships away from the urban sophistication, Alvy and Annie find their way outside the city despite Alvy's doubts about the romance of rural life. He associates the country with dead moths on screens and cult murderers.

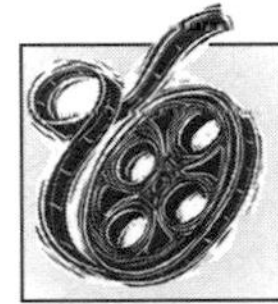

"Don't you see the rest of the country looks upon New York like we're left-wing, communist, Jewish, homosexual pornographers? I think of us that way sometimes and I live here."

Woody Allen as Alvy Singer in *Annie Hall* (1977)

In the kitchen at the beachhouse retreat, Annie and Alvy illustrate their ability to transcend adulthood's sex-specific behavior. Recapturing a sense of childhood innocence and play, in a moment that appears to transcend the film's encapsulating dialogues and the determinate nature of the film as medium, they shoo their lobster dinners toward a pot.

Later, Annie and Alvy leave the city again, but this time nature offers no escape, for the relationship is in trouble. Initially Annie and Alvy enjoyed making love. He found her "polymorphously perverse," for she responded so readily with every part of her body. In their second visit to the country, however, Alvy forbids Annie to smoke pot to relax, and she cannot achieve intimacy without it. Instead of pot, Alvy puts a corny red light bulb in their bedside lamp "for atmosphere," and quips that he and Annie could also develop photographs.

Although Annie and Alvy break up temporarily when Annie is caught arm in arm with her adult-education professor, they come to miss each other, and like many divorced screwball comedy couples, they reconcile. The difference is that this reconciliation does not last. Annie's moodiness, seen in memories from the last part of their relationship, indicates that she has learned self-consciousness from Alvy and has come to experience his discontent. While she has learned from experience with reading, analysis, adult education, and the films Alvy took her to, her whole background urges escape from the depression that accompanies Alvy's anhedonia. Thus, following a polished nightclub performance, she is flattered by an invitation from Tony Lacey (Paul Simon) to develop her career in California, and she and Alvy agree to end their relationship finally.

Alvy misses Annie and travels to California to propose, but Annie refuses. Back in New York, Alvy tries to deal with his loss through art; he writes a play about his love affair, but adds a happy ending. Art, he observes, is always more perfect than life. But art holds no more lasting meaning.

See Allen, Woody; Keaton, Diane

ANTHOLOGY FILM

An anthology film refers to a theme film constructed around a variety of existing sources. Various materials are brought together to explore a topic—such as the whodunit detective film genre, which is the title of an anthology film in the *Best of British Cinema* (1989) series. An anthology tribute to the MGM musical formed the documentaries *That's Entertainment, Part I* (1974), *That's Entertainment, Part II* (1976), and *That's Entertainment, Part*

III (1944). The latter anthology film expanded the MGM focus to include excerpts from outstanding comedy and drama films produced at the Hollywood studio.

APARTMENT, THE

A goad to a postwar American conscience gone soft with materialist complacency, *The Apartment* (1960), one of the many outstanding dramas in Billy Wilder's imposing oeuvre, presents a withering portrait of amoral self-seeking among corporate climbers. A commercial and critical success, the film earned Oscars for Best Picture, Best Director (Wilder), and Best Screenplay (I. A. L. Diamond).

The film's protagonist is C. C. Baxter (Jack Lemmon), a fawning, low-level insurance-company employee so addled with ambition that he will stop at almost nothing to advance his career, including currying favor with his superiors by lending out his apartment for their extramarital trysts. In exchange for turning his apartment into a hotel for amorous transients, he extracts promises of favorable reports to the head of the company, J. D. Sheldrake, played with a chillingly convincing blend of arrogance and cynicism by Fred MacMurray, who was cast against type before a movie audience accustomed to seeing him in more reassuringly affable roles.

The rewards are not long in coming for the scheming clerk. Baxter is soon exulting in his spacious office, secretary, and the coveted key to the executive bathroom. Sheldrake himself soon approaches Baxter about the possibility of availing himself of the corporate love nest, and the obsequious Baxter, of course, leaps at this opportunity to impress the big boss. Baxter and Sheldrake, although superficially alike in their pursuit of self-interest, are actually opposites. Sheldrake is the familiar suburban adulterer, the respectable husband and father who is never on time for dinner because he is with his secretary, or, when he tires of her, with the elevator operator. For all his panting ambition, however, Baxter is the least odious of the film's schemers, and it is because of Jack Lemmon's performance that audiences find him endearing. His efforts to advance only intensify his loneliness. He stands behind the stoop watching a colleague and a blonde race up the steps to his apartment while he must retire to a bench on Central Park South until they have finished. In an extreme long shot running the length of the screen, Baxter sits by himself, bundled in a raincoat; the wind drives the leaves along a row of benches that seems to stretch out to infinity. The camera tracks in, stopping short of a close-up and fading out instead.

"For awhile there you're kidding yourself you're going with an unmarried man. Then one day he keeps looking at his watch and asks you if there's any lipstick showing and then rushes out to catch the 7:14 to White Plains."

Shirley MacLaine as Fran Kubelik in *The Apartment* (1960)

Though hard won, Baxter's newfound prosperity has its attractions, such as an expensive, foppish wardrobe and the newfound confidence to pursue the woman of his dreams, Fran Kubelik (Shirley MacLaine), the engagingly shy and comely elevator operator in his office building. Just as his courtship begins to gain momentum, however, Baxter is stopped short by the devastating discovery that Fran is the woman that Sheldrake has been meeting in Baxter's apartment.

When, during one of their encounters, the guileless Fran makes it clear to Sheldrake that she views their liaison as a prelude to marriage, Sheldrake coldly disabuses her of that illusion with the perfunctory directness of a business transaction: "When you've been married to a woman twelve years you just don't sit down to a breakfast table and say, 'Pass the sugar. I want a divorce.' It's not that easy." After Sheldrake leaves her alone in Baxter's apartment, the despondent Fran attempts suicide by taking an overdose of

Despite his overly ambitious attempts to climb the corporate ladder, C. C. Baxter (Jack Lemmon) still manages to endear himself to audiences.

▼

sleeping pills. Baxter arrives home to find her inching toward death, and, during his desperate efforts to revive her, tells her that he loves her. He nurses her through a prolonged convalescence, cooking her meals and slowly restoring her ability to trust and love.

Transformed by the spectacle of Sheldrake's treachery and the power of Fran's love, Baxter comes to grips with the unacceptable costs of his unbridled ambition. In the face of still another request from Sheldrake for the use of his apartment with another woman, Baxter instead proffers the key to the executive washroom, brashly rebukes Sheldrake for his moral bankruptcy, and quits his job. When Fran hears that he has confronted Sheldrake and walked out of the company, she runs to join him at his apartment, where the final scene shows her and Baxter sitting on a couch, playing gin rummy. "I absolutely adore you," Baxter rhapsodizes. "Shut up and deal," Fran replies, checking his effusiveness with mock flippancy. "Shut up and deal" is the kind of one-liner that cannot be topped; just as *The Apartment* is the kind of film that cannot lead to a sequel or a remake. Naturally, one wonders if the couple will remain as incorruptible as they were at the fade-out.

See Wilder, Billy

A-PICTURE

The term A-picture originated in the 1930s and was used to denote the higher-quality film on a double-feature bill. The A-picture was usually made with popular stars and with careful attention to production values. Its counterpart, a lower-budget effort, was referred to as the B-picture.

See B-picture; Feature film

ART THEATER

The term art theater was frequently used in the 1950s and early 1960s to describe a motion-picture theater that exhibited films that were for the most part outside the commercial mainstream. Art theaters exhibited works that were considered important to the state of film expression regardless of their popular appeal: films by foreign directors, by independent filmmakers,

notable & quotable

"Billy Wilder grew a rose in a garbage pail."

Jack Lemmon, actor, 1960, referring to Wilder's humane handling of The Apartment*'s unsavory material*

FRED ASTAIRE

Born Frederick Austerlitz in Omaha, Nebraska, on May 10, 1899, Fred Astaire became a much beloved Hollywood star despite the verdict on his first screen test, taken in the early 1930s: "Can't act. Can't sing. Balding. Can dance a little."

It is true that Astaire was balding, and he was not a great actor or singer (though he introduced more hit tunes than any other crooner of his time, including "Night and Day" and "The Way You Look Tonight"). But Astaire was indisputably one of the greatest dancers and choreographers of all time. His smooth, innovative dance style, showcased in a series of popular musical comedies from the 1930s to the 1950s, epitomized grace and sophistication. Venerable composer Irving Berlin called Astaire "the purest talent I have ever worked with."

Astaire was known for his perfectionism. He would rehearse and film a dance number dozens of times until it was flawless—and the effort showed. It was very hard on his partners, however. (One, Nanette Fabray, called him a "dictator.") Astaire was just as demanding of himself as anyone else. He might rehearse a single dance for up to eighteen hours a day, for six to nine weeks at a time.

Astaire's versatility as a performer can be traced to his childhood. He was born to musical parents, who insisted on dance training (but little formal academic instruction) for their children early on. At age seven Fred traveled on the vaudeville circuit, paired with his sister, Adele, and dubbed "The Astaires." They made their Broadway debut in 1917 and soon became stars in the theater world.

When Adele married in 1931 and retired from performing, Fred gave Hollywood a try (accompanied by his wife, a young socialite named Phyllis Potter). Despite the infamous screen test, he was awarded a small part in *Dancing Lady* (1933).

In his next film, *Flying Down to Rio* (1934), he was paired with Ginger Rogers, a stroke of genius. Fred and Ginger went on to make ten musical-comedy films together, including *Top Hat* (1935), *Swing Time* (1936), and *Shall We Dance* (1937). The pair's magic on the dance floor was mesmerizing. Katharine Hepburn described their partnership this way: "Astaire gave her class; Rogers gave him sex."

Rogers eventually decided to undertake dramatic roles (perhaps encouraged by her uneasy relationship with Astaire, which one producer called "six years of mutual aggression"). Astaire continued to command an audience with such dancer/actresses as Cyd Charisse (*Silk Stockings,* 1957), Leslie Caron (*Daddy Long Legs,* 1955), and Eleanor Powell (*Broadway Melody of 1940).* His solo dance numbers, such as the Fourth of July firecracker dance in *Holiday Inn* (1942), were pure art.

Fred Astaire's demanding style resulted in some of the most memorable dance sequences ever captured on film.

Eventually Astaire followed Rogers's lead and turned to straight acting, winning accolades for his role in *On the Beach (1959).* He won a special Oscar for his performance in *The Towering Inferno* (1974). In 1949 the Academy gave him another special award, and Astaire was presented with the American Film Institute's (AFI) Life Achievement Award in 1981. In 1999 the AFI named him No. 5 on its Greatest Screen Legends men's list. His autobiography, *Steps in Time,* was published in 1960.

He had two children, Fred Jr. and Ava, and one stepson, Peter Potter. His much-loved first wife, Phyllis, died in 1954. In 1980 Astaire married Robyn Smith, a jockey, and much younger than he; it, too, was a happy marriage. Astaire died in her arms on June 22, 1987, of pneumonia, at age eighty-eight.

See Musical film; Rogers, Ginger

and works not released nationally. Art theaters also frequently presented programs that included film classics.

During the 1970s the term *art theater* was also often used by exhibitors who showed, exclusively, pornographic motion pictures. The adoption of this term by such exhibitors was a promotion gesture intended to call attention to specialized subject matter and to suggest serious purpose behind the showing of admittedly candid and controversial films. The "art theater" label implied that films being exhibited there had artistic merit, a criterion the Supreme Court had used after the *Roth* decision in 1957 in determining whether a sexually oriented motion picture possessed "redeeming social value," thereby meriting First Amendment protection.

See Avant-garde; Experimental film; Independent filmmaker; Psychodrama; Underground film

AUTEUR (CRITICISM)

A critical-theoretical term that comes from the French, meaning "author," as a theoretical concept the term *auteur* is used to describe motion-picture directors whose works are said to be produced with personal vision. Hence, an auteur is a director who "authors" a film by virtue of a driving personality and individual artistic control of the filmmaking process.

The auteur theory denies to some extent the idea that film criticism must examine the cinema as a collective art form and view each picture as the end result of a team of artists and technicians. While this is true in many cases, the auteur critics in expounding their theory claimed that many major directors carry with them from film to film individualized self-expression. As with an author, the filmmaker of vision incorporates into individual pictures a view of life through individual style. Therefore, the auteur critics judge motion-picture art by examining both the filmmaker (director) and the works that director has produced. A single film by a major director does not stand alone, but is viewed in relation to all the films by that director. The auteur critics claim that this critical procedure allows for the serious examination of lesser works by a given director that might otherwise be overlooked.

The auteur theory was first discussed by François Truffaut in an article, "Une certaine tendance du cinéma français," written in 1954 for the French film magazine *Cahiers due Cinéma.* Andrew Sarris, an American critic for the *Village Voice,* is given credit for bringing Truffaut's ideas of auteur criticism to the United States. The French critics, as well as Sarris and other subscribers to the auteur concept, developed lists of directors who were considered to have achieved auteur status. Among those directors: Alfred Hitchcock, Raoul Walsh, John Ford, Max Ophuls, Joseph Losey, Howard Hawks, and many others.

The major opposition to the auteur theory came from critics who pointed out that this procedure of criticism led certain motion pictures to critical acclaim when they were clearly poor films; others have argued that the approach tends toward hero worship and leads to a priori judgments.

At the same time, the auteur theory has served a number of useful functions in film criticism: (1) it provided a method for looking at film technique and style rather than content alone; (2) it stimulated, as a result of its controversial nature, provocative discussion of the motion picture as a serious art form; (3) it brought recognition to directors such as Alfred Hitchcock and John Ford who had previously been overlooked by the critics as serious artists; and (4) it reestablished the importance of the director in film art and criticism.

See Criticism; Director

AVANT-GARDE

Avant-garde is a term used to describe the first experimental film movement that began in Europe about 1920. In contemporary criticism, any film that employs new, original techniques and experimental approaches in expressing ideas on film is often referred to as avant-garde. The first avant-garde filmmakers produced two general types of films: those that employed techniques commonly associated with the Dada and surrealist movements in literature and art, and those that were nonnarrative and abstract in quality.

The impetus behind the first film avant-garde movement grew out of a revolt against cinema realism. The filmmakers embraced surrealism because of a "belief in the higher reality of certain hitherto neglected forms of association, in the omnipotence of the dream, in the disinterested play of thought," as stated by surrealism's principal spokesman, André Breton. The surrealist movement also gave filmmakers opportunities to parody painting, sex, psychology, contemporary politics, and the motion picture itself. The surrealists seized upon and photographed a variety of material phenomena and arranged these "word pictures" in disparate, illogical ways to effect subjective, dreamlike meanings. They did not want their images to have a mimetic life, but a spiritual life—to become images sprung free of a material existence. The films *Emak Bakia* (1927) and *L'Etoile de Mer* (1928) by

Man Ray and *Un Chien Andalou* (1928) by Luis Buñuel and Salvador Dali are representative of these surrealist impulses.

Surrealism by no means dominated the film avant-garde, either in practice or in theory. Within the movement there was a group of filmmakers who were advocates of *cinéma pur*, "pure cinema": artists who wanted to return the medium to its elemental origins. At the center of this group was René Clair, who wrote in 1927: "Let us return to the birth of the cinema: 'The cinematograph,' says the dictionary, 'is a machine designed to project animated pictures on a screen.' The Art that comes from such an instrument must be an art of *vision* and *movement*."

The cinema purists—Clair, Viking Eggeling, Fernand Léger, Hans Richter, among others—were interested in the rhythm, movement, and cadence of objects and images within a film—the building of an internal energy through which vision and movement would become both the form and the meaning of the film.

The film titles of the cinema purists suggest the musical-like emphasis on animated pictures: *Rhythmus '21, Ballet Mècanique, Symphony Diagonale, The March of the Machines, Berlin: The Symphony of a Great City.*

The pure-cinema interests were not limited to rhythmical abstractions alone, but also manifested themselves in the fiction film: in Jean Renoir's adaptation in 1926 of Emile Zola's *Nana,* a film where the original plot is incidental and where Renoir abstractly treats Zola's story; in Carl Dreyer's *The Passion of Joan of Arc* (1928), where the ordered use of extreme close-ups produces a spiritual response to the face; and in Jean Cocteau's *Blood of a Poet* (1930), a film made up almost entirely of visual transformations that take place in the mind of the poet.

See Art theater; Experimental film; Futurism; Independent filmmaker; Lynch, David; Psychodrama; Underground film

B

BARA, THEDA

Not until the age of fan magazines and feature pictures were conditions ripe for the creation of stars out of whole cloth, and the first great fabricated star, Theda Bara, reached the screen in January 1915.

She was born Theodosia Goodman, the daughter of a Jewish tailor who had emigrated from Poland to Cincinnati, Ohio. Her mother's family was Swiss, of French descent, and when the future star first tried the stage around 1908, she used her mother's family name, appearing as Theodosia de Coppet.

Theda, the diminutive by which her family traditionally addressed her, spent several years in New York attempting to gain a foothold in the theater. Her stage career never seems to have amounted to more than a handful of roles, but in 1924 she was spotted by Frank Powell, who decided to cast her as the seductress in *A Fool There Was* (1915), an important feature he was about to direct for William Fox. Powell and Fox had been considering a number of potential temptresses to play opposite Broadway star Edward José, but Robert Hilliard, who had produced the stage version, suggested signing an unknown. He claimed that the part would make an overnight success of anyone who appeared in it, and that by signing this actress to a long-term contract Fox could acquire a potential star at little cost.

The film version of *A Fool There Was* traced its genesis to a stage version that had appeared at New York's Liberty Theatre in 1909. This, in turn, was inspired by the Burne-Jones painting *The Vampire,* first exhibited in 1897, and the Rudyard Kipling poem of the same name. Painting, poem, play (and subsequent novelization) had already established a powerful image in the public's mind of the vampire-enchantress. What was needed was an angle, and after studying the performance Theodosia de Coppet delivered under Powell's direction, Fox put press agents Johnny Goldfrap and Al Selig on the job. They created the name Theda Bara, an anagram, they claimed, for "Arab Death." (Some historians believe that "Bara" derives from the name of Theda's maternal grandfather, François Baranger de Coppet.) The Fox publicity mill launched a bizarre campaign generating a detailed fantasy background for their new star: she was born in the shadow

notable & quotable

"Her success was primarily due Fox's publicity department; they created her image as a screen vamp and used it to titillate."

Ron Genini, author, 1997, from his book Theda Bara: A Biography of a Screen Vamp

of the Sphinx, played leads at the Théâtre Antoine, distilled exotic perfumes as a hobby, and was well versed in black magic. They informed readers that Theda Bara offscreen was identical to the character she played in *A Fool There Was,* destroying males and turning a cold shoulder to the pleadings of abandoned wives and children.

Bara did not always play the vamp; she appeared in *Romeo and Juliet* (1916), *The Two Orphans* (1915), *Under Two Flags* (1916), and *Kathleen Mavourneen* (1919) as well. But it was with this character that Fox's publicity identified her, and on which her career rose and fell. As late as December 1918 Bara was listed ninth in a popularity contest conducted by *Motion Picture* magazine, but the following year she parted company with Fox, and although she made several attempts, she never effectively revived her career.

Some critics see the Bara character simply as one pole of a standard male fantasy running from virgin to vamp, but this analysis fails to recognize the character's real popularity with women of the pre-flapper genera-

Theda Bara was one of the first film stars created almost solely by the Hollywood publicity machine.

tion. This character was one of the only females on screen who consistently demonstrated real power over men and who did not always have to pay the price for it.

See Brenon, Herbert; Negri, Pola

LAUREN BACALL

Actress Lauren Bacall, known for her tall, sultry good looks and husky voice, was born Betty Joan Perske in the Bronx, New York, on September 16, 1924. She received some training at the American Academy of Dramatic Arts after high school and found several small roles in Broadway plays. Bacall also began modeling and was quite successful at it. In 1943 the wife of powerful producer-director Howard Hawks saw Bacall's photograph on the cover of *Harper's Bazaar* magazine. Within a month, at age nineteen, Bacall was under contract to a Hollywood studio.

Her performance in her first film, *To Have and Have Not* (1944), won both popular and critical acclaim. In the movie, Bacall played the love interest of the star, Humphrey Bogart, twenty-five years her senior. The two hit it off, and in 1945 they married. (Though some people accused Bacall of marrying Bogart just to ride his coattails, most believe that theirs was a genuine love match.) The couple had a son and a daughter, Stephen and Leslie, and filmed three more movies together. After Bogart's death in 1957, Bacall was briefly engaged to Frank Sinatra. In 1961 she married Jason Robards Jr. They had a son, Sam, but later divorced.

Sultry Lauren Bacall was well known for her roles opposite leading man Humphrey Bogart, and the pair was affectionately dubbed "Bogie and Bacall."

Early in her career, Bacall was dubbed "The Look" for the come-hither expression in her eyes. People perceived it as sophistication, but Bacall later said that what viewers perceived as sexy actually stemmed from anxiety—to control her nerves while filming, she held her chin down and looked up at Bogie from under her eyelashes.

Bacall made several solid films in the 1940s, including *The Big Sleep* (1946) and *Key Largo* (1948). In the 1950s and 1960s, however, her roles were less substantive, in such movies as *How to Marry a Millionaire* (1953), *Designing Woman* (1957), and *Sex and the Single Girl* (1965). In later years Bacall would note that moviemakers did not seem to take her seriously as an actress.

Seeing the decline of her film career, Bacall turned to the Broadway stage and won Tony Awards for *Applause* (1970) and *Woman of the Year* (1981), both musicals. She returned to film in 1974 with *Murder on the Orient Express,* and in 1996 she won a Golden Globe award and her first Academy Award nomination for Best Supporting Actress in *The Mirror Has Two Faces.*

Besides occasional film and stage work, Bacall does voice-overs for television commercials, and is frequently seen out and about in New York. She has published two autobiographies: *Lauren Bacall by Myself* (1979) and *Lauren Bacall Now* (1994). In 1999 she was named to the American Film Institute's list of Greatest Film Legends.

See Bogart, Humphrey; Hawks, Howard

BELASCO TENDENCY

The Belasco tendency is a historical term once used to describe pictorial realism in theatrical art. In the late nineteenth century, when the theater was leaning progressively toward melodrama, romance, and spectacle, the stage setting and environment gained in importance. David Belasco, an American theater producer-director of the period, became obsessed with the idea of total verisimilitude on the stage. On one occasion, Belasco went so far as to transfer an entire hotel room, wallpaper and all, to a theater setting for realistic impact in a melodrama he was producing. These trends toward pictorial realism and the increasing appeal of more popular theater forms made the advent of the motion picture at the turn of the century especially timely. It has been noted by theorists and historians such as Nicholas Vardac (*Stage to Screen,* 1947) that the Belasco tendency could be more easily realized in the medium of film than on the stage.

BEN-HUR

Ben-Hur was one of the last great outsize gestures of the dying Hollywood studio system, a sprawling biblical extravaganza as epic in the making (the twenty-minute chariot race alone took three months to shoot) as it was in the telling. MGM bet its whole future on this cinematic leviathan and was repaid handsomely in the short term, sweeping the 1959 Oscars with eleven statuettes, including the award for Best Picture, and amassing $40 million in revenues against a cost of $12.5 million. Nevertheless, not even this sweeping tale of miraculous religious redemption could redeem MGM in particular or the big studios in general, whose long-term retrenchment was already irreversible.

The film's plot, adapted from Lew Wallace's novel, centers on Judah Ben-Hur (Charlton Heston), a child of aristocratic privilege in Roman-occupied Judea whose indignation at the oppressive cruelties of the occupiers has transformed him into an ardent anti-imperialist rebel. After he is imprisoned by the Romans, he receives a visit from the Roman legion Messala (Stephen Boyd), a childhood friend, who tries to extract the names of his fellow insurgents. Ben-Hur's adamant refusal sparks a burning animosity between the two.

Some days thereafter, as Ben-Hur and his sister, Tirzah (Cathy O'Donnell), take in a lavish parade celebrating the arrival of the new Roman governor, Tirzah inadvertently dislodges a roof tile that falls near the governor's horse. The startled animal throws the governor into a wall, severely injuring him. Messala seizes this pretext to arrest Ben-Hur's whole family.

On the long trek to Tyrus, Ben-Hur faints from thirst and exhaustion while being herded through Nazareth, and Jesus (Claude Heater) comes forward to offer him water. A Roman guard intervenes, but is overcome by the spiritual radiance of Jesus and backs away. Ben-Hur, his strength renewed by this infusion of spiritual light, is able to continue with the journey.

Ben-Hur is then pressed into service as a galley slave. When the ship is attacked by Macedonian pirates, the commander, Quintus Arius (Jack Hawkins), is hurled into the sea. Ben-Hur, who has already freed several slaves on the doomed vessel, dives into the water to rescue the commander. A grateful Quintus Arius rewards Ben-Hur's valor by taking him to Rome, adopting him, and sponsoring his training as a chariot driver, a field in which Ben-Hur soon achieves great eminence.

Years of accumulated wealth and glory as a chariot racer have not blunted Ben-Hur's pain over the loss of his sister and mother, so he travels back to Judea to enlist Messala's help in finding them. Messala, cognizant of his old friend's stature as a consul, promises to help. He seeks news of his loved ones from Esther (Haya Harareet), the daughter of his family's one-time servants (she eventually becomes his wife); not wanting him to know the terrible truth—that they are afflicted with leprosy because of years of harsh prison life—she tells him that they have died. Upon hearing this news, the enraged Ben-Hur vows to meet Messala in a chariot race to be sponsored by the wealthy Sheik Ilderim (Hugh Griffith).

A massive throng gathers in the great arena to witness this epic grudge match. Hurtling through the perilous, chaotic mass of racers, the malefic Messala pares down the field by shearing the wheels of competitors until only he and Ben-Hur are dueling for the lead, far ahead of the rest of the pack. Ben-Hur manages to avoid the deadly rotating blades on the axle of Messala's chariot, and, positioning himself behind Messala, sabotages the latter's chariot, which collapses, hurling the stunned and bloody Messala onto the track and to his eventual death under the remorseless thunder of dozens on oncoming hooves. With no more serious challengers, Ben-Hur surges on to victory.

After the race, Ben-Hur faces the nearly lifeless Messala in a room beneath the arena. Spiteful to the last, the fading charioteer informs his vanquisher that his mother and sister are indeed alive, inhabitants of the Valley of the Lepers. "The race is not over," Messala flares before dying.

"You can break a man's skull. You can arrest him. You can throw him into a dungeon. But how do you fight an idea?"

André Morell as Sextus in *Ben-Hur* (1959)

Ben-Hur sets out immediately for the Valley of the Lepers, furtively trailed by the ever loyal and loving Esther, who has been providing his mother and sister with food since their arrival there. Upon reaching the valley, Ben-Hur joyously and heedlessly embraces his mother, Miriam (Martha Scott), who tells him that Tirzah is dying. Determined to save her life, they embark for Jerusalem to find a miracle healer they have heard about, but once there they find him already bearing up a cross on the way to his execution. Recognizing him as Jesus, the man who offered him water when he was a desperately thirsty prisoner those many years ago, Ben-Hur manages to catch his eye, beaming gratitude for the grace and peace of this miraculous moment. As the family departs from the city, a sudden rain washes over his sister's and mother's flesh, from which the leprosy sores have just vanished. Understanding the source of this blessed miracle, they all rejoice. The film's last scene shows a shepherd and his flock passing an empty cross.

See Epic; Heston, Charlton; Wyler, William

BEST YEARS OF OUR LIVES, THE

The Best Years of Our Lives (1946) was the last film William Wyler made in collaboration with Samuel Goldwyn, and many consider it their finest joint achievement. Its eloquent delineation of the emotional dislocations facing returning World War II soldiers touched a nerve for an entire generation, and the film became the biggest box-office draw of the 1940s.

The initial inspiration for the film came when Goldwyn saw a *Time* magazine article on the difficulties faced by returning veterans. He then commissioned MacKinlay Kantor, a novelist and war correspondent, to write an original story on the subject. Kantor's blank-verse novel *Glory for Me* was converted into the shooting script by Robert Sherwood, a Pulitzer Prize-winning playwright.

The Best Years of Our Lives finds its structure through a series of parallels and contrasts centered around three veterans and their experiences. Although the men are always viewed as individuals, they are also meant to typify the generalized experiences of all servicemen. Each is drawn from a different branch of the service: Al (Fredric March) is an army sergeant; Fred (Dana Andrews) is an air corps bombardier; and Homer (Harold Russell) is a sailor. Each represents a different social class (Al, upper middle; Homer, middle; Fred, lower), but the lower-class Fred is an officer, while upper-class Al is an enlisted man. This scheme is only incidentally commu-

INGRID BERGMAN

Born in Stockholm, Sweden, on August 29, 1915, Ingrid Bergman would become one of the premiere actresses in the world, and, along with Greta Garbo, Scandinavia's most popular export. The camera loved her luminous face and tall, womanly figure; audiences were charmed by her accented English and accessible onscreen presence, whether she was playing a nun or a vamp.

Bergman was orphaned in early childhood and was raised by relatives. After graduating from high school, she enrolled in Stockholm's Royal Dramatic Theater School (attended in earlier years by Garbo), where she soon became its leading actress. Her first film performance, in the Swedish production of *Intermezzo* (1936), caught the eye of American producer David O. Selznick. He asked her to film an American version in Hollywood. The product of that collaboration was released in 1939 and was embraced by audiences. Selznick thereupon signed Bergman to a seven-year contract.

The 1940s were a golden time for the young actress. She starred in many popular and critically acclaimed films, including *Dr. Jekyll and Mr. Hyde* (1941), *Casablanca* (1942), *Gaslight* (1944), and *Notorious* (1946). Her role as the persecuted wife in *Gaslight* won Bergman her first Academy Award.

Once she was free of the contract with Selznick, Bergman was able to accept a variety of assignments. She performed on Broadway in *Joan of Arc* in 1946 and reprised the title role in the film version in 1948.

A personal matter threatened to destroy Bergman's career in American film in the late 1940s. She left her Swedish husband of more than a decade, Dr. Peter Lindstrom, and their daughter, Pia (later a New York television critic), for Roberto Rossellini, the Italian director of her film *Stromboli* (1949). Her passionate decision proved too much for the American audience of the era, and she was denounced on the floor of the U.S. Senate and barred from American film for seven years.

Bergman had three children with Rossellini (including actress/model Isabella Rossellini), but their marriage was annulled in 1958. That same year Bergman married for the third time, this time to Lars Schmidt, a Swedish stage producer. They divorced in 1975.

Swedish-born actress Ingrid Bergman was a favorite with movie audiences in the 1940s. She is best known for her role as Ilsa in the classic film Casablanca.

In 1956 Bergman won a second Academy Award for her role in *Anastasia*—the official sign that her American exile was over. Her "sins" had been forgiven. She then undertook a variety of roles in stage, film, and television. Her portrayal of a nursemaid in *Murder on the Orient Express* (1974) garnered her a third Oscar, as Best Supporting Actress. The much beloved actress's last role was as Israeli prime minister Golda Meir, in the television movie "A Woman Called Golda" in 1981. On August 29, 1982, her sixty-seventh birthday, Bergman died after a long battle with cancer. In 1999 she was named a Screen Legend by the American Film Institute.

See Bogart, Humphrey; Casablanca

nicated to the viewer, and the film's opening scenes are intent on expressing the three protagonists' common bond. Their journey home, nestled in the nose of a B-29, suggests not only the camaraderie that the shared experiences of war bring about, but also emphasizes, in the cramped space and tight frame they occupy, that the service and its symbols have provided them a home far more real, at least for the moment, than the home to which they are anxiously returning.

In a single-take scene, Homer (played by a serviceman who actually lost his hands during the war) explains to the others how he lost his hands. Later, they ride through Boone City in a taxi, gawking at the rapidly passing sights and sounds of a changed world captured in a lyrical montage of pans and traveling shots.

The three homecomings delineate simply but effectively the particular problems each man will face. Homer must come to terms with the shock of his parents and other family members over his physical trauma and his determination to find a path to a normal life. Al, who had been a well-

The American classic The Best Years of Our Lives *follows three veterans as they readjust to civilian life after World War II.*

▼

established banker before the war, comes home to a loving wife, Milly (Myrna Loy), but a much-changed household and grown-up children (his daughter, Peggy [Teresa Wright], has blossomed into a young woman, and his son, Rob, is already in college). These changes shake his confidence in himself and his way of life. Fred, who had endured poverty and dead-end jobs, comes home to a cold and demanding wife and bleak job prospects. The social milieu of Fred's world—his shabby home, his weary, dispirited mother, and his alcoholic father—underscores his desperation.

The script's careful but natural patterning allows a parallel development for the veterans' stories and also assures that the path of each man crosses and re-crosses those of the other two. *Best Years* divides into three unequal segments: homecoming, problems of adjustment (the major concern of the film), and, after a cathartic moment, resolution. Although it may seem coincidental that characters from quite different social spheres should cross paths in what appears to be a good-sized city, we seldom feel that their meetings have been contrived. Homer, early in the film, points out to his two new friends the bar owned by his uncle, Butch Engle (Hoagy Carmichael). Fred offhandedly suggests that they should all get together there sometime. But it is not simply dramatic structuring that brings them to Butch's place on their very first night home; rather, it is their common disappointments. Fred can't find his wife, Homer can't cope with the awkward concern of his family, and Al, almost afraid to be alone with his wife, needs a night on the town in order to relax. After a heavy bout of drinking, Fred is taken to Al's home, where, tormented by nightmares of his bombing missions over Germany, he finds himself being reassured by Al's daughter, Peggy, who is evidently taken with him. After apologizing for troubling the family, Fred goes home again and finally is reunited with his tawdry wife, who seems interested only in the surface glamour of the uniform he despises and in milking him for his veteran's benefits. Stymied in his job search, he dejectedly returns to the job he held before the war: working the soda counter at the local drugstore.

Homer appears at the bank where Al works as a loan officer and after they speak briefly, Al grants him a loan, even though Homer has no collateral. In approving the loan, Al is able to assert his independence from the conservative policies of the bank's management. Homer, meanwhile, is obliged to confront his insecurities over his physical debility when Wilma, the prewar girlfriend he has been avoiding, comes to visit him in hopes of convincing him to marry her. Attempting to repel her, Homer insists that she perform the nightly ritual of removing his mechanical hooks so she can see how helpless and dependent he is. Her loving, supportive response overwhelms him emotionally, reducing him to tears of gratitude.

At the drugstore, Fred's defense of Homer against an agitator's taunts ends up in fisticuffs and costs Fred his job. His marital slide steepens as his wife begins seeing another man and he begins courting Peggy, much to the

"I'm not an officer and a gentleman anymore, just a soda jerk out of a job."

Dana Andrews as ex-captain Fred Derry in *The Best Years of Our Lives* (1946)

consternation of her father, Al, who forbids her to see him again. Despondent, Fred decides to leave town and makes a plane reservation. Before his departure, however, he comes across a storage area for damaged war planes. Mounting the cockpit of one of the planes, he begins to imagine himself back in the thick of combat. Mercifully, his tormented reverie is dispelled by an attendant, who orders him out of the plane. When Fred learns that the aircraft are to serve as the raw material for new housing, he asks for a construction job and is hired. Fred then cancels his travel plans.

Homer marries Wilma, and at the ceremony Fred sees Peggy, and they embrace passionately. Promising her only lean years and struggle, he searches her face for a response, and her glowing smile assures him that their life together is about to begin.

See Goldwyn, Samuel; Wyler, William

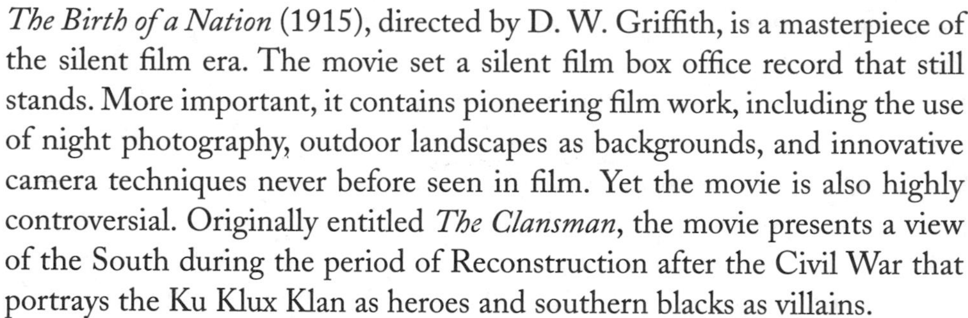

BIRTH OF A NATION, THE

"The bringing of the African to America planted the first seed of disunion."

Title from *The Birth of a Nation* (1915)

The Birth of a Nation (1915), directed by D. W. Griffith, is a masterpiece of the silent film era. The movie set a silent film box office record that still stands. More important, it contains pioneering film work, including the use of night photography, outdoor landscapes as backgrounds, and innovative camera techniques never before seen in film. Yet the movie is also highly controversial. Originally entitled *The Clansman*, the movie presents a view of the South during the period of Reconstruction after the Civil War that portrays the Ku Klux Klan as heroes and southern blacks as villains.

The story opens with a prologue that shows the introduction of slavery into America in the seventeenth century and the rise of the abolitionist movement in the 1800s. The tale then shifts to 1860 and introduces two families—the antislavery Stonemans of Washington, D.C., and the slave-owning Camerons of Piedmont, South Carolina. The two families know each other because their sons attend boarding school together.

While Phil and Tod Stoneman (Elmer Clifton and Robert Harron, respectively) are visiting the Camerons in South Carolina, romance develops between Phil and Margaret Cameron (Miriam Cooper), the eldest daughter in the family. Meanwhile, young Ben Cameron (Henry B. Wathall) becomes enchanted with the image of Phil's sister Elsie (Lillian Gish), whom he sees in a daguerreotype. As the Camerons entertain the Stoneman boys, the slaves in the household are hard at work on the plantation.

One evening Dr. Cameron (Spottiswoode Aitken) reads aloud news of the South's threat to secede from the Union. Soon after, the Stoneman boys return north. The outbreak of the Civil War then disrupts the relationship between the Stonemans and Camerons, as the boys of each family join the opposing armies of the North and South.

Two years pass, and Ben Cameron, who is on the march with the Confederate army, receives a letter from his sister Flora (Mae Marsh). In it, she tells him that Piedmont has been ravaged by the war and their home ransacked and burned. As he reads the letter, Ben's thoughts go to Elsie Stoneman. In the meantime, Duke Cameron (Maxfield Stanley) is about to bayonet a wounded Union soldier in battle and is shocked to see that it is his old friend Tod Stoneman. At that instant Tod dies, and Duke, shot by a bullet, falls down next to the body of his friend.

During the last days of the war, Stoneman and Cameron youth meet in battle again. During a desperate assault against Union troops commanded by Captain Phil Stoneman, Ben Cameron is seriously wounded. The war ends soon after, and the Camerons get word that their son Ben is near death

Although The Birth of a Nation *is highly regarded for its groundbreaking cinematic techniques, the content of the film is considered racist and inflammatory.*

▼

at a Union military hospital (the same one in which Elsie Stoneman is working). Phil Stoneman writes to his sister and asks her to take special care of Ben. Ben finally meets Elsie, the girl of his dreams.

Ben recovers and returns to South Carolina, kissing Elsie on the hand before he leaves. As he reaches home, weary and in despair, he finds his family anxiously awaiting his return.

The story now moves ahead to the period of Reconstruction. Southern blacks have gained their freedom, and northern carpetbaggers are flocking to the south to take advantage of the situation. In the north, Congressman Austin Stoneman (Ralph Lewis), the father of Phil and Elsie, is working to ensure equality for southern blacks. He sends his mulatto aide Silas Lynch (George Siegmann) to Piedmont, South Carolina, to enforce the new Reconstruction laws. As he leaves, Lynch shows an interest in Elsie. Stoneman leaves for South Carolina soon afterward, taking Elsie with him.

The Stonemans arrive in Piedmont, where Ben Cameron and Elsie meet again. While walking outdoors, they kiss as Silas Lynch spies on them. In the meantime, Phil Stoneman approaches Margaret Cameron, his former love. But she refuses to speak to him because she thinks about her brother Wade lying dead on the battlefield. Elsie and Ben are in love, but the bitter memories of the war remain a divide between them.

As Reconstruction proceeds, southern blacks take control in the south. The film depicts them as power crazed, disgraceful, lazy, and abusive toward whites and any blacks who pine for the good old days. White southerners grow increasingly angry at the actions of black legislators and white carpetbaggers.

Ben Cameron helps organize a secret vigilante group, the Ku Klux Klan, to frighten blacks and keep them in their place. When Elsie finds out that Ben belongs to this murderous group, she breaks off their relationship but promises not to let others know of his involvement. Ben's little sister Flora tries to console him and then goes out to fetch water.

While Flora goes to a spring with a bucket, Gus (Walter Long), a former black slave, follows her and makes advances. Flora runs away and scrambles up a rocky cliff. As he approaches she fears being raped or dishonored, so she leaps off the cliff. Ben finds her and she dies in his arms.

Ben enlists fellow townspeople to search for Gus, who has fled for his life. After a dramatic chase, Gus is captured and lynched by angry members of the Klan. When Silas Lynch discovers Gus's body, he orders black militia to fill the streets of Piedmont. He also dispatches spies to hunt out Klan members so they can be brought to justice.

The black militia storms the Cameron house and seizes the elder Dr. Cameron for harboring Klansmen. Ben and Margaret get away with the help of two loyal black servants. Together with Phil Stoneman, they rescue their father and flee from town.

Meanwhile, Elsie goes to Silas Lynch for help, not knowing his feelings toward her. When he proposes marriage, she threatens him with a horse-

B

HUMPHREY BOGART

Humphrey DeForest Bogart was born in New York City on January 23, 1899. "Bogie" was to develop a screen image as a world-weary, cynical toughie, but in actuality, he led a privileged early life. His father was a prominent surgeon in New York, his mother a magazine illustrator. He was sent to Phillips Academy, an exclusive college preparatory school in Andover, Massachusetts, but was expelled for an unknown reason.

Bogart joined the navy when the United States entered World War I. The story goes that Bogart was injured during a shelling on board a navy ship, resulting in his scarred and partly paralyzed upper lip and giving him the slight lisp that moviegoers would come to know so well. It is not clear if this story is fact or a concoction of a press agent. Another version claims that the impediment resulted when Bogart got into a fight with a naval prisoner he was escorting to jail. Whatever its cause, however, the fact is that this physical characteristic of Bogie's helped to define some of his most memorable film characters, such as detective Sam Spade and mercenary-turned-nightclub owner Rick Blaine.

After his stint in the navy, Bogart contacted a family friend, producer William Brady, for work. He subsequently performed various jobs in theater and Brady's film company, from office boy to stage manager. He began acting in small roles on stage in 1920 and in film in 1930, but it wasn't until 1936 that Bogart got his big break: the part of gangster Duke Mantee in *The Petrified Forest,* a reprisal of a role he had performed on Broadway. The film was a huge success, and it launched Bogart, finally, on the road to stardom.

For the next few years Bogart acted in several dozen films, usually as a gangster. One superb turn was opposite James Cagney in *The Roaring Twenties* (1939). In 1941 his performances in *High Sierra* and *The Maltese Falcon* electrified audiences, and he followed up with other great roles: in *Casablanca* (1942)—the film with which he is most associated, *The Big Sleep* (1946), *Key Largo* (1948), and *The Treasure of the Sierra Madre* (1948).

The 1940s were *the* decade of Bogart, but he acted in a few wonderful films in the 1950s, including *The African Queen* (1951), *Sabrina* (1954), and *The Caine Mutiny* (1954). His final movie appearance was in *The Harder They Fall* (1956). He died of cancer the following year.

Bogart, who apparently had a penchant for roughhousing and heavy drinking, was married four times, always to actresses. His marriage to Lauren Bacall, with whom he starred in *To Have and Have Not* (1944), was reportedly the best by far; it was "the stuff that legends are made of." They were together until his death in 1957. They had two children: a son, Stephen, and a daughter, Leslie.

Bogart won a Best Actor Academy Award for his role in *The African Queen* (the only Oscar he won despite several nominations during his career). In 1999 the American Film Institute named Bogart the Greatest Film Legend (number one on the men's list) of all time. He has been the subject of numerous film retrospectives and biographies.

See African Queen; *Bacall, Lauren; Cagney, James;* Casablanca; *Hepburn, Katharine;* Maltese Falcon; *Huston, John;* Treasure of the Sierra Madre

Humphrey Bogart's annual salary in 1942 was $114,125, while Abbot and Costello together earned $786,628.

whipping. But Lynch, lusting for power and Elsie, corners her and orders his aides to began preparing for a forced marriage. Elsewhere, Klansmen began to rally in the name of white womanhood, honor, and glory. They ride to rescue Elsie, the Camerons, and Phil Stoneman.

In the final climatic scenes of the movie, the Klansmen rescue Elsie, the Camerons, and Phil. White supremacy is restored. The Cameron and Stoneman families are also brought together as Phil and Margaret and Ben and Elsie reconcile their differences and renew their love.

See Epic; Ford, John; Gish, Lillian; Griffith, D. W.

BLAXPLOITATION FILM

notable & quotable

"They call her Coffy and she'll cream you!"

Tagline for blaxploitation film Coffy *(1973)*

Blaxploitation films were commercial-minded films of the 1970s made to appeal specifically to the interests of black audiences. The design of such films drew heavily on the popularity of black actors in screen stories that were often highly sensational. Tough crime plots with a superhero figure (*Shaft,* 1971) were common ingredients. The commercial success of *Shaft,* directed by black director Gordon Parks, generated many imitations that were made to capitalize on the drawing power of action films with black heroes. Other titles within the genre include *Melinda* (1971), *Superfly T.N.T.* (1973), *Black Belt Jones* (1974), *Three the Hard Way* (1974), and *Coffy* (1973).

BONNIE AND CLYDE

The controversial gangster film *Bonnie and Clyde* left an indelible mark on American cinema. When it opened in 1967, American moviegoers were confronted with a film unlike any they had seen before. Its scenes of graphic violence were unprecedented, and the hail of bullets that killed the title characters in the final scene permanently changed the way that movies depicted violence. Combining comedy, terror, love, and violence, the movie also redefined and romanticized the crime/gangster genre of film, allowing gangsters in future films to be portrayed as romantic fugitives and likable folk heroes.

The star of the film, Warren Beatty, was already quite well known, but his willingness to play a violent, sexually dysfunctional character was very

unusual for a 1960s leading man. The film's other star, Faye Dunaway, was an unknown actress who went on to become a huge star as a result of her work in the movie. *Bonnie and Clyde* also boosted the careers of several of its other little-known actors, including Gene Hackman, Estelle Parsons, Gene Wilder, and Michael J. Pollard. The film's inventive director, Arthur Penn, became forever remembered for his masterpiece.

Bonnie and Clyde is loosely based on the real-life characters Bonnie Parker and Clyde Barrow, two notorious outlaws and bank robbers whose gang terrorized parts of the midwest and southwest in the early 1930s.

The story begins in a small town in Texas, where Bonnie Parker (Faye Dunaway) is a beautiful but bored waitress in a Depression-era cafe. While looking out the window of her house, she sees a man attempting to steal her mother's car. She yells at him and rushes out to confront the thief, a handsome, well-dressed drifter named Clyde Barrow (Warren Beatty). Thcy

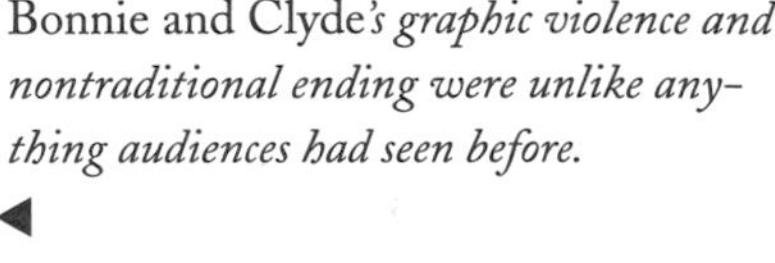

Bonnie and Clyde*'s graphic violence and nontraditional ending were unlike anything audiences had seen before.*

◀

start talking and before long Clyde is bragging to her about his stint in a state prison. Bonnie is intrigued by his charm and recklessness.

Clyde shows Bonnie his pistol, and to further impress her, he robs a small grocery store. As he runs to a car and hot-wires it to escape, Bonnie jumps in the front seat and they race off together, laughing hysterically. As they speed through the countryside Bonnie becomes sexually excited and she smothers Clyde with hugs and kisses. When Clyde pushes her away, Bonnie lashes out and says that he is not what he appears to be. Nevertheless, they go off together.

Over the next few days, Bonnie and Clyde pull off several small robberies and hide in deserted farmhouses at night. During their exploits they meet a dim-witted gas station attendant and mechanic named C. W. Moss (Michael J. Pollard), who fixes their stolen car. They invite Moss to join them and become a member of the Barrow gang.

"Your advertising is just dandy. Folks would never guess you didn't have anything to sell."

Faye Dunaway as Bonnie Parker, commenting on Clyde's lack of libido, in *Bonnie and Clyde* (1967)

The next robbery goes awry when Bonnie and Clyde have trouble finding C. W. and the getaway car. When they finally start driving away, Clyde kills the bank manager as he chases them. This is his first killing. Soon after, they are joined by Buck Barrow (Gene Hackman), Clyde's ex-con brother, and Buck's excitable wife, Blanche (Estelle Parsons). Together, the gang goes to Joplin, Missouri, where the outlaws settle down and rent an apartment over a garage. It is not too long before the police have discovered their hideout and begin to close in. While looking out the window, Clyde sees a police car. The excitable Blanche screams hysterically, and bullets begin to fly. The gang escapes the wild shoot-out, but several cops are killed.

After leaving Joplin, the Barrow gang drives cross-country searching for a safe haven. Along the way they steal a newspaper from a mailbox and read the news about their exploits, which makes them feel like celebrities. While parked beside a lake on a deserted road, the gang is discovered by a Texas Ranger, Captain Frank Hamer (Denver Pyle). They capture Hamer, handcuff him, and pose with him for pictures. When Bonnie kisses Hamer he spits in her face. Enraged, Clyde almost drowns the officer, but Buck stops him. They put the sheriff in a boat and push it into the lake.

Soon afterward, the gang commits another bank robbery. A police chase ensues, but the gang escapes by crossing the border into Oklahoma. When they discover that their stolen car is leaking oil, they steal a car belonging to mild-mannered Eugene Grizzard (Gene Wilder) and his fiancée, Velma Davis (Evans Evans). Eugene and Velma take chase in another car, but when they turn around to head for the police, the Barrow gang pursues and catches the terrified couple. Eugene and Velma are kidnapped and taken for a joyride. Along the way they talk, swap jokes, and eat hamburgers. Clyde asks if they would like to join the gang, but when Bonnie finds out that Eugene is a mortician she orders Clyde to leave them by the side of the road.

Bonnie feels a bit homesick now, so the gang goes to see her mother. During this clandestine reunion, Mrs. Parker voices concern for their safety, and Bonnie seems to realize that her days are numbered. They leave and drive to Iowa, where they hide out in a cheap tourist motel.

While staying at the motel, Blanche and C. W. are sent to get chicken dinners at a roadside cafe. One of the other customers notices a gun in C. W.'s pocket and notifies the sheriff. Within a short time the police have surrounded the hideout. During the bloody ambush that follows, Buck is shot in the face and Blanche is blinded by a bullet. They all manage to escape, however, and stop at a farm field.

By the next morning, the police have discovered the gang's trail and have surrounded the field. In another bloody shoot-out, Buck is killed and Blanche is captured. Bonnie, Clyde, and C. W. escape and head for the home of C. W.'s father in Louisiana. When they arrive, Mr. Moss (Dub Taylor) appears hospitable, but he is angered by his son's association with Bonnie and Clyde. Meanwhile, back in Iowa, Blanche inadvertently reveals C. W.'s last name to the police, allowing them to track Bonnie and Clyde.

The police arrive in Louisiana and secretly contact Mr. Moss, who agrees to help them get Bonnie and Clyde in exchange for a more lenient sentence for his son. A traitorous C. W., out of loyalty to his father, agrees not to accompany his friends when they leave.

Later, as Bonnie and Clyde drive down the road, they stop to help Mr. Moss change a flat tire (which he has faked). The police, meanwhile, are waiting in ambush behind thick shrubbery across the road. When Mr. Moss dives beneath his truck, the shooting begins. In a series of slow-motion and freeze-frame shots, the camera shows Bonnie and Clyde as they are gunned down and riddled by bullets. This beautifully filmed final scene is both horrifying and unforgettable.

When *Bonnie and Clyde* originally opened, many critics panned it, and the movie closed rather quickly. But some critics began to have second thoughts. The movie reopened and became one of the biggest box office hits of the year. Nominated for ten Academy Awards, the film won only two—Supporting Actress (Estelle Parsons) and Cinematography. Yet most critics and film historians consider the film much more important than the number of awards would suggest.

See Dunaway, Faye; Hackman, Gene; Kael, Pauline

BOW, CLARA

Did film make any real contribution to twentieth-century American culture? Most standard history texts are silent on the issue. For example, in Frank Freidel's *America in the Twentieth Century,* the impact of the cinema is reduced to the following:

> Motion pictures flamboyantly heralded the new moral code and together with tabloid papers helped fabricate false stereotypes of the period. An estimated 50 million people a week went to theaters to see the "It" girl, Clara Bow, the glamorous Rudolph Valentino, comedian Charlie Chaplin, gangster pictures, Westerns, and great spectacles like the first film version of *The Ten Commandments.* (*America in the Twentieth Century* [New York: Knopf, 1976], p. 154)

A further line about *The Jazz Singer* and the obligatory early mention of *The Birth of a Nation* are the limit of this text's acknowledgment of the motion picture. Other volumes might alter the supporting players, but Clara Bow, the "It" girl, remains a constant. When she died in 1965, her obituary was carried on the front page of the *New York Times.*

At the height of her popularity, the "It" girl, Clara Bow, received over 45,000 fan letters a month.

One would expect to see this importance reflected in numerous critical studies, monographs, and retrospectives, but such is definitely not the case. Clara Bow may be the cultural historians' idea of a silent star, but she rates hardly a mention from most film specialists.

There seems to be quite a difference of opinion here, and it turns on the real significance of Bow's position as a prototypical flapper. Colleen Moore was certainly the first to establish the screen archetype of the flapper, as early as 1923 in *Flaming Youth.* She was far more articulate than Bow, and with her own producing company, she had a degree of control over her roles to which Bow never even aspired. But Bow ensured her place in history in more spectacular ways. First, while Colleen Moore led a relatively decorous offscreen life, Clara Bow, in Adolph Zukor's words, "was exactly the same off the screen as on." More important, Bow was targeted by Elinor Glyn as the prime female possessor of "It," a fantastically successful promotional gambit that outlived Glyn and overwhelmed anything else one might say about Bow.

Madam Glyn, author of the scandalous best-seller *Three Weeks* (published in 1907 and filmed at least twice, most notably in 1924), had taken on herself the mission of instructing Hollywood society in proper standards of civilized behavior. Appalled by the various levels of vulgarity she found in Hollywood, Glyn formulated the concept of "It," an attractive aura of poise and self-confidence that she found all too rare among American film stars:

> To have "It," the fortunate possessor must have that strange magnetism which attracts both sexes. "It" is a purely virile quality, belonging to a strong character. He or she must be entirely unself-conscious and full of self-confidence, indifferent to the effect he or she is producing, and uninfluenced by others. There must be physical attraction, but beauty is unnecessary. Conceit or self-consciousness destroys "It" immediately. (quoted in James Robert Parish, *The Paramount Pretties,* p. 65)

"It" soon came to dominate the life and career of Clara Bow, which until then had been largely unexceptional. In 1921 she had entered one of many beauty contests then being sponsored by the fan magazines, from which she emerged with a screen test and a part in a real movie. Her scenes wound up on the cutting-room floor, but she eventually came under contract to B. P. Schulberg, a former Paramount executive then operating the "Poverty Row" studio, Preferred Pictures. Schulberg used her in some of his own films and skillfully built up her value by loaning her out to other producers. In 1924 she appeared in eight features, and in 1925 she was seen in fourteen, including Lubitsch's *Kiss Me Again* for Warners. When Schulberg rejoined Paramount late in 1925, he brought Bow with him, and with first-class stories, costars, and production values her popularity soared.

Surviving Bow films, especially *Mantrap* (1926), *Kid Boots* (1926), *Get Your Man* (1927), and *Red Hair* (1928), showed a natural comedienne,

notable & quotable

"Between 1922 and 1929 Clara Bow's vitality, sexiness, vivaciousness and acting naturalism defined the liberated woman of the 20's."

Diane MacIntyre, author, as quoted in The Silents Majority, *copyright 1996–99*

blending sexiness and humor. This accessible, home-grown sexuality, radiating the special magnetism that so captured the likes of Elinor Glyn, did offer a new screen vision of the American woman. But the whole "It girl" idea was so bound up with the ethos of the 1920s that Depression-era audiences rejected it, and Bow's career ended in 1933. It seems that the icons of one age can quickly become the "false stereotypes" of the next.

See Lubitsch, Ernst

MARLON BRANDO

Marlon Brando Jr. was born on April 3, 1924, in Omaha, Nebraska. His father, Marlon Sr., was a salesman, his mother an actress in local theater. Their son attended a military academy in Minnesota; after he was expelled (apparently showing an early penchant for causing trouble), he came to New York, where he studied acting with Stella Adler. He worked extensively with Lee Strasberg at the Actors Studio, where he, along with Kim Stanley, Montgomery Clift, Rip Torn, and Geraldine Page, became the leading representatives of "method acting."

People in the entertainment industry recognized quickly that there was something special about Brando. He was only twenty when he made his Broadway debut, as Nels in *I Remember Mama.* He acted in several other Broadway plays over the next few years, but it was his Broadway performance as the brutish Stanley Kowalski in *A Streetcar Named Desire* (1947) that made him a star.

With his dark, brooding good looks and naturalistic method-style acting, Marlon Brando has enjoyed a career that spans almost 50 years.

Brando's first movie role was as an angry paraplegic in *The Men* (1950). He "studied" for his performance by spending a month in a hospital rehabilitation ward—a common approach to a role today, but unique in that era. Over the next four years, Brando's naturalistic method style of acting, combined with his dark, brooding good looks and frank sexuality, brought him exceptional film roles—and Academy Award nominations for his acting as Kowalski in *A Streetcar Named Desire* (1951), Mexican revolutionary Emiliano Zapata in *Viva Zapata!* (1952), Marc Antony in *Julius Caesar* (1953), and Terry Malloy in *On the Waterfront* (1954). It was in the latter film that Brando uttered the lines that are most associated with him: "I coulda been somebody. I coulda been a contender." He later brushed off praise for his delivery, suggesting that the lines were so perfect that they were actor-proof. The Academy disagreed, finding something special in his performance and awarding him the Best Actor Oscar.

Brando's nonconformity was perfectly in sync with the interests of filmgoers in the 1950s. One would have thought that such an iconoclast would have excelled in the 1960s as well, but he chose to participate in a series of so-so movies, such as 1960's *One-Eyed Jacks,* which he also directed, *The Ugly American* (1963), and *Candy* (1968). His personal life was of more interest than his professional one. The story goes that while he was filming a remake of *Mutiny on the Bounty* (1962) in Tahiti, Brando—who always had a reputation as a womanizer—was involved in sexual liaisons with many local women, leaving behind a trail of venereal disease. In later years he would make his home on a nearby island and marry a Tahitian woman. (He married two other times; all three marriages ended in divorce.)

All in a 12-days' work: After his original $3.5 million for 10 minutes' screen time in *Superman* (1978), Marlon Brando was awarded an additional $15 million in a 1982 settlement out of court.

In the 1970s Brando's career revived when director Francis Ford Coppola hired him to play the title character in the blockbuster film *The Godfather* (1972). The studio initially opposed the casting, as Brando by then had an iffy reputation with producers, but Brando proved that Coppola had made the right choice when he won the Academy Award for Best Actor for that role. (Brando later refused to accept the statuette in protest of the treatment of American Indians.) Another film released in 1972, *Last Tango in Paris,* caused a sensation. Brando's gutsy performance in the film, which explored middle-aged sexuality, won him praise as well as derision (particularly in regard to his less-than-svelte body). Brando had pivotal roles in several other films during that decade, including *Superman* (1978) and *Apocalypse Now* (1979).

Brando performed in several mildly successful movies in the 1990s, such as *The Freshman* and *Don Juan DeMarco* (1995), but it was his personal life that riveted people's attention. His son Christian was arrested and convicted for killing the boyfriend of his half sister Cheyenne in Los Angeles; Brando's appearance on the stand during the trial caused a media frenzy. And tragically, Cheyenne committed suicide in 1994. In 1997 Brando again raised eyebrows when he stated in an interview that Hollywood is "run by Jews," setting off charges of anti-Semitism.

See Chaplin, Charlie; Coppola, Francis Ford; Godfather, The; *Kazan, Elia; Method actor;* On the Waterfront; Streetcar Named Desire, A

B-PICTURE

The term B-picture refers to a film that appeared on double-feature bills in the 1930s, 1940s, and 1950s. The B-picture was usually the second movie on a two-picture bill. It was characteristically inferior to the main picture (A-picture): low budget, lesser-known stars, reworked themes from familiar genres such as the western and science-fiction story. Production of B-pictures for theatrical release ceased in the late 1940s, although the characteristics of this type of film have continued in the form of made-for-television movies. The term is sometimes used in contemporary film criticism in a derogatory manner to describe a low-budget film or a film of inferior quality.

In recent years many film critics and historians have expressed an intense interest in the study of the B-picture category and its directors. They argue that this class of picture and its artists must be judged alongside the A-picture because of the important role each type played in motion-picture and cultural history, the economic system that produced the B-picture, and the perspective the B-picture provides in terms of both cinematic style and content with an art form that is ever-changing. Among the many memorable B-pictures are John Blystone's *Great Guy* (1936), Edgar Ulmer's *Detour* (1945), and Roger Corman's *Apache Woman* (1955).

See A-picture; Feature film

BREAKFAST AT TIFFANY'S

Breakfast at Tiffany's (1961), a drama with strong romantic and comedic components, is based on a novella of the same name by Truman Capote. The screenplay (by George Axelrod) lightened the dark tone of Capote's work and substituted a happy ending. Directed by Blake Edwards, *Breakfast at Tiffany's* was a box-office success.

As the film opens, it is very, very early in the morning. Holly Golightly (Audrey Hepburn), in black evening gown and sunglasses, climbs out of a cab on Fifth Avenue in New York City. She faces the imposing storefront of Tiffany's, her favorite jewelry store, and then meanders home.

A new resident is moving into Holly's small brownstone apartment building: Paul Varjak (George Peppard), a handsome young man who is "sponsored" in his writing ambitions by a rich older woman, Miss Thalan-

son (Patricia Neal). Paul introduces Miss Thalanson as his "decorator." Holly is skeptical; she guesses that Paul is a kept man. For his part, as he looks around her sparsely furnished apartment and gets to know something of her eccentric habits, Paul soon becomes aware that Holly, too, has her secrets. He learns that Holly receives money from men, her "rats" and "super-rats," and is paid to collect messages—"weather reports"—from Sally Tomato (Alan Reed), a notorious mobster who is imprisoned in Sing Sing.

Holly is beautiful and charming, and she has many acquaintances. But she seems attached only to her cat, named Cat, and to her brother, Fred, a sweet but slow boy who is away in the army.

When Holly has a party—one of the most entertaining party scenes ever filmed—Paul becomes acquainted with her social circle. Paul ends up

Audrey Hepburn delighted audiences as Holly Golightly, a gold-digging but ultimately lovable New Yorker. ◀

talking with O. J. Berman (Martin Balsam), a movie-producer type who likes Holly. He considers her "a phony, but a real phony." He tells Paul how he discovered Holly; she had style and class, but a hillbilly accent that it took him a year to help her get rid of. Holly opted to go to New York rather than audition for the movies in Hollywood.

Holly zeroes in on one party guest: Rusty Trawler (Stanley Adams). He is physically repulsive but has an unmistakable allure: he is "the ninth richest man in America under fifty," a statistic that Paul finds fascinating for a young woman to have at her fingertips. Later, when Trawler surprises her by marrying another woman, Holly takes up with Jose da Silva Perreira (Jose Luis de Villalonga), a handsome—and wealthy—Brazilian politico.

One day Paul's sponsor arrives, looking frightened: a man is lurking outside the brownstone, and she is concerned that she is being followed. Paul confronts him and learns that he is Doc Golightly (Buddy Ebsen), a veterinarian and farmer from Texas. Not only is Holly's name really Lula Mae, Doc explains, but she is Doc's wife and has four stepchildren. He wants her to come home. As they talk in the park, Paul keeps the prize from a box of Cracker Jacks that Doc had purchased: a plain ring, like a wedding band.

"If I found a real-life place that made me feel like Tiffany's, then I'd buy some furniture and give the cat a name."

Audrey Hepburn as Holly Golightly in *Breakfast at Tiffany's* (1961)

Holly is happy to see Doc, but she won't go back with him—she's not Lula Mae anymore. She and Paul see Doc off at the bus station. That night Holly gets drunk and cruelly mocks Paul for taking money from women.

Meanwhile, Paul has gotten serious about writing, and later he is elated to receive notice that his story has been accepted for publication. He and Holly go out to celebrate. They walk into Tiffany's to buy something, but the only thing they can afford is to have the Cracker Jacks ring engraved.

Paul breaks off the relationship with his sponsor and begins to hope that Holly might love him. But Holly has decided to go to Brazil. Jose, she says, is "absolutely cuckoo" for her, and she has every reason to believe he will marry her.

One evening Paul hears Holly screaming behind her apartment door. Jose doesn't know what is wrong, and Paul reads a telegram that has arrived from Doc: Holly's brother, Fred, has been killed in a Jeep accident. Paul explains the situation to Jose, and leaves him to take care of Holly.

Some months later, Paul climbs the stairs to Holly's apartment. He has moved elsewhere, and she has invited him for dinner. The next day, she tells Paul, she is to fly to Brazil; Jose still has not proposed, but she has no doubt that marriage is in their future. Paul offers his best wishes, and Holly congratulates him, as she has seen several of his stories published.

Holly ends up ruining the meal, so they decide to go out for dinner instead. When they return, they are surprised by the police, who take Holly to the police station to answer questions about her relationship with Sally Tomato, the mobster. Paul calls Mr. Berman, who uses his influence to get Holly released. Paul picks up Holly at the police station and ushers her into a waiting cab. As they drive along the rain-streaked streets, he tells the driver to head for a hotel, where Holly will be kept safe from the press. He has even brought Cat with him. But Holly directs the cab driver to go to the airport. Paul then gives her a note from Jose, who has decided that Holly is far too notorious for him—she will cause career and family problems for him in Brazil. Thus, Paul reasons, they will cash in her airplane ticket to Brazil.

Holly is upset, then straightens up. She surprises Paul by asserting that she is going to be on that plane to Brazil anyway; she wants him to send her the names of "the fifty richest men in Brazil. The fifty *richest*!" Paul protests that he loves her, and that she belongs to him. She responds by stopping the cab and throwing Cat out the door, onto the wet sidewalk, saying that she doesn't belong to anyone, just like Cat, who doesn't even have a proper name.

Paul, disgusted, gets out, telling her that she is in a cage of her own making. He tosses a jeweler's box in the door of the cab, telling her he has been carrying it around for months, but he doesn't want it anymore.

As the cab drives on, Holly, alone now, opens the box. It is the engraved Cracker Jacks ring. She slowly slips it onto her ring finger . . . and then stops the cab. She jumps out and runs down the street. Paul stands in the rain, looking for Cat. Holly, weeping, cries, "Cat! Cat!"

Finally, she hears a meow from one of the wooden boxes in the alleyway: it is Cat, wet and bedraggled. Holly bundles him to her chest, folding him in her trench coat. As she walks toward Paul, he opens his arms and embraces her, Cat snugly between them. To the swelling strains of the movie's theme song, "Moon River" (which won an Academy Award), Holly and Paul kiss.

Though some critics made fun of the contrived ending, audiences loved it. The movie, with its colorful characters and sophisticated themes, remains an enduring favorite to this day.

See Hepburn, Audrey

"But I am mad about Jose. I honestly think I'd give up smoking if he asked me."

Audrey Hepburn as Holly Golightly in *Breakfast at Tiffany's* (1961)

BRENON, HERBERT

The postwar period marked a watershed in silent-feature production, and few successful directors operated in the twenties who had been equally prominent in the early days of feature films. One of the most important was Herbert Brenon, a director originally noted as a pioneer of overseas location shooting and lavish spectacle who successfully adapted his style to the requirements of the postwar era. He developed a new reputation for his handling of actresses and adaptations of literary properties, and he closed out the silent era as one of its most popular and best-paid directors.

There was never a personality cult centered around Brenon and his work, however, and while the production of some of his films did make good copy, the man himself was too ordinary to capture the imagination of critics or acolytes. When he gradually stopped making films, he seems not to have been missed, and with so much of his key work gone, there is little possibility of reviving his reputation. Nevertheless, Brenon's career is crucial

Silent film director Herbert Brenon was equally at home with epic films and more restrained dramatic vehicles.

to understanding the development of the American studio system in this period.

Brenon was born in Dublin in 1880. He came to the United States in 1896 and looked for work in the theater, eventually finding a job directing a stock company in Minneapolis. He later found work as a scenario editor for the IMP studio. After five months behind a desk, Brenon was given the chance to direct his first film, *All for Her* (1912), which quickly established him as a director.

He made the first IMP three-reeler, *Leah the Forsaken* (1913), and later that year was sent to Europe, where he made important films in Britain, France, and Germany. The trip marked one of the few important attempts by American filmmakers to challenge the dominance of European producers by sending a complete crew right into their own backyard. Brenon's *Absinthe* (1913) appears to have been the first American film made in France, although French companies at the time were deeply involved in American production.

On his return to the United States, Brenon produced the seven-reel epic *Neptune's Daughter* (1914), an aquatic fantasy starring Annette Kellerman, which was a tremendous success. Moving to Fox, Brenon worked with Theda Bara for a time, then set out to top his success with the Kellerman picture through a kind of sequel, *A Daughter of the Gods* (1915–16). Taking over an entire corner of the island of Jamaica for eight months, he used 2,000,000 feet of lumber and 2,500 barrels of plaster to create vast, fantastic settings, and put 20,000 extras on the payroll. Far from Fox's supervision, Brenon shot 220,000 feet of negative and completely outstripped his budget. Worse, he began a war with William Fox over the personal publicity he was accruing (at Fox's expense), and when the company returned to New York, the film was taken from him and edited by the studio.

Brenon subsequently eschewed such spectacle, and *The Fall of the Romanoffs* (1917) was staged in his Hudson Heights studio. Becoming associated with more restrained dramatic vehicles, he directed some of the best films of Alla Nazimova, Norma Talmadge, and Pola Negri. Between 1923 and 1928 he was one of the key Paramount directors, and surviving films from this period, including the proto-feminist *Dancing Mothers* and the James M. Barrie adaptations *Peter Pan* (1925) and *A Kiss for Cinderella* (1926), reveal an exceptionally assured style. He closed out the silent era at the top of his form with *Beau Geste* (1926) and *Sorrell and Son* (1927) and was named the best director of 1927–28 in a massive *Film Daily* critics' poll.

But Brenon was unhappy with the talkies and labeled them a fad. An individualist in an increasingly producer-oriented system, Brenon found it harder to work in the manner in which he was accustomed and eventually returned to England, where he directed his last film in 1940.

See Bara, Theda; Negri, Pola; Talmadge, Norma; Vidor, King

B

BRIDGE ON THE RIVER KWAI, THE

In *The Bridge on the River Kwai* (1957) David Lean shows his ability to bring to life an epic tale filled with drama and psychological struggles of antagonists. The film takes on even greater meaning when the audience knows that the story of the bridge is based on real-life events.

The Bridge on the River Kwai is set in a World War II Japanese prisoner-of-war camp in Burma. The film centers around the conflict and psychological struggle between two power-obsessed commanding officers. On one side stands British colonel Nicholson (Alec Guinness); on the other, Japanese colonel Saito (Sessue Hayakawa). The film opens with Colonel Nicholson leading his men through the steaming jungle into the prison camp. As the British POWs march into the camp, they are watched by Shears (William Holden). Shears, an American sailor who has been a long-term

The Bridge on the River Kwai *is a psychological study of two power-obsessed commanding officers in World War II Burma.* ▼

inmate of the camp, has no respect for either commander and is only biding his time until he can escape. While Nicholson's goal seems to be retaining a sense of honor within the confines of the prison camp, Shears is looking only to survive.

The conflict between Nicholson and Saito emerges as Nicholson tries to apply his British rules of conduct to Saito. He contends that officers, under the Geneva Convention, are not required to carry out the manual labor needed to complete the bridge across the River Kwai. Saito, who must complete the bridge or commit suicide, forces the British officers to stand in the broiling sun as their troops set out to build the bridge.

With both commanders unwilling to compromise, Saito sends Nicholson off to sweat away in the "ovens"—small, corrugated tin boxes exposed to the tropical sun. While the two antagonists conduct their battle of wills, Shears and two British soldiers attempt escape. Only Shears is left alive as he falls into the river and is washed downstream. Shears eventually makes his way to a British hospital in Ceylon, where to obtain extra privileges he impersonates an officer.

Meanwhile, the conflict between Saito and Nicholson is resolved so that Saito is able to save face. Nicholson, portrayed as a stereotypical British officer with a stiff upper lip, sees the discipline of his men slipping away and arrives at a jarring solution. Rather than sabotaging the bridge building, he argues—in what could be considered a traitorous logic—that they should build the best bridge possible, a bridge they can be proud of. The switch between Nicholson and Saito becomes complete as Nicholson drives his men with more ferocity and determination than was ever shown by Saito.

While Shears passes the time in Ceylon impersonating an officer, he is confronted by Major Warden (Jack Hawkins). Warden is in charge of destroying the Kwai bridge and realizes that Shears's local knowledge of the area would be invaluable. Eventually, a reluctant Shears finds himself parachuting back into the Burmese jungle.

As the almost-complete bridge is destroyed, the story comes to its conclusion as the two commanders of opposing armies, both obsessed with the same objective, face the destruction of their dreams.

See Guinness, Alec; Lean, David

The first British film to be the top moneymaker in the U.S. was David Lean's *The Bridge on the River Kwai* in 1958.

"I hate the British. You are defeated but you have no shame. You are stubborn but you have no pride. You endure but you have no courage. I hate the British."

Sessue Hayakawa as Col. Saito in *The Bridge on the River Kwai* (1957)

BRINGING UP BABY

The legendary director Howard Hawks considered *Bringing Up Baby* (1938) to be his best comedy. The outrageous screwball film keeps up a hectic pace filled with zany antics, near perfect comic timing, a hilarious cast of

B

BRINGING UP BABY

characters, wild misadventures, pratfalls, impossible scenarios, and, of course, an unlikely romance. The film's screenplay by Dudley Nichols and Hagar Wilde is based on a short story by Wilde.

The film involves the perfect love/hate mismatch between a paleontologist, Dr. David Huxley (Cary Grant), and a madcap, eccentric heiress, Susan Vance (Katharine Hepburn). Grant and Hepburn are superbly matched in *Bringing Up Baby,* with Hepburn's ditzy socialite making an ideal foil for Grant's addled, absentminded professor. Charles Ruggles as Major Horace Applegate, a bumbling big-game hunter in suburbia, is but one of the fine supporting cast.

The film begins on the eve of Huxley's wedding day, as he tries to finish a painstaking, four-year labor of love: the reconstruction of a dinosaur skeleton at a museum. Only a single missing bone prevents completion of the monumental project. Without it, his museum will be denied a promised grant of $1 million. It is scheduled for delivery the next day, the date of Huxley's planned wedding to his fiancée, Alice Swallow (Virginia Walker).

Katharine Hepburn and Cary Grant play a madcap heiress and an absent-minded paleontologist in Billy Wilder's fast, funny screwball comedy Bringing Up Baby.

▼

But the hapless Huxley is now in the crosshairs of the cunning socialite Susan Vance, whose desperate schemes to entrap the bumbling scientist propel the plot on its delightfully improbable course. The indefatigable Vance tries everything to snare him: she swipes his golf ball, dents his car, and even steals his clothes to keep him near her.

By the end of the first day, Huxley tries to put Susan off and in doing so perfectly explains how she has turned his life upside down while at the same time admitting his attraction. He tells her, "Well anyway, I'm going to get married, Susan, and don't interrupt. . . . Now it isn't that I don't like you, Susan, because after all, in moments of quiet I'm strangely drawn toward you, but, well, there haven't been any quiet moments. Our relationship has been a series of misadventures from beginning to end." At the end of his speech, Huxley turns and falls headfirst into the pavement.

The next morning the bone that Huxley needs to complete his skeleton arrives in the mail. But Huxley is prevented from finishing the project when Susan convinces him to help her take a pet leopard, Baby, to her aunt's farm. In a rapid-fire sequence of hilariously implausible and outrageous scenes, Huxley ends up in a stolen car, loses his clothes, and ultimately learns that Susan's dog has buried his rare dinosaur bone in the backyard.

At Susan's Connecticut estate Huxley's quest for the million-dollar bone embroils him in still further insanity when a wild leopard escapes from a local zoo, and Susan, unable to distinguish her own Baby from the escapee, ends up inadvertently harboring the missing wild beast. Along with several locals and Huxley, Susan ends up in jail, where she scandalizes the local police by posing as a swaggering gun moll and taunting Huxley, threatening to expose the meek man of science as a dangerous criminal. Huxley is rescued from jail by his fiancée, but by this time she no longer wants to marry him.

In the end the bone is recovered, Huxley's museum gets its promised million, and Susan and Huxley end up together. But a final comic turn exemplifies the couple's relationship: Susan, as she places the prized bone in its place in the reconstructed dinosaur, causes the whole elaborate structure to come tumbling down atop her and Huxley.

See Hawks, Howard; Hepburn, Katharine

"There is a leopard on your roof and it's my leopard and I have to get it and to get it I have to sing."

Katharine Hepburn as Susan Vance in *Bringing Up Baby* (1938)

BROOKS, LOUISE

There is one actress who is destined to succeed Gloria Swanson some day in the hearts of movie fans. And, to our way of thinking, that actress

> is Louise Brooks. Her work in *A Social Celebrity* was a revelation. This girl has charm, experience, looks, personality, and BRAINS. (*Exhibitor's Trade Review,* 18 June 1926, p. 2)

In a sense, Louise Brooks did ultimately supplant Swanson in the hearts of movie fans, at least those who combined their nostalgia with a strong taste for the outré and the exotic. But the celebrity that Brooks achieved bears little relation to the Hollywood stardom of Norma Talmadge, Pola Negri, or Gloria Swanson. In her heyday at Paramount (1925–28) Brooks made few magazine covers, seldom achieved featured billing, and not infrequently appeared in support of W. C. Fields or Wallace Beery.

By no objective standard could Brooks be considered one of the major stars of the silent era, but today her status is unique. What historian Lotte

Although Louise Brooks is not considered one of the major stars of the silent era, today she enjoys a renewed popularity. ▶

Eisner once called "the miracle of Louise Brooks" became in the 1980s "the phenomenon of Louise Brooks." At a time not especially interested in silent film, a passion for Brooks and her work spread from a small circle of admirers to a broad international public. She became *The New Yorker*'s favorite silent-film star, published a surprisingly popular memoir, and saw festivals of her most obscure work reach museum screens around the world. Nonetheless, to view the silent film through the image of Louise Brooks is a substantial recasting of history.

Many reputations fall and rise over the years, but Brooks's renewed popularity was a rare instance of a major reordering of critical priorities. From the status of a minor entertainer, Brooks emerged as an icon of the decade. How this happened is not nearly so important as what it means to the study of film as a living art.

Initially, what critical reputation Brooks possessed was based on two films she made in Germany for G. W. Pabst, *Pandora's Box* (1929) and *Diary of a Lost Girl* (1929). Heavily censored and never widely released, they were known only to the cognescenti, who treasured the few prints collected in scattered archives.

Brooks entered film in 1925. Prior to this she toured as a dancer with the Denishawn Company (1922–24), then appeared in Broadway revues for George White and Florenz Ziegfeld. Her first films were made for Paramount in New York, but even the best of them, such as Frank Tuttle's *Love 'em and Leave 'em* (1926), fail to take full advantage of her radiant blend of innocence and sensuality. Nor is there much awareness of the character and intelligence in her face and eyes. In most of these films she is a traditional ingenue.

Her films improved when she transferred to Paramount's Hollywood studio in 1927–28, but the quality of her roles stayed about the same. Howard Hawks cast her as an anachronistic femme fatale in *A Girl in Every Port* (1928), and only in *Beggars of Life* (1928) did she have a role that brought out some of the contradictory elements of her screen personality. Tired of Hollywood life and the parts she was offered, Brooks left Paramount when the opportunity to work for Pabst arrived.

The acclaim Brooks later enjoyed was without direct parallel in film history. Revivals of interest in Humphrey Bogart, W. C. Fields, and Busby Berkeley were based on bodies of work widely applauded in their day, but Brooks had never made more than a minor splash. Artists or composers could pass their careers in silence, only to be "discovered" decades later, but until recently film lacked this kind of memory. Only when the work of scholars and archivists was sufficiently developed could such a reconsideration occur. That Brooks finally supplanted Gloria Swanson is due in no small measure to their efforts.

See Swanson, Gloria

BROOKS, MEL

Mel Brooks was born Melvin Kaminsky in Brooklyn, New York on June 28, 1926. One of the great masters of movie satire, Brooks is one of the most successful writers and directors of American film comedy.

The grandson of Russian Jewish immigrants, Brooks grew up in the predominately Jewish Williamsburg section of Brooklyn. Only two years old when his father died, Brooks and his three older brothers were raised alone by his mother. Brooks attributes her with instilling in him an "exuberant joy of living," which has been reflected throughout his career.

Mel Brooks, considered one of the most spontaneous comedians in the business, has made a career out of producing movie parodies such as Blazing Saddles *and* Young Frankenstein.

Brooks began clowning around as a youth, partly as a defense against abuse by his peers because he was small and sickly. It was years, however, before he considered pursuing comedy as a career. An early goal of becoming a pilot was put aside by thoughts of becoming a scientist. In the meantime, he learned to play the drums and became good enough to earn money playing after school and during the summer.

After attending Brooklyn College for a year, Brooks joined the U.S. Army and trained to be a combat engineer. He saw battle in Germany during the last years of World War II. After the war Brooks found jobs playing drums at nightclubs and Jewish resorts in the Catskill Mountains of New York State—the so-called Borscht Belt. It was at this time that he changed his name from Melvin Kaminsky to Mel Brooks to avoid being confused with another musician named Max Kaminsky. When a stand-up comic at one of the Catskill resorts became ill, Brooks took his place, launching a career as a stand-up comedian.

In the year of *Young Frankenstein* and *Blazing Saddles*—also known as 1974—the average film production cost was $2.5 million.

As a comic, Brooks gained a reputation for hilarious monologues and odd antics. He also tried his hand at acting, gaining roles in summer stock productions in New Jersey. In 1949 fellow comedian Sid Caesar, whom Brooks had met in the Catskills, asked him to help him write material for his TV show *Broadway Review*. This began a career in television. Brooks continued writing for Caesar for *Your Show of Shows*, and he occasionally appeared on that program as a comic as well. Brooks credits his years writing for Caesar as a great education for a comedian.

When Sid Caesar went off TV in 1958, Brooks tried his hand at writing for television specials. He also began working with writer-comedian Carl Reiner, making a series of "2,000-Year-Old Man" comedy recordings about funny, centuries-old men who knew many of the important people of history. These recordings earned Brooks a reputation as one of the most spontaneous comedians in the business. The spectacular success of the "2,000-Year-Old Man" recordings led to numerous television appearances as well as more TV writing assignments, including work on the popular satiric spy comedy *Get Smart*.

Brooks next ventured into film. His short film *The Critic*, which poked fun at modern art, won an Academy Award in 1963. Five years later his first feature-length film, *The Producers*, earned Brooks another Academy Award for best original screenplay. A hilariously funny satire on the Broadway theater world, the story in *The Producers* revolved around the production of a musical comedy called *Springtime for Hitler*. Considered vulgar and tasteless by many critics, the movie did poorly at the box office. But *The Producers* is now considered a classic American film comedy and one of the funniest films of all time. It also helped launch the career of comedian Gene Wilder, who starred in a number of Brooks's later films.

Brooks's next film, *The Twelve Chairs*, was released in 1970. A satire about post-revolutionary Russia, the film did poorly and seemed a setback to his career. Four years later, however, *Blazing Saddles* became a huge success. Brooks directed, cowrote, and costarred in this raucous satire of movie westerns. Its dark humor, racial epithets, and four-letter words outraged many critics, who felt that the movie went too far beyond the bounds of good taste. But the public obviously loved it, and it became one of the biggest moneymakers of 1974.

Blazing Saddles was followed by a remarkable series of comedies. Following right on its heels in 1974 was *Young Frankenstein*, a parody of the horror movies of the 1930s. This was followed by *Silent Movie* in 1976, *High Anxiety* in 1977, and *History of the World: Part One* in 1981. Each of these films was a parody on classic Hollywood films of the past. Once again the movies generally were panned by critics, but they proved quite popular at the box office. Beginning with *Silent Movie*, Brooks starred in his films as well as directing and producing them. This pleased his fans, but it was one reason for his disfavor with the critics.

"You've got to remember that these are just simple farmers. These are people of the land. The common clay of the new West. You know . . . morons."

Gene Wilder as Jim, the Waco Kid in *Blazing Saddles* (1974)

By the time *History of the World: Part One* was released, audiences had begun to grow weary of the typical gags and style of a "Mel Brooks movie." Nevertheless, Brooks continued to write, produce, direct, and star in comedies such as *Spaceballs* (1987), *Life Stinks* (1991), *Robin Hood: Men in Tights* (1993), and *Dracula: Dead and Loving It* (1995). Though less popular than earlier works, these films continued to showcase the special brand of screwball comedy for which Brooks is famous.

Although best known for his work in comedy, Brooks also produced a number of notable serious movies. These include *The Elephant Man*, which received eight Academy Award nominations in 1980, and *84 Charing Cross Road* (1986), which starred his wife, actress Anne Bancroft. Brooks also continued to work in the theater and to make cameo appearances on various television shows. For his role as Paul Buchman's Uncle Phil on the hit TV comedy series *Mad About You*, Brooks received an Emmy Award for Best Guest Actor in a Comedy Series.

Over the course of a career that spans nearly fifty years, Mel Brooks has made an indelible mark on American comedy—both on television and in movies. With their distinctive style and appeal, his madcap, "over-the-top" movie comedies have won the hearts of American filmgoers of all ages.

See Comedy; Producer

BUDDY FILMS

A type of film also popularly called "the buddy salvation" picture, a buddy film is so named because its stories involve male companionship. The term

came into use during the 1960s and early 1970s through the popularity of such films as *Midnight Cowboy* (1969), *Butch Cassidy and the Sundance Kid* (1969), *The Sting* (1973), *The Last Detail* (1973), *California Split* (1974), and *Freebie and the Bean* (1976). These were among the many films of the period dealing with men who help each other out during dramatic conflict and crisis. In these pictures women were relatively unimportant as pivotal characters. The popular, highly acclaimed *Thelma and Louise* (1991) successfully transferred the buddy film concept to female protagonists who celebrate companionship and who support each other emotionally. Presented in the form of a road picture, *Thelma and Louise* utilizes many of the action elements common to male buddy pictures such as *Butch Cassidy and the Sundance Kid* and *Freebie and the Bean.*

See Butch Cassidy and the Sundance Kid; Midnight Cowboy

BUTCH CASSIDY AND THE SUNDANCE KID

Butch Cassidy and the Sundance Kid (1969) is a western with a difference: While it is about two gunslinging outlaws, they are *endearing* outlaws. The audience can't help but root for these charming, good-natured rogues who thumb their noses at authority every chance they get. The film, directed by George Roy Hill, was a huge critical and commercial success, cementing the career of Paul Newman (Butch Cassidy) and making a star out of relative newcomer Robert Redford (the Sundance Kid).

The tale is based on the exploits of real-life characters who had long interested screenwriter William Goldman. The statement "Most of What Follows Is True" is posted after the opening credits, which are shown over a sepia-toned newsreel-type "film" about The Hole in the Wall Gang—our turn-of-the-century heroes.

As the action begins—still in sepia—Butch scopes out a bank at closing time; he's aware of every lock, latch, and bolt in the modernized building. He asks the guard about the old bank. The guard tells him it was robbed all the time—reason enough for the tightened security. Butch comments that frequent robberies were a small price to pay for beauty.

The film cuts to Sundance (Redford), who is handily beating some men at cards in a saloon. An opponent accuses him of cheating and threatens to draw his gun if Sundance doesn't forfeit the money. But when the man realizes whom he is dealing with, he apologizes and allows Sundance to leave with the money. As Sundance departs, the opponent asks him how good he is. Sundance gives him his answer: he turns and harmlessly shoots the man's belt off, sending his gun into the corner.

The third through fifth most popular films of the 1960s were *Butch Cassidy and the Sundance Kid*, *Mary Poppins*, and *The Graduate*, averaging $45 million.

BUTCH CASSIDY AND THE SUNDANCE KID

Butch and Sundance eventually make their way to their "hole in the wall" hideout. Butch, a talkative, intelligent schemer, tells Sundance, the quiet one, that they should go to Bolivia, where there are payrolls for mine workers to be robbed. But Butch hasn't been around much lately, and his gang has made plans to rob the Union Pacific Flyer train, a switch from holding up banks. One member of the gang, in an attempt to take over leadership of the group, challenges Butch to a knife fight. Fighting dirty, Butch sucker-kicks him, retaining his leadership. He also co-opts the gang's plan to rob the train.

As the Union Pacific Flyer approaches, Sundance jumps on top of it and forces the conductor to stop the train. The conductor is excited at this opportunity to watch the legendary gang in action, but a stubborn man named Woodcock (George Furth) is not: Woodcock was hired personally by E. H. Harriman, the head of Union Pacific, and out of loyalty he refuses to open the door to the money car. Unable to change Woodcock's mind, Butch resorts to blowing open the car with dynamite. Woodcock is injured but will survive. Butch and Sundance have struck again.

Robert Redford and Paul Newman played robbers with hearts of gold in the classic western Butch Cassidy and the Sundance Kid.

▼

After the robbery, the local sheriff tries to round up a posse to go after the gang, with no success. Sundance and Butch, amused, watch the ineffectual sheriff from a balcony of a nearby brothel. Butch is with a prostitute, so Sundance tells him he is going to go find a woman.

The Kid goes to the house of a beautiful young schoolteacher, Etta Place (Katharine Ross). Apparently unaware that he is there, she begins to take off her clothes. Sundance reveals himself and forces her, at gunpoint, to continue undressing. When she is almost naked, he approaches her and touches her, and she angrily asks what took him so long—the viewer realizes that this is a game between longtime lovers.

In the morning, Butch shows up on a bicycle (what a salesman earlier had called the future: the end of horses) and takes Etta for a ride on it. He does some silly stunts on the bike to impress her while "Raindrops Keep Falling on My Head" plays on the sound track. The scene ends with the telling words of the song "I'm free. Nothing worrying me." Etta and Butch wonder what might have happened between them if they had met before she and the Kid had.

Butch and Sundance later rob the Flyer again, this time tricking Woodcock into opening the door of the money car. But Butch uses too much dynamite to open the safe; the whole car is blasted open, and paper money flutters in the air. While the gang members dash about, trying to collect the money, a small train arrives with a professional armed posse. When two members of the gang are shot by the posse, Butch suggests they split up. The posse follows only Butch and Sundance.

Their tricks—splitting up, arranging for the posse to receive false information, scaring off the horses, and riding through water—fail to work against the dedicated posse. Butch and Sundance even visit an old acquaintance, a sheriff, in hopes that he will help them join the service in exchange for having the charges against them dropped. The helpless sheriff likes them but calls them two-bit criminals whose time is over. The posse is exceptionally good:

Butch: I think we lost 'em. Do you think we lost 'em?
Sundance: No.
Butch: Neither do I.

The posse pursues relentlessly—tracking them over rock, never slowing down, never falling out of formation. "Who *are* those guys?" Butch keeps asking, in awe. Eventually he and the Kid are cornered against a hundred-foot drop to a raging river. Rather than fight or surrender, Butch suggests that he and the Kid jump. Sundance demurs, finally admitting that he can't swim. Butch guffaws and assures him: "The fall'll probably kill you." The pair jumps off the cliff and are safely carried down the river.

Etta is relieved to learn that Butch and Sundance are alive. She tells them that E. H. Harriman of Union Pacific put the posse together, because

"Hey, I got vision and the rest of the world wears bifocals."

Paul Newman as Butch Cassidy in *Butch Cassidy and the Sundance Kid* (1969)

he thinks Butch's gang was singling him out. Butch wryly points out that the posse probably cost more than Butch ever stole from Harriman.

Because they know that the posse will chase them until they are dead, Butch and Sundance decide to go to Bolivia. Etta, who observes that an unmarried schoolteacher doesn't have much of a life, says she'll go and help to take care of them, but the one thing she won't do is watch them die.

A montage of sepia-toned pictures condenses their journey: Butch, Etta, and the Kid on trains, having fun in New York, on a boat to South America, and eventually arriving in a blighted section of Bolivia.

Etta teaches Sundance and Butch enough Spanish to rob banks (that "line of work requires a specialized vocabulary"). They then rob a series of banks—even using Etta to help them—but before long "Wanted" signs with their pictures begin to appear. One day Butch and Sundance catch sight of the leader of the posse that had pursued them so relentlessly, and they decide to go straight. Ironically, they take jobs as payroll guards. During this stint, Butch has to shoot somebody for the first time in his life. Realizing that they weren't meant to be payroll guards and that they are too old to become farmers, Butch and the Kid plan to go back to robbing. Disappointed, Etta decides to return home.

Butch and Sundance rob a payroll, but a foolish mistake leads to their eventual capture: a stolen horse with a brand on it gives them away when it is seen outside of the villa where they have holed up. A small group of lawmen have surrounded the villa, and Butch and Sundance are trapped. Knowing that their time is up, Butch and Sundance trade barbs and talk about how great it would be to go to Australia—because at least they speak English there. While they are chatting and loading their guns, a battalion of soldiers stakes out the tops of the surrounding buildings. Guns at the ready, Butch and Sundance burst out into the open, hoping to shoot their way to safety. The image of them in mid-step freezes as we hear the battalion leader's command to shoot, followed by the sound of several hundred shots. Butch and Sundance's bank-robbing days have come to an end.

Butch Cassidy and the Sundance Kid picked up an impressive seven Academy Award nominations. Goldman was awarded an Oscar for Best Screenplay, and Conrad Hall won for Best Cinematography. Two other awards went to Burt Bacharach for Best Song and Best Original Score.

See Hill, George Roy; Redford, Robert

CAMERA MOVEMENT

Camera movement refers to moving the motion-picture camera for the purpose of following action or changing the view of a photographed scene, person, or object. The camera and the base to which it is affixed may move together in order to move toward or away from a stationary subject (dolly shot); move behind, ahead, or alongside of a moving person or object (tracking shot/trucking shot); move up or down on an automatic crane for a lower or higher angle of view of a scene (boom crane shot). The camera may also be moved while the base to which it is attached remains stationary: a movement of the camera left or right on a fixed base is a pan, while one up and down is a tilt. A zoom shot can give the effect of camera movement, although it is the variable focal length of the lens rather than a moving camera that creates the effect.

Camera movement, in addition to following action and changing image composition, can be used to suggest a subjective point of view when the moving camera assumes character eye or body movements, as in Delmer Daves's *Dark Passage* (1947). A constant use of camera movement in a motion picture is often referred to as fluid-camera technique. American director Oliver Stone made the fluid camera a technical trademark of his cinematic style in such films as *Platoon* (1986), *Wall Street* (1987), *Talk Radio* (1988), and *JFK* (1991). In these films Stone's camera often appears to be charging through the stories' locations.

See Cinematographer; Stone, Oliver

CAMERA OBSCURA

The camera obscura is a device developed by Leonardo da Vinci in the sixteenth century that established the basic principle of photographic reproduction. The camera obscura (darkroom) allowed a small ray of light to pass through a hole into a totally dark space. An inverted and laterally reversed image of the outside scene appeared on a surface in the darkened room, thus producing the earliest form of a "camera." Da Vinci's image could be traced by the artist to achieve greater realism in artistic renderings. With the development of a photographic plate by Nicèphore Nièpce and Louis J. M. Daguerre in the 1830s, which would preserve the inverted image, still photography became possible.

JAMES CAGNEY

On July 17, 1899, James Francis Cagney Jr. was born to a working-class family in New York City. As a teenager Cagney worked at various jobs, including poolroom racker and female impersonator, to help his father, a bartender, support his family. (In his later years Cagney would continue to look after his family. His brother, William, and sister, Jeanne, would be involved in his professional life—the former as a producer of several of James's films, the latter as a costar in *Yankee Doodle Dandy.)*

The theater life appealed to Cagney, and in 1920 he joined the chorus of the Broadway show *Pitter-Patter* and traveled on the vaudeville circuit. Cagney began winning leading roles on Broadway in 1925, and Warner Brothers eventually took note of the young talent and signed him to a contract. He grabbed the spotlight with a starring role as a Prohibition mobster in *The Public Enemy* (1931). His performance as a brash, hot-tempered gangster—who, memorably, squashes a grapefruit in the face of gang moll Mae Clarke—defined him for a generation of moviegoers, and the rather small, average-looking Cagney became an unlikely film idol. Audiences loved his cocky self-confidence and his rat-a-tat, street-smart way of talking. His portrayal of the average guy who flies in the face of authority was tremendously popular and influential.

James Cagney's cocky, street-smart film roles made him a hit with audiences in the 1930s, '40s, and '50s.

Cagney enjoyed many career successes from the 1930s to the 1950s, starring in diverse roles in such films as *Lady Killer* (1933), *He Was Her Man* (1934), *A Midsummer Night's Dream* (1935), *The Fighting 69th* (1940), *Yankee Doodle Dandy* (1942), *13 Rue Madeleine* (1947), *What Price Glory?* (1952), and *Mister Roberts* (1955). He won the Best Actor Oscar for his portrayal of George M. Cohan in *Yankee Doodle Dandy*. He announced his retirement in 1961 but was occasionally lured from his upstate New York farm to perform in a film or television role. He last appeared in *Ragtime* (1981).

Cagney married Frances "Billie" Vernon early in the 1920s; their marriage endured until his death on March 30, 1986.

See Bogart, Humphrey; Gangster film; Yankee Doodle Dandy

CAPRA, FRANK

Born on May 18, 1897, Frank Capra spent his first six years in Bisaquino, a small village in Sicily. He immigrated with his family to the United States in 1903, settling in Los Angeles, California. Capra's status as an immigrant was one of the most important influences on his character.

Capra was ambitious, as are many children of immigrants, and he decided that getting an education was a prerequisite for making it in America. Thus, after graduating from Manual Arts High School, he enrolled in Throop Polytechnic (later the California Institute of Technology). Working at part-time jobs, and with the help of scholarships and loans, Capra graduated with a bachelor's degree in chemical engineering in 1918.

Upon graduation, Capra enlisted in the army. On his release in 1919, however, he was unable to find work as an engineer. He traveled around the west and southwest for a few years, working at various jobs. During this period of somewhat undirected wandering, Capra learned about dominant American attitudes, values, and behavior. He also had his first experiences at telling convincing stories to audiences.

He ended his wanderings and began his film career in San Francisco in 1922, where he convinced a Shakespearean actor-turned-movie producer that he could direct a film. The result was Capra's first film: *Fultah Fisher's Boarding House* (1922). The movie earned some positive reviews, and Capra began to develop a yearning to learn more about the movie business.

From 1922 to 1926 Capra worked at a wide range of movie jobs, which ultimately helped hone his skill as a director. At a film lab he not only developed, printed, and dried film, he gained valuable experience editing newsreels, amateur documentaries, and advertising footage. He became a propman for a time, but quickly returned to editing full time. Later, he was promoted to writing gags for silent comedies.

Capra won his first chance to direct a feature-length comedy in 1926, a time when the form was nearing its peak. He directed the two most successful of Harry Landon's features. These two collaborations, *The Strong Man* (1926) and *Long Pants* (1927), helped elevate Capra to a position of distinction as a film director.

A conflict at the end of shooting *Long Pants* led Capra and Langdon to dissolve their relationship. After four months of unemployment, First National offered Capra a job directing a feature called *For the Love of Mike* (1927), in which Claudette Colbert appeared in her first screen role. The film did not do well at the box office, and was later lost. In 1928 Capra moved to Columbia Pictures, where he directed fifteen feature films in less than four years. During this time he polished his visual and rhythmic sense while at the same time successfully making the transition to talking

In 1939 James Cagney was Warner Bros.' highest-paid actor, at $12,500 a week, and Bette Davis the highest-paid actress, at $4,000 a week.

pictures. Most of the features that Capra directed for Columbia were silent B movies, but he was unexpectedly given an opportunity to direct his first A film, *Submarine* (1928), the first of a trilogy of war films celebrating masculine friendship above all other values.

By 1931 Frank Capra's work on films like *Dirigible* (1930) and *The Miracle Woman* (1931) won him recognition as a director with wonderful talents. Capra's rise coincided with the beginning of his long and fruitful relationship with screenwriter Robert Riskin, who became his most constant collaborator. They worked together on *Platinum Blonde* (1931), *It Happened One Night* (1934), *Mr. Deeds Goes to Town* (1936), and others. *Platinum Blonde* remains significant in that it represents Capra's early attempt to speak in his own voice to a Depression audience.

Frank Capra's name will forever be associated with optimistic, sentimental films like It's a Wonderful Life.

The 1930s were Capra's peak years as a prestigious and successful director. His films from the early 1930s reveal at least two of his professional abilities. The first was his ability to coax strong performances from all of his actors, even the bit players. He also connected well with his audience because of his tendency to celebrate the common life of Americans and belittle the life of leisure. For example, *Lady for a Day* (1933), scripted by Riskin, combined the contrast between rich person and commoner and the topical references to the Depression. The film was an irresistible fairy tale about human kindness and good will.

Following *Lady for a Day*, Capra and Riskin again collaborated, this time on the quickly shot masterpiece *It Happened One Night*, one of the earliest and purest "screwball comedies." In it, Capra hit on a powerfully effective way to express his own moral inclinations within a feature film. At the 1935 Academy Awards, *It Happened One Night* was showered with the five major Oscars: Best Picture, Best Director, Best Screenwriter, Best Actress, and Best Actor. His next film, *Broadway Bill* (1934), is another example of the Capra-Riskin team developing its storytelling skills.

Capra was now one of the hottest directors around. He was elected president of the Motion Picture Academy, and in 1938 he became president of the Screen Directors' Guild. His five films between 1936 and 1941 were nominated for thirty-one Oscars, winning six, including two for Best Director and one for Best Picture. These major films include *Mr. Deeds Goes to Town*, in which the problem of unemployment during the Depression is raised; *Lost Horizon* (1937), a story of an ideal society free of social discord and civil strife; and *You Can't Take It With You* (1938), a fantasy of good will. In *Mr. Smith Goes to Washington* (1939), Capra dedicated his filmmaking talents to instructing audiences in what he perceived as the essence of Americanism; *Meet John Doe* (1941), Capra's darkest film, is about a fascist who desires to manufacture American idealism and then use it to dominate and control others; and *Arsenic and Old Lace* (1942) was a rip-roaring comedy about murder, in which Capra deviated widely from the method of filmmaking he had developed.

After Capra's run of successful films, the bombing of Pearl Harbor necessitated his draft into the army. He served in the armed forces until 1945, assigned to Special Services, where he was involved in a number of war department documentary films. He earned the Distinguished Service Medal, the highest noncombat award the army could give.

If Frank Capra is remembered for only one work, that film would be *It's a Wonderful Life* (1946), his first feature film after World War II. It is a story about a despondent George Bailey, who is given a chance to see what the world would be like had he not lived. Capra considered this his most personal film. Ultimately, the film did not do nearly as well at the box office as he hoped it would. Nevertheless, its popularity continues to grow to this day.

In September 1945 Frank Capra paid $10,000 for the rights to *The Greatest Gift*—a screenplay worked on by Clifford Odets, Dalton Trumbo, and Marc Connelly—which later became *It's a Wonderful Life*.

After the release of *It's a Wonderful Life*, Capra's career began a steady decline. His filmmaking formula from the late 1930s was no longer marketable. Two of his films during this time—*Riding High* (1950) and *Pocketful of Miracles* (1961)—were remakes of *Broadway Bill* and *Lady for a Day*, respectively. The others—*State of the Union* (1948), *Here Comes the Groom* (1951), and *A Hole in the Head* (1959)—were generally interesting films but not of the usual intensity of Capra's more important works.

Frank Capra died on September 3, 1991, at the age of ninety-six, in La Quinta, California. But his films, especially *It's a Wonderful Life*, are still enjoyed today, and the term "Capraesque" continues to be used to describe films of an optimistic, sentimental nature.

See Gable, Clark; It Happened One Night; It's a Wonderful Life; Mr. Smith Goes to Washington; *Stewart, James*

CASABLANCA

"Of all the gin joints in all the towns in all the world, she walks into mine."

Humphrey Bogart as Rick Blaine in *Casablanca* (1942)

Casablanca (1942), one of the best loved films of all times, is a tale of wartime intrigue in the French Moroccan city of Casablanca, on Africa's northwest coast. It won Academy Awards for Best Picture, Best Director (Michael Curtiz), and Best Screenplay (an adaptation by Julius J. Epstein, Philip G. Epstein, and Howard Koch of a never-produced play). The screenplay was written on almost a day-by-day basis; the actors did not know how the movie would end until the last day of filming.

Shot in black and white, the film is set in World War II. The movie opens with a map of Europe and North Africa, tracing the path of refugees fleeing the Nazis. A voice-over solemnly explains that Casablanca was a way station for those trying to reach the free world.

It seems that everyone in Casablanca eventually gravitates to Rick's Café Americain, owned by Rick Blaine (Humphrey Bogart), an American expatriate with a murky past rumored to include gunrunning in Africa and mercenary fighting in Spain. In his nightclub one finds glamorous women, hapless tourists, ominous Nazi officers, shady operators hawking bogus travel papers, and pickpockets. Customers quaff champagne while listening to Sam (Dooley Wilson), who plays the piano and sings quintessentially American tunes.

Casablanca is a city in turmoil. The exotic city represents the uncertainty of a world turned on its ear by the advance of Nazi Germany. Life there focuses on the daily flight to Lisbon, Portugal, from which a few lucky people may reach the safe haven of the Americas.

Thus, within minutes of the film's opening, the stage is set: we understand that this is a place of desperation. Anything is liable to happen.

Tensions rise as a Nazi commander, Major Heinrich Strasser (Conrad Veidt), arrives in Casablanca, in general to keep an eye out for enemies of the Nazis, and specifically to investigate the murders of two German couriers and the theft of the valuable letters of transit that they were carrying. Strasser is welcomed by the police chief, Captain Louis Renault (Claude Rains). Chief Renault leans whichever way is more favorable for him at the moment—Vichy (pro-Nazi), or Free French (anti-Nazi).

When a shady local character, a black marketeer named Guillermo Ugarte (Peter Lorre), asks Rick to hide two priceless exit visas for him, Rick believes him to be the culprit. Rick nevertheless agrees to hold the travel papers, stashing them in the club's upright piano.

That evening brings a special visitor to Rick's Café Americain: Victor Laszlo (Paul Henreid), a Czechoslovakian Resistance leader who recently

Former lovers Rick (Humphrey Bogart) and Ilsa (Ingrid Bergman) share a drink at Sam's piano in the classic film Casablanca.

escaped from a German concentration camp, and whose reputation for daring Rick greatly admires. He is accompanied by the beautiful Ilsa Lund (Ingrid Bergman).

Earlier, Captain Renault had spoken with Rick about Laszlo and his companion, "a lady." Renault predicts that Laszlo will be trying to get hold of the transit papers, at any price, as they will allow him to escape the Nazis. He tells Rick that Laszlo must not be allowed to leave Casablanca. Renault also warns Rick that the police will be making an arrest that evening at the café.

Soon another important visitor arrives at Rick's Café: Major Strasser. After some verbal sparring, he orders a rebellious Laszlo to meet with him for interrogation the following morning. During Strasser's visit, Ugarte is also detained by the police and charged with murder and with theft of the travel papers.

"I'm a drunkard."

Humphrey Bogart as Rick Blaine, when asked his nationality, in *Casablanca* (1942)

Ilsa, meanwhile, has noticed Rick's piano player, Sam. They met several years before in Paris, where Ilsa and Rick had been lovers. She presses Sam to play "As Time Goes By." Upon hearing it, Rick strides over to the piano player and says, "Sam, I thought I told you never to play that song!"—and sees Ilsa.

Flashbacks tell the story of how Ilsa broke Rick's heart in Paris. He is devastated to see her again: "Of all the gin joints in all the towns in all the world, she walks into mine." Her appearance has shattered Rick's carefully cultivated veneer of indifference and cynicism. He had never understood why she had disappeared from his life—she was supposed to meet him at the train station in Paris to flee the Nazis with him, but she never showed up, leaving only a cryptic letter.

Now, in Casablanca, Ilsa tells Rick that she is married to Laszlo. When they knew each other in Paris, she says, she thought Laszlo was dead. When she found out he was still alive—the day they were supposed to leave Paris—she had to go back to her husband. Rick finally understands why Ilsa abandoned him.

Ilsa does not know what to do. She is passionately in love with Rick. She left him once for honor's sake; now she is ready to forsake her honor in order to be with him. Rick, she tells him, must think for both of them.

And he must do it quickly. Ugarte has turned up dead in police custody—Renault can't say whether he committed suicide or was killed while trying to escape—and Strasser suspects Rick of hiding the stolen travel papers. The authorities have searched Rick's Café and then ordered it shut down while the investigation proceeds. Meanwhile, tensions have escalated between the Nazis and Laszlo, and he has been arrested.

Before there are no options left for Ilsa, Laszlo, or himself, Rick must decide what to do. He concludes that the cause of liberty that Laszlo stands for is more important than the love between him and Ilsa.

Craftily, Rick manipulates Captain Renault into bringing Laszlo and Ilsa to the airport in time to catch the plane for Lisbon. Renault could then cement his standing with the Nazis while arresting Laszlo and recovering the letters of transit. He thinks that Rick is going to leave on the plane with Ilsa.

Soon Renault learns that Rick has tricked him. At the airport, Rick forces Renault to sign the two letters of transit for Ilsa and Laszlo. Ilsa protests, and Rick explains that the cause of world freedom is more important than their own happiness: "The problems of three little people don't amount to a hill of beans in this crazy world." In the dense fog, Ilsa poignantly thanks Rick, and she and Laszlo turn toward the plane.

Major Strasser arrives, alerted on the sly by Renault. As the plane moves on the runway, he tries to stop it, and Rick shoots the Nazi dead. In a tense moment, Rick watches to see if Renault will betray him. Renault chooses to cover up for him, ordering his men to "Round up the usual suspects." As the film closes, Renault and Rick watch the plane take off for Lisbon. Renault discusses leaving Casablanca for good, intimating that he will join Rick in the anti-Nazi Resistance. Rick says, "Louis, I think this is the beginning of a beautiful friendship."

Although some people consider *Casablanca* manipulative and contrived, most others consider the film a true classic. Admirers cite the movie's tight, snappy dialogue, canny characterizations, atmospheric set design, rock-solid acting, and first-rate musical score, all of which have stood the test of time. And *Casablanca*'s timeless themes of honor and self-sacrifice continue to resonate with audiences.

See Bergman, Ingrid; Bogart, Humphrey

CENSORSHIP

Motion-picture censorship includes three kinds of regulation: (1) the suppression of film material intended for production, (2) the inspection of film material after the motion picture has been produced with the possible intention of denying public access to the material, and (3) the deletion of material from motion pictures by a censor, or the banning of a motion picture in its entirety because of "objectionable" content.

Statutory censorship began in the United States in the first decade of the new medium. By 1922 more than thirty states had pending censorship legislation.

In 1930 the Hollywood industry, under the guidance of Will Hays, drew up a self-regulatory code of moral standards to be used as a film production guide. This code and its administering organization, popularly called the "Hays Office," were designed as an internal means of combatting outside statutory censorship. The code contained a list of specific and general production taboos. Illicit sex, undue suggestiveness, illegal drug use, pointed profanity, and methods of crime were among the kinds of material forbidden by the code.

First Amendment guarantees of freedom of speech were given to the motion picture industry for the first time in 1952. *The Miracle* (1948), a film by Roberto Rossellini, had been charged by various Catholic organizations with being "sacrilegious." The U.S. Supreme Court ruled in 1952 that *The Miracle* could not be censored on the basis of a single group's interpretation of sacrilege. In so doing the Court reversed a 1915 decision that declared motion pictures to be a "business pure and simple" and not a vehicle for public opinion to be protected by the First Amendment.

Frankly, it's worth it: *Gone with the Wind*'s producer, David O. Selznick, agreed to a $5,000 fine for obscenity in Clark Gable's final line, "Frankly, my dear, I don't give a damn."

The rating system, devised by the Motion Picture Association of America in 1968, replaced Hollywood's self-regulatory code as a means of attempting to obviate statutory censorship of motion pictures. The rating system classified films according to their suitability for various age groups and offered four categories: G, general audiences; M, mature audiences, later changed to PG, parental guidance advised; R, restricted, adult accompaniment required for anyone 17 or under; X, no admittance for anyone under 18 years of age. PG-13 was added in 1984 as a special warning against viewing by very young children, and the X rating was changed in 1990 to NC-17, no children under 17 admitted.

Statutory regulation centered on the issue of obscenity increased in the United States after the Supreme Court ruled in *Miller* v. *California* (1973) that community standards, rather than state or national standards, would be applied in interpreting individual cases.

See Kazan, Elia; Losey, Joseph; Rating System

CHANEY, LON

Still known today as "the man of a thousand faces," Lon Chaney seemed to many the silent-film actor *par excellence.* He was a performer whose appeal lay not in his good looks, offscreen adventures, or lavishly mounted vehicles but in his traditional recourse to makeup and pantomime. Chaney whipped up his characters out of his makeup kit and applied his emotions with similar panache. Chaney's acting style was largely molded by his barnstorming years in stock and vaudeville, and his films are weakest when he is called upon to express any degree of subtlety.

Chaney certainly was at home, however, in the stylized world of the Grand Guignol. After 1919, and his great success in *The Miracle Man,* Chaney came to specialize in twisted minds and twisted bodies, objective correlatives of evil unmatched onscreen before or since. In *The Penalty* (1920) a careless surgeon leaves the young Chaney a legless cripple who grows up to avenge himself on society. In *West of Zanzibar* (1928) the target is Lionel Barrymore, who has not only stolen Chaney's wife but left him paralyzed after a brutal struggle. *The Blackbird* (1926) reverses this formula, with Chaney playing the role of a suave criminal who masquerades as a kindly but twisted Limehouse clergyman.

Actor Lon Chaney is shown here preparing one of his many wigs. Chaney is well known for his ability to transform himself through hair and makeup.

Irony and sacrifice are the punch lines of these films, typically played with all stops out. In *West of Zanzibar,* Chaney realizes too late that Barrymore's daughter, on whom he is extracting fiendish revenge, is in fact his own daughter. Time and again he makes great sacrifices for his leading lady, only to see her wind up in the arms of a handsome rival. The most baroque of these sacrificial ironies occurs in Tod Browning's *The Unknown* (1927), where Chaney has his arms amputated in fruitless pursuit of Joan Crawford, who has expressed an aversion to the romantic embrace. Browning proved to be the most sympathetic of Chaney's collaborators, although his most famous films were made for other directors.

Near the end of his career, Chaney starred, inevitably, in an adaptation of *Pagliacci* (*Laugh, Clown, Laugh,* 1928), thus capping a recurrent strain in his work that marked even his famous Quasimodo in *The Hunchback of Notre Dame* (1923). When Chaney allowed this sort of pathos to get out of hand, as he did in *Nomads of the North* (1920) or *Mockery* (1927), the result was an embarrassing display of silent-movie clichés, all broad gestures and eye-rolling. Any number of lesser actors could have demonstrated the restraint that these roles called for, but restraint was not a major element in Chaney's performing vocabulary.

His most famous film, *The Phantom of the Opera* (1925), does show Chaney at his best. Completely hidden behind a brilliant death's-head makeup, Chaney stalks the passages of an elegantly designed Paris Opera. Despite the efforts of two mediocre directors, Rupert Julian and Edward Sedgwick, the film manages to express much of the eerie texture of the original Gaston Leroux novel. With the chandelier sequence thrown away, and an unsatisfying chase at the end, only the authority of Chaney's performance holds the production together. Furiously pounding his pipe organ, or staring madly at Mary Philbin with eyes of fire, Chaney becomes a gargoyle unmatched in twenties cinema.

See Horror film

Bela Lugosi earned $3,500 for his role in *Dracula* in 1930, a year when an average of 90 million people went to the movies each week.

CHAPLIN, CHARLIE

Charles Spencer Chaplin was born in London on April 16, 1889. Not only is there no documentary evidence of his birth, but Chaplin himself told conflicting stories. At first he claimed to have been born in France; later he reduced the claim to conception in France and birth in London, and finally he dropped all foreign claims. His ethnic origins are uncertain as well. At various times and for various reasons, Chaplin claimed to be of Irish, Spanish, French, or Gypsy descent. He also sometimes claimed to be Jewish, while at other times he insisted he was not.

C

CHAPLIN, CHARLIE

Although he is best known for his role as the Little Tramp in silent films of the early 1900s, Charlie Chaplin was also a writer, director, producer, and even composer for some of his films.

What *is* fairly certain is that Charlie Chaplin was a figure of unique significance in the history of filmmaking. Besides writing, directing, and acting in all of his films after 1914, he became his own producer in control of his own studio and, after joining United Artists, had a hand in the distribution of his work. He even composed musical scores for his films and rigidly imposed his taste on subordinate craftsmen. Through some dazzling successes and occasional failures, he proved the possibility—despite the unlikelihood—of cinema being a one-man show.

Chaplin's first documented stage performance came in late 1898 at the age of nine, when he began to tour with the Eight Lancashire Lads. Remaining with this clog-dancing troupe until he was eleven, Chaplin then played a street waif in a touring production of *From Rags to Riches*. In late

December 1900, he demonstrated a talent for pantomime by playing a cat in *Cinderella* at the London Hippodrome. Shortly after his fourteenth birthday, Chaplin was offered contracts for two dramatic roles that would win him his first favorable press reviews. The first role was that of Sammy, a newspaper boy, in a short-lived touring production of *Jim: A Romance of Cockayne*. Shortly after, he began a tour as Billy, a pageboy in *Sherlock Holmes*. Chaplin was so successful in this latter role that two years and three tours later, he was still playing Billy and was the only original cast member left in the production.

In 1906 Chaplin joined a touring company of *Casey's Court*, a play about Cockney slum children. That was followed by a year with the Casey Circus, a vaudeville company. But Chaplin's breakthrough came shortly before his nineteenth birthday when his beloved older half brother, Sydney, who had become a featured player in one of Fred Karno's comedy troupes, talked Karno into giving the younger Chaplin a chance. Working for Karno meant an opportunity for Chaplin to learn and refine a variety of burlesque, slapstick, and pantomime techniques that would later prove useful in Hollywood. Equally important, Karno insisted on the mingling of comedy and pathos that would mark Chaplin's greatest films.

In 1914, the year World War I began, Charlie Chaplin's salary was $1,250 a week, and Mary Pickford's was $2,000. A year later, she was making $4,000 a week.

In the summer of 1908 Chaplin reached his first international audience in Paris when he appeared at the Folies Bergères in a Karno sketch. Back in England, he perfected his craft in leading and supporting roles in a variety of pantomime sketches. Finally, in late 1910, the twenty-one-year-old Chaplin arrived in the United States for the first of two American tours.

Chaplin's "discovery" by the infant film industry is the stuff of legend. The most popular version, told in various forms by Chaplin and Mack Sennett, is that Sennett spotted him as a drunken dandy in a sketch entitled *A Night in an English Music Hall.* However it happened, Chaplin ended nearly six years of association with Karno and signed a contract with Keystone for a starting salary of $125 a week—about five times the top salary a Ford Motor Company employee would have earned on a different kind of assembly line.

Without knowing it, Chaplin was entering the movie business at one of its most chaotic and creative periods. The star system was still in its infancy, a bare three years old, and the industry was on the verge of shifting from the short film to the longer format we now call the "feature."

Chaplin went on to play parts in nearly a dozen Keystone films. Finally, in April 1914, he was allowed to write and codirect *Caught in a Cabaret*. From that point on, he directed or codirected all but a handful of his remaining films with Keystone and was indisputably the central attraction in all but two.

Though Chaplin could have gone on writing and directing his own comedies at Keystone, he would have been under the heavy hand of Mack Sennett, fighting for control of his work. So he left Keystone for the

Essanay Company, where he was offered a salary of $1,250 a week and a bonus of $10,000. Essanay's northern California studio was run by G. M. Anderson (the "A" of Essanay), who was responsible for Essanay's "Bronco Billy" westerns, and George K. Spoor (the "S"), who ran the head office in Chicago. Chaplin made several comedies at the northern California studio—most notably *The Tramp*, in which he introduced the character he would forever be associated with: the wistful, ultimately selfless, long-suffering Little Tramp—before moving his base of operations to Los Angeles to avoid conflicts with Anderson over space and authority.

When Chaplin finished his contract with Essanay at the end of 1915, he sent his brother Sydney to New York to negotiate the best possible terms for a new contract. Sydney struck an astounding bargain with the Mutual Film Corporation: they would pay Chaplin $10,000 a week plus a bonus of $150,000. The salary was unprecedented in the world of entertainment, and there was some resentment that this recent immigrant would be earning almost as much in a single year as the entire United States Senate.

With the signing of the contract to deliver twelve two-reel comedies for Mutual, Chaplin entered what he later called the happiest period of his career. In only two years there, his films included *The Floorwalker, The Fireman, The Vagabond, The Pawnshop, The Cure, The Immigrant,* and *The Adventurer*, among others. Upon completing all twelve films, Mutual offered Chaplin a million dollars over and above his production costs for twelve more two-reelers. But Chaplin decided to gamble on himself by instead accepting an offer from the First National film company. In exchange for the delivery of eight two-reelers, Chaplin would receive a minimum of one million dollars—but he would have to pay all production costs. There were two advantages for Chaplin: he would share all profits after the distributors had covered their costs—and after five years, all rights to the films would revert to him. The disadvantage was that the contract put Chaplin under pressure to make short films quickly, when he really wanted to make long films slowly. Despite this, Chaplin regarded the First National deal as a better arrangement than his earlier contract with Mutual or the new contract Mutual offered because it meant he would no longer be expected to justify his expenditures to the front office. He was free to make films at any cost he wished, since he was now footing the bill.

Before starting work on his next film, Chaplin bought a five-acre lot on Hollywood's Sunset Boulevard and commissioned construction of the studio where he would make all of his films for the next thirty-five years. In April 1918, about six months after his last comedy for Mutual, he released his first new film: *A Dog's Life*. Generally considered to be Chaplin's first complete masterpiece, it was, at three reels, also the longest film he'd directed to date. He followed that film with *Shoulder Arms* (1918), *Sunnyside* (1919), *A Day's Pleasure* (1919), *The Kid*, and *The Idle Class* (both in 1921).

notable & quotable

"He always plays only himself as he was in his dismal youth. He cannot get away from those impressions and humiliations of that past period of his life. He is, so to speak, an exceptionally simple and transparent case."

Dr. Sigmund Freud, psychoanalyst, referring to actor Charlie Chaplin

Two years prior, in 1919, Chaplin had helped form United Artists with Mary Pickford, Douglas Fairbanks, and D. W. Griffith. A few years later—just following the release of his final film for First National, *The Pilgrim*—Chaplin's first film for United Artists, *A Woman of Paris*, was released. He followed that film with one of his most famous, *The Gold Rush*, in 1925, and in 1928 he released *The Circus*, for which he won a special award for "versatility and genius in writing, acting, and directing" at the first Academy Awards in 1929. In the 1930s and '40s Chaplin made several of his best-loved and most memorable films, including *City Lights* (1931), *Modern Times* (1936), and *The Great Dictator* (1940). But in 1952, tired of scandals (rumors in 1943 that he'd illegitimately fathered a child later turned out to be false) and publicity (Chaplin was married four times, most notably to actress Paulette Goddard), and plagued by tax collectors, Chaplin sold his Hollywood studio and left the United States for Switzerland. In 1957 he returned to filmmaking with the release of *A King in New York*, a film he made in England. Ten years later, Chaplin made what would be his last film: *A Countess from Hong Kong* with Sophia Loren and Marlon Brando. Chaplin returned to Hollywood in 1972 to accept a special Oscar honoring his lifetime contributions to the movies. He was also knighted in Great Britain in 1975. Charlie Chaplin died in his sleep of old age on Christmas Day, 1977.

See City Lights; *Comedy; Fairbanks, Douglas;* Gold Rush; *Keaton, Buster; Lloyd, Harold;* Modern Times; *Pickford, Mary; Sennett, Mack; Von Sternberg, Josef*

CHINATOWN

Chinatown (1974) is a lushly photographed and intricately plotted movie in the *film noir* genre, directed by Polish filmmaker Roman Polanski. Its original screenplay, written by Robert Towne (reportedly substantially restructured by Polanski for the filming) and based on a true event—the 1908 Owne River Valley scandal—won the Academy Award.

Chinatown was a huge critical and commercial success, with special attention given to Jack Nicholson's dead-on performance as Jake Gittes. Though the film is suffused with a warm, golden California light, the primary themes—of incest, betrayal, and corruption—are dark indeed.

The movie opens in the Los Angeles office of private investigator Jake Gittes (Nicholson), a former cop. Jake appears reasonably prosperous; he has several employees—a secretary and two operatives. The latter two sit in with Jake when the secretary ushers in a woman who identifies herself as "Mrs. Mulwray" (Diane Ladd). She asks Jake to find out if her husband, Hollis (Darrell Zwerling), is having an affair. He advises her to "let sleeping dogs lie," but she cannot.

Hollis Mulwray is an important man—the chief engineer of the city's Water and Power Company, in a town where access to water means everything. When Jake begins following Mr. Mulwray, he finds that nothing is as it seems.

Jake takes incriminating photos of Mulwray hugging and kissing a blonde girl, and he turns them over to Mrs. Mulwray. To his surprise, they are published in the papers a few days later, setting off a scandal. Jake will soon realize that "Mrs. Mulwray" was an impostor, sent to make trouble for Hollis and discredit him.

The papers identify Jake as being an investigator in the case, and now the *real* Mrs. Mulwray, Evelyn (Faye Dunaway), shows up in Jake's office,

Jake Gittes (Jack Nicholson) becomes entangled in a web of betrayal and corruption when he agrees to help Evelyn Mulwray (Faye Dunaway) in Roman Polanski's Chinatown.

◀

saying that she does not want him to pursue the matter. Evelyn Mulwray is a beautiful woman, much younger than Hollis. Jake suspects her of hiding something.

When Hollis Mulwray turns up dead—supposedly drowned—Jake finds that he was actually murdered because he found out that in the middle of the drought, someone had been illegally diverting thousands of tons of water from the city's reservoirs. Jake starts poking around for information and is soon jumped by some brutal thugs. One of them (played by Polanski) slices his nose open.

Evelyn Mulwray again appears to tell Jake to drop his investigation. But Jake, his nose swathed in bandages, coldly tells her that contrary to public belief, her husband was murdered. He wants to know why "half the city is trying to cover it all up" and why someone would go to such lengths as to threaten him physically. Eventually she will change her mind and hire him to find out the truth.

"Mr. Gittes, you think you know what you're dealing with, but believe me, you don't."

John Huston as Noah Cross in *Chinatown* (1974)

Slowly, Jake finds out the real story. Hollis Mulwray learned that corrupt developers were stealing water from farmers and channeling it to Los Angeles, sections of which they had been buying up at cheap prices, with the expectation that they would soon be able to cash in. As the movie makes clear—with shot after shot of brilliantly blue, cloudless sky—ready access to water is the key to prosperity in this region.

Jake learns that the most important figure in the water politics of Los Angeles is Noah Cross (John Huston, a famous director as well as actor)—the owner of the Water Department. Not only is Cross an old friend of Hollis Mulwray, but Cross is Evelyn Mulwray's father. With this stunning piece of information, the plot thickens.

It is not long before Jake has yet another client in the Mulwray matter: Noah Cross. Cross wants Jake to find the girl that Hollis was photographed with. Bemused, Jake pursues his parallel investigations. He uncovers the mastermind behind the land speculation deal: Noah Cross himself.

Meanwhile, at the Mulwray mansion one evening, Jake and Evelyn become lovers. She asks him about his past in Los Angeles's labyrinthine Chinatown. He tells her that he tried to keep something terrible from happening to a woman there whom he loved, but he could not help her. This tragedy caused him to quit the police force and become a private investigator.

The telephone rings. Evelyn answers, her voice becoming progressively more urgent and concerned. She hangs up and leaves, telling Jake to wait for her. But he follows her, tracking her to a small house. Through the windows, he sees her enter the room of a girl—the same girl with whom Hollis was photographed. Evelyn seems to administer some sort of drug to her, and leaves.

Once Evelyn reaches her car, she's unhappy to see Jake waiting in the front seat. When Jake presses her for information, she says that the girl who Jake thinks is Hollis's girlfriend is actually Evelyn's sister.

Jake realizes that the girl is a key to his investigation. Angry, he presses Evelyn for the truth:

> Jake (slapping her): I said I want the truth.
> Evelyn: She's my sister. (Slap.) She's my daughter. (Slap.) My sister, my daughter. (Slap. Slap.)
> Jake: I said I want the truth.
> Evelyn: She's my sister and my daughter! My father and I . . . understand? My father and I . . . understand? Or is it too tough for you?

Jake is stunned: the girl, Katherine (Belinda Palmer), is the result of incest between Evelyn and her father, the evil Noah Cross. Katherine wasn't Hollis's mistress—Hollis took care of Evelyn, who was only fifteen when she became pregnant, and then her daughter/sister, Katherine. Hollis's desire to protect Katherine from Cross was what really led to his murder.

Jake tries to help Evelyn and Katherine get out of town, through Chinatown. But when Evelyn drives off with Katherine in a convertible, a policeman—prompted by the powerful Mr. Cross?—shoots at the car. Evelyn is killed instantly, and the car comes to a stop, her head resting against the horn. Katherine cowers, screaming, while her father/grandfather, Noah Cross, arrives to claim her. As before in Chinatown, Jake is unable to save a woman he loves.

See Dunaway, Faye; Film noir; Huston, John; Nicholson, Jack; Polanski, Roman

CINEMA VERITÉ

Cinema verité is a stylistic movement in documentary filmmaking, and a term often applied to a fictional film that presents drama in a candid, documentary-like manner. In this type of film the filmmaker either seeks to use the motion-picture camera in an improvisational way or does so out of necessity. *Cinema verité,* meaning "cinema truth," attempts to avoid the slick, controlled look of studio pictures. Available lighting, hand-held cameras, long takes, in-camera editing, and natural sound recordings are techniques used to achieve a newsreel-like quality on film. The cinema verité method de-emphasizes the importance of artistic lighting, exact focus, perfect sound, and smooth camera movements in favor of an ostensibly more realistic, truthful recording of an event. Lighting is often intentionally "flat," and exposures may be less than perfect.

The documentaries of Frederick Wiseman have been described as cinema verité films because of their starkly naturalistic photographic styles. In his studies of American institutions, *Titticut Follies* (1967), *Hospital* (1969), and *High School* (1968), Wiseman used black-and-white film stock, natural sound, and available lighting to add a realistic impact to already shocking exposés. One of the intended effects of cinema verité is that of having the story appear to develop as it is being watched, thus adding to its candor.

Cinema verité filming techniques were widely used by the French New Wave film directors of the late 1950s and early 1960s. In the United States, John Cassavetes employed the approach in pictures such as *Faces* (1968), *Husbands* (1970), and *A Woman under the Influence* (1974). An early instance of this technique was that seen in the "News on the March" sequence of *Citizen Kane* (1941). A jerky, hand-held camera with telephoto lens is used to show Kane being pushed in a wheelchair about the grounds of his Gothic estate, effecting a sense of candor that resembles the cinema verité school of filmmaking.

See Actualité; Documentary; Neorealism; Realist cinema

CINEMATOGRAPHER (DIRECTOR OF PHOTOGRAPHY)

notable & quotable

"A cameraman cannot do a picture the way he wants to, because he's not the boss. It's a collaboration of the director, the art director, and the cameraman."

Lucien Ballard, cinematographer, 1971

Cinematographer is a title used to distinguish motion-picture photographers from still photographers. If the cinematographer in the filmmaking process is fully responsible for the artistic and technical quality of the screen images, that individual is known as the director of photography. The director of photography, working with camera operators and other technicians, has the larger responsibility for (1) exposure, (2) lighting, (3) color, (4) camera movement and placement, and (5) lens choice and framing of the screen image. The film director works closely with the director of photography to achieve the desired visual compositions and moods that enhance and carry the story.

A director of photography usually works to develop a visual style for a film. That style may be romantic or harshly realistic, or it may be standard studio photography. The stylistic and technical control of screen imagery by the director of photography (DP) is referred to colloquially within the film industry as "lensing."

See Camera movement; Composition; Director; Editor; Lighting; Montage; Producer

CITIZEN KANE

This epic film, made in 1941 and shot in black and white, was directed by wunderkind Orson Welles, just twenty-five years old at the time. Today it is widely considered one of the best movies of all time; in fact, many critics consider it to be *the* best film ever made.

From an original screenplay first entitled *American,* written primarily by Herman J. Mankiewicz but in collaboration with Orson Welles, the film tells the story of the limitless lust for power and the eventual decline of an American publishing tycoon, Charles Foster Kane (played by Welles).

In *Citizen Kane,* Welles and his cinematographer, Gregg Toland, used breathtakingly innovative, even revolutionary filming techniques. They

One of Citizen Kane*'s most innovative film techniques used the breakfast table to show how Kane (Orson Welles) and his wife, Emily (Ruth Warrick), have grown apart—literally.*

made "deep-focus" shots, from extreme close-ups to extreme backgrounds, in the process deepening and advancing the story line. They filmed long, unbroken sequences; employed unusual dissolves; and turned the world upside down with the use of low-angle shots. In addition, the unusual sound track was not mere background but actually moved the plot along.

The film opens on a foggy, damp night. A NO TRESPASSING sign dangles on a huge gate. A massive estate is revealed beyond the bars. We are at the home of Charles Foster Kane, a castle called Xanadu.

The camera moves ever closer to the castle, violating the warning sign, passing scenes of neglect. Clearly, something is amiss. A shot into a single lighted window shows a figure lying prone on a bed, unmoving.

Suddenly, snowflakes fill the screen, and we realize that we are seeing the inside of a glass globe, held in the hand of an elderly man. Grotesquely large lips are framed on the screen, uttering a single word: "Rosebud." The globe then falls and shatters on the floor. A nurse approaches the bed and sees that the man has died; she covers him with a sheet.

The man is Charles Foster Kane. Once revered and even projected to one day become president of the United States, he eventually was derided as being everything from a communist to a fascist, and mocked for his two marriages and two divorces. He has died alone in his disintegrating estate.

A newsreel of Kane's life sparks reporter Jerry Thompson's (William Alland) interest. He is determined to find out the details of Kane's life, and particularly the meaning of the word "Rosebud." Is Rosebud a woman, a thing?

Through Thompson's interviews with several key people in Kane's life, the film provides a kaleidoscope of impressions of Kane the man, told in the form of overlapping flashbacks.

We learn that Kane's mother (Agnes Morehead) ran a cheap boardinghouse in Colorado and became wealthy when the mining stock certificates given to her by a boarder paid off. In 1871 she put young Charles, just eight years old, under the guardianship of Walter Parks Thatcher (George Coulouris), a bank manager. The boy was sent away to school, traumatically separated from his parents.

At age twenty-five, Kane came into control of his fortune. He chose to run one particular part of his vast holdings: the *New York Inquirer.* Kane used the newspaper to attack trusts, including that of Thatcher, whom he despised. (For a time the film moves ahead to the year 1929, at the start of the Great Depression, when Kane signs away ownership of the newspaper. The paper has gone bankrupt.)

Bernstein (Everett Sloan), Kane's general business manager and devoted assistant, speculates that Rosebud may have been a woman. He reminisces about the day that Kane took over the *Inquirer,* along with his college buddy Jedediah Leland (Joseph Cotten). Kane planned to make the paper a champion for the downtrodden, a paper that would tell people the truth, "simply and entertainingly." It took years, but eventually the *Inquirer*

Merry Christmas, Mr. Hearst: On December 25, 1925, William Randolph Hearst moved into his $50 million castle at San Simeon, the model of *Citizen Kane*'s "Xanadu."

notable & quotable

"*Citizen Kane* is not based on the life of [William Randolph] Hearst or anyone else. On the other hand, had Mr. Hearst and similar financial barons not lived during the period we discuss, *Citizen Kane* could not have been made."

Orson Welles, director/writer

CITIZEN KANE

became the best-selling newspaper in New York. Kane became very powerful and began collecting precious things, such as sculptures—and a fiancée, Emily Norton (Ruth Warrick), the daughter of a senator. Kane also hoped to become president, but that dream gradually disintegrated, like his marriage to Emily.

Bernstein concludes that Emily was not Rosebud. "Maybe that was something he lost. Mr. Kane was a man who lost almost everything he had." Emily died in a car accident in 1918, not long after their divorce; their young son died in the crash as well.

Thompson interviews Leland, now a resident of a dreary retirement center. Leland says: "Guess all he really wanted out of life was love. That's Charlie's story, how he lost it. You see, he just didn't have any to give. Well, he loved Charlie Kane of course, very dearly, and his mother, I guess he always loved her."

Leland describes Kane's second marriage, to Susan Alexander (Dorothy Comingore), a salesgirl with ambitions to be a singer. (It is in Susan's boardinghouse room, after she and Kane first meet, that we first see the snowstorm glass paperweight.) Kane became involved with Susan while he was still married; this affair dashed his political hopes. Leland also describes his own falling out with Kane.

"I always gagged on that silver spoon."

Orson Welles as Charles Foster Kane in *Citizen Kane* (1941)

When Thompson interviews Susan, she explains that Kane's domineering traits, including forcing her to pursue an operatic "career," drove her to try to commit suicide and eventually caused the collapse of their relationship. Kane built Xanadu for her, in Florida, but bored in "retirement," and unhappy with Kane, Susan finally left him.

An interview with Kane's butler, Raymond (Paul Stewart), at Xanadu provides the final clues to the puzzle. After Susan left, says Raymond, Kane picked up the crystal paperweight and murmured, "Rosebud." Still, this doesn't help Thompson to find out who or what Rosebud is, and his look into Kane's life closes with a view of the extravagant material things that Kane accumulated in his lifetime.

At the film's end, only the film viewers are let into the secret: Rosebud is the name of the sled the young Charles abandoned in Colorado, right before he was separated from his mother and forced to go live with Thatcher. The sled is burned along with other "junk" from Kane's effects, its smoke trailing up into the sky.

The film criticizes not only the arrogance of powerful people like Kane, but also the fickleness of the public, who will raise a man up on a pedestal, only to abandon him and destroy him. *Citizen Kane* is widely believed to have been based on the life of newspaper magnate William Randolph Hearst, a man who had enormous influence in Welles's time. He was so powerful that the efforts of his employees, including gossip columnist Louella Parsons, on Hearst's behalf may have caused the collapse of the film at the box office.

Nominated for nine Academy Awards, *Citizen Kane* did not win a single one. In subsequent years, however, it achieved its currently high status. The film is credited with inspiring a generation of top film directors, including Martin Scorsese and Francis Ford Coppola, and today its technical innovations and unusual storytelling techniques are more thoroughly appreciated than when it was released.

See Coppola, Francis Ford; Lighting; MacGuffin; Scorsese, Martin; Welles, Orson; Writer

CITY LIGHTS

City Lights (1931), subtitled "A Comedy in Pantomime," is Charlie Chaplin's "silent film" released three years after the start of the talkies era of sound. It is the story of the difference between the reality of some sounds and the conclusions that people draw from them, and in the uncertainty of all surfaces, appearances, and arrangements.

City Lights opens with a shot of a city street at night. The next morning, a city official named Henry Bergman and some of his colleagues are dedicating a monument to peace and prosperity. The dropping of the veil reveals Chaplin's Tramp, asleep in the lap of a huge stone woman. He is awakened and the officials chase him off.

The scene cuts to a shabbily dressed blind girl selling flowers on a corner. When a limousine stops at the curb in front of her, the Tramp, to avoid a policeman, climbs through the empty passenger compartment and steps in front of her. Believing he is the owner of the limo, she offers him some flowers. Discovering she is blind, the Tramp accepts the flower and pays her. But before she can give him his change, the owner of the limousine gets in, slams the door, and drives away. She thinks the "rich man" has gone. The Tramp keeps his silence and tiptoes away.

Coming upon a suicidal millionaire (Harry Myers), the Tramp bolsters the man's confidence. The drunken millionaire is grateful, and begins treating the Tramp as a "friend." Coming upon the blind girl, the drunk lends the Tramp money to buy flowers from her. The Tramp then drives the girl home in the loaned limo, allowing her to believe he is rich.

When the Tramp returns to the mansion, the millionaire has sobered up and throws him out of the mansion. It seems he only recognizes the Tramp when he is drunk. But the next afternoon, drunk again, the millionaire meets the Tramp and greets him happily. Next morning when the millionaire wakes up sober, he again does not recognize the Tramp, tossing him out of the mansion.

Determined to help the blind girl regain her sight, the Tramp takes a job. Discovering an eviction notice at her apartment, he assures her that he will also pay the rent. But returning late to his new job, the Tramp is fired.

Again reunited, the drunken millionaire gives the Tramp $1,000 for the blind girl's operation. But suddenly robbers enter the mansion, assaulting the millionaire, and the Tramp calls the police. The robbers flee before they arrive and the police, finding the Tramp with the $1,000, mistake him for the thief. But before they can take him away, he snatches the money and rushes to the blind girl's house and gives her the money for the rent and the operation. Later, he is arrested by the police and sent to jail for nine months.

After the Tramp's release, by chance he comes upon the girl in her new flower shop, her sight restored. He is thrilled to see her, but she does not

Charlie Chaplin's Tramp must resolve several cases of "mistaken identity" before he finally gets the girl in City Lights.

recognize the bedraggled Tramp as her benefactor. Taking pity on him, she offers him a flower and, with her acute sense of touch, recognizes the familiar feel of his hand. She then recognizes him and accepts him for who he is. The famous final closeup is of the Tramp framed against a darkened background by the glowing nimbus of the girl's hair.

See Chaplin, Charlie; Sound

CLAY ANIMATION

Films incorporating animated clay have been produced in the United States from the early twentieth century. It was not until 1974, however, when Bob Gardiner and Will Vinton's clay film *Closed Mondays* (1974) won the Academy Award, that audiences took note of a clay animation revival that had been under way for some time among independent filmmakers. The last two decades have brought the rebirth of Gumby in a new television series, the production of the first clay animated feature film, the huge success of Will Vinton's California Raisins, and a new animated series, *The PJs*. Clay animation has developed from a cottage industry into one as visible as the cel animation industry, if not as pervasive. The resurgence of clay animation has made a basic survey of the medium's history a significant area of film study.

Clay—which is generally not "clay" at all, but rather oil-based modeling materials, usually plasticine—is relatively easy to animate. A mass of clay is animated by filming one frame at a time and by changing either the position of the mass in the frame or its appearance relative to some previous frame. Both of these methods can be very simple. A mass of clay—in any shape—can simply be moved between exposures to animate it, just as other objects are pixilated. Since clay is a plastic medium, there are many ways to change its appearance: it can be rolled, flattened, twisted, carved, kneaded, folded, smeared, ad infinitum. Clay can be animated using simple geometric objects, as in *Gumbasia* (Clokey, 1953), or by using human or animal characters, as in *Closed Mondays* (Gardiner and Vinton, 1974). Clay may also be animated in relief under a conventional rostrum camera, as in the "Penny Cartoon" series (Aardman Animations/Broadcast Arts, 1986–90) from *Pee Wee's Playhouse*. Clay vignettes can also be constructed and embedded by the so-called strata-cut method into "loaves," then cut away a layer at a time and filmed in stop motion, as in "The Declaration of Independence" (Daniels, 1987) and "Christopher Columbus" (Daniels, 1987) from *Pee Wee's Playhouse*.

Yet, like other forms of animation, clay does have its limitations, notably, its inherent weight and the difficulty in achieving deeply saturated colors. The sheer weight of clay makes larger clay forms sag, sometimes imperceptibly, over successive frames during filming. When projected, such sagging is often clearly visible to the viewer. While the cel animator has at his or her disposal a complete range of richly saturated colors, those who work with plasticine must accept it for what it is, a low-saturation medium. Because of the density of plasticine, it can hold only so much pigment and its surface tends to soak up rather than reflect light, creating a rather limited range of saturated colors.

See Animation

CLOCKWORK ORANGE, A

A Clockwork Orange (1971) is a disturbing film that questions whether society has a right to condition people for the good of the overall society and, if so, whether an individual's basic nature can be changed at all. The screenplay, by director Stanley Kubrick, was adapted from the Anthony Burgess novel of the same title. *A Clockwork Orange* was nominated for Academy Awards for Best Picture, Best Director, and Best Screenplay.

"It was a bit from the glorious Ninth by Ludwig Van."

Malcolm McDowell as Alex in *A Clockwork Orange* (1971)

People today are accustomed to media depictions of violence without conscience or remorse. But in the era that the movie was released, Kubrick's intense, highly stylized portrayal of youth gangs run amok—set sometime in the modernistic near future—was a sensation, if not a scandal.

A Clockwork Orange has one of film's most memorable opening shots: gang leader Alex de Large (Malcolm McDowell, looking, it must be said, a trifle older than the high school boy he portrays) smirks at the camera, his face painted with extravagant eyelashes surrounding one eye, and wearing a bowler hat. He and his pals live in England and speak a hybrid English of author Burgess's design called Nadsat. Their world is one of loud music and gaudy design—hyper-modernistic furniture and trappings in lurid primary colors.

Alex is the narrator of the film as well as the main "protagonist." His followers are Georgie (James Marcus), Dim (Warren Clarke), and Pete (Michael Tarn). As the film opens, the four youths sit in the nightclub-like Korova Milkbar, which is outfitted with tables in the shape of naked women. Alex and his gang are drinking drug-laced concoctions and plotting an evening of mayhem.

The boys steal a car and escape into the night, driving like maniacs. They approach the home of a couple and talk their way in. The husband,

Frank Alexander (Patrick Magee), sits typing, while Mrs. Alexander (Adrienne Corri) reads.

Wearing grotesque masks, the gang terrorizes the couple, raping the woman in front of her husband. Alex beats Mr. Alexander, all the while singing the cheerful lyrics of "Singin' in the Rain."

Later Alex goes home to the dilapidated Municipal Flatblock where he lives with his parents. He lies on his bed and relaxes to a tape of Beethoven's Ninth Symphony—the "perfect ending" to his "wonderful evening."

The next afternoon, he finds his gang in a mutinous mood; Georgie is trying to wrest control of the group. Alex quickly reasserts his dominance but acquiesces in Georgie's plan to rob and plunder the Woodmere Health Farm. There Alex barges in on Miss Weathers, known as the "Catlady" (Miriam Karlin), and kills her. Before he got into the room, however, she managed to call the police, and they arrive in time to arrest Alex. He is sentenced to fourteen years in prison for first-degree murder.

Two years into his stint, Alex volunteers for a new "reprogramming" treatment, which is meant to transform young hoodlums "out of all recognition." If it is successful, he will be cured of his urges for sex and violence and will be released early from prison. The program involves injecting Alex with drugs that make him feel nauseous and pairing those effects with violent film images, played to Beethoven's Ninth. He is rapidly pronounced cured of his antisocial nature. The prison chaplain protests that the treatment has made Alex "a clockwork orange"—a robotlike being—and deprived him of free will.

Malcolm McDowell (center) portrays Alex, the leader of a violent youth gang who is later "reprogrammed" to cure him of his urges for sex and violence in Stanley Kubrick's A Clockwork Orange.

▼

Once released back into society, Alex is unable to defend himself against violence. His parents no longer provide him with a buffer zone, either. They have found themselves a substitute son, and so he has, in essence, lost his home. His old gang members Georgie and Dim are of no help; ironically enough, they have become policemen in the increasingly totalitarian government.

Alex is on his own. As he walks down a road at night, in a drenching rain, he comes across a sign that speaks to his needs: HOME.

It is the Alexander home. Frank Alexander is now confined to a wheelchair. Because Alex wore a mask when he went to the home before, Mr. Alexander does not immediately recognize him. He does know, though, that Alex is the "poor victim of this horrible new technique" (the brainwashing), and warmly welcomes him. He offers Alex a bath, which Alex acccpts.

In the bathtub, Alex starts humming "Singin' in the Rain"—and now Mr. Alexander knows who he is. Over dinner, he drugs Alex and explains, intensely, that his wife died as a result of the pain and suffering she endured when some vicious young hoodlums assaulted her in this very house. Alex collapses into his plate of spaghetti, and later tries to commit suicide.

The politicos, who are concerned about public perception of the police/government as inhumane, take Mr. Alexander prisoner. Alex, however, is told that he will be given a job if he will be "instrumental in changing the public's verdict." Alex agrees and gives the thumbs-up sign.

As the movie ends, we see Alex's fantasy: he is nude, with a woman wearing only black silk stockings, making love to her—or is he raping her? An audience looks on, applauding. His leering voice says, "I was cured all right."

Viewers tend either to hate *A Clockwork Orange* or to love it. Critics have called it overindulgent and manipulative; admirers maintain that the movie was prescient and that its message merited the melodrama. What all can agree on is that the film is visually stunning. It sealed Kubrick's reputation as a master filmmaker.

See Kubrick, Stanley; Singin' in the Rain

notable & quotable

"I think it fascinated him [Kubrick] that ordinary people could turn into monsters without much pushing."

Adrienne Corri, actress, 1999 (Mrs. Alexander in A Clockwork Orange*)*

CLOSE ENCOUNTERS OF THE THIRD KIND

Close Encounters of the Third Kind (1977) is a science fiction/fantasy tale of contact between humans and friendly alien beings. It was directed by Steven Spielberg, who also wrote the screenplay, based upon the book *The*

UFO Experience by J. Allen Hynek. It is unusual among its genre in its optimistic and affectionate portrayal of aliens. Audiences and critics responded warmly to the movie. In addition to its massive commercial success, *Close Encounters* won eight Academy Award nominations. It won the Oscar for Best Cinematography (Vilmos Zsigmond).

The story begins as a group of men make their way through Mexico's Sonoran Desert in a swirling dust storm. The men are astounded to come upon pristine World War II fighter planes in this bleak terrain. The planes were reported missing in 1945. An old man tells an incredible tale of the sun coming out in the dead of night and singing to him. The French scientist Lacombe (played by Francois Truffaut, a famous director much admired by Spielberg) interprets this as the activity of alien beings.

The scene shifts to a black, murky sky. Clouds are massing ominously over a small, secluded house in rural Indiana. Inside the house, a single mother, Jillian Guiler (Melinda Dillon), and her four-year-old son, Barry (Cary Guffey), are asleep. Clanking cymbals wake the boy, who pops out of

Roy Neary (Richard Dreyfus) in inexplicably compelled to build models of Devil's Tower—this one in his living room—in Steven Spielberg's Close Encounters.
▼

bed to investigate. He finds his toy trucks and cars mysteriously zooming about while a record player blares; his eyes widen in awe. In the kitchen, the mysterious force is wreaking havoc. The refrigerator door opens and food pours out all over the floor. Glasses and dishes fall from cabinets while furniture lurches violently. The world is full of sound and light—a pairing that occurs again and again in the film.

Barry's mother is finally awakened by the noise, and she goes to investigate. Jillian hears her son talking from outside the house and looks out the window. Barry seems to be following something into the woods. Jillian runs outside in hot pursuit.

The action jumps to the Neary household. Roy Neary (Richard Dreyfuss) lives in a middle-American tract home with his wife, Ronnie (Teri Garr), and their three children. Roy is called to work by the power company that employs him: there is a massive power outage in the area. During his investigation, his car is overtaken by an enormous spacecraft giving off an intense shaft of light, catching Roy in its white glare. When the spacecraft abruptly disappears, Roy impulsively follows it.

Rounding a curve in pursuit of the spacecraft, Roy almost hits a small child who is walking alone along the dark road. It is Barry, who is snatched up at the last minute by his mother. After checking that Barry is all right, Roy looks around to see a mass of people gathered on the hillside near the road. They watch in amazement as a procession of large alien craft is followed by a small, red ball of light. The vehicles zoom with astounding speed and ease out over the horizon and toward the heavens, like a trio of fighter jets breaking formation.

Back home, as Roy is getting ready for work, he squirts shaving cream into his palm, idly shaping the cream into a mountainlike structure. He is not sure what it means or why he has done that, and he asks his wife if it reminds her of anything. She looks at him suspiciously and is upset when he wants to tell others about his UFO experience. Just then, Roy's company calls, giving the word that he has been fired from his job.

In the Gobi Desert, meanwhile, an international team is investigating another bizarre find: a lost ship that has simply appeared in the desert. Lacombe and fellow researchers are studying chanting Indians, who are pointing toward the sky. Their chant is a distinctive five-note melody. Lacombe's team busily records the sounds. He soon plays the recordings for fellow scientists in a large auditorium; he believes the tones to be a form of communication from alien beings.

The cartographer Laughlin (Bob Balaban), Lacombe, and other members of the team investigate pulses received from outer space. Composer John Williams's five notes register when the pulses are converted by computers into numbers, generating musical tones. Laughlin interprets the numbers as map coordinates.

Back at Jillian's house, half a world away from the chanting Indians, Barry is playing the same five-note sequence on his toy xylophone. Jillian is

"This means something. This is important."

Richard Dreyfuss as Roy Neary, making a model of Devil's Tower with his mashed potatoes at dinner, in *Close Encounters of the Third Kind* (1977)

outside hanging clothes when lights appear in the sky; clouds rush toward her like a freight train. She runs inside, bolting all doors and windows. The light attempts to enter through the fireplace, but Jillian is quick to shut the flue. The house is under siege. The stove begins to glow bright red, and the vacuum cleaner starts up of its own volition and roars around the living room.

In terrified awe, Jillian watches the screws from the floor furnace vent undo themselves: the force, whatever it is, is trying to get in from under the house.

Jillian loses sight of Barry, who is trying to get out of the house through the back door. He wants to play with the aliens—he, unlike Jillian, is not afraid. Jillian runs into the kitchen to save her son. He is halfway out the door when she grabs him, but Barry is pulled through the door. Jillian runs out of the house, only to see an alien craft part through the clouds and disappear with her son.

Meanwhile, preparations are underway to move the scientific team and all their instruments to the top of Devil's Tower, the exact location the map coordinates have indicated. The scientists believe that a meeting with the aliens will take place. Back at the Neary household, things are beginning to fall apart. The children are not sure what to make of Dad, who appears "different." He obsessively forms the mountainlike structure out of anything he can. He even attempts to build the structure out of dirt—in the house. Ronnie can't take it anymore; she packs up the kids one morning and drives off to her sister's.

In the lonely days that follow, Roy tries to make sense out of his experience. What is this structure that he feels compelled to create? When he sees a television news report about events at Devil's Tower, he compares the television image to his own sculpture and excitedly sees the similarity. A parallel scene shows that Jillian also has the implanted vision of the mountainlike structure; she has compulsively created countless drawings of it, which litter her house. Although their journeys to Wyoming begin separately, Roy and Jillian eventually find each other at the train depot and finally make it to Box Canyon, on the other side of Devil's Tower. At the base of the plateau, an array of technicians, machines, and instruments is assembled to record the alien encounter.

Finally, the same alien spaceships that Roy and Jillian spotted on that lonely roadside in Indiana fly past them again. The craft hover on the runway facing the technicians, who initiate communication by playing the five tones. After a moment of tense silence, the spaceships respond with similar tones and then quickly fly off. Soon a huge mother ship comes into view and descends toward the runway. Slowly it positions itself above the scientists, who begin communication through the electronic organ and light display by playing the five-note theme over and over. Eventually, the mother ship responds, in fantastic, booming fashion.

Once these formalities are over, a hatch in the mother ship opens, and an intense, blinding light sprays out of the opening. The scientists pull back, not knowing what to expect.

The first beings to march out of the alien spaceship are humans—various military personnel and civilians who have been missing for years, taken away by the aliens long ago. To Jillian's surprise and delight, Barry also appears.

By this time, Roy has managed to reach the activity center stage. Meanwhile, a team of men and women has assembled to go with the aliens. Jillian decides to stay behind, but Roy joins this group of hopeful space travelers, suiting up in a bright orange outfit.

A small group of childlike aliens descends from the opening, gently and lovingly surrounding Roy as if he were a specially invited guest. He is led, smiling and happy, up into the spaceship, after which an adult extraterrestrial descends from the hatch ramp to greet his earthly hosts. When the alien returns to the mother ship, the hatch closes and the spaceship begins to lift off the runway. Jillian looks on while her son, Barry, waves his arm and utters a touching "Good-bye, good-bye."

See E.T.; *Special-effects film; Spielberg, Steven*

COMEDY

Comedy refers to lighthearted drama designed to amuse and provoke laughter. Most screen comedies end on a happy note, although the plotting situations that generate the humor may, as Walter Kerr notes in *Tragedy and Comedy* (Simon & Schuster, 1967), simply end arbitrarily as if the writer suddenly decided to send "everyone off to bed." Kerr also emphasizes the fine line between the tragic and the comic. The most physical types of comedy, for example, slapstick, have their roots in harmless cruelty. The term *slapstick* comes from a stage device made of two pieces of bound wood that produces a loud sound when struck against a character or another object. Slapstick came to mean any form of harmless cruelty or horseplay designed for laughs. An early Lumière film, *Watering the Gardener* (1896), exploits slapstick humor when a lad steps on a water hose, enticing the gardener to look down into the hose's end just as the water is released to spray the man in the face. The Three Stooges took the physical elements of slapstick cruelty in film to a comic-book extreme by effecting bodily harm on one another to the accompaniment of stylized sound effects.

Much of screen comedy depends on exaggeration of situation, language, action, and character. The screenwriter and filmmaker capitalize on incongruities within character and situation for laughter, engaging the audience in the merriment of observing the foibles and deficiencies of other human beings. Charlie Chaplin's "little tramp" character displayed visual incongruity in his pretentious but ill-fitted tuxedo-like costume; situational incongruity occurred in the efforts of the tramp character to survive the social environment around him. Buster Keaton was incongruously stoic as a comic screen figure doing battle with man-made objects and the physical laws of the world. The silent screen by nature exploited the visual and physical components of comedy.

"Talking" motion pictures added verbal wit to screen comedy, ranging from the absurdist view of language evident in many of the Marx Brothers' films (the reading of an employment contract in *A Night at the Opera,* 1935) to the cruel verbal barbs of W. C. Fields. Mae West's film comedy capitalized on dialogue retorts filled with deflating sexual innuendo. On a higher level Ernst Lubitsch employed witty, urbane dialogue, obliquely innuendoed, in the creation of sophisticated romantic comedies, for example, *Trouble in Paradise* (1932), *Design for Living* (1933), and *Ninotchka* (1939).

In the late 1940s the Ealing Studios in Britain took advantage of the country's many gifted writers and actors to make black comedies, many involving crime and murder. The Ealing comedies *Kind Hearts and Coronets* (1949) and *The Ladykillers* (1955) represent in subject matter and stylistic toning the nature of black comedy at its best: droll, satiric treatment of otherwise deadly serious subject matter.

Filmmakers have continued to perpetrate the classic traditions of screen comedy, usually in a highly eclectic manner, for example, Woody Allen, in *Sleeper* (1973) and Charles Chrichton and John Cleese in *A Fish Called Wanda* (1988). Sight gags, physical slapstick humor, verbal absurdity, character incongruity, topical satire, and sexual innuendo all appear as comic elements in these popular films. Mel Brooks's *Silent Movie* (1976) offers itself as a parody in tribute to the traditions of silent screen comedy.

See Allen, Woody; Brooks, Mel; Chaplin, Charlie; Keaton, Buster; Lloyd, Harold; Screwball comedy; Slapstick comedy

In 1971, when the average ticket price was $1.65, Sean Connery earned $1.2 million for *Diamonds Are Forever.*

COMPOSITION

The use of light (including color), camera angle, movement, and object and character blocking within the film frame for photographic and dramatic expression is called composition.

The impact of these elements in a film shot depends on certain psychological and learned facets of visual perception. Lighter objects attract the

SEAN CONNERY

The durable favorite Sean Connery was born Thomas Sean Connery in Edinburgh, Scotland, on August 25, 1930. His family was working class, and when young Connery dropped out of school at age fifteen (some sources say thirteen), it seemed his options would be limited. He joined the British Navy, and in a few years took such diverse jobs as lifeguard and even a coffin polisher.

Connery—already exceptionally good-looking—had an interest in bodybuilding, and his workouts paid off when he got work modeling swimming trunks. He joined bodybuilding competitions and was rewarded by representing Scotland in the 1950 Mr. Universe contest.

In 1951 Connery moved in another direction: toward acting. He won a part in the chorus of a London theater production of *South Pacific,* and over the next few years gained more experience in small roles on the stage, and eventually in film. His career went nowhere in particular in the 1950s, but all that would change with the role that would make him famous: James Bond.

Beating out several contenders, Connery played the British agent in the first Bond movie, *Dr. No* (1962). His smoldering portrayal of the suave yet dangerous agent 007 catapulted him to stardom, and he reprised the role in several other Bond films over the next decade, and beyond. (*Never Say Never Again* was released in 1983. Reportedly, Connery later said that he hated making that movie, but it was well received by filmgoers.)

While the financial rewards and public acclaim were certainly welcome, Connery tried to break from the mold of the Bond role, not wishing to spend his entire career typecast as a sexy secret agent. He accepted a variety of roles and eventually became accepted as an actor of range, in comedies and dramas as well as adventure films. His many "non-Bond" films of note include *The Man Who Would Be King* (1975), *Robin and Marian* (1976), *A Bridge Too Far* (1977), *Highlander* (1986), *The Name of the Rose* (1986), *The Untouchables* (released in 1987, for which Connery won an Oscar for Best Supporting Actor), *Indiana Jones and the Last Crusade* (1989), *The Russia House* (1990), and *The Hunt for Red October* (1990).

Though he is nearing seventy, Connery's sex appeal is still bankable. In 1999 he played the romantic lead opposite siren Catherine Zeta-Jones in *Entrapment.*

Connery is said to be a family man, with the words "Scotland Forever" and "Mom and Dad" tattooed on his arm. Since 1975 he has been married to Micheline Roquebrune, a French painter. An earlier marriage to actress Diane Cilento ended in divorce. Connery has one son, Jason, also an actor.

See Lumet, Sidney

notable & quotable

"As for looking to the future, I always wanted to be an old man with a good face, like Hitchcock or Picasso."

Sean Connery, actor, 1999

eye more readily than darker objects; therefore, light can be used as a means of achieving compositional emphasis. Mass, volume, and movement also have importance for emphasis in frame composition. A single figure separated from a crowd will usually stand out as significant. Similarly, a moving actor will draw attention away from static figures. Because of the kinetic nature of the motion picture, composition is rarely static, and hence emphasis and psychological impact through composition are in a state of constant flux.

A straight-on view of a scene in which actors and objects are harmoniously arranged so as to fill with equal "weight" all areas of the screen frame is said to be formally balanced. In a deathbed scene, formal composition can be achieved by photographing the scene from a straight-on view taken at the foot of the bed. The placement of a nurse on one side of the bed and a doctor on the other side adds further formality to the scene that would be lost if both nurse and doctor were placed ("weighted") on the same side of the bed, or if a sharp side angle were chosen for the camera's positioning. The "balanced" arrangement of characters and objects and the straight-on photography cause the deathbed scene to appear "at rest."

Whereas formal composition connotes harmony and an at-rest feeling in a scene, a slanted, or Dutch angle, shot produces a sense of unrest.

See Camera movement; Cinematographer; Director; Lighting; Montage

GARY COOPER

Gary Cooper, an actor who would become known as the face of American frontier justice and integrity, was born Frank James Cooper on May 7, 1901, in Helena, Montana. Cooper's father was a state supreme court justice. As a youngster, Cooper was sent to boarding school in England, and he attended several private colleges in Montana and Iowa.

As a young man, Cooper's first love was cartooning. He submitted some political cartoons to a local newspaper, the *Helena Independent,* and then moved to California, hoping to become a cartoonist. He had little success in his goal, having to work as a door-to-door salesman and other jobs to make ends meet. In 1925 he found work in Hollywood films, usually as an extra in westerns. The next year Cooper got a break when he was cast at the last minute as the second lead in a Ronald Colman film called *The Winning of Barbara Worth.* The movie was a big hit and gave Cooper the influence he needed to get meatier roles.

Over the next decade Cooper improved his acting skills and became known and respected by film audiences. His tall, lanky good looks and unassuming way of talking appealed to men and women alike, who chose to see in Cooper's quiet style—highlighted in such films as *The Texan* (1930) and *A Farewell to Arms* (1932)—all that was good about America. While most of his films during this period were westerns and other dramas, Cooper also showed an aptitude for comedy, as in *Mr. Deeds Goes to Town,* (1936), which was a huge commercial and critical success—and which won Cooper an Academy Award nomination.

By the early 1940s Cooper was a movie icon, revered by audiences and peers alike. He received two more Oscar nominations, for *Sergeant York* (1941) and *The Pride of the Yankees* (1942). He won the Best Actor Award for his work in *Sergeant York*.

Gary Cooper's private life was followed closely by the public, and his escapades with women were of particular interest. In 1936 a daughter, Maria, was born to Cooper and his wife, socialite and occasional actress Veronica Balfe. Cooper reportedly had a variety of "manly" hobbies, including fishing, swimming, hunting, and even taxidermy.

Cooper won a second Best Actor Oscar in 1952 for his work in *High Noon*, generally considered his best film, and in 1960 he was given a special Academy Award for his "many memorable screen performances." It was accepted on his behalf by his friend and fellow actor Jimmy Stewart, who had recently learned that Cooper was battling cancer. Gary Cooper died the following month, in May 1961.

Actor Gary Cooper, shown here with the spoils from one of his big game hunts, had a variety of "manly" hobbies, including taxidermy.

◀

COPPOLA, FRANCIS FORD

Francis Ford Coppola was born on April 7, 1939, in Detroit, Michigan. He grew up in Queens, New York, where he was surrounded by creative influences. His father was the solo flutist for Arturo Toscanini, and his older brother introduced him to literature at a very early age. When Coppola was stricken with polio at age ten, he amused himself by creating puppet shows, making 8mm films, and playing with a tape recorder.

His interest in the storytelling arts flourished when he attended Hofstra College on Long Island, where he wrote the book and lyrics for several musicals and received a scholarship for playwriting. After seeing Sergei Eisenstein's *Ten Days That Shook the World*, he turned his attention from theater to film.

Production costs for *Apocalypse Now* were projected at $12 million, but ended up at $30 million. Its U.S. gross in 1979 was $37 million.

He went to graduate film school at UCLA where he won the Samuel Goldwyn screenwriting award for *Pilma* in 1962. Although criticized for selling out, Coppola took whatever chance he could to direct—he directed a soft porn movie titled *Tonite for Sure* in 1962, and worked on some other exploitation films at the time as well. Roger Corman, who would later give a first break to young filmmakers like Martin Scorsese, Jonathan Demme, and Peter Bogdonavich, gave Coppola the opportunity to direct a low-budget horror feature, *Dementia 13*. In 1967 he directed *You're a Big Boy Now*, which also served as his master's thesis project. That film helped him earn a shot at directing two other features: *Finnian's Rainbow* (1968) and *The Rain People* (1969).

After accumulating a savings of approximately $20,000, Coppola was frustrated that although it was a large sum for the time, he was far short of the money needed to make a movie. Indicative of the brash, if not sound, business decisions that would constantly plague his career, Coppola sunk his money into Scopitone, a jukebox for showing short films, which turned out to be a bad investment. Totally broke, Coppola was redeemed when he was offered payment for adapting the screenplay for *Patton*, which would earn him a shared Oscar for Best Adapted Screenplay.

His Oscar led him to helm *The Godfather*, which, despite conflict at every level of production, was an enormous financial and critical success. Coppola humanized Vito Corleone (possibly to a fault), drawing the audience into sympathy for the cold-blooded murderer who heads a Mafia family.

In 1974 he released a very personal film, *The Conversation*, about a surveillance expert, played by Gene Hackman, whose voyeuristic obsession destroys his life. Not so much a meditation on paranoia as much an homage to movie making and the subjectivity of sound, *The Conversation* influenced many later films, including the popular adaptations of writer John Grisham's paranoid thrillers. The film also served as an obvious model for the 1998 movie *Enemy of the State,* which reinstated Hackman as essentially the same character.

If winning the Golden Palm Award at Cannes for *The Conversation* wasn't enough for 1974, Coppola also released *The Godfather: Part II,* which many believed surpassed the quality of the first. By crosscutting from young Vito Corleone's story to that of his son Michael, Coppola created a complex film with a less sentimental treatment of Michael and his father. Coppola won or shared three Academy Awards for directing, producing, and cowriting the film. *The Godfather: Part II* also stands as the only sequel ever to win a Best Picture Oscar.

His next critical hit was *Apocalypse Now* (1979), a loose adaptation of Conrad's *Heart of Darkness* in a Vietnam War setting. Its power as film may have been overshadowed by the production nightmare of the movie. Several sets were destroyed by storms, and the movie went over budget by millions

Best known for the Godfather *trilogy, director Francis Ford Coppola has also served as producer on many films in collaboration with director George Lucas, known for a trilogy of his own—the first three* Star Wars *films.*

◀

of dollars, much of which was Coppola's own money. Coppola would spend most of the 1980s as a "work for hire" in an attempt to alleviate his poor financial situation.

Among some of his 1980s films were the underappreciated light time-travel comedy *Peggy Sue Got Married* (1986) and *Tucker: The Man and his Dream* (1988). The latter detailed a bold visionary's brash challenge against the established Detroit automobile industry. The topic seemed to have autobiographical echoes for Coppola, whose career has alternated between commercial and critical hits and misses, creating a tumultuous relationship between Coppola and the Hollywood studios.

Forever the champion of the arts, Coppola has also published magazines like *City* and *Zoetrope*. He has produced and executive produced a bold and eclectic mix of projects for his talented friends and peers, including George Lucas's *American Graffiti* (1973) and *THX 1138* (1970); Paul Schrader's *Mishima; A Life in Four Chapters (*1985); Carroll Ballard's *The Black Stallion* (1979); and Agnieszka Holland's *The Secret Garden* (1993).

Coppola began the 1990s with the final installment of his trilogy: *The Godfather: Part III.* When actress Winona Ryder, who played the key role of Michael's daughter, withdrew from the film due to exhaustion, Coppola was severly criticized for replacing her with his daughter Sophia, an inexperienced actress. Most recently Coppola directed a strikingly visual if not overwhelming adaptation of *Bram Stoker's Dracula* (1992). He also directed the comedy *Jack* (1996), starring Robin Williams, and wrote and directed John Grisham's *The Rainmaker* in 1997.

See American Graffiti; *Brando, Marlon;* Citizen Kane; Godfather, The; Godfather: Part II, The; *Hackman, Gene; Lucas, George; War film*

CORMAN, ROGER

Roger Corman was born in Detroit, Michigan, on April 5, 1926, to William and Ann Corman. The family moved to Beverly Hills, California, while Corman was still a teenager, and he attended Beverly Hills High School and then Stanford University, where he obtained a degree in engineering. Corman believed that a son should follow in his father's footsteps, but unlike his father, Corman worked only briefly as an engineer after graduation. Like many future directors, the young Corman was an avid moviegoer, recalling with special fondness the films of John Ford *(My Darling Clementine)* and fantasy efforts like Hal Roach's *One Million* B.C. Indeed, Corman evinced a general interest in fantasy from his earliest youth that

embraced the extremes of popular culture, from films to magazines like *Astounding Science Fiction*. Much of his future film work would derive from this early preoccupation, with about half of his films falling into the genres of science fiction and horror.

Corman began what could be considered his creative life during his college days, when he combined practical, technical expertise with self-expression by writing freelance articles for magazines like *Popular Mechanics* and *Science and Mechanics*. This early experience of earning money through creative ventures—particularly writing—influenced his initial decision to become a writer (his first Hollywood credit is as writer rather than director). He also spent three years in the navy, followed by a semester at Oxford University in England studying English literature. Returning to America, Corman began writing scripts, but he received little recogni-

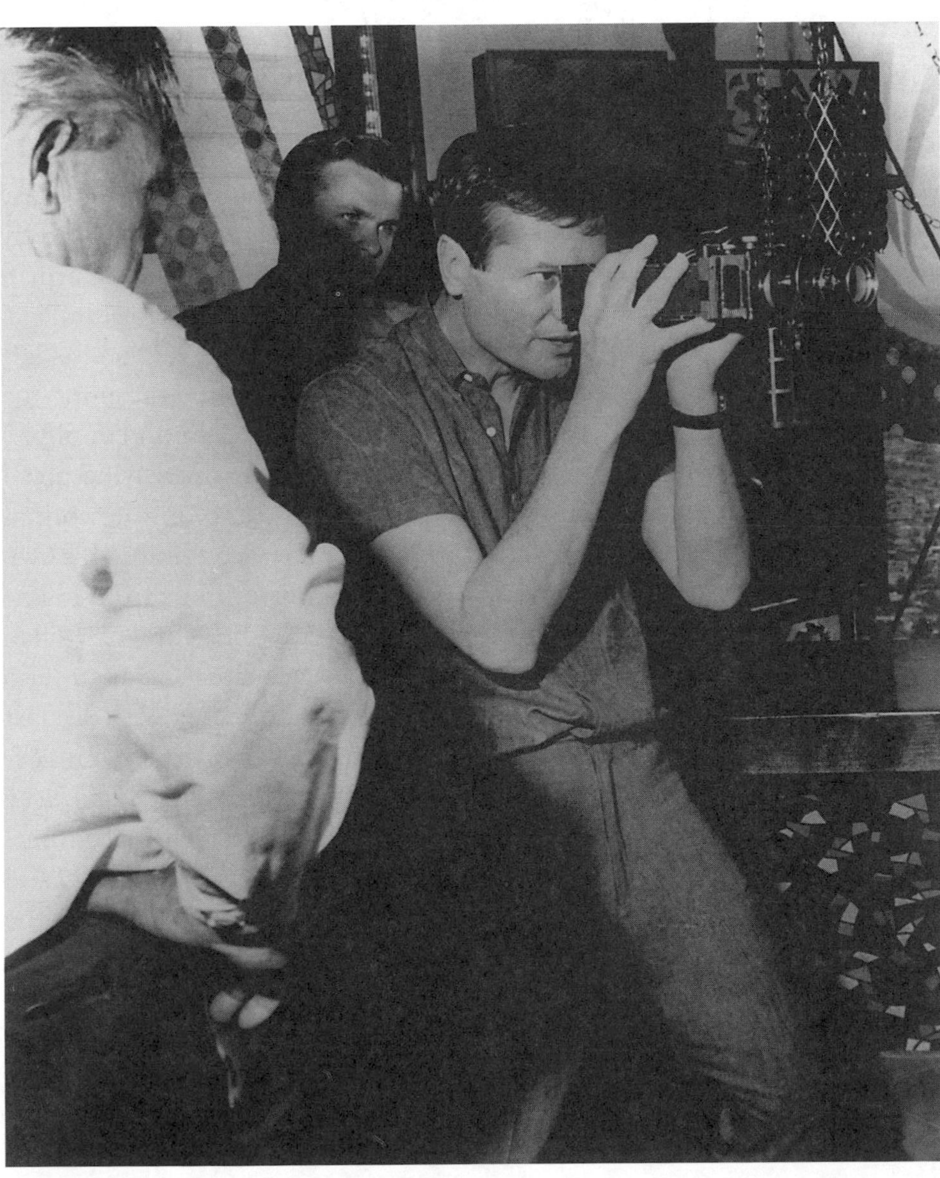

Independent filmmaker Roger Corman was nicknamed "King of the Bs" for films that depicted drug use and graphic violence.

◀

tion. He took a job as a messenger at Fox and worked his way up to story analyst before selling his first script, "House by the River," to Allied Artists, which retitled it *Highway Dragnet* to capitalize on the popularity of a 1950s television show with a similar name. Corman's insistence on receiving an associate producer credit in addition to the writer credit showed his sound business sense and gave him a foothold in the industry. In 1954, after producing several low-budget genre films, Corman became the silent third partner in a fledgling low-budget film company, American Releasing Corporation. Resisting offers of employment from Republic and Lippert Studios, Corman agreed to supply the films that James Nicholson, a sales manager for Realart Pictures, and Samuel Arkoff, an industry lawyer, would finance and distribute. Corman's earliest efforts for the company were straightforward genre films—westerns, adventure pictures, science fiction—but his fast and efficient shooting methods (six-to-ten-day schedules were the norm) guaranteed profits, and Corman was able to set up his own unit that he used not only for American Releasing Corporation—which changed its name to American-International Pictures in 1956—but for films he produced and directed for other studios as well. This unit consisted most frequently of Corman as director/producer, Charles Griffith as writer, Floyd Crosby as cinematographer, and people like Francis Doel as story editor and Chuck Hanawalt as key grip. The group worked so cohesively that it developed a strong reputation around Hollywood, and Corman rented them out to other studios when they were not working for him.

notable & quotable

"The difference from working for a studio was that, if Roger paid for a script, it got made—his only rule was, don't go overbudget."

John Sayles, independent filmmaker, 1999, as quoted in "How John Sayles Learned to Stop Worrying and Love the Studio," by Harry Stein, Premiere, *July 1999*

Corman's association with AIP lasted from 1955 to 1969, when he left them to start his own studio, New World Pictures. (A previous attempt, the Filmgroup, lasted from 1960 to 1962 and produced only a handful of films.) Corman was somewhat invisible during the 1950s but gained widespread prominence beginning in 1960 with a series of films based on the work of Edgar Allan Poe. His rejuvenation of the horror genre—combining his own sensibility with the influence of a series of sensual horror films from Hammer Studios in England (and cross-pollinated with the work of Italian director Mario Bava)—resulted in widespread acclaim. Corman also became controversial during his second decade as a director with a court battle over the denial of an MPAA Seal to his racially progressive film *The Intruder,* a near-scandal over the submission of the violent *The Wild Angels* as the American entry at the Venice Film Festival in 1966, and a continuous alienation of the critics with his "endorsement of drugs" *(The Trip)* and his graphic use of violence *(Bloody Mama).* Corman's low profile during the 1950s changed radically in the sixties and his reputation as a maverick independent earned him several nicknames including "King of the Bs" and "Schlockmeister." Like Jerry Lewis, Corman received a more favorable response in Europe—especially in France, where the French Film Institute held the earliest retrospective of his work in 1964—than in America, where critics tended to see him as a man who recognized the talents of *others,* rather than an artist in his own right. His early use of people like Peter Bogdanovich, Martin Scorsese, Jack Nicholson, Robert De Niro, and most of what came to be known as "the New Hollywood" solidified this reputation.

In 1970 Corman started New World Pictures, a company he headed until 1983, when he sold it. Corman developed New World as a sort of miniature AIP, though he split its format between producing low-budget genre pictures *(The Big Doll House)* and distributing foreign prestige films like Bergman's *Cries and Whispers* and Fellini's *Amarcord,* a dichotomy that further fixes his reputation as more a patron than an artist.

Corman married one of his assistants, Julie, in 1975, and they have three children. In 1983 Corman started a new company, Millennium Films. The name paid tribute to the first serious book about Corman's films, the Edinburgh Film Festival's *Roger Corman: The Millennic Vision,* a seminal work in the recasting of Corman's place in history as a film artist; but the company's name was later changed to Horizon Pictures.

See De Niro, Robert; Ford, John; Nicholson, Jack; Scorsese, Martin

COSTUME FILM

A costume film is the motion-picture genre characterized by historical pageantry and spectacle. Since the beginning of the film narrative, the costume spectacle has been a commercial mainstay of the screen. One of the earliest films made by Thomas Edison was a brief costume drama entitled *The Execution of Mary Queen of Scots* (1896). The feature-length costume drama originated in Italy with pictures like *Quo Vadis?* (1913) and *Cabiria* (1914). Bible-inspired spectacles on a much larger scale were popularized in the 1920s through the work of Cecil B. DeMille (*The Ten Commandments,* 1923, and *King of Kings,* 1927). Costume-action spectacles of a swashbuckling variety were given impetus by the great popularity of films starring Rudolph Valentino (*Blood and Sand,* 1922) and Douglas Fairbanks (*The Mark of Zorro,* 1920). The development and use of wide-screen processes in the early 1950s brought about a new rash of costume dramas displaying spectacle, color, and stereophonic sound. The genre went into a demise in the 1960s after the failure of *Cleopatra* (1963); occasionally more modern variations of the costume film appear, for example, *The Three Musketeers* (1974), *Excalibur* (1981), *Robin Hood: Prince of Thieves* (1991)—films that have brought added touches of realism along with the costume film's expected spectacle and pageantry.

TOM CRUISE

Thomas Cruise Mapother IV was born in Syracuse, New York, on July 3, 1962. By the time he was in his early twenties, he was one of the hottest film stars in the world, using the screen name Tom Cruise.

Cruise came from a broken family often described as "nomadic." He attended numerous schools in Canada and the United States, including a Franciscan seminary in Cincinnati, Ohio. Cruise was introduced to acting in high school in New Jersey and started pounding the pavement in nearby New York City after he graduated, paying the bills by working as a janitor and busboy. He did not have long to wait for success as an actor. He soon won small roles in several movies, including *Endless Love* (1981), and *Taps,* also in 1981. But with his 1983 starring roles in the brilliant and wildly successful *Risky Business* and *All the Right Moves,* Cruise was on his way to the big time.

By the end of the 1980s Cruise was a bona fide superstar, having starred in the popular and critically acclaimed movies *Top Gun* and *The Color of Money* (1986), *Rain Man* (1988), and *Born on the Fourth of July* (1989). Cruise was nominated for an Oscar for his performance as a paraplegic Vietnam veteran in this last film.

In the 1990s Cruise was one of the highest paid actors in the world, with hit after hit: *Days of Thunder* (1990; Cruise also cowrote), *A Few Good Men* (1992), *Interview with the Vampire* (1996), and 1996's *Mission Impossible*, which he also coproduced. As the sports agent who learns to love in *Jerry Maguire* (1996), he was nominated for a Best Actor Academy Award.

Tom Cruise's usually savvy career choices and good manners have led him to be well regarded in the movie industry. He was married for several years in the 1980s to actress Mimi Rogers; that marriage ended in 1990. That same year he married another actress, Australian Nicole Kidman, with whom he has worked in several movies, including his latest, Stanley Kubrick's last film, *Eyes Wide Shut* (1999). Cruise and Kidman have two adopted children, Isabella and Connor. Predictably, the couple is fodder for gossip columnists' and tabloids' cannons. They have lodged (and won) several lawsuits to fight against untrue stories, considering it their right not to be misrepresented in the press.

See Hoffman, Dustin; Kubrick, Stanley; Nicholson, Jack; War film

notable & quotable

"The most important thing is not to do things that don't interest or excite you, no matter how heavy the pressure or what the price may be. It's not what I've tried to do. It's what I've done."

Tom Cruise, as quoted in "Ready for the Dark Side?" by Richard Rayner, Harper's Bazaar, *July 1999*

CRITICISM

Criticism is the interpretation and evaluation of film; the study and elucidation of film form and content.

Many approaches to film criticism can be taken. Films may be grouped for study by director (as in auteur criticism), by genre (the gangster, western, war film, etc.), by studio (Warner Bros., Paramount), by subject matter (social themes), by technical evaluation (quality of cinematography), by time period (the studio years), or by nationality (French, German, Japanese), and lend themselves to new and differing insights in each instance. Films may also be analyzed for their cultural significance, how they serve as a mirror of or commentary on a given society at a given point in time. A critical approach of this latter type is structuralism, an anthropological method of evaluating what films reveal about broad cultural patterns of human behavior.

Subjective film criticism judges motion pictures by their aesthetic and emotional qualities. In general, criticism strives to enrich and deepen the film experience by increasing the reader's understanding of what happens in a motion picture and of how its effects are brought about in a cinematic way.

See Auteur; Cultural criticism; Ebert, Roger; Kael, Pauline; Maltin, Leonard; Newspapers; Siskel, Gene; Trade papers

CRUZE, JAMES

James Cruze was one of the highest-salaried directors of silent pictures, and many of his films were among the most popular of the postwar decade. Cruze's reputation is largely bound up with that of his best-known film, *The Covered Wagon* (1923). During the twenties, however, he was initially applauded for a series of lively and unpretentious Wallace Reid and Fatty Arbuckle films made between 1918 and 1921. In commercial terms, these pictures capped Reid's career as a matinee idol and helped Arbuckle move successfully from shorts to features. But the rise of both stars ended abruptly, and in revamping the script of a proposed Arbuckle vehicle to suit Will Rogers, Cruze hit upon a new style of satirical comedy, one that he would continue to develop over the next several years. *One Glorious Day* (1922) was the story of a mild-mannered professor temporarily possessed by a mischievous spirit sent from Valhalla. What might have been a straightforward situation comedy was shaped by Cruze into a canny satire of politics and spiritualism. Audiences resisted the film, but critical support moved Cruze further in the direction of satirical comedy. His *Ruggles of Red Gap* (1923) and *Merton of the Movies* (1924) established him as a master of this form before it was taken over by the Lubitsch school. Cruze adopted the expressionistic theater staging of *Beggar on Horseback* (1923) for his film version and continued with this style in *Hollywood* (1923), a much-praised satire of life in the young movie colony. Cruze's current reputation might be different if he were more identified with films like these, but when Lubitsch's work captured the public's imagination, Cruze's efforts were forgotten. Today, nearly all these films have disappeared, and it is impossible to judge Cruze's real contribution to the genre.

With the Reid and Arbuckle films also out of sight, Cruze's reputation rested on a handful of outdoor epics that followed the success of *The Covered Wagon,* namely *The Pony Express* (1925), *Old Ironsides* (1926), and the talkie *Sutter's Gold* (1935).

The Pony Express and *Sutter's Gold* have had few defenders, and their occasional screenings do little to help Cruze's image. *Old Ironsides,* considered a costly flop on release, was still being damned a decade later as "a dismal failure."

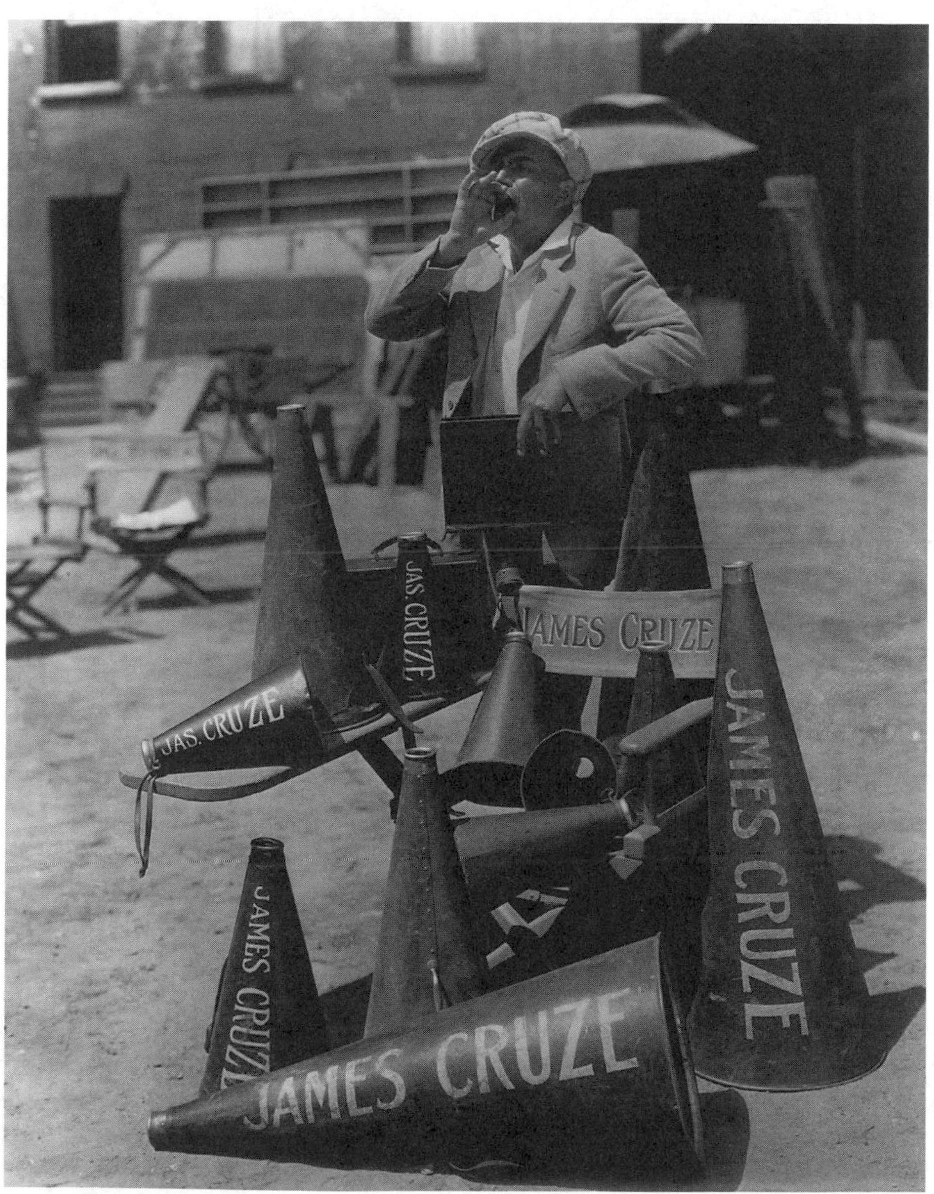

Director James Cruze, surrounded by megaphones provided by his crew, preferred to shout his directions. Many of Cruze's films were among the most popular of the postwar decade.

This leaves us with *The Covered Wagon,* a film whose value, even at the time of its initial release, was the subject of some debate. Jesse Lasky had acquired the rights to Emerson Hough's *Saturday Evening Post* serial and felt that he could revive the western genre by shifting the emphasis from stars (like William S. Hart) to scenery and situations. Accordingly, he authorized Cruze to take a large unit on location and to expend considerable sums in capturing a degree of physical authenticity previously unknown in westerns. Largely thanks to the camerawork of Karl Brown, who photographed most of Cruze's silent films, *The Covered Wagon* set a visual standard for western epics to come and was the dominant critical and commercial success of the season. Victor Freeburg's *Pictorial Beauty on the Screen,* perhaps the most sophisticated analysis of film aesthetics until then published in America, was dedicated to Cruze that year, and a still from *The Covered Wagon* served as the frontispiece. Many were impressed by the palpable authenticity of props and locations in this pageant of American history, but details of the action were criticized by a knowledgeable few, while others found the casting of J. Warren Kerrigan and Louis Wilson in the leads a serious mistake. But the film's very success in launching a cycle of epic westerns soon began to cut into its reputation. John Ford's *Three Bad Men* (1926), for example, seems far more satisfactory by any possible standard, especially when compared with the truncated prints of *The Covered Wagon* available today.

When Cruze was unable to repeat its success, his standing at the studio began to fall, and he especially bore the brunt of the costly failure of *Old Ironsides.* In addition, he was the sort of director who preferred to work with a small unit, loyal primarily to himself. As in the case of Erich von Stroheim and Marshall Neilan, this approach did not suit the developing production practices of the studios and his contract was dropped in 1928.

See Neilan, Marshall; Reid, Wallace; von Stroheim, Erich; Western

CUKOR, GEORGE

George Cukor was born of Hungarian immigrants in New York City on July 7, 1899. Although his family hoped he would follow the family tradition of becoming a lawyer, Cukor always wanted to pursue a career in the theater. From the second balcony, he saw all the great theatrical luminaries of the day.

After graduating from De Witt Clinton High School in 1918, Cukor enlisted in the Students Army Training Corps, where he served until the end of World War I. His professional career in the theater began in 1919 when he became an assistant stage manager, eventually moving up to stage manager for several productions by various Broadway producers. He gained invaluable experience by directing plays in summer stock in Rochester, New York, from 1920 to 1928, and on Broadway from 1925 to 1929.

With the advent of talking pictures, Cukor headed to Hollywood in 1929. Paramount offered him the job of dialogue director, a position designed to help make the transition from silent to talking pictures. His first film was *River of Romance* (1929).

On loan from Paramount, Cukor acted as dialogue director on Universal's distinguished World War I epic *All Quiet on the Western Front* (1930). During the shooting of this picture, he learned how to use a motion picture

Director George Cukor, right, instructs Ruth Hussey and James Stewart on the set of The Philadelphia Story. *Cukor was known for his "women's pictures" such as* Little Women *and* Gone with the Wind.

camera: everything from maintaining visual continuity from shot to shot to choosing camera angles. He was sorely dismayed, however, when director Lewis Milestone was unwilling to give Cukor screen credit, because he did not want to "divide" his own directorial credit. Upon his return to Paramount, Cukor was assigned to codirect three films.

Moving to RKO in 1931, Cukor became a full-fledged director. His first film was a satire on the amorality of New York high society, *Tarnished Lady* (1931). It was noteworthy for two reasons: first, it was the movie debut of Tallulah Bankhead, and second, it was Cukor's first collaboration with screenwriter Donald Ogden Stewart, who was to lend his talents to several screenplays for Cukor films over the years.

Given more creative freedom at RKO, Cukor showed that he knew how to use his camera with equal dexterity both indoors and outdoors. He was aware that motion pictures by their very nature must appeal primarily to the eye rather than to the ear as plays do. Among his first films for RKO was *Rockabye* (1932), one of a cycle of "confession films" that was enormously popular in the early 1930s. Also in 1932, he directed *What Price Hollywood?* and *A Bill of Divorcement*. This latter film was the first of ten pictures he made with Katharine Hepburn. He also made *Our Betters* (1933), based on a sophisticated play by Somerset Maugham.

In 1933 Cukor moved to MGM, marking the beginning of an association with that studio that was to last for nearly a quarter of a century. His first project at MGM was *Dinner at Eight* (1933), a comedy featuring a stellar cast, including John Barrymore, Jean Harlow, Wallace Beery, and others. With this film, Cukor at last hit his stride as a director of significance. He followed with Louisa May Alcott's *Little Women* (1933), and went on to direct several other star-studded MGM productions like *David Copperfield* (1935), *Romeo and Juliet* (1936), *Camille* (1937), and *Holiday* (1938).

As early as 1937 Cukor began long-term preproduction work on David O. Selznick's Civil War epic *Gone with the Wind* (1939), but after three weeks' shooting on the film, he was dismissed by Selznick on February 13, 1939. Replaced by Victor Fleming at the behest of the film's male lead, Clark Gable, Cukor believed that he was replaced most likely because "Gable took seriously my reputation for being a good director of actresses." Cukor was immediately reassigned, this time to direct *The Women* (1939), about a group of gossipy New York socialites.

His next project was producer Joseph L. Mankiewicz's *The Philadelphia Story* (1940), another Katharine Hepburn vehicle for which she won the New York Critics Award for her portrait of a domineering, supersophisticated young socialite, who nevertheless retains a disarming vulnerability. The film also earned Oscars for Jimmy Stewart for Best Supporting Actor and Donald Stewart for Best Screenplay.

Cukor's two films of 1941, *A Woman's Face* and *Two-Faced Woman*, starred, respectively, Joan Crawford and Greta Garbo. While Cukor was more than satisfied with Crawford's performance, Garbo's last picture was a disappointment.

During World War II, his first project was *Her Cardboard Lover* (1942), his only work that he directed on both stage and screen. *The Keeper of the Flame* (1943) teamed Katharine Hepburn with Spencer Tracy. In 1944 Cukor directed *Gaslight*, earning Ingrid Bergman an Oscar for her performance, and later that same year he directed *Winged Victory*, which Cukor considered a high-class kind of training film.

After the war Cukor directed two films in a row with Spencer Tracy as the male lead: *Edward, My Son* (1949) and *Adam's Rib* (1949). The latter included Katharine Hepburn as the female lead.

In 1950 Cukor convinced Columbia that Judy Holliday would shine in *Born Yesterday*. In *The Marrying Kind* (1952) and *It Should Happen to You* (1954), he cast Holliday again as a character who was at once both humorous and sympathetic. *Pat and Mike* (1952) was another Tracy-Hepburn collaboration.

Cukor's first musical, *A Star Is Born*, was shot in 1954. Two years later, he returned to the stage to direct *The Chalk Garden* (1956), his only theatrical production after 1929. He did another musical, *Les Girls* (1957), his most explicit film in dealing with the conflict of fact and fantasy in people's lives. *Heller in Pink Tights* (1960), Cukor's only western, was based on a Louis L'Amour novel. Then came another musical, *Let's Make Love* (1960), starring Yves Montand and Marilyn Monroe. He started another film with Monroe in 1962, *Something's Got to Give*, but it was ultimately canceled as her mental health deteriorated to the point where she could no longer work. Just two months later she committed suicide.

My Fair Lady (1964), his engaging musical comedy, marks the peak of Cukor's career in terms of official recognition by the industry. After receiving five nominations over the years for both Best Picture and Best Director, this movie brought him, at long last, Oscars in both categories, as well as six others.

The movies Cukor directed in the last decade of his career included *Travels with My Aunt* (1972), *Love Among the Ruins* (1975) and *The Corn Is Green* (1979). Cukor's last film, *Rich and Famous* (1981), directed when he was eighty-one years old, marked him as having the longest continuous career in movies and television of any previous director.

Credited with having directed fifty films in his long and illustrious career, George Cukor died on January 24, 1983, at the age of eighty-three.

See All Quiet on the Western Front; *Garbo, Greta;* Gone with the Wind; *Hepburn, Katharine; Mankiewicz, Joseph; Milestone, Lewis; Monroe, Marilyn;* My Fair Lady; Philadelphia Story; *Tracy, Spencer;* Wizard of Oz, The

CULT FILM

A cult film is a motion picture of limited but special appeal to a particular group of filmgoers. Devotion to the film is such that its followers attend showings time and again, often frequenting theaters that program late-night screenings of cult favorites, for example, *Harold and Maude* (1972), *The Rocky Horror Picture Show* (1975), *Hairspray* (1988). The quirky, often outrageous nature of these films is the source of their peculiar attraction. *My Own Private Idaho* (1991), a serious film, achieved cult status through its offbeat and sometimes surreal portrayal of male hustling and friendship in the Pacific northwest. The film's following was limited but intense. Mainstream gay and lesbian films, in part because of their relative obscurity, also often gain cult-film status, for example, *Desert Hearts* (1985), the story of a developing relationship between a female professor and a young woman on a Nevada ranch.

See Harold and Maude; Hairspray; *Lynch, David;* My Own Private Idaho; Rocky Horror Picture Show

CULTURAL CRITICISM/ CULTURAL STUDIES

Cultural criticism is a movement in film and literary analysis that seeks to incorporate cultural and historical context. Cultural criticism takes into account a variety of theories and critical strategies that are seen to cross-fertilize one another; hence, the movement may be described as interdisciplinary in intention. In its embracing of pluralism, cultural criticism has drawn upon Marxist theory, psychoanalysis, semiotics, feminism, and gay-lesbian study, among other strategies. Cultural criticism avoids any recognizable set of criteria and in this sense may be seen as a reactionary response to previously developed, hardbound practices of analysis.

See Criticism; Gaze (look); Postmodernism; Psychoanalysis and cinema

DAGUERREOTYPE

A daguerreotype is the name given to a photographic image retained on silver or silver-covered copper plates, successfully realized through the efforts of Nicèphore Nièpce and Louis J. M. Daguerre. Daguerre publicly displayed examples of the daguerreotype in Paris in January 1839, signaling the arrival of still photography. The development of still photography constituted an important step in the progress toward motion pictures.

DANCES WITH WOLVES

Kevin Costner coproduced (with Jim Wilson), directed, and starred in this 1990 film about the end of the free way of life of Native Americans. The screenplay was based on a book of the same name; both were written by Michael Blake. The three-hour epic was wildly popular with audiences and applauded by most critics. It won the Best Picture Academy Award for 1990.

Costner plays John Dunbar, a lieutenant in the Union Army in 1863, during the Civil War. In his desperation to escape the amputation of his injured foot, Dunbar accidentally leads the Union troops to a victory against the Confederates in Tennessee. As a reward for his "heroism," Dunbar is allowed a new posting of his choice. He asks to go to the western frontier, which he wants to see "before it's gone." He is sent to Fort Sedgwick in the Dakotas, the farthermost outpost.

Dunbar is provisioned, and Timmons (Robert Pastorelli) is assigned to get him to Fort Sedgwick by horse and wagon. Dunbar, who narrates the movie and relates events from his point of view, notes that he would have greatly enjoyed the trip were it not for Timmons, the "foulest man I have ever met."

"Only a white man would make a fire for everyone to see."

Wes Studi as a Pawnee brave in *Dances with Wolves* (1990)

When they arrive at Fort Sedgwick, they find it deserted. Supplies are abundant, but the post is a mess. Timmons turns the wagons back toward Tennessee; he is killed and scalped by Indians on his return journey.

Dunbar sets about cleaning up the post. In a nearby river, Dunbar is repulsed to find a submerged deer. He burns the carcass, which sends up massive amounts of smoke. A local tribe of Sioux Indians notices it; they comment that only a white man would be so foolish as to alert others to his presence in the territory. They decide to keep an eye on Dunbar.

Dunbar is happy in his new home, and he quickly makes a new friend, a wolf that he calls Two Socks. The animal comes closer each day, taking Dunbar's measure and learning to trust him. (Later the Indians will name Dunbar Dances with Wolves.)

A relationship soon develops between the local Sioux and Dunbar. One day he comes across a woman from the tribe, Stands with a Fist (Mary McDonnell). She is bleeding, and tries to run away from him. He catches her and carries her on his horse to her people. He delivers her safely, and then wisely retreats. Stands with a Fist, he will learn, is a white woman who was stolen as a child by the rival Pawnee Indians but raised by the Sioux.

"In trying to produce my own death, I was elevated to the status of a living hero."

Kevin Costner as Lt. Dunbar (narration) in *Dances with Wolves* (1990)

In their first true meeting—appropriately enough, out on the open prairie—Dunbar and the Indians discuss buffalo. They "speak" in pantomime, since they do not speak each other's language. The fierce Wind in His Hair (Rodney A. Grant) thinks Dunbar is a little crazy, but Kicking Bird (Graham Greene), a holy man, wishes to withhold judgment until they get to know this particular white man better.

Dunbar keeps a journal, describing through words and drawings what he is learning about the Indians. The learning process is helped along by Stands with a Fist, who remembers some English from her childhood and serves as translator for Dunbar and the Sioux while they get to know each other's language. And slowly, she and Dunbar fall in love.

One night Dunbar is awakened by an uncanny shaking and pounding of the earth: A huge buffalo herd is running by. He leaps on his horse and alerts the Sioux, who have been wondering where the buffalo have gone. They return and find many buffalo carcasses strewn about, unused but for the skins. White buffalo hunters have been here, and have wasted the animals they killed. The Sioux know better how to utilize the resources of the prairie, and Dunbar is invited to participate in their hunt. When he kills a buffalo that is threatening a young Sioux, he proves himself to be a true friend to the tribe. In a fight with the rival Pawnee to protect the Sioux's land and people, Dunbar understands what it means to be willing to fight and die for something. He knows who he is: Dances with Wolves.

But the inevitable occurs: the white man arrives in force. An army detachment arrives at Fort Sedgwick, and Dances with Wolves experiences firsthand the trauma that the Indians of the frontier already know so well.

The soldiers senselessly kill his horse and Two Socks, the wolf; they beat Dances with Wolves and mock him for having "gone Injun."

The Sioux friends of Dances with Wolves soon free him, killing many of the troops in the process. As a result, Dances with Wolves faces a heartbreaking dilemma. He realizes that the army will not rest until he is caught, and if he remains with the Sioux, they will all be killed. Thus he must leave them.

Stands with a Fist, now his wife, asserts that her place is with him, and the two ride away into the wilderness, hoping that their people will remain safe—at least for a while.

Dances with Wolves, Costner's directorial debut, is a highly visual film; much of the story is told through the lens of cinematographer Dean Semler. The prairie scenery is glorious, and the camera helps to reveal the deepening relationship between Dunbar and the Sioux. While Dunbar's narration is in English throughout, a substantial portion of the dialogue is spoken in Lakota (Sioux), with English subtitles.

The tale is told at a leisurely pace. It is all the more affecting because we know that the Indians, presented so sympathetically in this film, ultimately do not stand a chance against the advancing hordes of white men.

DAVIES, MARION

The screen career of Marion Davies is of course inextricably bound up with the name of William Randolph Hearst. While this fact has always been recognized, the critical treatment of this particular partnership has shifted considerably over the years. When Hearst and Davies were still actively producing films, none dared mention the personal side of their relationship.

The emphasis in all periods has been to suggest that Davies's screen career was manufactured, then foisted on unwilling audiences and exhibitors. But the current high regard for Davies as a comedienne is largely a modern fashion, and her accomplishments in the bulk of her silent features are much more varied than is generally admitted.

Hearst's interest in film predated his encounter with Davies. He operated the International Newsreel, an animation studio, and produced several of the most important early serials, including *The Exploits of Elaine* (1915). He spotted Marion Davies in the 1916 Ziegfeld Follies and after seeing her performance in a cheaply made feature called *Runaway Romany* (1917) decided to fold her into his own motion-picture empire. Under the Cosmopolitan banner, Hearst was already producing a series of features with

Alma Rubens, but because of his special interest in Davies, he now became involved on a much more personal level.

The bulk of Davies's Cosmopolitan productions, which were made in New York until Hearst shifted his center of operations to California in 1924, are light romantic melodramas. Some are more tearful than others, but one finds a wartime spy plot (*The Burden of Proof,* 1918) a comedy (*Getting Mary Married,* 1919), and a flapper-era morality tale (*The Restless Sex,* 1920). These films do not seem to have been especially successful, and Hearst was already being chided in print for his string of Davies features.

Why these films failed is not at all clear. Perhaps the use of second-rate directors like Julius Steger or George D. Baker had something to do with it.

Although William Randolph Hearst was credited with "manufacturing" Marion Davies's film career, her performances as an actress are quite capable of standing on their own.

One of the few films to survive from the period, *Beauty's Worth* (1922), suggests that Davies's screen persona was not a problem. Yet the public did not respond to these films. Only when Hearst began production of costume spectacles in the wake of the 1921–22 revival of this genre was he finally able to sell Davies to audiences. Their initial effort, *When Knighthood Was in Flower* (1922), proved to be one of the season's big hits, although seen today it suffers from its overstuffed period detail and lackluster direction by Robert Vignola. The film did utilize the full resources of the vast International studio, an old Harlem beer garden that had been taken over by Hearst when Prohibition arrived. It was followed by the equally successful (and similarly dull) *Little Old New York* (1923). This featured even more lavish settings, including an entire neighborhood of nineteenth-century Manhattan rebuilt inside a vast Brooklyn armory. But the spectacles that followed reverted to the original run of bad luck. *Yolanda* (1924), a still more elaborate medieval pageant, gorgeously designed by Hearst's house art director, Joseph Urban, was a complete failure. So was the lavish American Revolutionary War melodrama *Janice Meredith* (1924) and the Hollywood-produced *Lights of Old Broadway* (1925). Hearst could hardly be blamed for trying to duplicate the success of his earlier hits, but he did cease production of these costume epics after 1925.

Davies's late silents, produced on the MGM lot, are as varied as those of any silent star. They include a large group of comedies, among them the still underrated *The Fair Coed* (1927), and such literary adaptations as *Quality Street* (1927) and *The Red Mill* (1927).

In viewing her films today one finds a bright, engaging performance style so often lacking among silent-screen actresses. While Hearst's backing certainly provided the wherewithal to get Davies onscreen and keep her there during periods of public apathy, the performances we see today are quite capable of standing on their own.

DEER HUNTER, THE

The Deer Hunter (1978) is a searing look at the meaning of friendship, the fragility of life, and the futility of the Vietnam War. Directed by Michael Cimino, the screenplay was written by Derik Washburn, from a story by Washburn, Cimino, Louis Garfinkle, and Quinn K. Redeker.

The Deer Hunter is the tale of three Russian-American friends from a dreary Pennsylvania steel town. The young men—Michael (Robert De Niro), Nick (Christopher Walken), and Steven (John Savage)—have grown up together; their lives are closely intertwined.

The average ticket price in 1978—the year of *The Deer Hunter* and *Close Encounters of the Third Kind*—was $2.34.

BETTE DAVIS

The larger-than-life Bette Davis, whom some filmgoers regard as the most accomplished actress in American screen history, was born Ruth Elizabeth Davis on April 5, 1908, in Lowell, Massachusetts. In the late 1980s, looking back on her long and interesting life, she suggested that her tombstone would read "She did it the hard way."

Davis had some advantages, but she did have to fight for her career. She had a comfortably middle-class background, but her parents—her father was a patent lawyer, her mother a photographer—divorced when she was a young girl, which was quite uncommon in those days. Davis knew early in high school that she wanted to be an actress—in her era, not a welcome ambition, especially for a woman.

Davis gained some acting experience in school and local theater, and finally she enrolled in a drama school. Throughout the 1920s she had to work hard for roles. She did not have a conventional sort of beauty, and her personality was quite forceful. Her determination paid off, however, and in 1929 she debuted on Broadway in the play *Broken Dishes.*

Finally, Hollywood beckoned, and Davis soon conquered it. In 1930 she won a six-month contract with Universal (the story goes that a studio representative was sent to meet her train but left when he didn't see anyone who looked like a movie star). That contract led to a seven-year deal with Warner Brothers. During that tenure—working pictures back-to-back—Davis became a huge star, in such movies as *Of Human Bondage* (1934) and *The Petrified Forest* (1936). She won Best Actress Oscars for *Dangerous* (1935) and *Jezebel* (1938); during her career, Davis would be nominated eight other times for Academy Awards.

During the 1940s Davis's star appeared to be on the decline. She had plenty of work, including *Now Voyager* (1942), a film that is particularly associated with her, but she was not as popular as she had been. That changed, at least momentarily, with the release of *All About Eve* in 1950. Her brilliant performance as a stage star who is dogged by a ruthless young actress was right on the money, and Davis's stock in Hollywood was soaring again.

But unfortunately her renewed success did not translate into great parts. Again, Davis always had film work, but she had to wait until 1962 for a really juicy part, in the horror movie *What Ever Happened to Baby Jane?*

Dramatic actress Bette Davis was nominated for ten Academy Awards over the course of her long career; she won twice, for Dangerous *(1935) and* Jezebel *(1938).*

By then Davis was hardly an ingenue—she was solidly middle-aged—but her performance reminded filmgoers of the long-time star's particular charisma. For the next three decades Davis performed often enough in films (and sometimes television) and appeared frequently on TV talk shows, to the point that her by then very grand persona was lampooned regularly by *Saturday Night Live* and various comedians. Davis stayed in the public eye until her death on October 6, 1989.

Davis was married four times and had three children; in 1985 her daughter Barbara Davis Hyman published a scandalous biography of her mother entitled *My Mother's Keeper.*

The American Film Institute awarded Davis its Lifetime Achievement Award in 1977 and in 1999 named her one of its "Greatest Film Legends."

See All About Eve

As the film opens, it is a time of change. The friends, all steelworkers who are used to the searing heat and fire of the steel mill, are preparing to go to Vietnam. They are excited and proud. They have no idea how profoundly their experiences in the war will affect their lives, and the lives of their loved ones.

Steven marries his girlfriend, who is expecting a baby, and it is a time of ritual and celebration for all the friends. As the story unfolds, Michael's admiration for Nick's girlfriend, Linda (Meryl Streep), becomes evident: he only has eyes for her; he always seems on the verge of kissing her. Michael would not be so disloyal to his friend, however. During the wedding reception, where a banner announces "Serving God and Country Proudly," Nick asks Linda to marry him when he returns from the war. She accepts.

Michael (Robert De Niro) drags his friend Steven (John Savage) from a river that they floated down to escape the Vietcong in Michael Cimino's The Deer Hunter.

While Steven is on his honeymoon, Michael and Nick, along with some of their other friends, go off on a last hunting trip. There they discuss their understanding of the nature of death, the purity of a single gunshot in killing a deer.

Once the young men arrive in Vietnam, everything they know about life and death, honor and patriotism becomes irrelevant. The world is turned upside down in that dark and terrifying place. Under harrowing circumstances, the three friends are taken prisoner by the enemy, the Vietcong.

Held in a hut on a river, the men are tortured. The Vietcong force them to play Russian roulette, a game in which each is made to spin the cartridge of a pistol, point the gun at his head, and pull the trigger. There is a single bullet in the chamber. The Vietcong make bets on which of the prisoners will, or will not, kill himself. Russian roulette serves as a symbol for a war in which nothing seems to make sense or have purpose.

Michael is the one who proves most able to endure the circumstances in which they find themselves, and he tries to encourage and protect Nick and Steven. The men grab an opportunity to escape, and they float away down the river, clinging to a fallen tree. Michael can see that Steven's legs are badly damaged, and he carries him up the riverbank toward safety. He is not able to save them all, though, and Nick is left behind.

"You have to think about one shot. One shot is what it's all about. The deer has to be taken with one shot."

Robert De Niro as Michael in *The Deer Hunter* (1978)

When Michael returns to his hometown, he is welcomed as a hero. He is a proud man who keeps his feelings to himself, and no one can understand how profoundly he has changed. Linda comes to realize that he has been deeply hurt, and she asks him to become her lover, so that they can comfort each other.

He finally gets up his courage to visit Steven, who is recuperating in the veteran's hospital—Steven lost both of his legs, and he is emotionally wounded as well. There, Michael learns that Nick is still in Vietnam and may still be alive.

Michael returns to Vietnam to find Nick, honoring an adolescent promise he made long ago. But there is nothing adolescent about Michael now.

Once back in Vietnam, Michael does find Nick—and learns that his friend now plays Russian roulette professionally, for bets. Nick recognizes Michael, and Michael sees the needle tracks on the veins of Nick's forearm, indicating drug use. Michael, desperate to reach Nick, plays Russian roulette with him, amid a shouting crowd in the gambling den, hoping that Nick will be shocked into reality. But Nick is too far gone to understand what is at risk. He points the gun at his head and pulls the trigger—and loses.

After his funeral, Nick is remembered at a small gathering back in Pennsylvania. Michael, Linda, and his other friends make a toast to him: "Here's to Nick." The film ends poignantly, and ironically, as the group sings "God Bless America."

DORIS DAY

Doris Day, the singer/actress who epitomized the image of the wholesome, perky American "girl-next-door" popular in the 1950s, was born Doris von Kappelhoff in Cincinnati, Ohio, on April 3, 1924. She enjoyed a successful singing career, performing with big bands in the 1940s and making popular recordings. Upon being cast in the musical *Romance on the High Seas* (1948), she became a favorite with film audiences as well.

Day quickly won major roles in film after film, including *Young Man with a Horn* (1950), *April in Paris* (1952), *By the Light of the Silvery Moon* (1953), *The Man Who Knew Too Much* (1956), *The Pajama Game* (1957), and *Pillow Talk* (1959). In the 1960s she starred in *Please Don't Eat the Daisies* (1962), *Send Me No Flowers* (1964), and *With Six You Get Eggroll* (1968). Whether drama or comedy, her parts were typically of an innocently sexy, seemingly ditzy but ultimately down-to-earth blonde.

Day's real life was far more eye-opening than her film roles (and, starting in the late 1960s, her television work). Even her childhood was melodramatic. She was hospitalized for a year as a young teen, and later a car accident derailed her hopes to be a dancer. She married for the first time at age seventeen—in her autobiography *Doris Day: Her Own Story* (1975), she described her first husband as a "psychopath." She married for the second time at age twenty-two, again unsuccessfully. Her third marriage, to Marty Melcher, lasted for seventeen years, but upon his death in 1968 Day learned he had embezzled or mishandled all of her money—many millions of dollars. In 1974 a court awarded Day $22 million in damages from the lawyer who helped Melcher squander her fortune. Since her last film in 1968, Day has enjoyed occasional success in television and has gained a reputation as an animal-rights advocate.

notable & quotable

"I knew Doris Day before she was a virgin."

Oscar Levant, humorist/actor

The Deer Hunter, filmed in both the United States and under very difficult conditions in Thailand, was a critical and commercial triumph. It was nominated for nine Academy Awards and won five, including Oscars for Best Picture and Best Director. Christopher Walken won for Best Supporting Actor.

See De Niro, Robert; Streep, Meryl; War film

DEMILLE, CECIL B.

Cecil B. DeMille arrived in Los Angeles on December 20, 1913. He was the newly appointed director general of the Jesse L. Lasky Feature Play Company and was traveling with the firm's entire production unit. The journey had been undertaken in order to film Edwin Milton Royle's western play *The Squaw Man* in surroundings of greater authenticity than those available in New Jersey. The company soon acquired a lease on the property at 6284 Selma Avenue, a renovated barn and adjacent grounds in the suburbs of Hollywood. They were not the first filmmakers in Hollywood, but they were the first company to specialize in feature pictures.

DeMille constructed an open-air stage on the lot and here managed to film the studio scenes of *The Squaw Man* (not inside the barn, as some would have it, since he had no lights). Despite a series of misadventures,

Legendary filmmaker Cecil B. DeMille distanced himself from other producers through his arresting visual style and gift for self-promotion.

including a problem with variant framelines (still visible in existing prints of the film), the picture was successful.

Over the next three years, DeMille directed the twenty-nine features on which his early reputation was based. Made for the Lasky Company, and later Famous Players–Lasky, these films were closely tied to their theatrical sources and the performances of their Broadway stars.

DeMille was able to distance himself from rival producers of canned theater by an arresting visual style and a true genius for self-promotion. Although he was never very successful at articulating screen space through the use of such devices as editing or camera movement, from the beginning he was quite concerned with pictorial composition and won immediate attention for his lighting effects. Working with cameraman Alvin Wyckoff, DeMille pioneered a style of illumination soon known as "Lasky lighting" or (when DeMille was speaking) "Rembrandt lighting." His concern with visual style was relatively advanced at a time when most companies were satisfied to record a clean, detailed image.

DeMille's artistry reached its peak in *The Whispering Chorus* (1918). Although relatively successful at the box office, it marked the end of his early period of artistic experimentation. He followed it with *Old Wives for New* (1918), the first in a series of titillating melodramas designed to capture postwar audiences. This series, especially *Male and Female* (1919) and *Why Change Your Wife?* (1920), inspired a flock of screen imitations, reflecting Hollywood's vision of postwar American social mores. The postwar films became those on which his later reputation was to build (especially his first version of *The Ten Commandments* [1923], with its portents of later spectacles), and the early years of innovation were soon forgotten. When he began to film Gloria Swanson in golden beds and golden bathtubs, DeMille moved permanently from artistic pioneer to cultural phenomenon.

See Goldwyn, Samuel; Lighting; Lubitsch, Ernst; Reid, Wallace; Sunset Boulevard; *Swanson, Gloria; Wilder, Billy*

ROBERT DE NIRO

Robert De Niro, the man whom many critics have called the greatest actor of his time, was born into an artistic family in New York City on August 17, 1943. He grew up in New York's Little Italy—an experience that likely has informed much of his acting work—and attended the High School of Music and Art. De Niro later studied with Stella Adler and Lee Strasberg, appearing on the off-Broadway stage in the 1960s.

De Niro acted in a number of films in the late 1960s and early '70s, but it was not until 1973 that his work drew particular notice. His heartbreaking performance as a dying baseball player in director John Hancock's *Bang the*

D

DENIRO, ROBERT

Method actor Robert De Niro formed his own production company, TriBeCa Productions, in 1989. De Niro also co-owns a successful restaurant in the New York City neighborhood for which his production company was named.

▶

Drum Slowly and his portrayal of a smarmy hoodlum in Martin Scorsese's *Mean Streets* captured the attention not only of audiences but also of film directors and producers. From then on De Niro's star was on an explosive upward trajectory, thanks not only to his talent but also to his savvy in choosing good parts (though *New York New York,* in 1977, was a mistake).

In 1974 De Niro received the Best Supporting Actor Oscar for his performance as the young Vito Corleone in *The Godfather: Part II.* Soon on the heels of that role came the one that is most associated with De Niro, as the violent psychotic in Scorsese's *Taxi Driver* (1976). With that film De Niro solidified his standing as one of the premier actors of his generation. The Academy gave De Niro another Oscar nod for his moving portrayal of a Vietnam vet in *The Deer Hunter* (1978), this time for Best Actor.

De Niro gained a substantial amount of weight in order to play boxer Jake La Motta in *Raging Bull* (1980), another Scorsese film. That was the last truly classic film that De Niro has performed in to date, though he has since made many good movies, including *The Untouchables* (1987), *Midnight Run* (1989), *GoodFellas* (1990), *A Bronx Tale* (1993; De Niro also directed), *Casino* (1995); *Heat* (also in 1995), and *Analyze This* (1999).

See Deer Hunter; Godfather: Part II, The; GoodFellas; Raging Bull; *Scorsese, Martin;* Taxi Driver

DETECTIVE FILM

A motion picture whose plot centers on the prowess of a confident, diligent private eye is called a detective film. This individual is usually shown carrying out a mission of seeking evidence against and tracking down a criminal in a big-city environment. Cool and methodical, the detective-hero eventually gets the job done—succeeding where local police officers and law officers could not.

The detective film differs from a gangster picture. Emphasis and sympathy within the detective film are directed toward the heroic powers of a law-enforcing intermediary, whereas in the gangster film the principal character is often an antiheroic figure living and working in the underworld.

The detective film was widely popular during the 1930s and 1940s, varying in style from the lighthearted *Thin Man* series (1934–44) to the more serious film noir effort, for example, *The Maltese Falcon* (1941). Long-running television series programs, such as *Columbo, Murder, She Wrote,* and *Matlock,* testify to the genre's continued popularity.

See Bogart, Humphrey; Film noir; Gangster film; Maltese Falcon, The

DIEGESIS/DIEGETIC SOUND

Diegesis is a word derived from Greek origins meaning narration or a recitation of narrative facts. As a film term diegesis refers to everything that is occurring on screen: characters' actions and dialogue, visible onscreen space (the frame mise-en-scène), and ambient sounds/music that originate from the screen environment. Together these form the diegesis (fictional narrative). Sound or music that has a recognizable source (character speech, a radio, a musical instrument being played on screen) is termed diegetic sound. Nondiegetic sound refers to sounds that do not originate from the onscreen space, for example, supplied musical scoring, expressive sound effects, voice-over narration. Intradiegetic sound is a term that is often used to describe sounds that have an apparent relationship with the diegesis but are not actually "visible" on screen. An example is the use of voice-over narration by a character in a fictional narrative, for example, the voice-over narration of the character Mark Renton (Ewan McGregor) in Danny Boyle's *Trainspotting* (1996).

See Sound; Trainspotting

DIRECTOR

That individual in the filmmaking process who serves the principal function of developing the film story into an engaging experience that is artfully constructed is the director. The artful construction of a film story involves the appropriate use of motion-picture techniques, the development of a consistent film style, and control of the dramatic elements of acting, pace, and blocking.

A second but equally important function of the film director is the coordination of the various technicians who must support the film's concept. The director usually confers on such important considerations as costumes, lighting, makeup, camera movement, locations, and special effects. Script changes, including additions and deletions, are often within the jurisdiction of the director, who in filming the story must determine whether a scene will or won't "play" and whether plot and character development are clear.

In a general way, it is possible to divide the motion-picture director into two broad types: the craftsman director and the personal director.

notable & quotable

"Only an artist who has mastered all of the rules can break them properly and make the fullest use of the medium he has chosen."

Robert Wise, director, 1971

The Craftsman Director

That individual who is skillfully efficient at taking a motion-picture script and bringing it to life on the screen, the craftsman director knows all facets of film production thoroughly and is able to function with both dramatic and technical ease. A shooting script is closely followed as the director works with the actors and other technicians. The craftsman director is one employed to guide and coordinate the filming of a story with professional skill.

The Personal Director

An individual whose degree of involvement in the filmmaking process is pervasive, most often the personal director selects the film idea and either alone or with other writers develops the idea into a screen scenario and eventually into a shooting script. The idea is chosen because the director has a strong artistic urge to bring the story to the screen. The personal director often both generates and develops the film idea.

See Cinematographer; Editor; Producer; Writer

DISASTER FILM

A disaster film is a type of screen melodrama characterized by a narrative plot that is centered on the efforts of a number of characters to escape a man-made or natural disaster. In its primary goal of providing mass-appeal escapism, the disaster film usually combines extensive action sequences with a story containing character types that are chosen to represent a broad spectrum of society. Technical virtuosity in the display of screen special effects is also a critical element in the disaster film's formulaic design. The genre achieved popularity during the 1930s with such works as *San Francisco* (1936) and *In Old Chicago* (1938) where an earthquake and a fire, respectively, generate calamity. Beginning with *Airport* (1970) and *The Poseidon Adventure* (1972), the disaster film experienced an impressive revival that lasted through most of the 1970s.

See Special-effects film; Titanic

DR. STRANGELOVE, OR: HOW I LEARNED TO STOP WORRYING AND LOVE THE BOMB

Stanley Kubrick's *Dr. Strangelove, or: How I Learned to Stop Worrying and Love the Bomb* (1964), an acidulous deconstruction of the insanities of war in general and the nuclear age in particular, is widely regarded as one of the greatest comedies ever made. Its bravura directorial technique, a daring swirl of surreal comedy and heart-stopping suspense, combines with the high-wire acting brilliance of Peter Sellers (in three roles), George C. Scott, and Sterling Hayden to create one of the classics of American cinema.

The average ticket price in 1964—the year of *Dr. Strangelove*, *My Fair Lady*, and *Zorba the Greek*—was 93 cents.

As the film opens to an oddly serene image of the midair refueling of a B-52 bomber, a narrator somberly warns of a top-secret "Doomsday Device" developed by the Soviet Union (Russia). The camera moves across heavy cloud cover; mountain peaks are just visible in the distance. This isolated place is where the terrifying device is said to exist—that is, if it exists at all.

At Burpelson Air Base, a B-52 bomber lands. Group Captain Mandrake (Sellers), a British liaison officer, receives a call from his supervisor, Strategic Air Command general Jack D. Ripper (Sterling Hayden). Ripper

D

DR. STRANGELOVE

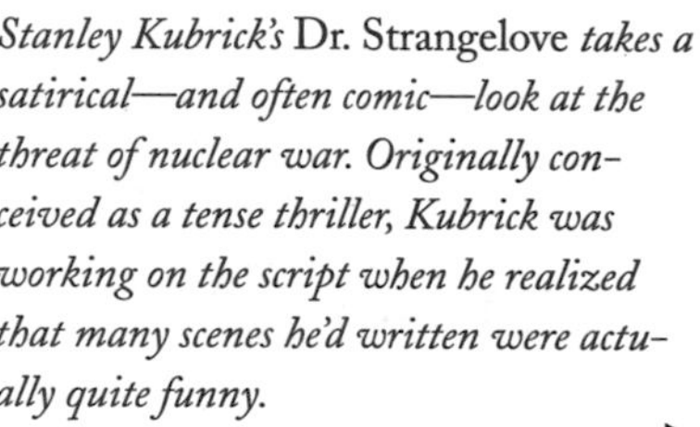
Stanley Kubrick's Dr. Strangelove *takes a satirical—and often comic—look at the threat of nuclear war. Originally conceived as a tense thriller, Kubrick was working on the script when he realized that many scenes he'd written were actually quite funny.*

says something to Mandrake about "a shooting war." He is putting the base on Condition Red: "I'm afraid this is not an exercise." He continues, "My orders are for this base to be sealed tight, and that's what I mean to do, seal it tight." General Ripper eventually seals the base so tight that even the president cannot get a message through—with dire results.

The United States keeps a large fleet of B-52 bombers in the air at all times. In one such plane, the crew is going about its daily routines. The superior officer is Major T. J. "King" Kong (Slim Pickens), a plucky cowboy type with a thick twang. The plane receives orders that decode to "Wing Attack Plan R, R for Romeo." A nuclear bomb is to be deployed. Kong puts on a ten-gallon hat and says, "Well, boys, I reckon this is it, nuclear combat, toe-to-toe with the Ruskies." The song "When Johnny Comes Marching Home" plays in the background.

The phone now rings in the hotel room of General "Buck" Turgidson (George C. Scott). His secretary, Miss Scott (Tracy Reed, a *Playboy* centerfold), answers it from her perch on the bed, where she has been lying in her bathing suit under a tanning lamp. When Turgidson emerges from the bathroom, he learns that "all communications are dead" with Ripper at the Command Base. He is called to the Pentagon's underground war room.

Back at the Air Force base, Mandrake goes to Ripper's office, where he realizes that Ripper has gone mad. The orders for the bomber attack originated not from the U.S. president, as Mandrake initially thought, but from Ripper, who believes that his orders will subvert a communist "plot" to fluoridate the drinking water in the United States.

His British sangfroid barely concealing his enveloping panic, Mandrake asks Ripper, "We don't want to start a nuclear war unless we really have to, do we?" He tries to coax Ripper into rescinding the order, only to find that Ripper is holding him captive, dithering on about a demented theory of bodily purity that entail his denying his "essence" to his many loves.

In the war room, President Muffley (Sellers again) presides. He and various advisors sit at a large round table, dominated from above by the "Big Board," a strategic map showing the progress of the bombers to their targets in the Soviet Union.

Turgidson briefs the president on the airborne exercise that General Ripper has set in motion. The planes, armed with nuclear weapons, will penetrate Russian radar cover within twenty-five minutes. Turgidson concedes that "General Ripper exceeded his authority." The Plan R that Ripper is functioning under, Turgidson admits, lacks "the human element."

President Muffley realizes that the systems put in place to prevent an accidental nuclear war have actually set off an attack. He is appalled by Turgidson's suggestion that they might consider letting the attack just proceed and reap the benefits. Turgidson proudly declares, "Mr. President, I'm not saying we wouldn't get our hair mussed, but I do say not more than ten or twenty million killed tops, depending on the breaks."

Desperate to find a solution, President Muffley calls in the Soviet ambassador. Turgidson, scrambling to gather up his secret documents, protests: "He'll see the Big Board!" Muffley also orders U.S. soldiers to attack Burpelson so that they can capture Ripper and force him to recall the B-52s, which are streaking ominously toward their targets; at the helm of his bomber, Major Kong dutifully checks the contents of his survival kit, which includes four days' emergency rations, three lipsticks, a condom, and a miniature combination Russian phrase-book and Bible. Then the Russian ambassador, De Sadesky (Peter Bull), arrives at the tense war room, and Turgidson accuses him of trying to clandestinely photograph the Big Board, and they get into a scuffle. The president intervenes: "Gentlemen, you can't fight in here. This is the war room!" Muffley then attempts to con-

"You can't fight in here. This is the war room!"

Peter Sellers as the U.S. president in *Dr. Strangelove* (1964)

tact Soviet premier Kissof on the hot line, finally tracking him down in the midst of a drunken revel at a brothel and informing him, "One of our generals went and did a silly thing."

Meanwhile, at Burpelson Air Force Base, the guards think that some American troops are actually Russians in disguise. A gun battle ensues. After the ambassador speaks with Kissof, he warns that something terrible is going to happen: "The fools . . . the Doomsday Machine . . . a device which will destroy all human and animal life on earth." The device is designed to trigger itself automatically if a nuclear bomb strikes anywhere in the Soviet Union.

Muffley now consults with Dr. Strangelove (Sellers again), an ex-Nazi German nuclear scientist, now an American citizen and a nuclear weapons strategist. Strangelove sits in a wheelchair, constantly wrestling into submission a seemingly autonomous black-gloved right hand that ever yearns to uncoil into a Nazi salute. The Doomsday Machine, Dr. Strangelove explains, really exists. He asks why the Russians kept it a secret, since the whole point of the machine is nuclear deterrence. The ambassador responds, "It was to be announced at the Party Congress on Monday. As you know, the premier loves surprises."

"Well, boys, I reckon this is it—nuclear combat toe-to-toe with the Rooskies."

Slim Pickens as Major T. J. "King" Kong in *Dr. Strangelove* (1964)

Back at the base, General Ripper is exchanging gunfire with the attacking troops. His office is now a bullet-riddled disaster, but he rants on to Mandrake about the dangers of fluoridation to his "life essence" as his overpowered defending troops surrender the base. Mandrake tries to get Ripper to give him the code that can stop the nuclear operation. But before he can talk him into it, Ripper walks into the bathroom and shoots himself to death. Mandrake finds written clues to the lifesaving recall code but with all communications to the base severed has no way of relaying them to the president. Mandrake convinces the commander of the invading forces, Colonel "Bat" Guano (Keenan Wynn), to shoot the change out of a Coca-Cola machine so he can call the White House from a pay phone. Guano solemnly warns him, however, that if Mandrake is lying, he will have to answer to the Coca-Cola company.

A brief surge of elation in the war room follows the successful transmission of the recall code to all the planes until it becomes evident that one plane, Kong's, has not received the code and is proceeding toward its target. Muffley then gives the Soviets whatever information they need to shoot down the plane. Kong, learning that a Soviet missile is tracking his B-52, tries to evade it, and it detonates just a mile from the plane, almost knocking the B-52 out of the sky. Three engines are out, and the plane is leaking fuel. Forced to choose a closer target, his crew selects a nuclear missile site in Russia. Kong climbs astride a bomb to fix some circuitry. At the same time, the crew opens the bomb doors and releases the missile. The last we see of Kong he is riding the bomb like a cowboy on a bronco, shouting, "Yahoo! Yahoo!" as it descends toward its target. A rising nuclear mushroom cloud signals a successful hit.

Back in the war room, the men are still looking for ways to survive the coming nuclear holocaust. Dr. Strangelove proposes a hundred-year plan for reconstituting the population, with women breeders chosen for their sexual desirability. The Soviet ambassador says, "I must confess, you have an astonishingly good idea there, Doctor."

Meanwhile, Doomsday is approaching. The Doomsday Machine sets itself off, and, just before the world is incinerated to the anomalously dulcet strains of the ballad "We'll Meet Again," Strangelove's arm springs into a triumphant Nazi salute as he rises from his wheelchair and exclaims, "Mein Führer! I can walk!"

See Chaplin, Charlie; Duck Soup; *Kubrick, Stanley; War film*

DOCTOR ZHIVAGO

Although it became one of the biggest box-office draws in movie history, *Doctor Zhivago* (1965), David Lean's follow-up to the magnificent *Lawrence of Arabia,* struck many critics as a disappointment—a physically impressive production that never transcended the feel of a lumbering, epic

Hundreds of extras were used in the filming of Doctor Zhivago, *David Lean's epic tale of war and revolution.*

▼

soap opera. The Motion Picture Academy was somewhat more charitable in its assessment, if somewhat more reserved than it had been with more successful historical epics: the film won Oscars in only five of the ten categories in which it was nominated (screenplay, music, cinematography, art direction, and costumes).

The film is based on Boris Pasternak's acclaimed novel of the same name. Edmund Wilson, a preeminent American critic, heralded Pasternak's banned-in-the-USSR novel as "one of the great events in man's literary and moral history," comparing Pasternak to Pushkin and Tolstoy; literary posterity has not so far corroborated this clarion declaration, even though Pasternak was awarded the Nobel Prize for literature in 1958, mostly on the strength of *Doctor Zhivago.*

"One day she [Lara] went away and never came back. She died or vanished somewhere in one of the labor camps—a nameless number on a list that was, afterwards, mislaid."

Alec Guinness as Gen. Yevgraf Zhivago in *Dr. Zhivago* (1965)

Pasternak's book tells the story of Yuri Zhivago (Omar Sharif), a nineteenth-century Russian doctor/poet who lives through the great social upheavals of war and revolution while balancing obligations to his family and a passion for his mistress. In adapting Pasternak's novel for the screen, Lean and his scenarist, Robert Bolt, strove to remain true to the spirit of the sprawling novel but were obliged to forge their own path, despite their high regard for the source. The screenplay Bolt and Lean together fashioned retains the central characters (more or less altered), an outline of the plot, and some of Pasternak's major thematic concerns. However, the film's structure, many of the characterizations, most of the specific episodes, and virtually all of the dialogue are either original with the filmmakers or highly imaginative transformations of details from the novel.

Zhivago was born to an aristocratic family that fell into poverty. Orphaned, he is raised by a warm family of wealthy nobles with whom he passes a privileged childhood in their house in St. Petersburg and, during the summers, on their vast country estate. The talented young Zhivago develops into an accomplished poet and falls in love with the family's daughter Tonya (Geraldine Chaplin), who eventually becomes his wife. The film traces the ways in which this serene, elevated way of life is disrupted and eventually destroyed by the wars and revolutions that convulsed the social fabric of Russia in the early twentieth century: the revolution of 1905, World War I, the revolution of 1917, and the fierce civil war that followed.

During World War I, Zhivago, trained as a medical doctor, is drafted into military service. During his stint in the army he meets and is drawn to the captivating and dedicated nurse Lara (Julie Christie), whose heroically unflagging devotion to her calling makes a powerful emotional impression on Zhivago. But after the war, his loyalty to his wife, Tonya, prevails, and he returns to the family estate, where aristocratic gentility has given way to upheaval and despair in the wake of the Bolshevik seizure of the property. When Zhivago encounters Lara once again at the estate, their wartime affinity blossoms into a passionate affair.

The tempests of history intervene to separate the lovers when Zhivago is captured by the Bolsheviks during the civil war. He is now permanently

separated from his family, all of whom have fled to Paris in the wake of the Red Terror. Zhivago endures a brutal two years as a prisoner of the Bolsheviks, including forced marches across desolate winter steppes, after which he manages to escape and return to the abandoned estate, where he rejoins Lara. Their time together is a period of creative flowering for Zhivago, who writes his most inspired poetry during this brief interlude.

But their bliss is interrupted when Lara's estranged husband, Pasha (Tom Courtenay), is declared an enemy of the state, thus casting a stigma on all of his associates. Following Pasha's suicide to avoid execution at the hands of the Bolsheviks, Lara is obliged to leave the estate and seek safety elsewhere, relying on the help of a lover from her youth, the lawyer Boris Komarovsky (Rod Steiger). Komarovsky is Zhivago's antithesis in every respect: he is a brutish, cynical, but powerful political operative who becomes Lara's only hope of eluding arrest by the Bolsheviks. Despite her enduring love for Zhivago, she accepts Komarovsky's help in fleeing to safety—the price of which, presumably, is enduring his sexual predations—and leaves the estate, never again to see her beloved Zhivago, whose pride prevents him from accepting any help from the despicable Komarovsky.

Eight years later, Zhivago, his health ruined by a weak heart, is riding a streetcar in Moscow when he sees Lara through the window. After a frantic scramble to exit the car, he staggers after her on the street, but before he can overtake her, he suffers a heart attack, collapses, and dies. The oblivious Lara disappears around a corner, eventually to perish in a Stalinist labor camp. The film ends with the image of Zhivago's funeral drawing a large crowd of admirers despite the state's official ban on his work.

See Guinness, Alec; Epic; Lean, David

DOCUMENTARY

Documentaries are nonfiction films that are usually shot on location, use actual persons rather than actors, and focus thematically on historical, scientific, social, or environmental subjects. Their principal purpose is to enlighten, inform, educate, persuade, and provide insight into the world in which we live.

The World Union of Documentary defines the documentary film genre in this manner: "By the documentary film is meant all methods of recording on celluloid any aspect of reality either by factual shooting or by sincere and justifiable construction (reenactment), so as to appeal either to reason or emotion for the purpose of stimulating the desire for, and the widening of, human knowledge and understanding, and of truthfully posing problems and their solutions in the spheres of economics, culture and human relations." Newsreel essays and informational films with unifying themes are often categorized as a type of documentary film.

A documentary, more often than not, is a recording of physical reality that the filmmaker interprets for us by the edited arrangement of the material: "a creative treatment of actuality," according to John Grierson in his essay "First Principles of Documentary," published in *Cinema Quarterly* (1932–34). Among the early significant creative documentary filmmakers were Robert Flaherty (*Nanook of the North,* 1922) and Pare Lorentz (*The River,* 1937). Flaherty's films deal with humans in their environment. Lorentz in *The River* and *The Plow That Broke the Plains* (1936) produced poetic films aimed toward social persuasion about ecological problems of the decade. These films established the traditional documentary. In recent decades many subschools of documentary filmmaking have developed, for example, cinema verité, direct cinema, docudrama, ethnographic film.

notable & quotable

"You photograph the natural life, but you also, by your juxtaposition of detail, create an interpretation of it."

John Grierson, pioneering documentary producer, 1932–34

With the advent of television, the documentary film genre acquired the two principal elements needed to sustain the form: a mass audience and financial support through institutional sponsorship. On television, the genre is seen in a variety of different orientations: (1) journalistic: intended to provide information and analysis (*CBS Reports, NBC White Papers*); (2) social: designed to reveal social problems and to persuade (*Harvest of Shame,* 1960; *I Want It All Now,* 1978); (3) poetic, educational: intended to entertain and teach (*America,* 1972); (4) magazine: composed of a variety of short documentaries and newsreel essays, with a studio host or hosts introducing and commenting on different segments (*60 Minutes, 20/20, Prime Time*).

See Actualité; Cinema verité; Feature film; Neorealism; Newsreels; Realist cinema

DOUBLE INDEMNITY

Double Indemnity, Billy Wilder's 1944 film about deception and double crosses, helped establish the genre French critics later dubbed *film noir,* a type of American melodrama set mostly in stygian nightworlds of heartless cities where women with a past and men with no future are driven by lust and greed to desperate schemes of treachery and murder. No film evoked this uniquely modern sense of the sinister better than *Double Indemnity,* a masterpiece of hard-edged cynicism laced with Raymond Chandler's masterfully dark, edgy dialogue. It earned Academy Award nominations for

Best Picture, Best Actress, Best Director, Best Screenplay, Best Cinematography, Best Score, and Best Sound.

The film begins as a figure on crutches walks into the frame, blackening it with his shadow. The darkness spreads over the screen, disappearing into the early morning fog. The wounded man, Walter Neff (Fred MacMurray), lurches into an office, where he begins dictating a memorandum to his supervisor in which he confesses to the murder of one of his clients. With Walter Neff telling his own story, the film takes the form of a series of flashbacks. Wilder returns to Neff periodically, and every time he does, the bloodstain on Neff's suit jacket gets larger.

The flashback reveals that Neff is an insurance salesman who has been lured to his doom by a cynical seductress, Phyllis Dietrichson, whom he first meets on a seemingly minor house call concerning her husband's auto insurance. Mr. Dietrichson is out, so Neff instead confronts his wife, Phyl-

Double Indemnity *was originally supposed to end with the trial and execution of Walter Neff (Fred MacMurray), but the Hayes office insisted that those scenes be cut, calling the footage "a blueprint for murder."*

lis (Barbara Stanwyck), just returned from a sunbath and draped only with a towel and a wanton leer. Their animal attraction is immediately evident, and she invites him back to discuss the matter further. Upon Neff's return, not only is the husband absent, but this time the maid is also gone. Phyllis, now in a dress but oozing the fulsome carnality of the pathologically greedy, outlines a plan to take a huge double-indemnity insurance policy on her husband's life that her spouse is to know nothing about. Although hooked by the brazen erotic allure of this overture to murder, the conflicted Neff at first rebuffs the whole idea; for days afterward he wrestles with his conscience, but his repulsion is gradually overcome by the insistent power of Phyllis's siren song.

In a chillingly effective series of scenes set in mundane settings such as a grocery store, the pair develops a plan designed to make Dietrichson's demise appear accidental, with Neff confident that his insider's knowledge of the business will guarantee their success. She even convinces him to undertake the task of murdering her husband (Tom Powers), whose leg is in a cast from an accident. Neff then boards a train, impersonating Dietrichson right down to the cast. He leaps from the train at a prearranged spot, where Phyllis waits with the dead man's body, which the pair places on the tracks, thus completing an apparently perfect crime.

"The border? You won't make the elevator, Walter."

Edward G. Robinson as insurance investigator Barton Keyes, after hearing the pleas of his friend Fred MacMurray (as confessed murderer Walter Neff) to escape, in *Double Indemnity* (1944)

The engine of justice is set in motion by the suspicions of the insurance company's claims adjuster, Barton Keyes (Edward G. Robinson), who tells his colleague Neff that he is convinced that Phyllis has murdered her husband. Keyes, dedicated and relentless, informs Phyllis of his suspicions, but he initially believes that her accomplice is Nino (Gig Young), the lover she has wooed away from her stepdaughter, Lola (Jean Heather), who has already informed Neff that Phyllis, then a nurse, murdered her mother in order to marry her father.

Keyes's steady, methodical investigation gnaws at Neff, who decides that the only way to escape detection is to murder his accomplice. He enters Phyllis's bedroom intent on murder, but she grabs a gun from under her pillow and shoots him first. Paralyzed by an uncharacteristic spasm of feeling, she cannot summon the will to finish the job. He grabs the gun and coldly slays her.

Having staggered to the office to give his dictation, Neff notices Keyes listening to his confession. Neff begs Keyes to allow him sufficient time to get past the border to Mexico, but Keyes gives no quarter, responding that Neff will not even make it to the hallway. After calling the police, Keyes bends down beside his dying colleague and lights his cigarette; Neff drags on it with his last breath.

Double Indemnity is designed to be seen from a particular point of view—Neff's. Wilder keeps everything within Neff's range of vision. Thus we not only see what Neff sees; we also see it his way, refracted through the vision of a fast-talking, slick insurance agent. *Double Indemnity* reeks of sleaze brought there by the narrator. Neff lives in a sparsely furnished and harshly lit one-room apartment. He spends his time on the road, a hustler with an enviable sales record because he knows how to talk his way into a house, pushing past the maid to con the mistress. Wilder films Neff's scenes either streaked with shadow or overlit, sinister, or garish.

Phyllis is always seen from Neff's perspective. When she first appears in the film descending the stairs toward Neff, she is little more than a pair of long legs and a gold ankle bracelet. Her allure alternates with crassness; a blonde ice woman melting into vulnerability. Wilder dresses her in white for the crucial scenes: in a white bath towel when she meets Neff, a white cashmere sweater with a slip strap showing when she seduces Neff, and during the shoot-out where she dies, blood-spattered white lounging pajamas. The only time Phyllis reveals the human side of her personality is when she fires at Neff; for a short second she has a sense of regret—a moment that gives Neff the chance to kill her first.

The only pure relationship in the film is between Neff and his supervisor, Barton Keyes. Their relationship is like that of father and son, with Neff looking up to Keyes because he has integrity. That Neff loves this man is not surprising. As Wilder presents it, one loves what one lacks. Keyes's integrity puts the conspirators at risk as he begins to suspect foul play. The theme of father and son is played out to the end. Wilder created one of the most powerful images of male love ever portrayed on the screen: a pietà in the form of a surrogate father lighting the cigarette of his dying surrogate son.

See Film noir; Wilder, Billy

DRIVE-IN THEATER

A form of open-air movie theater that increased in number and popularity in the decade following World War II, the development and growth of drive-in theaters resulted in part from the postwar baby boom and the increasing auto culture of new, family-oriented suburbanites. Drive-in theaters were designed and equipped to make motion-picture viewing possible from inside a parked automobile. The average drive-in theater would hold 300–500 automobiles; larger ones held as many as 1,500 cars. In a period when box office revenues were diminishing, drive-in theaters spurred new interest in filmgoing by making group attendance possible at a lower cost. The number of drive-in theaters decreased after a peak in the late 1950s.

FAYE DUNAWAY

An actress known for her cool blonde beauty, Faye Dunaway was born in Bascom, Florida, on January 14, 1941. According to most reports, Dunaway's father was an army officer, and the family moved around frequently in the United States and Europe; in several interviews, however, Dunaway has referred to herself as a poor southern country girl. As is often the case in the movie business, it is hard to separate fact from the fiction of the public relations machine.

After graduating from high school, Dunaway reportedly attended the University of Florida and Boston University's School of Fine and Applied Arts. In 1962 she was accepted into the competitive Lincoln Center Repertory Company in New York City, where she had roles in *A Man for All Seasons* and several other plays.

She did not have long to wait for stardom. Dunaway had a banner year in 1967, when she won parts in three movies: *The Happening, Hurry Sunday,* and *Bonnie and Clyde.* In this last film, playing opposite Warren Beatty ("Clyde Barrow"), Dunaway's portrayal of gangster Bonnie Parker won her an Academy Award nomination for Best Actress.

Over the next few years Dunaway was in great demand, acting in one or two films a year, but she did not make another big splash until 1974, when she played a complicated, tragic character in the well-reviewed movie *Chinatown.* Again she won a nomination for Best Actress—and again she did not win. Dunaway's antagonistic relationship with *Chinatown* director Roman Polanski gave credence to rumors that she was "difficult" to work with, an unpleasant reputation that has dogged her ever since.

It was for her role in the film *Network* (1976) that Dunaway finally won an Academy Award, for Best Supporting Actress. A few years later her chilling portrayal of actress Joan Crawford in *Mommie Dearest* (1981) also earned rave reviews.

In the 1980s Dunaway spent much of her time in Europe, raising her son, Liam, from her marriage to photographer Terry O'Neill. They eventually divorced; she was also married for a time to rock singer Peter Wolf. Toward the end of the decade she returned to Hollywood to revive her flagging career, taking a gutsy role as a drunk in *Barfly* (1987). Since that time she has had a series of roles in small films and done television work.

Gorgeous blonde Faye Dunaway was nominated twice for an Academy Award before she finally won for her portrayal of a driven network executive in the film Network *(1976).*

See Bonnie and Clyde; Chinatown; *Nicholson, Jack; Polanski, Roman*

DUCK SOUP

Duck Soup (1933), a short film starring the Marx Brothers (Groucho, Harpo, Chico, and Zeppo), is a comedy with a decidedly political bent, a lampoon of the totalitarian government style of Nazi leader Adolf Hitler and other dictators. *Duck Soup* was directed by Leo McCarey.

Through songs and constant sight and verbal gags, the film lampoons the idiocy of high government and the meaninglessness of war. The story, music, and lyrics were created by Bert Kalmar and Harry Rubin, with additional dialogue by Arthur Sheekman and Nat Perrin.

After the opening credits (four quacking ducks symbolizing the four Marx Brothers) the audience is introduced to the mythical kingdom of Freedonia, a country somewhere in the Balkans.

Freedonia has gone bankrupt. Mrs. Gloria Teasdale (Margaret Dumont), a wealthy dowager whose late husband once was president, offers $20

The Marx Brothers' Duck Soup, *a flop when first released, is now considered a masterpiece of satirical comedy, complete with sight gags.*

million to the government to bail out the country, but she requires that certain demands be met before she will cough up the money. She claims that the government has been mismanaged, and she insists that a new leader be named. Thus, the pompous Rufus T. Firefly (Groucho Marx) is appointed as the new head of Freedonia.

Trentino (Louis Calhern), the ambassador of the rival country Sylvania, tries to subvert Mrs. Teasdale's plans, hiring the seductive dancer Vera Marcal (Raquel Torres) to distract Firefly. Trentino thinks he'll be able to marry Mrs. Teasdale and thus take over Freedonia. He also hires some spies to subvert Firefly, little realizing that they will soon be members of Firefly's cabinet (Chicolini, a peanut and hot dog vendor played by Chico Marx, will be Firefly's secretary of war, while Pinkie, played by Harpo Marx, will be the official chauffeur).

In Firefly's first cabinet meeting, he keeps his governmental aides and ministers waiting while he finishes a game of jacks. His secretary of war resigns, frustrated with Firefly's refusal to discuss any real governmental matters, and the president offers the vendor Chicolini a government job:

"*I have a good mind to join a club and beat you over the head with it.*"

Groucho Marx as Rufus T. Firefly in *Duck Soup* (1933)

Chicolini: What job?
Firefly: Secretary of War.
Chicolini: All right, I take it.
Firefly: Sold!

When President Firefly goes to a tea party at Mrs. Teasdale's residence, he is greeted by the national anthem. There, he vies with Trentino for Mrs. Teasdale's affection. The tensions between the two men threaten to plunge their countries into war. Mrs. Teasdale tries to reconcile the two, but to no avail. Therein begins a comic set of misunderstandings, mistaken identities, and insults that climaxes in an absurd parody of war. In a spectacular musical ensemble, "The Country's Going to War," the Marx Brothers and the people of Freedonia hail the coming of battle.

Freedonia wins the war when Ambassador Trentino gets stuck in the door of the Freedonian headquarters—he finally surrenders on behalf of Sylvania when he is pelted with apples.

Duck Soup was a flop at the box office. Both critics and general audiences rejected the movie—at that time, the height of the Great Depression and the rise of fascism in Europe, its political irreverence was viewed as not only disrespectful, but downright scandalous. Today the film is perceived as daring and prescient, warning people of the cataclysm to come under the Nazis.

See Comedy; Dr. Strangelove; *Kubrick, Stanley; War film*

E.T.: THE EXTRATERRESTRIAL

E.T.: The Extraterrestrial, the most profitable movie in history until trumped by Spielberg's own *Jurassic Park* (1993), became an instant classic among latter-day high-tech Hollywood blockbusters. Breaking the bank by cannily casting a cross-generational spell of innocent wonder and intergalactic good vibes, Spielberg's star went supernova as he confirmed his status "as a master storyteller of his medium," in the words of *Time*'s Richard Corliss. The Oscar voters seconded the ticket-buyers and critics, awarding top honors to *E.T.* for best original score and best visual effects, and conferring nominations for Best Picture, Best Direction, Best Screenplay, Best Cinematography, Best Sound, and Best Sound Effects.

The story is a blend of tried-and-true elements: large helpings of *Old Yeller* and *Peter Pan* and a dash of New Testament. The film opens as a spaceship lands in a California forest, and its small passengers disembark in order to collect plant samples. When local authorities are alerted to a disturbance in the woods, the spaceship makes a hasty takeoff—accidentally leaving one of its passengers behind.

"*How do you explain school to higher intelligence?*"

Henry Thomas as Elliott in *E.T.: The Extraterrestrial* (1982)

Later, a young boy, Elliott (Henry Thomas), discovers the "goblin" in his backyard and lures him into the house with Reese's Pieces. Once in Elliott's room, the extraterrestrial, or "E.T.," as Elliott calls it, begins scanning the various toys and objects scattered around, initiating a learning process between the alien and an earthbound boy. From this gentle point of departure Spielberg fashions a touching tale that all kids—especially suburban children, of which Spielberg was one—might fantasize during those lonely, isolated periods of youth.

Elliott introduces E.T. to his brother and sister. Gertie (Drew Barrymore) is startled when she meets the ugly but strangely cute creature that Elliott has found. She immediately blurts out a scream that alarms E.T.: he cranes his neck up in fear and belches out an unearthly screech. Eventually, Gertie takes an interest in E.T. and teaches him to talk.

E.T.'s living space is a large closet off Elliott's room filled with clothes, toys, and stuffed animals. E.T. experiences Halloween with other neighborhood kids, a sequence that is both funny and touching. For E.T.'s disguise, the children dress him up in a sheet, and one of the first creatures he sees is outfitted in a "Yoda" costume (from director George Lucas's *Star Wars* series).

E.T.'s glowing finger, we learn, can heal wounds, and he uses it to heal Elliott's cut finger. E.T.'s heartlight also causes his chest to glow at various times, either in dire fear or because he has been warmly touched. In addition, a symbiotic relationship between the creature and the boy develops, so that whatever E.T. experiences, Elliott does too. In one scene, for example, E.T. becomes intoxicated on beer and Elliott exhibits the effects at school. E.T. watches a love scene on television between John Wayne and Maureen O'Hara in John Ford's film *The Quiet Man* (1952). At the same time, Elliott, now in science class and under the spell of E.T.'s symbiotic extrasensory perception, quickens his nerve and kisses the prettiest girl in the class. Noticing that his friend E.T. looks like the frogs he and his classmates are about to dissect, Elliott is suddenly compelled to free all the frogs from their glass enclosures, putting himself in trouble with the science teacher.

E.T.: The Extraterrestrial (1982) has been seen by over 240 million people, as estimated by its distributor, MCA.

Meanwhile, unidentified government agents are quietly on the prowl for the little alien. They listen in to neighborhood conversations with ultrasensitive sound equipment, use radiation detectors to pick up traces of the extraterrestrial, and eventually begin a house-to-house inquiry.

Fortunately, E.T. manages to build a transmitter contraption out of spare parts (a Speak 'n' Spell computer toy, an umbrella, a circular saw blade, bobby pins, and a record player) and places it on a hillside with help from Elliott. While the contraption is bleeping out signals into the heavens in an attempt for E.T. to "phone home," Elliott falls asleep, and E.T. stands guard over the machine. E.T. eventually begins to feel ill. He walks off into the forest, and when Elliott awakens in the morning, the contraption is still functioning, but E.T. is gone! Feeling depressed and ill himself, Elliott walks home to a worried mother, and sends his brother Michael (Robert MacNaughton) out to find the lost creature. E.T. is found in the forest and brought home. Life has begun to leave E.T., who becomes afraid for Elliott, because his life seems to be draining away, too—the result of the symbiotic relationship. The children fetch their mother for help, and it is the first time she sees the creature. Her first thought is to protect her children, and in doing so, attempts to usher them out of the house, away from E.T. But when she opens the door, she encounters a man in a space suit.

Outside the house, government workers have enveloped the house in a plastic tent to decontaminate it. A makeshift emergency room is set up, and E.T. and Elliott are placed alongside each other on long tables. When E.T. is pricked with a needle, Elliott responds in pain. But E.T.'s life is fading, and so is Elliott's. Elliott implores E.T. to heal himself, but apparently he cannot. When it appears hopeless for the extraterrestrial, the doctors turn their attention to saving Elliott, but even that now appears futile.

E.T. dies, but Elliott miraculously comes back to full health. He looks at his dead friend and pleads for him to come back to life, but the alien remains pale and motionless. Later, viewing his friend for the last time, Elliott notices E.T.'s heartlight glowing. Overjoyed that his friend is not dead, he knows he must help E.T. escape the government workers. He gets Michael to recruit his friends for help. Pretending E.T. is still dead, Elliott closes the lead tomblike container and follows it through the plastic tunnel to the waiting van.

Once inside, he opens the tomb, brushes away the ice, and helps E.T. out. Michael, meanwhile, sneaks into the cab of the van, starts the engine, and zooms off, dragging along the plastic tunnel with the two men still inside it. When the men begin to climb forward, Elliott unfastens the tunnel, dropping the workers in the middle of the road. Michael, although too young to have a license, succeeds in driving the van to the meeting placc, where his friends are waiting with bicycles. Elliott places E.T. in his bike's basket, and the bicyclists head for the rendezvous location where E.T.'s spaceship will pick him up. When government workers and police trap the bikers with a roadblock, E.T. miraculously makes the bicycles fly off the ground (in classic Disney style) and past the moon (recalling *Peter Pan*).

At the rendezvous site, there is a touching good-bye betwen E.T. and Elliott, while the others—Gertie, Michael, and their mother—look on in wonder and amazement. Gertie gives E.T. a geranium plant that had died but that E.T. brought back to life, and E.T. tells her to be good. Then he waddles up the ramp of the ship, the hatch quickly closes, and the ship rises. E.T. is finally going home after his adventure on planet Earth.

See Spielberg, Steven

CLINT EASTWOOD

The phenomenally successful actor, director, and producer Clint Eastwood was born on May 31, 1930, in San Francisco, California. His father worked in gas stations and moved his son (named Clinton Eastwood) frequently during the lean years of the Great Depression.

After Eastwood graduated from high school, he worked for a few years at odd jobs, then served in the army from 1950 to 1954. The story goes that while he was on leave, his plane crashed into the Pacific and he swam three miles to shore. He was then assigned as swimming instructor for boot camp, thereby being spared combat action in Korea.

After his stint in the army, Eastwood sought and won a modest contract at Universal Studios and was given a few small roles in B movies. But when some studio executives decided that the young man's Adam's apple was too big, they dropped him from the contract. He worked odd jobs for a few years to pay the bills, but he continued to try to find work in show business.

In 1964, the year Julie Andrews was paid $125,000 for *Mary Poppins*, Clint Eastwood earned $15,000 for his role in *A Fistful of Dollars*.

In the late 1950s he was cast as Rowdy Yates in *Rawhide*, a long-running western television series. That portrayal won him starring roles in several "spaghetti westerns" (so-called because they were made by Italian director Sergio Leone), including *A Fistful of Dollars,* 1964, and *The Good, the Bad, and the Ugly,* 1966. These films were internationally popular and established the rugged, tight-lipped actor as a star.

The year 1971 was a banner one for Eastwood. He starred in and directed *Play Misty for Me,* which established him as a versatile actor, capable of more than just westerns. Eastwood also played the title character in *Dirty Harry,* the first of what would be a string of popular movies about the San Francisco cop who has his own brand of vigilante justice. Eastwood became closely associated with the strong, silent character, whose tag line was "Go ahead. Make my day."

Eastwood was a top male star throughout the '70s, appearing in (and often directing or producing) such fare as *High Plains Drifter* (1973), *The Outlaw Josey Wales* (1976), *The Eiger Sanction* (1976), *Every Which Way but Loose* (1978), and *Escape from Alcatraz* (1979).

Eastwood's magic touch continued into the 1980s, with turns in such movies as *Honkytonk Man* (1982), *Sudden Impact* (1983), and *Pale Rider* (1985). His direction of *Bird* (1988) earned critical raves.

In 1992 Eastwood—whom many filmgoers consider as attractive as ever—won Best Picture and Best Director Oscars for his western *Unforgiven.* (The film was also credited by some critics as having single-handedly revived the genre.) His roles in *In the Line of Fire* (1993), *The Bridges of Madison County* (1995; he also directed), *Absolute Power* (1997), and *True Crime* (1999) were welcomed by his fans.

Eastwood was married from 1954 to 1980 to Maggie Johnson, but had romantic entanglements on the side (he had a daughter with actress Roxanne Tunis in 1964). Eastwood also had two children with Johnson during their marriage. In the late 1970s Eastwood became involved with actress Sondra Locke; their bitter breakup a decade later led her to file a "palimony" lawsuit against Eastwood and Warner Brothers (the lawsuit was settled out of court), and she wrote a nasty tell-all book, which one critic suggested be taken with "a boulder of salt." Eastwood later had a daughter with actress Frances Fisher, and he married television news broadcaster Tina Ruiz in 1996. They have one child.

Eastwood has served as mayor of Carmel, California. He has also been given many awards by the film community for his many professional accomplishments during his long career.

See Streep, Meryl; Unforgiven; *Western*

Clint Eastwood is one of the few actors who have made a smooth transition from actor to director. His film Unforgiven *won the Oscar for Best Picture, and Eastwood won for Best Director.*

EASY RIDER

Easy Rider (1969) is a "biker flick" or "road movie" whose theme is the high price of freedom in the midst of an increasingly paranoid and bigoted America. The names of the two protagonists, Wyatt (or "Captain America," played by Peter Fonda) and Billy (Dennis Hopper), derive from two rebellious figures from the Wild West, Wyatt Earp and Billy the Kid.

The film's screenplay was reportedly written by Fonda, Hopper, and Terry Southern (though Hopper later tried to claim all the credit); it received an Academy Award nomination. In addition to Fonda and Hopper costarring, Fonda produced and Hopper directed.

By all accounts, it is astounding that the film ever made it to the screen, as its production was remarkably slapdash. Fonda and Hopper were part of the wave of "New Hollywood," and the rules for making movies, like the times, were in flux. Hopper had never directed before and is said to have been significantly drug impaired during the filming. The shooting of the Mardi Gras scene was particularly haphazard.

Easy Rider opens with Wyatt and Billy conducting a cocaine deal. (Hopper later claimed that his role in this film was responsible for the eventual widespread use of cocaine in the United States.) Wyatt hides some drugs and the money from the deal in a transparent plastic tube in the gas tank of his Harley, and he and Billy take off for parts unknown.

Besides the fact that they are from Los Angeles, we learn nothing of these men except what we see onscreen. With his cool head, soft-spoken manner, and slim elegance (despite his omnipresent black leather pants, which would seem unbearably uncomfortable, given the steamy terrain he is riding through), Wyatt/Captain America is the natural leader of the pair. By contrast, Billy is a hothead and a slob, constantly smoking, drinking, or snorting something. Billy seems to revere Wyatt, almost to the point of sexual obsession.

Early on their cross-country odyssey, Wyatt and Billy are turned away when they ask for a room at a motel; apparently the manager is alarmed by their disheveled appearance. Subsequently the bikers begin camping out. During their journey, they run into a number of interesting strangers. A rancher who has made his own way in the world, out of the mainstream, helps them when Wyatt has a flat tire. A commune of city kids who are trying to make it on the land welcomes them for a short stay.

While passing through a small town, Wyatt and Billy fall in line with a parade. The "longhairs" on their Harleys stand out like a sore thumb, and they are rounded up by the local police. In jail they meet a drunken lawyer,

"Well, they got this here, see, scissor-happy 'Beautify America' thing going on around here. They're trying to make everybody look like Yul Brynner."

Jack Nicholson as George Hanson in *Easy Rider* (1969)

George Hanson (Jack Nicholson). He helps Wyatt and Billy get out of jail and subsequently joins them on their cross-country trek, riding behind Captain America and wearing a gold football helmet. They set off for Mardi Gras in New Orleans, expecting the trip to take two or three days.

George never makes it to Louisiana. When the men stop for a bite to eat at a diner along the road, they attract attention from the local police and assorted bigots. That night, in their camp, they are attacked, and George is killed as he lies in his bedroll.

Instead of packing it in, Wyatt and Billy decide to carry on. Once they reach Mardi Gras in New Orleans, they head for Madame Tinkertoy's House of Blue Lights, reputedly the best whorehouse in the south. There they hire two prostitutes, Mary (Toni Basil) and Karen (Karen Black). The four go out on the town and take LSD. The film chronicles their hallucinogenic trip in a cemetery.

Wyatt and Billy drive onward toward Florida. Billy is just happy to have made some money by selling drugs and having traveled cross-country on

Wyatt (Peter Fonda) and Billy (Dennis Hopper) bring drunken lawyer George Hanson (Jack Nicholson) along on their cross-country adventures in the '60s biker flick Easy Rider.

▼

his bike. Wyatt, however, wishes there had been a better way to search for their freedom. "We blew it," he says.

The next day, they are driving along a two-lane road when a pickup truck approaches. Inside are two redneck southerners, who decide to take their rifle off the rack and have some fun with the longhairs on the motorcycles. One shoots at Billy—and kills him. Wyatt, horrified, drives down the road for help, but before he can get away, he, too, is murdered by the rednecks.

The film won the 1969 Cannes Festival award for the best film by a new director. Nicholson's breakthrough performance met with rave reviews. He earned an Academy Award nomination as Best Supporting Actor.

See Nicholson, Jack

EBERT, ROGER

Motion-picture reviewer Roger Ebert was born in Urbana, Illinois, on June 18, 1942. The portly partner in the reviewing team of Siskel and Ebert, he is one of the best known and respected movie critics in the United States. He is also the only film critic ever to have won a Pulitzer Prize for criticism.

A movie buff from an early age, Ebert remembers going to the movies as a child and paying just nine cents to see a double feature of cartoons and a featured film. The first film he ever saw was *A Day at the Races*, one of the classic comedies of the Marx Brothers.

After high school Ebert enrolled at the University of Illinois, where he became editor of the student newspaper. While in college he wrote articles for the *Chicago Sun-Times*, one of Chicago's leading daily newspapers. He began working on a Ph.D. at the University of Chicago in 1964, but left two years later to take a full-time job with the *Sun-Times*. A year later, at age twenty-four, he became the paper's film critic. He credits his assignment to the fact that young audiences were flocking to the movies in the 1960s, and the newspaper's management wanted its film critic to present a youthful slant on the movies being released.

Although he had been an avid filmgoer, Ebert actually had only limited knowledge of movie making and the film industry when he began his career as a critic. But he learned quickly. He gained a great deal of knowledge about filmmaking while writing a screen adaptation of *Beyond the Valley of the Dolls*, a novel by Jacqueline Susann. The movie, which opened in 1970, received many negative reviews from other critics because of its sex and violence. Ebert the critic thus found himself on the receiving end of harsh movie reviews.

notable & quotable

"I value television because it allows me to exchange views with a colleague I respect. I value print because it allows me to be uninterrupted."

Roger Ebert, critic, 1997, as quoted in Roger Ebert's Video Companion–1997 Edition

EBERT, ROGER

During the late 1960s and early 1970s Ebert's work for the *Sun-Times* attracted a great deal of attention nationwide, and his reviews were soon syndicated in more than 100 newspapers across the country. He won the Pulitzer Prize in 1975. Soon after winning that distinguished award, Ebert was invited to appear on television in Chicago as cohost of a weekly program dedicated to reviewing movies. Interested by the offer, he was somewhat shocked to discover that the person slated to be his cohost was Gene Siskel, an archrival film critic at the *Chicago Tribune*, Chicago's other major newspaper. Both critics were hesitant to accept the offer because of their animosity toward each other, but they eventually agreed.

The TV program *Opening Soon at a Theater Near You* premiered on WTTW in Chicago in 1977. Soon after, its name was changed to *Sneak Preview*. An instant hit in Chicago, within a year the program was being aired on public broadcasting stations throughout the nation. *Sneak Preview* soon became the highest rated weekly entertainment series on public TV.

In 1982 Siskel and Ebert accepted a deal to put their program on commercial network TV under a new name—*At the Movies*. Four years later, they sold syndication rights to the program to Buena Vista Entertainment, which renamed it *Siskel & Ebert*.

The *Siskel & Ebert* show garnered a weekly audience of millions, most of whom were attracted by the insightful reviews and good-natured bickering of the cohosts. The format of the program was the same from week to week: the two critics would take turns introducing a movie, showing clips from it, and then giving an opinion of the film. The other critic would then give his review, after which they would discuss their differences of opinion. Sometimes, these exchanges became rather heated. Siskel and Ebert would then give the movie a "thumbs up" or "thumbs down." The pair eventually became famous for these thumbs up or thumbs down assessments, and film studios often displayed a two thumbs up in their promotions for a film. In fact, the reviews by Siskel and Ebert became a well-accepted endorsement or criticism that could have a serious impact on the commercial success or failure of a movie.

The death of Gene Siskel in 1999 has made the future of *Siskel & Ebert* uncertain. The two reviewers started out as archrivals, and there was considerable animosity between them over the years—at least according to the official view of their relationship. However, in interviews after Siskel's death, Ebert acknowledged that the two had become friends and that he would greatly miss working with his longtime partner. Although *Siskel & Ebert* will no longer be the same, Roger Ebert plans to continue doing the work he loves so much.

In addition to writing reviews for the *Chicago Sun-Times* and appearing on television, Ebert attends many film festivals as guest and film juror. He also lectures and hosts various seminars on movies and film making. Ebert is the author of several books, including *Roger Ebert's Video Companion*, a best-selling compendium of more than 1,000 movie reviews, interviews with celebrities, and essays that is updated annually.

See Criticism; Kael, Pauline; Maltin, Leonard; Newspapers; Siskel, Gene; Trade papers

EDITOR

That individual responsible for the aesthetics of film construction in the postfilming stages is called the editor. In dramatic filmmaking the editor determines cutting style, transitions, and the development of the narrative. Astute rearrangements of scenes to aid dramatic effect and enhance tempo, as well as the deletion of undesirable material, are within the jurisdiction of the film editor. It is not uncommon for the director and the producer to work closely with the editor in making editorial decisions or in approving both the rough cut (first assemblage) and final cut of the motion picture.

See Cinematographer; Director; Montage; Producer

EPIC

An epic is a motion picture characterized by its extensive narrative form and heroic qualities. The epic film generally covers a large expanse of time as it follows in an episodic manner the continuing adventures of a hero or set of heroes. Often the heroes of epic films are boldly courageous figures whose deeds are presented in the course of great historical events, for example, *The Birth of a Nation* (1915), *Gone with the Wind* (1939), *War and Peace* (1956), *Doctor Zhivago* (1965), *Gandhi* (1982), *Dances with Wolves* (1990), *Gettysburg* (1993), and *Schindler's List* (1993). Other epic films are more picaresque in quality, chronicling an extended portion of a roguish character's life story, for example, *Tom Jones* (1963), *Barry Lyndon* (1975), and *Reds* (1981).

The production of epic films usually involves elaborate settings, authentic period costumes, and a large cast of characters. These elements are considered necessary in achieving the romantic aura expected of epic films.

See All Quiet on the Western Front; Ben-Hur; Birth of a Nation, The; Dances with Wolves; Doctor Zhivago; Gone with the Wind; Schindler's List

notable & quotable

"The epic film neither deals with a problem nor offers a solution. True, it also can seize upon the great discords of life, which create human suffering, but, unlike the dramatic film, it limits itself to describing their manifestations."

Rudolf Arnheim, film theorist, 1957

EXPANDED CINEMA

Expanded cinema is a general term referring to an inquiry into highly technological approaches to film art. Ranging from the use of multiple projectors to computer-generated films to simple shadow plays, the artist attempts to create moving, kinetic art experiences and mixed-media environments that affect the senses. Often expanded-cinema artists deal with the essence of motion that has always intrigued the filmmaker, and also seek a reexploration of three basic principles of cinematic art: light, time, and space. Removing itself from the popular concept of a "canned" film projected onto a screen in a movie house, expanded cinema seeks to make each production a totally self-sufficient and original experience. Expanded-cinema programs included mixed-media presentations, sometimes with "live" performers; video technology; and multiprojection systems. The term *expanded cinema* was first used by the critic Gene Youngblood.

EXPERIMENTAL FILM

The term avant-garde is generally used to describe the first experimental film movement, which began in France in the 1920s. Many of the avant-garde filmmakers were artists who came to the cinema from other arts, particularly from painting and literature. The movement began as a reaction against the narrative motion picture of the time. It was also an extension of contemporary art into the medium of cinema, where artists such as Hans Richter, Viking Eggeling, Salvador Dali, and Fernand Léger could continue their experiments with abstract, expressionistic, and surrealistic art. Painters such as Richter and Léger were particularly interested in the motion picture as a means of bringing their abstract images to rhythmic life. In *Rhythmus '21* (1921) Richter rhythmically alternated black and white geometric shapes on film. Léger in *Ballet Mécanique* (1924) placed common objects into rhythmical and mechanical motion. These films are also commonly classified as abstract films.

Because they believed that the film story was too closely allied with the theater and literature, the avant-garde filmmakers experimented extensively with cinematic techniques and camera tricks—an approach referred to as *cinéma pur* (pure cinema).

Leading a second experimental film movement was Maya Deren, a Russian-born director whose important work was done in the United States in the 1940s. Her *Meshes of the Afternoon* (1943) is a subjective self-study that mixes dream and reality in an ambiguous manner. Deren's work stimulated numerous filmmakers to create highly personal self-projections on celluloid, including Curtis Harrington (*Fragments of Seeing,* 1946) and Kenneth Anger (*Fireworks,* 1947). The frank quality of these films and the necessity of self-distribution and exhibition led to the use of the term underground film in the 1950s to denote the work of experimental American filmmakers. By the time the term came into use, however, the range of experimental approaches was far greater than the subjective model introduced by Deren. *Underground* came to mean any film that was made for noncommercial, personal purpose; that sought to break with the traditions of commercial cinema; that treated subject matter considered taboo in commercial films; and that exploited the pure-cinema possibilities of the medium.

Other terms emerged in the 1960s to denote experimental film. New American Cinema appeared briefly in reference to works by an organized group of filmmakers, most of whom were located in New York City. The term expanded cinema was coined by critic Gene Youngblood in reference to multimedia experiments, often including live performance. Generally speaking, contemporary experimentalists—whatever their intentions or their methods of cinematic expression—are referred to as independent filmmakers.

See Art theater; Avant-garde; Independent filmmaker; Lynch, David; Psychodrama; Underground film

EXPRESSIONISM

A stylistic movement within film, drama, painting, fiction, and poetry, expressionism uses unrealistic, unnaturalistic methods in an attempt to reveal inner experience. In the expressionistic film, and in expressionistic drama, actors, objects, and scenic design are treated not as representational but as elements that function to convey mood, emotion, and psychological atmosphere. *The Cabinet of Dr. Caligari* (1919) is a well-known film that employs expressionistic devices. In this German motion picture the settings are wildly distorted. The actors move in concentric circles, and lighting is unusually dark and somber. The mise-en-scène of *The Cabinet of Dr. Caligari* underscores in a psychological rather than a realistic manner the film's story, which occurs in the mind of an inmate in a mental hospital. Similar in expressionistic and thematic interests is Alain Resnais's *Last Year at Marienbad* (1961), a film presenting the viewpoint of a single character. The use of stylized settings, costumes, and special effects (fast motion) also lend an expressionistic quality to Stanley Kubrick's *A Clockwork Orange* (1971). Dark, somber toning of the cardboard-like settings of *Batman* (1989) gives the production design of this Tim Burton film an expressionistic feeling.

See Clockwork Orange, A; *Kubrick, Stanley; Psychodrama*

FAIRBANKS, DOUGLAS

One of the most popular American stars throughout the period of silent features, Douglas Fairbanks was idolized overseas as well and mobbed by thousands in London, Paris, and Moscow. His subject was always the American Everyman, and even when this was masked behind the veil of a costume picture, the source of his character's energy and optimism was unmistakable.

Fairbanks was a stage actor of minor reputation when he was brought into films in 1915 by Triangle's Harry Aitken, who offered him a starting salary of $2,000 per week. Aitken had been assembling a stable of Broadway celebrities to appear in Triangle features under the supervision of D. W. Griffith, but when such high-salaried performers as Weber and Fields or Sir Herbert Beerbohm-Tree failed to register with film audiences, the entire project began to seem hopeless and ill advised.

Griffith himself had no sympathy for "the jumping jack" or his style and foisted him off on Christy Cabanne, one of the least-imaginative directors on the lot. Aitken nervously slipped the first Fairbanks picture, *The Lamb*, onto the premier Triangle program, which opened with considerable attention at New York's Knickerbocker Theatre on September 23, 1919. Billed with an Ince picture and a short Sennett film, *The Lamb* captured critical attention and proved to be Triangle's first real hit. Frank Woods, the head of Triangle's scenario department, had a better grasp of Fairbanks's potential than did Griffith and teamed him with writer Anita Loos and director John Emerson. Over the next two years, this group would fashion a series of popular light comedies that defined the early Fairbanks persona. Their hero was a bright young representative of the moneyed classes who realizes his dreams through a witty application of initiative and physical agility. At a time when many films still featured working-class heroes, Fairbanks often appeared as a young broker or businessman, a fact that made the realization of these dreams that much easier. Audiences approved.

In 1919, in an effort to gain complete control over the financing and distribution of his pictures, then in the hands of Adolph Zukor, Fairbanks became one of the founders of United Artists. Within a year he had dropped the character of the American Everyman and reappeared in the guise of Zorro, beginning a series of costume adventures that lasted

throughout the twenties. What might have been a wrenching change of image for a lesser star only served to increase Fairbanks's popularity, for his new Don Diego character was simply Doug's old American aristocrat dressed up for a costume party. Behind Zorro's mask was the Fairbanks his fans had come to adore, now fully liberated through the simple expedient of the period setting. *The Three Musketeers* (1921) and *Robin Hood* (1922) were more of the same, and even when Fairbanks played a rogue, as in *The Thief of Bagdad* (1924) or *The Black Pirate* (1926), he was building on the old prewar virtues of self-reliance, initiative, and responsibility.

Douglas Fairbanks was one of the 36 founders of the Academy of Motion Picture Arts and Sciences as well as the organization's first president. ▶

These films were among the most commercially successful of the silent era. Fairbanks's popularity grew throughout the twenties, and the care he lavished on his productions bespoke his position as true Hollywood nobility.

As Fairbanks aged, he realized that the ability to continue in this genre was finite. In *The Iron Mask* (1929) he bade a formal farewell to the swashbuckler, and to the silent drama that had nurtured and developed it. In one of the most elegantly mounted of costume epics, a film that labors over the correctness of every setting and costume design, he kills off D'Artagnan and the Three Musketeers, annihilating his ageless screen persona. Fairbanks, who had once brought new vigor and imagination to silent films, became the first to offer the medium a melancholy elegy.

See Academy of Motion Pictures; Chaplin, Charlie; Griffith, D. W.; Pickford, Mary; Valentino, Rudolph

FANTASIA

The 1940 animated feature *Fantasia* was the result of Walt Disney's desire to be considered something more than a mere cartoon maker. In 1937 Disney proposed that he and Leopold Stokowski, conductor of the Philadelphia Symphony Orchestra, collaborate on an animated version of Paul Dukas's symphonic poem "The Sorcerer's Apprentice." Stokowski agreed. The resulting "Sorcerer's Apprentice" cost $125,000, a huge amount of money for the time. To justify the expense, Disney decided to expand the cartoon into a full-length feature. The result was *Fantasia*, an experimental film that set the standard for future animation and prefigured MTV.

The film is comprised of seven animated sequences illustrating eight works of classical music. Stokowski conducting the Philadelphia Orchestra is the cement that holds the film together. He is shown between each segment, a dark silhouette against a blue background. Deems Taylor, a radio announcer for the New York Philharmonic, narrates. The first sequence in the film is set to Bach's Toccata and Fugue in D Minor. As the music begins, orchestra members are illuminated with colored lights as their instruments are featured in the music. The colors resolve into abstract and naturalistic shapes that shift in hue and shape in response to the music.

Tchaikovsky's music for *The Nutcracker* inspires the second sequence, a celebration of the beauty of nature from summer to winter. Multicolored fairies awaken flowers. The web of an orb spider is touched with shining pearls of dew. Chubby red-capped mushrooms morph into Chinese dancers. Fish with impossibly long diaphanous tails perform seductive

underwater dances. Thistles perform a wild Russian dance. Finally, the fairies return and transform the landscape into fall, then winter.

The third segment, "The Sorcerer's Apprentice," is the most famous. Mickey Mouse is the hardworking apprentice to a grim and mysterious sorcerer. When the master is done for the day, he leaves his hat glowing magically on a table. Mickey, who has been hauling water into the sorcerer's cavern from a pool outside, dons the hat and casts a spell on an old broom. The broom sprouts hands, and Mickey teaches it to fetch the water. Assured that his work is being done by the robotlike creature, Mickey flops down on the sorcerer's chair and falls asleep. In his dream, he imagines himself on a promontory, conducting— not an orchestra but the stars and the seas. As the waves lap at his feet, Mickey awakens to discover that the broom has done its job too well. The room is flooded and the broom cannot be stopped. Mickey grabs and axe and hacks the broom to pieces, but each piece becomes another broom carrying more and more water into the cavern. As the water whirls, the sorcerer reappears and parts the waters. A sheepish Mickey dusts off the hat, returns it to the Sorcerer, and picks up his buckets again.

Stravinsky's *The Rite of Spring* is the musical background to Disney animators' vision of earth's first billion years. From beyond a spiral nebula, the earth forms, a violent molten mass. Life begins under the sea, as one-celled animals evolve into a fish whose fins develop into legs. Dinosaurs come to dominate the earth, then die in a drought that transforms the earth into a desert. The piece ends with earthquakes and an eclipse of the sun.

Beethoven's *Pastoral* Symphony is illustrated with a mythological romp. Centaurs and nymphs court, satyrs gambol and play their pipes, flying horses and unicorns herd their young through the skies. Bacchus, a roly-poly fellow with a conspicuously red nose, rides a unicorn-mule and supervises an orgy of wine making while the other creatures dance. The gathering is interrupted by a huge storm provoked by Zeus hurling lightning bolts. When the storm ends, peace returns to the land and the creatures fall asleep under the moon and stars.

Amilcare Ponchielli's *Dance of the Hours* is illustrated by the most unlikely ballet imaginable. Gawky ostriches perform *tours jetés* and tutu-wearing hippos pirouette. Elephants blow pastel bubbles for a comic bubble dance. Leering alligators in capes hoist hippos over their heads and collapse under the weight.

Fantasia's finale combines two works that the narrator says paint a "picture of the struggle between the profane and the sacred," as Mussorgsky's *Night on Bald Mountain* segues into Shubert's "Ave Maria." At the summit of an evil-looking mountain sits Chernobog, the monstrous lord of evil and death, who calls forth the evil spirits from the village below and tosses them into the fiery depths. As day dawns and the church bells ring, the monster reacts with horror and enfolds himself in his wings. To the strains of "Ave Maria" tiny figures holding huge globes of light walk through a gray and

misty morning. The tall thin trees bend to form gothic arches, and the mist clears as the sun rises. In the end, good triumphs over evil.

See Animation; Snow White and the Seven Dwarfs

FANTASY

A fantasy is a type of film story or film experience that occurs within the imagination, dreams, or hallucinations of a character or within the projected vision of the storyteller. Film theorist Siegfried Kracauer defines film fantasy as storytelling or visual experience that is "outside the area of physical experience." The term *fantasy* is also often used to describe a work that is set in an unreal world or that includes characters that are incredible in conception. Many of the early trick films of George Méliès, such as *A Trip to the Moon* (1902), are fantasy films, as are George Cukor's *The Blue Bird* (1976) and George Lucas's *Star Wars* (1977). Fantasy has been used both for light entertainment (*Mary Poppins,* 1964) and as a vehicle for social commentary (*It's a Wonderful Life,* 1946; *Heaven Can Wait,* 1978; *Defending Your Life,* 1991).

See E.T.; It's a Wonderful Life; Star Wars

FARGO

This 1996 film by Ethan and Joel Coen is a macabre black comedy set in the flat, white, snow-covered landscape of northern Minnesota. An odd little tale about the banality of evil, *Fargo* is loosely based on a real crime gone awry in Minnesota in 1987.

The film opens with a long shot of dark telephone poles against a white ground and a white sky. Driving along the road is a car towing another car. Jerry Lundegaard (William H. Macy) has traveled from Minnesota to Fargo, North Dakota, to meet with two low-life thugs, Carl (Steve Buscemi) and Gaear (Peter Stormare). In exchange for the car, a new tan Ciera, and $40,000, Jerry wants Carl and Gaear to kidnap his wife, Jean (Kristin Rudrud). He plans to extort ransom money from his rich father-in-law to invest in a get-rich-quick scheme to build a parking lot. He tells

"You know, it's proven that second-hand smoke is, uh, carcin—uh, you know, cancer related."

Steve Buscemi as Carl Showalter in *Fargo* (1996)

the kidnappers that he'll split the $80,000 ransom with them, although he actually plans to set the price for his wife's return at a million.

Jerry, his wife, Jean—a chirpy housewife with an adenoidal voice and a staggeringly flat Minnesota accent—and his son, Scott—who has a poster of "The Accordion King" on his bedroom door—live in the shadow of Wade Gustafson (Harve Presnell), Jean's wealthy father. Wade is a self-made millionaire who has nothing but disdain for his weak son-in-law. Jerry runs a car dealership for Wade, who never lets him finish a sentence. But to Jerry's amazement, on the morning after Jerry arranges for the kidnapping, Wade calls him to say that the parking lot proposal looks "sweet." Jerry takes this to mean that Wade will lend him the money he needs to cinch the deal and tries to call off the kidnapping, only to realize that he doesn't have the kidnappers' phone number.

"Oh, he was just funny-looking. More than most people even."

Hooker describing Carl Showalter (Steve Buscemi) in *Fargo* (1996)

While Jerry meets with his father-in-law and learns that Wade wants the deal for himself, the kidnappers break into the Lundegaard home and snatch Jean. Gaear cuts his finger as he breaks a window and lumbers around the house muttering "unguent," while Carl chases the screaming Jean all over the house. Jean eventually gets herself entangled in a shower curtain and falls down the stairs, making it an easy job for the kidnappers to roll her up and cart her off.

Near Brainerd, Minnesota, a trooper stops Carl and Gaear because the Ciera still bears dealer plates. Carl—who looks and acts like a chihuahua—tries to slip the trooper a bribe. When the trooper refuses the bribe and asks the two to step out of the car, Gaear—a silent, sullen lump of a man—calmly reaches across Carl, shoots the trooper in the head, and orders Carl to pull the body off the road. As Carl is dragging the body, a car drives by and its passengers gape at the bloody sight along the side of the road. Gaear leaps into the driver's seat and speeds off after the car. He finds it, upside down, off the side of the road. A woman in pinned inside the car and the driver is running across a snow-covered field. Gaear shoots both passengers and drives back to pick up Carl.

Called to the scene to investigate the crime is Brainerd police chief Marge Gunderson, played by Frances McDormand, who won the Best Actress Oscar for her portrayal. Marge is sweet, cheerful, seven months pregnant, and a crack police officer. Like just about everyone else in the movie, she speaks Minnesotan and sprinkles her conversation with "you're dern tootin," "ya betcha," and "oh geez." She immediately deduces what must have happened and sets off to solve the crime. She traces the car to Jerry and stops in to question him, saying that she's "investigating some malfeasance."

Meanwhile, much to Jerry's dismay, Wade insists on delivering the ransom money himself. He meets Carl on a hotel roof with a suitcase containing a million dollars. Like the cowboy he is, Wade pulls a gun on Carl, but Carl shoots him. Wade's gun goes off as he falls and the bullet grazes Carl's cheek.

Jerry arrives on the scene a few minutes later to find Carl and the money gone, his father-in-law and the parking attendant dead.

Carl is on the way back to the kidnapper's hideout at Moose Lake, when he stops to count the money and realizes that there's a lot more in the suitcase than a mere $80,000. He takes $80,000 out and stops to bury the suitcase in a snow-covered field, along a fence that stretches in dreary sameness for as far as the eye can see. He tries to spy something distinctive in the landscape, gives up, and plants an ice scraper in the ground to mark the spot.

When he returns to the cabin, he finds that Gaear, annoyed with Jean, has broken a chair over her head and killed her. He splits the money with Gaear but they fight over who gets the Ciera.

Meanwhile, Marge is driving around Moose Lake on a tip when she spots the car. She walks up the driveway to see Gaear disposing of Carl's body in a wood chipper. Only Carl's foot is still visible, and the snow around the chipper is covered with bloody dust. Marge pulls her gun and calls out "police," but Gaear can't hear her over the chipper. Eventually, though, he catches sight of her and she yells "police" again, this time pointing to the badge on her hat to be sure Gaear gets the message. He does, and takes off across a frozen lake. Marge takes aim and wounds him.

She gets him in the back of her car and on the way to the station, she lectures him about his bad behavior. "There's more to life than a little money, ya know."

Jerry Lundegaard is caught hiding in a cheap motel.

In the final scene of the film, Marge snuggles up in bed next to her husband, Norm. If evil is banal, good, it seems, is simple, ordinary, and speaks with a flat midwestern accent.

FEATURE FILM

A feature film is a full-length motion picture made and distributed for release in movie theaters as the principal film for any given program. The evolution of the feature film in the period 1913–16 brought with it larger, more comfortable movie theaters and refined systems for motion-picture exhibition. By the early 1920s the economic success and popularity of feature-length films had led to the development of movie-house chains owned and operated by the major Hollywood production studios. A typical movie theater program runs for approximately two hours. Until the 1960s, it was common practice to run a short-subject film, or short, with the feature film to fill out the two hours.

See Acting; A-picture; B-picture; Documentary; Newsreels; Star system

SALLY FIELD

Actress Sally Field was born in Pasadena, California, on November 6, 1946. The child of actors—her mother was Margaret Field (also known as Maggie Mahoney), and her stepfather was Jock Mahoney—Field knew early on what she wanted to do with her life.

Field attended an acting workshop at Columbia Studios and was eventually chosen over 150 contenders to star in *Gidget*, a television series about a perky teenager. The show ran from 1965 to 1966 and led to Field's casting as the star of another popular TV series, *The Flying Nun* (1967–70). Reportedly Field has struggled to overcome the typecasting of these "cutesy" roles ever since. In 1977 she received an Emmy Award for her portrayal of a schizophrenic in the television movie "Sybil." The well-received performance helped her to be considered for other dramatic roles.

Field had acted in various movies, but in 1979 she received the recognition she had been seeking with her role as a union organizer in the film *Norma Rae,* which won her the Academy Award for Best Actress. A few years later, in 1984, she won the Oscar again (for *Places in the Heart),* an unanticipated victory that prompted her to say in her acceptance speech, "You like me, you really like me!"—a public burst of spontaneity that Field would probably rather forget.

Since her Oscar victories, Field has performed in a number of popular films, including *Murphy's Romance* (1985), *Steel Magnolias* (1989), *Mrs. Doubtfire* (1993), and *Forrest Gump* (1994). The actress, twice divorced, is the mother of three children, Peter, Elijah Craig, and Samuel Greisman.

See Forrest Gump; *Hanks, Tom*

FILM NOIR

Films noirs—literally, "black films"—derive their name from their unusual tone and atmospherics. Characterized by heavily low-key lighting schemes, the term film noir is often applied to detective films and crime stories of a pessimistic nature. Film noir evolved in the 1940s when black-and-white film stock, standard at that time, allowed a wide range of black-to-white shadings and permitted directors to experiment with the darker end of the scale in photographing stories and characters of a sinister, brooding quality. The interior light in these films gives them a dark and gloomy look, as if photographed at night. Exteriors were often shot at night to add to the dreary environments. Story locations in films noirs are commonly the dark streets and dimly lit apartments and hotel rooms of big cities.

The inspiration for film noir came in part from Orson Welles's bold, expressive use of low-key lighting in *Citizen Kane* (1941) and *The Magnificent Ambersons* (1942). Film noir also had earlier precedent in German expressionism and in the psychological films of the German directors E. A. Dupont, G. W. Pabst, and F. W. Murnau, where mood is often matched by shadowy lighting and darkly oppressive settings.

Writing in 1946, Nino Frank was the first to use the term film noir in print. Having just seen John Huston's *The Maltese Falcon* (1941), Billy Wilder's *Double Indemnity* (1944), *Laura* (Otto Preminger, 1944), and *Murder, My Sweet* (Edward Dmytryk, 1944), Frank estimated that these four films had rendered obsolete the traditional detective film, with its "thinking machine" protagonist, long explanations of the initially inexplicable crime, and one-dimensional, stereotypical characters.

The film noir style is also found in film adaptations of Raymond Chandler novels, in many of the private-eye films of Humphrey Bogart, and in works by Howard Hawks (*The Big Sleep*, 1946), Robert Aldrich (*Kiss Me Deadly*, 1955), and Orson Welles (*The Lady from Shanghai*, 1948, and *Touch of Evil*, 1958).

See Chinatown; Citizen Kane; *Detective film;* Double Indemnity; *Huston, John; Lupino, Ida;* Maltese Falcon, The; *Wilder, Billy*

ERROL FLYNN

Errol Leslie Thomson Flynn was born in Hobart, on the island of Tasmania near Australia, on June 20, 1909. Flynn would become notorious for his "swashbuckling," on film and off, during his short lifetime. Flynn never did things halfway, always being involved in some adventurous scheme. To the dismay of his father, a distinguished marine biologist and zoologist, Flynn was expelled from schools in both Australia and England. At age sixteen he went to New Guinea and tried his hand at gold mining—to no avail. He returned to Australia for a time, bought a boat, and sailed back to New Guinea with several friends (he described this journey in his book *Beam Ends,* published in 1937).

Back in New Guinea, the young man worked for a time as a manager of a tobacco plantation, and he wrote columns for the Sydney (Australia) *Bulletin.* When he returned to Australia he was offered the role of First Mate Fletcher Christian in a semidocumentary film, *In the Wake of the Bounty.* (Flynn reportedly was descended from one of the midshipmen from the real *Bounty.)* In 1933 Flynn went to England, where he got more acting experience, on stage as well as in film, which led to a Hollywood contract in 1935.

Flynn was an immediate success in the United States, his tall good looks gaining him work in several good movies (including *Captain Blood,* 1935, and *The Charge of the Light Brigade,* 1936) and a wife, actress Lili Damita. He seemed to like a measure of consistency, usually working with the same two directors, Michael Curtiz and Raoul Walsh, and often with actors Alan Hale (who later played Skipper in *Gilligan's Island*) and Olivia De Havilland (who played Melanie in *Gone with the Wind).*

FLYNN, ERROL

During the late 1930s and the '40s Flynn cranked out several films per year, including *The Adventures of Robin Hood* (1938), *The Sea Hawk* (1940), *They Died with Their Boots On* (1942), and *Adventures of Don Juan* (1949). He also became renowned in the gossip columns for his hard living—chasing women, drinking, and brawling. The marriage of "The Charming Rogue" (as he was called) and Damita collapsed in 1942; they had one son, Sean, who later disappeared while serving in southeast Asia as a war journalist. In subsequent marriages Flynn had more children: two daughters with Nora Eddington and one daughter with Patrice Wymore.

In 1942 Flynn was charged with statutory rape of two teenage girls. He was acquitted, but the notoriety of this incident led to the catch phrase "in like Flynn." His lifestyle became ever more frenetic, but the partying caught up with Flynn in the 1950s. His acting suffered along with his health, and he was swimming in debt. He played alcoholics in several of his last films, including *The Sun Also Rises* (1957) and *Too Much Too Soon* (1958).

Flynn's autobiography, *My Wicked, Wicked Ways,* was published in 1959. In 1980 a scandalous biography about the star was published, in which Flynn was accused of being a Nazi.

Notorious womanizer Errol Flynn was known as the king of the swashbuckler films, a title he inherited from actor Douglas Fairbanks. ▶

JANE FONDA

Actress Jane Fonda was born in New York City on December 21, 1937. Her father was actor Henry Fonda, her mother a socialite, Frances Seymour Brokaw. In 1950 Frances committed suicide, leaving behind not only her husband but also Jane and her younger brother, Peter (who in later years would also become an actor).

Though saddled with this tragic personal history, Jane was fortunate enough to inherit the best of her father's delicate, soulful good looks, an advantage that served her well as a model as a young woman and then in her film career and personal life. But she has never been content to sit back and reap the rewards of her privileged background; Jane Fonda has always pushed the envelope, which has won her both fans and foes.

Fonda was brought up on the west coast until she was age ten, at which time she and her brother were relocated to their grandmother's home in Connecticut while their father was performing on Broadway. She attended Vassar College for a time and then studied art in Paris, France. Upon her return to the United States, Fonda began modeling, with no small success: she appeared on the cover of *Vogue* magazine twice. Around that time Fonda also began studying at the Actors Studio in New York City.

In 1960 Fonda debuted both on Broadway and in Hollywood. Over the next few years she acted in several movies, but she did not make much of an impact until she was cast in the popular films *Cat Ballou* (1965) and *Barefoot in the Park* (1967). In 1968 she starred in the futuristic sex farce *Barbarella* (1968; directed by her then-husband Roger Vadim); while silly, it brought the young actress lots of attention.

In the next fifteen years or so, Fonda became a bona fide star in her own right, apart from her father's legend, and leaving her sex-kitten image behind. She starred in such major films as *They Shoot Horses, Don't They?* (1969), *Klute* (1971), *Julia* (1977), *Coming Home* (1978), *The China Syndrome* (1979), *On Golden Pond* (1981), and *The Morning After* (1986). She earned many Academy Award nominations and won two Best Actress Oscars, for *Klute* and *Coming Home.* Fonda also became an exercise guru during this period, earning millions of dollars through sales of her workout videos.

Over the years, Jane Fonda has played many roles: model. actress, political activist, exercise maven, and most recently, wife of a media mogul.

Fonda's personal life has always been as interesting as her film career. She has been as politically oriented as many of her films have been, and her strong opinions have occasionally met with controversy. Fonda particularly drew fire during the Vietnam War for embracing the North Vietnamese communist regime (she apologized for this many years later, but some people will not forgive "Hanoi Jane").

Jane was married to French director Roger Vadim from 1965 to 1973; they had one daughter. Her second husband was Tom Hayden, whose political career Fonda generously financed. They had one son, and divorced in 1989. Fonda is currently married to media mega-mogul Ted Turner. She retired from filmmaking in the early 1990s, not long after marrying Turner.

FOLEY ARTIST

A foley artist is a sound effects person who specializes in the creation of sounds that enhance the ambient effects of a film scene, especially the development of sounds that coordinate with character body movements, footsteps, and interaction with props and setting (turning a door knob and opening a door, for example). The art of enhancing and coordinating such character-related sounds is named for recordist Jack Foley, a pioneer in the field.

See Lighting; Sound

FORD, JOHN

John Ford's career as a film director spanned almost sixty years. His 130 movies included silent films, westerns, and classics such as *The Grapes of Wrath*. Ford's contribution to the film industry's evolution came in the form of his use of the camera, composition, the careful development of characters, and a realism that permeated most of his work.

There is some controversy over where John Ford was born and what name his parents gave him at birth. Some biographers state that he was born in Ireland, while most others report he was born in Cape Elizabeth, Maine. The various birth names biographers have attributed to him include John Martin Feeney, Sean O'Feeney, John Sean O'Feeney, and Sean Aloysius O'Fearna. The Lilly Library at Indiana University, which holds the John Ford collection, states that he was born in 1895 in Cape Elizabeth, Maine, with the birth name of Sean Aloysius Feeney.

It is known that Ford was the youngest of thirteen children born to Irish immigrant parents. Within a few years of his birth, his family moved to Portland, Maine, where his father owned a saloon. Ford said that his fascination with movies began as a child going to nickelodeon theaters. He graduated from high school in 1913, and briefly attended the University of Maine.

Ford got his start in films in 1914 after he followed his older brother, Francis Ford, an actor, writer, and director, to Hollywood. Francis Ford had spent several years on the vaudeville circuit and then moved on to Hollywood, eventually making over 600 movies. After moving to Hollywood

HARRISON FORD

Harrison Ford was born July 13, 1942, in Chicago, Illinois. One of the biggest box-office draws in film history, Ford usually plays rugged heroes and good guys.

Ford began acting as a student at Ripon College in Wisconsin. He subsequently did some local summer stock and then headed to Hollywood to try his luck there. Although Ford got some work—a few minor roles in films and on television shows, usually playing a cowboy—he finally concluded that his acting career was going nowhere. He was a good carpenter, so he adopted that as his second-choice career.

A role in a small film by newcomer director George Lucas brought Ford back to the movie business: *American Graffiti* (1973). No one seemed to expect the movie to do much business, but it was a big commercial as well as critical success.

A few years later Ford landed a movie role that would prove to spread seismic-level shock waves in his life: Han Solo in Lucas's *Star Wars* (1977). He followed that up with roles in some humdrum films (*Force 10 from Navarone,* 1978; *The Frisco Kid,* 1979) and another blockbuster (*The Empire Strikes Back,* 1980). But it was Ford's casting as archaeologist Indiana Jones in Steven Spielberg's adventure movie *Raiders of the Lost Ark* (1981), another wildly successful film (and its sequels), that cemented the actor's status as a bona fide movie icon.

Ford's handsome yet craggy looks and generally calm demeanor—reminiscent of such American movie heroes as John Wayne and Gary Cooper—have won audiences' affection and ensured his place in the pantheon of all-time favorite actors. He has not always made great choices in roles (*Regarding Henry,* 1991, and *Sabrina,* 1995, for example), but his successes have far outweighed the clunkers. Ford has an impressive list of films to be proud of besides the ones already mentioned, including 1985's *Witness*, which earned him an Academy Award nomination, *Presumed Innocent* (1990), *Clear and Present Danger* (1994), and *Air Force One* (1997).

Ford was married from 1964 to 1979 to Mary Marquardt Ford, whom he met at Ripon College. They have two children. He also has two children with his second wife, screenwriter Melissa Mathison, whom he married in 1983.

See American Graffiti; *Lucas, George;* Raiders of the Lost Ark; *Spielberg, Steven;* Star Wars

Actor Harrison Ford, who typically plays rugged heroes, appears rather similar offscreen: he maintains a ranch in Wyoming that he built himself, and he is also an accomplished private pilot who owns several planes.

notable & quotable

"I'll make you a deal. I'll try to keep making films that put people in your theater seats and you try to keep their shoes from sticking to the floor."

Harrison Ford, to cinema owners in Las Vegas

F

FORD, JOHN

Director John Ford was honored in 1973 as the first recipient of the American Film Institute's Life Achievement Award.

Sean Aloysius Feeney followed his brother's example and took the name John Ford.

For the first few years, Ford worked as bit part actor, prop manager, and stuntman. Among the bit parts he played was that of a Klansman in D. W. Griffith's *The Birth of a Nation*. After just two years in Hollywood, Ford began to work as an assistant director. At times, he made a movie a week. In 1917 he was hired to direct westerns starring Harry Carey. His first film as writer/director was *The Tornado*, a bank robbery western. By 1924 he made about fifty silent films, mostly westerns, nearly all of which have been lost. Only twelve of his silent films still survive, including his best silent works, *The Iron Horse* (1924) and *Four Sons* (1928).

In 1920 Ford married Mary McBride Smith, formerly a lieutenant in the Army Medical Corps. The couple had two children, Patrick Roper, born in 1921, and Barbara Nugent, born in 1922.

While Ford had made his reputation in silent movies, his greatest contribution as a director was in talking movies. His first talkie, *The Informer* (1935), a film about the 1922 Irish rebellion, is considered one of the first creative sound films. *The Informer* was enthusiastically received by the public and received critical acclaim, including an Academy Award for Best Director and the New York Film Critics Award for Best Motion Picture.

In 1936 Ford began directing the first of ten films for Twentieth Century-Fox. In 1939 he directed three classics: *Stagecoach*, *Young Mr. Lincoln*, and *Drums along the Mohawk*. *Stagecoach*, for which he won the New York Film Critics Award for Best Direction, is credited for helping revitalize the western genre and launching John Wayne's career.

Ford claimed another Academy Award in 1940 when he directed the film version of John Stienbeck's novel *The Grapes of Wrath*. The harsh naturalistic style of the film is a hallmark of Ford's cinematography. He followed this film with another Academy Award-winning effort, *How Green Was My Valley* (1941), a film about a coal mining town in Wales.

The outbreak of World War II found Ford, an enthusiastic member of the Naval Reserve, promoted to the rank of commander. He formed the Naval Field Photographic Reserve in early 1940. His new unit was assigned to the Office of Strategic Services and Ford was ordered to report to Washington on September 11, 1941.

He spent the war years doing documentary work in the Pacific, North Africa, Europe, and India. Ford received Oscars for two documentaries that he directed during the war, *The Battle of Midway* and *December 7th*.

In February 1945 Ford took a leave of absence from the navy to film the war movie *They Were Expendable*. He used the salary he received from the picture to start the Field Photo Home, a club for the veterans of the Field Photographic Unit. He was released from the navy on September 28, 1945.

The following March, Ford and producer, Merian C. Cooper, formed Argosy Productions. This company produced eight pictures, seven of which were directed by Ford. Among these were three of Ford's most famous and commercially successful films—the trilogy of cavalry stories: *Fort Apache* (1948), *She Wore a Yellow Ribbon* (1949), and *Rio Grande* (1950). Ford won his fourth and final Academy Award for Best Director for *The Quiet Man* (1952).

Between 1952 and 1956 ford directed *Mogambo*, *The Sun Shines Bright*, *The Long Gray Line*, *Mister Roberts*, and *The Searchers*. *The Searchers*, a tense psychological western about pioneers searching for a girl captured by the Indians, is often cited as Ford's greatest film.

Ford continued making films throughout the 1950s and early 1960s. His last film, *7 Women*, was completed in 1966. He received the American Film Institute's first Life Time Achievement Award in 1973, the same year President Nixon presented him with the nation's highest civilian honor, the Medal of Freedom. John Ford died a few months later in Palm Springs, California, on August 31, 1973.

notable & quotable

"Ford had the whole company [film crew] in his pocket. They said Ford was a mean old son-of-a-b****, but he was *their* son-of-a-b****."

Maureen O'Hara, actress, as quoted in "America Goes Hollywood," Newsweek, *June 28, 1999*

Two documentaries about Ford and his work were made in 1971: *The American West of John Ford* coproduced by Ford's grandson, Daniel Sargent Ford, and director Peter Bogdanovich's *Directed by John Ford.*

See Birth of a Nation, The; *Corman, Roger;* Grapes of Wrath, The; *Griffith, D. W.; Location shooting; Murnau, F. W.;* Searchers, The; Stagecoach; *Tracy, Spencer; Vidor, King*

FORREST GUMP

Robert Zemeckis's 1994 Oscar-winning film *Forrest Gump* makes brilliant use of computer-generated imaging to place its title character in the middle of nearly every major event in American history from the 1950s to the 1980s.

The film opens with a feather that drifts on a breeze and lands on the scuffed shoe of a man waiting at a bus stop. Forrest Gump (Tom Hanks) tells whoever sits beside him the story of his extraordinary life. Like the feather, Gump has drifted, going where fate takes him, an innocent observer of sorrow and joy.

"I'm not a smart man but I do know what love is."

Tom Hanks as Forrest Gump in *Forrest Gump* (1994)

Young Forrest Gump has an IQ of 75 and must wear leg braces to straighten his back, which the local doctor says is as "crooked as a politician." Gump's mama, played by Sally Field, is determined that her son have as normal a life as possible, and she teaches him simple precepts to help him cope. When people ask him if he's stupid, Forrest replies, "Mama always said, 'Stupid is as stupid does,' " and his guiding philosophy is "Life is like a box of chocolates; you never know what you're gonna get." Gump begins his enchanted life of influencing cultural events by teaching the youthful Elvis Presley how to dance in a style that suits Gump's limited use of his legs.

As he climbs onto the bus on his first day of school, Forrest encounters the cruelty of children; no one will allow the boy in leg braces to sit with them. Finally, a little girl named Jenny, the abused daughter of a poor tobacco farmer, invites him to sit beside her. On the way home from school one day, Forrest is chased by bullies. Jenny yells, "Run, Forrest, run," and, as he does, he discovers his genius. His leg braces fracture and fly apart and Forrest easily outruns the boys on bicycles. As if to compensate for his mental slowness, Gump is extraordinarily quick at everything else. His speed even wins him a place on the University of Alabama football team, where he runs touchdowns but doesn't know enough to stop after he's crossed the goal line.

While at the university Gump watches George Wallace bar the door to the first African-American students. As a member of the All-American football team, he is invited to the White House to meet John Kennedy.

FORREST GUMP

After college Gump joins the army and is sent to Vietnam, where his literal-minded obedience makes him the perfect soldier. His best friend, Bubba (Mykelti Williamson), is as sweet and slow as Gump himself; all he wants is to return to the family shrimp business. Of the war Gump says that he and his buddies take "these long walks . . . looking for a guy named Charlie." When the platoon is attacked, Gump single-handedly rescues the wounded, even though he himself is hit in the "butt-ox," as he pronounces "buttocks." Bubba dies but his platoon leader, Lieutenant Dan (Gary Sinise), survives as a double amputee. He is furious with Gump, whom he feels robbed him of his destiny to die honorably. While recovering in a camp hospital, Gump learns to play ping-pong, a sport in which his lightning quickness again works in his favor.

Upon his return to the United States, Gump is awarded the Medal of Honor by Lyndon Johnson. Left to wander around Washington after the ceremony, Gump stumbles into the middle of a peace rally where he encounters Jenny (Robin Wright). Attracted to abusive men and drugs, Jenny refuses Forrest's proffers of love and leaves on a bus for Berkeley. As Gump lives out a version of the American dream, Jenny's life becomes a countercultural nightmare.

The two top-grossing films in 1994 were *The Lion King*, at $306 million, and *Forrest Gump*, at $301 million.

Gump goes to China on the American ping-pong team. When he returns, he appears on the Dick Cavett show with John Lennon and inspires him to write "Imagine." As he leaves the studio, he runs into Lieutenant Dan—long-haired, disheveled, drunk, and still angry about being saved. Gump plans to buy a shrimp boat, and he invites Lieutenant Dan to be his first mate. Dan refuses. Leaving him in New York, Gump joins his ping-pong teammates in Washington as they are introduced to Richard Nixon, who suggests that Gump stay at a new hotel, called the Watergate. That evening Gump calls the police when he notices suspicious activity in an office across from his room.

Gump's attempts at shrimping are a disaster until Lieutenant Dan decides to join him. When the pair is caught in a hurricane, Lieutenant Dan climbs the mast and defies God to come and get him. Because they stayed offshore, theirs is the only shrimp boat that survives the storm, and they become rich. Gump invests his share of the company profits in a "fruit company" called Apple Computer.

When Mama dies Forrest returns home. One afternoon, Jenny shows up. After they live platonically together for a period, Forrest again declares his love and asks her to marry him. She refuses but makes love with Forrest that evening. She leaves the next morning while he is still sleeping.

Gump, devastated, begins to run. For the next three years he runs constantly, crisscrossing the nation and becoming a popular culture phenomenon. Admirers join him on his run and wait for him to utter words of wisdom. His casual comments yield the yellow happy face icon and other pop-culture icons.

When he stops running, Gump receives a letter from Jenny asking him to visit. In fact, he confides to the woman sitting next to him on the bench, that's why he's waiting for the bus. When he arrives at Jenny's apartment, he learns that their sexual encounter produced a son. His eyes tear as he struggles to ask the most pressing question, "Is he smart or . . . ." Jenny confirms that the boy is smart. Later she confesses she is dying of a mysterious virus and asks Forrest to marry her. The year is 1982; presumably the virus is AIDS.

When Jenny dies, Forrest raises his son, fishing, playing ping-pong, and reading to him from *Curious George*. In a repeat of a scene early in the film, Forrest takes his son to the bus on the first day of school. As the bus departs, a feather that lands on Forrest's foot catches the breeze and floats away.

See Field, Sally; Hanks, Tom

FRANKENSTEIN

More than a dozen films have been inspired by Mary Shelley's 1818 novel *Frankenstein*, including one made in 1910 by Thomas Edison. Still, the 1931 film directed by James Whale and featuring Boris Karloff is probably the best-known version of the story.

"Now I know what it feels like to be God."

Colin Clive as Dr. Henry Frankenstein in *Frankenstein* (1931)

Though filmed in black and white and lacking modern special effects, Whale's *Frankenstein* continues to inspire viewers with horror and pathos. In just over an hour Whale tells the classic tale, incorporating unforgettable images enhanced by the interplay of light and shadow.

The movie opens with an eerily symbolic graveyard scene, shot from below so the mourners and tombstones loom large against the mottled evening sky. As mourners weep and church bells toll, Frankenstein and his assistant, Fritz, peer through iron fence palings at the proceedings. The camera pans across the graveyard catching images of crucifixes and a statue of the grim reaper. When the gravedigger completes his work, the scientist and his hunchbacked assistant creep from their hiding place and disinter the coffin. On the way home, the pair recover a hanged man from a gibbet. When Fritz climbs the pole to cut the body down, Frankenstein is disappointed. The man's neck is broken, rendering the brain useless for his purposes.

The scene shifts to Goldstadt Medical College where Dr. Waldman illustrates the difference between a normal brain and the one just removed from a murderer. When students and teachers file out of the classroom leaving the two brains in jars at the front of the room, Fritz, who has been watching through a window, enters and steals the normal brain. Startled by the sound of a gong, however, Fritz drops the jar. Leaving the normal brain

on the floor, he takes the container marked "Dysfunctio Cererbi—Abnormal Brain."

The scene changes. Victor Moritz has come to visit the obviously distraught Elizabeth, Frankenstein's fiancée. She has asked Victor to help her investigate Henry's strange behavior: he has left the university to live in an abandoned watchtower and pursue mysterious experiments. Victor and Elizabeth decide to question Dr. Waldman, Henry's former teacher at the university, from whom they learn that Henry has become obsessed with the idea of creating life. Elizabeth and Victor persuade Dr. Waldman to accompany them to rescue Frankenstein.

At the ruined watchtower a thunderstorm rages. Inside, Frankenstein prepares to electrify the creature he has assembled from stolen body parts. The laboratory is deeply shadowed; lightning flashes through an opening in the ceiling animating electrical equipment that crackles in response. Just as Frankenstein is about to trap the "electrical secrets of heaven," there is loud knocking at the door. Elizabeth, Victor, and Dr. Waldman have arrived. Frankenstein begs them to leave him alone, but his friends insist they be admitted. When Victor tells Frankenstein he's crazy, the scientist reacts defensively. "Crazy, am I? We'll see whether I'm crazy or not," he says, as he leads the group to his laboratory.

Bela Lugosi was originally offered the role of the monster, made famous by Boris Karloff in the 1931 version of Frankenstein.

▼

As the storm intensifies, Frankenstein and Fritz crank the table on which the cadaver rests up through the opening in the ceiling. When the table descends, Frankenstein rushes to his creation. A huge, scarred arm hangs down from the table. Slowly, the fingers move, and Frankenstein exults, "Look! It's moving. It's alive. . . ." His voice is drowned out by thunder and the howling wind.

Later, conversing with Dr. Waldman, Henry reveals that he has kept the monster completely in the dark and is anxious to see his response to light. As the monster enters the room, Henry opens a skylight, and the monster reaches heavenward, as if to grasp the sun. When the skylight is closed, he appears distraught and reaches out as if to embrace the doctor. The scene ends as Fritz torments the monster with his torch. The monster, in fear of the flame, reacts violently, and the men bind and drag him into a dungeon-like room.

After they leave, Fritz returns to further torment the monster. Upstairs, Henry and Dr. Waldman hear screaming and rush to the dungeon only to discover Fritz, dead and hanging from a hook on the rafter. The monster breaks out but is again subdued, this time by an injection. Henry's father, Elizabeth, and Victor arrive and persuade Henry to leave. Dr. Waldman assures his former student that he will find a painless way to destroy the monster. While Henry rests at his father's home, Dr. Waldman prepares to dissect the sedated monster. When he leans over to listen to the heart before making the first cut, the monster's hand rises slowly—just as it did when he first came to life—and strangles Dr. Waldman.

As the Frankenstein family celebrates the wedding of Henry to Elizabeth, the monster roams the countryside. In a scene deemed too horrible for audiences in 1931 but restored to the film in 1987, the monster encounters a little girl named Maria who invites him to play with her. She hands him a bunch of daisies and the two joyfully toss blossoms into a pond. When the monster runs out of daisies, he gently lifts the girl and lofts her into the water, clearly expecting her to float like the daisies. When she begins to scream, he runs away in terror.

The scene shifts to the Frankenstein home. Victor announces that Dr. Waldman has been killed and that the monster is on the loose.

Outside, the wedding festivities continue until Maria's father walks through town carrying his dead daughter in his arms. In his grief, he walks as stiffly as the monster and his face has the same inhumane impassive expression. When they learn what has happened, the men of the village, including Henry, take torches and dogs and set out to capture the monster. Henry, separated from his party, confronts the monster on a rocky promontory. They fight, and the monster drags Henry to an old abandoned windmill. The angry crowd catches sight of the monster and follows. Inside the windmill, Henry struggles with the monster, who throws him out a window. The villagers set fire to the old wooden building. As the windmill burns, the monster howls piteously. The arms of the windmill form a cross against the conflagration.

The movie ends happily, with Henry recovering from his injuries.

See Horror film

FRENCH CONNECTION, THE

Considered by many to be the best detective film ever made and featuring one of the all-time great movie car chases, William Friedkin's 1971 Best Picture Oscar winner *The French Connection* is an unsparingly realistic look at undercover police work. The film is based on Robin Moore's best-selling book about the real-life adventures of Harlem narcotics officers Eddie Egan and Sonny Grosso, both of whom play small roles in the film. *The French Connection* has the appearance and feel of a documentary: many scenes were shot with a handheld camera on location in New York City's slums and tenements; much dialogue is obscured by traffic and other noise; and Popeye Doyle (Gene Hackman), the protagonist, is one of the least heroic heroes imaginable. He is bigoted, profane, brutal, and completely obsessed with his work.

"I'm going to bust your a** for those 3 bags and I am going to nail you for picking your feet in Poughkeepsie."

Gene Hackman as Jimmy "Popeye" Doyle in *The French Connection* (1971)

The film opens in Marseilles, France. Pierre Nicoli (Marcel Bozzuffi) shoots a French detective in the face. He steps over the body, tears a piece of bread from the man's just-bought loaf, and walks away eating it. The scene shifts to Brooklyn, where Popeye Doyle and his partner, Buddy Russo (Roy Scheider), dressed as a skinny Santa Claus and a hot-dog vendor, chase down and rough up a small-time drug dealer. Doyle questions the man, interspersing legitimate questions with what becomes his trademark non sequitur, "Have you ever picked your toes in Poughkeepsie?"

On a hunch, Doyle and Russo follow a candy store owner, Sal Boca (Tony Lo Bianco), who has a good deal more money to spend than he should, and discover a connection between Boca and Joel Weinstock (Harold Gary), who is suspected of being the money behind the importation of illegal drugs into the city. In a shakedown in a bar, Doyle and Russo discover from an informant that a big shipment of drugs is due to arrive within a week.

Back in Marseilles, Pierre Nicoli's boss, Alain Charnier (Fernando Rey), pays French actor Henri Devereaux (Frederic de Pasquale) to transport a brown Lincoln Continental into the United States. Devereaux doesn't know what is going on, though he is vaguely aware it is illegal. Charnier arrives in the United States also, and soon Doyle, Russo, and two FBI agents, Mul-

Popeye Doyle (Gene Hackman), still in his Santa suit, and partner Buddy Russo (Roy Scheider) rough up a small-time drug dealer in The French Connection.

derig and Klein (played by Bill Hickman and real-life cop Sonny Grosso), are tailing everyone involved—still on Popeye's hunch.

The scene shifts to a suite at the Westbury Hotel, where a chemist hired by Weinstock indicates that the sample he tested is "absolute dynamite. Eighty-nine percent pure junk. Best I've ever seen. If the rest is like this, you'll be dealing this load for two years." Boca wants to make the buy right away, but Weinstock urges caution.

One morning Doyle notices Charnier leaving his hotel unobserved by the agents who are supposed to be watching him. Doyle tails him through New York streets and into the subway system. It soon becomes clear that Charnier knows he's being followed, and he manages to trick Doyle by rapidly moving in and out of subway cars. As his car moves away, Charnier waves at Doyle still standing on the platform, signaling to him that his cover has been blown. He later orders Pierre Nicoli, the hit man who murdered the French detective, to kill Doyle.

Frustrated that the deal has not yet happened, Captain Simonson (played by Grosso's real-life partner, Eddie Egan) takes Doyle and Russo off special assignment. On his way home, Doyle passes a woman walking a baby in a carriage. A shot is fired and the woman falls. Doyle looks up and sees a sniper atop a nearby building. He realizes that the shot was meant for him and proceeds to chase the shooter, who turns out to be Nicoli. Nicoli manages to evade Doyle by boarding the elevated train, and Doyle appropriates a car and gives chase underneath the el at breakneck speed, causing several accidents by weaving in and out of lanes. A scene in which Doyle barely misses a woman wheeling a baby carriage is all too real; not realizing a film was being made, a woman wandered onto the set and got the scare of a lifetime.

Nicoli hijacks the train and shoots two conductors. When the engineer has a heart attack and the train crashes, Nicoli takes off on foot. Doyle eventually catches up with him and shoots him at the top of the train depot stairs.

Eventually Doyle and Russo impound the Lincoln and have it towed to a police garage to be searched. After two hours spent in tearing the car apart, they find 120 pounds of heroin in the rocker panels. The car is put back together and the deal is allowed to proceed.

The film's final scene takes place on Wake Island. As the drug deal is completed, Boca and Charnier drive away only to find their path blocked by a police barricade. Doyle waves to Charnier but Boca backs the car up and the police chase the two back to the warehouse where the drugs were sold. Boca is shot and Doyle chases Charnier through the abandoned building. Russo joins him and they see a figure in a doorway in front of them. Doyle shoots, but the target turns out to be Mulderig, the FBI agent. Doyle runs out of the building and a shot is heard. Still photographs with subtitles end the film. Charnier escapes and the case is not proved against Weinstock. Only Henry Devereaux, the actor, serves time for conspiracy. Doyle and Russo, the subtitle says, "were transferred out of the Narcotics Bureau and reassigned."

See Documentary; Gangster film; Hackman, Gene; Realist cinema

FROM HERE TO ETERNITY

From Here to Eternity won eight Oscars, more than any film since *Gone with the Wind.* The 1953 release was distinguished by several sterling perfor-

F

FROM HERE TO ETERNITY

This illicit love scene between Sergeant Warden (Burt Lancaster) and Karen (Deborah Kerr) is one of the sexiest ever captured on film.

mances—including one by Frank Sinatra as Angelo Maggio that many say revived his sagging career—and it is still famous for its realistic portrait of military life and a steamy love scene between Burt Lancaster and Deborah Kerr on a Hawaiian beach.

As the film opens, Private Robert E. Lee (Prew) Prewitt (Montgomery Clift) arrives at Schofield Barracks near Pearl Harbor and runs into old friend Angelo Maggio. Prewitt has been demoted and transferred from the Fort Shafter bugle corps for refusing to give up his position as first bugler to a friend of the top sergeant. Prew is introduced to Captain Holmes (Philip Ober), who tells him he pulled strings to have Prew reassigned to his command because his boxing team needs a good middleweight. But Prew declines to fight. He has given up the sport, he says, because he accidentally blinded a friend in a sparring match. When it becomes clear that Prew cannot be persuaded to change his mind, the captain issues a subtle threat. Later he encourages the other boxers to make Prew's life miserable.

Witness to this interchange is First Sergeant Milt Warden (Burt Lancaster), who runs the company while Captain Holmes devotes his time to boxing and philandering. As Warden says of the captain, "He'd strangle in his own spit if he didn't have me to swab his throat out for him." Warden tries to convince Prew not to be stubborn but he admires the young man's grit.

On their first weekend pass, Maggio takes Prew to the New Congress Club where Prew meets and falls in love with one of the hostesses, Lorene (Donna Reed). Prew quickly becomes jealous as Lorene entertains other men; he refuses to accept her explanation that she is merely doing her job. Meanwhile, Maggio, who is quite drunk, criticizes the piano playing of Fatso Judson (Ernest Borgnine), the sergeant of the guard at the stockade. The two fight and have to be separated. They fight a second time some weeks later, and Warden intervenes when Judson pulls a knife on Maggio.

Sergeant Warden visits Captain Holmes's wife, Karen (Deborah Kerr), when he knows her husband will be away, and the two are immediately attracted to each other. Later, they meet on a beach, where they embrace as the waves roll over them. As they kiss, Warden begins to question Karen angrily about former lovers, but she silences him with the story of her marriage and the tragic loss of a child.

It is some weeks before Prew can see Lorene again. At the last minute, Maggio is assigned to guard duty. As Lorene and Prew talk in a bar, Maggio shows up, AWOL and quite drunk. He is arrested by the MP and sentenced to the stockade. As he enters the jail, Fatso is waiting for him, billy club in hand.

Prew proposes to Lorene but she rejects him because she doesn't want to be a soldier's wife. She tells him that she is saving so she can meet a "proper man with the proper position to make a proper wife who can run a proper home and raise proper children. And I'll be happy because when you're proper, you're safe."

At the same time, Karen and Warden discuss a plan so they can be together. Karen says she will ask for a divorce and suggests that Warden apply to become an officer. He protests, "I hate officers. I've always hated officers," but reluctantly agrees to do as Karen suggests.

Prew's hazing continues until one day he is pushed past the breaking point by Sergeant Galovitch (John Dennis), one of the company's boxers. A fistfight breaks out. At first Prew restrains himself, refusing to punch Galovitch in the face. Eventually, he fights back with all his might and knocks Galovitch out. As he walks away, he says, "If you guys think this means I'm steppin' into a ring, you're wrong." Captain Holmes watches the fight but does nothing to intervene; his actions are witnessed by senior officers, and he is eventually reprimanded for his behavior and for his cruelty toward Prew. To avoid a court martial, he resigns.

The evening after the fight, Prew and Warden sit in the middle of a road drinking. Maggio, who has escaped from the stockade, stumbles onto the scene, barely able to walk. He describes the repeated beatings he received at Fatso's hands and dies.

Prew waits for Fatso outside the New Congress Club. They fight and both men pull knives. Prew kills Fatso and, wounded, escapes to Lorene's

"He ain't like the others. He'll make it tough on you but he'll draw himself a line he thinks fair and he won't come over it."

Jack Warden as Cpl. Buckley, referring to Sgt. Warden (Burt Lancaster) in *From Here to Eternity* (1953)

apartment. Warden, suspecting the truth, covers Prew's absence for three days.

A calendar on the wall reveals the date. It is now Saturday, December 6—the day before the Japanese strike on Pearl Harbor. Warden tells Karen that he cannot go through with the plan to become an officer. The two separate.

The next morning the soldiers are at breakfast. It is ten minutes to eight as the Japanese planes fly overhead. The barracks is in chaos until Warden begins to bark orders. Eventually he and some of his men climb to the roof and shoot down a plane; the attack on the ships at Pearl Harbor is shown in authentic documentary footage.

While recovering at Lorene's, Prew hears about the attack and insists on going back to his company. On the way, he is mistaken for a saboteur and killed by guards. Warden is nearby and sums up Prew's life, "He was always a hardhead . . . but he was a good soldier. He loved the Army more than any soldier I ever knew."

The film ends with Karen and Lorene standing next to each other on a luxury liner bound for the mainland. Lorene tells Karen that her fiancé was a bomber pilot who was killed during the attack; Karen listens sympathetically until Lorene says his name, which Karen recognizes. She doesn't reveal her knowledge but throws two leis overboard, citing a legend that if the leis float to shore the visitor will return.

See War film

"I never like to disturb a man when he's drinking."

Burt Lancaster as Sgt. Milton Warden in *From Here to Eternity* (1953)

FUTURISM

An artistic movement, closely associated with cubism, futurism originated in Italy in the early 1900s and was characterized by an interest in giving expression to the movement and energy of mechanical processes. In 1906 futurist painter A. G. Bragaglia produced a film, *Perfido Incanto,* in which he posed actors before futurist settings. Futurist interests can be assessed as closely allied with the interests of later avant-gardists, who placed objects in motion for formally expressive intentions, for example, *Ballet Mécanique* (1924). The movement also had an impact on Russian filmmakers of the 1920s.

See Avant-garde

GANGSTER FILM

A hard definition remains elusive, yet everyone, including moviegoers, thinks he or she can easily recognize a gangster when he appears onscreen. The academic community, as well as mainstream film critics, certainly don't agree on what transforms an ordinary crime film into a gangster film. Nor do they agree if such films should be lumped together to form a genre.

The gangster has a timeless quality, just like the sins he commits. He's been described as possessing the leftover anguish of a character from classical Greek tragedy. He's also been dubbed a twentieth-century Macbeth armed with a smoking gun. Those who dabble in the social sciences have called the gangster a fitting metaphor for the battered myth of the American dream—especially among downtrodden immigrants who found that dream wanting.

Romanian-born actor Edward G. Robinson appeared in over twenty gangster films in the 1930s. He is shown here in a scene from Little Caesar *(1930).*

◀

CLARK GABLE

Clark Gable, an actor who played a roguish, good-humored type in most of his films, was born in Cadiz, Ohio, on February 1, 1901. Given the name William Clark Gable, he left home and school at age fourteen and began working at a tire factory in Akron, Ohio. While there, Gable began volunteering backstage at a theater and was eventually offered small parts in some of the theater's productions. Later, Gable's father, a farmer-turned-oil-driller, took the younger Gable with him when he moved to start work in the oil fields of Oklahoma. When Gable was twenty-one, he joined a traveling acting troupe, and in 1924 he found his way to Hollywood.

Gable got a few bit parts in films, but not enough to earn a living, so he went on the road again, eventually landing a few roles on Broadway. One play, *Love Honor and Obey,* took him back to California in 1930. This time Gable had more success with the movie studios. He was cast in a western, *The Painted Desert* (1931), and soon was signed by MGM, which cast him in film after film. His good-natured bullying of star Norma Shearer in *A Free Soul* (1931) won him many fans, and MGM began casting him in more important roles.

Clark Gable is best known for his role as Rhett Butler, the handsome southern scoundrel in Gone with the Wind.

Within a few years Gable was entrenched at MGM, popular with both men and women filmgoers, but he began to complain about being cast over and over in gangster roles. To punish him, studio head Louis B. Mayer lent him out to Columbia for "some movie about a bus." That "little" production, released in 1934 as *It Happened One Night,* was the first film to win the five major Academy Awards, including the Best Actor Oscar for Gable. He was now a bona fide movie star, being given plum roles in such films as *The Call of the Wild* (1935), *Mutiny on the Bounty* (1935), *San Francisco* (1936), and *Saratoga* (1937). Gable became known as "The King of Hollywood."

Gable had been married twice, briefly, in the mid-1920s and again in the 1930s. In the late 1930s he fell in love with star Carole Lombard; they married in 1939, delighting fans and leading to all sorts of romantic legends about "Gable and Lombard."

The year 1939 was also notable for Gable in another way: he won the male lead in what promised to be the biggest film of the year: *Gone with the Wind.* His portrayal of the irresistible, handsome scoundrel Rhett Butler would come to be viewed as his defining character.

In 1942 Gable's world fell apart when Lombard was killed in a plane crash. He subsequently joined the air force and fought in Europe during World War II, winning several medals for distinguished service. But some people claim that Gable never recovered from the loss of his beloved wife.

After the war Gable began performing again, with 1945's *Adventure.* But Gable's popularity had waned; he was drinking too much and was no longer the dashing, trim young lead that audiences had so admired. His roles became gradually more varied, in such movies as *Command Decision* (1948), *To Please a Lady* (1950), *Lone Star* (1952), *Mogambo* (1953), *Soldier of Fortune* (1955), *Band of Angels* (1957), and *Run Silent, Run Deep* (1958).

Some critics consider Gable's best acting to be in *The Misfits* (1960), a mature drama in which he played opposite Marilyn Monroe. It was her last role—as well as Gable's. He died of a heart attack before the film was released. He left behind his fifth wife, Kay, and his only child, John Clark Gable, who was born after the star's death.

See Capra, Frank; Cukor, George; Gone with the Wind; It Happened One Night; *Leigh, Vivien; Monroe, Marilyn;* Mutiny on the Bounty; *Screwball comedy*

What's in a Gangster Film?

A gangster, more so than other criminal types, belongs to a collective, a gang, a mob, a syndicate. That can mean a loosely gathered group such as the Dillinger gang or an organization as widespread as the Mafia. More important, though, the gangster and his cohorts think of themselves as more than a collection of professional accomplices. They tend to bond on a personal level and rely on one another as if they were extended family members.

Although the gangster film's story line includes criminal activities and "rackets," the backbone of a gangster film story is the metamorphosis of the gangster character. He will rise spectacularly and then fall horrendously until he's finally destroyed. His downfall occurs either physically, mentally (he ends up as a Corleone-type "living corpse"), or he's redeemed and transformed into something more virtuous than a gangster.

Moreover, although he's usually exterminated by outside forces (rival gangsters or law enforcement), the seeds of his destruction have already been sown within himself. He possesses a fatal flaw, and the very personal qualities that enable him to bully his way to the top ultimately destroy him. In other words, he's his own worst enemy and does himself in long before anyone else fires a shot.

In 1933 Clark Gable, the year's #7 most popular film star, was earning $2,500 per week.

The genre's best films wallow in this psychic purgatory; the worst ignore the character development and interior torment and go for the bloodletting. Although violence is an integral part of the gangster life, the best films use violence for punctuation, symbolism, historical accuracy, and indispensable shock value. But if violence is allowed to overwhelm the human drama that underpins the story, the film drifts into the territory of the "action" film, robbing the gangster of his essential tragedy.

The gangster genre has evolved over the years—owing to fashion, morality, and the prevailing definition of what constitutes illegal and immoral activities. There's even a recognizable gangster "look," regardless of the era, that depends on an insatiable appetite for flamboyant clothes that marks him as a strutting peacock and a social misfit. Moreover, from Cagney to the boyz, screen gangsters, hoods, wise guys, and homeboys forever mistake conspicuous consumption (lavish cars and voracious materialism) as a surefire measure of success at the expense of personal growth.

The faces of the gangsters have also changed over the years, not just because movie stars shine and fade away, but because the images of real-life criminals have changed. Gangsters have nearly always come from the bottom of society and get their start in the gangs that thrive on America's meanest streets. The personnel of gangs has changed over the years to reflect the newest wave of underdogs who stir together anger and unrealized ambition to cook up the gangster persona. In a society that doesn't value these people, they find employment, stature, and abundant reward

GRETA GARBO

Greta Garbo, an actress whose very name has become synonymous with mystery and glamour, was born Greta Louisa Gustafsson in Stockholm, Sweden, on September 18, 1905. As a young woman she attended the Royal Dramatic Theater School (as did fellow Swedish icon Ingrid Bergman some years afterward).

Garbo's first onscreen appearances were as an advertising model, though she did some feature work while still in her teens. Her first leading role was in the silent film *The Atonement of Gosta Berling* (1924). The director of that movie, Mauritz Stiller, changed Gustafsson's name to the easier Garbo. The following year, after costarring with Asta Nielsen in *The Joyless Street*, Garbo followed Stiller to Hollywood in 1925 and signed up with MGM.

MGM initially was not too keen on the young actress, giving her run-of-the-mill parts in several films just to please Stiller, but when Garbo garnered favorable attention with the release of *Flesh and the Devil* (1927), she had some leverage. She demanded a substantial raise (reportedly from $600 to $5,000 per week—certainly impressive now, but absolutely astronomical at that time), and at first MGM balked. Unfazed, Garbo returned to Sweden. The actress's placid refusal to return to Hollywood until MGM met her demands contributed to the iconoclastic image that eventually came to define her.

Once MGM bent to her will, it had no choice but to accede to all her demands. When Garbo returned to Hollywood, she was given the ultimate in "star treatment." She would work with only the most prestigious directors, and she usually demanded that the studio's best cinematographer, William Daniels, work on her films. The filmmakers had ample material to work with: Garbo's face, with her huge eyes, generous mouth, and stark planes, is often likened to a great canvas.

In films such as *A Woman of Affairs* (1928), *The Kiss* (1929), *Wild Orchids* (1929), and *Anna Christie* (1930—her first "talkie" film), audiences reveled in Garbo's aloof exoticism. When MGM tried to pass her off as an American in *Two-Faced Woman* (1941), they rebelled.

Filmgoers were happiest when Garbo played a glamorous but tragic heroine. Her roles in *Grand Hotel* (1932), *Mata Hari* (1932), *Anna Karenina* (1935), and *Camille* (1937) remain favorites among film devotees and perfectly capture the mysterious essence that made her a star. She never received a regular Academy Award but in 1954 was granted an Oscar for her "unforgettable screen performances."

Despite her great popularity, much of Garbo's private life remains a mystery. She never married; though her love life was much speculated about, not much of substance is known. She retired from film at a very young age (just thirty-six), in 1941, perhaps partially in response to the poor critical and commercial reception that year of *Two-Faced Woman.* Garbo subsequently dropped out of sight—not because of lack of interest on the part of the public, but out of personal choice. She kept homes in France, New York City, and Switzerland. When she died at age eighty-four, Garbo was viewed as a recluse. She left an estate reported to be worth $200 million.

See Cukor, George; Gilbert, John

(however short-lived) in the Underworld. And after the women's movement was launched in the 1960s, a woman's finger has more often been placed on the trigger.

Gangster films, like those that comprise other genres, run the gamut. Some strongly affected, reflected, or stimulated the genre. Others merely demonstrate what happens when a genre gets stale and formula replaces creativity. And still others boldly delighted moviegoers despite leaving Hollywood unimpressed and uninterested. Some of the most popular gangster films—with audiences and critics alike—include Arthur Penn's *Bonnie and Clyde* (1967), Francis Ford Coppola's epic *Godfather* trilogy (1972, 1974, and 1990), John Cassavetes's *Gloria,* and Martin Scorsese's *GoodFellas* (1990).

See Bonnie and Clyde; *Cagney, James; Coppola, Francis Ford; Detective film; Film noir;* Godfather, The; GoodFellas; *Scorsese, Martin*

GAZE (LOOK)

Gaze or look is a concept in cinematic discourse that theorizes that directed awareness and accompanying visual pleasure can be derived from the "gaze" of the film spectator, as controlled by the camera's eye. The position of the camera onto the scene and screen characters is said to "set" the spectator's gaze (look) in such a way that responses to the character(s) are affected in an unconscious manner. Feminist theorists have maintained that the screen gaze has traditionally been directed toward the male spectator—the camera's eye favoring male voyeurism (visual pleasure) in the perusal of screen imagery, while limiting female gaze. The theorist Laura Mulvey has asserted that the prevalent male gaze in narrative cinema in effect permits the male spectator indirectly to "possess" the female as an onscreen object. Others (e.g., D. N. Rodowick) have taken issue with these assertions by arguing that the gaze may in fact render the male submissive to the screen female rather than possessive.

See Criticism; Cultural criticism; Postmodernism; Psychoanalysis and cinema

GENRE

Genre refers to any group of motion pictures that reveals similar stylistic, thematic, and structural interests. There are numerous narrative film gen-

JUDY GARLAND

Judy Garland, the now-legendary actress and singer, was born to a vaudeville family in Grand Rapids, Minnesota, on June 10, 1922. She was named Frances Ethel Gumm, and she made her theatrical debut at age three and performed regularly through her childhood with her sisters, as part of the "Gumm Sisters Kiddie Act." Apparently her mother was horrifically ambitious; as an adult, Judy Garland would refer to her mother as the "Wicked Witch of the West" (a reference to a nasty character in *The Wizard of Oz).*

Frances eventually changed her name to Judy, and the whole family converted to "Garland." The child's special singing talent was recognized early on; she was billed as "the little girl with the great big voice." At just thirteen she was signed to a contract with MGM under Louis B. Mayer, who auditioned her personally.

In 1937 Garland made a splash in the film *Broadway Melody of 1938* (singing a love song, "Dear Mr. Gable/You Made Me Love You" to a photograph of the movie star) and was paired with Mickey Rooney (for the first of many films together) in *Thoroughbreds Don't Cry* (both in 1937). At age sixteen she won the coveted role of Dorothy in *The Wizard of Oz*. A director's suggestion to go for a more natural look helped her to win people's hearts as the ingenue from Kansas. She was awarded a special "juvenile" Oscar for her work.

Actress and singer Judy Garland will forever be associated with her role as Dorothy, the ingenue from Kansas, in The Wizard of Oz.

As a teenager, Garland began having weight problems, and the studio put her on diet pills. She also began taking pills to help her sleep. The considerable strain of stardom was taking its toll, and this dependency on drugs only added to her unhappiness. Today Garland is remembered as much for her deterioration into chronic abuse of alcohol and prescription drugs, and several attempts at suicide, as for her superb acting and singing. Audiences responded warmly to the vulnerability of her persona, whether in film or on stage.

During the 1940s Garland performed in such memorable films as *Meet Me in St. Louis* (1944), *Ziegfeld Follies* (1946), and *Easter Parade* (1948). But at the end of the decade, MGM, frustrated by the star's unreliability, terminated her contract. Despite her personal troubles, Garland had a tremendous following, and she was able to keep in the public's eye by performing onstage at the London Palladium and New York's Palace Theater. In 1954 she returned to the screen with *A Star Is Born* (1954). Her last significant film role was in *Judgment at Nuremberg* (1961).

Garland married five times and had three children, Liza Minnelli (with Italian director Vincente Minnelli) and Lorna and Joey Luft (with manager Sidney Luft). Her fifth husband, a London discotheque manager named Mickey Deans, found her dead on the bathroom floor on June 23, 1969. Her death was attributed to an accidental overdose of sleeping pills.

An interesting side note regarding Garland's death came when New York City's gay community jammed bars to pay tribute to Judy Garland during the week of her death. The police raided one of the bars, the Stonewall Inn, and the resulting "Stonewall Riots" became one of the pivotal moments in the history of gay rights.

See Wizard of Oz, The

res: the western, the gangster film, the musical, the screwball comedy. *Genre* is also often used to distinguish other film classes, such as the documentary, the experimental film, and the animated film.

The study of the various film genres has given rise to genre criticism. By isolating the various filmic elements that characterize a particular motion-picture genre, it is possible to employ those elements in evaluating a film that falls within the genre. Through an examination of the manner in which the recognizable generic elements have been copied or varied, genre criticism seeks to determine how the film's thematic intentions have been achieved. Many western films, for example, make topical statements by their varied arrangements of generic elements. *High Noon* (1952), a film about the bravery of a small-town marshal, makes a statement about individual courage that was especially timely during the era of the McCarthy committee investigations. *Lonely Are the Brave* (1962), a western film story placed in a modern time and in modern settings, makes a statement about loss of individual freedom in a technological society, as does *The Electric Horseman* (1979).

See Animation; Buddy films; Detective film; Documentary; Experimental film; Gangster film; Horror film; Science-fiction film; War film

The weekly salary of the dog that played Toto in *The Wizard of Oz* (1939) was $125, while Judy Garland's was $500 for playing Dorothy.

GIANT

Directed by George Stephens and based on the novel by Edna Ferber, 1956's *Giant* is a sprawling melodrama. The film received ten Academy Award nominations, including a posthumous nomination for James Dean, who was killed in a car accident shortly before shooting was complete (another actor had to provide the voice for some of Dean's lines). Rock Hudson was nominated for Best Actor, for what many believe was the best performance of his career—the portrayal of the highly complex rancher Bick Benedict. Elizabeth Taylor shines in her role as a strong woman who ages more than thirty years during the course of the film, and Carroll Baker, Sal Mineo, and Dennis Hopper can all be seen at the very beginning of their careers.

The three-hour epic opens in the early 1920s as Jordan "Bick" Benedict (Hudson), the owner of a 595,000-acre Texas ranch called Benedict Reata, is on his way to Maryland to buy a prize stallion. There he meets and falls in love with Leslie Lynnton (Taylor), the independent-minded, highly principled daughter of a wealthy doctor. The two marry and travel back to Reata together as husband and wife.

Leslie has a lot to adapt to on the ranch. The Benedict home is a huge, gothic mansion far out on the Texas range. The landscape is dry, brown, and unnervingly flat, roasting under a bright blue sky. Except for the Mexican servants who live in a dilapidated village on the Benedict property, the nearest neighbor is fifty miles away. And Bick is a typical Texas rancher of the day—disdainful of Mexicans and steeped in a code of male superiority.

Leslie also has to adjust to marriage, as does Bick. His is a more chauvinistic society than Leslie is used to, and she continues her independent ways despite Bick's displeasure. She infuriates her husband by befriending Jett Rink (Dean), a surly, no-account ranch hand who is drilling for oil on a small piece of property left to him by Bick's sister. Jett is very attracted to the beautiful Leslie, but knows she is unattainable, which only makes him more hostile toward Bick. Leslie further antagonizes Bick by visiting and trying to help the Mexican villagers and by daring to join in political discussions.

Bick is delighted when Leslie announces she is pregnant; he envisions his son as the next owner of Reata. Leslie bears twins, Jordan Jr. and Judy, and two years later the couple's third child, Luz, is born.

The strains between Leslie and Bick continue as the years go by. On the twins' fourth birthday, Bick forces a terrified Jordy to ride a horse. This is the last straw for Leslie, and she asks for a separation and takes the children to live with their grandparents in Maryland. After several lonely months, Bick journeys to Maryland to try to revive his marriage. Leslie agrees to return home as long as Bick understands that she intends to express her opinions and do what she believes is right.

Rock Hudson (center) and James Dean (right), shown here with Giant *costar Elizabeth Taylor, were both nominated for Best Actor Oscars for their roles in the film.*

In the meantime, Jett has struck oil and achieved a Texas-sized fortune, but he fails to find happiness in wealth. Over the years, he becomes an uncouth, mean alcoholic who envies Bick his family.

As his wells dry up, Jett tries to convince Bick to join him in the business of drilling for oil, but Bick is committed to preserving the ranch for his children. However, the Benedict children refuse to live out Bick and Leslie's dreams. Leslie wants Judy (Fran Bennett) to attend an exclusive college in Switzerland, but Judy wants to marry a cowboy and operate a small ranch. Bick wants the now grown-up Jordy (Dennis Hopper) to run Reata, but Jordy wants to follow in his grandfather's footsteps and study medicine. Jordy also angers Bick by marrying Juana (Elsa Cardenas), a woman of Mexican descent. Worse, Bick and Leslie's youngest child, Luz (Carroll Baker), is attracted to Bick's much-despised rival Jett. Finally, discouraged by his children's lack of interest in the ranch, Bick drops his opposition to drilling for oil and becomes fabulously wealthy, as does Jett, as a result.

Later, when the now-rich Jett throws a huge party to celebrate an airport's being named after him, the entire Benedict family and many of their friends—in order not to be outdone—show up for the celebration in a private airplane and stay at a luxury hotel owned by Jett. When Juana is refused service at a beauty salon at the hotel because she is Mexican, Jordy confronts the staff, only to be told that the discriminatory policy was specifically set by Jett.

Infuriated, Jordy interrupts the party and challenges Jett. While bystanders hold Jordy back to keep him from fighting, Jett lands several punches—a cowardly tactic he had earlier used in a conflict with Bick. Bick invites Jett outside to finish the fight on his son's behalf, but ends up walking away in disdain because Jett is too drunk to fight. The Benedicts leave the party and Jett climbs the dais to speak. But before he can begin, he passes out in front of the entire crowd, his head ignominiously lolling in his plate. Much later Luz, feeling sorry for Jett, returns to the dining room and overhears him delivering an incoherent speech to an empty room. The speech reveals Jett's lifelong love for Leslie.

While some of the Benedict entourage return to Reata by plane, Bick, Leslie, Luz, and Juana drive home. When they stop at a restaurant for a hamburger, the proprietor refuses to serve Juana and her baby son, Jordan II. Bick, who up until this point in the film has continued to express racist views, has a sudden insight into the pain of discrimination, and challenges the proprietor to a fight. In what must be one of the longest movie brawls ever, the two men slug at each other until Bick, who is much older than his opponent, gets knocked down and ends up lying in a pile of pies and salad greens. His opponent, who apparently admires Bick for his grit, pulls a sign reserving the right to refuse service off the wall, and tosses it on top of Bick.

In the final scene of the film, Bick and Leslie are babysitting for their two grandsons, one fair and blue-eyed, the other dark and brown-eyed, and

notable & quotable

"Jimmy [Dean] and Rock [Hudson] didn't get along. Jimmy was thoroughly 'Method.' Rock was riddled with an inferiority complex."

Elizabeth Taylor, actress, 1999, as quoted in "America Goes Hollywood," Newsweek, *June 28, 1999*

Leslie tells Bick that she never respected him more than when he was lying in the salad. The audience is satisfied that Leslie and Bick's relationship has endured and deepened over the years despite their differences.

Although *Giant* was named by the American Film Institute as one of the 100 Best Films of all time, most critics believe that it does not quite merit such a lofty claim. Much of its stature today derives from the fact that it was James Dean's last performance.

See Epic; Taylor, Elizabeth

GILBERT, JOHN

By the time of Rudolph Valentino's death, the mantle of "great lover" had already begun to pass to a local contender, Metro-Goldwyn-Mayer's popular new star John Gilbert. Gilbert had been working in pictures for a decade, first as a bit player, later as a writer and director, and by the early twenties as the lead in a series of inexpensive melodramas for William Fox. But even his elegant performance in John Ford's *Camero Kirby* (1923) had failed to arouse much public response. In 1924 Gilbert moved to the new MGM, and his sudden acclaim for films such as *His Hour* (1924) and *He Who Gets Slapped* (1924) made him seem an overnight success.

Release of *The Merry Widow* and *The Big Parade* in 1925 firmly established his popularity as well as his value to MGM. Although his onscreen lovemaking was as dark and passionate as Valentino's, Gilbert projected a different image of a romantic idol. The hearty, good-natured American values that he projected made him the first successful link between the romantic traditions of Valentino and Wallace Reid.

However, according to King Vidor, who directed five Gilbert features between 1924 and 1926 and was a close friend, Gilbert was never able to handle the emotional stress that came with Hollywood celebrity:

> Jack Gilbert was an impressionable fellow, not too well established in a role of his own in life. The paths he followed in his daily life were greatly influenced by the parts that some scriptwriter had written for him. When he began to read the publicity emanating from his studio which dubbed him the "great lover," his behavior in real life began to change accordingly. It was a difficult assignment to live up to. (*A Tree Is a Tree*, p. 134)

Gilbert was not the only Hollywood star to behave in an erratic and self-destructive fashion, but the reasons for his ultimate decline seem directly bound up with his personal and emotional problems. He made more than his share of powerful enemies (most notably Louis B. Mayer), while his romantic entanglements with such stars as Greta Garbo, Leatrice Joy, and Ina Claire, the last two of whom he married, seem hopelessly neurotic and immature.

It is a convention of Hollywood history that John Gilbert's career was destroyed by the talkies, but why this was allowed to happen is still a controversial issue. Critics report that audiences laughed at his lovemaking in the first talkie he released, *His Glorious Night* (1929), but the conclusion that his voice was at fault is no longer generally accepted. Rather, Gilbert seems to have been the victim of inappropriate scripting and direction. As Vidor suggests, "The literal content of his scenes, which in silent films had been imagined, was too intense to put into spoken words."

Supporters of a conspiracy theory lay the blame at the feet of Louis B. Mayer. According to this group, Mayer had sworn to destroy Gilbert as early as September 8, 1926, when the actor assaulted him over an insult to Greta Garbo, whom Gilbert was scheduled to marry that day. When talkies arrived, Mayer took advantage of the confusion to sabotage Gilbert's films and ruin his career. But the conspiracy buffs attribute too much wisdom and foresight to Mayer. The fact is, most silent stars were very badly presented in their early talkies, even those producing their own films. Pickford, Gish, Swanson, Talmadge, Lloyd, Keaton, and Gilbert were only some of those whose talking picture debuts were far below their usual standard. Only Garbo and Chaney, who chose to make eccentric talkie debuts, came through unscathed.

John Gilbert was a victim of the inability of Hollywood's best minds to predict a method of pushing silent stars into the age of talkies. Any vendetta on the part of Louis B. Mayer was simply another nail in the coffin.

See Ford, John; Garbo, Greta; Reid, Wallace; Sound; Valentino, Rudolph; Vidor, King

GISH, LILLIAN

Lillian Gish was a disciple, some say a creation, of D. W. Griffith. From the time she and her sister, Dorothy, first appeared at the Biograph studio in 1912 (to visit their friend Mary Pickford) Lillian Gish was Griffith's most important performing tool. From short films like *The Musketeers of Pig Alley* (1912), through nearly all of his great features, Gish delivered the needed balance of strength and fragility. The heroines Griffith offered might have appeared helpless in the face of melodramatic onslaught, but they were not about to whimper and collapse. Sustained by an inner strength, they justified Griffith's vision of a world in which spiritual values always overcame

G

GISH, LILLIAN

Actress Lillian Gish was arguably silent film's biggest star, as well as the industry's most dedicated proponent.

the forces that threatened them. The vision found its greatest exponent in Lillian Gish.

This notion was writ large in *The Birth of a Nation* (1915), *Hearts of the World* (1918), and *Orphans of the Storm* (1922). But consider Gish's work in *True Heart Susie* (1919), a nostalgic pastoral where her sacrifices go unnoticed and her opponent is only an uncaring city vamp. The same strength of character serves her here, and without the distractions of rides to the rescue, the clarity and sophistication of her performance are all the more evident.

Gish had remained with Griffith through the production of *Orphans of the Storm,* but he sent her out on her own when her fame began to exceed his financial resources. For Inspiration Pictures she made two lavish costume romances in Italy, *The White Sister* (1923) and *Romola* (1925). Then, in 1925, she signed with Metro-Goldwyn-Mayer for two years at $8,000 per week. From Griffith she had learned the importance of personally supervising each detail of her films, and the attention she lavished on her MGM pictures was soon the talk of Hollywood. She had left the West Coast five years earlier to work with Griffith in New York and had contin-

notable & quotable

"I never approved of talkies. Silent movies were well on their way to developing an entirely new art form. It was not just pantomime, but something wonderfully expressive."

Lillian Gish, attributed

ued her career in Europe. Returning to Hollywood, she was shocked at the rigidity of studio production.

Gish's contract gave her not only the right to choose stories and directors but the ability to rehearse the entire film in advance, as Griffith did. Such working methods were far from standard at MGM, and Mayer and Thalberg seemed unhappy, especially when the returns on her pictures proved disappointing.

Griffith had created for her an image of virginal purity, but at MGM Gish began to explore more mature characterizations. While her conception of the love scenes in *La Bohème* (1926) was based on keeping the lovers always apart (playing on what she called their "suppressed emotion"), the next subject she selected was *The Scarlet Letter* (1926).

Choosing a Swedish director, Victor Seastrom, and a Swedish costar, Lars Hanson, Gish succeeded in giving the picture the aura of the early Swedish cinema classics. Time and place became powerful characters, compensating for the necessarily delicate handling of the adultery theme. But by 1928 MGM was actively trying to rid itself of Gish's contract.

In a controversial discussion of MGM's handling of Greta Garbo and Gish, Louise Brooks suggests that MGM tried to build up the Swedish actress (over whom they had more effective control) in an effort to damage Gish's position in the industry. Not only was Gish earning a fabulous salary, but she was exercising the sort of control over her pictures that the studio preferred to reserve for itself. At one point, Louis B. Mayer asked her to sign, without legal consultation, a release that would take her off salary until the studio found a suitable vehicle for her. When she demurred, Mayer threatened, "If you don't do as I say, I can ruin you." Gish made one last, ineffective film for MGM, then signed with United Artists for $50,000 a picture.

She returned to the stage, and to a social circle that included Joseph Hergesheimer, George Jean Nathan, F. Scott Fitzgerald, and Carl Van Vechten. Although her later film appearances were few, she continued working into the 1990s as the last great survivor of her generation. Most remarkable of all, Lillian Gish became a roving ambassador for the silent cinema, traveling to distant campuses and film festivals with only one purpose—to bear witness to the "universal language" of film.

See Birth of a Nation, The; *Griffith, D. W.; Pickford, Mary; Thalberg, Irving*

GODFATHER, THE

The Godfather tells the tale of the powerful Corleone "family" and its struggle to stay intact as a criminal organization as well as a collection of blood relatives. The film opens with a lavish wedding and ends with a courtly baptism. Each celebration is violated by violence and betrayal. It is a tale of contrasts and the consistent matching of emotional and visual opposites. Murky, somber interiors with characters' eye sockets shrouded in darkness and swarthy men who seem monstrous are juxtaposed with white wedding gowns, rainbow-hued gardens, and the sun-washed starkness of Sicily. While grown-ups whisper death threats and order men to kill, children giggle and wives serve heaping bowls of pasta. The life of *la famiglia* and its rituals seems everlasting. So do its lies.

Interrupting the opening wedding scenes is a grim business meeting between the bride's father, Vito Corleone (Marlon Brando), and a man who asks that his daughter's brutal beating be avenged. A Sicilian tradition directs that Vito cannot refuse any request on his daughter's wedding day. After the man grovels, the don agrees to do "the favor." But it may have to be reciprocated someday, he warns.

"My father made him an offer he couldn't refuse. My father assured him either his brains or his signature would be on the contract."

Al Pacino as Michael Corleone in *The Godfather* (1972)

While other guests feast, sing with the orchestra, dance the tarantella, and gulp red wine, Mafia leader Barzini (Richard Conte) assaults a photographer for taking his picture, and the eldest Corleone son, Santino (James Caan), spits on an FBI badge held out by an agent as identification outside the estate's front gates.

Vito refuses to have the family portrait taken until his youngest son, Michael, arrives. When Michael (Al Pacino) makes his entrance, dressed in uniform and adorned with medals as a war hero, he's accompanied by Kay Adams (Diane Keaton), a WASP New Englander. Soon Michael tells the story behind the ominous hulk she's ogling. "His name is Luca Brasi," Michael says and explains Luca's part in Johnny Fontane's career. The famous crooner (Al Martino) has just arrived and is delighting shrieking females with a love song. Michael says that Luca helped the don make a bandleader "an offer he couldn't refuse." Luca held a gun to the man's head while the don "assured him either his signature or his brains would be on the contract." While Kay gapes over her plate of lasagna, Michael reassures her, "That's my family, Kay. It's not me." Michael also explains how the fair-haired Tom Hagen (Robert Duvall) became his adopted brother: when Sonny was a kid, he brought the orphan Tom home to the Corleones, who raised him as one of their own.

The tone and style abruptly change for the next sequence, in which Tom—who's quickly on his way to becoming the don's *consiglieri*—arrives in the plastic world of Hollywood. (*Consiglieri* is a Mafia term for the family's key business advisor.) Tom has been sent to deal with Woltz, a studio czar who has refused the don's godson Johnny a contract in Woltz's new movie. Tom also hints to Woltz that he could make union problems "disappear." But Woltz is angry that Johnny spoiled one of his protégés and made him look ridiculous. After Woltz shows Tom his mansion's prize amenities, including a $600,000 stallion named Khartoum, he refuses the don's request. The next morning, in one of the film's most famous and horrific scenes,

Woltz wakes up to find his pajamas covered in blood. He frantically searches the bedclothes until he discovers he's in bed with Khartoum's severed head.

After the Corleones meet with a mobster named Sollozzo, an attempt is made to assassinate the don. Sollozzo (Al Lettieri) had offered Vito a 30 percent return for a $1 million investment in a drug partnership. But Sollozzo really wants to tap into the don's connections. Before the meeting, Tom advised the family that "narcotics is the thing of the future," but the don warned that officials on his payroll "wouldn't be friendly very long if they knew my business was drugs instead of gambling, which they regard as a harmless vice."

Sonny tipped his hand at the meeting and showed interest, which gave Sollozzo the idea to kill the don and work with Sonny. Sollozzo and his backer, Bruno Tattaglia (Tony Giorgio), first garrot Luca, then kidnap Tom, and finally order an ambush of the don while he's buying fruit from a street vendor in Little Italy.

Until this point Michael has remained outside the family business, but now he begins to be drawn into the fold. While enjoying Manhattan's Christmas ambience with Kay, he's devastated by a newspaper headline that reports his father's murder. He rushes home and finds the homestead transformed into Sonny's war room. Armed men patrol the gates, and the hotheaded Sonny and his *caporegimes* (captains) plot their revenge.

As Michael Corleone, Al Pacino goes from the quiet, sensitive youngest son to ruthless godfather in a chilling yet virtually seamless transformation.

Once released, Tom tries to barter a truce between Sonny and Sollozzo to avoid a full-scale war between the Mafia families. Sonny accuses Tom of not wanting revenge because he's not a real son to the don. Sonny quickly apologizes, but the insult remains a sore spot between the two men. Mafia rules maintain that a *consiglieri* or other family power broker should be another Sicilian.

Michael goes to see his father at the hospital but finds the place deserted. His father's bodyguards have been sent away, and Michael knows that his father is vulnerable to attack. The hospital sequence, which ends with Michael telling the don, "I'm with you now," changes Michael from "civilian" to family player. Rather than panic as Sonny fears, Michael takes control. He warns the nurse that men are coming to kill his father, whom she helps move out of the room. He then enlists the help of Enzo the baker, who unwittingly arrives with flowers to pay his respects. Michael and Enzo stand outside the hospital entrance pretending to have guns to scare off the assassins, who eventually drive on when they see the entrance guarded.

The Turk's bodyguard, a corrupt police captain named McCluskey (Sterling Hayden), arrives and ends up breaking Michael's jaw. In the next scene, in the family library, Michael makes the formal leap into the family trade. First, he sits quietly in the background, listening to Tom and Sonny fight over strategy. Sonny brags about the "hundred button men on the street," referring to the soldiers who carry out the killing. Michael finally speaks, slowly outlining a calculated scenario that ends with him murdering Sollozzo and the police captain. After a long silence, the other men burst into laughter. They're amused not only at who's suggesting the double homicide but that one of the victims should be a cop. The fallout from killing a cop is too dangerous, Tom warns, fearing that the family would be an outcast within the Underworld.

The Godfather dwarfed the competition in 1972: at #1, it earned $81.5 million; *Fiddler on the Roof* made $25 million, and *Diamonds Are Forever* $21 million.

Michael remains unruffled. He soon convinces them that feeding a story to the reporters on their payroll about a "crooked cop who got mixed up in the rackets and got what was coming to him" will deflect the fallout.

Michael's murder of Sollozzo and McCluskey in the restaurant is a taut orchestration of anxiety, anticipation, and swift violence. After the blood of Michael's victims mixes with sumptuous food and purplish wine, Michael flees looking both stunned and deliberate.

When Vito is brought home from the hospital, he learns that Michael murdered his enemies and is now hiding in Sicily. The Sicilian sequence shows Michael roaming the idyllic countryside with two armed bodyguards, eventually visiting the village where his father was born: Corleone. It became the family name when Vito arrived in America. Interspersed between Michael's courtship of a *signorina* named Apollonia are ferocious episodes involving Sonny and Connie back home. Connie's husband, Carlo, angry that he's been shut out of the family business, stages a cruel row with Connie to entrap Sonny. Sonny has come to his beaten sister's aid before, savagely thrashing Carlo on the street while his hoods kept the crowds back. But Connie (Talia Shire) had begged Sonny not to seek revenge, shrieking that the fight was her fault. This time, taunted by Carlo's mistresses and his abuse, a very pregnant Connie performs an orgy of destruction in her own home, smashing china and glass and waving a butcher knife at Carlo. He knocks the knife away, corners her in the bathroom, and beats her with a belt. Afterward Connie calls Sonny, who drives off without bodyguards and becomes trapped at a deserted Long Island tollbooth, where he's mowed down by a waiting squad of machine gunners.

Meanwhile, in Sicily, Michael marries Apollonia. Michael patiently abides by the village customs and treats Apollonia with tenderness. However, shortly after their nuptials, she's blown up by a car bomb meant for him.

In the wake of Sonny's death, Vito orders Tom to call a meeting of the heads of the five families. In an opulent boardroom fit for any corporate power broker in America, Vito ensures Michael's safe return from Sicily in exchange for his political links to launch the interfamily drug business. But Vito warns, "I believe this drug business is going to destroy us in years to come."

After Michael has been back a year, he goes to see Kay outside the school where she teaches. He explains that he's working for his ailing father, and she reminds him that he vowed never to get involved. Michael argues that his father is no different from other powerful men, likening Vito to a senator or president. Kay tells him how naïve he sounds, noting that such leaders "don't have men killed." He explains that his father's way of doing business is over. "In five years the Corleone family is going to be completely legitimate," he adds. "Trust me. That's all I can tell you about my business."

Seduced by the memory of an idealistic Michael and his caressing, intimate words that now reassure her, Kay finally climbs into the back of his black limousine and becomes a Corleone.

Eventually taking a seat behind his father's regal desk, Michael seems agitated and frosty as he listens to Tessio (Abe Vigoda) and Clemenza (Richard Castellano) complain bitterly to Vito about other families eating into their territories. They also are hinting that Michael is too inexperienced to run the family. But Michael, in his pricey three-piece suit, doesn't have his father's tact or ability to subdue people. Rather than reassure his *capi*, Michael tells them little about his plans. He also abruptly fires Tom as *consiglieri* but keeps him on as family lawyer.

Soon Michael goes to Las Vegas, where Fredo was sent to lie low during the street wars. Fredo has changed from the meek, invisible Corleone son to a garish dresser who barks at bellboys in order to appear tough. Neither camouflages his basic docility or self-loathing. As such, he has become a lackey for mobster Moe Greene (Alex Rocco), whom Michael intends to strong-arm into selling his casino to the Corleone family. After Michael pushes for a buyout price on the casino, Moe storms off, leaving Fredo to scold Michael for being disrespectful. Michael is barely able to contain his

notable & quotable

"I always thought of *The Godfather* as a story of a great king with his three sons. The oldest was given his passion and aggressiveness; the second, his sweet nature and child-like qualities; the third his cunning and coolness."

Francis Ford Coppola, director, 1992

rage and further humiliates Fredo by ordering him never to take sides against the family again.

As Vito putters around his garden sipping wine, he and Michael go over the plan to wrestle back power for the Corleones, in particular, from the Barzini family. In between tender musings between father and son about the family legacy, they plot Michael's next move. Later, while Vito is playing the monster for his grandson's amusement, he has a heart attack and drops dead in his vegetable garden.

At Vito's funeral, Michael recalls his father's advice that the capo who approaches him with a Barzini meeting will be the traitor, who turns out to be Tessio. Michael also explains to Tom at the funeral that he plans to meet with the heads of the five families after the baptism of Connie's baby; he has agreed to become a godfather.

The film's finale has become one of the most celebrated in the history of the cinema. Playing on the contrasting structure, the last sequence juxtaposes the rituals of the baptism with the preparations of Michael's henchmen to massacre his enemies. In one scene, the priest dabbles ointment on the infant's lips while the face of a Corleone soldier is smeared with shaving cream before his appointment to kill. As the sequence progresses, the baby moves from peaceful slumber to frantic wailing, the organ from melodic tones to frenzied noise, with Michael answering the priest's query: "Do you renounce Satan?"

As Michael answers his vows, each boss of the five families is summarily executed. Barzini is shot and rolls down the steps. Moe Green is shot in the eye, another boss is blasted at close range by Clemenza's shotgun, a revolving door becomes a cage for another victim, and the remaining kingpin is riddled with bullets alongside a naked and equally bloodied woman. Moreover, Michael orders Tessio and Carlo killed as revenge for their betrayals. Carlo is garroted by Clemenza, and realizing he's about to die, Tessio tells Tom, "Tell Mike it was only business. I always liked him."

In the last sequence, a hysterical Connie bursts into Michael's office and howls about the massacre, which included her husband. "Want to know how many men he had killed?" Connie shrieks at a confused Kay. "Read the papers. . . . That's your husband."

Michael is anxious about Connie's hysterics. He tries to put his arms around her, but she quickly pulls away and wails more ferociously than before. Michael avoids Kay's eyes and nervously paces around his office. She keeps asking if Connie's accusations are true until he shouts a reminder that she's not to ask about his business. Soon he quiets himself and permits her to ask him "just this once." Fearfully, she repeats her question, and Michael looks her straight in the eye and utters a convincing "no." Her face relaxes and they embrace. After she leaves to fix them a drink, remaining out of focus in the front of the frame, Michael is in the background surrounded by his underlings, including his father's workhorse Clemenza. Clemenza then kisses Michael's hand and calls him "Don Corleone." Just as the door is about to shut on Kay's view, the last shot shows her face flushed with dread as she comprehends the unfolding ritual.

The Godfather won the Academy Award for Best Picture in 1972, and its star, Marlon Brando, won for Best Actor. The film's director, Francis Ford Coppola, was nominated for Best Director.

See Brando, Marlon; Coppola, Francis Ford; Gangster film; Keaton, Diane; Pacino, Al

GODFATHER: PART II, THE

The sequel to *The Godfather* takes the theme of contrasts to new heights—juxtaposing not only violence with family devotion but one era with another. The film switches back and forth between Vito's humble life in Little Italy in the early 1900s to Michael's new-world success in the 1950s. The two plots comment on the escalating corruption of gangsters as well as their connection to modern-day America.

The sequences that involve a nostalgic look back at the young Vito are filmed in rich sepia tones that accentuate their historical perspective (with period costumes created by Theadora Van Runkle of *Bonnie and Clyde* fame). Vito is easily able to dominate the Italian universe created within America, whereas Michael, *la famiglia*'s new patriarch, seems out of place in the western frontier of Nevada and the carnival colors of Havana's nightlife.

"*I don't feel that I have to wipe everybody out, Tom. Just my enemies, that's all.*"

Al Pacino as Michael Corleone in *The Godfather: Part II* (1974)

The plot of the 200-minute film—also coauthored by Puzo and Coppola—focuses on betrayals as well. But it's often difficult to know who's forsaking whom and why. In the end, Michael's goal, as in part 1, is to avenge his enemies and maintain control over his domain. Young Vito's struggle is to gain power despite starting out a disadvantaged immigrant hemmed in by poverty. He eventually blends Sicilian customs with American opportunity and becomes a crime czar. Michael, on the other hand, is threatened by forces his father never had to deal with: the loss of family and deteriorating respect for traditions.

The film opens with the last scene of part 1, in which Michael is revered as the new godfather. The story shifts abruptly to Sicily around 1901. The nine-year-old Vito accompanies his mother to his father, Antonio's, funeral. His brother, Paolo, is soon gunned down by his father's murderer—the local Mafia chieftain, Don Ciccio. Ciccio refuses to heed the widow's pleas to spare her remaining son, the "weak, dumb-witted" Vito. Ciccio says Vito will "come for revenge" when he becomes a man. (After becoming an American Mafia boss, Vito does in fact return to Sicily to kill Ciccio personally.) Hearing Ciccio's refusal, his mother puts a knife to his throat and orders her son to run for his life. She's killed before Vito's eyes, but the townspeople hide him despite warnings of Mafia reprisals. He's soon smuggled out of the country and arrives at Ellis Island, where his name is mistakenly changed from Vito Andolini from Corleone, Sicily, to Vito Corleone. He also is quarantined for three months for smallpox. The quiet boy takes each setback with quiet resignation and unblemished innocence.

As a grown man with a wife and son, Vito (Robert De Niro) works at Abbandando Grosseria. But a series of events start him down a different path. First, he loses his meager job because the grocer is forced to hire the nephew of the Black Hand—the local extortionist named Fanucci who makes everyone in the neighborhood pay protection money. After meeting Clemenza (Bruno Kirby), Vito learns the tricks of stealing to gain material wealth and clout. When Fanucci approaches them for a cut of their profits, Clemenza and his associate Tessio agree to pay, but newcomer Vito votes no. He instructs them to give him the money, ask no questions, and trust him to "make him an offer he don't refuse." He stalks Fanucci during the San Gennaro festival in Little Italy and shoots him three times, the last time with the gun's barrel jammed in the blackmailer's mouth. Completely composed, Vito then joins his wife and three sons on their brownstone stoop for the rest of the festival. As Vito's reputation in the "import business" continues to grow, so does his prestige in the neighborhood.

"If anything in this life is certain, if history has taught us anything, it is that you can kill anyone."

Al Pacino as Michael Corleone in *The Godfather: Part II*

The opening sequence for the modern era is the Holy Communion of Vito's grandson Anthony in Lake Tahoe in 1958. In addition to showing many familiar faces, the sequence also introduces new players: Pentangeli, an old-timer who worked for Vito; Hyman Roth, the legendary Jewish mobster from Miami; Johnny Ola, Roth's "Sicilian messenger boy"; and a U.S. senator named Geary.

At the Communion party, Pentangeli (Michael Gazzo) demands that Michael stop the Rosato brothers' encroachment on his New York territories. He complains that the Rosatos ignore the gambling business until they have spent themselves on drugs and whores. Michael says that the Rosatos remain unharmed because they answer to Roth, with whom Michael is working on a deal.

Also at the Communion party, Geary (G. D. Spradlin) accepts a handsome endowment check from the Corleones. Michael wants the senator to help him with the gaming license on a new casino that the Corleone family wants to take over. But Geary tries to extort money from Michael instead.

Geary is later caught with a bloodied, dead prostitute at one of Fredo's brothels. When Tom shows up and offers the shamed, shocked senator the Corleones' help, he's permanently drawn into their service. Although Geary was a willing partner, he can't remember how the prostitute was murdered. The circumstances point to a Corleone frame as Tom assures Geary that the woman had no family. "It'll be like she never existed. All that's left is our friendship."

Besides the legal gaming license, Michael must deal with Roth, who's the casino's true owner along with a partner. Roth, however, gives Michael approval to oust the partner and remain in business with him. As the plot unfolds, however, Roth double-crosses Michael several times while pretending to be his mentor.

The first time Roth tries to have Michael killed is in his bedroom at the Nevada homestead. Michael is led to believe that Pentangeli attempted the murder for revenge. At first Michael believes this theory but ultimately realizes that Roth set him up. Later, while Michael and Roth are in Cuba working on a deal that will make them "bigger than U.S. Steel," Roth tries again. He first wants the Corleone's $2 million investment, but Michael is stalling for time and sends his henchman to kill Roth first. While in the act of smothering Roth in his hospital bed, however, Michael's man is mysteriously shot by Cuban soldiers. Part of Michael's reluctance to consummate the deal is his astute observations about Castro's unfolding revolution, which threatens the entire structure of Cuba's gambling kingdom.

When Fredo arrives in Cuba with the Corleone money, he's dressed in a white suit with black shirt and a coordinating hat, looking every inch the pimp. Fredo also is on hand to perform his specialty—arranging entertainment for Michael's business associates, including Geary. But Fredo resents being treated like an errand boy. Michael finds out how deep Fredo's outrage goes when he learns that Fredo is the one who betrayed him and nearly got him killed in his bedroom. During Havana's colorful New Year's Eve celebration, he tells Fredo he has arranged to flee and has a plane waiting to take them both away. Then he forcefully grabs Fredo, kisses him on the mouth (the kiss of death) and hisses, "I know it was you Fredo. You broke my heart."

Fredo had tried to confess his betrayal to Michael earlier when the two shared a drink at a Cuban bistro. Fredo admitted that he had been mad at Michael when he was "stepped over" so that Michael could head the family. Fredo also regrets not marrying a woman like Kay, instead of the showgirl Deanna—whom Michael's men frequently have to subdue.

Back in Nevada, Fredo, who disappeared in Cuba, is found and brought to Michael. He explains how he was lured with the promise of a deal of his own, not a hand-me-down from Michael. But he swears he knew nothing about a hit. Michael banishes Fredo, telling him that he's no longer a brother or a friend. But during the interrogation, Fredo divulges a useful item: Roth has a Senate lawyer on his payroll and has arranged for Michael to be exposed before a congressional committee investigating organized crime. At the hearing, a nervous Geary gets a former family soldier to admit that he never took orders directly from Michael and that the godfather claims are speculation. But prosecutors have a star witness who worked under Michael with no "buffers": Pentangeli. The Corleones believed Pentangeli had been killed by the Rosato brothers on Roth's orders, but Pentangeli survived the attack and was told Michael ordered the hit. When nabbed by the feds, Pentangeli agreed to testify against the Corleones out of revenge.

While in Washington, Kay announces she's leaving Michael. When he tries to sweet-talk her back into the fold, she plays her trump card, revealing that she didn't have a recent miscarriage as he believes, but had an abortion. With bitter relish, she explains how she refused to "bring another one of your sons into this world. . . . This Sicilian thing" must end. Michael strikes her and leaves her cowering in fear. He assumes custody of their children, Anthony and Mary, and allows Kay to visit only when he's not home.

Connie is put in charge of Michael's children. Connie was shown at the film's start as a party girl and a lousy mother. She arrived at the Communion with the blond gigolo Merle (Troy Donahue) in tow; she was hoping Michael would give her enough money to marry Merle and leave for Europe. But later in the film she comes to Michael on her knees, whispering, "I'd like to stay close to home right now if it's all right." She admits that she did things to harm herself because she was mad at him but now realizes he was just being strong like Papa and taking care of business.

"Fredo, you're nothing to me now. You're not a brother, you're not a friend. I don't want to know you or what you do."

Al Pacino as Michael Corleone in *The Godfather: Part II*

When Mama Corleone dies, the last obstacle is removed for Michael's final sweep of revenge. He had vowed to spare Fredo while she was alive, but at the funeral, hugging Fredo at Connie's insistence, Michael glares at his henchman and signals Fredo's murder. Michael also orders Roth to be shot. Roth is trying to flee Castro's Cuba and go to Israel but is refused entry, as in every country he tries to bribe for a resident's permit. And although Roth has only six months to live, Michael wants him assassinated at the Miami airport. Tom asks Michael, "Is it worth it? You won. . . . you wanna wipe everybody out?" Michael says, barely above a whisper, "Just my enemies."

He has distanced himself from Tom as well. When Michael had left for Cuba, he affectionately called Tom "his brother." He also appointed Tom the acting don in his absence, noting Fredo has "a good heart . . . but he's weak. And he's stupid. And this is life and death." Tom wept that day, moved by Michael's love and trust. As the story comes to a close, Tom asks, "Why do you hurt me? I've always been loyal to you."

To save Michael the trouble of murder, Pentangeli kills himself. First, he gets "amnesia" during the government hearings when he spots his older brother from Sicily seated next to Michael. The message: your family will be killed if you testify. Tom visits Pentangeli in prison, and they discuss how traitors were handled during the Roman empire (the structural model for the Mafia). If they committed suicide, their families were taken care of for life by the Roman regime. Pentangeli explains how they took a bath, "opened their veins and bled to death," prefiguring his own demise.

Michael once again settles the family business, but this time the victory leaves him totally isolated. A final flashback shows the day when the Japanese bombed Pearl Harbor and Michael enlisted in the Marines. It was also Vito's birthday. While the children wait to surprise their father, Sonny tells Michael that soldiers are saps "because they risk their lives for strangers. . . . your country ain't your blood." Michael answers derisively, "That's Pop talking," implying that his allegiance is to America and not to an antiquated code from the Old Country. Michael is ultimately left alone in the room—as he is in life. He never felt he belonged to the family nor did he want any part of its criminal business. Yet after a dozen years, he has become its leader and the most ruthless of them all. The last scene shows Michael, still wearing a wedding ring—another hollow symbol of his pose as a family man. He's sitting alone outdoors as winter overtakes the Nevada landscape. The film ends with an extreme close-up—Michael's eyes now dark and desolate.

The Godfather: Part II is the only sequel to ever win the Academy Award for Best Picture.

See Coppola, Francis Ford; De Niro, Robert; Gangster film

GOLD RUSH, THE

Charlie Chaplin's 1925 silent picture, *The Gold Rush*, is a comedy epic of lasting fame. Chaplin created this remarkably gentle and forgiving film

The Gold Rush *was one of many films that Charlie Chaplin wrote, directed, produced, and starred in over his long career.*

about two prospectors, partners in the Alaskan gold rush, who survive cold and hunger to discover a mountain of gold and love.

The film opens on the image of a long line of prospectors stretched out across a snow-covered Alaskan mountain. One prospector, Charlie (Chaplin), has collapsed from exhaustion. But he forges on until a storm blows him into a cabin. Moments later, the wind blows a large, bearlike figure, Big Jim McKay (Mack Swain), into the cabin as well. Charlie goes in search of food, but returns empty-handed. Starving, Big Jim attacks Charlie, but a bear ambles in and scares him off. Charlie recovers to shoot the bear and they eat, their friendship cemented.

Charlie decides to give up prospecting and finds his way to a local bar. There he notices a dance hall girl, Georgia (Georgia Hale), just after she tears one of her photographs trying to get it back from Jack (Malcolm Waite), a prosperous patron. To make Jack jealous, Georgia chooses the startled Charlie, who has no idea he is simply a pawn in her game. Georgia gives Charlie a wilted rose and he is smitten.

Charlie has been loaned a snug cabin to use, so he invites Georgia to visit. Georgia, sitting on his bed, discovers the torn photograph and wilted rose under his pillow. When Charlie joins her on the bed, she makes fun of him. Nevertheless, Charlie asks her to dinner. She sets a date she has no intention of keeping, for it is a busy night in her trade: New Year's Eve.

"Chicken or no chicken, his friend looks appetizing."

Title revealing starving Mack Swain's (as Big Jim McKay) feelings toward Charlie Chaplin (as the Lone Prospector) in *The Gold Rush* (1925)

The night of the dinner, Charlie fantasizes that he is a success as host, but predictably, Georgia never shows up. Later that night, abruptly remembering her dinner date, the callous Georgia proposes to Jack that they go to the cabin to tease Charlie. Meanwhile, Charlie has disconsolately left the cabin. At the cabin, Georgia feels remorse when she discovers how much loving care Charlie has put into preparing for her. When Jack forces a kiss, Georgia slaps him and flees the cabin.

Back at the dance hall a repentant Georgia writes a note without salutation, asking for forgiveness. But she intends the note for Jack, who sneers at it and passes it on to Charlie, who cares only for the message and knows nothing of how it has reached him. In search of Georgia, Charlie goes to the dance hall. There he meets up with Big Jim, and they decide to prospect again.

So, Charlie and Big Jim settle back into their old "home." During the night, a storm blows the cabin to a mountain of gold. When Big Jim climbs out of the cabin, he discovers the gold, and he and Charlie embrace.

Later, on a ship, a reporter asks the elegantly dressed Charlie to be photographed in his old tramp outfit. The film cuts to Georgia, down in steerage, as she watches the crew searching for a stowaway. Cutting back to the ship cabin, Charlie reappears in his old rags, and obeying the photographer, steps back and falls down into steerage. The last scene shows Charlie and Georgia embracing, as the two successful survivors are voyaging home in luxury.

See Chaplin, Charlie

GOLDWYN, SAMUEL

Samuel Goldwyn, one of the most powerful and influential studio chiefs in Hollywood history, was born Samuel Gelbfisz in Warsaw, Poland, on August 27, 1882. After going to work at age eleven as an office boy, a few short years later Goldwyn sensed the limits imposed on him by the poverty, political upheaval, and anti-Semitism of his native land, and he decided to leave Poland. After a brief and restless sojourn with relatives in England (who Anglicized his surname to Goldfish), he set out for the United States, which he viewed as the true land of opportunity.

After his arrival in New York City in 1896, Goldwyn quickly found work in a glove factory in upstate New York. Befriending the owner's son and showing a competitive knack for the business, he soon became one of the most successful salesmen in the company. During his life as a salesman, Goldwyn fell in love with a woman who eventually married Jesse Lasky, a famous theatrical producer. Despite this marriage, the woman Goldwyn loved, Bessie Ginzburg, remained friends with him and soon arranged for him to meet her husband's sister, Blanche Lasky.

Goldwyn and Blanche Lasky were married in 1910. Goldwyn's motives in the marriage were questioned by some who felt he was using Blanche as a stepping-stone to a career in show business. Still restless and searching, he set out to acquire the culture that had been denied him as a child, attending the theater and opera and reading widely. He grew fascinated with the idea of a career in show business.

By 1912, Arthur S. Friend, a lawyer, was suggesting that Goldwyn take seriously the idea of a career in motion pictures. When a change in tariff laws led Goldwyn to fear a downturn in the domestic glove business, he held serious discussions about the movie industry with Lasky, who was desperately in need of money and was searching for a way out of his own business, in which he was partnered with the talented but mercurial Cecil B. DeMille.

And so in December 1913 the Jesse L. Lasky Feature Players company was founded by Lasky, DeMille, and Goldwyn. Goldwyn's quest was to improve the quality of motion pictures, and their first effort, *The Squaw Man* (1913), made film history: it was the first full-length feature film produced in the United States and the first major film produced in Hollywood. An immediate box-office success, the venture encouraged the new company to produce a rapid succession of equally successful feature-length films.

In July 1916 the Lasky Company merged with its larger competitor, Adolph Zukor's Famous Players, to form the Famous Players-Lasky Corporation. Goldwyn and Zukor were at odds from the start, and when Zukor threatened to leave if Goldwyn stayed, the latter accepted $900,000 in exchange for his resignation.

notable & quotable

"Pictures are for entertainment; messages should be delivered by Western Union."

Studio head Samuel Goldwyn, attributed

G

GOLDWYN, SAMUEL

Director Samuel Goldwyn was well known for his witty, intentional malapropisms, such as "Include me out."

In December 1916 Goldwyn entered into a partnership with four people, two of whom—brothers named Edgar and Arch Selwyn—were Broadway producers. The company was named the Goldwyn Pictures Corporation (from the first syllable of Goldfish and the second syllable of Selwyn). Goldwyn, who did not legally change his name from Goldfish until 1919, liked the new name and began to use it as his own.

The new Goldwyn company strove early for quality in all areas of production, hiring well-known playwrights and production designers. To create good stories for the screen Goldwyn formed Eminent Authors, Inc., in 1919, as a separate part of the company to attract the best writing talent. To publicize Eminent Authors, Goldwyn hired Howard Dietz, who selected a roaring lion peering through a porthole on which was engraved the Latin inscription *Ars Gratia Artis* (Art for Art's Sake) as the trademark for the Goldwyn Pictures Corporation.

Despite his artistic successes, Goldwyn's stockholders and partners were unhappy with the company's profit margin. In March 1922 Goldwyn was forced out of office as president of his own company. After settling with the Goldwyn Pictures Corporation for roughly a million dollars, he decided that he would produce movies entirely on his own. By taking responsibility for his films, Goldwyn could then guarantee that here would be no aesthetic compromises in any of his future projects. Goldwyn formed his new company in 1923, naming it Goldwyn Productions, Inc., Ltd.

No longer tethered to quarreling partners and meddlesome stockholders, Goldwyn was free to pursue his own vision of quality—and profitability—in the burgeoning movie business. From his first production, *The Eternal City* (1923), to his last, *Porgy and Bess* (1959), Goldwyn combined canny commercial instincts with a quest for taste that became known as "the Goldwyn touch." His determination to acquire the best talent ranged over every aspect of film production. Over the years his roster of acting talent included such names as Ronald Colman, Vilma Banky, Gary Cooper, Anna Sten, Will Rogers, David Niven, and Merle Oberon; among his stable of writers were Sinclair Lewis, Ben Hecht, Lillian Hellman, and Sidney Kingsley; and he attracted top directors such as as King Vidor, Lewis Milestone, Norman Z. McLeod, Howard Hawks, Otto Preminger, and, preeminently, William Wyler. Wyler became Goldwyn's favored collaborator and directed what many consider to be the summit of Goldwyn's career, *The Best Years of Our Lives* (1946), a widely admired drama of World War II soldiers returning to civilian life that garnered seven Oscars, including the award for Best Picture of the year.

Other notable Goldwyn productions were *Wuthering Heights* (1939), *Dodsworth* (1936), *Stella Dallas* (1937), *Ball of Fire* (1941), *The Pride of the Yankees* (1942), *Come and Get It* (1936), *The Little Foxes* (1941), *My Foolish Heart* (1949), and *Guys and Dolls* (1955).

Goldwyn's contributions to the art and business of film were recognized in 1947, when the Motion Picture Academy awarded him the Irving Thalberg Memorial Award; in 1957 the academy honored him again with the Jean Hersholt Humanitarian Award; and in 1971 President Nixon presented him with the Medal of Freedom. Goldwyn died at home on January 31, 1974. In its obituary *Variety* wrote, "Dean of the independent producers, and the only true indie, he began bucking the majors at a time when they dominated the industry . . . and emerged as a dominant personality among giants . . . having met his competition with a long string of superior quality pictures."

See Best Years of Our Lives, The; *Cooper, Gary; DeMille, Cecil B.; Hawks, Howard; Milestone, Lewis; Producer; Vidor, King;* Wuthering Heights; *Wyler, William*

GONE WITH THE WIND

A great many superlatives have been attributed to 1939's *Gone with the Wind*. At the time of its release, it was the longest and most expensive film ever made. It was also the first major motion picture filmed in color. It won eight Oscars, including Best Picture and Best Actress for Vivien Leigh. And the Best Supporting Actress Oscar for Hattie McDaniel was the first ever awarded to a black performer.

Based on Margaret Mitchell's blockbuster novel, the film is a sentimental tribute to the "Old South." Despite its unrealistic portrayal of slavery, *Gone with the Wind* is still a remarkable film, full of brilliant performances, good storytelling, and flamboyant cinematography.

"I can't go all my life waiting to get you between husbands."

Clark Gable as Rhett Butler to Vivien Leigh as Scarlett O'Hara in *Gone with the Wind* (1939)

The heroine of *Gone with the Wind*, sixteen-year-old Scarlett O'Hara of Tara plantation, is in love with Ashley Wilkes. Beautiful and flirtatious, but also spoiled, unscrupulous, and strong-willed, Scarlett is consumed with jealousy when she learns that Ashley plans to marry his meek cousin, Melanie Hamilton. When Scarlett corners Ashley in the library and confesses her love for him—only to be gently rebuffed—she discovers that her embarrassing confession has been overheard by Rhett Butler, a handsome, cynical rogue from Charleston. When she chastises him, "Sir, you are no gentleman," Rhett responds, smiling and clearly entranced, "And you, miss, are no lady."

Suddenly a horseman arrives to announce that Fort Sumter has been fired upon, and the men prepare to leave for war. Out of spite, Scarlett flirts with Melanie's brother, Charles, steals him from Ashley's sister India, and convinces him to marry her. They wed on the day after Ashley and Melanie, just before the men leave for the front.

Charles is killed early in the war and Scarlett is devasted—not because her husband is dead but because she must wear black and behave like a widow. To ease her situation, her mother offers her a trip to Altanta to stay with her Aunt Pittypat. Scarlett jumps at the chance because Melanie lives in Atlanta, and Scarlett wants to be there when Ashley comes home on leave.

At a fund-raising ball in Atlanta, Scarlett, still wearing widow's attire, enjoys the proceedings from the sidelines until Rhett Butler, now a Confederate blockade runner, proposes an auction "for the cause." Most of the young men bid $20 or $25 for a dance with the girl of their choice, but Rhett scandalizes Atlanta society by bidding $250 for a dance with the young widow. When Scarlett accepts, a horrified Aunt Pittypat faints dead away.

Ashley, home on leave, extracts from Scarlett a promise that she will take care of the now-pregnant Melanie. Not long after he returns to the front, the situation in Atlanta becomes more and more dangerous. By the time the city is on the verge of falling to Sherman's army, Melanie is about to give birth. Scarlett wants to escape but cannot because of her promise to Ashley. On her way to find a doctor for Melanie, Scarlett must walk across the Atlanta railroad yard, where thousands of Confederate soldiers lie wounded and dying. The doctor refuses to abandon the wounded to deliver a baby, so Scarlett returns to the Wilkes's house where she and her black slave, Prissy, deliver Ashley's son.

Rhett Butler comes to the rescue of Scarlett and Melanie as Atlanta burns to the ground. He takes them out of the city, then leaves them on the road to Tara so he can return to fight for the cause he already knows is lost. Although the plantation is still standing when Scarlett and Melanie arrive, Scarlett's homecoming is a shock. Her mother has died of typhoid, the plantation has been looted, and her father has been driven insane by his losses. Of the former slaves only Pork and Mammy have stayed on. As she scrabbles in the dry ground for a raw turnip to eat, a desperate Scarlett

Scarlett, horrified to learn that her eighteen-inch waist is now twenty inches, vows never to have another child in this scene from Gone with the Wind.

vows, "If I have to lie, steal, cheat, or kill, as God is my witness, I'll never be hungry again."

As the once-pampered younger O'Hara sisters pick cotton, a Union soldier breaks into the house. When he comes toward Scarlett, intending to rape her, Scarlett shoots him in the face. She and Melanie steal money from his haversack, then hide the body. The money is enough for the women to live on, and there's even some left to help feed the returning soldiers when the war ends. Before long, Ashley returns and helps the women to rebuild the plantation, but despite their efforts, they learn that unless they can come up with three hundred dollars, Tara will be sold for taxes. Scarlett convinces Mammy to make her a dress out of her mother's velvet curtains so that Scarlett will be suitably dressed for a trip to Atlanta, where she hopes to sweet-talk Rhett into lending her enough money to keep the plantation. At first Rhett is delighted to find that Scarlett has "grown a woman's heart," but he soon realizes that she is merely using him and sends her away. Despondent, Scarlett bumps into Frank Kennedy, her sister's fiancé, who now runs a store and a sawmill in Atlanta. She convinces him to marry her instead of her sister and uses his money to pay the taxes on Tara.

In *Variety*'s count of Top-Grossing Movies of All Time, *Gone with the Wind* is #1 with $1,299.4 million and *Titanic* #19, with $427 million earned.

Under Scarlett's management, Kennedy's store and lumber business prosper, and she makes Ashley a partner. A tough and independent businesswoman, Scarlett travels all over town by herself. One day, riding through Shanty Town, she is assaulted by two men. That evening Frank, Ashley, and some of their friends conduct a vigilante raid to avenge the assault. Frank Kennedy is killed, and Scarlett is a widow once again.

On the day of Frank's funeral, Rhett proposes that Scarlett marry him "for fun." She accepts, though she warns him that she will always love Ashley. Rhett lies, "I'm not in love with you any more than you are with me. Heaven help the man who ever really loves you." Rhett has become fabulously wealthy as a result of his dealings during the war, and he and Scarlett live in gaudy splendor. After the birth of their daughter, Bonnie Blue Butler, Scarlett is horrified to find that her eighteen-inch waist is now twenty inches and vows never to have another child. She tells Rhett she intends to lock her bedroom door against him.

On Ashley's birthday, Scarlett visits him at the sawmill. They talk and Ashley hugs Scarlett to comfort her. India Wilkes witnesses the embrace; having always hated Scarlett, she spreads the story of what she's seen all over town. Scarlett, ashamed, takes to her bed, but Rhett forces her to put on a bright red dress and attend the party Melanie is hosting for Ashley that evening. Melanie treats Scarlett as kindly as ever and will not allow any of their friends to believe India's interpretation of the embrace. When Scarlett arrives home after the party, she finds Rhett drinking in the library. They argue, and Rhett, in a combustible mixture of alcohol, anger, and passion, kisses Scarlett fiercely and carries her off to bed.

The next morning Scarlett is a changed woman; as she luxuriates in bed, she is clearly ready to resume marital relations with Rhett. But he fails to notice her mood and tells her that he's leaving with Bonnie for an extended stay in London. A couple of months later, when they return, Scarlett tells Rhett she is pregnant, but he is still angry with her. The couple exchange heated words, and as Scarlett reaches out to slap Rhett, she falls down the stairs. The injuries from her fall result in a miscarriage.

When Scarlett recovers, Rhett tells Scarlett that he loves her and asks her forgiveness. As they talk, Bonnie, who has been riding her pony, takes a dangerous jump, falls, and breaks her neck.

Later, Melanie dies giving birth to her second child. Rhett watches in anger as Scarlett comforts Ashley, who confesses to Scarlett how much he loved Melanie. Scarlett suddenly realizes what a fool she has been and runs after Rhett. She finds him at home and tells him she loves him, but it is too late. Rhett takes his suitcase and walks out the door. As he leaves, Scarlett cries, "If you go, where shall I go? What shall I do?" Rhett responds with the famous line "Frankly, my dear, I don't give a damn."

Scarlett weeps pitiably for a moment, then decides she'll go crazy if she thinks about what just happened. She'll think about it tomorrow; she'll go home to Tara to "think of some way to get him back. After all, tomorrow is another day."

See Cukor, George; Epic; Gable, Clark; Leigh, Vivien

Gone with the Wind (1939) held the box-office championship from 1940 until 1966, when it was replaced by *The Sound of Music* (1965).

GOODFELLAS

GoodFellas (1990), a sprawling tale of real-life hoodlum Henry Hill's odyssey through the ranks of the New York mob, has often been taken as Martin Scorsese's counterpoint to Francis Ford Coppola's *The Godfather* and its romanticizing of the gangster's life. *The Godfather*'s stately images of the Mafia—reverent familial hierarchies, sacred internal codes of honor, and charismatic patriarchs—are here blown sky high in a melange of cheating husbands, desperately unhappy, assertive wives, homicidal psychotics, and staggering brutality and greed. This unflinching probe into the heart of organized crime's darkness won an Oscar for Best Supporting Actor (Joe Pesci) and was nominated for five other Academy Awards.

In the opening nighttime scene, it is 1970 and three mobsters are driving down a freeway—Henry Hill (Ray Liotta) behind the wheel, Jimmy Conway (Robert De Niro) in the passenger's seat, and Tommy De Vito (Joe Pesci) in the back. Thumping sounds coming from the car's trunk lead them to pull over—in the trunk is Batts, a mob member, who is bloodied but still alive and wrapped in a tablecloth. To finish off Batts, Tommy stabs him repeatedly, and Jimmy pumps four bullets into the body.

"Whenever we needed money, we'd rob the airport. To us it was better than Citibank."

Ray Liotta as Henry Hill (narration) in *GoodFellas* (1990)

A flashback to 1955 shows Henry as a teenager, dreaming of acquiring the power and prestige of the neighborhood "wiseguys," or gangsters. He curries favors with the mobsters by parking their gleaming Cadillacs, running numbers for them, and eventually, selling smuggled untaxed cigarettes, a venture that leads to his first arrest and the first test of his criminal mettle, which he passes by maintaining the mob's code of silence. Although young Henry's half-Irish heritage precludes him from entering the mob's most powerful circles, he impresses a local Mafia boss, the brutal and unscrupulous Paulie Cicero (Paul Sorvino), who takes Henry under his wing. Under the tutelage of Paulie and his wiseguys, Henry's criminal activities proliferate in league with his idol, Jimmy (Robert De Niro), Paulie's hitman. Tommy (Joe Pesci), Henry's age, is Jimmy's homicidally volatile and paranoid apprentice.

"When I was broke, I'd go out and rob some more. We ran everything. We paid off cops. We paid off lawyers. We paid off judges. Everybody had their hands out. Everything was for the taking."

Ray Liotta as Henry Hill (narration) in *GoodFellas* (1990)

By 1963 Henry, now a full-fledged member of Paulie's crew, has begun dating Karen (Lorraine Bracco), a nice Jewish girl who is unaware of his background. The relationship between Henry and Karen blossoms, and they are married. Karen eventually learns what Henry's world is about, and she rationalizes his criminal vocation, fascinated by the glamour and excitement of their life together. The couple is also newly rich, as Henry and Tommy have successfully executed an airport heist of more than $400,000.

The narrative then jumps back to 1970 in order to explain the film's opening scene. In a typically volcanic explosion of temper, Tommy beats a fellow mobster, Batts, nearly to death, enlisting Jimmy's help in what they both know is an imprudent break with mob protocol, since this is not an officially authorized whack. They wrap the body in a tablecloth, and we return to the film's opening scene in which Batts is in the car trunk. Soon the Mafia launches a search for the missing Batts.

Meanwhile, Henry and Jimmy are arrested for beating up a bookie and sentenced to ten years in prison. As he serves his time in federal prison, Henry secretly starts dealing drugs to other inmates to support his family. When he is released four years later, he goes back to work for Paulie, ignoring his boss's warnings to quit dealing drugs.

Henry continues to deal drugs, and he also joins Jimmy and Tommy as they plan another airport heist, the famous Lufthansa job at JFK airport, which yields some $6 million. Although Jimmy has warned everyone involved to lie low with the money to avoid arousing suspicion, some of the heist accomplices start recklessly flaunting their newfound wealth. Paranoid, Jimmy orders the accomplices killed in order to sever any links between him and the robbery.

Later, Tommy is about to be ceremoniously accepted into the Mafia as a made man. But when he is ushered into an empty room to take the oath, he is shot in the back of the head—retribution for Batts's death, and especially vicious: Tommy's mother will be forced to have a closed casket at his funeral because of the head wounds.

Meanwhile, in the film's charged final scenes, a paranoid, drugged-out Henry frenetically attempts to close a drug deal while simultaneously managing the chaotic scene at his home. But his paranoia turns out to be real, and he is arrested for the deal. Out on bail, he knows his life is on the line: Paulie and his wiseguys, threatened by Henry's arrest, are watching. Henry clandestinely meets with the FBI and negotiates a deal to expose his Mafia colleagues in return for entrance into the FBI's witness protection program. The last scene shows the arrests of Paulie's wiseguys—Henry has ratted on them all. After testifying against the Mafioso, Henry and Karen, under government protection, retreat to what appears to be a safe but dull life in the midwest. The final shot shows us the new Henry, sadly defeated, just another suburban jerk walking out on his lawn to get the morning paper.

See De Niro, Robert; Gangster film; Scorsese, Martin

GRADUATE, THE

Few films have both reflected and shaped the temperament of a generation as decisively as Mike Nichols's *The Graduate* did in 1967. Dustin Hoffman, in his first major feature film-star turn, portrays Benjamin, who has just graduated from college and who, upon arriving at his parents' lavishly appointed house, tells his father that he is concerned about his future, that he wants it to be different. But his father is interested in getting him downstairs, where a welcome-home/graduation party awaits him. Benjamin drifts uncomfortably through the chic assemblage, as though he had just landed from another planet. He is really alone, suddenly disoriented and disaffected by the values and mores of his parents' materialistic generation, with their swimming pools, color television, and raffish cars. The values of that culture, often described in those years as a "plastic" society, score a direct hit on him when one of the party guests, a slickly attired, middle-aged businessman, shepherds Benjamin to one side, fixes him with an earnest stare, and tells him that he is going to utter only one word of advice about Ben's future: "plastics."

"Oh no, Mrs. Robinson, I think you're the most attractive of all my parents' friends, I mean that."

Dustin Hoffman as Benjamin Braddock in *The Graduate* (1967)

Benjamin is jolted from his reverie of anomie when his neighbor Mrs. Robinson (Anne Bancroft), clad seductively in a shiny black dress, asks Benjamin to drive her home. At the Robinson home, Mrs. Robinson confides in Benjamin, confessing that she is an alcoholic, subtly luring him into her web. She asks Benjamin to unzip her dress. As Benjamin stares at her daughter's glass-covered portrait, he suddenly sees the reflected image of the nude body of Mrs. Robinson, who has just entered the room, telling him that she will always be available to him. As she opens the door, her image blots out the daughter's face, and a flustered Benjamin, hearing Mr. Robinson's car outside, bolts from the house.

Next seen languishing in the family pool in his new diving gear—sinking to the bottom, symbolically drowning—Benjamin decides to save himself by calling Mrs. Robinson from a phone booth at a hotel, where she meets him for a drink before they repair to the room for their first encounter. The ever-anguished Benjamin temporizes, voicing his guilt over the meeting, until Mrs. Robinson tosses off the taunt that he must be a virgin. Goaded to action, Benajmin slams the door, and the screen goes black. A series of scenes cut between the hotel room and Benjamin at home indicate that time is passing as the affair continues.

When Benjamin tries to talk out his feelings with Mrs. Robinson, she makes it clear that she wants him only for sex. In an especially brutal scene she makes him promise not to take her daughter, Elaine, out, saying that he is not good enough for her daughter. Benjamin calls her a broken-down alcoholic whom he sees out of boredom. They apologize to each other, and Benjamin agrees not to take Elaine out. But when his parents

The Graduate*'s theme of an older woman's adultery with a much younger man helped define the mores of the 1960s "free love" generation.*

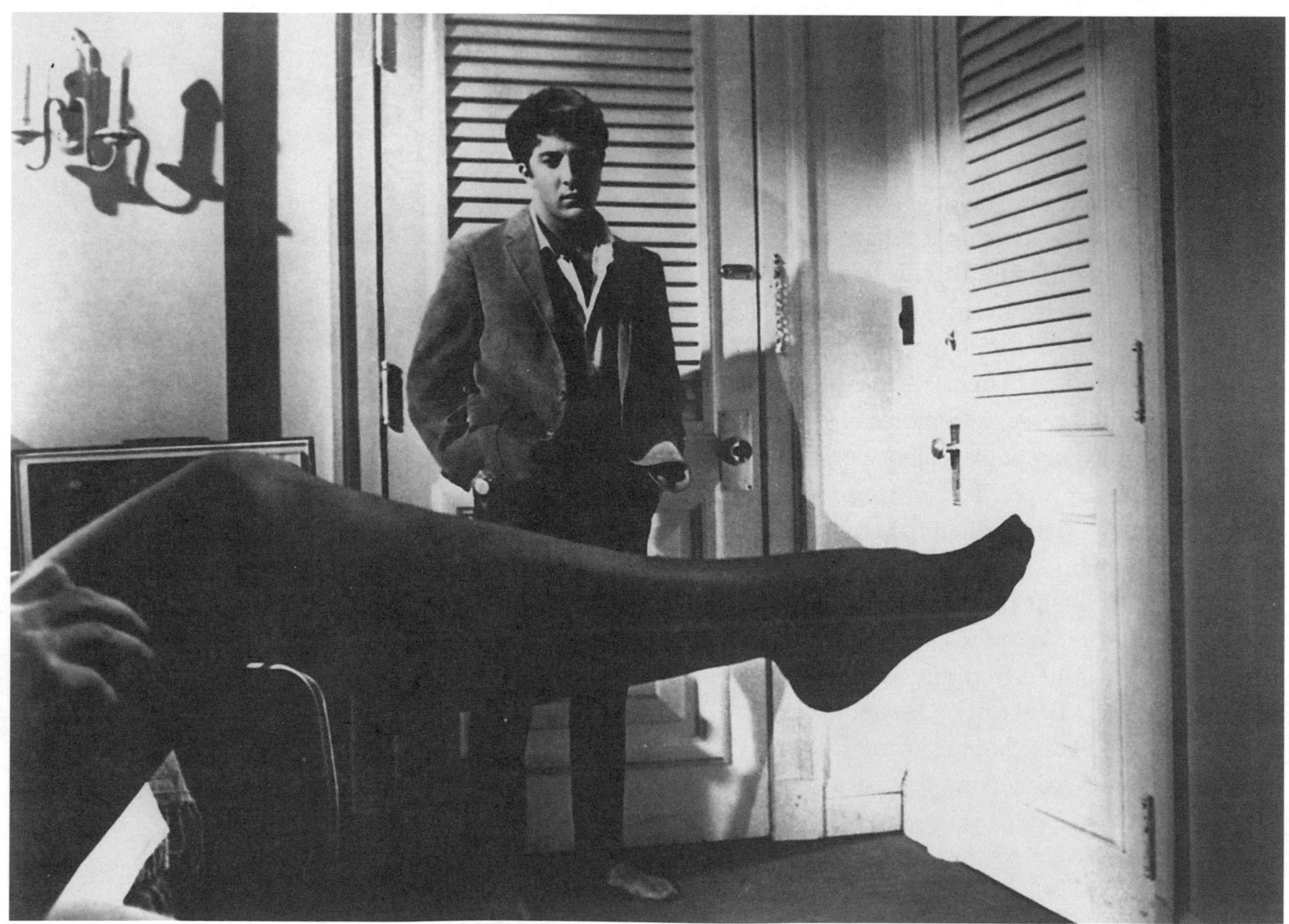

threaten to have the Robinson family over for dinner unless he sees Elaine, he asks her out, apparently to avoid that excruciatingly awkward circumstance.

Benjamin takes Elaine to a strip joint deliberately to humiliate her. His motivation may be to preserve his relationship with Mrs. Robinson, but it also allows him to hurt her as he has been hurt by others. The horrified Elaine flees, and Benjamin catches up with her, telling the crying Elaine that he is not really what he seems to be, and they kiss—a very loving, tender kiss that contrasts with the impersonal lust he has known with her mother.

At a drive-in restaurant, he opens up to her about his feelings, and she listens and understands. They go to Elaine's house, but do not kiss each other goodnight. They agree to meet the next day. When Benjamin drives up to Elaine's house that day, it is raining. Mrs. Robinson, dressed in black, gets in the car, soaking wet. She tells Benjamin never to see Elaine again, or she will tell Elaine everything. Benjamin immediately runs out of the car, into the Robinson's house, and up the stairs to Elaine's room.

When Elaine realizes that Benjamin has been having an affair with her mother, she screams at him to get out. The desolate Benjamin lurks on the periphery of her life until she leaves for college in the fall, at which point he snaps out of his emotional paralysis and resolves to drive to Berkeley to propose marriage to her. Arriving at the campus, he observes Elaine from afar, noticing that she is dating a handsome medical student named Carl Smith. Determined to understand Ben's motivations, Elaine visits Benjamin in his rooming house. She learns from Benjamin that her mother lied to her; that he had not initiated the affair. Upset but newly receptive to the devoted Benjamin, she gives him a very tender kiss and leaves, neither accepting nor rebuffing his offer of marriage. After several days of coaxing, he goes back to his room and is surprised by Mr. Robinson, who tells Benjamin that he and his wife are getting a divorce and that he is taking Elaine away where Benjamin cannot get to her. Benjamin runs to Elaine's dorm, and, in a note brought to him by her roommate, she tells him that although she loves him, it would never work out.

Panicked over the thought of losing Elaine, Benjamin drives to her home in Los Angeles. He tears into the house, goes upstairs, and finds Mrs. Robinson in the bedroom. She icily tells him that she can't invite him to Elaine's wedding and calls the police to report Benjamin as a burglar. "I'll find her," vows Benjamin, who drives back to Berkeley and to Carl Smith's fraternity, where his "brothers" tell him that Carl, "the makeout king," is getting married in a church in Santa Barbara. Extracting the address of the church, he tears off for the service, running out of gas and making the last leg on foot.

Arriving at the white church, he climbs the stairs and peers through the glass on the balcony overlooking the ceremony and communicates his

notable & quotable

"He [Ben] needed a weapon and he needed something to bar the door with. In a church what do you use? I always use a cross."

Buck Henry, co-screenwriter, 1992

anguish by crying out to Elaine and banging on the church window. Touched by his ardor, Elaine answers with a desperate cry of "Ben," and rushes to him. The two flee the church together and board a bus and sit in the back. As the bus pulls off, we see Benjamin and Elaine sitting in silence. The sound track is playing "Hello darkness, my old friend" ("The Sound of Silence"). The film ends on this minor chord, leaving the audience to wonder whether the young couple will find an authentic path of their own or come full circle and replicate their parents' way of life. Nichols's verdict is this: "In my mind, it's always been that in five miles she's going to say, 'My God, I haven't got any clothes.'"

See Hoffman, Dustin; Nichols, Mike

GRAPES OF WRATH, THE

"Fella ain't got a soul of his own, just a little piece of a big soul, one big soul that belongs to everybody."

Henry Fonda as Tom Joad in *The Grapes of Wrath* (1940)

Director John Ford's famous 1940 film adaptation of John Steinbeck's Pulitzer Prize-winning novel *The Grapes of Wrath* is also his most acclaimed. This moving Depression-era drama follows the migration of workers from the Oklahoma dust bowl through their subsequent disillusionment upon reaching California, the "Promised Land."

The film's opening image depicts a flat, paved highway road in rural Oklahoma lined by telephone poles. A man, Tom Joad, (played by Henry Fonda), walks out of the distance. He is hitchhiking to his family's sharecropping farm after serving a short prison term.

When Tom, joined by an itinerant ex-preacher named Casy (John Carradine), finds the Joad shack, it is seen at dusk through a howling dust storm. Like its only inhabitant, Muley (John Qualen), it emerges from the darkness surrounded by a lonely, ghostly aura. Inside, it is completely dark. Tom's family seems to have disappeared. Then a sound, followed by a disembodied voice, then a shadowy face appears. The scene continues with only a candle flickering, giving Muley and the entire scene a sense of nightmarish, spatial disorientation. The film suggests by the power and centrality of the Muley episode that it is his face and nightmare that motivates the Joads in their quest to keep the agrarian dream alive.

The story continues, focusing only on the Joads as they prepare to leave for California. When their truck enters the main highway, they slip in among a caravan of other Okies hitting the road. Once the Joads reach California, dubbed the "land of milk and honey," they discover that others have already claimed this last frontier. There is no land left for the agrarians or Ma Joad's "people." For Ma (played by Jane Darwell) there is nothing left but blind faith in their Darwinian survival.

The second half of the film follows the Joads as they move from one migrant camp to another. As their truck enters the Hooverville Camp, the camera emphasizes the Joads' isolation from the misery of the camp inhabitants. The blank, indifferent gazes of these people and the mechanical movement of the Joads' truck through them gives the impression of the Joads' seeing them as mere objects to be passed through. However, it is the eyes of these people that shame the Joads into reaching out by feeding hungry children at their first meal. From this point, the Joads' sense of community intensifies as the family's disintegration increases.

While at the Hooverville Camp Tom gets into a fight with a sheriff who just killed an innocent woman. Tom is now an outlaw. Force to flee before he is caught by the deputies, the family packs up and drives to a second camp. As the Joads drive into the next camp, they are confronted with shotgun-toting guards. They are offered low-wage work, but are not told that some of the workers are on strike and are attempting to organize a union.

Tom finds that Casy, living in a nearby camp, is involved in the union movement. Casy and the striking workers plead with Tom to help organize

John Ford's adaptation of John Steinbeck's classic novel The Grapes of Wrath *is a moving tale of Depression-era Oakies moving from the dust bowl to California.*
▼

the ranch's pickers and join the strike against their exploitation, but Tom declines. When a guard mortally wounds the ex-preacher, Tom steps up to his defense. In the fight that follows Tom kills the attacking guard.

Again, circumstances force the Joad family to move on, this time to a government camp. When they arrive at the camp a wary Ma Joad and family listen as they hear how the government camp is democratic and self-governing. The Joad family's hope that they have at last found peace is shattered when Tom realizes that the deputies are close behind him and he must again flee.

In the famous final farewell scene with his mother, Tom talks about wanting to do something about "what it is that's wrong." He says, "Well, maybe it's like Casy says. A fella ain't got a soul of his own, just a little piece of a big soul—the one big soul that belongs to ever'body. Then . . . then, it don't matter. I'll be all around in the dark. I'll be ever'-where—wherever you can look. Wherever there's a fight so hungry people can eat, I'll be there. Wherever there's a cop beatin' up a guy, I'll be there. . . . An' when the people are eatin' the stuff they raise, and livin' in the houses they build—I'll be there, too."

Ma doesn't understand Tom's decision, and as she watches, he walks away with his only possessions rolled into a bundle. Ma Joad vows that she will never be afraid again. As the key figure in the film, the matriarch has optimistically faced the challenges of almost-certain destruction, and led the family with dignity through life's situations with a transcendent attitude, will, and feminine life force. The final shot of the film shows a line of migrant trucks moving along through the countryside.

See Ford, John

GRIFFITH, D. W.

David Wark Griffith was born January 22, 1875, on a 264-acre farm in Oldham County, Kentucky. His father, Jacob, was a colorful man who set up a medical practice, fought in the Mexican War, prospected for gold in California, then enlisted under the Confederacy during the Civil War at age forty-two. Griffith remembered that his father dressed in his old colonel's uniform, thrusting a saber at imagined enemies to amuse his seven children. The son would emulate his father, becoming a leader who sought an adventurous life.

In his childhood, Griffith was surrounded by people who would help form his later melodramas. His father read Shakespeare, Poe, and Longfellow out loud at night, laying the foundation for the younger Griffith's mastery of story sequence. There was a pompous politician cousin who was a terrific orator; a smart, energetic aunt who sent four children to college, repaired her own buggy, and had a thriving business selling butter and eggs; and a Jewish peddler who told stories of his travels and played the accordion. Some of Griffith's best and most strongly felt passages in later movies were of country people like those he knew.

Griffith didn't have an easy childhood. The farm, known as Lofty Green, had to be sold to pay off debts when his father died when Griffith was only ten. He walked more than two miles each way to school in every kind of weather, and the Griffiths didn't have much money for food. The family eventually moved to Louisville, where his mother took in boarders to help make ends meet. An intelligent boy, Griffith skipped two grades, but had to leave high school at fifteen to help support the family.

Running an elevator at the J. C. Lewis Dry Goods Store in Louisville wasn't the most inspiring beginning, but the work allowed Griffith time to think and read. It also gave him access to the city's many theaters. Ameri-

Legendary director D. W. Griffith has been called "the father of film technique" and "the man who invented Hollywood."

▼

cans wanted stimulating entertainment and culture even then. Touring companies performed classics like *Hedda Gabler, Henry VIII*, and *The Scarlet Letter*, and Griffith attended a play a week. He also spent a lot of time in the Polytechnic Library, immersing himself in Dickens, Browning, and Civil War history. A performance of *Romeo and Juliet* ignited a desire to act, and Griffith's first role was in an amateur production of the play *The District School*, where he played an unlikely character: the dunce.

A cousin who was leaving Flexner's, Louisville's leading bookstore, introduced Griffith to Benjamin Flexner, and he was hired on there as a clerk in 1893. The Flexners were intellectual and artistic leaders in the community and their shop was a magnet for other cultural thinkers, visiting actors, and celebrities. They would meet in a back room after hours to talk and share their views. The young clerk lingered, dusting shelves, unloading books, working at anything that enabled him to listen to the fascinating discussions. Flexner's was a haven for Griffith. He was surrounded by wonderful books and stories, people with analytical views and thoughts, and theatrical managers and press agents who gave out free passes to new shows.

Of films made before 1930, *The Birth of a Nation* (1915) was the biggest seller, with $10 million in rentals; next was King Vidor's *The Big Parade* (1925), at $5.5 million.

By 1896 the Flexners had sold their shop to Charles Dearing, a new employer who wasn't as kind or as stimulating. Griffith found work as a super on two plays with leading lady Sarah Bernhardt, the star of her day, then signed on as an actor with a touring company. He acted with different companies for about a decade, playing mostly minor roles for low pay, and met his first wife, Linda Arvidson, in San Francisco when they both worked for the same touring company.

Two important incidents led directly to his work behind the camera. In 1906 Griffith sold a play he'd written, *A Fool and a Girl*, for $700. It was a substantial sum of money at the time, and the sale pushed him to write another about the American Revolution, called *War*. Battle scenes were a big part of the story and *War* became his first attempt to create the spectacle, a theme he would become known for. In 1908, after looking for a job as a screenwriter at the Edison studio in the Bronx, New York, Griffith was hired to play a leading role in a film, *Rescued from the Eagle's Nest*. His work with the studio ended with that one role and as he made the rounds for another, the manager and co-owner of the Kalem studio sent him to Biograph.

Biograph, on East 14th Street in New York City, was known for its newsreel coverage, from the Spanish Civil War to McKinley's funeral, as well as its catalogue of well-known actors miming famous stage and vaudeville routines for the camera. At the time, the movies had been introduced in the United States just twelve years before and the industry was growing. By 1908 an estimated one hundred million Americans were paying a nickel or a dime each week to watch a sixty-minute program of short films in little storefront theaters called nickelodeons. Biograph was producing two "one-reeler" fiction films a week and wanted to strengthen the quality of its stories. Griffith was hired as an actor and writer. After three months, Biograph's lone director became ill and Griffith was asked to step in.

Over the next four years, Griffith directed about 420 films, mostly one-reelers approximately fifteen minutes long. In his first film, *The Adventures of Dollie*, Griffith unleashed his natural instincts. In the story, a child is stolen from her yard by gypsies, nailed up in a barrel, and floated down a river over a waterfall before being rescued. Griffith was thoughtful in shaping the narrative. He shot the barrel sequence, not in the nearby Bronx River, but in Hackensack, New Jersey, and Sound River, Connecticut, matching the footage. The river appears in the opening shot, where Dollie is carried by her loving family on a Sunday walk. Two boys pass in the opposite direction with fishing poles. Dollie will be in peril on that river later on, and the boys will eventually rescue her. The film had swift, strong, action sequences with a coherent pattern and *Dollie* surpassed house sales records. Griffith cranked out sixty movies during the last six months of 1908.

Before Griffith, films were basically unedited shots spliced together in consecutive order. But in his hands, camera techniques were used to build emotion and theme. For suspense, he panned in on a gun that was set to go off and aimed at a heroine, then the camera would zoom in on a ticking clock. The scene would then crosscut between the frightened heroine and her frantic saviors. When he noticed audiences giggling at a long kiss, the standard clinch ending all comedies and romances, Griffith used fade-outs.

In 1914 Griffith directed *Judith of Bethulia*, America's first four-reel film. It was a cinematic spectacle with impressive visual settings, a preliminary to films like *The Birth of a Nation*, the first blockbuster in film history. *The Birth of a Nation*, which opened in 1914, chronicled two families torn apart by the Civil War. While the film conveys antiwar sentiment, it was horribly prejudicial. It glorified the Ku Klux Klan as the savior of the South, condoned a lynching, promoted Aryan birthright, and skewered Reconstruction. In spite of the unsavory underlying theme, Griffith's techniques were visionary. He utilized the iris in a scene where a small circle of light shows war refugees, then grows larger with a view of Sherman's army and widespread destruction. He panned the camera to emphasize battle scenes, and his step-by-step representation of Lincoln's assassination was mesmerizing. The film made him a famous public figure, and he financed his next film, *Intolerance*, with the profits from *The Birth of a Nation*.

Intolerance was a gargantuan spectacle that interestingly addressed the theme of bigotry and topped *The Birth of a Nation* in effect. A 1916 *New York Times* film review cites Griffith as "a real wizard of lens and screen," but *Intolerance* was a commercial flop.

In 1919 Griffith—with Douglas Fairbanks, Mary Pickford, and Charlie Chaplin—formed United Artists as a way to guarantee artistic freedom and for actors to profit from their work. A careless businessman, he eventually sold his interest. Griffith also went on to make several other films after *Intolerance*. *Abraham Lincoln* (1930), his first sound film, was a hit. His next, *The Struggle*, released in 1931, was not. It was his last film.

Griffith lost his Midas touch with film in the 1930s. Although he received a special Academy citation for his life's work in 1936, the public was no longer interested in his sentimental melodramas. He started drinking heavily, and increased his womanizing. While not financially destitute, he did die alone in a hotel room in 1948. Known more for his techniques than for the content of his films, Griffith's legacy was substantial. The techniques he perfected are taken for granted now, but he was ahead of his time, and he is credited with elevating motion pictures to an art form.

See Birth of a Nation, The; *Chaplin, Charlie; Director; Fairbanks, Douglas; Ford, John; Gish, Lillian; Ince, Thomas; Montage; Pickford, Mary; Sennett, Mack; Vidor, King; von Stroheim, Erich*

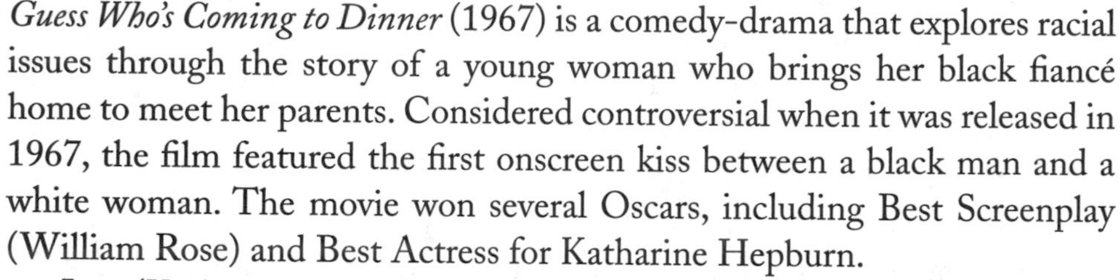

GUESS WHO'S COMING TO DINNER

Guess Who's Coming to Dinner (1967) is a comedy-drama that explores racial issues through the story of a young woman who brings her black fiancé home to meet her parents. Considered controversial when it was released in 1967, the film featured the first onscreen kiss between a black man and a white woman. The movie won several Oscars, including Best Screenplay (William Rose) and Best Actress for Katharine Hepburn.

"You're two wonderful people who happened to fall in love and happen to have a pigmentation problem."

Spencer Tracy as Matt Drayton in *Guess Who's Coming to Dinner* (1967)

Joey (Katharine Houghton, Hepburn's real-life niece) is the lovely, treasured daughter of Matt and Christina Drayton (played by Spencer Tracy and Hepburn), a well-to-do, liberal couple. Matt is the owner of a San Francisco newspaper; Christina (Chris) owns an art gallery. The film opens as Joey arrives home unexpectedly early from a trip to Hawaii, to introduce her fiancé, John Wade Prentice (Sidney Poitier), to her parents. Prentice is worried that Joey's parents will not accept a black son-in-law. But Joey assures him that her parents will have no difficulty at all with an interracial marriage.

When Christina arrives home, Prentice is in another room making a phone call, and Joey proudly and excitedly announces her engagement. She tells her mother that although she and Prentice have known each other for only ten days, they intend to marry. She is about to mention the question of race when Prentice enters the room. Christina is visibly shocked, so much so that Prentice suggests that she sit down. Joey comments, "He thinks you're going to faint because he's a Negro."

When Matt Drayton comes home, he is equally shocked. He retires to his study to let his old friend Monsignor Ryan (Cecil Kellaway) know he will not be playing golf that day. He also calls his secretary and asks her to find out everything she can about Prentice. Chris joins him, and moments later Prentice asks to speak with both of them privately. He tells them that he has resolved not to marry Joey unless both her parents can approve the marriage without reservation. When he leaves, Chris tells Matt, "The way she is, is just exactly the way we brought her up." She reminds him that they taught her discrimination was "always, always wrong." And, she says, "when we said it we did not add 'but don't ever fall in love with a colored man.' "

When Matt's secretary calls back with the information he requested, he learns that Dr. Prentice is an "important guy." He is a graduate of Johns Hopkins and has taught at Yale and the London School of Tropical Medicine. He has written two textbooks and has a list of monographs and honors "as long as your arm." Matt is clearly disappointed that he cannot find any reason to dislike Prentice, but he remains uncomfortable with the idea of the marriage.

Well ahead of its time, Guess Who's Coming to Dinner *(1967) addressed race relations long before it was considered politically correct to do so.*

GUESS WHO'S COMING TO DINNER

Earlier, when he arrived at the Drayton house, Prentice had called his parents to tell them about the engagement, but he could not bring himself to mention that Joey was white. He apologized that he would not be able to visit them in Los Angeles before his departure for Switzerland. Later they call back and volunteer to make the short flight to San Francisco to see him. Joey grabs the phone and invites them to come and meet her parents. She immediately tells her mother and runs off to tell Tillie (Isabel Sanford), the black maid, that two more will be coming for dinner.

In the short time she has known him, Chris has come to be very impressed with Prentice. Having had a little time to adjust to the idea, she is now completely supportive of the marriage. Matt, however, still has his doubts. His primary concern is how society reacts to interracial marriage and biracial children. However, he has no doubts about Prentice personally. As he tells Chris, he considers Prentice to be a remarkable man. What kind of parents, he wonders, raised such a fine son? Chris responds: "You'll get to know this evening. Guess who's coming to dinner?"

In the following scene, Matt's friend Monsignor Ryan drops by the house, and, when he is apprised of the situation with Joey and Prentice, he is immediately in favor of the marriage. Jokingly, he suggests to Matt that he is a "phony broken-down liberal come face to face with his prejudices." The Monsignor has to leave for now, but he offers to join the group for dinner.

Later, Prentice and Joey meet Prentice's parents at the airport. When Mr. and Mrs. Prentice (Roy E. Glenn Sr. and Beah Richards) see the red-haired, very white-skinned Joey, they are quite as shocked as the Draytons had been. Mrs. Prentice, however, soon comes around, just as Chris did. Mr. Prentice, however, is against the marriage. Sharing Matt's concerns, he is fearful that his son will have a tough time because of society's opposition to interracial couples.

When Monsignor Ryan arrives for dinner, Chris sends Ryan upstairs to talk with Matt—she is sure that Matt intends to withhold his approval of Joey and Prentice's marriage. In a humorous scene, Matt and Ryan argue about the issue as Matt tries to dress. He pulls on his sock only to find a huge hole. When he yanks out his sock drawer to grab another pair, the whole thing falls on the floor, and all his ties slip off the rack. When he refuses to accept Ryan's arguments, the exasperated priest calls him a "pontificating old poop."

Finally Matt comes downstairs and calls everyone together. He delivers a charming, comic summary of the day and finally gives his blessings to the couple. It is clear that all of the parents have decided to give their support to the loving young couple. The film ends as Matt turns to Tillie and says good-naturedly, "Well, Tillie, when the hell are we going to get some dinner?"

This was Spencer Tracy's last onscreen line. He died three weeks after shooting on the film was completed.

See Hepburn, Katharine; Poitier, Sidney; Tracy, Spencer

ALEC GUINNESS

Alec Guinness was born in London, England, on April 2, 1914, with the full name Alec Guinness de Cuffe. As an adult, the extremely versatile, almost chameleon-like actor has riveted audiences with his film performances, whether in comedy, drama, or science fiction.

As a young man, Guinness worked as an advertising copywriter. Making a career shift, he studied acting at the Fay Compton Studio of Dramatic Art in London, making his stage debut in a small, walk-on part in 1934. He gained experience at the venerable British theater the Old Vic, performing in works by the masters of theater such as Shakespeare and Chekhov. He subsequently began appearing regularly on the British stage. But World War II began, and Guinness joined the British Navy in 1941. The following year he was given leave in order to appear in a play in New York to support the war effort.

The year 1946 marked the beginning of Guinness's film career, with his role as Herbert Pocket in *Great Expectations;* in 1948 he performed in another Dickens piece, as Fagin in *Oliver Twist.* The following year he played eight parts in the film *Kind Hearts and Coronets.* Subsequently Guinness appeared in a variety of movies, including *The Lavender Hill Mob* and *The Man in the White Suit* (both in 1951), *The Bridge on the River Kwai* (1957), *Our Man in Havana* (1959), *Lawrence of Arabia* (1962), *Doctor Zhivago* (1965), and *Scrooge* (1970). In the 1970s and 1980s Guinness became familiar to younger filmgoers as Obi Wan-Kenobi in *Star Wars* (1977), *The Empire Strikes Back* (1980), and *Return of the Jedi* (1983). But he didn't neglect more serious work, performing in such movies as *A Passage to India* (1984) and *A Handful of Dust* (1988).

In 1938 Guinness married Merula Salaman, an actress. They had one child, Matthew, who eventually became an actor himself. In 1959 Queen Elizabeth II knighted Guinness in recognition of his substantial achievements on stage and screen; henceforth he was known as Sir Alec.

Guinness won the Best Actor Oscar for *Bridge on the River Kwai* and was nominated for Academy Awards four other times. In 1985 he published an autobiography, *Blessings in Disguise.* His 1997 autobiography best expresses this actor's modest self-deprecation: *My Name Escapes Me.*

H

HAIRSPRAY

John Water's first PG-rated film, *Hairspray,* is a campy, kitschy stroll through the early 1960s. Starring some members of Water's repertoire group, Dreamlanders—such as Divine and Mink Stole—*Hairspray* also stars pop icons Ricki Lake, Sonny Bono, Debbie Harry, Pia Zadora, and Jerry Stiller. Everyone gives an over-the-top performance in this outrageous film about the triumph of the underdog.

Set in Waters' hometown of Baltimore in 1962, *Hairspray* chronicles the attempt of Tracy Turnblad (Lake), a chubby teenager with a blatantly bouffant hairdo, to dance on the Corny Collins show, the local version of American Bandstand. Tracy's parents, Edna (played by Divine, a 300-pound transvestite) and Wilbur (played by the diminutive Stiller), don't particularly like their daughter's music, but they are tolerant of Tracy's tastes. Not so with Mrs. Pingleton (JoAnn Havrilla), the paranoid puritanical mother of Tracy's best friend, Penny (Leslie Ann Powers), who stalks her daughter in order protect her from the various dangers of adolescence.

"Tracy, our souls are black even though our skin is white."

Michael St. Gerard as Link Larkin in *Hairspray* (1988)

Tracy manages to audition for the program, where her dancing ability and perky personality win over everyone on the student advisory group except the unscrupulous and jealous Amber Van Tussel (Colleen Fitzpatrick). When Amber, who is the top-rated dancer on the show and candidate for Miss Auto Show, asks during Tracy's audition "Isn't she a little fat for the show?" Tracy, unfazed, answers, "I'm sure many of the other home viewers out there are pleasantly plump or chunky."

Tracy is a hit on the show, and her parents are impressed by their daughter's celebrity. In a hilarious scene, Edna, who to this point wears nothing but housedresses, and Tracy go shopping. To the tune of "Momma Didn't Lie," the two waddle identically down the street to the Hefty Hideaway, where the manager, Mr. Pinky (Alan J. Wendl), asks Tracy to model his clothes on the show. Edna and Tracy buy outrageous new dresses and then waddle on down the road to get their hair done.

At school, Tracy is sent to the principal's office because, as her teacher says, her "ratted hair is preventing another student's geometry education." She is demoted to special education classes, where the school warehouses

GENE HACKMAN

Enduring character actor Gene Hackman was born Eugene Allen Hackman in San Bernardino, California (near Los Angeles), on January 30, 1931. He was raised in a rural part of Illinois. His father, a press operator, abandoned the family when Hackman was thirteen—he simply drove away, casually waving goodbye. The traumatic event understandably created a big impression on the young Hackman. At sixteen, shy in school and under pressure to provide fatherly care for his younger brother, Hackman quit school and lied about his age in order to join the Marines. He served in China, Japan, and Hawaii; during his years in the Corps, Hackman completed a high school equivalency course and was assigned as a broadcaster on the Armed Forces Network.

After his discharge from the Corps in 1952, Hackman traveled around the United States. He briefly studied journalism at the University of Illinois, then moved to New York City, where he enrolled in the School of Radio Technique. He took a few jobs in radio but was not much interested in the field, so he went on to study commercial art for a time.

Hackman eventually made his way to California and tried to pursue an acting career, enrolling in the Pasadena Playhouse. There, he and fellow student Dustin Hoffman were voted "least likely to succeed." Frustrated, Hackman returned to New York and took some odd jobs while occasionally getting work on the stage. After years of struggle, Hackman finally got a good break: a small but memorable role in the film *Lilith* (1964). Fellow *Lilith* actor Warren Beatty cast Hackman three years later in his hit film *Bonnie and Clyde* (1967). Hackman's gritty performance as Clyde's outlaw brother Buck earned him an Academy Award nomination, and his film career was on its way.

In 1970 Hackman received another Best Actor nomination for *I Never Sang for My Father,* and the following year he won the Oscar for the most pivotal role of his life, as the dour detective Popeye Doyle in *The French Connection.*

In subsequent years Hackman's many film roles have been amazingly varied—from comic turns in *Young Frankenstein* (1974), *Superman* (1978), and *Get Shorty* (1995) to intense drama in *Mississippi Burning* (1988; Oscar nomination), *Unforgiven* (1992; Oscar for Best Supporting Actor), and *Absolute Power* (1997).

Hackman has many diverse interests in his private life as well. In his earlier years he was known as something of a daredevil, enjoying stunt flying and motorcycling; more recently he has pursued painting and sculpting.

Because Hackman is one of the most in-demand actors in film, he is offered roles despite his absence in Hollywood—since 1981 he has made his home in New Mexico. He was married for nearly thirty years to Fay Maltese; they divorced in 1985. They have three children. In 1991 Hackman married Betsy Arakawa, a concert pianist.

See Bonnie and Clyde; *Coppola, Francis Ford; Eastwood, Clint;* French Connection, The; *Hoffman, Dustin;* Unforgiven

black students. Tracy immediately becomes friends with Seaweed (Clayton Prince), the son of a black broadcaster, Motormouth Mabel (Ruth Brown), and learns that blacks can only appear on Collins's show one Thursday a month, on "Negro Day." Tracy's best friend, Penny, and Seaweed eventually fall in love.

As Tracy's star rises, Amber cannot contain her jealousy and continues to harass her rival, claiming that she has roaches in her hair and calling her names. Eventually, Amber is suspended from the show for a day. Sulking as she watches the show in her passionately pink bedroom, Amber discovers that her boyfriend, Link (Michael St. Gerard), is dating Tracy.

Link, Tracy, and Penny journey to Motormouth Mabel's radio station to learn some dance moves from the black kids. They are followed there by Mrs. Pingleton, who is dropped off by a taxi before she realizes she is in a black neighborhood. Her terror is a source of amusement for the people on the street as they watch her approach Mabel's door. She bursts in, grabs Penny, and screams hysterically at Mabel, "Don't you try any of your voodoo on me you . . . you NATIVE WOMAN!"

When "Pre-Teen" day on the Corny Collins show arrives, Seaweed tries to gain admission for a young friend, Inez, and is told that blacks

Shock director John Waters's first PG-rated film, Hairspray, *is a nostalgic satire of 1960s integration of a teen dance program.*

▼

are not allowed in. Although Corny (Shawn Thompson) wants to end discrimination on the show, the grotesque station manager (also played by Divine) refuses to change his policy. Tracy joins the protest outside and is arrested.

Penny continues to date Seaweed until she is kidnapped by her mother and a deranged psychiatrist, played by Waters himself, who tries to cure Penny of her attraction to black boys with a psychedelic pinwheel and a blue neon cattle prod.

Meanwhile, Motormouth Mabel leads a march to demand that blacks be admitted to Tilted Acres, the amusement park owned by Amber's parents and the location of a special edition of the Collins show. When Tracy joins the protest, she is arrested again and sent to reform school.

Tracy has the votes to win the Miss Auto Show title, but because she cannot be at the ceremony, Amber is declared the winner by default. But Motormouth Mabel and Inez handcuff themselves to the governor of Maryland until he agrees to pardon Tracy. Freed, Tracy and an entourage of friends dance down to the studio, where she claims her crown and dons the gown designed for her by Mr. Pinky—a pink satin sheath decorated with huge black roaches. Amber's parents smuggle a bomb into the studio hidden in Mrs. Van Tussel's (played by Debbie Harry) extremely large hairdo, which they intend to detonate if Amber doesn't win. In a moment of poetic justice, the bomb goes off while the wig is still in place, and the hairdo itself flies across the room and lands on Amber's head. The police haul the Van Tussles away as everyone else dances.

See Cult film

"That's the bed I've made, and it's very comfortable."

Tom Hanks, actor, on his likable image

TOM HANKS

The boyishly appealing actor Tom Hanks was born in Concord, California, on July 9, 1956. His parents divorced when he was a young child, and he was raised by his father, a cook. Eventually they settled in Oakland, where Hanks began acting in high school. Later, at nearby California State University at Sacramento, Hanks studied drama. He acted in summer repertoire, then settled in New York.

Hanks first became known to a wide audience as one of the stars of the television comedy series *Bosom Buddies* (1980-82). His first film *(He Knows You're Alone,* 1980) sank, but he made a "splash" in his second, the mermaid-themed *Splash* (1984). Over the next few years Hanks performed in a number of passable but unremarkable movies, such as *Volunteers* (1985) and *The Money Pit* (1986), before hitting his stride in *Big* (1988). His endearingly comical performance as a boy-wrought-large earned him an Academy Award nomination.

Another few years passed before Hanks had another hit, *A League of Their Own* (1992), in which he played the alcoholic manager of a women's baseball team. That was followed in 1993 by the smash romantic comedy *Sleepless in Seattle,* with actress Meg Ryan. That same year, playing a lawyer with AIDS in the drama *Philadelphia,* Hanks won a Best Actor Oscar.

The year 1994 brought yet another golden (as in Oscar-winning) performance, in the title role of *Forrest Gump*. Hanks endeared himself to audiences with his portrayal of the slow-witted Gump who nevertheless manages to live a remarkable life. His performance in *Apollo 13* was well received in 1995 by critics and audiences alike, as was his performance in the war film *Saving Private Ryan* (another Academy Award nomination) in 1998.

Hanks tried his hand at directing and screenwriting in *That Thing You Do.* It was respectfully received by his peers—a measure of the esteem he is held in within the film industry—but not particularly popular with filmgoers. He has also done some directing of television programs.

Hanks was married from 1980 to 1987 to actress/producer Samantha Lewis. They had one son and one daughter. In 1988 Hanks married actress Rita Wilson (with whom he appeared in *Sleepless in Seattle*), the couple has two sons.

See Field, Sally; Forrest Gump; Saving Private Ryan; *Spielberg, Steven*

HAROLD AND MAUDE

Harold and Maude (1971) is a "small" but poignant film that has become a cult classic. Directed by Hal Ashby, it tells the story of a morose young man, Harold (Bud Cort), who is taught how to live by Maude (Ruth Gordon), a vibrant and zesty septuagenarian.

As the film opens, Harold is preparing himself for a staged "suicide"—just another one of fifteen or so he has performed, primarily for the benefit of his mother, Mrs. Chasen (Vivian Pickles). As the scene unfolds, Harold steps off a stool and, it appears, hangs himself. At this point, Harold's mother walks in—and acts as though absolutely nothing is out of the ordinary. The viewer can now see that the "suicide" is a sham; Harold has not really killed himself. He is just looking for attention. He lives in a lavishly appointed mansion, well-tended by servants, but he is utterly ignored.

Harold is profoundly interested in the topic of death. His favorite pastime, besides his phony suicides, is attending funerals—anyone's funeral. This week, Harold begins noticing an old lady at the funerals he attends in his Northern California area. When at a church service she scoots over and offers him some licorice, they begin to get acquainted. Her name is Maude, and she is a very unusual person.

Maude announces that next week she'll turn eighty years old. Seventy-five is too early to die, she says, but by eighty-five, you're just "marking time." Maude, like Harold, is attracted by the subject of death, but not in the morbid way that Harold is—she's interested in it because it is a part of life.

Maude is a revelation to the sheltered young man. She routinely steals cars, considering them public property, and drives like a maniac, proving adept at escaping from the police. She poses for an artist in the nude. She encourages Harold to learn how to play an instrument. Music, she says, is the "cosmic dance." The music of Cat Stevens winds throughout the film.

Over the next few days, Maude initiates Harold into the art of living. Being too moral, she contends, keeps one from truly experiencing life. She introduces Harold to dancing, the banjo, marijuana, and lovemaking. She may be old, but Maude is unmistakably sensuous, even sexy. She alludes briefly to her life before she came to America, and one day Harold notices traces of tattooed numbers on her forearm—the only indication he has that she was a victim of the Nazi concentration camps in Europe during World War II.

"It's best not to be too moral. You cheat yourself out of too much of life."

Ruth Gordon as Maude in *Harold and Maude* (1971)

In the meantime, Harold's mother has entered him in a computer dating service, and she introduces him to a series of potential mates. It is for naught: Harold is falling in love with Maude, and he sabotages the meetings. Finally he announces to his mother that he has decided to marry. When Mrs. Chasen sees a picture of Maude, she is horrified and sends him to have some sense knocked into him by a psychiatrist, a priest, and his military-officer uncle. They fail to dissuade him from pursuing this relationship with a woman old enough to be his grandmother.

On Maude's eightieth birthday, Harold plans to ask her to marry him. But Maude has made other plans. She has taken some pills to commit suicide, considering eighty the perfect age to die. Harold rushes her to the hospital, but it is too late: Maude is dead.

Despondent, Harold races along in his sports car, which he has modified to look like a hearse. Next we see it fly off a cliff and land upside down, flattened, on a beach. The camera pans away from this image of death and moves slowly up the cliff—and there is Harold, alive, picking at his banjo strings, and then beginning to sway and dance.

Viewers could perhaps be forgiven for not flocking to a movie with this unusual love story as its premise, but the film's many admirers find that it is full of timeless charm, humor, and wisdom. Both Gordon and Cort won Golden Globe Awards for their performances.

See Cult film

HAWKS, HOWARD

Director Howard Winchester Hawks was born into a successful Midwestern family on May 30, 1896, in Goshen, Indiana. In 1908 he moved to Pasadena, California with his parents, Frank and Helen Hawks, and two brothers, Kenneth and William. (Both of Hawks's brothers entered the movie industry as well; William as a producer and Kenneth as a director.) Hawks enjoyed a relatively privileged childhood, attending the exclusive

Howard Hawks made his debut as a director in 1926, after having worked as a plane pilot and race car driver in his late teens.

boy's high school Philips Exeter Academy in New Hampshire and becoming a professional car and plane racer by the time he was sixteen.

Hawks's first exposure to the film industry was during his summer vacations from Exeter, where he worked during summer vacations in the property department of the Famous Players-Lasky (later Paramount) Studio.

When the United States entered World War I in 1917, Hawks put his flying experience to use by joining the Army Air Corps. He was sent to Europe where he served as lieutenant and flight instructor. While he was in the Air Corps, he received his degree in engineering from Cornell University.

After leaving the army in 1922, Hawks returned to Hollywood, where he independently produced films for directors as Marshal Neilan, Allan Dwan, and Allen Holubar. During this same period he worked on production, scripts, and casting for Paramount and MGM. He is credited with contributing to *Quicksands* (1923) and *Tiger Love* (1923). His first films as director and writer were the silent films *The Road to Glory* (1926) and *Fig Leaves.*

notable & quotable

"She put up with terrible things. I don't think she had the fun she was capable of having."

Blake Edwards, director, 1999, referring to Audrey Hepburn, as quoted in "America Goes Hollywood," Newsweek, *June 28, 1999*

For the next few years, Hawks continued to make silent movies for Fox. His first talking film came in 1930 with *The Dawn Patrol.* The same year he filmed *Scarface* (released in 1932), a film he considered one of his favorites. *Scarface* marked Hawks's return to his role as independent director; he made the film with financing from Howard Hughes. *Scarface* also brought a new harsh psychological realism to the screen that had not been seen before. In many ways it is the progenitor of later gangster movies.

For the next forty years, Hawks continued to direct dozens of adventure, western, and comedy films. These included *The Crowd Roars* (1932), *Twentieth Century* (1934), *Bringing Up Baby* (1938), and *Only Angels Have Wings* (1939). In the 1940s Hawks directed *His Girl Friday* (1940), *Sergeant York* (1941), *Ball of Fire* (1941), *To Have and Have Not* (1944), *The Big Sleep* (1946), *A Song Is Born* (1948), and *Red River* (1948). The next two decades brought *The Thing* (1951), *Gentlemen Prefer Blondes* (1953), *Rio Bravo* (1959), *Hatari!* (1962), *Man's Favorite Sport?* (1963), *Red Line 7000* (1965), and *El Dorado* (1967). He made his last big screen production at the age of seventy-four, with a western called *Rio Lobo.*

During most of his lifetime, Howard Hawks was largely ignored by the critical establishment. His films were neither epics nor sensational box office hits. The honor of discovering Hawks goes to the French critics of the Truffaut generation. His films were regularly reviewed in French periodicals and film journals from the early 1950s onward.

The real breakthrough in Hawks criticism, however, occurred in 1962 and early 1963. During the summer of 1962 Peter Bogdanovich organized a Hawks retrospective for the Museum of Modern Art, in connection with which he prepared a monograph on Hawks. At the same time, Andrew Sarris was at work on his long overview article on Hawks. In December of

AUDREY HEPBURN

Edda van Heemstra Hepburn-Ruston was born near Brussels, Belgium, on May 4, 1929. As actress Audrey Hepburn, she would win the hearts—and the respect and admiration—of filmgoers throughout the world. Her early death (to cancer) in 1993, when she was just sixty-four, was met with the same shock, dismay, and solemnity that are typically reserved for beloved royalty and heads of state, not entertainers.

When she was a young girl, Hepburn's parents—an English banker and a Dutch baroness—sent her to a boarding school in England after their divorce. Audrey spent the years during World War II in Arnhem, the Netherlands, which was occupied by the Germans. She attended a local public school and received ballet training at the Arnhem Conservatory. In later years she would talk about the hardship of her war years, explaining that no one in the town had enough to eat, and discuss how that experience affected her life and worldview.

After the war Hepburn went to London on a ballet scholarship. The slim, long-legged young woman with a "gamine" look soon found work modeling. Eventually she took acting classes and acted in small roles in several British films.

While working on *Monte Carlo Baby* (1951), Hepburn met Colette, the notorious French novelist, who thought Hepburn would be perfect for the title role in *Gigi* in an upcoming Broadway stage adaptation of Colette's work. Hepburn was a huge success in the role in New York, and she was soon signed to play opposite Gregory Peck in the movie *Roman Holiday* (1953). To say that she was welcomed by Hollywood is an understatement: Her role as a princess on the loose in Rome won Hepburn an Academy Award as Best Actress. She was just twenty-four years old.

Following that success, good film roles came fast and furious for Hepburn. Her greatest successes were *Sabrina* (1954), with Humphrey Bogart, and *Funny Face* (1957), with Fred Astaire.

The film that is probably most associated with Audrey Hepburn, *Breakfast at Tiffany's* (1961), came at a good time in her career. The actress still had legions of fans, but she needed a hit. The movie provided that, and more—she won another Academy Award nomination for her portrayal of Holly Golightly, as she had received for *Sabrina* and *The Nun's Story* (1959). (Later she was nominated for *Charade,* in 1963, and *My Fair Lady,* in 1964.)

Beautiful Audrey Hepburn personified class and elegance for generations of movie fans. Her signature sunglasses and capri pants were all the rage in the 1960s.

Hepburn's private life was full as well. Besides starring opposite some of the biggest male stars of all time (including Humphrey Bogart, Cary Grant, Fred Astaire, and Sean Connery, the latter in *Robin and Marian* in 1976), she married actor Mel Ferrer in 1954 and had a son; they divorced in 1968. She later married Dr. Andrea Dotti, an Italian psychiatrist, with whom she also had a son. After they divorced Hepburn became acquainted with Dutch actor Robert Wolders, with whom she maintained a close relationship until her death. She lived for most of her adult life in Switzerland.

Beginning in the late 1980s Hepburn became well known, and well loved, for her role as the special ambassador for UNICEF, a charitable United Nations organization that had helped her during the war years. In 1999 Hepburn was named No. 3 on the American Film Institute's women's list of Greatest Screen Legends.

See Astaire, Fred; Bogart, Humphrey; Breakfast at Tiffany's; My Fair Lady; *Wyler, William*

1962 the British journal *Movie* published a special Hawks issue containing articles by several critics.

While the world of critics finally brought Hawks the acclaim he deserved, he was never awarded an Academy Award for any of his films. He was, however, was finally recognized for his work when he was awarded an honorary Oscar in 1975 for his cumulative work in films. Howard Hawks died in Palm Springs, California, on December 12, 1977.

See Bringing Up Baby; *Goldwyn, Samuel; Hepburn, Katharine; Screwball comedy*

The year 1940's highest payment for film rights for a novel was $150,000 to Ernest Hemingway for *For Whom the Bell Tolls.*

KATHARINE HEPBURN

Katharine Houghton Hepburn was born to a socially prominent and well-to-do family in Hartford, Connecticut, in 1907 (the precise date varies from source to source). She would become the most celebrated actress in the world—nominated for twelve Academy Awards, and winning four of them.

As a child Hepburn performed in local amateur theater. After attending Hartford School for Girls, she majored in drama and participated in theatrical productions at Bryn Mawr College. After graduating in 1928 Hepburn moved to Baltimore, Maryland, to join a theater company and fulfill her long-time ambition to be a great stage actress. (Reportedly, her parents, who were otherwise quite liberal, were not thrilled with their headstrong daughter's goal.) She made an impact immediately and within the year had appeared in a few small roles on Broadway.

Hollywood came calling, in the form of a contract offered from RKO Pictures. At that point Hepburn wasn't much interested in a film career, so she demanded an exorbitant salary. To her surprise, RKO agreed. By 1932 the athletic young actress with the aristocratic bearing was making a staggering $1,500 a week—during the height of the Depression. Her movie debut was in *A Bill of Divorcement,* a huge hit.

Hepburn was an anachronism in Hollywood. She was not the typical young "starlet" and did not fit into the usual categories of young actresses of the era—narrow variations on the themes of sweet-girl-next-door or vamp. She was arrogant and demanding, but usually got her way because of the success of many of her films. They were not *always* well received, however; Hepburn was sometimes labeled box-office poison. And early in the 1930s Hepburn did not fare so well with a Broadway production of *The Lake.* Her performance in that play prompted Dorothy Parker's now famous sarcastic remark that Hepburn "ran the gamut of emotions from A to B."

In 1933 Hepburn won her first Best Actress Oscar, for *Morning Glory.* That year she also triumphed in the pivotal role of Jo in *Little Women.* She made several films a year throughout the 1930s, including *Spitfire (*1934) and *Stage Door* (1937). In 1938 she appeared in *Bringing Up Baby* and *Holiday;* and in 1940 she delighted audiences with *The Philadelphia Story,* which she had perfromed on the Broadway stage and for which she owned the movie rights. Hepburn sold the movie rights to MGM and was able to name her director (George Cukor) and costars (Cary Grant and Jimmy Stewart) for the movie version.

The film *Woman of the Year* (1942) opened a new era for Hepburn—in it she was paired with actor Spencer Tracy. He would be her life companion until his death in 1967, and they would do nine mostly memorable films together, including *Adam's Rib* (1949), *Pat and Mike* (1952), *Desk Set* (1957), and *Guess Who's Coming to Dinner* (1967). She won a second Academy Award for the latter film.

Tracy was devoutly Catholic—and married. While he apparently did not have a problem with having an affair, divorce was out of the question. His relationship with Hepburn was an open secret in the entertainment industry, but gossip columnists largely respected the couple's privacy—a perk that Hepburn had not enjoyed during her earlier liaisons with agent Leland Hayward and tycoon Howard Hughes. Hepburn was married once, from 1928 to 1934, to Ludlow Ogden Smith.

In the 1950s Hepburn's most memorable films were *The African Queen* (1951), *Summertime* (1955), and *Suddenly Last Summer* (1958). In the 1960s she excelled in *Long Day's Journey into Night* (1962), the aforementioned *Guess Who's Coming to Dinner*, and *The Lion in Winter* (1968; third Best Actress Oscar). Her most important role since then—and her fourth Oscar nod—was in *On Golden Pond* (1981).

Hepburn has an apartment in New York City and spends much of her time in a large home on the Connecticut shoreline. She has published two memoirs: *The Making of the African Queen* (1987) and *Me* (1992).

See African Queen, The; *Bogart, Humphrey;* Bringing Up Baby; *Cukor, George;* Guess Who's Coming to Dinner; *Lumet, Sidney; Mankiewicz, Joseph;* Philadelphia Story, The; *Poitier, Sidney; Tracy, Spencer*

HIGH NOON

High Noon (1952), directed by Fred Zinnemann and produced by Stanley Kramer, is widely considered to be one of the best westerns of all time. Carl Foreman wrote the screenplay based on *The Tin Star,* a story by John W. Cunningham. The film received Academy Awards for Best Actor (Gary Cooper) and Best Song ("High Noon," sung by Tex Ritter). *High Noon* is said by some to have been written as a metaphor for the McCarthy era, in which many Hollywood writers and other filmmakers were blacklisted and few stood up for them.

H

HIGH NOON

The movie, filmed in black and white, takes place on a hot summer day in 1875. In the small western town of Hadleyville, lawman Will Kane (Gary Cooper) has just gotten married. His bride is a young Quaker woman, Amy Fowler (Grace Kelly). She has strong pacifist beliefs, and she has convinced Kane to put down his marshal's badge, a tin star. She and Kane have decided to move to a new town and start a family.

During the marriage party, the train stationmaster rushes in and pulls Kane aside. He has learned that Frank Miller (Ian MacDonald), a murderer whom Kane put behind bars five years ago, has been pardoned. Miller's gang of gunslingers is already at the train station, and Miller will be arriving in Hadleyville on the noon train.

The marshal is urged to get out of town right away, but he decides that he can't turn his back on what he considers to be his moral duty. He doesn't want to be a coward, to be run out of town by an outlaw.

The pained expression on Gary Cooper's (as Kane) face throughout the film is entirely realistic, as Cooper had a bleeding ulcer at the time High Noon *was filmed.*
▼

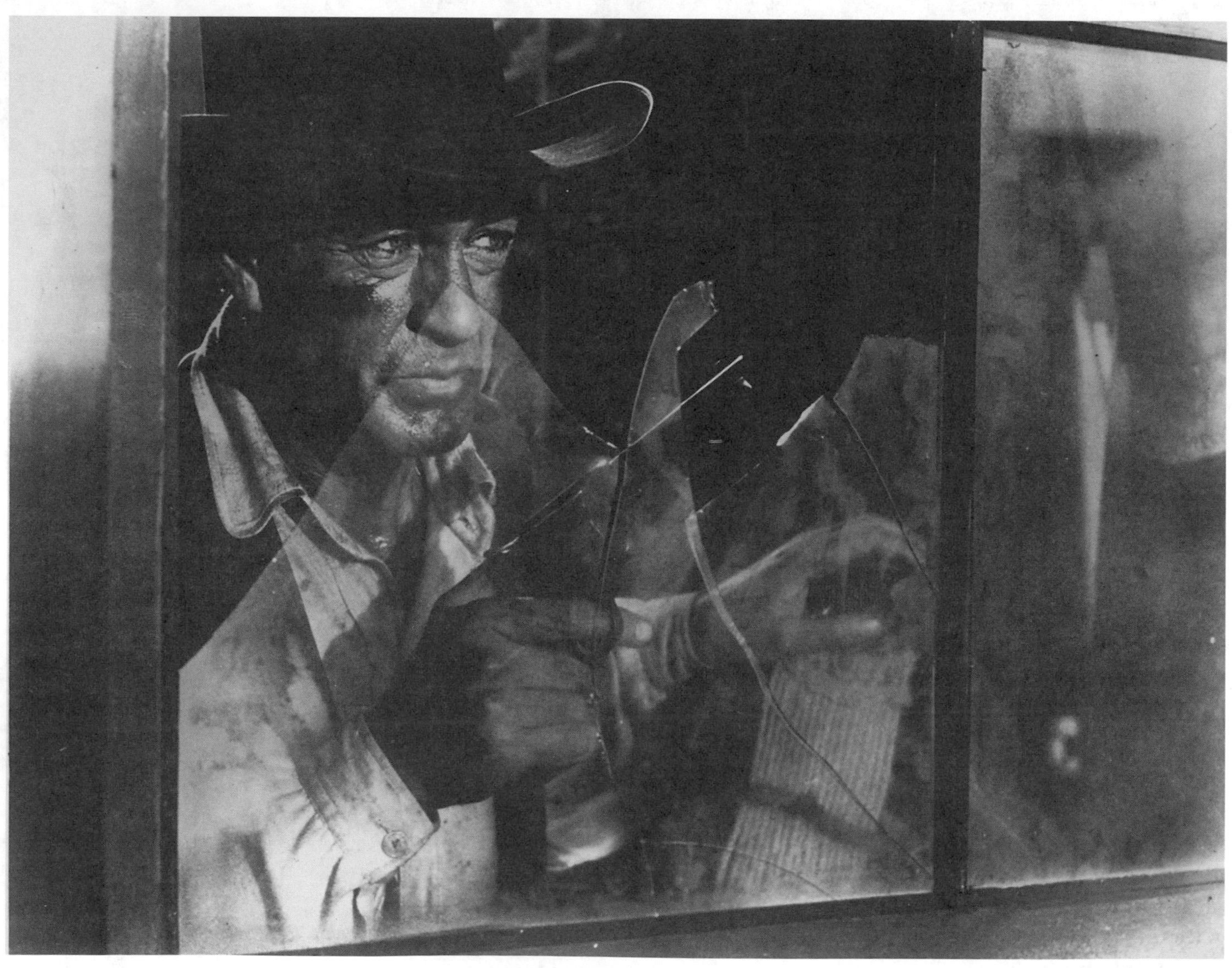

Kane explains to his new wife that Miller was supposed to be hanged, but his sentenced was commuted. Miller "was always wild and kind of crazy," Kane says. "He'll probably make trouble." Amy tries to convince him that Miller is now the responsibility of the new marshal, but Kane is resolute. Miller has sworn to kill him, he notes, and will try to do so no matter where Kane goes. Besides—he points to his badge—"I'm the same man with or without this."

Amy feels that she has no choice but to go—she refuses to stand by and see whether she is "going to be a wife or a widow." Given this ultimatum, however, Kane still refuses to budge from what he believes is the right thing to do.

The townspeople gear up for trouble. Many decide to leave town until the dispute between Miller and Kane is resolved. Tension builds. Everyone's attention is riveted on the clock, counting down the minutes to high noon.

Kane presumes that he will have some support in fighting the outlaws, but he is soon disappointed. His deputy marshal, Harvey Pell (Lloyd Bridges), will not help, still angry because Kane did not support him as his successor. The judge who sentenced Miller, Percy Mettrick (Otto Kruger), not only refuses to join Kane in the confrontation, but plans to get out of town. And while Kane has his admirers, there are some people who feel that Kane is due to be knocked down a peg. Meanwhile, others are concerned about the impact of a shootout on the town's image and financial prospects. At the Ramirez saloon men busy themselves placing bets on the outcome of the showdown between Kane and the outlaws.

The marshal speaks to his former woman friend, saloon owner Helen Ramirez (Katy Jurado), to warn her that Miller—with whom she was also involved at one time—is coming to town. Helen respects Kane's decision to stay and face his enemy, but she too prepares to depart. She advises Amy, however, to support her new husband in whatever he chooses to do.

Kane searches the town for men who will assist him as special deputies, but he finds not a single volunteer. Ex-marshal Matt Howe (Lon Chaney Jr.), old and arthritic, sums up every lawman's dilemma: "You risk your skin catchin' killers and the juries turn 'em loose so they can come back and shoot at ya again." Howe understands the townspeople's apathy: when it comes to law and order, "deep down they don't care."

As high noon approaches, the tension is so thick it can be cut with a knife. Kane, fully expecting to die, sits alone in his office, writing his last will and testament. At twelve o'clock the deep silence is punctuated by the train's whistle. Kane folds his will into a sealed envelope, writing on it: "To be opened in the event of my death."

Kane, alone, walks along the deserted streets to meet Miller and his three gangmembers. The shootout begins, and Kane manages to kill two of them. Kane is wounded in the arm, and Frank Miller and another man are still to be dealt with. Suddenly, Kane learns he has an ally: Amy. She has

"You're asking me to wait an hour to find out if I'm going to be a wife or a widow."

Grace Kelly as Amy Kane in *High Noon* (1952)

decided that protecting her husband is more important than honoring the letter of her religious convictions. She sneaks up behind Miller's fellow outlaw and shoots him through a broken window.

Now only Miller remains alive. He grabs hold of Amy and pulls her into the middle of the dusty street, threatening to kill her unless Kane shows himself. To save Amy, Kane will do anything Miller asks, but Amy again comes to Kane's rescue: She claws at Miller's face, distracting him. In pain, he pushes her to the ground, at which point Kane is able to shoot him without endangering Amy.

Kane helps Amy up, and they embrace. As the townspeople gather and stare, silent, Kane and Amy climb into a buggy. Kane takes off his marshal's badge and throws it into the street. Without a word or backward glance, the newlyweds ride out of town.

High Noon is celebrated not only for its technical merits but also for the depth and meaning of the psychological themes that are explored through the storytelling. In so doing, *High Noon* gave new resonance to the genre of westerns.

See Cooper, Gary; Kelly, Grace; Western

CHARLTON HESTON

Charlton Heston, sometime-director, writer, and political activist, was born Charles Carter in St. Helen, Michigan, on October 4, 1924. (Some sources identify Heston's real name as John Charlton Carter, his birthplace as Evanston, Illinois, and his birth year as 1923.)

While studying drama and speech at Northwestern University, Heston performed on Chicago radio stations and starred in a student film production of *Peer Gynt* (1942). Subsequently Heston served for three years in the military before trying his hand at stock theater. He debuted on Broadway in *Antony and Cleopatra* in 1947 with Katharine Cornell's theater group, which in earlier years had included Orson Welles. Heston made his professional film debut in 1950, in *Dark City.*

Heston's robust frame and noble, craggy features soon drew national attention, and soon he was offered the chance to play larger-than-life characters, from president (Andrew Jackson in *The President's Lady,* 1953), to adventurer (William Clark of the Lewis and Clark expedition in *The Far Horizons,* 1955), to biblical figures (Moses in *The Ten Commandments,* 1956). He also played a Latin hero in Orson Welles's innovative film *Touch of Evil* in 1958. In 1959 his portrayal of the title character in *Ben-Hur* won the Best Actor Academy Award.

In the 1960s Heston was on top of the movie world. His more important roles included the title character in *El Cid,* in 1961; John the Baptist in *The Greatest Story Ever Told,* in 1965, and Michelangelo in *The Agony and the Ecstasy,* also in 1965. He had starring roles in two *Planet of the Apes* movies during that decade.

But Heston was not content to rest on his laurels. In the 1970s, 1980s, and 1990s he remained a viable screen presence, in such films as *The Omega Man* (1971), *Airport* (1975), *The Awakening* (1980), *Wayne's World 2, Tombstone* (1993), and *Hamlet* (1996).

In recent years Heston's greatest influence has been in the political arena. As a six-term president of the Screen Actors Guild, and as a chairman of the American Film Institute, he became known for his conservative political beliefs. In 1996 Heston was named president of the National Rifle Association (NRA), which has brought him considerable notoriety among the more liberal in Hollywood. Heston has been married to wife Lydia Clarke since 1944; they have two children.

See Ben-Hur; *Wyler, William*

Rugged actor Charlton Heston was president of the Screen Actors Guild from 1966 to 1971. He is currently active in the Republican party and the National Rifle Association.

◀

HILL, GEORGE ROY

George Roy Hill has never been accorded the status given to such older American directors as John Ford, Frank Capra, or Howard Hawks, nor is he ranked with more recent luminaries such as Francis Ford Coppola, Martin Scorsese, or Robert Altman. Such a judgment, however, is neither final nor accurate. A skilled craftsman, Hill created some of the true gems that define the "American movie" genre.

Perhaps one reason Hill is overlooked is that his career as a director seems an afterthought to his work in television and on the stage. He did not direct a film until he was forty, and did not commit himself full time to films until he was forty-five. He was not an avid filmgoer as a youngster, and thus the obsession with films that is often evident with younger directors is not apparent in Hill's work.

Hill started as a music student at Yale University, where he participated in the Glee Club, was a member of the Whiffenpoof Society, and headed the Yale Drama Club. After graduation in 1943, he entered the Marine Corps and served in the Pacific theater. After the war, Hill studied music and literature at Trinity College in Dublin, Ireland, and acting with Cyril Cusack at the Abbey Theater. Although Hill took a bachelor's degree in literature from Trinity, acting eventually won out, and he returned to New York to make his mark in that profession. While Hill was able to find work as an actor, he never achieved any great success. Instead, Hill, a very private person, eventually found that the stress he felt before a performance outweighed the satisfaction of performing. As he approached his thirtieth birthday, Hill was still struggling to establish himself in his chosen field.

The Korean War interrupted that struggle, for Hill was recalled to active duty and spent eighteen months at the Marine Corps jet-pilot training center at Cherry Point, North Carolina. Since off-duty recreational activities were scarce, Hill began writing in his spare time. He sold his first teleplay, *My Brother's Keeper,* to the *Kraft Television Theater* in 1953, and after his discharge he returned to New York to work as a writer and a director. Moving from in front of the camera to behind it was Hill's proverbial turning point; it was the discovery of a vocation that called forth all of his creative energies and opened new worlds of exploration. Within a short time Hill established himself as one of television's leading producer/writer/directors. In 1956 he was nominated for two Emmy Awards (for writing and direction) for *A Night to Remember,* one of the most complex live television dramas ever presented. He was also responsible for *The Helen Morgan Story* (1959) and over fifty dramas in television's golden age.

Yet television changed as the networks discovered the financial benefits of the series, and the opportunities to do meaningful work were reduced.

HILL, GEORGE ROY

Some of director George Roy Hill's best known films include Butch Cassidy and the Sundance Kid *(1969),* The Sting *(1973), and* The World According to Garp *(1982).*

Like other television directors (Arthur Penn, Sidney Lumet, and Franklin Schaffner), Hill searched for other media that might offer him the kind of material and the degree of control he needed to work effectively. Theater was Hill's first new venture, and in 1957 he directed his first play, an adaptation of Thomas Wolfe's *Look Homeward, Angel.* He also received several offers to direct films, but he turned most of these down. Only two projects ever reached the preparatory stage, and both of these fell through. It was not until he was offered the chance to direct *Period of Adjustment* (from the Tennessee Williams play that he had directed on Broadway) that Hill was able to make the leap to film.

After *Period of Adjustment* (1962) Hill directed Lillian Hellman's *Toys in the Attic* (1963). Though both were fairly well received, they were not indicative of great cinematic virtuosity. *Period of Adjustment* is essentially a filmed play. *Toys in the Attic* is a step forward cinematically, for the camera begins to move, the close-up is discovered, and the lighting helps convey ideas and character. But in two of Hill's next three films, *Hawaii* (1966) and *Thoroughly Modern Millie* (1967), there is little evidence of further growth. Only *The World of Henry Orient* (1964) received widespread approval, garnering praise for its unusual story, the fresh performances Hill evoked from the teenage actresses, and its skillful cinematic presentation of adolescence.

After these first five films, Hill remained virtually unknown. In the increasingly film-conscious world of the 1960s, Hill's efforts seemed part of an outdated commercial tradition. American directors like Scorsese and Bogdanovich were touted, early directors rediscovered, critical theory was pushed in new directions, and politics was made a criterion of film excellence. Commerical films like Hill's seemed to belong to an appreciated but no longer relevant past.

In 1969 Hill released *Butch Cassidy and the Sundance Kid,* an enormously popular and successful western with Paul Newman and Robert Redford that seemed proof of Hill's commerical ingenuity and conventionality. His subsequent efforts—*Slaughterhouse-Five* (1972), *The Sting* (1973), *The Great Waldo Pepper* (1975), *Slapshot* (1977), *A Little Romance* (1979), *The World According to Garp* (1982), *The Little Drummer Girl* (1984), and *Funny Farm* (1988)—all received similar critical treatment: perfunctory acknowledgment of the craftsmanship and an occasional sigh that such efforts were being put into commercial exploitation. Hill's position as a talented, "studio" type director seemed fixed, and he is currently relegated to the status of a Herbert Ross or Arthur Hiller, or older studio reliables like Mervyn LeRoy and Michael Curtiz.

See Butch Cassidy and the Sundance Kid; *Redford, Robert*

HITCHCOCK, ALFRED

Alfred Hitchcock was born in London, England, on August 13, 1899. He was one of the very few directors in the history of motion pictures whose name has always been as important on a movie marquee as that of any actor appearing in one of his films. He firmly believed that his first obligation as a filmmaker was to entertain his audience.

Hitchcock had a strict Catholic upbringing. He attended London's St. Ignatius College, a preparatory school run by the Jesuits, where corporal punishment was commonplace. From St. Ignatius College Hitchcock went

on to the London School of Engineering and Navigation, majoring in engineering and draftsmanship before switching to fine arts.

After graduating in 1920, he entered the film industry by designing inter-titles for silent films at studios in London that later became Paramount Pictures. Between 1922 and 1925, Hitchcock continued his apprenticeship in motion pictures by acting as art director, scriptwriter, production manager, and assistant director on various films.

Hitchcock's first solo directorial assignment was *The Pleasure Garden* (1926), for which British reviewers hailed him as a promising new director. *The Mountain Eagle* (1926) was met with little enthusiasm, but his next

British director Alfred Hitchcock is well known for his hard-to-spot cameos in many of his films. His directorial style has inspired the term "Hitchcockian" in reference to taut, noirish thrillers.

film, *The Lodger* (1926), which demonstrated for the first time his talent for telling a taut suspense tale, opened to both critical and public acclaim and established him at the forefront of British directors. *Downhill* (1927) was all too appropriately titled, mainly due to a predictable plot. Hitchcock then directed *Easy Virtue* (1927), based on the Noel Coward play *The Ring* (1927), considered one of his top silent films. *The Farmer's Wife* (1928), based on a long-running play, *Champagne* (1928), marked the lowest ebb of his career and was his last silent picture, while *The Manxman* (1929), too, was insignificant. The film *Blackmail* (1929) was the first British talkie.

Hitchcock's movies of the 1930s started with *Murder!* (1930), a whodunit, followed by *Juno and the Paycock* (1930), based on a Sean O'Casey play, which elicited ecstatic reviews. His film of John Galsworthy's *The Skin Game* (1931) was recognized as a polished piece of cinema, but *Rich and Strange* (1932) was not well received. *Number Seventeen* (1932) was the precursor of the superior thrillers that constituted the peak of his British period. But he was disenchanted with *Waltzes from Vienna* (1933), a musical about Johann Strauss, Senior and Junior, believing that melodrama was his forté.

With *The Thirty-Nine Steps* (1935), one of Hitchcock's finest achievements ever, his critical reputation and popularity reached well beyond Britain to the world at large. Another chase movie followed, *Young and Innocent* (1937). Between directing those two films, Hitchcock directed two movies that had a decidedly darker, more disturbing tone to them: *Secret Agent* (1936) and *Sabotage* (1936).

The Lady Vanishes (1938) enjoyed popular and critical acclaim in the United States, as demonstrated by the New York Critics' Award to Hitchcock as Best Director. The last film he made in England before going to the United States was *Jamaica Inn* (1939), a suspense yarn. Although it was a hit in England, it failed to find an audience just about everywhere else.

With his arrival in Hollywood in the 1940s, Hitchcock began to turn out longer, more costly motion pictures that allowed him greater screen time for probing the psychology of his characters. Starting out in the David O. Selznick studios, he directed *Rebecca* (1940), a story about a wealthy, aloof widower who marries the youthful heroine. The film was hailed as Best Picture by the Motion Picture Academy. *Suspicion* (1941) reunited him with Joan Fontaine, the young heroine of *Rebecca*, and she won the Best Actress Oscar for *Suspicion*.

As the public clamored for more chase melodramas, Hitchcock obliged first with *Foreign Correspondent* (1940), which was nominated for but did not win the Oscar for best picture of the year—only because *Rebecca* did. Another manhunt melodrama was *Saboteur* (1942), a story about treasonous activities against the United States.

When comedienne Carole Lombard asked Hitchcock to direct her in a screwball comedy, he agreed because of his admiration for her. *Mr. and Mrs.*

notable & quotable

"A lot of people think I'm a monster. I'm more scared than they are in real life."

Alfred Hitchcock, director, 1973

Smith (1941) was about a feisty married couple who try different ways to rejuvenate their sagging relationship. But after directing this comedy, he gladly returned to the thriller genre.

Shadow of a Doubt (1943), always one of Hitchcock's personal favorites, had a richness of characterization rarely equaled in the director's other films. *Lifeboat* (1944), a story of survivors of a torpedo attack, all but sank under the weight of its verbose screenplay, while *Spellbound* (1945) was a superb thriller. *Notorious* (1946), a romantic thriller, starred Cary Grant, Claude Rains, and Ingrid Bergman, all turning in outstanding performances. Hitchcock's last film for Selznick, *The Paradine Case* (1947), was trounced by critics and avoided by the public. *Rope* (1948), his first film in color, was a pace-setter in the director's innovative experiments with protracted takes and in its treatment of homosexuality. *Under Capricorn* (1949) was both a popular and critical failure.

The 1950s were peak years for Hitchcock in Hollywood. He directed *Stage Fright* (1950); *Strangers on a Train* (1951), a truly masterful film; *I Confess* (1953), his tribute to the priesthood; *Dial M for Murder* (1954), an authentically cinematic film; *Rear Window* (1954), a wonderful thriller; *To Catch a Thief* (1955), an exhilarating action film; and *The Trouble with Harry* (1955), which exploited the fine line between comedy and tragedy. *The Man Who Knew Too Much* (1956) was a remake of a movie with the same title that Hitchcock had originally done in England. In the late 1950s Hitchcock directed *The Wrong Man* (1957), a factual movie with a religious dimension; *Vertigo* (1958), about a man tortured by bouts of vertigo, and *North by Northwest* (1959), starring a debonair Cary Grant.

Sandwiched between the 1950s and the 1960s were Hitchcock's television years. He introduced some 365 segments of his weekly television series that he supervised from 1955 to 1965, some of which he directed himself.

The 1960s and 1970s were vintage years for Hitchcock. His masterpiece, *Psycho* (1960), a thriller about the fiendishly deranged Norman Bates, was a supreme triumph of the motion picture art. His next movie, *The Birds* (1963), involved a great deal of technical trickery to realistically simulate the bird attacks. *Marnie* followed in 1964, *Torn Curtain* in 1966, and *Topaz* in 1969. *Frenzy* in 1972 marks Hitchcock's return to London where the director's career had begun. *Family Plot* (1976) was shot after he had suffered a mild heart attack, and turned out to be his final film.

In 1979 Hitchcock received the prestigious American Film Institute Life Achievement Award. A few months before his death in 1980, he was knighted by Queen Elizabeth II. Sir Alfred Hitchcock died on April 20, 1980 at the age of 80.

See Kelly, Grace; Lubitsch, Ernst; MacGuffin; North by Northwest; Psycho; Rear Window; *Stewart, James;* Vertigo

notable & quotable

"The horror genre is too important to be left to the kids. It speaks to every doubt and guilt we silently share; it lends a seductive form to fear and leaves us with a dread not easily shaken off."

Richard Corliss, critic, as quoted in Time, *July 12, 1999*

H

HOFFMAN, DUSTIN

DUSTIN HOFFMAN

Dustin Lee Hoffman, born August 8, 1937, in Los Angeles, California, had acting ambitions early on. A born ham, he was a class clown who first performed onstage in a junior high school production of *A Christmas Carol.* During high school, however, Hoffman was less outgoing, apparently embarrassed by the twin indignities of acne and braces.

After graduation from Los Angeles High, he attended both the Los Angeles Conservatory of Music and Santa Monica City College. Eventually he landed at the Pasadena Playhouse, where he and fellow classmate Gene Hackman (later, both Oscar winners) were voted "least likely to succeed." Instead of pursuing an acting career in Hollywood, just around the corner, Hoffman followed Hackman to New York City. His primary motivation for getting into the business, Hoffman later said, was to meet girls.

Hoffman worked a variety of odd jobs while looking for acting work in New York. He first appeared on Broadway in 1961 in the play *A Cook for Mr. General*. Over the next few years he grabbed acting assignments wherever he could, on stage and on television.

It wasn't until 1967 that Hoffman appeared in a movie: *The Tiger Makes Out.* Unfortunately, it sank without a trace. His next role was to prove more memo-

Dustin Hoffman, 30, was paid $17,000 for his role in *The Graduate*, which earned $39 million in 1968. (Anne Bancroft was 35.)

Once voted "least likely to succeed," Dustin Hoffman has won the Best Actor Oscar twice—for Kramer vs. Kramer *(1979) and* Rain Man *(1988).*

rable: as confused rich boy Benjamin Braddock in *The Graduate*, reportedly beating out Robert Redford for the role. *The Graduate* was a huge hit, and Hoffman was off and running. He played an entirely different part—as the down-and-out Ratso Rizzo—in his next film, *Midnight Cowboy.* He was given Best Actor Academy Award nominations for his work in both *Graduate* and *Cowboy.*

To say that Hoffman had a good start in the movie business is an understatement. He received Oscar nominations for six of his first twenty films (and two wins). Among the best of these outings were *Little Big Man* (1970), *Straw Dogs* (1971), *Lenny* (1974; Oscar nomination), *All the President's Men* (1976), *Marathon Man* (1976), and *Straight Time* (1978). He finally won the Academy Award with the commercial and critical success *Kramer vs. Kramer* (1979), and audiences went wild for the comedy *Tootsie* (1982), in which Hoffman plays an out-of-work actor who dresses as a woman to get roles. He won his second Best Actor Oscar for his work in *Rain Man* (1988), in which he plays an autistic idiot-savant. Hoffman increasingly had to battle whispers that he was excessively temperamental and demanding on the set.

In the 1990s Hoffman acted in a variety of films. Some were mediocre at best *(Hook,* 1991; *Hero,* 1992), while others were more popular *(Mad City* and *Wag the Dog,* both in 1997; he received a seventh Oscar nomination for the latter film). In 1999 he was given a Lifetime Achievement Award by the American Film Institute.

Hoffman was married from 1969 to 1980 to dancer-turned-actress Anne Byrne, with whom he has two daughters. He married lawyer Lisa Gottsegen in 1980. They have four children.

See Cruise, Tom; Graduate, The; *Hackman, Gene; Lumet, Sidney;* Midnight Cowboy; *Nichols, Mike;* Tootsie

HORROR FILM

A horror film is one whose plot is centered on strange, alarming events that threaten the principal character or characters. The terrorizing threat often occurs as a result of extraterrestrial powers (the devil in *The Exorcist,* 1973), at other times the result of scientific experimentation that gets out of hand (Proteus 4, the deviant, computerized brain in *The Demon Seed,* 1977). Conflict within the horror film pits these monsters—supernatural or man-made—against the naïve and the weak. Superhuman effort (the priest in *The Exorcist*) is necessary to destroy the evil that resides in the monster and that threatens those less strong. Horror films aimed at teenage audiences were highly popular in the 1980s, often appearing in multisequel form, for example, *Friday the 13th.* The gruesome murder of young people in isolated settings (summer camp, a cruise ship) typifies these cheap thrillers.

See Chaney, Lon; King Kong

Highest-paid author: William Peter Blatty, as novelist and producer of *The Exorcist* (1973), earned 40 percent of the gross, which had passed $90 million within 15 years of its release.

Jamie Lee Curtis was paid $8,000 for her (debut) role in *Halloween,* which opened October 25, 1978.

ANTHONY HOPKINS

Anthony Hopkins was born on December 31, 1937, in Port Talbot, South Wales. His was a modest family—his father was a baker—and the young Hopkins grew up during World War II, when danger was close and luxuries few. He was withdrawn as a schoolboy but realized that he wanted to act when he joined a community drama group at age seventeen.

Hopkins studied at the Welsh College of Music and Drama in Cardiff in 1955. Later, in 1961, he attended the Royal Academy of Dramatic Art in London. He graduated two years later and then joined the Phoenix Theater Company in Leicester, England. In 1965 Hopkins applied for a spot in the prestigious Old Vic (the National Theatre), where he auditioned before the great actor Laurence Olivier, one of his idols. Hopkins won the position and began appearing regularly on the London stage. Early on he was recognized as an extraordinary talent.

In 1968 Hopkins won the role of Richard the Lionhearted in the film *The Lion in Winter,* starring Peter O'Toole and Katharine Hepburn. He acquitted himself well and began acting in movies on a regular basis; he appeared in such films as *A Doll's House* (1974), *A Bridge Too Far* (1977), and *84 Charing Cross Road* (1987). He has also done many miniseries and television movies.

While his work has always been greatly admired, it was his no-holds-barred performance as the diabolical Hannibal "the Cannibal" Lecter—a serial killer with good taste—in 1991's thriller *The Silence of the Lambs* that captured the public's imagination. It brought him a Best Actor Oscar and an invigorated film career. Since that time he has worked regularly in both British and American cinema, starring in such movies as *Howards End* (1992), *Bram Stoker's Dracula* (1992), *The Remains of the Day* (1993), *Shadowlands* (1993), *Legends of the Fall* (1994), *Nixon* (1995), *Surviving Picasso* (1996), *Amistad* (1997), and *The Edge* (1997). To all of his roles he brings a riveting intensity.

Hopkins was married from 1967 to 1972 to Petronella Barker, with whom he has a daughter, Abigail, born in 1969. In 1973 Hopkins married Jennifer Lynton. (Two years later the actor, said to have a hot temper, stopped drinking alcohol.) Lynton and Hopkins separated in 1995 and reconciled in 1996; however, in 1999 a divorce reportedly was in the works.

See Hepburn, Katharine; Silence of the Lambs, The

HUSTON, JOHN

John Huston's autobiography, *An Open Book*, reveals his literary side, a side that he took full advantage of during his career. He was equally adept at turning both literary classics and pulp fiction novels into some of his greatest films. The most compelling thread that Huston weaves through his best films is that of the quest.

H

HUSTON, JOHN

Director John Huston won the Best Director Oscar in 1948 for The Treasure of the Sierra Madre. *Huston was nominated thirteen other times, for awards as varied as Best Screenplany and Best Supporting Actor.*

◀

He was born August 5, 1906 in Nevada, Missouri. As the son of well-known stage actor Walter Huston and Reah Gore Huston, a journalist, John got his first taste of show business as a juvenile actor on the vaudeville circuit. A few years after his birth Huston's parents divorced and he spent the rest of his childhood traveling between two homes. When he was eleven he moved to Arizona with his mother in an effort to improve his health. A prescription of exercise and good food proved to be the remedy.

Huston and his mother later left Arizona for Los Angeles. Huston quit school at age fifteen and first pursued a career as a boxer, then gave that up to enter art school. In 1924 he left California for New York where he began his acting career on the stage. His first movie appearance consisted of eight lines in a two-reeler titled *Two Americans* (1929), a film in which his father played the dual roles of Abraham Lincoln and Ulysses S. Grant.

Huston's return to California came when he was hired as a writer for the Goldwyn Studio. After a few months without producing anything at Goldwyn, he went to work for Universal Pictures. The first two films he co-wrote, *A House Divided* (1931) and *Law and Order* (1932), starred his father, Walter Huston.

These two films, along with *Murders in the Rue Morgue* (1932), did little to enhance his reputation as a writer. He describes this period of his life as a "series of misadventures and disappointments." Looking for success but not finding it, Huston moved around, writing for various studios and magazines in the United States and Europe. Finally, in 1938 his life took a turn

HELEN HUNT

Helen Elizabeth Hunt, born on June 15, 1963, in Los Angeles, California, is a rare bird: not only is she a onetime child performer who has been even more popular in adulthood, but she is equally popular in both television and movies, having excelled in both. She also has had success on the stage.

Becoming an actress was a natural for Hunt. Her father, Gordon Hunt, is an acting coach and a director; her mother, Jane Hunt (she and Gordon divorced in 1981), a photographer; her grandmother, Dorothy Fries, a voice coach; and her uncle Peter Hunt, a director.

Hunt started appearing on television at age ten; she was in her first film at age thirteen *(Rollercoaster,* 1977). She played minor roles in a number of subsequent movies—including *Girls Just Want to Have Fun* (1985), *Peggy Sue Got Married* (1986), *Next of Kin* (1989), and *Bob Roberts* and *Mr. Saturday Night* (1992)—then captured the starring role in the blockbuster *Twister* (1996).

But in the late 1990s Hunt's star really began to rise. It was as a harried waitress and overprotective mother in *As Good as It Gets* (1997) that Hunt received the ultimate in accolades: she won the Best Actress Oscar the following year in 1998. That year proved a banner year for Hunt: she also won the Golden Globe for best actress in *As Good as It Gets*, and she took home an Emmy for her work on the television series *Mad About You.* (Hunt was nominated for her role as Jamie Buchman on the series every year from 1993 to 1998, and she won in 1996, 1997, and 1998.) The final episode of *Mad About You* aired in 1999, and Hunt's fans look forward to seeing her in another role soon, whether on the big screen or the small one.

See Nicholson, Jack

for the better when he began work as a contract writer for Warner Brothers. Over the next few years he was a collaborator on a number of successful film scripts including *Jezebel,* for which he was nominated for an Academy Award, and the acclaimed *High Sierra* (1941).

Among the first films he worked on was *The Amazing Doctor Chitterhouse* (1938). The film's significance in Huston's career has less to do with its quality than the lead actor, Humphrey Bogart. The film proved to be the start of a long working relationship between the two. Bogart and Huston worked together on eight films, including three now-classics: *The Maltese Falcon* (1941), *The Treasure of the Sierra Madre* (1948), and *The African Queen* (1952). *The Maltese Falcon* was Huston's directorial debut. Warner Brothers had no hesitation about letting Huston make the low-budget *The Maltese Falcon*, a film on its third remake. His directorial debut, starring Bogart and little known actors Mary Astor, Peter Lorre, and Sidney Greenstreet, proved to be one of Hollywood's all-time classics and earned him another Best Screenplay nomination.

HOLLY HUNTER

Actress Holly Hunter was born in Conyers, Georgia, on February 2, 1958, the youngest of seven children. Their father was a part-time sales representative who farmed a 250-acre tract of land. Holly was encouraged to develop her acting talent from an early age; her first part was as Helen Keller in a school play in fifth grade.

In 1976 the new high school graduate moved to Pittsburgh, where she studied drama at Carnegie Mellon University. She graduated in 1980 and went immediately to New York City to pursue her acting dreams.

Hunter reportedly had the great good fortune to meet playwright Beth Henley when they were stuck together in a broken elevator. The playwright was intrigued by the young, frenetic actress with the pronounced southern twang; she seemed perfect for playing roles in Henley's plays, centered in the south. Subsequently Henley used her influence to help the budding actress get parts in her plays *Crimes of the Heart* and *The Miss Firecracker Contest,* playing in New York in the early 1980s.

In 1981 Hunter had her first film role—four words ("Hey Todd, over here") in a modest effort called *The Burning.* After a few more years of plodding along, trying to make a living in her chosen career, Hunter won a part in the film *Swing Shift* (1984). The exceptionally petite actress (a very slim 5′2″), not the average femme fatale, did not get another film role until 1987, when she struck gold, being cast in three movies: *Raising Arizona, End of the Line,* and *Broadcast News.* Over the next few years Hunter enjoyed modest successes in *Miss Firecracker* and *Always* (1989), *Once Around* (1991), and *The Firm* (1993).

In 1993 *The Piano* was released, a very unusual movie in which Hunter played a mute English widow who travels to New Zealand with her daughter. Hunter had to fight for the quirky role, and it paid off: she won the Academy Award for Best Actress. Since that triumph she has performed in several forgettable films, including *Home for the Holidays* (1995) and *A Life Less Ordinary* (1997). However, in 1998 she had a big success with *Living Out Loud,* costarring Danny DeVito.

After following up *The Maltese Falcon* with *In This Our Life* (1942) and having started *Across the Pacific* (1942), World War II interrupted Huston's career: he was called to serve as a filmmaker in the Signal Corp. During his tenure in the Signal Corp he made three documentaries, *Report from the Aleutians* (1943), *The Battle of San Pietro* (1944), and *Let There Be Light* (1946). *The Battle of San Pietro* so accurately depicted the horrors of battle that the War Department declared it an antiwar film. It was eventually used as a training film. *Let There Be Light,* an account of psychological dysfunction among American soldiers, was also so brutally honest that the government refused to release it until 1980.

Once Huston was released from military service, he returned to the Broadway stage to direct *No Exit.* In 1948 he returned to Warner Brothers to film *Treasure of the Sierra Madre*, starring Walter Huston, Humphrey Bogart, and Tim Holt. This dark psychological portrait of men under stress won Huston his first Academy Award for Best Screenplay. His father also won an Academy Award for Best Supporting Actor.

Key Largo, another film starring Bogart, was Huston's last film under contract with Warner Brothers. For the next six years Huston directed some of his best movies including *The African Queen* (1951), *The Red Badge of Courage* (1951), *Moulin Rouge* (1952), and *Moby-Dick* (1956). Of these the most successful was *The African Queen.* The movie received three Academy Award nominations, and Huston directed Humphrey Bogart to his only award for Best Actor.

The end of the 1950s also signaled the end of Huston's ability to produce one great work after another. Between 1958 and 1975 Huston directed a mix of good, fair, and failed films. During this period, he also returned to his acting roots with roles in films as varied as *Chinatown* (1974), *Battle for the Planet of the Apes* (1973), and a Mexican release film, *The Bridge in the Jungle* (1979). While some of his choices in acting roles were questionable, two nominations for Best Supporting Actor proved his prowess in front of the camera.

In 1975 Huston's legendary skill in adapting literary classics for the screen returned with his film adaptation of Rudyard Kipling's short story, *The Man Who Would Be King*. He followed this success with *Wise Blood* (1979), an adaptation of Flannery O'Connor's gothic novel about a fanatical southern preacher. For the next decade Huston acted, wrote, narrated, or directed over a dozen films, the most memorable being *Prizzi's Honor* (1985). In *Prizzi's Honor* Huston directed his daughter Angelica Huston and Jack Nicholson. The film earned him his last award, for a Golden Globe best director, as well as an Academy Award nomination. John Huston's last films include *The Dead* (1987), an adaptation of a James Joyce short story that he directed, and *Mr. North* (1988), his last film as a screenwriter.

John Huston died August 28, 1987, in Middletown, Rhode Island.

See African Queen, The; *Bogart, Humphrey;* Chinatown; Maltese Falcon, The; Treasure of the Sierra Madre, The

I

INCE, THOMAS H.

Thomas H. Ince was established as a leading American film producer by 1915. Once a small-time stage actor, he appeared in one of D. W. Griffith's Biography films in 1910, then won a contract with the IMP Company, for which he directed Mary Pickford throughout 1911. On the strength of these films, he was hired by the New York Motion Picture Company to take charge of their Edendale studio later that year.

In a lengthy series of one- and two-real films, Ince took advantage of the spectacular California landscapes and the services of the Miller Brothers 101 Wild West Show to breathe new life into the traditional western and Civil War action genres. More important, he was one of the first to systematize film-studio production in a practical and efficient manner.

Soon after arriving in California, Ince split his forces into two units, maintaining personal control of one and assigning the other to Francis Ford, an experienced actor-director who already specialized in outdoor action pictures. Instead of using the relatively open scenario form common in 1911, Ince provide Ford with highly detailed shooting outlines. Over the years, these outlines evolved into formal blueprints (perhaps a better allusion would be to a musical score) that the director was expected to film without change.

As his operation expanded, Ince learned to delegate more and more authority to his staff and ultimately retreated from the specific writing, directing, and even editing functions, although he maintained careful supervision of each of these procedures.

While Ince's films were highly successful domestically, in Europe he was hailed as an artist. Ince began distributing through Paramount-Artcraft. He now supervised fewer releases each year, but somehow the mechanical qualities of his productions began to overwhelm the creative elements.

In fact, Ince's vaunted system was merely an extension of his personal taste and style. A mature production line, such as the one Irving Thalberg developed at MGM, can function effectively despite changes in top management. But when Thomas Ince died suddenly in 1924, operations at the Ince plant shut down completely. His system failed to survive him.

See Griffith, D. W.; Pickford, Mary; Sennett, Mack; Thalberg, Irving

INDEPENDENT FILMMAKER/FILM

A more recent designation for the avant-garde, underground, or experimental filmmaker, the term *independent filmmaker* has come to mean any filmmaker who works outside the commercial mainstream, creating films of personal styling and expression. The resultant film may or may not be distributed for commercial purposes.

See Art theater; Avant-garde; Experimental film; Lynch, David; Redford, Robert; Underground film

INGRAM, REX

If there was one director who gave Louis B. Mayer of the MGM studio almost as much trouble as Erich von Stroheim, it was certainly Rex Ingram. The problems these two had with Mayer quickly became a major part of early Hollywood lore, but such stories have more than merely anecdotal value. When Mayer positioned himself against this pair (and, to a lesser extent, Marshall Neilan), he was asserting not just his personal authority but the authority of MGM's entire production system. Ingram and von Stroheim championed the position of freewheeling directors operating within a supportive industrial framework. Mayer felt the need to establish a hierarchical power structure, with authority flowing down from key studio executives. There is no question as to who won this battle, but how it was waged reveals much about the position of key Hollywood filmmakers in the early and mid 1920s.

Ingram was a European who arrived in America during the nickelodeon era and dabbled in other media before entering films as an actor, changing his name, and eventually directing his first film at Universal. He was born Reginald Hitchcock in Dublin in 1893, and he arrived in the United Sates in 1911 to study art at Yale. As Rex Hitchcock, he began acting for Edison in 1913, transferred to Vitagraph the following year, and by 1915 was working on scripts for Fox. He also adopted his mother's maiden name, Ingram.

Ingram began directing before America's entry into World War I and completed his first feature for Universal in 1916. He enlisted in the Royal

Canadian Flying Corps as an aviation instructor, saw no action, but was severely injured in a crash. Making his way back to Hollywood, he was appalled to see Erich von Stroheim occupying "his" spot as a director on the Universal lot. Years later, von Stroheim remembered how uncomfortable it made him feel to have "yesterday's wonder boy," now an injured veteran in uniform, glaring at him from the sidelines the first day they met. But the pair soon became friends and found that their attitudes toward film, and the process of directing, were remarkable similar. Within a short time they were competing for the industry's accolades, with von Stroheim's *Foolish Wives* winning the sort of attention for Universal that Ingram's *The Four Horsemen of the Apocalypse* (1921) had garnered for Metro the previous season (although the Ingram film was vastly more profitable).

Ingram's vision of a director gradually shaping a film, with the contributions of other collaborators being reduced to the merely technical, is in the direct tradition of D. W. Griffith and von Stroheim. Like both of these men, Ingram preferred to avoid professionally trained actors and actresses, convinced that he could "discover" a personality and then shape it to fit. He made a star of Valentino (although who actually did the discovering is open to question), and when Valentino left him, he set out to do the same with Ramon Novarro. His wife, the actress Alice Terry, was another of his discoveries, and her passive blond beauty glides through most of Ingram's greatest films.

Ingram also had an obsession with atmosphere, believing that a convincing mood on the set could affect actors and audience alike. To help achieve this mood, he might ask his principals to speak to one another in French if the silent film they were making was set in France. He would film many takes of the same scene, hoping to achieve one magical synthesis of all the elements he sought to bring out.

Von Stroheim had to deal with Louis B. Mayer in Hollywood, but when the Metro-Goldwyn merger occurred Rex Ingram was in North Africa filming *The Arab* (1924). Thus he was able to negotiate a new contract directly with Nicholas Schenck in the New York office of the parent company, Loew's, Inc. This contract allowed him to acquire the Victorine studio in the south of France and base his operations there. More surprisingly, his films were not to carry Louis B. Mayer's name on the credits, a unique concession that infuriated the Hollywood mogul.

Working away from the studio and away from Mayer, Ingram was able to make his films according to his own standards, although there were some difficulties regarding the length of *Mare Nostrum* (1926). According to Whytock, the films were generally inexpensive enough to remain profitable, but as Mayer gradually increased his authority, MGM decided that it had little use for such working arrangements, and the contract was not renewed. Again like von Stroheim, Ingram made only one talking picture, which was scarcely distributed and soon forgotten. Failing health and a lack of interest in necessary studio politics kept him from directing again. The Victorine solution offered only a temporary answer to the creative struggles of 1920s Hollywood.

See Griffith, D. W.; Valentino, Rudolph; von Stroheim, Erich

IT HAPPENED ONE NIGHT

“*Remember me? I'm the fellow you slept on last night.*”

Clark Gable as Peter Warne to Claudette Colbert as Ellie Andrews in *It Happened One Night* (1934)

It Happened One Night (1934) is one of the greatest romantic comedies in film history. This “screwball comedy,” recounting the unorthodox courtship between a mismatched couple, was a huge hit. It won the top five Academy Awards, an astounding accomplishment. The screenplay, cowritten by Robert Riskin and director Frank Capra (uncredited), was based on “Night Bus,” a story by Samuel Hopkins Adams.

As the film opens, heiress Ellie Andrews (Claudette Colbert) is having an argument with her wealthy father, Alexander Andrews (Walter Connolly). They are on a yacht moored in the waters off the Florida shoreline, and he has just learned that she has married a worthless playboy, King Westley (Jameson Thomas). Mr. Andrews is so angry that he has Ellie kidnapped, planning to hold her captive until he can get her unconsummated marriage annulled.

Ellie manages to escape, diving off the yacht and swimming to freedom in Miami. Mr. Andrews hires detectives to track her down, but they don't look hard enough: Ellie is at the bus station, but the detectives never think that a high-class woman would take a bus. Ellie has someone buy a ticket for her, and she gets on a bus bound for New York, planning to meet her husband there.

Peter Warne (Clark Gable) is also traveling on the night bus, because that is all he can afford. Peter has recently been fired from his job as a reporter for what he calls a “scandal sheet.” He and Ellie are thrown together, literally, when they must compete for the last seat on the bus. They end up having to share it. They bicker constantly—the gruff newspaperman versus the spoiled brat.

When the bus makes a stop, Ellie's purse is stolen, leaving her with just four dollars. Peter urges her to report it to the police, but she refuses: “Would you please keep out of my affairs?”

At the next stop, Ellie misses the bus. Peter pretends to have missed the bus, too, because he has learned who she really is—a wealthy heiress.

On the next bus, their bickering continues, but Ellie is forced to rely on Peter to protect her from an obnoxious salesman, Shapeley (Roscoe Karns)—"Shapeley's the name, and that's the way I like 'em!"

When the bus passengers have to spend the night at a motel, Ellie and Peter pretend to be married, thereby saving money by sharing a room. Peter reveals that he knows who she is—and that he is a newspaperman. He plans to sell an "exclusive" story about her "Mad Flight to Happiness," with the hopes of getting his job back. Peter promises to help her reach King Westley if she will stay with him for the rest of the trip. If she refuses, he will contact her father.

Ellie and Peter settle down for the night, and they must find a respectable way to sleep in the same room. Peter rigs up "the walls of Jericho"—a blanket slung over a clothesline between the twin beds. Ellie is suspicious about this arrangement and is reluctant to go to her side of the "wall," so Peter begins undressing in front of her, discussing the various

Director Frank Capra's It Happened One Night, *starring Claudette Colbert and Clark Gable, swept the top five Academy Awards in 1934.*

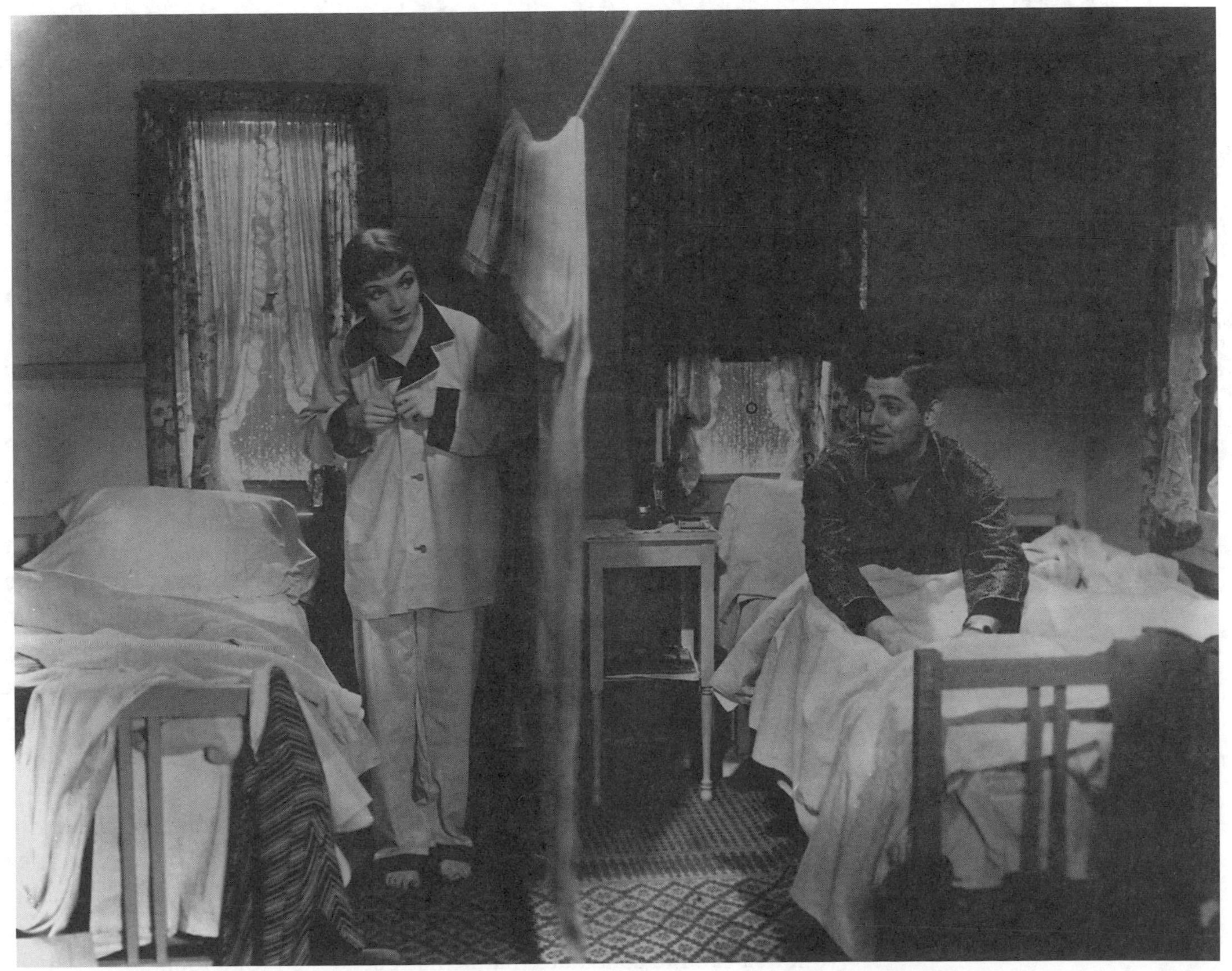

ways men undress. (When Clark Gable took off his shirt and revealed that he was not wearing an undershirt, they went out of fashion and sales plummeted.) When he reaches for his belt buckle, Ellie flees behind the "wall."

At breakfast in their room the next morning, Ellie explains how she sees herself: "You think I'm a fool and a spoiled brat. Well, perhaps I am, although I don't see how I can be. People who are spoiled are accustomed to having their own way. I never have. On the contrary. I've always been told what to do, and how to do it, and when, and with whom. Would you believe it? This is the first time I've ever been alone with a man!"

Back on the bus, Shapeley recognizes Ellie's face from a newspaper story, and Peter and Ellie decide they must find another way to New York. That night they stay in a deserted barn. Peter starts complaining about the pickle he has gotten himself into: "Taking a married woman back to her husband. Hm-mmm. I turned out to be the prize sucker." He walks off to find some food, and Ellie starts talking (she thinks) to him: "If being with me is so distasteful to you, you can leave. . . . I can get along." Her independence falters, however, when she turns and sees that Peter is not there, and she hugs him fiercely when he returns. Peter and Ellie are falling in love.

"What she needs is a guy that'd take a sock at her once a day, whether it's coming to her or not. If you had half the brains you're supposed to have, you'd have done it yourself, long ago."

Clark Gable as Peter Warne in *It Happened One Night* (1934)

The next day, they decide to hitchhike. When Peter brags about his technique but fails to get a single car to stop, Ellie reveals her superior ability: In one of the most famous scenes of all filmdom, she hoists her skirt above her knee and displays her shapely leg when an automobile approaches. The car comes to a screeching halt, the camera focusing in on the driver's feet slamming on the breaks and on the skidding wheels.

The driver (Alan Hale) stops for a meal and then tries to steal Peter's suitcase by driving away without them. Peter runs after him and soon returns with the car—sans the driver.

In New York, meanwhile, Mr. Andrews has decided to withdraw his objections to Ellie's marriage; now he just wants his daughter back. But Ellie has begun to have doubts.

On their last night together, again in a rented room with a blanket between their beds, Ellie confesses her love for Peter, but he rejects her. She cries herself to sleep, while he begins to realize that he loves her, too. He leaves quietly, planning to sell his story to his former boss—a "scoop" that will give him the money to "tear down the walls of Jericho" (to give him a leg to stand on when proposing marriage to Ellie). The scoop is that the missing heiress is going to have her marriage annulled and marry someone else—Peter.

Meanwhile, Ellie has woken up. She thinks Peter has abandoned her in order to sell her out. Defeated, she calls her father, and he and Westley come to collect her. Their entourage of limousines passes Peter, also on his way toward Ellie. But his car breaks down, and he sees her heading to New York in a car. He concludes that he has been taken for a fool.

Over the next few days, newspapers herald Ellie and Westley's plans for a proper church wedding. But Ellie is miserable, and she confesses to her father that she loves Peter, not Westley. When Peter writes Mr. Andrews, requesting a meeting over a financial matter, he and Ellie think that Peter wants the $10,000 reward money. But Peter just wants to be reimbursed for what Ellie cost him on the road: $39.60. Mr. Andrews knows that Peter really loves his daughter.

That day, as Mr. Andrews walks Ellie down the aisle to be married, he whispers the truth about Peter. When it comes time to say "I will" to marrying Westley, Ellie flees, to the arms of Peter. The two outwardly mismatched lovers have learned that they have a lot in common. And with their marriage, the "walls of Jericho" that separate them come tumbling down.

See Capra, Frank; Gable, Clark; Screwball comedy

IT'S A WONDERFUL LIFE

Given the mixed critical reception and box-office failure that greeted the original release of Frank Capra's *It's a Wonderful Life* (1946), no one could have predicted that this Christmas parable of despair and redemption would become not only one of the most popular and critically revered films in Hollywood history but a cultural touchstone for successive generations of Americans. In fact, Capra's frankly immodest celebration of this film echoes the sentiments of countless viewers and critics: "I thought it was the greatest film I ever made. Better yet, I thought it was the greatest film anybody ever made. It wasn't made for the oh-so-bored critics or the oh-so-jaded literati. It was my kind of film for my kind of people." Often dismissed for its mawkish sentiment, it is precisely the film's uncompromisingly dark vision of small-town American life that stirs such a deep response to the protagonist's eventual redemption.

When the film opens, it is Christmas Eve in Beford Falls—an Anytown, USA—in 1946. Two angels in heaven are listening to the prayers of George Bailey (James Stewart), a despairing man driven to the brink of suicide by a lifetime of compounding frustrations that have culminated in the impending failure of his savings and loan bank. An extended flashback then recounts the life story that has brought George to this desperate pass.

The flashback starts in 1919, when George is twelve years old. His kid brother, Harry, plunges through the ice on a frozen pond, and George jumps in to save him. Although he saves Harry from drowning, George's heroics cause him to go deaf in his left ear. We also see him at his job at Mr. Gower's (H. B. Warner), where George catches the drunken druggist in an error that would have resulted in the death of a patient; the irrational Gower boxes George in the ears before acknowledging his error and pleading for the boy's forgiveness.

Each succeeding chapter of George's life is a tale of thwarted hopes. In the summer of 1928 George is about to leave for Europe on his dream trip, after which he will go on to college. George does not plan to return to Bedford Falls and is determined to achieve boundless worldly success. But before he is to leave, George meets up with an old childhood friend, Mary Hatch (Donna Reed). Their first date is interrupted when George gets the tragic news that his father has died. Knowing that his affable but hapless Uncle Billy (Thomas Mitchell) cannot run the bank, George agrees to

To this day Frank Capra's sentimental It's a Wonderful Life *remains the classic Christmas film for many movie fans.* ▶

remain in Bedford Falls to operate his father's loan company. The selfless George pays for the college education of his younger brother, Harry (Todd Kearns), planning to finish his own schooling when Harry returns to Bedford Falls to take over the bank. But Harry marries a woman whose father offers him an opportunity in the family business, so once again George is stymied.

His despair is temporarily assuaged by his rediscovery of his love for Mary. Their wedding bodes a hopeful turning point in his life, but malign fate strikes again: as Mary and George are about to board a train for New York for their honeymoon trip, a bank panic seizes the town, and a menacing mob storms the savings and loan company, demanding all their deposits. George and Mary are forced to use their $2,000 to pay off the angry depositors, and with the $2,000 goes George's last chance to leave Bedford Falls.

George and Mary thus go on with their lives in Bedford Falls. They have four children, and George, although never entirely comfortable in his role as the town's good samaritan, continues his daily struggle to provide the means for the town's honest wage earners to own homes of their own. He also faces the task of keeping the business from being taken over by Mr. Potter (Lionel Barrymore), the town's surly robber baron and gouging landlord. With the coming of World War II, George is ineligible for military service because of his bad ear, but he spearheads the local war-support effort while his brother, Harry, a navy pilot, is awarded the Congressional Medal of Honor for his valor in combat.

The story has now caught up to the day of George's suicide attempt—Christmas Eve. Uncle Billy enters Potter's bank to deposit $8,000 to the savings and loan's account. While taunting the glowering Potter, Uncle Billy inadvertently tosses aside the newspaper in which he has wrapped the cash. Potter seizes the money, stuffs it in a drawer, and smirks with satisfaction as the panicked Uncle Billy scrambles in vain for the funds.

Uncle Billy, now babbling with panic, staggers back to the bank, where an examiner has just arrived to check the books. George has Uncle Billy retrace his steps back to the bank, but to no avail. In desperation he turns to Potter for a loan, but the old man derisively offers only to call the police to have George arrested for embezzlement, reminding him that with a $15,000 life insurance policy, he is "worth more dead than alive."

George goes out to Martini's saloon, where he drinks heavily and offers the desperate prayer that is heard in heaven. Concluding that his suicide would be the best solution for everyone, he heads for the bridge over the river. But before George can jump, an elderly stranger (his guardian angel, Clarence) throws himself into the icy water. George instinctively jumps in to save the eccentric old man.

Drying out in the bridge house, the old man (Henry Travers) identifies himself as Clarence Oddbody—angel, second class. He tells the incredulous George that he has been sent to save George's life as his prerequisite

notable & quotable

"It wasn't made for the oh-so-bored critics or the oh-so-jaded literati. It was my kind of film for my kind of people."

Frank Capra, director, from his autobiography, The Name Above the Title

for earning his wings. When Clarence hears the contemptuous George mutter that everyone would have been better off if he hadn't been born, Clarence seizes on the idea as the perfect redemptive device and grants the wish so that George can see how everyone would have fared in his absence.

What follows is a protracted journey into a hell that makes George's current life seem like paradise. Harry, he learns, died on that lake because there was no George to save him; all the men that Harry saved in the war also perished because there was no Harry. Because George was not there to prevent Gower from mixing poison into the prescription, the patient perishes and Gower goes to jail, only to be released as a drunken, broken panhandler. George then lurches down Main Street to see that Bedford Falls has become the tawdry, seedy Pottersville, studded with bars and girlie shows, with the town's workers living in shacks they rent from Potter. His mother (Beulah Bondi), an embittered old woman, doesn't recognize George. She is running a shabby boardinghouse, and when George asks about Uncle Billy, she tells him that he was committed to an insane asylum before slamming the door in George's face. Now in a frenzy of terror, he dashes off to the safety of his house, only to find it a ghostly ruin. Informed by Clarence that Mary has become an old-maid librarian, he runs to find her, but the wan and mousy Mary of this inverted world screams in terror at his approach, and he flees as Burt (Ward Bond), the local cop, tries to shoot him.

"One man's life touches so many others, when he's not there it leaves an awfully big hole."

Henry Travers as Clarence in *It's a Wonderful Life* (1946)

George runs back to the bridge and tearfully begs Clarence to restore him to the life he had tried to end just hours earlier. As he mutters his prayer, the police squad car pulls up, but the Burt who emerges is not the pursuer of his nightmares but his old friend, expressing concern over George's alarming behavior. Realizing that Clarence has restored him to life, an exultant George runs back to his house, gleefully and heedlessly expecting arrest and scandal but no longer caring as long as he can be reunited with his family. There, to his delight and surprise, he finds the entire community assembled to pour their precious savings into rescuing George and the savings and loan. His learns that his old friend Sam Wainwright, now a wealthy businessman, has authorized a loan of $25,000. Harry makes a surprise appearance, raising a toast in tribute to his redeemed brother: "To my big brother George—the richest man in Bedford Falls." To the strains of "Auld Lang Syne" the sheriff tears up the warrant for George's arrest, and the bank examiner drops a dollar into the pot. Hearing a bell ring on the Christmas tree, George's little daughter says that her teacher told her that every time a bell rings, an angel gets his wings. George looks skyward, winks, and says, "Attaboy, Clarence."

See Capra, Frank; Stewart, James

J

JAWS

For a director who has churned out blockbuster megahits as efficiently and reliably as a short-order cook dispatching cheeseburgers, *Jaws* doubtless occupies a special place in Steven Spielberg's heart as his "first time." A relatively unknown with only one feature film to his credit when he was offered the 1974 shark shocker, he piloted the project into a suspense classic that became one of the biggest-grossing films up to that time and launched the young Spielberg on the path to directorial stardom.

Jaws was the 1970s' second-biggest seller, with $129 million in rentals. *Close Encounters of the Third Kind* was seventh, at $82 million.

The opening shot of the nighttime beach party sets the time and place for *Jaws*. In the next scene, two of the partygoers, a young man and woman, run down the beach for an intimate swim. What begins as harmless fun soon turns into a nightmare when the young woman, who has left her drunken companion behind on shore, is attacked in the water. Only the girl's nude body is seen thrashing in the murky water. Early the next morning, Police Chief Brody (Roy Scheider) and his deputy, Meadows (Carl Gottlieb), discover the young woman's body. In a scene shortly after the body is found, Brody is shown trying to type the police report in a police station bustling with distractions. Spielberg is manipulating the audience by letting them in on Brody's excitement visually and aurally. A close-up of the hastily typed report in the typewriter reveals that Brody is terribly flustered (or a terrible speller), for he has typed "corner" for "coroner."

Brody, frantically buying materials for signs to close the beaches, bumps into Mayor Vaughn (Murray Hamilton), who is comically decked out in a sport coat festooned with anchors, obviously happily anticipating a prosperous tourist season. A scene on Amity's ferry is used to suggest the island's isolation and dependence on tourists for survival. The confining atmosphere of the ferry effectively shows the mayor and town leaders' avarice in forbidding Brody to close the beaches.

Scenes rush along, creating a feeling of time passing rapidly, until an episode on the beach just before the Fourth of July holiday jamboree. The Fourth is Amity's big event, the day the beaches are officially opened for the tourist season. Brody is shown carefully scanning the horizon and waterline while everyone else is enjoying the beach. Next we see a dog swimming with a stick in its mouth. Several shots later, the dog is nowhere to be seen, only the stick floating atop the waves. In the distance, the dog's owner can be heard calling to it. Then we see a young boy, Alex Kintner (Jeffrey Voorhees), afloat on his rubber raft. Spielberg takes us below for a suspense-building underwater shot where Alex's legs are vulnerably flapping off the back of the raft. A long shot shows the raft turn upside down and a gush of red liquid spurts up. "Did you see that?" a surprised vacationer ask his wife, who is basking in the sun. Brody, eyes wide, inches forward. There is another spurt of blood. Several screams are heard from the boy before he disappears from the camera's view. Brody leaps to his feet and yells for everyone to get out of the water.

Brody enlists the help of a shark expert, Hooper (Richard Dreyfuss), and the two embark on a nighttime boat ride to hunt for the shark on the theory that sharks are "night feeders." They come across an abandoned fishing boat. Hooper investigates by diving into the water in scuba gear. Brody, who cannot swim, waits uneasily on the surface. The murky underwater shots provide claustrophobic tension while Hooper investigates a hole in the boat's hull. He finds a shark's tooth and, after examining it, goes in for a closer look. At any moment we expect the shark to spring forth and devour the

*Because the shark is actually shown only briefly in the film—the result of problems with the mechanical beast—*Jaws *relies on the viewer's imagination and fear of the unknown for the real scares.*

▼

ichthyologist like a gumdrop. Instead, Spielberg floats the head of the dead fisherman through the hole in the bow, scaring Hooper (and the audience).

The scene after Brody tells the mayor of their discovery shows tourists flocking to the beaches. The mayor has decided "the beaches will be open"—commercialism reigns. People are pouring into Amity from everywhere. The beach sequence ends with the bathers rushing from the water when an ominous fin is spotted. Spielberg shows the fin coming toward potential victims, who register sheer horror. Just as guns are aimed at the menace from patrolling boats, the cardboard fin flops over and up come two young tykes attired in wetsuits and snorkles. This scene is a clever distraction, for the "real" shark fin is soon spotted on the other side of the bay, where Brody's son, Michael, and a playmate are boating. The shark attacks a man in a boat nearby. The turbulence capsizes Michael's boat, throwing him and his playmate into the water. He is immobilized by fear. Still unseen, the huge shark seems to brush the boy before it leaves the cove. This incident is capsuled in a hospital confrontation with the mayor, who finally agrees to authorize a shark hunt.

In a storytelling session in the cabin of the *Orca*, a boat belonging to a local shark hunter called Quint (played by Robert Shaw), the three protagonists reveal their personalities. Brody is shown to be the real hero of the piece, because he has gone out to hunt the shark in spite of his acknowledged fear of water and his inability to swim. Quint reveals that his desire to kill sharks is for revenge. He recounts a hideous World War II incident in which he and eleven hundred shipmates, on a ship returning from delivering the atom bomb dropped on Hiroshima, were torpedoed and left to swim helplessly in shark-infested waters.

Suddenly, the shark rams the *Orca*. The men are stunned by the jolt and silently question its origins. Seconds later, the shark rams the boat again, breaking several planks in the hull. With the attacker clearly identified, they jump to their feet to retaliate. Hooper is lowered in a shark cage with a spear gun tipped with poison in a last-ditch effort to kill the shark. The shark's attack on the cage causes Hooper to drop his spear gun, forcing him to escape through the twisted bars when the shark retreats momentarily. He quickly swims to the ocean floor where he hides in a coral reef to escape the shark's fury. On deck, meanwhile, Brody and Quint are aware of the shark's attack on the cage, and desperately try to retrieve it. They eventually raise it from the ocean, but the battered shark cage is empty and Hooper is feared dead. A close-up focuses on blood spurting from Quint's mouth as he is devoured by the shark

With Quint's demise, only Brody is left to do battle with the shark. After several attacks on the boat, Brody manages to lodge one of Hooper's diving tanks in the shark's mouth. With the boat now completely underwater except for the mast, which Brody clings to for life, the shark begins its final attack. Armed with his rifle, Brody carefully aims it at the oncoming shark, screaming, "Smile, you son of a b****!" He fires and hits the air tank,

"What we are dealing with here is a perfect engine, an eating machine. It's really a miracle of evolution. All this machine does is swim, eat and make little sharks, and that's all."

Richard Dreyfuss as Hooper in *Jaws* (1975)

which explodes violently and tears the shark to pieces. Brody heaves a sigh of relief, but is given a deathly scare when Hooper miraculously appears from the water. Hooper inquires about the fate of Quint, but Brody merely shakes his head. But despite the loss of the brave shark hunter, in Amity it is once again safe to go back in the water.

See Spielberg, Steven

JAZZ SINGER, THE

The film that emblematizes the birth of the talkies is *The Jazz Singer.* Al Jolson's blackened face, tear-jerking performance, and unabashed vocal gusto are understood to signal the end of Hollywood's silence. The 1927 film enjoys this stature not only in popular opinion but in academic discourse. An insightful article about *The Jazz Singer,* for example, has described the musical "as a summation of those various elements which came to distinguish the musical genre." *The Jazz Singer* was an enormous Broadway hit but movie producers, having been burned by promoters of sound systems too often, were skeptical of its success and slow to convert to sound.

For Jolson, *The Jazz Singer* was a once-in-a-lifetime casting opportunity. The entertainer, who sang jazzed-up minstrel numbers in blackface, was at the height of his phenomenal popularity. Anticipating the later stardom of crooners and rock stars, Jolson electrified audiences with the vitality and sex appeal of his songs and gestures, which owed much to African-American sources. In September he had grossed $57,286 for a one-week personal appearance at the Metropolitan Theater in Los Angeles. The crowds were so wild that Jolson gave three extra performances without pay. His songs in the 1926 Vitaphone short "Plantation Act" had amply demonstrated the singer's celluloid appeal. And having auditioned the competitors Jessel and Jolson together on the same Vitaphone program and compared audience reactions certainly must have made the Warners imagine how nice it would be to sign Al.

notable & quotable

"Everyone was mad for the talkies. I remember 'The Jazz Singer,' when Al Jolson just burst into song, and there was a little bit of dialogue. And when he came out with 'Mammy,' and went down on his knees to his Mammy, it was just dynamite."

Gregory Peck, actor, 1999

Jolson filmed the silent scenes in June and the eight sound sequences in August 1927 at the Hollywood Vitaphone studio. The film opened on October 6, 1927. Warners set the Broadway premiere on the day before Yom Kippur as a show business flourish, since the film's plot centers on that holiday.

The story of this legendary film is one of generational conflict and atonement. A prologue shows young Jakie Rabinowitz (Bobby Gordon) singing ragtime renditions of "My Gal Sal" and "Waiting for the Robert E. Lee" in a Lower East Side saloon. His father (Warner Oland), a cantor at the synagogue, catches him, they argue over his profane singing, and Jakie leaves home. The story jumps ten years and "Jack Robin" is now eking out a living as a jazz singer. He finds success, partly through the influence of a talented vaudeville performer, Mary Dale (May McAvoy). He and Mary are scheduled to appear together in a big Broadway show. Jack goes to visit his mother, Sara Rabinowitz (Eugenie Besserer), and performs "Blue Skies" for her. Cantor Rabinowitz enters unexpectedly, yells "Stop!" and makes Jack leave. Opening night of the show falls on Yom Kippur, but the cantor has not recovered from his shock and cannot sing. Jack answers his mother's appeal to come visit and is so moved by his fathers suffering and the call of his own reawakened religion that he sings the Kol Nidre in his father's place. The cantor dies, but his lifelong dream of hearing his son sing the ancient hymn has been fulfilled. In an epilogue, Jack appears onstage at the Winter Garden theater and sings "Mammy" to his mother in the audience.

The first movie ever to feature audible dialogue, The Jazz Singer *tells the story of singer Jakie Rabinowitz, played with gusto by Al Jolson.*

▼

In the screenplay, there was considerable room for improvisation owing to the lack of precedents for writing a part-talking film. In an early scene, Jack performs "Toot, Toot, Tootsie" in Coffee Dan's club. When it is over Jolson exclaims, "Wait a minute! Wait a minute! You ain't heard nothin' yet." These lines, among the most famous in film history, are also among the most misrepresented. First, Jolson does not say them to Besserer aloud in the later scene, as is widely believed; rather, that line is repeated in a conventional silent intertitle: "Mama—You ain't heard nothing yet." Second, though the lines do not appear to have been scripted, they were planned for deliberately and calculated to spark recognition and applause from his fans in the audience, since "You ain't heard nothin' yet" was the signature tag line Jolson always repeated during his stage act.

There was little advance publicity for *The Jazz Singer,* and little response (enthusiastic or otherwise) in the daily reviews. In the trade papers, the premiere was overshadowed by the sudden death of Sam Warner, at age forty, the previous day.

Reviewers acclaimed Jolson's singing but panned his acting style. "*The Jazz Singer,*" according to *Exhibitors Herald,* "is scarcely a motion picture. It should be more properly labeled an enlarged Vitaphone record of Al Jolson in half a dozen songs." Within months the film would make a great sum for Warners, but at the time it was not the biggest hit of the season. The film was represented as a triumph for Jolson, and for Warners in hiring him, but not for talking cinema. Nevertheless, the message was clear to small exhibitors outside of New York. Though the price of wiring for Vitaphone was exorbitant, the prospect of having Al Jolson "play" in the local theater made it a surefire investment.

See Sound; Vitaphone

JURASSIC PARK

Jurassic Park (1993) is a fantasy-adventure film based on the book of the same title by Michael Crichton, with screenplay by Crichton and David Koepp. Directed by superstar director Steven Spielberg, *Jurassic Park* was a blockbuster at the box office, earning hundreds of millions of dollars on its first run alone, and in merchandising circles, as it set off a frenzy of interest (and spending) in dinosaurs among the young people. It even led to a highly profitable theme ride and exhibition park being built by Universal Studios.

While critics mocked the exceptionally lackluster characterizations and lame acting in the movie, they couldn't deny that the special effects—the dinosaurs—were fantastic. The special effects were created by the company Industrial Light and Magic (ILM), particularly known for its work on the *Star Wars* films.

The film centers on a one-of-a-kind "theme park"—an isolated island off the Pacific coast of Costa Rica, where John Hammond (Richard Attenborough), a wealthy and eccentric entrepreneur, has managed to clone and raise a diverse colony of dinosaurs—raptors, Tyrannosaurus Rexes, and other prehistoric beasts—cloned from sixty-five-million-year-old DNA of mosquitos (who fed on dinosaur blood) preserved in amber. Hammond hopes to open the park to a well-heeled paying public, which will be understandably astounded by this amazing peek into earth's past.

To give his theme park some scientific credibility, Hammond invites two dinosaur experts, paleontologist Alan Grant (Sam Neill) and paleobotanist Ellie Sattler (Laura Dern), and a mathematician with a bent toward the philosophical, Ian Malcolm (Jeff Goldblum), to experience the island firsthand. Various other people will also converge on the island to experience its unique treasures, including a lawyer and Hammond's two grandchildren, Lex (Ariana Richards) and Timmy (Joseph Mazzello).

The visitors are predictably slack jawed when they catch sight of the dinosaurs. The camera closes in on their faces as they first lay eyes on the beasts. With their falling jaws, sharp intakes of breath, and widening eyes, the actors heavy-handedly relay their awe and amazement. When they express their concern about the safety of visitors, they are told that the park's 10,000-volt electric fences, which are computer controlled, will keep the animals in their place, placidly frolicking in the lush natural terrain of the island, their every need provided for.

The scientists are told how the animals were cloned, and they are shown around the theme park's "brains"—a high-tech command center that controls the electrified fences and services such as the remote-control utility vehicles. There are discussions of the impact of tampering with Mother Nature, but the scientists are assured that the state-of-the-art resources in this command center will keep everything under control, for the maximum pleasure of the theme park's guests.

Predictably, however, things go horribly awry. An employee tries to steal some dinosaur embryos and shuts down the computer system that controls, among other things, the electrified fences. A fierce storm lashes the island, further weakening the systems that are meant to manage the theme park, and the dinosaurs go berserk. They knock down the fences and get loose, quickly traveling off their carefully segregated squares of turf, and fiendishly wage war on one another and on the humans on the island. The good guys (such as Dr. Grant and the children) manage to survive, but the more dis-

"Genetic power is the most awesome force the planet has ever seen, but you wield it like a kid who found his dad's gun."

Jeff Goldblum as Dr. Ian Malcolm in *Jurassic Park* (1993)

posable and less sympathetic characters (such as the lawyer) are killed by the beasts.

The mayhem reminds viewers that fooling with nature's design is an unpredictable and dangerous undertaking. And as things settle down on the island, a group of those cuddly, ravenous raptors are seen alighting on another shore, thereby setting up an ominous scenario for a profitable sequel.

See Spielberg, Steven; Special-effects film

KAEL, PAULINE

Film critic and writer Pauline Kael was born in Petaluma, California, on June 19, 1919. She attended the University of California at Berkeley from 1936 to 1940, graduating with a bachelor's degree in philosophy. She stayed in Berkeley and over the next two decades held a variety of jobs there, including managing movie theaters. Her appreciation for the art of filmmaking grew as she made several experimental short films and wrote reviews of movies. For a time she had a weekly show at a Pacifica radio station, talking about film.

In the 1960s Kael began to reach a national audience; she moved to New York City in 1965. She did some writing for *The New Republic,* and when that magazine refused to print a 9,000-word piece on the movie *Bonnie and Clyde* (1967), she took it to *The New Yorker,* which agreed to publish it. Her glowing review has been credited with giving *Bonnie and Clyde* the critical push that the controversial film needed to succeed at the box office.

Kael began working full time for *The New Yorker* in 1968, as resident film critic. Though the weekly magazine did not have a huge circulation, its readership was very influential, and Kael's reviews helped to shape the emerging film culture—called New Hollywood—of the era. She became known as an advocate for young, innovative directors and pushed for their independence of the big movie studios, which she felt constrained filmmakers' creativity. Kael's detractors considered her to be too close to certain film directors of the '70s, such as Robert Altman, to be able to give objective reviews of their work.

But, subjective or not, Kael earned many fans (some so devoted they were dubbed "Paulettes"). Her writing style at *The New Yorker* was punchy and vigorous, drawing the reader into the subject matter. And whether or not one agreed with her opinions of individual films, Kael's reviews always managed to impart her great enthusiasm, even passion, for movies. In addition, her work helped to develop respect for filmmaking as a valuable and unique art form; her work even lent a new legitimacy to the "art" of criticism itself.

Kael earned a reputation for spotting trends and people to watch in the movie industry. In 1974, for example, she suggested that television was eroding the viewing audience's taste. Also that year, in writing about Steven Spielberg's debut movie, *The Sugarland Express,* she observed that he was "that rarity among directors—a born entertainer."

Kael became known as one of the most important film critics in the United States, if not *the* most. In the 1970s her reviews were so influential that studio executives even began to fear her. When studios started using television to advertise their releases in the late 1970s, however, her influence on moviegoers began to wane, along with that of other print critics, and her reviews became more commercially oriented, of the "thumbs up/thumbs down" variety.

In 1979, in response to Kael's criticism of his film *Reds,* Warren Beatty, a powerful director who had substantial clout at Paramount Studios, challenged her to come to Hollywood to make movies: "If you think it's so easy, you ought to try it yourself." Kael thus accepted a position to produce a film called *Love and Money* at Paramount, taking a leave of absence from *The New Yorker.* After six weeks, however, the director, James Toback, had her fired, claiming that she was overly competitive with him, trying to rewrite the script over and over again. She allegedly also took to calling Beatty's then-girlfriend Diane Keaton, trying to get Keaton to persuade Beatty not to make *Reds*—not a usual activity of film critics.

When Kael returned to *The New Yorker,* she wrote a scathing analysis of the future of the movie business, presumably based upon her experiences in Hollywood. She stayed at the magazine until her retirement in 1991.

Kael has published a number of books, including collections of her reviews, including *I Lost It at the Movies; Kiss Kiss Bang Bang; Going Steady; Deeper into Movies; Reeling; When the Lights Go Down; Taking It All In;* and *Movie Love.* She has also issued several editions of a general guide to film, entitled *5001 Nights at the Movies.*

See Altman, Robert; Bonnie and Clyde; *Criticism; Ebert, Roger; Maltin, Leonard; Newspapers; Siskel, Gene; Trade papers*

KAZAN, ELIA

Elia Kazan was born Elia Kazanjoglous in Constantinople (Istanbul), Turkey, on September 7, 1909. Of Greek ancestry, Kazan directed a number of very successful plays on Broadway in the 1940s and 1950s, as well as some of the most critically acclaimed motion pictures in the history of American film. But he is also one of the most controversial figures in the performing arts because of his actions during the McCarthy "communist-hunting" era in the 1950s.

When Kazan was four years old, his family moved from Turkey to America, first to a Greek neighborhood in New York City and then suburban New Rochelle, New York. Kazan spent much of his childhood reading. While attending Williams College in Massachusetts, where he majored in English, he saw the classic film *Potemkin* by Russian director Sergei Eisenstein. Awed by the film's drama and impact, he decided to pursue a career in the performing arts.

Upon graduation in 1930, Kazan enrolled in the drama school at Yale University. However, he did not finish his studies at Yale. Instead, armed with a letter of introduction from Yale faculty member Philip Barber, Kazan began working at the recently formed Group Theater in New York City. His early apprenticeship at the theater included backstage work and bit parts in several productions. His first significant role was as a taxi driver in the 1935 production of *Waiting for Lefty*, a play by Clifford Odets.

Kazan wanted to direct rather than act. But his success in *Waiting for Lefty* revealed an unusual talent for acting and led to increasingly important roles. His performance in such plays as *Paradise Lost* and *Golden Boy*, both by Clifford Odets, earned him great praise from a number of theater critics, including the famous Brooks Atkinson of the *New York Times*. Kazan continued acting into the early 1940s, but at the same time he became increasingly involved in directing.

Kazan first began to direct in the mid-1930s at the Group Theater. But it was not until the 1940s that his efforts became noticed. His first great success was as director of the play *The Skin of Our Teeth* by Thornton Wilder, for which he won the New York Drama Critics Award in 1942. Over the next few years, the director had a number of stage triumphs, and critics began to hail him as one of Broadway's finest directors. In 1947 Kazan won another New York Drama Critics Award, as well as a Tony Award, for directing Arthur Miller's *All My Sons*. In 1947 Kazan began collaborating with playwright Tennessee Williams on his play *A Streetcar Named Desire*, which earned Kazan more awards for direction and Williams a Pulitzer Prize.

In 1948 Kazan joined with several alumni from the Group Theater, including famed teacher Lee Strasberg, to found the Actors Studio. Although an acting school, the Studio also became a spiritual refuge for actors. Kazan's teaching there helped mold the careers of such famous actors as Marlon Brando, Paul Newman, James Dean, and others.

Kazan continued to direct plays on Broadway while teaching at the Actors Studio. Among his greatest successes in the late 1940s was Arthur Miller's *Death of a Salesman*, which earned Miller the Pulitzer Prize and Kazan another Tony Award and the New York Drama Critics Award in 1949. In the 1950s Kazan's continuing collaboration with Tennessee

K

KAZAN, ELIA

Originally a director of Broadway plays, Elia Kazan made a name for himself in film by directing such movies as On the Waterfront *(1954),* East of Eden *(1955), and* Splendor in the Grass *(1961).*

Williams resulted in memorable stagings of *Cat on a Hot Tin Roof* (1955) and *Sweet Bird of Youth* (1959), which proved to be his last work on Broadway.

While working on Broadway, Kazan had also become active as a film director. His first film was *Pie in the Sky*, a short comedy he codirected with Ralph Steiner in 1934. He collaborated with Steiner again on *People of the Cumberlands*, a short documentary about miners in Tennessee that was released in 1937. Kazan's first solo directing effort was on a wartime informational film about food rationing called *It's Up to You* (1941).

Kazan's first feature-length Hollywood film was *A Tree Grows in Brooklyn* (1945), a story about growing up in the slums of New York City. By this time, he had a considerable reputation as a director for the stage, and his

work on this movie showed Kazan's great skill as a film director as well. His film *Boomerang* won a New York Film Critics Award in 1947, and in the same year Kazan won his first Academy Award as director of *Gentleman's Agreement*.

In these early feature films, Kazan took a theatrical approach to directing, focusing on the characters and dialogue. With his next film, the urban thriller *Panic in the Streets* (1950), he began to display a more cinematic approach, with greater concern for camera angles, movement, and other cinematic effects. In the screen adaptation of *A Streetcar Named Desire* (1951), starring his former student Marlon Brando, Kazan used the camera to expand the single set in which the story takes place and to focus on the performances of the actors.

In 1952 an episode occurred in Kazan's life that made him the controversial figure he subsequently became. During the early 1950s U.S. senator Joseph McCarthy chaired a series of special congressional hearings aimed at exposing communists in the United States. In 1952 Kazan testified before the House Un-American Activities Committee, naming several people in theater and film who he claimed were, or had been, members of the Communist Party. Kazan himself had been a member of the party in the 1930s, but he ultimately broke with it and became fiercely anticommunist. Kazan's naming of names, including former friends and colleagues, caused people to lose their careers and be banned from working in the theater or film, at least in the United States. His action infuriated many people, and he became a highly controversial figure, one both admired and hated.

Although shunned by many, Kazan was able to continue working in the film industry. In fact, two years after testifying in Congress, Kazan reached a milestone in his career as a film director. In 1954 his movie *On the Waterfront*, a gritty drama about labor corruption among dockworker unions starring Marlon Brando, won six Academy Awards, including Best Actor, Best Picture, and Best Director. The film, perhaps Kazan's best known and most widely acclaimed work, also marked the culmination of two of the most defining aspects of his directing—a realistic style and strong, naturalistic performances by his actors. Kazan became famous as an "actors' director" because of his rapport with them and his ability to draw out brilliant performances.

The films that Kazan directed in the 1950s made a considerable impact on American cinema. His skill in filming in urban locations, attempt to deal with difficult social issues, and handling of actors helped to establish new attitudes in Hollywood. Between 1955 and 1976 Kazan directed only nine more films, including classics such as *East of Eden*, starring James Dean, and *Splendor in the Grass*, with Warren Beatty and Natalie Wood, as well as *America, America* and *The Arrangement*, both of which were based on bestselling novels written by Kazan.

Kazan directed his last movie, *The Last Tycoon*, in 1976. He continued writing, however, and published several works, including an autobiography, *Elia Kazan: A Life*, in 1988. In March 1999 Kazan was awarded a Lifetime Achievement Award at that year's Academy Awards ceremony. Still a center of controversy, he accepted the award amid both applause from supporters and stony silence from some who regard him with contempt because of his actions during the McCarthy era.

See Brando, Marlon; Losey, Joseph; Method actor; On the Waterfront; *Ray, Nicholas;* Streetcar Named Desire, A

KEATON, BUSTER

Many vaudevillians and music-hall comedians were attracted to the cinema during the silent era, from Charlie Chaplin and Harry Langdon to Stan Laurel and W. C. Fields. Most were content to transfer the style or character of their theater work to the screen in relatively unchanged fashion. In Chaplin's case, this meant inserting more mood and characterization into his films than Mack Sennett felt comfortable with. For Langdon or Fields, it was an opportunity to film the most popular of their stage routines. Only Buster Keaton took the trouble to master the essential mechanics of the cinema. From the day he first set foot in Roscoe "Fatty" Arbuckle's studio, he began to study the function of the camera in screen comedy. Where other comics were content to record their own performances on film, Keaton involved the camera (and all other technical elements of the cinema) as a key participant, not just an observer.

While an artist and craftsman of consummate skill, Keaton was politically and socially unable to play the Hollywood game. When working conditions were good, he produced the most graceful and hilarious of his films; when conditions were bad, he drew a blank. Control of those conditions was typically shaped by a more experienced friend or associate, one who could set up a production situation within which Keaton could operate, thus freeing him from administrative details and allowing him, if he so desired, to continue spending his time on impromptu baseball games.

Arbuckle was the first of these mentors. In 1917 he invited Keaton, who had recently broken up the family act "The Three Keatons" to join his Comicque Film Company in New York City. Keaton writes in his autobiography:

Roscoe . . . took the camera apart for me so I would understand how it worked and what it could do. He showed me how film was developed, cut, and then spliced together. But the greatest thing to me about picturemaking was the way it automatically did away with the physical limitations of the theatre. On the stage, even one as immense as the New York Hippodrome stage, one could show only so much. (*My Wonderful World of Slapstick,* p. 93)

With his years of stage experience and fine baritone voice, Buster Keaton was one of the few silent film stars eager to work in "talkie" pictures.

Showing everything soon became a Keaton trademark. Under Arbuckle's tutelage, Keaton quickly learned to build on the mock violence and knockabout of his vaudeville act. The contained pratfalls of the stage comedian soon grew into the expansive, sweeping trajectories of films like *Our Hospitality* (1923) and *Seven Chances* (1925).

It was Joseph Schenck who made it possible for Keaton to develop these skills on his own. Schenck had been producing Arbuckle's films and noted Keaton's growing success in the short films made between 1917 and 1919. When Arbuckle moved to features, Schenck promoted Keaton to head Arbuckle's unit, where Keaton continued to work with much of his familiar technical staff and supporting company. Keaton had married Natalie Talmadge, the sister of Schenck's wife, Norma, and the business relationship took on the cozy familiarity of a family affair. Keaton flourished under this supportive arrangement, and his series of two-reelers quickly established him as the screen's fastest-rising young comedian. During 1921 and 1922, when Chaplin films were few and far between, a new Keaton two-reeler was onscreen every other month. In 1923 Keaton himself moved to features, although not until he released *The Navigator* (1924) did he have a hit of sizable proportions.

Modern acclaim tends to obscure the fact, but in box-office terms Keaton's films were not in the same league as those of Chaplin and Lloyd. Keaton's contract paid him a salary of only $1,000 per week, plus 25 percent of the profits of his pictures, but these were slim and occasionally nonexistent.

Joseph Schenck became a partner in United Artists in 1924 and president two years later. All of Keaton's features had been distributed through Metro or Metro-Goldwyn-Mayer, but Schenck moved him over to United Artists and gave the go-ahead for Keaton's most ambition production, *The General* (1927). In his scrupulous account of Keaton's finances, Tom Dardis shows how the film, now regarded as perhaps the single greatest achievement of silent comedy, was both a critical and commercial failure in 1927. Two additional United Artists features, *College* (1927) and *Steamboat Bill, Jr.* (1928), were nearly as disappointing. Unable to continue backing the sagging Keaton production company, Schenck advised the comedian to move his operation to MGM. Here, his old unit dissolved, he was assigned a production supervisor, and MGM screenwriters dared to concoct his scripts. While the first of these films, *The Cameraman* (1928), was certainly up to standard, no critics today will defend the later MGM features (1929–33) against the earlier output. Keaton's lack of involvement is palpable, but his own personal problems, especially his growing alcoholism, must bear most of the responsibility.

Happily, however, Buster Keaton became the first great screen artist to be rehabilitated through film restoration. After decades as a Hollywood ghost, he got a tumultuous reception at the 1965 Venice Film Festival that not only restored his own reputation but helped trigger a wholesale reassessment of the entire silent era, a period that had suffered as much as he had from many years of patronization and neglect.

See Chaplin, Charlie; Comedy; Lloyd, Harold; Slapstick comedy

DIANE KEATON

Born into a comfortable middle-class family in Los Angeles on January 5, 1946, Diane Keaton (born Diane Hall) has made a successful career out of playing charming but somewhat ditsy types (like the title character in *Annie Hall*) or lovable, reliable girls-next-door (such as her role as the mother in the 1990s versions of *Father of the Bride*). Whatever her role, audiences seem to find something comforting about the actress's offbeat screen persona, though critics have not always been kind.

Keaton got her start in the late 1960s when, after spending a couple of semesters attending a junior college, she decided to head for New York City, where she studied acting at the Neighborhood Playhouse. She did some summer stock and played several roles (including the lead part) in the Broadway musical *Hair*. In the Broadway production of *Play It Again, Sam,* she played opposite Woody Allen. The two became a couple, and in the 1970s she starred in several of his movies, including the film version of *Play It Again Sam* (1972) and *Sleeper* (1973). She also played the title character in Allen's bittersweet romantic comedy *Annie Hall* (1977), for which she won the Best Actress Academy Award. She later starred in another Allen production, the "dramatic comedy" *Manhattan* (1979).

Keaton found steady work playing the girlfriend-turned-wife of Michael Corleone (played by Al Pacino) in the three *Godfather* movies (1972, 1974, and 1990). At various times over the years she and Pacino have had a personal relationship.

In 1981 Keaton starred in *Reds* opposite Warren Beatty, with whom she was romantically linked for a number of years. In the mid 1980s she performed in several passable but not spectacular films, including *The Little Drummer Girl* (1983) and *Mrs. Soffel* (1984). The year 1987 saw a resurgence in her career, with roles in *Radio Days* and *Baby Boom.* She starred opposite Steve Martin in two *Father of the Bride* movies (1991 and 1995), and made a splash as a jilted middle-aged wife in *The First Wives Club* (1996). She received an Oscar nomination for her performance in the drama *Marvin's Room* in 1996.

At an age when most American actresses have long since been put out to pasture, Keaton has had steady, high-profile work. Keaton has also tried her hand at directing (an eccentric documentary entitled *Heaven,* 1987, and a feature film, *Unstrung Heroes,* 1995), and has published two books of photography (*Reservations,* 1980, and *Still Life,* 1983). Keaton has one daughter, Dexter.

See Allen, Woody; Annie Hall; Godfather, The; Godfather: Part II, The; *Pacino, Al*

KING KONG

King Kong (1933) has reigned for decades as one of the greatest fantasy/adventure films of all time. Producer/director Merian C. Cooper created the Beauty and the Beast-type story of a gigantic apelike monster who falls in love with a beautiful young woman. The screenplay was written by James Creelman and Ruth Rose.

As the film opens, it is 1932 in New Jersey. On the waterfront, a watchman confirms that nearby is the "moving picture ship." Filmmaker Carl Denham (Robert Armstrong), known for his fearless risk taking and exciting jungle movies, is getting ready for another "crazy" adventure. The ship is carrying an unusually large cargo of some sort (it turns out to be gas bombs).

"Oh no, it wasn't the airplanes. It was beauty that killed the beast."

Robert Armstrong as Carl Denham in *King Kong* (1933)

No one on ship, not even First Mate John ("Jack") Driscoll (Bruce Cabot), knows where the ship is going or what its mission is. They only know that it has something to do with a movie.

Denham's agent has not found a leading lady for such an unorthodox assignment, but he feels that one is necessary to serve as a love interest in this movie. So Denham decides to do some scouting in New York. At one spot, he passes the soup lines brought about by the Great Depression. At a small outdoor stand, he notices a young woman, Ann Darrow (Fay Wray), stealing a piece of fruit. He buys her a meal and begins talking to her. When he asks her what has happened to her to bring her to the point of having to steal food, she says, "Bad luck."

Ann has acting ambitions, and Denham persuades her to go along on his voyage. "It's money and adventure and fame. . . ." When she hesitates, he tells her that it's "strictly business." She agrees to go.

The next day, the S.S. *Venture* sets off for the South Pacific. First Mate Driscoll is initially disgruntled that a woman is on board, but he eventually falls in love with Ann, and she with him.

When they reach a mysterious, uncharted island called Skull Island, Denham, Ann, Jack, and a number of crewmembers disembark. The natives are having a ceremony of some sort, near a huge wall. The wall was built very long ago, apparently, to protect the islanders from some terrifying creature. Soon, the crew learns that this powerful being is called Kong. Denham has every intention of capturing this creature on film.

When the natives notice the interlopers, the chief is fascinated by Ann. He proposes a trade: Six of his women for Ann. The discussion is interrupted by the earthshaking arrival of King Kong, a huge, apelike being. In the melee of people running for their lives, Kong scoops Ann up and carries her off into the jungle.

Denham, Jack, and the rest of the crew follow, encountering a spectacular landscape of prehistoric jungles, swamps, and dinosaurs. They pursue Kong and try repeatedly to free Ann, but Kong is too strong. During their battles with him, a dozen men die. It becomes clear that Kong will do anything to keep Ann.

Eventually, Jack foils Kong and escapes with Ann. Kong comes pounding back to the village in pursuit, only to be felled by Denham's gas bombs.

Somehow Denham manages to bring King Kong to New York, and he reveals this "Eighth Wonder of the World" at a gala theater presentation. The audience is astounded at the sight of the enormous creature, chained to a huge platform. Denham introduces Ann and Jack—now engaged—to the audience, and he says of King Kong and Ann: "There the Beast. And here the Beauty."

Denham invites the press on stage, but the flashing bulbs of the photographers, along with the sight of Ann, drives Kong into a frenzy. He breaks free and charges out of the theater, where he creates havoc in New York. Eventually, in the window of a skyscraper, he finds the object of his

The models of King Kong were only 18 inches high, but on film Kong appeared huge and menacing.
▼

desire: Ann. He pulls her through the window and eventually makes his way up to the spire on the top of the Empire State Building, with the young woman clutched firmly in his fist.

Four navy biplanes are sent to do away with Kong. They shoot at him relentlessly, with their machine guns mounted fore and aft. He swats at them like flies, but eventually succumbs to their bullets. He gently strokes Ann one last time, then tumbles off the building. Seconds later, Jack scrambles to the top of the spire and rescues Ann.

Far below, the crowds gather around Kong's body. A policeman says, "Well, Denham, the airplanes got him." Denham shakes his head and corrects him: "Oh, no. It wasn't the airplanes. It was Beauty who killed the Beast."

Decades after *King Kong* was made, the film's technical innovations still dazzle. Even in the digital age, the special effects (by Willis O'Brien) impress. And the tale still retains its ability to create sympathy for the Beast who died for his love of Beauty.

See Horror film; Special-effects film

GRACE KELLY

The filmography of actress Grace Kelly is short but impressive. Born into a wealthy and socially prominent Philadelphia, Pennsylvania, family on November 12, 1928 (some sources say 1929), Kelly made quite a splash in Hollywood before retiring from the movies in 1956 to marry Prince Rainier III of Monaco, a tiny European principality.

Kelly was educated at Raven Hall Academy and the Stevens School in Philadelphia. She then studied acting at the Academy of Dramatic Arts in New York City. The classically beautiful blonde with the regal bearing was offered modeling jobs and started appearing in television commercials for cigarettes. Between that exposure and her occasional stage work, particularly on Broadway in 1949 in the play *The Father,* Kelly drew notice in Hollywood. In 1951 she appeared in the film *Fourteen Hours.*

Kelly's first starring role came in only her second film, as the prim but ultimately gutsy Quaker wife of a sheriff (played by Gary Cooper) in *High Noon* (1952). In her next role, in *Mogambo* (1953), Kelly did an about-face and played an adulteress. It won her an Academy Award nomination for Best Actress.

In 1954 Kelly starred in four films: *Dial M for Murder, Rear Window, Green Fire,* and *The Country Girl.* She won the Best Actress Oscar for the latter film. She turned in other memorable performances in *To Catch a Thief* (1955) and *High Society* (1956).

When Kelly married Prince Rainier, her fans' enthusiasm for the fairy-tale aspects of her wedding was dampened by her decision to retire from filmmaking. Kelly and Rainier had three children, but reportedly their marriage was not always happy. In 1982 the world was shocked and saddened when Princess Grace died in a car accident on a narrow, winding road in Monaco—ironically, it was reportedly the same road that provided a stunning backdrop for the elegant young actress in *To Catch a Thief.*

See Cooper, Gary; High Noon; *Hitchcock, Alfred;* Rear Window; *Stewart, James*

Actress Grace Kelly's regal bearing became reality when she married Prince Rainier III of Monaco in 1956.

◀

KUBRICK, STANLEY

American filmmaker Stanley Kubrick was born in the Bronx, New York, on July 26, 1928. Though not prolific in his work, he is considered one of the most imaginative and talented filmmakers of the twentieth century. Kubrick also had a reputation as a recluse and eccentric because of his desire for privacy and avoidance of the Hollywood limelight.

Intelligent but a poor student, Kubrick was sent by his father to Pasadena, California, in 1941 to stay with an uncle and attend school in a different environment. The move did little to improve his attitude toward school, though, and Kubrick returned to the Bronx in 1941. In an effort to find something that might interest his son, Kubrick's father introduced him to chess. Kubrick quickly developed a love for the game and became a skilled player. He also became passionate about photography after his father gave him a camera for his thirteenth birthday. Kubrick often wandered around New York for hours taking photos.

While still in high school, Kubrick began selling photos to magazines, including *Look*. He became friendly with many of the staff photographers for that magazine, and landed a job there as an apprentice photographer during his last year of high school. Over the next few years, Kubrick was given numerous assignments for *Look*, and the work took him all over the United States. His travels stimulated a hunger for knowledge, and he began courses at Columbia University. At the same time he became enamored with the movies, and spent much of his free time watching films.

In 1950 Kubrick and a friend, Alexander Singer, decided to make a movie of their own. They used their meager life savings to finance a sixteen-minute documentary called *Day of the Fight*, about boxer Walter Cartier. The film, which Kubrick directed, filmed, and edited, was purchased by RKO and played at a theater in New York, earning a small profit for Kubrick. This film was followed by two other low-budget documentaries—*Flying Padre* (1951) and *The Seafarers* (1952).

Another low-budget film, *Fear and Desire* (1953), was Kubrick's first full-length feature. Despite mixed reviews from the critics, Kubrick was singled out for his efforts. It was his next two films, however, that began to establish Kubrick's reputation as a talented director. *Killer's Kiss*, a low-budget feature released in 1955, told the story of an over-the-hill boxer who falls in love with the girlfriend of a gangster. Shot on location at a boxing arena in New Jersey, the film combined gritty realism with symbolic film imagery. *The Killing*, a story about robbery and murder at a race track, was released in 1956. The film's documentary-like realism, fresh approach, and attention to detail won the applause of critics as well as the attention of Dore Shary, the head of production for MGM studios in Hollywood.

notable & quotable

"Kubrick really made the same movie over and over again—vivid, brilliant, emotionally unforgiving, imagistically unforgettable variations on the theme . . . man, his illusions of order stripped away, is left to fend with the sometimes deadly, always devastating consequences of that loss."

Richard Schickel, critic, from "All Eyes on Them," by Richard Schickel, Time, *July 5, 1999*

KUBRICK, STANLEY

Director Stanley Kubrick made his last film, Eyes Wide Shut, *a sexual thriller starring husband and wife Tom Cruise and Nicole Kidman, in almost total secrecy.*

MGM offered Kubrick and James Harris, who had produced *The Killing*, a chance to undertake a project for the studio. Kubrick decided to make a film adaptation of *Paths of Glory*, a powerful antiwar novel by Humphrey Cobb. Unfortunately, MGM and every other major studio rejected the idea until actor Kirk Douglas agreed to star in it. Released in 1957, *Paths of Glory* proved to be Kubrick's first film classic, and many critics regard it as one of the finest films about war ever made. The movie is about French generals in World War I who order a costly attack for their own personal gain and then execute three soldiers for cowardice.

In 1959 Kirk Douglas offered Kubrick the job of directing a historical epic about a slave rebellion in ancient Rome. The film, *Spartacus*, was Kubrick's first box-office hit. Many critics commended him for his camera work, skill in directing thousands of extras, and film editing. Behind the

scenes, however, some of the crew of the movie complained about Kubrick's directorial style.

At about this time Kubrick became disenchanted with Hollywood and decided to move permanently to England. He remained there for the rest of his life and filmed all his movies there or in Europe. The first movie he made in England was *Lolita*, a story about a middle-aged professor obsessed with a young girl. Based on the highly controversial novel by Vladimir Nabokov, the movie was released in 1962.

Kubrick's next project was a comic satire about technology and the future called *Dr. Strangelove, or: How I Learned to Stop Worrying and Love the Bomb*. Starring the popular English actor Peter Sellers, the movie became both a critical and commercial success after it was released in 1964. It garnered Kubrick Academy Award nominations as coauthor, director, and producer, and its success gave him the financial and artistic freedom to pursue only those projects he most desired.

Following the success of *Dr. Strangelove*, Kubrick teamed up with noted science-fiction writer Arthur C. Clark to create *2001: A Space Odyssey* (1968). The most technically advanced film of the decade, it presents a view of man controlled by technology. The movie not only set the standard for future science-fiction films, it also changed people's views about time and space. Lauded by the critics, and beloved by film buffs, the movie is considered by many to be one of the greatest films ever made as well as a landmark in the history of the cinema. The movie *2001* also earned Kubrick his only Academy Award, for Best Visual Effects.

Kubrick's next project was *A Clockwork Orange* (1971), a highly controversial film about the future based on a novel by Anthony Burgess. The film's graphic portrayals of youthful violence generated a great deal of outrage in Britain, and Kubrick withdrew the film from theaters there. Despite an initial X rating in the United States, the film did well and earned Kubrick three Oscar nominations as writer, director, and producer.

After the controversy over *A Clockwork Orange*, Kubrick changed direction and created *Barry Lyndon*, an eighteenth-century historical piece based on a novel by English author William Makepeace Thackeray. Once again, Kubrick's work gained several Oscar nominations, although the film did poorly at the box office. By this time, Kubrick's demands for perfection from cast and crew had become legendary. He would often make actors perform dozens of takes and retakes without any break. He also paid meticulous attention to every detail of the filmmaking process.

Kubrick's next film, *The Shining*, which opened in 1980, received poor reviews but did well at the box office. Based on a novel by best-selling author Stephen King, the horror movie starred Jack Nicholson. *Full Metal Jacket*, a movie about the Vietnam War, became both a critical and box office success when it opened in theaters in 1987.

Kubrick had always taken his time in developing projects, but now his work almost ground to a halt. In the early 1990s he began developing another science fiction project called AI (Artificial Intelligence), but the technical requirements of the movie were so complex and advanced that by 1995 the project was put on hold. In the meantime, Kubrick began planning another project, a film called *Eyes Wide Shut,* which would star husband-and-wife team Tom Cruise and Nicole Kidman. Shooting on the film began in late 1996 under intense secrecy and took fifteen months to complete, making it the longest shoot in modern film history. *Eyes Wide Shut* was scheduled to open in the summer of 1999 but Kubrick died of a heart attack on March 7, 1999, before he could see this last movie brought to the screen.

See Clockwork Orange, A; *Cruise, Tom;* Dr. Strangelove; *Nicholson, Jack;* 2001: A Space Odyssey

L

LAWRENCE OF ARABIA

Director David Lean's *Lawrence of Arabia* (1962) is widely regarded as one of the great epics of the cinema, a gripping story of stunning visual sweep based on a modern literary classic, *The Seven Pillars of Wisdom,* in which T. E. Lawrence recounts his evolution from a British colonial functionary to a political-spiritual visionary who helped to galvanize the Arab world into modern political self-consciousness. The film's power was reflected at the Oscar ceremony, where it won awards for Best Film, Best Director, Best Original Score, Best Color Cinematography, Best Art Direction, Best Sound, and Best Editing.

The film begins with T. E. Lawrence's (Peter O'Toole) fatal motorcycle crash in 1935. The rest of the film's four hours reel forward from a flashback that begins with Lawrence's early service to the British empire in Cairo, where he is a cartographer in British headquarters during World War I. He eagerly accepts an assignment from the British Arab Bureau to transfer to Constantinople to investigate the causes and strength of the Arab revolt there. Lawrence's character begins emerging as a vacillating combination of keen intelligence, charisma, and barely concealed madness soon after he receives permission to go into Arabia in search of Prince Feisel (Alec Guinness) and the bedouins. Facets of all these qualities, and more, flash from O'Toole's performance, showing Lawrence's commitment to the dream of uniting the fractured bedouin tribesmen.

"So long as the Arabs fight tribe against tribe, so long they will be a little people, a silly people—greedy, barbarous and cruel."

Peter O'Toole as T. E. Lawrence in *Lawrence of Arabia* (1962)

Upon his arrival in Arabia the suddenly energized Lawrence undertakes the task of forging a united front among the competing Arab tribes who are revolting against the Turks. Facing fearful logistical and political obstacles, he persuades Prince Feisal to furnish a contingent of soldiers. Lawrence and Sharif Ali ibn El Kharish (Omar Sharif) lead the soldiers across the Nefud Desert, joining up with the army of Auda Abu Tayi (Anthony Quinn) to seize the port of Aqaba from the more numerous but less disciplined Turks. On the road to this victory, however, Lawrence confronts an ethical dilemma: one of the men has acted in a way that might incite division among the tribes, and Lawrence knows that killing him will help to ensure

JESSICA LANGE

Jessica Lange was born on April 20, 1949, in Cloquet, Minnesota, one of four children born to Al Lange, a traveling salesman and teacher, and Dorothy (Dodie) Lange. The family moved frequently during Jessica's early years. After high school, she attended the University of Minnesota for a couple of years and then studied mime in Paris, France. There she also danced in the chorus at the Opéra Comique.

Lange found modeling work in New York upon her return to the United States, and she snagged the starring female role in the Dino De Laurentiis version of *King Kong* (1976). It was a campy movie, but it served to get her noticed. She next performed in *All That Jazz* (1979), the semiautobiographical story of the difficult choreographer/director Bob Fosse, with whom she had been romantically involved. In 1980 Lange played a role in *How to Beat the High Cost of Living,* and the following year she appeared opposite Jack Nicholson in a steamy remake of *The Postman Always Rings Twice.*

Lange had a banner year in 1982, with the release of *Frances,* the biography of the tragic actress Frances Farmer, and *Tootsie*, a comedy about an actor who pretends to be a woman in order to win a soap-opera role. *Frances* won Lange an Academy Award nomination for Best Actress, but she won the Best Supporting Actress Oscar for *Tootsie,* the film that, perhaps more than any other, showcased her fresh, sensual beauty. That was the first year since 1942 that an actress had been nominated for two Oscars in the same year.

In subsequent years Lange has concentrated more on her family life—including three children (a daughter with ballet star Mikhail Baryshnikov, and a son and daughter with actor/playwright/director Sam Shepard) than on acting. She has appeared in a film every year or two, however, including *Crimes of the Heart* (1986), *Music Box (*1989), *Cape Fear* (1991), *Blue Sky* (1994), *Rob Roy* (1995), and *A Thousand Acres* (1997). Lange was awarded the Best Actress Oscar for her portrayal of an emotionally unbalanced wife and mother in *Blue Sky.*

See Hoffman, Dustin; Nicholson, Jack; Tootsie

unity and thus victory. After executing the man, Lawrence experiences not the expected guilt but rather an odd exhilaration in the act of killing.

Lawrence's successes have earned him a glowing reputation among his superiors in Cairo, where General Allenby (Jack Hawkins) persuades Lawrence to capitalize on the Arabs' trust in him by pursuing further military campaigns in the desert. Lawrence's experiences force him to question his own actions and motives: he knows that war is progressively corrupting him and that he has failed to gauge how much his own dreams and plans involve bloodshed. Most frightening of all, as he confesses to General Allenby, he has come to enjoy the bloodshed.

Now amply provisioned with men and materiel, Lawrence begins a prolonged guerrilla campaign, during which he emerges as a legendary figure to both his fighting men and to a wider public, which learns of his exploits through the firsthand accounts of an American reporter, Jackson Bentley (Arthur Kennedy), who is accompanying Lawrence through the desert. Here, at the midpoint in the film, the intense young hero turns into a cynical and vainglorious poseur. Bentley's appearance underlines the shift in focus between the film's two major parts. Lawrence is by now a public figure, a "hero" created by Bentley; ironically, his fame seems to have diminished his responsibilities. Now more of a sideshow than anything else, he and his guerrilla bands derail and loot Turkish trains. A hero in the eyes of the Arabs, Lawrence appears vain and childish to the movie audience.

Lawrence's renown does not render him invincible, however, and the Turks eventually capture him and arrest him. During his imprisonment he

Stunning, sweeping visuals characterized director David Lean's Lawrence of Arabia, *regarded as one of the great epics of cinema.* ▼

Year of the Big Picture: Four of 1963's top five box office hits were *Cleopatra*, *The Longest Day*, *Lawrence of Arabia*, and *How the West Was Won*.

is subjected to a variety of tortures, including sexual abuse, at the hands of a sadistic Turkish bey (José Ferrer).

After his release, Lawrence returns to Cairo, where General Allenby is waiting with a new assignment: Lawrence ("El Aurens" to the Arabs) is to lead an attack on Damascus. Lawrence undertakes the task, and after successfully marching into Damascus, he endeavors to forge unity among the victorious factions in the Arab council. But this time he is unsuccessful, and the council breaks up in discord. As General Allenby and Prince Feisal struggle to unify the bickering Arabs, Lawrence retreats to England, feeling a failure in the wake of British and French plans to divide Arabia between them.

Lawrence's relationship with the Arabs epitomizes imperialism. Idealist or not, Lawrence wishes to dominate, to impose his will, his vision, his understanding of what is good for them on the Arabs whose life he shares and whose aspirations he claims to value.

Having no identity of his own (he is, as he explains to all, a bastard), he is willingly adopted—literally—by his Arab friends. But identities cannot be acquired so easily; he is not, after all, an Arab, and the more he tries to be one, the more emphatic his alienation becomes. Having failed in his paradoxical goal to lead the Arabs to unity and independence—but an independence inspired by a non-Arab leader—Lawrence can now only retreat from heroism, put aside his Arab dress, and return to England, where he meets the absurd, perhaps not entirely accidental death with which the film began.

See Guinness, Alec; Lean, David; Roeg, Nicolas

LEAN, DAVID

David Lean was born in Croydon, England, on March 25, 1908, the youngest of two sons of Francis William le Blount Lean, a chartered accountant in a London firm, and Helena Annie (Tangye) Lean.

David Lean began his film career at the age of nineteen as a bottom-rung apprentice for the Gaumont-British company at London's Gainsborough Studios. The son of strict Quakers, Lean had been encouraged by his father to study accounting, but he soon discovered his interests lay elsewhere, and spent most of his spare time at the movies. "I was fascinated by films," he would later recall, "but it took me a long time to realize that one could actually work in them." One is less surprised by Lean's youthful naiveté than by his having had the courage to give up a secure career in accounting for something as chancy as the British film industry. His arrival

at Gainsborough in 1927 coincided with one of the worst of the periodic crises that plagued British films. The year 1926 had been disastrous: the amount of screen time devoted to British films in British cinemas, which had been steadily shrinking since the end of World War I, had dwindled to 5 percent. Lean was presumably unaware of or undeterred by the bleak prospects ahead.

At Gainsborough, Lean underwent a varied apprenticeship. Initially attached to a unit filming Maurice Elvey's *Quinneys* (1927), his job was to hold up the number board in front of the camera at the beginning of each take. Subsequently, he worked as a camera assistant and as a third assistant director, the latter job consisting almost entirely of carrying tea and calling actors onto the set. However, his interests soon focused on the editing process. He was made a full-fledged editor while working on newsreels and by 1930 he had been promoted to chief editor of Gaumont British News. Over the next several years, Lean performed the same function for both British Movietone News and Paramount British News.

Director David Lean, shown here attempting a shot for 1970's Ryan's Daughter, *is as well known for his all-male adventures like* The Bridge on the River Kwai *(1957) as he is for literary adaptations and "women's films."*

▼

Lean did not continue long with newsreels. In 1934, Paramount moved him over to its feature film division. It was here that he met Merrill White, an American who had been chief cutter for Ernst Lubitsch. "I learned all about [editing] from Merrill White," Lean would claim many years later. After editing *Escape Me Never* (1935), *As You Like It* (1936), and *Dreaming Lips* (1937), Lean had become Britain's best known and highest paid editor.

Lean's opportunity to move from film editing to directing came from Noël Coward. When Coward was asked to direct his first movie, *In Which We Serve* (1942), he hired Lean as codirector. The choice of Lean, himself a beginner behind the camera, was perfect from Coward's point of view. He was able to take advantage of an experienced technician without having to accommodate the ego of an established filmmaker. Coward turned out to be so impressed with Lean's work that he gave Lean permission to direct any of his plays.

In 1944 Lean formed Cineguild, an independent production company, with Ronald Neame, Noel Coward, and Anthony Havelock-Allan. The company's first production, *This Happy Breed* (1944) adapted from Coward's play, was Lean's directorial debut. Lean then followed with Coward's comedy *Blithe Spirit* (1945), which received an Oscar for its special photographic effects, and *Brief Encounter* in 1945 brought him his first Oscar nomination as Best Director.

notable & quotable

"Lean was a romantic about himself, and these rewards may have persuaded him that he was too grand for small things. It was the Selznick syndrome."

David Thomson, author, 1994

In 1946 Lean turned to Charles Dickens's *Great Expectations* for inspiration. Lean's mastery behind the camera and Dickens's superb storytelling brought the film three Academy Award nominations. Lean then continued his success with Dickens in a 1948 adaptation of *Oliver Twist*.

The opening of *Oliver Twist* in the United States was delayed for several years because some argued that the characterization of Fagin was anti-Semitic. When it was finally released in 1951 eleven minutes had been edited out. It was not until 1982 that the original movie was made available in the United States.

The Cineguild production company, with Lean as director, made two more films *The Passionate Friends* (1948) and *Madeleine* (1950) before dissolving.

In 1950 Lean joined Alexander Korda's London Films and directed *The Sound Barrier* in 1952. The film was released in the United States as *Breaking the Sound Barrier*. In 1954, Lean directed *Hobson's Choice,* and in 1955 filmed *Summertime* (*Summer Madness* in its British release), his third and last film for London Films. *Summertime* earned both David Lean and Katharine Hepburn Academy Award nominations.

A year after completing *Summertime*, Lean began work on *The Bridge on the River Kwai* (1957). The movie, starring Alec Guinness and William Holden, was filmed on location in Ceylon (Sri Lanka). It was awarded six Oscars, including Best Director for Lean, Best Actor for Guinness, and Best Picture. *The Bridge on the River Kwai* introduced Lean to the world of extravagant and high-cost filmmaking.

His next film, *Lawrence of Arabia* (1962), was equally ambitious. The story of World War I hero T. E. Lawrence was based on Lawrence's autobiography, *The Seven Pillars of Wisdom*. Lean hired two little-known actors to star in the film, Peter O'Toole and an Egyptian actor named Omar Sharif. Lean took three years to produce the film shooting on location in Jordan and Spain. When it opened in 1962, its instant success earned it seven Academy Awards, including Best Director and Best Picture.

With two monumental successes to his credit, Lean was considered one of the most successful box office directors of the time. With his reputation at an all time high, Lean then went on to make another epic film, *Doctor Zhivago*. When it opened in 1965, critics were not nearly as charmed. It was only through an additional million dollars in promotion funding that the film became an eventual box office hit. While the movie did receive five Oscars, none were in the top categories.

Doctor Zhivago was the second-biggest seller of the 1960s, with $60.9 million in rentals, after *The Sound of Music*, at $79.9 million.

Lean's next film, *Ryan's Daughter* (1970), turned out to be a $13 million, 206-minute love story that critics hated. With *Ryan's Daughter*, Lean's magic touch and his confidence seemed to disappear. It would another fourteen years before he returned to directing.

When he did return with *A Passage to India* in 1984 his reputation as an epic filmmaker was reestablished. The film, starring Judy Davis, Alec Guinness, and Dame Peggy Ashcroft, was adored by the public and critics alike. After its release the film was nominated for eight Oscars, including Lean's seventh for Best Director and Best Picture. Besides his Academy Award honors, David Lean was also knighted in 1984.

A quick glance over Lean's filmography suggests a director with no particular center of interest or coherent vision. Literary adaptations like *Great Expectations* and *Oliver Twist* rub elbows with so-called women's films like *Brief Encounter* and *Summertime* and with all-male adventures like *The Bridge on the River Kwai* and *Lawrence of Arabia*. A close look at the films themselves, however, reveals unsuspected patterns. Stylistic and thematic motifs recur with surprising frequency among quite unrelated genres. Most of Lean's films, in fact, fall into two large categories: adventure and romance. The adventure films include *In Which We Serve*, *The Sound Barrier*, *The Bridge on the River Kwai*, and *Lawrence of Arabia*. Among the romances are *Brief Encounter*, *Madeleine*, *The Passionate Friends*, *Summer Madness*, *Doctor Zhivago*, and *Ryan's Daughter*. The first group concentrates on the world of men, and the second group on the world, or at least the consciousness, of women. However, even this distinction turns out to be superficial. Nearly all of his films have at their center a passionate intelligence: in Lean's hands, adventure and romance are very much the same thing.

David Lean died in London on April 16, 1991.

See Bridge on the River Kwai, The; Doctor Zhivago; *Editor; Guinness, Alec;* Lawrence of Arabia; *Roeg, Nicolas*

In 1936 Margaret Mitchell sold the movie and television rights to *Gone with the Wind* to David O. Selznick for $50,000—$20,000 more than Vivien Leigh was paid to play Scarlett O'Hara.

VIVIEN LEIGH

Vivien Leigh was born in Darjeeling, India, on November 5, 1913, and named Vivian Mary Hartley. Her parents were British—her father, serving in the military, was stationed in India. The young beauty who would conquer the British stage and American screen was educated in convents in Britain and on the European continent and studied at the Royal Academy of Dramatic Arts in London, England.

Leigh made her first appearance in a film in 1934—a British effort entitled *Things Are Looking Up.* In 1935 she debuted on the stage in London and acted in several other movies: *The Village Squire, Gentleman's Agreement,* and *Look Up and Laugh.* Over the next few years she would perform in numerous films, including *Dark Journey* (1937), *A Yank at Oxford* (1938), and *21 Days/21 Days Together* (released in 1939).

In *Fire Over England* (1937), Leigh played opposite Laurence Olivier, a much-respected British actor. Leigh and Olivier, though both married (she to Herbert Leigh Holman, a businessman), began a love affair. The romance was no secret to anyone; indeed, it was reported in the press. The two eventually obtained divorces from their spouses and married in 1940.

When Leigh accompanied Olivier to Hollywood, she was introduced to the producer of a new film in production, *Gone with the Wind.* The lead part, of calculating southern belle Scarlett O'Hara, had not yet been cast, though hundreds of actresses had been auditioned. Leigh auditioned for the plum part and won it—and the Best Actress Oscar for 1939.

In subsequent years Leigh's most memorable work was in *That Hamilton Woman/Lady Hamilton* (1941), *A Streetcar Named Desire* (1948), *The Roman Spring of Mrs. Stone* (1961), and *Ship of Fools* (1965). She won a second Best Actress Oscar for her performance in *Streetcar*.

In 1960, after many tempestuous years together, Leigh and Olivier divorced, due at least in part to Leigh's battles with mental illness and tuberculosis. Her illnesses also got in the way of her professional life. Leigh died in 1967, reportedly of complications from tuberculosis.

See Brando, Marlon; Gable, Clark; Gone with the Wind; *Olivier, Laurence;* Streetcar Named Desire, A

LIGHTING

Lighting refers to the control of light in a motion picture for purposes of exposure and artistic expression. Motion-picture light may come from either available-light sources or from artificially produced sources.

Light coming from an already existing source of illumination, as opposed to that provided by the filmmaker through portable or studio lighting instruments, is referred to as *available light.* Until interior studios and artificial lighting instruments were developed, dramatic films were photographed outdoors, with interiors shot in boxlike settings built with an open front and no roof. The available light provided sufficient illumination for satisfactory exposures, but little creative use was made of the light. For this reason the dramatic and documentary films made in the first decade or so of motion-picture history have a flat, bland look. In flat lighting the light is evenly washed across the scene without artistic relief, and the light has not been controlled to achieve a sense of depth by aiding in the separating of areas or actors.

To provide depth and visual dimension through lighting in a scene, film artists control the quality, amount, and placement (angle) of light. Light as a quality may be described as soft light or hard light. Soft light is an evenly diffused, unfocused light that washes softly over a scene. Hard light is a focused, highly directed light that will produce intense shadows as it strikes objects or characters in a scene.

Set Light

The combination of controlled hard and soft light in a lighting scheme allows the filmmaker to achieve satisfactory illumination for exposure while adding artistic shadings to the setting. Architectural detail in the setting is achieved by throwing a hard light at a 90-degree angle across the set. The hard light produces shadows at points where there is varied texture and structural shape on the set wall. Lighting technicians frequently begin with this setting light as the first step in arranging light to create the desired atmosphere for a scene. The moody, gothic quality of the Xanadu scenes in *Citizen Kane* (1941) is in large part attributable to Gregg Toland's artful use of setting light.

"How can you act and think about the key light at the same time?"

Conrad Hall, cinematographer, 1971, in reference to actresses who demanded that they be lit a certain way

Actor Light

The characters in a scene may also be lighted for dimensional interest and for artistic shading. The general procedure in actor lighting with artificial instruments is to provide the character with a key light, a back light, and, depending on desired mood, additional fill light for purposes of general illumination. The key light, generally a hard light, is the light that indicates the principal source and angle of illumination. It is the most intense light in the scene. If a character reads by a table lamp, and that is the major source of illumination, the lamp becomes what is referred to as the "ostensible" source of illumination, or the "apparent" source of light. Although the light in the scene might be further controlled or added to by technicians, the aesthetic guide for light quality and light angle becomes the table lamp. The *key light* is focused on the actor to match the throw of light from the lamp. A *back light*, which may have no apparent source of illumination, is then added. This light falls on the head and shoulders of the character. It comes from the back, usually at a 45-degree angle, and serves to add dimension to the scene by separating the actor from the background. A *fill light,* usually a softer light than key, back, or setting light, may then be used to add some general illumination to the scene and to reduce the harsh shadows produced by the hard light sources.

High-Key, Low-Key Lighting

High-key and low-key describe the quality of illumination in motion-picture lighting schemes. When a scene has a bright general illumination, the lighting is referred to as *high-key lighting.* This is a lighting scheme designed so that illumination of the scene has a bright, general quality. *Low-key lighting* has the opposite quality. There is less general illumination in the scene, heavier shadows, and a more atmospheric quality.

By tradition, high-key lighting is employed for comedies, musicals, and standard dramatic situations where dialogue and action are the critical concerns of the scene or film. Low-key lighting is used to add atmosphere to dramas and suspense stories where visual underscoring of mood is a critical consideration. Whether high key or low key, the lighting sets the dramatic mood of the scene.

See Cinematographer; Citizen Kane; *DeMille, Cecil B.; Location picture; Sound; Studio picture*

LLOYD, HAROLD

Harold Lloyd was not only the most popular comedian of the 1920s but, by the close of the silent era, the biggest box-office draw in motion pictures. He far outgrossed Buster Keaton (whose best films sometimes lost money) and surpassed even Chaplin over the long run, since there was always at least one new Lloyd feature each year. Richard Schickel reminds us that when *Variety* ranked the twenty wealthiest members of the entertainment industry in 1927, Lloyd was the only performer on the list. While his decline in popularity was rapid when the industry converted to sound, it seems strange that Lloyd was so quickly consigned to oblivion in the classic film histories.

In his introduction to the 1971 reissue of Lloyd's 1928 autobiography, Museum of Modern Art curator Richard Griffith suggested an explanation for the dearth of interest: "The lack of a definitive late book on Lloyd reflects the disesteem in which he has traditionally been held by the movie highbrows. They do not like his optimism" (*An American Comedy,* p. v).

Griffith wrote this just a few years too soon. Not only would the film-book explosion of the 1970s and 1980s produce several important studies of Lloyd and his work, but the public mood itself began to change dramatically; eventually, it became difficult to find anyone who would hold Lloyd's prosperity and optimism against him. Lloyd's bespectacled "glass" character was the quintessential achiever in the era of Harding normalcy and Coolidge prosperity. Onscreen, he applied wit, perseverance, and guile in an exhausting effort to better himself and achieve the American dream. Off-screen, Lloyd made it clear that comedy making was a business with him, and in discussing his work with reporters, he concentrated almost exclusively on the mechanics of gag construction. He pioneered "scientific" methods of audience research that included charting gags and plotting viewers' chuckles and titters on elaborate graphs. Using this data to recut and reshape his features, he crafted them into laugh-provoking entertainments of unparalleled efficiency.

Of all the major silent comedians, Lloyd was the only one with no prior reputation as a stage comic. In fact, his theater experience was limited to backwater stock companies, and when he entered films it was not as a featured player but as an extra. He fell in with another extra, Hal Roach, who was about to set himself up as a producer on the strength of a small inheritance. When he began working for Roach in 1915, Lloyd looked around at the other comedians onscreen and saw a collection of clowns in funny costumes and makeups. There were remnants of the ethnic stereotypes of vaudeville days, fat comics and thin comics, an assortment of ill-fitting suits and pants, and a forest of pasted-on moustaches. He stole from the best. Lloyd created the character of "Lonesome Luke," an inverted Chaplin figure. "All his clothes were too large, mine were too small. My shoes were funny, but different; my moustache funny, but different."

But in 1917 Lloyd and Roach dropped Lonesome Luke, substituting a new character whose mannerisms were completely natural and whose costumes were comfortably off the rack. A pair of black horn-rimmed glasses completed the look, and the famous Lloyd "glass character" was born. With the stylized Sennett tradition already fading, the situation comedy based on realistic characters and events took its place. Lloyd's genius was to shape his character in such a way that it seemed to merge with the postwar generation's developing self-image.

The twenties adopted Lloyd as a special icon. In *Safety Last* (1923) his character hopes to rise to the top of the department-store business, a dream that comes true when Harold is forced to climb the outside of the building. The shot of Lloyd dangling from a clock face in this film is the most famous image in silent comedy.

Many suggestions have been offered to explain Lloyd's decline after 1928, from poor material to his own inability to continue playing the same character, eternally youthful and optimistic. What has been overlooked is that Harold Lloyd, like the jaunty boater he often sported, was an ingrained element of twenties culture. Depression-era America turned its back on all that, and blotted out its love affair with artists like Lloyd.

See Chaplin, Charlie; Comedy; Keaton, Buster; Sound

LOCATION SHOOTING (PICTURE)

The shooting of a film or film scenes in a real setting as opposed to the controlled environment of a Hollywood shooting stage or studio back lot is called location shooting. The term came into use after the establishment of the studio system and the arrival of talking pictures had forced film production almost entirely indoors. Better technical control of sound recording and lighting was possible within the studio setting, thus greatly diminishing the outdoor shooting that had dominated early film production. Occasionally, important directors of the 1930s and 1940s would venture off the studio lot for location scenes, for example, John Ford (*Stagecoach,* 1939), Jean Renoir (*Swamp Water,* 1941).

Following World War II, location shooting became increasingly common, spurred by the experiences of filmmakers who had served in the armed forces during the war and by the inspirational work of Italy's neorealists, who broke from the studio altogether. With improved technology and a growth of independent production since the 1950s, the number of films made entirely on location has continued to grow.

See Ford, John; Lighting; Sound; Stagecoach; *Studio picture*

LOSEY, JOSEPH

Joseph Losey was one of the finest American directors, but he never made a major film in America. Blacklisted during the political witch-hunts of early 1950s McCarthyism, Losey moved to London and in time created a body of serious work that most likely would never have emerged, ironically, within the constraints of the Hollywood studio system from which he was driven.

Losey was born to a wealthy family in the American heartland, in La Crosse, Wisconsin, in 1909. His snobbish, anti-Semitic Wasp family provided a model against which Losey rebelled. "When my father died," Losey said, "I decided not to have anything to do with my family." He went to Dartmouth instead of Princeton, which was his father's alma mater, and he shied away from the politics that so entrenched his family.

During the Depression, separating himself politically and economically from his family, Losey came "in direct contact with political life. I had to work. I met *engagé* people, who told me: 'Do political cabaret, workers' theater. It doesn't matter that you are an Anglican snob from Dartmouth. If you do the theater you will become "engaged" and enter the Communist Party.'" Though it took him many years to realize it, Losey had replaced one kind of tyranny with another. His belief in radical politics, like his

Summoned by the House Un-American Activities Committee in the early 1950s on suspicion of communist leanings, Joseph Losey moved to London and made nearly all of his major films in Europe.

upbringing in a severe Wasp family, was something he had to outgrow in order to claim his independence.

Losey graduated form Dartmouth in 1929. In 1930, after he received an M.A. in English literature from Harvard, he began writing theater and book reviews for the *New York Times, Theater Arts Monthly,* and the *Saturday Review of Literature.* In 1931 he was the stage manager of Charles Laughton's American production of *Payment Deferred.* He staged the first variety shows at Radio City Music Hall in 1932. A year later he directed a problem drama on Broadway called *Little Ol' Boy* (which made Burgess Meredith a star) about a reformatory school. Shortly after, he directed a political play by Sinclair Lewis called *Jayhawker.* The following year Losey went to Moscow, where he attended film classes conducted by Eisenstein and staged a well-received English-language production of Clifford Odets's *Waiting for Lefty.*

In 1936 Losey was hired by the Federal Theater to direct several entries in the Living Newspaper series. As the most radical and explicitly political branch of the project, the Living Newspapers were later investigated by the House Un-American Activities Committee. Losey's association with the Living Newspaper productions was one of the reasons, a decade later, as his career in Hollywood was taking off, that he was considered politically suspect.

Because his acclaimed work for the Living Newspaper had stamped him as a political activist as well as an antirealist, Losey was chosen to direct the American premiere of German playwright Bertolt Brecht's *Galileo* in 1947, in a production starring Charles Laughton. *Galileo* was first produced at the Coronet Theater in Los Angeles in the summer of 1947 and then in New York the following December. In the interim, Brecht was investigated by the House Un-American Activities Committee. Clearly Losey's career in America was on a collision course with the gathering forces of reaction, but before he was hounded out of America, he was able to direct five feature films between 1948 and 1951.

Galileo's sold-out limited engagement in New York attracted the attention of Dore Schary, then head of production at RKO, who hired Losey to direct a political fable called *The Boy with the Green Hair.* Losey's subsequent brief Hollywood career was confined to low-budget pictures at a time when they had real vitality, when formulaic material was embellished with personal style, when directors and screenwriters used well-worn movie stories to make insinuating or subversive statements about the escalating hysteria of contemporary politics. Thus, although not overtly political, all of Losey's films of this period—*The Boy with the Green Hair* (1948); *The Lawless* (1949); *The Prowler* (1950); and *M* (a remake of the Fritz Lang classic,

1950)—critically evoked the increasingly menacing tone of America's political culture, which was soon to scuttle Losey's career in Hollywood.

When Losey left Hollywood hurriedly in 1951, before he had completed postproduction work on *The Big Night,* he did not know that he would never return. He had left in order to do a film in Italy with Paul Muni. Subpoenaed at the time to appear before the House Un-American Activities Committee, he decided to remain in London, a decision that ensured his blacklisting in the American film industry. Thus stigmatized, at first Losey was unable to get any assignments in England at all. When he finally did secure work, he was not allowed to sign his own name to his first two English films, *The Sleeping Tiger* (1954) and *Finger of Guilt* (1956), because fear of the blacklist had penetrated the British film studios. Not until 1956, with *Time Without Pity,* would English producers permit him to place his own name on the credits.

Long saddled with routine scripts in England, in 1962, with *Eve,* Losey finally undertook a project with full enthusiasm, because the story and characters had a personal significance to him. But it wasn't until the following year, with Harold Pinter's exquisite screenplay for *The Servant,* that he was given material that did not have to be extensively remodeled before Losey felt prepared to begin filming. The collaboration was a fruitful one for both men. In mounting Pinter's dark, claustrophobic study of masochism and repressed sexuality, Losey was obliged to "correct" his early social didacticism with a large dose of Pinter's unremitting introspection and gnawing ambiguity. From Pinter Losey took his feeling for mystery and shading, and his work became noticeably more subtle thereafter.

His two subsequent collaborations with Pinter are widely regarded as his best efforts in the ensuing years: *The Accident* (1967) and *The Go-Between* (1971). In his other features through the mid-1970s—*King and Country* (1964); *Modesty Blaise* (1966); *Boom* (1968); *Secret Ceremony* (1968); *Figures in a Landscape* (1970); *The Assassination of Trotsky* (1972); *A Doll's House* (1973); *Galileo* (1973); and *The Romantic Englishwoman* (1975)—he remained the fastidious auteur whose cerebral approach to his subjects engaged the respect of critics and audiences but never their unalloyed enthusiasm.

Losey moved to France in 1976, where he made four films, all in French: *Mr. Klein* (1977), *Roads to the South* (1978), *Don Giovanni* (1979), and *The Trout* (1982). In the early 1980s, two projects that would have brought him back to America fell through at the last minute. Losey died on June 22, 1984, in London. His final film, *Steaming,* was released in 1985.

See Censorship; Kazan, Elia

LUBITSCH, ERNST

Before 1914 America had been the world's most important film market, but by the close of World War I it was the most important film producer as well. The French and the Italians were no longer viable as international competitors, but even before the Armistice, a potential new rival had arisen. Backed by the Alfred Hugenberg fortune and masterminded by impresario Paul Davidson, the German film industry had pulled itself out of the cultural wreckage that hung over Berlin in 1918. In a dramatic turnaround, German films were sent off to conquer foreign capitals so recently denied to German troops.

It was not until 1920 that this wave was allowed to break on American shores. But when the presentation of *Madame Dubarry* (renamed *Passion*) at New York's giant Capitol Theatre successfully overcame the firmly entrenched anti-German hysteria among American audiences, the domestic market once more seemed vulnerable to foreign infiltration. This was an intolerable and utterly surprising development for Hollywood. Reporting on the vast crowds being turned away from the theater by extra policemen summoned for the occasion, the *New York Times* marveled that "none of the hostility that has greeted attempts to revive German opera and drama" was still in evidence. The success of *Dubarry* was matched a few months later by that of *Deception (Anne Boleyn)* and one or two others. But not all German films were greeted so warmly. *The Golem* (1920) flopped with American audiences, while *The Cabinet of Dr. Caligari* (1919) inspired picket lines of disgruntled war veterans. Only those films directed by Ernst Lubitsch seemed surefire successes.

Lubitsch's first American employer was Mary Pickford, for whom he directed a Spanish costume romance called *Rosita* (1923). Warmly received by critics but generally ignored by audiences, it was later suppressed by Pickford, who hated the film, hated Lubitsch, and hated the whole experience of working with the man. Pickford had expected to be well served by Europe's greatest director and was unwilling and unable to bend herself to his wishes. She, after all, was producing this picture.

Lubitsch had been trying to get himself to America for years. Now he appeared to have ruined his big opportunity, antagonized one of the world's most powerful stars, and sullied his box-office reputation. But Lubitsch was a survivor. In a dazzling change of pace, he dropped the large historical canvas that had brought him his greatest success since his days with Max Reinhardt and turned to the comedy of manners.

Moving from Pickford to the small Warner Bros. studio, Lubitsch quickly produced a series of films, including *The Marriage Circle* (1924),

Kiss Me Again (1925), and *Lady Windermere's Fan* (1925), which redefined sophisticated American screen comedy. Early efforts in this genre by James Cruze and others were forgotten, and for many critics, DeMille himself was "swept aside" by a man with more style and better taste.

The films were characterized by clever bits of business, soon referred to as "Lubitsch touches," which illuminated character or situation and cast ironic (never sentimental) reflection on the action. Threatened with a palace revolt, Adolphe Menjou in *Forbidden Paradise* (1924) reaches for his hip—and draws out a checkbook to quell the disturbance. In the same film, Pola Negri surreptitiously moves a footstool into position so as to better plant a kiss on handsome Rod La Rocque. That these touches were often associated with aggressive female sexuality only added to their mild titillation.

It should be noted that Lubitsch was not an easy director to work for. He planned out every shot, every gesture, far in advance of shooting, and set a pattern for Alfred Hitchcock in his subjugation of actors.

At the end of the silent period, Lubitsch returned to the historical spectacle. United with Emil Jannings for the first time since their Berlin days, he made *The Patriot,* a tale of Czar Paul, which proved a failure with audiences. But with talkies on the horizon, Lubitsch did not need to change. Sound held no terror, and the microphone only provided opportunities for more Lubitsch touches.

See DeMille, Cecil B.; Hitchcock, Alfred; Murnau, F. W.; Negri, Pola; Pickford, Mary; Vitaphone

LUCAS, GEORGE

George Walton Lucas Jr. was born in Modesto, California, on May 14, 1944. Best known as the writer and director of the *Star Wars* series of movies, Lucas is also a prolific film producer and creative genius who has done much to advance the technology for developing visual special effects for the movies.

Lucas grew up in a typical middle-class family in suburban California. An intelligent but shy youngster, he loved watching cartoons on TV and reading comic books. As a teenager, Lucas became interested in cars, and he spent hours tinkering with old hot rods and cruising the streets of Modesto with friends. These joyriding experiences would later contribute to his early success as a filmmaker. But at the time, his parents worried that their son lacked direction in his life. They tried to encourage him to do better in

L

LUCAS, GEORGE

Director George Lucas provided all of the funding for three of his biggest blockbusters: The Empire Strikes Back *(1980),* Return of the Jedi *(1983), and* Star Wars: Episode I—The Phantom Menace *(1999).*

▶

The Empire Strikes Back, at $120 million the top-selling film of 1980, earned double the gross of its nearest competitor, *Kramer vs. Kramer.*

school, but Lucas was not interested in academics or in pursuing a practical career—he wanted to become either a race car driver or an artist.

Only a few days before his high school graduation, Lucas was involved in a car crash that nearly took his life. The accident left him shaken but also determined to pursue other interests and do something important with his life. While a student at Modesto Junior College, Lucas discovered the joys of photography; he especially liked devising trick shots. Still interested in auto racing—but not as a career—he often went to the race track to photograph the races. It was there that he struck up a friendship with Haskell Wexler, a pioneering Hollywood cinematographer. Wexler encouraged Lucas's interest in filmmaking and helped him gain admittance to the film school at the University of Southern California (USC).

Lucas entered USC in 1964 and gained experience in all aspects of filmmaking—writing scripts, directing, working with sound and cameras, and film editing. The school gave students ample opportunities to create short films, although it emphasized educational films and documentaries. After only his first year at USC, Lucas had become well known for his very creative and innovative films. His student film *Look at Life*, which presented contrasting images of the Vietnam War, won several awards at student film festivals and drew attention to his talent.

Lucas graduated from the undergraduate program at USC in 1966. Certain that he would be drafted to fight in the Vietnam War, he tried to enlist in the Air Force, where he hoped to work in aerial photography. But the air force rejected him, as did the army, because it was discovered that he had diabetes.

In 1967 Lucas took a job making educational and propaganda films for the United States Information Agency. At the same time, he enrolled in the graduate film program at USC. During this time Lucas made a short film that later would help launch his career—*THX 1138:4EB*, a simple but powerful story about a futuristic, totalitarian society. The film captured the attention of director Francis Ford Coppola, who hired Lucas to work on his next film, *The Rain People*. While working on the Coppola film, Lucas made a highly acclaimed documentary called *Filmmaker*.

Soon after, Lucas began working full time at Coppola's film company, American Zoetrope. It was there that he reworked and expanded his earlier, award-winning student film into the full-length feature *THX 1138*. Released in 1970, this futuristic tale of a dehumanized world and one man's attempt to escape it did not awe the critics, but they recognized the brilliance of the director. The film earned Lucas a cult following among young film buffs and a reputation for making artistic science-fiction films.

Lucas's second feature film, *American Graffiti*, established his reputation when it opened in 1973. It also launched the careers of many actors who went on to become stars, including Richard Dreyfuss and Harrison Ford. A smash box-office hit and a favorite of the critics, *American Graffiti* was based on Lucas's teenage experiences cruising the streets of Modesto in his car. Nominated for five Academy Awards, the film also won several other awards, including a Golden Globe for best motion picture comedy.

Even before he had begun filming *American Graffiti*, Lucas had started thinking about a science-fiction fantasy focusing on the struggle between good and evil. He worked on the screenplay for more than three years, and in 1977 the movie *Star Wars* was released. The story of Jedi Knights, a mystical "force," strange creatures, comical robots and androids, and an evil empire "in a galaxy far, far away," *Star Wars* became an instant and enormous hit. Unlike anything seen before, the movie combined a simple story of good versus evil with spectacular visual special effects.

Appealing to all age groups, *Star Wars* became a cultural phenomenon. The movie also changed the future direction of film, ushering in an era of

notable & quotable

"You go from a warm, secure, uninvolved life into the later sixties, which was involvement, anti-war stuff, revolution and a different kind of rock 'n' roll."

George Lucas, director, 1996

action adventure and the increasing use of special effects. Lucas later wrote and produced two sequels—*The Empire Strikes Back* in 1980 and *Return of the Jedi* in 1983. He envisioned this trilogy to be part of a nine-film series that would tell a saga spanning many years.

After *Star Wars* Lucas began to direct his energies to screenwriting, producing, and developing new film technologies. Among the movies he wrote and produced were the wildly successful Indiana Jones movies, which were directed by Steven Spielberg. Starring Harrison Ford, whom Lucas had introduced to movie audiences in *American Graffiti*, the three movies—*Raiders of the Lost Ark* (1981), *Indiana Jones and the Temple of Doom* (1984), and *Indiana Jones and the Last Crusade* (1989)—featured the death-defying adventures and exploits of a swashbuckling archaeologist combined with dazzling special-effects wizardry. In 1992 Lucas created a TV show based on the movies, *The Young Indiana Jones Chronicles*, which followed Indy's adventures as a young man.

Not all of Lucas's films have achieved the same success as the *Star Wars* and *Indiana Jones* series. *Howard the Duck* (1986), *Labyrinth* (1986), *Willow* (1988), and *Radioland Murders* (1994) were all financial disappointments. Such letdowns have not had much effect on Lucas's career, however. Since *Star Wars*, he has increasingly focused on other types of projects.

The two top-selling movies of the 1970s were *Star Wars* (1977) with $193.77 million and *Jaws* (1975) at $129.55 million.

The money Lucas earned from *Stars Wars* enabled him to build Skywalker Ranch, an idyllic 3,000-acre retreat in northern California where young filmmakers can develop their skills and where experienced filmmakers can use state-of-the-art equipment. During the making of *Star Wars* Lucas set up several companies to create special effects for movies. Industrial Light & Magic, which designed and developed visual effects, helped revolutionize filmmaking. Skywalker Sound created special sound effects. These two companies later combined into Lucas Digital Ltd., recognized as the best and most innovative special effects company in the world.

In 1982 Lucas established LucasArts Entertainment Company, which develops and publishes educational computer software. Lucasfilm Ltd., a production company that Lucas founded in 1971, produces feature films and movies for TV. Lucas also established an educational foundation in 1992 aimed at improving education as it relates to the use of technology.

Calling himself a northern California filmmaker, Lucas does not consider himself a part of the Hollywood establishment. He jealously guards his independence, and his financial success has allowed him to maintain complete control over his projects, without interference from the major Hollywood studios that control most filmmaking in the United States.

In recent years, Lucas has found himself drawn back to his dream of expanding the *Star Wars* series. He is now working on writing screenplays for the "prequel" films, set in a time period forty years before the original *Star Wars*. The first film in the new prequel series, *The Phantom Menace*, directed and produced by Lucas, opened in theaters across the United States in May 1999 to mobs of expectant fans and amid enormous hype. The next two episodes are scheduled for release in 2002 and 2005.

See American Graffiti; *Coppola, Francis Ford; Ford, Harrison; Lynch, David;* Raiders of the Lost Ark; *Spielberg, Steven;* Star Wars

LUMET, SIDNEY

Director Sidney Lumet, known as much for the sensitivity and intelligence of his work as for his complex, socially relevant films, was born in Philadelphia, Pennsylvania, on June 25, 1924. His father, Baruch, was an actor, and his mother, Eugenia, a dancer. In 1926 Baruch Lumet moved his family to New York City, where the senior Lumet joined the Yiddish Theater. Sidney Lumet made his show business debut acting alongside his father in a Yiddish Theater production at the age of four. Several years of roles as a child and adolescent actor followed in the 1930s and early 1940s.

In 1942 Lumet entered the U.S. Army, serving as a radar repairman in the China-Burma theater of operations. After military service, Lumet returned to acting on the New York stage, taking over the role of David in Ben Hecht's *A Flag Is Born* in 1946.

Although he had occasionally directed small stage productions, Lumet's directing career began in earnest in 1950, as a staff television director at CBS. Between 1951 and 1953 Lumet directed about 150 episodes of an adventure series called *Danger* and twenty-six episodes of *You Are There*, a program featuring dramatic recreations of historical events. Lumet also directed a number of live productions on CBS's *Playhouse 90* and NBC's *Kraft Television Theater* and *Studio One*.

In 1957 Lumet helmed his first film, *Twelve Angry Men*. The movie is considered one of Lumet's best works. It features a powerful performance by Henry Fonda as a principled juror who becomes the lone voice holding out for an acquittal. The movie received Academy Award nominations for Best Picture, Best Director, and Best Adapted Screenplay.

Lumet followed with two unimportant films, *Stage Struck* (1958) and *That Kind of Woman* (1959). He returned briefly to television in 1960, directing two highly respected teleplays, *The Sacco and Vanzetti Story* and *The Iceman Cometh*. Both earned Emmy nominations, and Lumet won the Best Director Emmy for the latter.

L

LUMET, SIDNEY

Although born in Philadelphia, director Sidney Lumet chooses New York City as the backdrop for many of his films.

During 1960 Lumet's film career continued with direction of *The Fugitive Kind*, a screen adaptation of the Tennessee Williams play *Orpheus Descending*. In 1962 he released *A View from the Bridge,* the critically praised film version of the Arthur Miller play about a Brooklyn longshoreman's star-crossed love for his wife's niece. That same year, Lumet also directed *Long Day's Journey into Night,* starring Katharine Hepburn, Sir Ralph Richardson, Jason Robards Jr., and Dean Stockwell. Hepburn received an Oscar nomination, and Lumet won the 1963 Directors Guild of America Award for the film.

Two years later Lumet directed *The Pawnbroker* (1965), about a concentration camp survivor who operates a Harlem pawnshop that is a front for criminal activity. The film won critical praise, and its star, Rod Steiger, won the Oscar for Best Actor. That year, Lumet also released *The Hill,* starring Sean Connery. In 1967 Lumet completed the espionage thriller *The Deadly Affair,* with James Mason and Maximilian Schell. That was followed in 1968 with *Bye, Bye Braverman,* a comedy centering on four friends reminiscing about a deceased friend. At the time, Lumet called it his most personal film. A few box-office disappointments ensued, but Lumet finally struck gold with the Oscar-nominated documentary about Martin Luther King Jr. entitled *King: A Filmed Record . . . Montgomery to Memphis* (1970), which he codirected with Joseph Mankiewicz. Lumet had another box-office hit in 1971 with *The Anderson Tapes,* a caper movie starring Sean Connery.

Lumet began the most commercially successful portion of his filmmaking career in 1974 with *Serpico,* the first of many films about police corruption in New York City. Star Al Pacino won a Golden Globe, and the film earned two Oscar nominations. After the less successful *Lovin' Molly* (1974), Lumet hit again with *Murder on the Orient Express* (1974). The whodunit featured an all-star cast including Albert Finney, Lauren Bacall, Martin Balsam, and Ingrid Bergman. It garnered six Oscar nominations, and one Oscar win for Bergman. *Dog Day Afternoon,* an Al Pacino film about a bank robbery in New York City, followed in 1975. It was nominated for six Oscars, including Best Director. The following year *Network,* a dark media satire with Faye Dunaway, William Holden, and Peter Finch, earned ten Oscar nominations, including Best Picture and Best Director.

Lumet's 1977 adaptation of the play *Equus* was a critical success and won Oscar nominations for Richard Burton and Peter Firth. The unsuccessful musical *The Wiz* (1978) was then followed in 1980 by the uneven comedy *Just Tell Me What You Want.*

Lumet returned to his familiar theme of police corruption with *Prince of the City* (1981) starring Treat Williams. The next year, he made the thriller *Deathtrap* with Michael Caine and Christopher Reeve, and the riveting courtroom drama *The Verdict,* with Paul Newman, James Mason, and Charlotte Rampling. *The Verdict* earned several Academy Award nominations. The 1983 film *Daniel,* about two young people whose parents were put to death for spying, was not a critical or box-office success. But it is one of Lumet's favorites.

Lumet followed in the mid-1980s with some unremarkable films: *Garbo Talks* (1984), *Power* (1986) and *The Morning After* (1986). During this time, Lumet made one of his best but least known films, *Running on Empty* (1988). It starred Judd Hirsch and Christine Lahti as parents on the run from the FBI with their children. *Family Business* (1989) was an entertaining mob comedy with Sean Connery, Dustin Hoffman, and Matthew Broderick. *Q & A* (1990) returned to the familiar territory of corruption in New York City; it featured fine performances by Timothy Hutton and Nick Nolte.

Lumet seems to have lost his touch in the 1990s, however, with films such *A Stranger Among Us* (1992), *Guilty as Sin* (1993), and *Night Falls on*

Manhattan and *Critical Care* (1997) leaving critics and audiences unimpressed. Lumet's latest film, *Gloria* (1999), a remake of the 1980 film starring Gena Rowlands, starred Sharon Stone as a streetwise woman who takes in a suddenly orphaned boy.

Despite this recent string of disappointments, Lumet remains an influential director, lauded for his willingness to experiment with a range of techniques and styles and for his respect for actors and writers.

See Connery, Sean; Dunaway, Faye; Hepburn, Katharine; Hoffman, Dustin; Network

LUPINO, IDA

Ida Lupino was born February 4, 1918, in London, England. At that time, the Lupinos had been a highly regarded theatrical family for over 300 years, ever since their debut in England as traveling puppeteers. The family home was regularly filled with actors, producers, and others involved in the theater. Ida's father, Stanley Lupino, was a popular stage comedian who wrote the books and music for most of the musical comedies he starred in. Connie Emerald, Ida's mother, was an actress with a similar stage heritage.

Given her background, it's not surprising that Lupino wrote and produced her first play at age seven for her classmates. Later on, after she became a well-known Hollywood star, Lupino commented that her main reason for becoming an actress was not wanting to let her father down. But it was clearly her decision early on. As a youngster Lupino was already improvising and acting out scenes with her younger sister, Ruth, and by age ten, she convinced her father to build a miniature theater for them. Stanley, who must have recognized his daughter's creative bent, actually built an elaborate 100-seat structure, complete with a pit and electrical equipment. It was here that Lupino emoted as Juliet, Hamlet, and Camille in front of invited audiences well before her teen years.

At age thirteen, after announcing her plans to begin a professional career, Lupino began studying at the Royal Academy of Dramatic Arts. Two years later, when her mother auditioned in London for a part as an adulterous flapper in the film *Her First Affair* (1933), it was Lupino who got the role instead. Later Lupino played both a tough gold digger and a sweet, innocent girl in *Money for Speed* (1933). After these first two efforts, Paramount Pictures offered Lupino a contract and she left England for Hollywood shortly after, accompanied by her mother.

Lupino was clearly talented, but the studios were more interested in capitalizing on her beauty than on her acting prowess, and she was cast in minor

Actress and director Ida Lupino defied 1940s and 1950s stereotypes by directing movies and later, episodes of such television shows as The Twilight Zone, Gilligan's Island, *and the long-running program* The Fugitive.

ingenue roles for five years. Lupino didn't want easy parts, and it was a disappointing time for someone who had tackled tough classical roles in childhood. Frustrated, Lupino took a year off from the screen to study acting.

Later, it was her riveting interpretation of complex, neurotic, hard characters in the 1940s and '50s for Warner Bros. and RKO films that attracted attention and respect from both the movie industry and audiences. Lupino's professionalism and mastery won support from directors and studio heads when she finally did branch out. Her first challenging break came in the role of Bessie Broke, the vengeful Cockney prostitute who destroys the masterpiece of an artist who is losing his sight, in *The Light That Failed* (1940). Ronald Colman, the leading man at the time, wanted someone else as his costar for the film. Well known for his retentive memory, Colman tried to sabotage Lupino's performance during a key scene by twice pretending to forget his lines. Director William A. Wellman put a stop to Colman's behavior by threatening the star with character actor parts for the rest of his career.

Lana Carlsen, an adulterous murderer who later goes mad on the witness stand, was Lupino's next character, in *They Drive by Night* (1940). Lupino's favorite role was the murdering housekeeper who kills her employer, then uses the home as a refuge for her two insane sisters in *Ladies in Retirement* (1941). In 1943 Lupino won the New York Film Critics Circle best actress award for playing the ruthless manager who pushes her sister to stardom in *The Hard Way* (1943). Lupino also took several roles without a dark side, including the eccentric Emily Brontë in *Devotion* (1946). Overall, Lupino was a brilliant, intuitive actress who conveyed a stunning range of emotions with just a glance. Her portrayals were always memorable and she accumulated over fifty screen credits including her last movie, *My Boys Are Good Boys* (1978).

Her emotional understanding of women on the edge, as well as an early attraction to the classics and how their stories unfolded, no doubt helped her direct several successful, low-budget films. In 1949, a year after Lupino married Columbia Pictures executive Collier Young, the couple founded a production company called the Filmmakers. *Not Wanted* (1949), a drama about an unwed mother, was Lupino's first project. Lupino was initially producer and co-scriptwriter, then stepped in as director when Elmer Clifton became ill. Her position was significant for its time. Many women who were active as directors in Hollywood's early years had been pushed out by the 1930s. Dorothy Arzner, whose first directorial assignment was in 1927, was the sole female who continued directing motion pictures until the early 1940s, and Lupino would pick up the gauntlet.

Just as she was drawn to challenging characters, Lupino chose unusual and difficult subjects. *Never Fear* (1950) poignantly addressed the realities a young dancer faced when stricken with polio. *Outrage* (1950), a joint venture with RKO, was about rape and its awful aftereffects for the victim. In 1950 Lupino and Young divorced, but they continued to work together. *Hard, Fast and Beautiful* (1951), their next production, dealt with the exploitation of a young tennis star by her greedy mother. Lupino even directed a film noir called *The Hitch-Hiker* (1953). This time the psychopath was a man who holds two vacationing businessmen hostage. In 1953 Lupino played a dual role, directing and acting in *The Bigamist*.

Lupino didn't direct another Hollywood film until 1966. But she did return to acting in films and directed television episodes during the 1950s that included such series as *Have Gun, Will Travel*, *The Donna Reed Show*, *Mr. Novak*, and *Dr. Kildare*. Lupino also produced and starred in a television sitcom, *Mr. Adams and Eve*, with her new husband, Howard Duff.

In 1966 Lupino directed her last film. It was a comedy about nuns in a convent, an unusual switch for the noir-ish director. *The Trouble with Angels* starred Rosalind Russell, Hayley Mills, and Gypsy Rose Lee. After that film, Lupino continued to act in television and film, but health problems after 1975 forced her to cut back on work and finally retire. A varied and prolific visionary who was always ahead of her time, Ida Lupino died on August 3, 1995.

See Director; Film noir

LYNCH, DAVID

David Lynch is one of the very few avowedly avant-garde directors to have cracked not only the big Hollywood studios but also network television without watering down his darkly comic, at times gruesomely unsettling, vision.

David Keith Lynch seems to have been the all-American boy. He was born in Missoula, Montana, on January 20, 1946. Lynch remembers a rural childhood: "My father was a research scientist for the department of agriculture in Washington. We were in the woods all the time. I'd sorta had enough of the woods by the time I left, but still, lumber and lumberjacks, all this kinda thing, that's America to me." Lynch grew up in the Pacific northwest, in small towns in Montana, Idaho, and Washington and lived for a time in North Carolina.

Lynch attended the Corcoran School of Art in Washington, D.C., from 1963 to 1964. He studied at the Boston Museum School from 1964 to 1965, where he was attracted to works by artists ranging from Francis Bacon to James Hopper. He was drawn to the expressionists, who sought an objective representation of inner feelings. The student artist enthusiastically abandoned the confines of the classroom and set off for Europe to study with the expressionist painter Oskar Kokoschka.

Lynch's first trip to Europe in 1965 fell apart after only fifteen days. He returned to the United States to continue his study of painting at the Pennsylvania Academy of the Fine Arts in Philadelphia, where he lived through 1970. Renting an apartment across from Philadelphia's city morgue exposed Lynch to urban brutality, which blended with his art studies to shape his fascination with life's corroded underbelly. "I never had an original idea until I came to Philadelphia," Lynch has said.

Lynch began making films while in art school in Philadelphia, where his talent was immediately recognized in a prize-winning student film *Six Men Getting Sick,* a thematic forerunner of *Eraserhead* and his later works. His next film, *The Alphabet,* done on a commission from a gallery owner, blends animation and live action to unsettling effect. This striking effort earned Lynch an American Film Institute grant to continue filmmaking. His next film, *The Grandmother,* about a disturbed boy nurturing a grand-

L

LYNCH, DAVID

Avant-garde director David Lynch is equally at home—and his vision just as darkly comic—in movies and in network television.

mother he plants from a seed bag, already has the look and, more particularly, the sound, of Lynch's later works.

That project won Lynch a spot in the American Film Institute's Center for Advanced Film Studies in Los Angeles, where he spent most of the next five years realizing his first full-length film, *Eraserhead* (1978), which he began shooting in 1972. This "altogether amazing, sensuous film" (Pauline Kael), which ranges from chilling grotesqueries of mind and body to the exaltation of spiritual quest, positioned Lynch in the first echelon of avant-garde filmmakers. It also brought Lynch to the attention of Mel Brooks, who was mounting a film of the life of John Merrick, a Victorian Englishman of noble character and elevated mind whose grotesquely physical deformations condemned him to a life of isolation and ridicule. It was a project begging for Lynch's visonary gifts, and his restrained, compassionate direction of *The Elephant Man* (1980) resulted in a critical and commercial triumph that garnered eight Academy Award nominations, including one for best director.

Spurning an offer to direct George Lucas's *Return of the Jedi,* Lynch instead pitched his own sci-fi script, *Johnnie Rocket,* at Zoetrope Studios, but the project never left the launching pad. Instead Lynch accepted an offer to direct an adaptation of Frank Herbert's labyrinthine science fiction epic *Dune,* a prodigious undertaking that flopped at the box office when it was finally released in a studio-trimmed version in 1984.

With *Blue Velvet* (1986) Lynch not only regained his footing but vaulted into the cinematic stratosphere. In the words of Stephen Schiff, "Brilliant and unsettling . . . this is the work of an all-American visionary—and a master film stylist." Jeffrey, the film's protagonist (and Lynch's semi-autobiographical alter ego) is the very image of the handsome, affable, foursquare American boy who, upon returning from college, plummets through the looking-glass of small-town America into a swirl of murder, betrayal, lust, and sadism. Lynch insinuates fear into the most pedestrian shot and tinges the most brutal shot with a hint of sly humor; it is a world in which the standard dualities of waking and dreaming, serenity and fear, innocence and decadence blur and dissolve.

This Dantesque vision of the deathly horror that smirks just beneath the settled surface of middle-class appearances also permeated Lynch's next major project, the televised miniseries *Twin Peaks* (1990), for which he was full-time producer and occasional director. The series, which lingers with ritual menace over the heart of darkness lurking beneath a grisly small-town murder, was an unprecedented expansion of network television's normally stunted aesthetic horizons.

Since then Lynch's creative energies seem to have stalled. *Wild at Heart* (1990) and *Lost Highway* (1997) struck many critics as self-derivative exercises that at times bordered on self-parody. *Driven to It* is planned for 1999 release, and many Lynch fans are hoping that it will signal his return to form.

See Avant-garde; Cult film; Experimental film; Independent filmmaker; Lucas, George; Underground film

M

M*A*S*H

*M*A*S*H* (1970) is Robert Altman's funniest film, quick, witty, offhand, and completely realistic. The story has no conventional plot but is made up of a series of disjointed episodes, revolving around two renegade doctors serving in a MASH unit during the Korean conflict.

Upon their arrival to the 4077th MASH unit, surgeons Hawkeye Pierce (Donald Sutherland) and Duke Forrest (Tom Skerritt) each intend to establish themselves as renegades, unwilling to conform to any army protocol or regulations. The atmosphere of the camp is relaxed and informal; everyone is on a first-name basis.

In addition to the problem of being understaffed, Hawkeye and Duke must live and work with Major Frank Burns (Robert Duvall), who is not only a hypocrite and a religious fanatic but also an incompetent surgeon. They bully Colonel Blake (Roger Bowen) into moving Burns from their tent. Upon the arrival of surgeon Captain "Trapper" John McIntyre (Elliott Gould) as their new bunkmate, Hawkeye and Duke offer the man a martini, to which he agrees. His initiation to their circle is completed when he removes a jar from his coat pocket and offers them an olive.

The team is now complete, and immediately the antics of the threesome escalate, particularly with the entrance of the new head nurse, Major Margaret "Hot Lips" Houlihan (Sally Kellerman). Hawkeye is at first attracted to her, but he is warned that he is encountering an alien perspective when Houlihan observes that "Major Burns is not only a good technical surgeon, he is also a good military surgeon." Hot Lips and Frank Burns develop a sexual attraction for each other, but one day Hawkeye teases Frank about his affair with her, pushing him to the breaking point. Ultimately, the pitiable Frank is removed from camp.

Once Burns is gone, the film is more loosely episodic. In the Last Supper sequence, "Painless Pole" (John Shuck), the dentist, feels compelled to kill himself because of his occasional impotence. The surgeons invent the black capsule and conduct an irreverent eulogy before settling him in his coffin. Once he is asleep, a beautiful nurse slips in with Painless and he is cured.

"Frank, were you on this religious kick at home or did you crack up over here?"

Donald Sutherland as Hawkeye Pierce to Robert Duvall as Maj. Frank Burns in *M*A*S*H* (1970)

The surgeons' next scheme is to expose Hot Lips in a craftily rigged shower. The timing and execution of the stunt result in revealing Hot Lips naked in the shower to the entire camp. When she threatens Colonel Blake with resigning her commission, he calls her bluff.

On the occasion of Ho-Jon (Kim Atwood) being inducted into the Korean Army, Hawkeye tries to help his friend by drugging him. But Ho-Jon is drafted anyway, and tender Hawkeye is shocked and dismayed at the loss of his friend.

Later, Hawkeye and Trapper are invited to operate in Tokyo. After the operation, the two surgeons go out on the town. In between shenanigans, the two illegally operate to save the life of a Japanese infant. Having saved two lives in Tokyo they arrive back at the 4077th wearing new golf clothes.

In the final scene, Hawkeye tells Duke that their tour is up and they can leave. He has mixed feelings: elation at the prospect of going home, and sadness about leaving his friends. The two surgeons leave as they had arrived—with Hawkeye driving the Jeep.

*M*A*S*H*, at $22 million 1970's second-biggest seller (after *Airport*), won the Palme d'Or at Cannes and Best Picture (Musical/Comedy) in the Golden Globe Awards.

See Altman, Robert; War film

MacGUFFIN (McGUFFIN)

The term MacGuffin is attributed to Alfred Hitchcock, who used it to describe a plotting device for setting a story into motion. The term is frequently applied to that object or person in a mystery film that at the beginning of the plot provides an element of dramatic curiosity. The MacGuffin can be something that all the characters are trying to get their hands on, for example, a falcon in *The Maltese Falcon* (1941) or a gem in *The Pink Panther* (1963). The MacGuffin can also be someone or something that is lost and is being sought. In Hitchcock's *Family Plot* (1976) the MacGuffin is a missing heir. The ensuing search for the heir leads to a larger, more involved mystery story. Once the dramatic plot is under way in a Hitchcock film, the MacGuffin often ceases to be of major importance.

notable & quotable

"The MacGuffin is a thing that the spies are after but the audience doesn't care."

Alfred Hitchcock, director, 1973

The search for the meaning of "Rosebud" in *Citizen Kane* (1941) is described by some critics as a plotting device like that of the MacGuffin. *Rosebud* becomes the element of dramatic curiosity that motivates the mosaic investigation that helps explain the meaning of Kane's life.

See Citizen Kane; *Hitchcock, Alfred;* Maltese Falcon

MAGIC LANTERN

A magic lantern is an amusement device that predates the motion-picture projector. In the seventeenth century, Athanasius Kircher, a German priest-scientist, employed mirrors and candlelight to cast images onto a wall from a boxlike apparatus labeled a *magic lantern.* Later, Kircher added a lens so that the projected images, usually drawn on slides, could be focused. The magic lantern served as a popular source of visual entertainment well into the twentieth century, with many refined models allowing the presentation of highly sophisticated slide programs. Photographs were added to magic-lantern shows during the 1850s.

See Nickelodeon; Zoëtrope

MALTESE FALCON, THE

With *The Maltese Falcon* (1941) John Huston made a smashing directorial debut with a twisty crime thriller that featured Humphrey Bogart's first turn as the flinty, semiscrupulous, but ultimately incorruptible private detective Sam Spade. Based on a novel by Dashiell Hammett, the film received Oscar nominations for Best Picture, Best Screenplay, and Best Supporting Actor (Sydney Greenstreet).

The densely plotted film begins with this scroll: "In 1539 the Knights Templar of Malta paid tribute to Charles V of Spain by sending him a Golden Falcon encrusted from beak to claw with rarest jewels. But pirates seized the galley carrying this priceless token, and the fate of the Maltese Falcon remains a mystery to this day." The scene then shifts to the San Francisco office of private eye Sam Spade, which he shares with his partner Miles Archer (Joe Cowan). The proverbial beautiful woman in distress, Ruth Wonderly (Mary Astor), arrives and implores Spade to help her find her sister, who has gone missing in the company of an unsavory character named Thursby. Sam explains the predicament to Archer, whom he tells to accompany Ruth on a planned meeting with her sister that night.

"I couldn't be fonder of you if you were my own son. But, well, if you lose a son it's possible to get another. There's only one Maltese Falcon."

Sydney Greenstreet as Kasper Gutman in *The Maltese Falcon* (1941)

As Archer approaches the agreed-upon meeting place, he is shot dead. Rushing to the murder scene, a police detective, Tom Polhaus (Ward

Bond), informs Sam that Archer must have been on the trail of Thursby. When Sam calls Ruth at her hotel, he is informed that she is no longer there.

Back at his apartment, Sam is interrogated by Polhaus and Lieutenant Dundy (Barton Maclane) about his involvement in the case, but Sam refuses to divulge the identity of his client, even when provoked by the suggestion that he committed the murder. They inform Sam that Thursby has also been murdered.

Archer's widow, Iva, visits Sam the next morning and makes a pass at him, which he gruffly spurns. Later he receives a telephone call from Ruth, who now identifies herself as Brigid O'Shaughnessy, asking him to meet with her. At their encounter Sam tells her that he has withheld her identity from the police but that he knows that her tale about her missing sister was a fabrication. Brigid claims to have been with Thursby and claims that he most likely was Miles's murderer, but she is baffled by Thursby's own mur-

The Maltese Falcon *is a twisty crime thriller featuring Humphrey Bogart, left, in his first role as detective Sam Spade.*
▼

der. Spade agrees to investigate the murders, but only after he receives another substantial payment.

Back at his office, Sam is surprised by a mysterious man exuding a strong scent of cologne, Joel Cairo, who is willing to put up $5,000 if Spade can help him find a precious black sculpture of a bird. He suddenly waves a gun at Sam and begins to look around the office, but Sam is able to knock him out and examine his wallet, in which he finds French and British passports and a ticket to the Geary Theater. When Cairo regains consciousness, he asks Sam if he has the bird, but Sam bemusedly dismisses him as a crank.

Sam informs Brigid about the episode with Cairo, suspecting that she knows more than she is telling him. Together they meet with Cairo at Sam's place, where Brigid's curiosity is piqued with Cairo's talk about the black bird and "the Fat Man." After Cairo leaves, Sam grills Brigid about the statue, but she evades his inquiries. Peering through his window, Sam notices a man lurking outside who had been following him earlier.

Determined to pierce the enveloping mystery, Sam heads for Cairo's hotel, where he again notices the same shadowy figure he had spied on the street. Sidling up to the man, Wilmer Cook (Elisha Cook Jr.), Sam asks him what he is up to and where Cairo is, but he is met with a sharp rebuff. Returning to his office, Sam finds a message from the Fat Man, Kasper Gutman (Sydney Greenstreet). He immediately heads to Kasper's hotel suite, where the first figure he encounters is Wilmer, who turns out to be one of Kasper's bodyguards. He is received buoyantly by Kasper, who makes him a drink; Sam, however, homes in on the matter of the black bird. When Kasper evades his questions, Sam erupts in anger, hurling his glass aside and demanding that Kasper come up with some answers—and soon.

Later on the street, Wilmer, his pocket bulging with his gun, summons Sam back to a meeting with Kasper. Sam easily disarms the thug and humiliates him by handing his pistol to Kasper upon arriving back at the suite. Warming to his task over drinks, Kasper now explains the long, convoluted history of the Maltese Falcon, first relating the tale told in the opening scroll and adding that centuries after its disappearance, the bejeweled artifact turned up in Paris, where it was enameled in black. The bird later fell into the hands of an antique dealer from whom the bird was stolen after he was murdered. The trail of the falcon then ran cold in Istanbul. Kasper believes that the statuette is in San Francisco and offers Spade $25,000 and a 25 percent cut of the sale price if he can find it. As Sam rises to leave, he passes out, drugged by Kasper's drinks.

After regaining consciousness to find that he is alone in Kasper's suite, Sam calls his secretary and is told that Brigid has vanished. As he looks around the suite he notices a newspaper in which a ship's arrival time has been underscored. Deciding to follow up on the lead, Sam heads to the dock. But when he arrives, he finds that the ship, *La Paloma* from Hong Kong, is ablaze. An exhausted Sam returns to his office. While he is enjoy-

"When you're slapped, you'll take it and like it!"

Humphrey Bogart as Sam Spade in *The Maltese Falcon* (1941)

ing a soothing shave by his secretary, a man bearing a package bursts into the room. He hands the package to Sam, sputtering that it is "the falcon," and then falls dead. An inspection of the dead man's wallet reveals that he is Captain Jacobi, skipper of *La Paloma.* At last Spade holds the coveted statuette.

At that moment Brigid calls, blurts out the address 26 Ancho Street, and then screams as the call is cut off. Sam then instructs his secretary to notify the police of the captain's death but to say nothing about the falcon. He checks the package in a baggage room, mails himself the claim ticket, and hops a taxi to 26 Ancho Street, which turns out to be a vacant lot. Sam later finds Brigid at her apartment and brings her over to his place, where he is surprised by Cairo, Wilmer, and Kasper, who hands Sam $10,000 and asks for the falcon. After retrieving a missing $1,000 bill from Kasper, Sam agrees to hand over the bird, just delivered by his secretary. When Kasper cuts away the black enamel covering, however, he finds no jewels and declares it a fake, accusing Brigid of having substituted the phony and keeping the real one for herself. Cairo, in turn, spews abuse at the Fat Man, rebuking him for having botched the transaction. At gunpoint the exasperated Kasper demands his money back from Sam, who agrees but keeps $1,000 for his trouble.

After the three men exit, Sam calls the police and puts them on the trail of the sinister trio. He then tells Brigid that he now knows that she killed Miles to incriminate Thursby and then killed Thursby as well. He tells her, "Well, if you get a good break, you'll be out of Tahatchapi in twenty years, and you can come back to me then. I hope they don't hang you, precious, by that sweet neck." Desperate, Brigid turns up the steam and tries to coax Sam into taking the fall for her, but Sam dismisses her pleas, explaining that he is duty-bound to redress the wrong inflicted on his longtime partner.

The police arrive and Sam turns over Brigid, the falcon, and the $1,000 he accepted from Kasper. Noticing the unusual heft of Sam's package, Polhaus asks Sam what's inside. Retrieving the bird, Sam replies, "The—er—stuff that dreams are made of." As the distraught Brigid is hustled off by the police, Sam, gripping the notorious falcon, walks into the night.

An antihero elevated to the status of near-myth in America's popular culture, Spade is a complex character torn by his own greed but doing what is right because that is what his personal code demands, even when he is hounded by temptation—erotic or pecuniary—or danger. The deftly shaded rendering of Sam's inner conflict, his continual wavering between heroism and villainy, makes his character a mirror held up to the viewer's own uncertain conscience and helps to transform this engrossing film noir into a lasting contribution to the art of American film.

See Bogart, Humphrey; Film noir; Huston, John; MacGuffin

MALTIN, LEONARD

Leonard Maltin was born December 18, 1950, and grew up in Teaneck, New Jersey. He has appeared on the long-running syndicated TV show *Entertainment Tonight* since 1982, as its enthusiastic, bearded historian and film critic. His passion for films began with television in the 1950s and '60s when old movies were regularly scheduled at prime time. Back then, Fred Astaire and Ginger Rogers tore up the dance floor in glamorous films like *Top Hat;* Claudette Colbert, Jennifer Jones, and Robert Walker tugged heartstrings in *Since You Went Away;* and Cary Grant played his bent for comedy to the hilt in *I Was a Male War Bride*. These and other greats all aired at times that didn't require setting an alarm clock. "When I was a kid," Maltin told Alan Dumas in a Scripps-Howard News Service interview, "old movies were inescapable. You couldn't avoid them."

While Maltin's parents weren't movie buffs themselves (his father was a lawyer; his mother, a singer), both encouraged their son's interest. He began poring over books about Charlie Chaplin and Walt Disney as early as grade school. Maltin's writing career was launched at thirteen. *Famous Monsters of Filmland* was *the* boys' magazine of the time, and when Maltin read about *Film Fan Monthly* and *8 Millimeter Collector* in one fateful issue, he decided to pitch his services to both periodicals.

"I had the incredible cheek to propose a column, 'Research Unlimited,' like the answer man," explained Maltin in a telephone interview. "It was only after the editor said he liked my submission that I told him how old I was." Maltin wrote "Research Unlimited" for *8 Millimeter Collector*, which was based in Indiana, Pennsylvania. For *Film Fan Monthly*, a Vancouver-based publication, Maltin produced a review of new home movie releases. After two years, *Film Fan*'s editor approached Maltin. Would he take over as editor and publisher? Maltin did. He was fifteen.

In 1969 New American Library, a Signet imprint, hired Maltin for its first collection of capsule reviews, *TV Movies*. "There was an English teacher at Teaneck High School who had seen my magazine. She told me, 'I have a friend whom I think would enjoy meeting you,'" Maltin explained. The friend was editor Patrick O'Connor, and a meeting was arranged.

Maltin brought copies of *Film Fan Monthly* to the meeting, but O'Connor knew it already. O'Connor wanted to publish *TV Movies* as a volume to rival Bantam's book on films. When O'Connor asked Maltin what he would do to make their volume different, Maltin replied, "I would add things like the name of the director, running time, whether it was in color or black and white, and cast names." O'Connor offered him the job on the spot, and this time Maltin didn't conceal his age—he was seventeen years old. "I was eighteen when that first book came out," Maltin told Dumas. "I went to college at NYU studying journalism, writing movie books in my spare time. It was great."

Since then, *TV Movies* has become the annually revised *Leonard Maltin's Movie & Video Guide*, celebrating its thirtieth anniversary in 1999. *TV Movies* is no small undertaking; the recent version had 19,000 reviews.

While Maltin credits some of his success to breaking in before publishers (and readers) were inundated with movie books, he nonetheless provides an expertise film buffs appreciate. His mostly celebratory approach, which mirrors his on-air style, is a pleasure to read. But just as important, Maltin is a stickler for the correct and little-known fact because he cares so much about film. In his foreword for *Leonard Maltin's Movie Encyclopedia* is a revealing anecdote. Maltin's wife once encountered the actress Kim Darby in the ladies' room of a local theater and told her husband that if he had any questions for Darby, now was the time. Maltin, who was in the thick of his 1994 thousand-page tome, waited for Darby, then asked her why some filmographies listed that she'd starred in *Red Sky at Morning* (1970), although Maltin couldn't find her in the cast listings.

Darby explained she was under contract for the film, but got out of her commitment to act in *The Grissom Gang*, a Robert Aldrich film, instead. A reference book researcher apparently culled the information from an early cast announcement. The error was compounded over and over and never corrected. Maltin was glad to have the correct information—he and his staff are known for placing calls to unions, agents, managers, publicists, parents, halls of records, and, at times, the celebrity, to confirm and reconfirm information. His goal is always to get all of his information exactly right.

Maltin is also particular about films, rarely giving four stars. As for his own personal favorites, Maltin has a soft spot for old movies. "Old movies just push certain buttons for me," he told Patricia Brennan of the *Washington Post*. His top two favorites are *Citizen Kane* and *Casablanca*. "The first time, I saw both in the theater," he remembered. "I was really lucky to see them in revivals on the big screen. There's no better way. I feel bad for young people who see them on video." The musical *Singin' in the Rain* (1952), the affectionate spoof of Hollywood when it switched to talkies, starring Gene Kelly, Debbie Reynolds, and Donald O'Connor, is also a Maltin favorite, as is the comedy *Modern Times* (1936), in which Charlie Chaplin hilariously demonstrates the new "efficient" eating machine. "I used to be considered a freak in that I saw three or four movies a day or in a weekend," he told Brennan. "Now everyone is doing it."

Maltin has authored, edited, and contributed to over two dozen film history books. His skilled prose and meticulous research has brought forgotten, but important, film periods to life. *Of Mice and Magic: A History of American Animated Cartoons* (New American Library, 1987) went into depth about the early days of animation. Movie shorts were explored in *The Great Movie Shorts* (Crown, 1972, published as *Selected Short Subjects*, Da Capo Press, 1983) and *The Little Rascals: The Life and Times of Our Gang* (Crown, 1994). Maltin wrote about many brilliant and important comedians we see rarely on film, if at all, in *The Great Movie Comedians* (Crown, 1978), *Movie Comedy Teams* (New American Library, 1970; revised edition, 1985), and *Carole Lombard* (Pyramid Publications, 1976).

The old radio broadcast shows that preceded television in importance were covered in *The Great American Broadcast* (E. P. Dutton, 1997), Maltin's most recent film history book. "I got hooked on old-time radio, but it came later in my life," explained Maltin. "When my wife and I moved to L.A. there were a lot of broadcast veterans still alive and they had wonderful stories. I spent eleven years working on that book. There was an interesting crossover because so many from the movies did both." Maltin also writes regularly for well-known periodicals such as *Playboy*, the *Los Angeles Times*, and *Disney Magazine*. His latest book, *Leonard Maltin's Family Film Guide* (published by Signet), is a parents' guide, with 1,000 all-new reviews.

But, as rumored, does Maltin really have theater seats in his living room where he watches films? "Yes," he says. "I have two seats from the old Paramount Theater in Times Square on Broadway, before they tore it down."

See Auteur; Criticism; Ebert, Roger; Kael, Pauline; Newspapers; Siskel, Gene; Trade papers

MANCHURIAN CANDIDATE, THE

The Manchurian Candidate (1962) is a very dark satire about political extremists. The screenplay was written by George Axelrod, adapted from the novel of the same name by Richard Condon. John Frankenheimer directed.

Laurence Harvey plays Sergeant Raymond Shaw, an American soldier during the Korean War who, captured along with his platoon by enemy soldiers, is brainwashed into becoming the perfect assassin—only he doesn't know it. He goes about his affairs, unthinkingly awaiting the call to action from his mysterious controller in the United States.

When Shaw returns to the United States, he is welcomed at the Washington, D.C., airfield by an admiring crowd and a handful of generals, sent to meet this very highly decorated soldier. Shaw's mother (Angela Lansbury) also meets him there, carefully coifed and in a fur coat, accompanied by her husband, Senator John Iselin (James Gregory). Politically ambitious, to

"It's a terrible thing to hate your mother. But I didn't always hate her. When I was a child, I only kind of disliked her."

Laurence Harvey as Raymond Shaw in *The Manchurian Candidate* (1962)

M

MANCHURIAN CANDIDATE, THE

Laurence Harvey stars in The Manchurian Candidate, *a taut political thriller about a Korean War hero and his mother's scheming plans to promote her husband's career. Angela Lansbury, who plays Harvey's mother in the film, was actually only three years older than him.* ▶

say the least, Mrs. Iselin has made sure that the press is present, and she thrusts a banner that says "Sen. Iselin's boy!" over her son's head. (Raymond repeatedly and angrily asserts that Iselin is his stepfather, not his real father.) The senator is a hopeful presidential candidate for the Republican party, and Raymond's mother will do anything to help him achieve that spot.

When boarding a private plane to go home, Raymond is moody, and his mother urges him to have a drink and relax. He explodes, telling her that he hates her and her new husband and all that they stand for. He announces that he has decided to take a job in New York City with a newspaper publisher who is an ardent foe of Senator Iselin's. After speaking his mind, Raymond leaves the plane, leaving his mother and stepfather to digest the news.

Soon we see Raymond, with other members of his platoon, sitting on a podium while fussily dressed middle-aged women discuss hydrangeas. The men, dressed in their fatigues, gaze off in all directions, looking quite bored, but not necessarily unhappy. This setting, which appears several times in the film, is juxtaposed with another view of the men, this time amid a roomful of foreign military types who are talking about the men as if they are laboratory rats. Are the military men Koreans? Chinese? Soviets? It is initially unclear what regime is at work here. We see, however, that the men think they are at a garden party, when in fact they are completely under the thrall of the foreign military. At one point Raymond is called upon to demonstrate his loyalty to his new masters: At their bidding, he strangles one of his men, while the rest of the platoon looks placidly on.

But once they are back in the United States, several of the platoon members start having nightmares about their experiences in Manchuria, and one of them, Bennett Marco (Frank Sinatra), begins to understand what really happened. He is terribly upset and bewildered, and on a train to New York City, his resulting erratic behavior attracts the attention of a young woman, Rosie (Janet Leigh). She presses her address and telephone number on him, repeating them several times to make sure that he remembers them. We are never quite sure what her motivation is. Does she just find Marco attractive, or could she be an enemy agent and Marco a backup assassin?

"There are two kinds of people in this world: Those that enter a room and turn the television set on, and those that enter a room and turn the television set off."

Laurence Harvey as Raymond Shaw in *The Manchurian Candidate* (1962)

Eventually the U.S. government decides to use Marco to try to find out the truth about Shaw and his controllers. What Marco eventually learns is an ugly story. Raymond Shaw has been so brainwashed that he will kill anyone who gets in the way of what his controller wants—he even kills the newspaper publisher who hired him in New York, at his controller's bidding. He goes so far as to murder his new wife and her father, a big man in the Republican party, who despises Raymond's stepfather, Iselin, and vows to do everything in his power to keep Iselin from getting anywhere near real power. The trigger that is used to set Raymond off is the queen of diamonds. Raymond is still completely unaware that he has been brainwashed.

Marco sets out to "decondition" Raymond, who has become so miserable and confused that he is like a zombie, but Raymond's controller—who turns out to be his loathsome and smothering mother, working for the Soviets—turns out to be more powerful. Marco cannot completely decondition him. Yet Raymond's own will seems to be surfacing to some degree. When his mother orders him to assassinate the Republican party candidate for president, Raymond kills her and his stepfather instead. Then, before Marco can stop him, poor Raymond turns the gun on himself.

The Manchurian Candidate was unavailable for viewing for some twenty-five years after its first run, due to a dispute between Sinatra and United Artists. It reportedly was locked up in a vault in Sinatra's home. It was finally released in the late 1980s on video.

MANKIEWICZ, JOSEPH

Joseph Mankiewicz was born on February 11, 1909, in Wilkes-Barre, Pennsylvania, where his German-emigré father was a language instructor. Mankiewicz would begin his directorial career rather late, after World War II, when he was thirty-seven years old and had already enjoyed successful careers as a producer and as a screenwriter.

The family moved to New York City from Germany in 1913. Mankiewicz graduated from Stuyvesant High School in 1924, and entered Columbia University. After graduating from Columbia in 1928 with a major in English, he contemplated a life in letters, envisioning a career that combined university teaching with playwriting. He expected to make the "grand tour," then return to his alma mater as a specialist in the literature of the English Renaissance. But the grand tour ended in Berlin, where Mankiewicz was dazzled by a decadence that appealed as much to the mind as it did to the senses. He found a job at UFA providing English translations for inter-titles in German films intended for British and American release, thus beginning in the movie business as a titler.

On the basis of his UFA experience, Mankiewicz was working in Hollywood within a year, writing titles for Paramount films that were made as talkies but would be shown in theaters that were not yet equipped for sound. But with the advent of sound came the spoken word and, with the spoken word, dialogue.

Pursuing the only course a writer could in the early days of sound, Mankiewicz moved from titling to dialogue and finally to screenwriting. Between 1929 and 1932 he contributed to the scripts of fourteen films, winning an Oscar nomination for *Skippy* (1931). But the film of that period with which he is most commonly associated is *Million Dollar Legs* (1932), an anarchic comedy. Mankiewicz's next screenplay, *Diplomaniacs* (1933), imitated the loose structure and comic techniques of its predecessor, *Million Dollar Legs*. In *Dilpomaniacs* the anarchy was undisguised bedlam that exploded into silliness. But Mankiewicz soon outgrew this varsity show humor. What followed was a superior example of his comic writing, *If I Had a Million* (1932), an anthology film for which he wrote three episodes.

It was the opportunity to work on the screenplay *Manhattan Melodrama* (1934) that brought Mankiewicz to MGM. *Manhattan Melodrama* centered on boyhood friends who end up on opposite sides of the law. However, after writing the screenplays of *Forsaking All Others* (1934) and *I Live My Life* (1935) for MGM, Mankiewicz realized that he wanted to direct his own work. But because MGM was essentially a producer's studio, he settled for producing and quickly evidenced a quality associated with creative producers: he supervised each film, refusing to be intimidated by the

Before making his name as a director, Joseph Mankiewicz worked as a translator of intertitles in Berlin, then later as a dialogue writer and screenwriter for Paramount. He also produced films for MGM and Fox in the 1940s.

credentials of the screenwriter or the director. Humility was not one of Mankiewicz's virtues.

Of the nineteen films he produced at MGM, several were sophisticated comedies, including *Double Wedding* (1937), *The Philadelphia Story* (1940), *The Feminine Touch* (1941), and *Woman of the Year* (1942). Mankiewicz had the unique ability to impart a vulnerable quality to actresses like Bette Davis and Ava Gardner, whose screen personae militated against vulnerability.

In 1943 he parted company with MGM, and shortly after, Twentieth Century-Fox offered him a five-year contract that allowed him to write, produce, and direct. Significantly, he produced only one film, *The Keys of the Kingdom* (1944), during his eight-year association with Fox once he realized that Fox, unlike MGM, was a studio of directors and writers, but not of producers.

His directorial debut was neither promising nor spectacular. *Dragonwyck*'s (1946) paradigm was of conjugal terror. The film had a weak plot, the performances were uninspired, the dialogue archaic or unsuitably glib. But *Dragonwyck* embodied a theme that became Mankiewicz's trademark: class consciousness that is so universal that it transcends gender, profession, and time.

The second film he directed for Fox fared somewhat better. *Somewhere in the Night* (1946), about a soldier who suffers amnesia when a grenade explodes in his face, at least challenged Mankiewicz's abilities as a screenwriter and allowed him to experiment with subjective camera work. But he added so many details that he succeeded only in making the film more of a study in the art of a thriller than an expression of that art.

"I think it can be said fairly that I've been in on the beginning, rise, peak, collapse, and end of the talking picture."

Director Joseph Mankiewicz, attributed

A collaboration with screenwriter Philip Dunne resulted in three films: *The Late George Apley* (1947), *The Ghost and Mrs. Muir* (1947), and *Escape* (1948). Dunne's career paralleled that of Mankiewicz, and both men considered themselves "writers who direct." In *The Ghost and Mrs. Muir*, Mankiewicz achieved a realism where the film acquired the lifelikeness of representational art and the wholeness of stage action without a stagey look.

Mankiewicz's first popular success, *A Letter to Three Wives* (1949), won him Oscars for Best Screenplay and Best Director. A later film, *The Honey Pot* (1967), had a similar plot but was a failure. But both films illustrated his penchant for working literature and music into the story. His next films for Fox, which were undistinguished, included *House of Strangers* (1949), *No Way Out* (1950), and *People Will Talk* (1951).

Mankiewicz's outstanding gift, and at the same time his chief frustration, was his ability to express life in terms of theater. His finest film, *All About Eve* (1950), has become a major part of movie mythology. Although it portrayed life in the theater, it did so in a way that was cinematic. The story is about the stagestruck Eve, who charms herself into the good graces of Broadway star Margo Channing, exploiting her as a means of furthering Eve's own career.

His later films included *Five Fingers* (1952); *Julius Caesar* (1953), for which Mankiewicz won an Oscar for Best Art Direction-Set Direction; *The Barefoot Contessa* (1954), his first film as producer, director, and screenwriter, and also his most personal; the musical *Guys and Dolls* (1955), both adapted and directed by Mankiewicz; *Suddenly, Last Summer* (1959), his portrait of the commoner victimized; and *Cleopatra* (1963), starring Elizabeth Taylor and Richard Burton. Mankiewicz's last film was *Sleuth* (1972), a story of adultery.

Joseph L. Mankiewicz died on February 5, 1993, less than a week before he was to turn eighty-four years old.

See All About Eve; *Cukor, George; Hepburn, Katharine;* Philadelphia Story, The; *Stewart, James*

MANN, ANTHONY

Attempts to research Anthony Mann's background bear little fruit. What is known about him is not only shadowy, but largely contradictory. His real name is known not to have been Anthony Mann, but the original is variously listed as Emil Bundsmann and Anton Bundsman. It is certain that he was born in California, but whether the birthplace is Point Loma or San Diego is in doubt. Mann's date of birth is thought to be approximately 1907, and his parents are thought to have been two schoolteachers, Emil and Bertha Bundsmann.

Although the early years are shadowy, it is clear that the Bundsmanns encouraged Mann's interest in the theater. When the family relocated to New York City when he was about ten years old, the young boy was able to attend Broadway plays, an experience that made him determined to become an actor. After his father's death, which occurred during Mann's high school years, Mann left his formal education behind and sought work in his chosen profession. He made his Broadway debut as a walk-on, and went on to become a leading actor in various stock companies. On Broadway, the name "Anton Mann" can be found listed in the casts of *The Dybbuk* (1925) and *The Little Clay Cart* (1926).

Mann did not limit himself to acting. He tried his hand at every role in the theater, including assistant production manager, stage manager, and set designer. His first big break came when he was hired as production manager for the prestigious Theater Guild. It was during his years with the Guild he discovered that his greatest interest was in directing, not acting. He made a minor success as director of such productions as *Thunder on the Left* (1933), *Cherokee Night* (1936), *So Proudly We Hail* (1936), and *The Big Blow* (1938), the latter produced by the WPA Federal Theatre.

Mann's minor Broadway success came to the attention of Hollywood. From that point onward, his professional life is more fully documented. Producer David O. Selznick hired him to come to California to work as a talent scout, which helped Mann develop his excellent skill at casting. More important, it gave him his first taste of directing actors on film, for Selznick assigned him the job of directing new talent in screen tests for various productions, among them *Gone with the Wind*, *Intermezzo*, and *Rebecca*.

In 1939 Mann left Selznick to work for Paramount as an assistant director. He spent three years in this capacity, serving many prominent directors, among them Preston Sturges. Finally, Mann was assigned to direct his first film, *Dr. Broadway*, largely through the efforts of his friend MacDonald Carey, who was to star in the low-budget feature for Paramount.

MANN, ANTHONY

Mann's obituary notices fill in the remainder of the details of his private life. He had been married three times, first to Mildred Kenyon, by whom he had two children, Nina and Anthony. Their twenty-five-year marriage ended in divorce in 1956. The following year, he wed Mexican actress Sarita Montiel, who had starred in his film *Serenade*, based on James M. Cain's novel. Their marriage was annulled in 1963. At the time of his death in 1967, Mann was married to a former ballerina, listed in the obituaries as Anna Mann. The couple had one son, Nicholas.

It is a scanty biography, and one that sheds little light on his work. To understand Anthony Mann, it is necessary to look to his films. Although Mann came to Hollywood from Broadway, unlike many who made that transition, he did not think of film as an extension of theater. He wasted no time trying to bend movies into plays. Instead, he saw film as an entirely different medium, with specific properties of its own. As soon as he was allowed to direct, he set about the task of exploring those properties and playing with them for various kinds of effects and meanings. From the very beginning of his career, Mann made films that were inherently cinematic.

notable & quotable

"Mann probed beneath the surface of his male heroes with real psychological insight resulting in powerful and occasionally violent work."

Joel C. Findler, author, 1985, as quoted in The Movie Directors Story *by Joel C. Findler, Crescent Books, 1985*

Mann evolved the concept of the total image, one that contained story (content) and presentation of story with the tools of cinema (form) as a unified event. His career follows a clear progression toward purity and simplification. Mann spent five years, from 1942 to 1947, learning the fundamentals of his craft in a series of low-budget features for Paramount, RKO, Universal, and Republic. The six films he directed were typical "B" film projects of two types—musicals and atmospheric thrillers, made with little money, minor stars, and an abbreviated running time of under seventy minutes. Designed to help fill the enormous demand for movies—any kind of movies—from escape-hungry audiences during World War II, they were meant to be made quickly and cheaply.

Assessing his chances to turn these liabilities into films good enough to keep him working in the medium, Mann decided it was up to him to create story depth and characterization where none existed. He formed two rules for himself on how to direct a picture: (1) select a clear and simple story; (2) make the story better.

Throughout his career, Mann never wavered from these two ideas. Even after he became a top-name director and could choose his own scripts and actors, he looked for stories that were, in his own words, "simple and pictorial." He always considered himself a storyteller, and he endeavored to present his story to the audience as clearly and directly as possible. Of the first ten films directed by Mann, the most interesting are *Strangers in the Night*, *The Great Flamarion*, and *Strange Impersonation*, in addition to his very first full-length feature, *Dr. Broadway*.

Mann's films between 1947 and 1950 all lie within a body of work known as *film noir*. It was a tradition that stressed the darker side of American life, and thus was perfect for Mann's developing sensibility. It afforded him a wide range of possibilities in using studio work and location shooting. By 1950 Mann's cinematic world contained a hero who is linked in the narrative to someone else. *In Side Street* and *Desperate,* it is a woman he loves. In *T-Men* and *Border Incident*, it is to a fellow government agent. The audience is aligned with the hero, who is established for them as the center of the film. Although he may be weak, criminal, or psychotic, the audience is set up to identify with him and his situation. The hero's position in the narrative dictates the emotional situation the audience is going to be put through.

By the end of his film noir period, Mann had achieved a remarkable technical mastery and was ready to move into westerns.

In 1950 Mann directed his first western, *Devil's Doorway*. With his westerns, Mann found the freedom to simplify and to express in purely formal terms what most of his predecessors in the genre had expressed in content. The previously established set of characters and conventions associated with the genre allowed him the freedom not to explain in words various kinds of information. Viewers understood and accepted a man who came from nowhere, and a revenge based upon a conflict never shown.

It is in this decade that Mann's work unifies completely. He centered his films around a basic narrative pattern, involving a recurring set of characters: the hero, villain, old man, woman, and secondary villains.

Mann's westerns, which began with *Devil's Doorway*, followed by *Winchester '73* and *The Furies*, present a story about a hero who is undergoing a psychological change. The landscape, or background, is aligned with him and used to illustrate his internal change through the device of the journey. This internal change, demonstrated visually by background (and position in frame) and revealed by plot, causes the hero to demonstrate his emotional stress through action. The action, usually culminating in violence, creates an emotional effect on the audience, which is like that the hero is undergoing in the narrative. The story, the internal and external life of the hero, and the effect on the audience are all unified.

With his epic films between 1960 and 1965, Mann stripped away characterization in the conventional sense. Since the people of an epic film (particularly *El Cid*) are legends, or mythical figures, the need to develop them as ordinary heroes with psychological problems was unnecessary. Their problems were historical, and the personal was sacrificed to the epic. With his final films, Mann almost returned to his original position as a director, in which he enhanced cardboard characters with form. In his final great film, *El Cid*, his simplicity was almost primeval. He removed the last vestiges of literary meaning from his work, and *El Cid* stands as an example of what might be called "pure cinema."

Mann broke from his four main "periods"—his beginning films, films noirs, westerns, and epics—only twice. *Men in War* (1956) is a war film, and *God's Little Acre* (1958) is Mann's only real literary adaptation.

In 1960, just before his own epic production of *Cimarron*, Mann worked on another big-name, big-budget production, *Spartacus*. He directed all the scenes taking place in the desert, and all those in the school for gladiators (except those with Jean Simmons). These scenes are notably done in Mann's familiar compositional style, and are markedly superior to many in the remainder of the picture.

When asked why he abandoned *Spartacus*, which obviously had such great possibilities and which he had begun shooting with such promise, Mann explained, "Kirk Douglas was the producer of *Spartacus*. He wanted to insist on the message angle. I thought that the message would go over more easily by showing physically all the horror of slavery. A film must be visual. Too much dialogue kills it. From then on, we disagreed."

In the winter of 1966 Mann began work on what was to be his final film, a spy-who-came-in-from-the-cold story based on a Derek Marlowe novel, *A Dandy in Aspic*. On April 29, 1967, after a few weeks of shooting, Mann suffered a fatal heart attack, leaving the film to be finished by its star, Laurence Harvey. As a result, the last film to bear Anthony Mann's name was sadly unworthy of his career: cold, confusing, and not up to the standard associated with his best work from the past.

See Epic

MATHIS, JUNE

Many silent scenarists exercised a degree of power that extended far beyond the drafts emerging from their typewriters. Frances Marion had the ear of Mary Pickford, and the prolific C. Gardner Sullivan skewed the character of Ince releases by the sheer quantity of his own output. But the most influential screenwriter of the day was undoubtedly June Mathis.

She was born in Leadville, Colorado, in 1890 and was onstage from the age of eleven. Well known on the touring circuits in various ingenue roles, she was with the Julian Eltinge company in 1912–13 as the only woman in the cast of *The Fascinating Widow*. When road-company business declined, she turned to writing and soon settled in New York with a place on the staff of the Metro studio. Few film writers had been able to exercise any degree of creative control in this period, when most significant producers and directors were either drafting their own scripts or isolating their writing staffs behind a bureaucratic curtain. But Mathis won the attention of Metro president Richard Rowland and soon began shaping the course of Metro releases. She had a flair for the romantic and the exotic, and frequently emphasized elements of mysticism and spiritualism in her films. In a 1917 *Moving Picture*

June Mathis was arguably the most influential screenwriter of the silent era. Many of her films emphasized elements of mysticism and spiritualism.

World article, she advised prospective authors not to think about their works too long before setting them down on paper in order to prevent the ideas from being stolen by those with conscious or unconscious telepathic powers.

Inevitably, Mathis joined forces with Metro's mysterious Russian star Alla Nazimova, mistress of her own occult circle. Together they made such films as *Out of the Fog* (1919) and *The Red Lantern* (1919), which proved too exotic for general tastes, although Mathis maintained her own commercial standing with a series of successful potboilers. Her most important film was *The Four Horsemen of the Apocalypse* (1921), which she convinced Metro to produce on an elaborate and spectacular scale. Not only did she adapt the Ibáñez novel, but she also selected director Rex Ingram and was responsible for casting the relatively unknown actor Rudolph Valentino in the main role.

Mathis, Ingram, and Valentino then made *The Conquering Power*, an adaptation of Balzac's *Eugénie Grandet,* but Valentino soon quarreled with his director and aligned himself with Mathis, with whom he shared an interest in the occult. She would be the most significant creative figure in his career. He appeared in the *Camille* she wrote for Nazimova, then signed with Famous Players–Lasky. Mathis, too, had outgrown Metro. For a time she followed Valentino to Famous Players–Lasky, where she scripted *Blood and Sand* (1922), one of his greatest successes. But *The Young Rajah* (1922), a steamy travesty of Hindu mysticism, was ridiculed by critics and damaged Valentino's career.

Mathis was later appointed editorial director of Goldwyn Pictures. She was to set studio production policy, pass on contracts, and involve herself personally with the most important films. Soon the Goldwyn studio was populated by such directors as King Vidor, Victor Seastrom, Marshall Neilan, and Erich von Stroheim, but its financial status only grew less secure.

What occupied most of her time was the protracted filming of *Ben-Hur* (1926). She ordered the entire production to be shot in Italy, but this time adequate preparations were never executed. Her director of choice, Charles Brabin, shot reels of useless footage and refused the suggestions she made when she journeyed to Rome to oversee production. Ultimately the Goldwyn company was absorbed in the Metro-Goldwyn-Mayer merger, and the new executives fired Brabin, Mathis, and George Walsh.

Mathis emerged from this debacle relatively unscathed and became editorial director at First National. Here she concentrated on stories for Colleen Moore and Corinne Griffith, comedies and melodramas such as *We Moderns* (1926), *The Marriage Whirl* (1925), and *Irene* (1926). Although none of these films had the impact of the best of her early work, Mathis was able to demonstrate her successful supervision of a major studio's entire output, personally handling some of the most important titles. Perhaps Frances Marion's filmography is more impressive, but June Mathis was the only screenwriter ever to achieve this degree of control.

Mathis died on July 26, 1927, in New York during a performance of *The Squall.*

See Valentino, Rudolph; Vidor, King

MELODRAMA

Any type of film, play, or television program characterized by a sensational plot designed principally to provide thrills and to appeal to the emotions of the audience is called a melodrama. The term *melodrama* translates literally as a "play with music," a throw-back to the origins of the genre in English theater during the nineteenth century. As the form developed it became customary to include incidental music with the dramatic action to enhance the emotions and thrills, thus "melodrama."

Film melodramas similarly seek to engage the emotions of the audience and provide thrills; often they are characterized by the liberal use of music to underscore the developing plot. The form has been popular in the motion picture since the evolution of the fictional film, particularly in mystery thrillers and in westerns. In melodramas characters are often one-dimensional, appearing in action plots in which good eventually triumphs over evil.

METHOD ACTOR

"Method actor" is a popular term used to describe actors who have studied the Stanislavsky method of naturalistic acting. Popularized in the United States in the 1930s by director Richard Boleslavski and Stella Adler, and eventually a principal approach at the New York City Actors Studio under Lee Strasberg and Elia Kazan, method acting seeks to combine a psychological attitude with learned technical skills. The ultimate goal is greater realism in character interpretation. Method acting began to make an impact in Hollywood with the arrival of Actors Studio graduates (Marlon Brando, Julie Harris, James Dean, Karl Malden, Kim Stanley) in the early 1950s. This new acting style coincided appropriately with a partial move in American filmmaking toward more psychological, introspective stories: *A Streetcar Named Desire* (1951), *East of Eden* (1955), and *The Goddess* (1958).

See Brando, Marlon; Kazan, Elia; Streetcar Named Desire, A

METONYMY

Metonymy is a film term derived from the Greek "metonymia," meaning "change of name." Metonymy refers to the use of the name of an object or concept to imply something of related meaning, for example, "the brass" for

"high-ranking military officers." Metonymy in a motion picture can refer to an object that serves narrative and thematic functions through implied correlation. In Vittorio De Sica's *The Bicycle Thief* (1947) a stolen bicycle acts as a metonymical device for implying the desperation of post–World War II Italians in a context greater than that of Antonio's (the protagonist) own individual plight. The missing bicycle signifies an overall sense of desperate need and can be seen as representing, metonymically, "a paradise lost."

MIDNIGHT COWBOY

Midnight Cowboy (1969) is the only X-rated film to have ever received the Best Picture Oscar. (In later years—more permissive times—the movie was rerated, upgraded to an R.) It received seven nominations and three Oscars, including statues for Best Director (John Schlesinger) and Best Adapted Screenplay (written by Waldo Salt, based on James Leo Herlihy's novel of the same title). *Midnight Cowboy,* a term used to refer to a male hustler, is a drama of the friendship that develops between two drifters in New York City and the searing realities of their lives.

The average ticket price in 1969—the year of *Midnight Cowboy*, *Butch Cassidy and the Sundance Kid*, and *The Love Bug*—was $1.42.

Joe Buck (Jon Voight, who, although unknown at the time, won a Best Actor nomination for his performance) is a dishwasher at Miller's Restaurant, a little joint in a dusty, dreary Texas town. He decides that with his tall, blond good looks, he can make a fortune with the love-starved rich women in New York City.

Decked out in cowboy boots, a Stetson hat, and a fringed-leather jacket, Joe boards a Greyhound bus and begins the long trip east. On the journey, and throughout the film, Joe has occasional flashbacks to his life in Texas. He thinks back to when he was a boy, being spanked, naked, by his creepy grandmother, Sally Buck (Ruth White), a woman who has a parade of boyfriends. Joe also has flashbacks to when he is making love with Annie (Jennifer Salt), who keeps asking, "Do you love me, Joe? Do you love me? . . . You're the only one, Joe. . . . You're better, Joe." Later we will see Joe and Annie being attacked by a group of men while necking in a car.

Joe's excitement mounts as the bus approaches New York. He's convinced that he'll climb off the bus and immediately be besieged by admiring women. He's in for a big disappointment: no one pays him the slightest bit of attention. He takes a room in a second-rate hotel, decorating his grimy room with a magazine picture of a topless woman and a poster of Paul Newman in the movie *Hud.*

Back on the street, Joe runs into Cass (Sylvia Miles), an older woman—probably a prostitute. He accompanies her to a penthouse apartment,

Dustin Hoffman (left) and Jon Voight were both nominated for Best Actor Oscars for their performances in Midnight Cowboy *(1969). Though neither won the award, the film did win Best Picture, and its director, John Schlesinger, won for Best Director.*

◀

thinking that this will be his first paying customer, but the crafty Cass turns the tables on him. Joe ends up giving *her* money when she makes him feel guilty and asks him for cab fare. He displays the bills in his wallet, and she plucks out a twenty.

Joe is quickly learning that life in New York isn't going to be a piece of cake. His funds are dwindling at an alarming rate when he meets Enrico "Ratso" Rizzo (Dustin Hoffman, in a role that earned him a second Academy Award nomination for Best Actor) in a sleazy bar. Ratso is a puny, sickly-looking bum with a chronic cough who walks with a limp and talks in a whine. Ratso, ever the opportunist, sees how naïve Joe is. He offers to become his "street manager" and introduce him to a pimp who will get Joe on his way to making some serious money. He sends Joe—after collecting $20 in fees—to see Mr. O'Daniel (John McGiver). Joe admits that although he is not a "for-real cowboy," he is quite a stud. O'Daniel, a deranged religious fanatic, says, "I'm gonna use ya. . . . You and me can have fun together. It doesn't have to be joyless." Joe flees, furious at being taken advantage of yet again.

Things become desperate for Joe. He can't pay his hotel bill and is thrown out, his belongings confiscated until he settles up. At the end of his rope, with nothing to eat, he tells himself, "You know what you gotta do, cowboy" and sells himself to a male student. During their assignation in a darkened movie theater, he thinks of making love to Annie, then helplessly witnessing her rape.

But this turning point in the "education" of Joe Buck has a bad end: the student has no money to pay him. Joe has lost yet again, and in more ways than one.

The next day Joe runs into Ratso, who has no money either. Ratso invites Joe to move into his place—a filthy, crumbling apartment in a condemned building. Ratso tells Joe of his dream to go to Florida, and he teaches the young Texan the ways of surviving on the street. His clothes, he tells Joe, have got to go if Joe wants to hook up with a rich woman; the cowboy garb is more appealing to homosexuals than to women. "And I'll tell ya another thing. Frankly, you're beginning to smell. And for a stud in New York, that's a handicap."

Joe defends himself: "I like the way I look. . . . And women like me. . . . Women go crazy for me. . . . Crazy Annie, they had to send her away."

Joe is convinced that the only reason he hasn't scored is because he needs management. Ratso agrees to take him in hand. He spruces up his appearance and tries to get him dates with women, but they fail miserably.

Ratso and Joe become bonded in their desperation and share more of their life stories: Ratso's father was an illiterate shoeshine man. Joe has been let down and abandoned.

The weather turns colder, and Ratso's cough seems to be worsening. He and Joe are in desperate straits. They have no money, and then they can only watch helplessly as their home is torn down.

Finally, at a party, Ratso gets Joe gets a date with a rich woman named Shirley (Brenda Vaccaro). At first Joe cannot perform sexually. Shirley says, "Maybe if you didn't call me ma'am, things might work out better." She suggests that he is gay; affronted, he sets out to prove he is really a man.

Shirley recommends Joe's services to a girlfriend of hers, and Joe is elated. Here is his chance, finally, to achieve what he set out to do when he left Texas. But Ratso says he must get to Florida now—he's getting sicker by the minute.

Desperate for cash to buy bus fare and fulfill his friend's dream of going to Florida, Joe prostitutes himself to a man in town for a convention. Afterward, when offered only $10 and a St. Christopher's medal for his services, Joe breaks: he goes berserk and beats and robs the man.

"I'm walking here! I'm walking here!"

A spontaneous ad lib (left in the final cut) by Dustin Hoffman as Enrico "Ratso" Rizzo, to an aggressive taxi driver in the street during filming of *Midnight Cowboy* (1969)

Ratso and Joe finally get on a bus to Florida. Ratso's health, however, is failing with each passing mile. Joe buys them new clothes and talks of his own expectations of Florida, planning to find an easier way of making a living than hustling, perhaps getting some outdoor work. But as the palm trees flash by outside the bus windows, he realizes that Ratso has died. In the last shot, he puts his arm around Ratso and holds him.

See Hoffman, Dustin

MILESTONE, LEWIS

Lewis Milestone achieved a rare combination of eminence and longevity among Hollywood directors, spanning the transition from silent cinema to sound and excelling in projects as diverse as the stirring antiwar epic *All Quiet on the Western Front* and the madcap farce *The Front Page.*

He was born Lewis Milstein to a prominent and prosperous family of Russian Jews in Odessa on September 30, 1895, and spent his youth in Kishinev. His parents, although liberal, discouraged his interest in the theater. Sent off to engineering school in Germany, the teenage Milestone, bored by his studies and flunking his courses, joined two equally adventurous classmates on a trip to New York in 1913. After a sojourn with an aunt, he decided to stay and pursue a theatrical career, taking on a series of odd jobs, the most useful of which was a stint as a photographer's assistant that taught him technical and aesthetic tricks of the trade that would soon prove useful in Hollywood.

Milestone's first encounter with film was in the photography section of the Army Signal corps during World War I, during which he worked on training films and edited combat footage in New York and Washington, D.C. These assignments also brought him into contact with other future directors such as Victor Fleming and Josef von Sternberg. Upon his discharge from the army in February 1919, he officially changed his name from Milstein to Milestone and returned briefly to the photographic business, which he found depressing. When he heard about an opening in Hollywood for an assistant editor at $20 per week, he eagerly withdrew his meager savings and boarded a train for Hollywood. After a brief stint at Hampton Studios, Milestone became the assistant to the director Henry King and shortly thereafter, a gag writer, double, and assistant editor at Mack Sennett's Comedy Studio. Later, working at Ince Studios, he met the director William A. Seiter, for whom Milestone served as assistant director

M

MILESTONE, LEWIS

Director Lewis Milestone won the Oscar for Best Director twice: in 1929 for Two Arabian Knights *(1927) and again in 1931 for* All Quiet on the Western Front *(1930).*

on several projects, learning the director's craft while continuing work as a freelance editor and writer and acquiring a reputation as one of Hollywood's bright young men.

Milestone followed Seiter to Warner's, where, in 1925, he directed his first feature film, the comedy *Seven Sinners.* Another comedy, *The Caveman* (1926), soon followed, and Milestone was on his way. After a salary dispute with Warner's, he moved to Paramount, where a string of his directorial successes attracted the attention of millionaire Howard Hughes, who hired Milestone to direct for his Caddo Company. It was here that the young director crossed the bridge to the sound era: his last silent film, *Betrayal,* and his first sound film, *New York Nights,* were both released in 1929.

His next project for Hughes was *All Quiet on the Western Front* (1930). This stirring adaptation of Erich Maria Remarque's antiwar novel, which earned Oscars for Best Film and Best Director, is generally considered Milestone's masterpiece. During the ensuing decade Milestone continued to work in the theater, choosing his cinematic projects carefully and succeeding in a wide array of genres: the comedy *The Front Page* (1931), the musicals *Hallelujah, I'm a Bum* (1933) and *Anything Goes* (1936), the thriller *The General Died at Dawn* (1936), and a highly regarded adaptation of John Steinbeck's novella *Of Mice and Men* (1939).

Ironically, during the 1940s Milestone, who had established his reputation with a poignant indictment of war, was obliged to churn out a series of World War II projects that glorified the battlefield: *The North Star* (1943), *The Purple Heart* (1944), and *A Walk in the Sun* (1946). With the war's end, finally freed from the formulas of guts-and-glory battlefield yarns, Milestone presided over his signal achievement of the 1940s, the richly atmospheric film noir thriller *The Strange Love of Martha Ivers* (1946).

Milestone recreated the battlefield twice more in the fifties but with no greater distinction than he had during the war years: *The Halls of Montezuma* (1950) and *Pork Chop Hill* (1959), set in the Korean War, were competent if pedestrian efforts. By the mid-1950s, as he devoted more time to television directing, his feature film output dropped markedly. In 1960 he steered Frank Sinatra's Rat Pack in the Las Vegas caper *Ocean's 11,* and in 1961 his efforts on his last feature film, *Mutiny on the Bounty* (1962), foundered on the bitter animosity between Marlon Brando and Richard Harris on the set.

After directing a few more television projects in the early 1960s, Milestone eased into retirement, suffering from a host of chronic health problems. In 1978 he endured the death of his wife and a debilitating stroke. The Director's Guild honored him with a Pioneer Tribute on July 28, 1979. After a succession of illnesses, Lewis Milestone died on September 25, 1980, at the UCLA Medical Center, five days before his eighty-fifth birthday.

See All Quiet on the Western Front; *Brando, Marlon; Cukor, George; Goldwyn, Samuel;* Mutiny on the Bounty; *von Sternberg, Josef; War film*

MR. SMITH GOES TO WASHINGTON

Mr. Smith Goes to Washington (1939), directed by Frank Capra, was released less than two months after World War II broke out in Europe. The film

M

MR. SMITH GOES TO WASHINGTON

earned the second largest domestic box-office gross (only *Gone with the Wind* earned more) in 1939. The story argued that although America did have its problems, it also had political traditions and ideals worth preserving.

The idealistic and patriotic Jefferson Smith (Jimmy Stewart), leader of the Boy Rangers, is named to the United States Senate after a senator's sudden death. Scorned by his cynical secretary, Saunders (Jean Arthur), and mocked by newsmen when he arrives in Washington, the wide-eyed Smith eagerly attempts to introduce a bill establishing a boys' camp in his state. He is portrayed as a childlike innocent in the world of experience. He grows to manhood through the film, doubting yet ultimately retaining his patriotic idealism.

A powerful and corrupt newspaper and industrial magnate, James Taylor (Edward Arnold), and Smith's state's senior senator, Joseph Paine (Claude Rains), learn about the proposed boys' camp. It is to be built on

As relevant today as ever, Frank Capra's Mr. Smith Goes to Washington *follows one man's attempts to address corruption in the U.S. Senate.*
▼

land that Taylor has quietly bought and planned to sell at a huge profit under the provisions of another pending bill, endorsed by Paine. They try to buy Smith off, then to break him. To that end, Paine falsely accuses Smith of owning the land himself, then urges the Senate to oust him.

Disillusioned, Smith almost leaves Washington. His deepest moment of self-doubt occurs at the steps of the Lincoln Memorial, but it is the image of the Capitol Dome that is particularly affecting to him; it reminds him of the American commitment to liberty. In addition, Saunders, through her memory of her doctor father's altruism and her observation of Smith's vulnerability in Washington, has become charmed by Smith's simple idealism. With her assistance and support, Smith decides to remain and fight. Gaining the Senate floor, he filibusters for twenty-four hours, hoping to bring news of Taylor's corruption to his home state.

Though Taylor's newspapers carry only negative reports of Smith, Senator Paine cracks under the pressure. He wistfully recalls that thirty years earlier, he and Smith's father, a newspaper editor who was murdered for printing exposés of a corrupt mining company, had been "twin champions of lost causes." Paine, after attempting suicide, confesses his complicity in Taylor's scheme of corruption, which brings about the ritual victory and the vindication of Smith's idealism.

Nevertheless, Taylor, the villain of wealth and power, remains unconverted at the end, making Smith's victory a tentative and limited one at best. This film, made at a time when many Americans were searching for the essence of America, due largely to the threat of Nazi aggression and tyranny, was Capra's powerful tribute to Christian love and American liberty.

See Capra, Frank; Stewart, James

notable & quotable

"It showed the Senate made up of crooks, led by crooks, listening to a crook. . . . It was so vicious an idea it was a source of disgust and hilarity to every member of Congress who saw it."

Sen. Alban W. Barkley, 1939

MIX, TOM

Adult audiences began deserting the western genre after 1915. It was abandoned by serious filmmakers like DeMille and Ince (apart from his Hart releases), and tradepaper criticism grew increasingly condescending. But an underclass of western films, and the popularity of a few individual western stars, did continue to grow. During the late teens, William S. Hart dominated the western market, but by the close of the war he was being eclipsed by Tom Mix, a rival who actually predated him in the motion-picture business.

Cowboy actor Tom Mix developed a comical style, emphasized action and thrills, and even performed his own stunts in westerns of the 1920s.

Some have argued that it was Mix's heavy use of stunts, comedy, and outlandish western garb that somehow stole away the Hart audience, an explanation that implies an increasing frivolity among postwar filmgoers. But it was not the individual moviegoers who changed. The adult audience who had supported the gravity of a Hart film like *The Darkening Trail* (1915) had long since abandoned the genre. Children now made up the bulk of the western audience, and the relatively mature themes of the Hart films had little interest for them. Tom Mix, who offered "action and excitement spiced with a boyish sense of fun," captured this young audience, and with it the western market.

Whatever his audience, Mix was highly successful in appealing to it throughout the mid 1920s. The appeal of a Mix film was straightforward and direct. In 1920 the *Photoplay Plot Encyclopedia,* which analyzed the story lines of one hundred recent features, noted about *The Cyclone* (1920), in which Mix played a Canadian mountie, that the film's simplicity as a limiting factor was somehow overcome by Mix's athletic ability. The powerful appeal of an uncomplicated narrative (and uncomplicated hero) is hardly considered. But it is precisely this quality that separated Mix from William S. Hart, and on which much of his appeal to unsophisticated audiences was based. While Hart offered the ambiguity of a "good bad man," and emotionally wrenching "soul fights" from the pen of C. Gardner Sullivan, Mix avoided such dramatics. Uncomplicated characterizations and simple narratives put no strain on his histrionic abilities and made his films much more accessible to young audiences.

Such behavior laid the foundation for the B-western genre, a category identified not merely by budgetary limitations but by an entire Mix-inspired, "code of the West." B-western heroes often sported outrageous dude-ranch versions of western garb, fantasies of cowboy life that drew their inspiration from circuses and Wild West shows.

For Mix, it all led inevitably back to the circus (he toured with his own for several years before his death) and to life as a media cowboy in vaudeville, comic books, and radio.

See DeMille, Cecil B.; Ince, Thomas; Western

MARILYN MONROE

Screen legend and goddess Marilyn Monroe was born Norma Jean Mortenson in Los Angeles, California, on June 1, 1926. Her unmarried mother, Gladys Baker, was abandoned by the baby's father, Edward Mortenson, even before she was born. Gladys was a mentally fragile woman, and from the age of nine Norma Jean grew up in a series of orphanages and foster homes. It was an unhappy, traumatic childhood—one that included sexual abuse—that would leave many emotional scars on Norma Jean.

At sixteen Norma Jean married a young factory worker; that union lasted four years. She started working in the Radio Flier Company factory, and around this time she bleached her hair and started modeling bathing suits and posing for pin-up shots. Photos from that period reveal the innocent, vulnerable, but definitely sensual quality that came to define her.

In 1954 Norma Jean—now using the name Marilyn Monroe—was signed to a contract by 20th Century-Fox. But the studio clearly did not know what

Once asked by a reporter what she wears to bed, sex goddess Marilyn Monroe coyly replied, "Chanel No. 5."

to do with Monroe and soon dropped her. She found work in a few films over the next several years, but it was not until 1950 that she was given parts in *The Asphalt Jungle* and *All About Eve* that, while small, brought her notice. The Fox studio, now realizing her star potential, reassessed their apparently rash decision to drop the incandescent starlet, and re-signed her to a more lucrative contract. Her burgeoning appeal was surprisingly helped, not hindered, by the late-breaking discovery of the series of nude calendar shots she had posed for in 1948 when she was out of work (the photos were published in the debut issue of *Playboy* in December of 1953). Few could hold them against her when she related that the $50 she received for the photo session kept her out of the breadline. When asked whether she had anything on at all in the photos, Monroe replied, "Yes, the radio." Audiences and exhibitors were set atwitter by the huge amount of publicity generated from the photographs, so much so that Monroe's name on a billboard was estimated to add $500,000 to a film's gross. Consequently, the studio handed her plum assignments, in the Cary Grant comedy *Monkey Business* (1952), and in three 1953 features that would cement her celebrity: *Niagara, Gentlemen Prefer Blondes*, and *How to Marry a Millionaire*.

The following year marked Monroe's marriage to legendary baseball player Joe DiMaggio, whom she had met on a blind date two years earlier. The marriage lasted a scant nine months, failing largely because Monroe

Marilyn Monroe's 23 films between 1950 and 1961 grossed $200 million.

didn't turn out to be the baby-making housewife that the retired, celebrity-shirking slugger had in mind when he wed her. For her part, Monroe reveled in the adulation of her very public life, and her constant headline making caused friction in their relationship. The now-famous scene from Billy Wilder's *The Seven Year Itch*, in which a gust of air from a subway grating sends Monroe's skirt billowing up well past her waist, was the final straw for the straitlaced DiMaggio. The couple remained close friends following their divorce, and for twenty years after Monroe's death, DiMaggio faithfully sent roses to be placed on her grave three times a week.

Monroe's screen persona in all her films dovetailed closely with the voluptuous dumb-blonde archetype, but she always managed to invest what could otherwise have been cardboard-cutout roles with an appealing combination of innocence and overt, yet vulnerable, sexuality. Her *Clash by Night* (1952) director, Fritz Lang, remarked of this knowing naiveté, "She was a very peculiar mixture of shyness and uncertainty and—I wouldn't say 'star allure'—but . . . she knew exactly her impact on men." In an effort to move beyond the confines of her perennial employment as a sex object, Monroe moved to New York, where she studied acting under Lee and Paula Strasberg, announced the formation of her own production company, Marilyn Monroe Productions, and fell in with a circle of intellectuals that included playwright Arthur Miller, whom she married in 1956, after converting to Judaism.

Back under a lucrative contract with Fox in 1955, Monroe continued to mature as an actress and to polish her fine comic sense—most notably in 1956's comedy-drama *Bus Stop*, and in the 1959 classic *Some Like It Hot*. Also around this time, Monroe's many personal troubles began exacting their toll on her always fragile mental and physical health. She succumbed to increasingly narcissistic behavior, relying on stimulants and sleeping pills to keep her going, and undergoing frequent treatment in psychiatric clinics for her chronic depression. Her marriage to Miller ended in early 1961, one week prior to the release of what was to be her last film, John Huston's *The Misfits*. Written specifically for her by Miller, the film represented her finest dramatic performance, which resonated poignantly due to the fact that she was so obviously on the verge of mental breakdown. In fact, Monroe entered a hospital for psychiatric care several weeks after the film premiered. Her reputation for professional unreliability finally reached insupportable levels on the set of 1962's *Something's Got to Give*: out of thirty-two days of shooting, she showed up only twelve times. Refusing to indulge her, the studio fired her and subsequently slapped her with a $750,000 lawsuit for unprofessional conduct.

One month later, in August of 1962, Monroe was found dead from an overdose of barbiturates at her Los Angeles home. Though medical examination concluded that the blonde bombshell had taken her own life, many people suspected—and continue to suspect—that foul play was involved, largely due to rumors that she had been romantically entangled with both President John F. Kennedy and his brother Attorney General Robert Kennedy in the months preceding her death.

See All About Eve; *Cukor, George; Gable, Clark;* Some Like It Hot; *Wilder, Billy*

notable & quotable

"She could never get there on time [the set of *The Misfits*]. Getting to that set was opening her up to all the anxiety, all the hate, all the pain."

Eli Wallach, actor, 1999, as quoted in "America Goes Hollywood," Newsweek, *June 28, 1999*

MODERN TIMES

Modern Times (1936), with no traditional dialogue, just voices and the sounds of machines, is Charlie Chaplin's last full-length "silent film." Starring Chaplin as the Tramp, it is a story of industry and of individual enterprise—humanity crusading in the pursuit of happiness.

From a thematic montage suggesting that factory workers are like sheep, the scene cuts to a worker, the Tramp (Charlie Chaplin), who is holding up production. When he steps away from the line to take a break, he cannot stop tightening nuts and bolts. He twitches mechanically for several moments until he is able to shake himself back into something approximating human form. Under the pressures of the assembly line, he slowly goes "nuts."

Released from a hospital after his nervous breakdown, he is without a job. Innocently retrieving a danger flag that has fallen from the back of a passing truck, he is mistakenly arrested as a communist agitator. The Tramp finds himself in a prison that echoes the regimentation of the factory. He

Charlie Chaplin's Modern Times *used sound in a unique way: we hear spoken voices only when they come from mechanical devices, in keeping with the film's theme of technology and dehumanization.*

languishes there, but when he inadvertently manages to avert a jailbreak, he is released.

On the street, the Gamine (Paulette Goddard) steals a bunch of bananas. She returns home to share her food with her motherless younger sisters and her unemployed father. Days later, when her father is killed in a riot, the authorities come to take away her sisters. The Gamine escapes their clutches.

The Tramp finds work in a shipyard, but leaves when he sinks a half-finished ship. Hungry and scared, he is determined to get arrested again to go back to the safety of jail. His attempts are in vain; he even tries to take the blame when the Gamine is caught stealing a loaf of bread. The ploy fails and she is arrested instead.

Finally succeeding in getting arrested, the Tramp meets the Gamine in the paddy wagon on the way to jail. The two manage to escape, and they team up. As they get to know one another, the Tramp fantasizes aloud about having a happy life with her in a nice home. He becomes inspired to make the dream a reality.

He finds a night watchman job in a department store, where he sneaks in the Gamine, feeds and clothes her, and puts her to bed, promising to wake her before the store opens the next morning. She awakens in time to get out, but the Tramp is found asleep on the job and is jailed for ten days.

The Gamine is waiting for him upon his release and shows him their dream home, a dilapidated shack. They settle down and establish a loving relationship. Trying to find a job, the Tramp is picked up for loitering and sent to jail for another week.

Meanwhile, the Gamine finds a job as a café dancer. She then secures the Tramp a job as a waiter in the same cabaret. Failing at that, he becomes a smashing success singing in the cabaret. But when the juvenile officials show up to take the Gamine away, the Tramp grabs her and they escape.

The last scene shows them walking arm in arm into the sunrise. Free of assembly lines and impersonal social processes at last, the Tramp and his love have finally escaped the vast machine and are walking toward the future together.

See Chaplin, Charlie; Sound

MONTAGE

Montage is a French word meaning "mounting," frequently used to describe the assemblage of a film through editing. Numerous subcategories of montage have developed to denote particular methods of editing. Among them are the following terms:

MONTAGE

Accelerated Montage

The use of editing to add to the effect of increased speed of action in a motion picture is called accelerated montage. By decreasing the length of individual shots in an action or chase sequence, it is possible to impose an external pace on the rhythm of the film. The quickening of pace through editing is termed *accelerated montage.* The climax to a screen chase is often accompanied by accelerated montage, where the excitement of the event seems to quicken with shorter shots and staccato editing. In D. W. Griffith's *The Lonedale Operator* (1911) accelerated montage is achieved through rapid crosscutting among three locations until a young engineer on a speeding train arrives to rescue his girlfriend from invading robbers. The scene in Jean-Luc Godard's *Breathless* (1959) in which Jean-Paul Belmondo kills a policeman seems unusually fast because of accelerated montage. Three quick shots are cut together in a brief four-second span of time.

American or Hollywood Montage

American or Hollywood montage is sometimes used to refer to a scene in which a series of short, quick shots are edited so as to suggest in a brief period the essence of events occurring over a longer span of time. The cinematic cliché of newspaper headlines presented in a rapid succession of shots to capsulize in time the major developments in an event and to serve as a transition between dramatic sequences is an example of American montage. *Citizen Kane* (1941) employs this type of device on several occasions.

Conceptual Montage

The cutting together of shots for the purpose of creating meanings that exist only by the arrangement of the various shots is called conceptual montage. The theories and application of conceptual montage were major concerns of the Russian filmmakers of the 1920s, particularly Sergei Eisenstein and V. I. Pudovkin. These filmmakers believed that montage (editing) was the very essence of film art and sought to exploit its most expressive possibilities. Eisenstein and Pudovkin were less interested in matched-cut editing and more interested in the overall effect of an assortment of shots. They arranged their material for emotional-intellectual impact as well as for narrative flow.

In the Odessa steps sequence of *The Battleship Potemkin* (1925) Eisenstein intentionally distorts time and space by expanding the actual time of the scene and employs dramatic long shots of the fleeing victims beside close-up shots of the pounding boots of the Cossacks. The contrast provided by this editing of close shots of marching feet and helpless victims becomes a powerful visual metaphor for authoritarian persecution in Russia. To end the scene a shot of a soldier lifting his rifle saber to slash a baby in a perambulator is followed by a dynamic cut to a startled woman who has just been hit in the eye by a Cossack's bullet. The woman's shocked expression of horror serves as a realistic one for her own fate and a symbolic, conceptual one for the baby's fate, as it is edited in immediately after the stabbing that is not visualized. The joining of the two shots magnifies the horror and tragedy of the event.

Montage of Attraction

Montage of attraction is a metaphorical editing method whereby two separate images on the screen become related to one another because of visual and contextual similarities. In *Ten Days That Shook the World* (1928) Eisenstein employed this method of montage of attraction so extensively as to make the film a virtual burlesque. For example, a shot of an arrogant czarist politician is followed by a shot of a peacock spreading its proud tail feathers. This type of satirical editing is common throughout Eisenstein's film.

Relational Montage

Relationship montage is a form of narrative montage whereby two or more shots create meaning by their relationship to one another. In the early 1920s a Russian film experimenter, Lev Kuleshov, edited a single shot of an actor's expressionless face between shots of an empty soup bowl, a dead woman in a coffin, and a child playing with a toy. In each return to the shot of the actor's face film viewers who were shown the short film said that the actor's emotions had changed. They saw hunger on the face after the shot of the empty bowl, sadness after the shot of the coffin, and happiness after the insert of the playful child. The belief that the actor had changed expressions was a direct result of relational editing.

Narrative Montage

The editing together of shots and scenes that have been arranged in a desired chronological order according to a prescribed shooting script or master-shot procedure is called narrative montage. The editor's goal is to reconstruct the semblance of events and to structure the narrative flow of the film story. Narrative montage is more concerned with the development of a story, whereas conceptual montage seeks to produce ideas and effects through the joining or collision of shots.

Rhythmic Montage

Editing for rhythmic variation to effect the thematic intentions of a film or a film scene is known as rhythmic montage. The length of shots, movement within a frame, and types of transitions employed between scenes most significantly affect editing rhythm. The actual length of shots determines external rhythm, while movement within a frame determines internal rhythm. Eisenstein employed the term *rhythmic montage* to describe editing methods used in his films. The Odessa steps sequence, for example, combines external and internal rhythms to create a montage of powerful effect.

A short film called *Values and Interpretations,* produced by the American Society of Cinematographers in 1963, illustrates the role of the film editor in determining dramatic effect through cutting rhythms. *Values and Interpretations* shows a sequence being filmed for the television series *Gunsmoke.* The scene opens with a man assaulting a young woman and concludes with a fistfight between the man and the town marshal. The woman and various other townspeople watch the action. The director of the scene, Ted Post, employs a standard approach in filming the material. He begins each action with long shots and then repeats the action for closer views and reaction shots of the onlookers.

The *Gunsmoke* sequence of shots is then given to three different film editors and we are allowed to see how each edits the scene. The most striking and revealing contrast occurs between the work of the first two editors. The first editor breaks the material into short, staccato shots, frequently cutting in the middle of sentences of dialogue rather than at the end of sentences. As a result the pace of the action is dynamic and metronomic. Obviously this editor interpreted the scene as intense and active and sought to use quick cutting to complement that interpretation.

The second editor is less dynamic. He makes extensive use of close-up reaction shots and "holds" on these shots for a more extended period of time than the first editor. Because of this less dynamic approach, the second version appears more contemplative. The onlookers seem to be absorbing the impact of the violent action rather than passively viewing it.

The length of the shots is the key difference between the tempos of the two variations of the theme.

Russian Montage

Russian montage refers to the various editing approaches of prominent Russian directors during the 1920s, namely, Sergei Eisenstein, Lev Kuleshov, V. I. Pudovkin, and Dziga-Vertov. Spurred by extensive post-Revolutionary experimentation in all the arts, Russian film directors sought new methods of expression to achieve their assigned tasks of educating and rallying the country's citizens. Montage—expressive editing—was viewed as the very essence of cinematic art, particularly the linkage and collision of shots to produce emotional, physical, and ideological meaning. Reflecting his effort to produce socially useful statements, Dziga-Vertov's early editing experiments in the *Kino-Pravda* newsreels (1922–25) often juxtapose scenes of the past (taken from vintage footage) with newly recorded shots of more favorable current conditions. Kuleshov's creative geography and relational montage experiments reveal how separate shots—when linked together through editing—can suggest geographic and emotional realities that in fact do not exist. Pudovkin developed a theory of "constructive edit-

ing" in which the precise selection and arrangement of narrative details are seen as the primary means by which the filmmaker seizes attention and guides the viewer's "thoughts and associations." Eisenstein advocated "montage of collision"—the clash and contrast of shots for a dialectical effect. Montage of collision, Eisenstein said, could be achieved through rhythmic clash, temporal-spatial conflict, and within image composition, including the clash of mass or volume. The application of these latter methods appears most noticeably in Eisenstein's *The Battleship Potemkin* (1925).

By employing editing as their primary means of film expression, Russian directors of the 1920s gave new meaning to the concept of montage, while establishing themselves through their dynamic methods as important motion-picture formalists.

See Editor; Griffith, D. W.

MURNAU, F. W.

"The camera is the director's sketching pencil," F. W. Murnau wrote in 1928. "It should be as mobile as possible to catch every passing mood, and it is important that the mechanics of the cinema should not be interposed between the spectator and the picture." Long before Alexandre Astruc, Murnau was aware of the principle of the *caméra stylo.* He articulated the doctrine of the long take, and seemed to recoil from the lavish studio fabrications that marked the early days of the German expressionist film. While other directors working in Hollywood, even Erich von Stroheim or Ernst Lubitsch, built their work around scenarios of substance, Murnau approached his art from another direction.

Murnau was brought to America by William Fox in 1926. He made three films for the Fox Company, none of which was commercially successful. Yet the impact of his method of working changed the entire direction of the American cinema in this period. Hollywood had absorbed and Americanized such talents as Lubitsch and Benjamin Christensen, but Murnau proved to be the one European filmmaker of the era who succeeded in changing Hollywood.

Murnau's *The Last Laugh* (1924) had been a great critical success in America, though a box-office catastrophe. William Fox, eager to enhance his industry position and be seen as the peer of Adolph Zukor, signed Murnau to a luxurious four-year, four-picture contract. The salary began at $125,000 and rose in annual increments to $200,000.

But in signing Murnau, Fox had not just bought himself a German director, he had acquired a substantial segment of the German film indus-

M

MURNAU, F. W.

Friedrich Wilhelm Plumpe, better known as F. W. Murnau, brought German film techniques—as well as a substantial segment of the German film industry's players—to Hollywood.

try as well. For the first film, *Sunrise* (1927), a script came in from Carl Mayer, scriptwriter of *The Cabinet of Dr. Caligari* and *The Last Laugh.* To build the sets, designer Rochus Gliese was imported, and so were Herman Bing and Edgar G. Ulmer, who acted as Murnau's assistants and intermediaries. Even one of the film's American cinematographers, Charles Rosher, had just spent a year with Murnau in Germany.

A vast city set was constructed in diminishing perspective on the Fox lot. Inside the stages was built a great marsh, with the camera suspended from tracks in the studio ceiling. As it moved with actor George O'Brien through the bullrushes, Karl Struss, Rosher's associate, had to hang from the ceiling with one eye glued to the inverted image in his Bell & Howell viewfinder. Most elaborate of all was the village set, constructed at Lake

Arrowhead. *Sunrise* became a demonstration project of German film techniques applied with Hollywood budgetary resources.

Soon even those directors most closely associated with cozy Americana subjects, men like Brown, Frank Borzage, and John Ford, had absorbed the lessons of Murnau and his style. Ford actually shot much of *Four Sons* (1928) right on the old *Sunrise* village sets. Too costly to be profitable, too arty to be popular, *Sunrise* made no money but left a deep mark on the final few years of silent film in Hollywood. Shadows, camera movements, artfully stylized settings and gestures, all became the mark of true film art in Hollywood during 1927 and 1928.

But Murnau failed to benefit from the impact of his work. His next film, *The Four Devils* (1928), caused little stir, and his final effort for Fox, *Our Daily Bread,* shot largely on a farm outside Pendleton, Oregon, in 1928, was not even released in the form he left it. Remarkable mainly for its sensuous tracking shots sweeping through fields of wheat, *City Girl* (as it was called on its release in 1930) at least moved Murnau off the back lot again. When he broke with Fox, he teamed with Robert Flaherty. The Murnau-dominated film that emerged, *Tabu* (1931), remains the last great achievement of the silent cinema.

See Ford, John; Lubitsch, Ernst; von Stroheim, Erich

MUSIC (FILM MUSIC)

Music appearing as a part of the sound track of a motion picture is called film music. Film music may be either realistic or functional, sometimes both. Realistic film music, generally, is music that appears on a film as a part of the story, and its source is visible, or made known, to the viewer. A filmed concert, ballet, or opera is an example of realistically recorded music. The music here is fully or partly derived from the dramatic action. Functional film music, on the other hand, is most often a background score designed to enhance mood, to intensify emotions and actions, and to aid film structure by supplying aural unification. In achieving these goals the music serves several expressive functions. Scenic music sets the scene for the action that will follow. The musical cliché of the French cancan sets the scene for a Paris location; the sound of American Indian music, suggested by the overused rhythmic beat of a tom-tom, signals the Old West while sounding an ominous note; the music coming from the flute of an Indian snake-charmer suggests the exotic nature of the Far East. Stephen Foster's music often accompanies film stories set in the old South.

Time periods may also be a functional goal of film music. Film stories set in Renaissance Europe are often scored with music dominated by blaring trumpets, cornets, and other brass instruments. Later periods, set in the more genteel seventeenth and eighteenth centuries, utilize harpsichords and harps to suggest the time. Contemporary films with modern themes, such as *Medium Cool* (1969) and *Mickey One* (1965), both set in Chicago in the 1960s, contain modern jazz scores to suggest both their contemporaneity and their urban settings.

In addition to its scenic functions, film music may also punctuate and reinforce screen action. A chase scene is often accompanied by a rhythmic, dynamic piece of music, which is coordinated to match the pace of the dramatic action, and is thus reinforcing. Music to reinforce action may be generally synchronized to the scene, or it may be synchronized precisely. This exact synchronization of visual image with an associative musical sound is a common technique in many of Walt Disney's cartoon films. Mickey Mouse and other Disney characters often have musical sounds accompany their every movement. This technique, when prominent in coordinating music with image, is sometimes referred to as Mickey Mousing or "Mickey Mousing the music."

Another function of film music is to heighten dramatic tension and to convey mood. Music for mood and dramatic tension is common in suspense scenes, romantic scenes, and landscape scenes. These scenes are often intensified by unobtrusive background music, which, without calling attention to its presence, becomes the principal element that establishes and maintains the mood of the scene.

Another function of music is to provide a musical motif for a motion picture. The various parts of *Gone with the Wind* (1939) are unified by the lyrical music of "Tara's Theme." "Lara's Theme" in *Dr. Zhivago* (1965) provides a unifying musical motif throughout the picture. Musical motifs, or leitmotifs, are sometimes used for character association and are often employed to bridge segments of the story while sustaining mood and film flow. In epic films such as *Gone with the Wind* and *Dr. Zhivago,* motif music plays an important part in conveying the epic quality of the story.

Film music can provide a method for structural unity in scenes that are visually fragmentary. An American montage sequence, which presents rapid shots of dramatic actions for the purpose of condensing a period of time into a brief, capsulized view, is usually accompanied by a unifying piece of music. This is the case with the kinestatic interludes used between sequences in *Same Time, Next Year* (1978). The sustained quality of a musical selection gives structural unity to the brief, fragmentary images.

Because music is present on the filmstrip and can be coordinated precisely with any single film frame, it is also possible to use music to change dynamically the scene or the mood and to "key" essential dramatic information. Soft, romantic music may accompany a fireside living-room scene where a man and a woman are enjoying an evening together. A psychopathic killer makes his way down a corridor leading to the living room. The editor crosscuts between the couple and the killer's feet, and each time inserts dramatic suspense music for the feet shots and returns to the romantic music for the fireside shots. The intercutting has both visual and aural impact. The crosscutting of music serves as a means of rapidly indicating for the viewer different qualities of mood in abrupt scene changes.

The direct coordination of film music with image allows music to serve as an expressive sound effect. Frequently musical notes are substituted for the human voice for a stylized, comic effect.

A single, sustained musical note or combination of notes used to punctuatc a dramatic moment in a film is called a *stinger* because of the aural conclusion it provides. A stinger calls dramatic attention, in a heightened manner, to a moment of information. An electronic stinger effect is used throughout John Sayles's *Passion Fish* (1992) as an abrupt transitional bridge.

Film music often conveys psychological and subjective states not communicable by pictures alone. Musical instruments in film may evoke impressions of happiness, gaiety, sadness, or depression. The film music may convey mood; it may also suggest interior states through its associative relationship with characters and with the emotional climate of a story. A confused state of mind can be conjured up by using a cacophonous, chaotic piece of electronic music. In Carol Reed's *The Third Man* (1949), the confused political state and personal ethics in Vienna during the period following World War II are indicated by a musical score played on a zither.

See Gone with the Wind; Doctor Zhivago; Fantasia; *Musical film; Sound*

MUSICAL FILM

Two definitions exist for musical film. The first is a fictional motion picture that deals in a significant manner with the subject of music and that uses musical performance as an integral part of the narrative, for example, *Yankee Doodle Dandy* (1942), *The Great Caruso* (1951), *The Buddy Holly Story* (1978). In the second definition, a musical film is a motion picture that

incorporates the conventions of song and dance routines into the film story and that uses the musical numbers as an accepted element in the film narrative, for example, *An American in Paris* (1951), *Hello, Dolly!* (1969), *Grease* (1978).

The conventions of the musical genre, in general, include liberal use of musical numbers, choreographed dance, expressive costuming and scenery, and abstract color and lighting—particularly in the song-and-dance routines.

A subcategory within the musical-film genre is the backstage musical, a type of film in which the plot centers on characters who are stage performers. The dramatic plot in backstage musicals invariably develops around the intricacies and tensions of producing a successful stage musical. Integration of elaborate musical numbers into this type of film is justified by the nature of the story, for example, *42nd Street* (1933). The backstage musical was especially popular during the 1930s.

See American in Paris, An; *Astaire, Fred; Rogers, Ginger;* Singin' in the Rain; West Side Story; Yankee Doodle Dandy

The stylish musical Cabaret *won eight Academy Awards, including Best Actress for singer Liza Minnelli and Best Director for Bob Fosse.*

▼

MUTINY ON THE BOUNTY

Mutiny on the Bounty (1935) is considered by many to be one of the best adventure films of all time. An MGM picture, it tells the story—based loosely on real events—of the rebellion of the crew of the H.M.S. *Bounty* against the malevolent Captain William Bligh (Charles Laughton). The screenplay (by Talbot Jennings, Jules Furthman, and Carey Wilson) was adapted from a popular series of books called *The Bounty Trilogy* (composed of *Mutiny on the Bounty*, *Men Against the Sea*, and *Pitcairn Island*), written by Charles Nordhoff and James Norman Hall. The film, directed by Frank Lloyd, won the Academy Award for Best Picture.

The film opens in 1787, as the H.M.S. *Bounty* is preparing to set sail from Portsmouth, England, for a two-year voyage. The king's ship has been charged with collecting breadfruit trees in the South Pacific island of Tahiti and delivering them to British plantations in the West Indies, to provide cheap food for the slaves.

The crewmembers, even Midshipman Roger Byam (Franchot Tone), a gentleman who views the journey as a bit of a lark, soon realize that this will be a punishing voyage. Captain Bligh quickly shows himself to be cruel and maniacal in his imposition of rules and regulations. His fleshy face is set in a perpetual frown. He enjoys humiliating the seamen, doling out arbitrary and brutal punishments, often for no reason beyond that he doesn't like a man's face. Says Bligh's first officer, Master's Mate Fletcher Christian (Clark Gable), "He likes to see men crawl."

Bligh is obsessed with discipline and "duty," and he will tolerate no dissent. Bligh tells Christian that the men "respect but one law—the law of fear. . . ." He adds, "I expect you to carry out whatever orders I give, whenever I give them."

After months at sea, during which Christian has become more and more disgusted by Bligh's treatment of the men, the *Bounty* finally arrives at the beautiful island of Tahiti. Midshipman Byam is warmly welcomed by Hitihiti, the island's chief. Byam soon falls in love with Tehani (Maria Castaneda-Movita). For a long time Bligh does not allow Christian to leave the ship, but as soon as he does Christian becomes enamored of Maimiti (Mamo Clark), Hitihiti's granddaughter.

After some months, during which time many of the men of the H.M.S. *Bounty* have become happily involved in Tahitian life, it is time for the ship to set sail for the West Indies. Once back at sea, Captain Bligh's tyranny immediately comes to the fore. He forces the ship's sick, elderly surgeon, Dr. Bacchus (Dudley Digges), a favorite with the crew, to come up to the deck to watch five crew members be whipped for attempting to jump ship

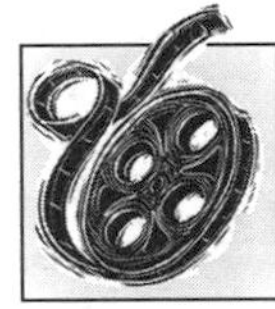

"I'll take my chance against the law. You'll take yours against the sea."

Clark Gable as Fletcher Christian in *Mutiny on the Bounty* (1935)

and return to Tahiti. When Dr. Bacchus dies, the crew turns mutinous, led by Master's Mate Christian.

The men respond eagerly, tying Bligh to the mast and threatening him with death. Christian restrains them from killing Bligh, warning them not to be as cruel as the captain himself.

The captain and some of his followers are loaded into a small launch. Byam and several others who are not part of the mutiny remain on board the *Bounty* due to lack of room in the boat. Astonished, Bligh says, "But you're taking my ship. My ship." Responds Christian: "Your ship? The King's ship, you mean. And you're not fit to command it. Into the boat!"

Bligh, unrepentant, cannot believe that he is being cast adrift in the middle of the ocean in an open boat, and he vows to survive and get his revenge. Bligh and his followers somehow manage to sail to Timor, an

Clark Gable, shown here as Fletcher Christian in MGM's Mutiny on the Bounty *(1935), appeared in over 80 films in his long career as an actor.* ▶

island in the Dutch East Indies, thousands of miles away. Meanwhile, the mutineers sail the *Bounty* back to Tahiti. There, Christian marries Maimiti, and Byam weds Tehani.

A year later the mutineers' worst fear is realized: Bligh returns, commanding another British ship, the *Pandora.* He is bitter and has come to exact his revenge.

Christian and the other mutineers take their Tahitian families and sail away on the *Bounty;* they will establish themselves far away, on another island where they can live their lives in peace. Byam and a few others who did not support the mutiny stay behind, expecting Bligh to welcome them. Instead, Bligh shackles them and sails them to England to stand trial.

Five years after the *Bounty* sailed from Portsmouth, Byam is sentenced to hang. Invited to give a statement, the midshipman who once refused to mutiny against his commanding officer now has no qualms about revealing the truth about Captain Bligh. He tells how Bligh "led" men to their duty not by merit or honor, as befits an agent of the king, but by brutality and terror. He urges lenience for the other men who have been on trial. Byam's plea is successful. The king pardons him, and he returns to serve in the British Navy.

Mutiny on the Bounty has its flaws. It's very long and is filmed almost entirely on the ocean—a strain for many viewers. The actors have a disconcerting variety of accents—for the King's Navy, a surprising number of seamen, including Christian, speak in distinctly American cadences. And the idyllic scenes on Tahiti strain credulity. Still, the movie's themes of pride and honor continue to resonate with audiences—and in film, a rousing good adventure is always timeless.

See Gable, Clark

MY FAIR LADY

My Fair Lady (1964), a musical romantic comedy based on George Bernard Shaw's 1923 play *Pygmalion*, was directed by George Cukor. The film garnered eight Academy Awards, including Best Picture, Best Director, and Best Actor, among others. It is the story of a speech teacher who transforms a Cockney flower girl into the belle of the ball.

Professor Henry Higgins (Rex Harrison) is an egotistical phonetics expert who prides himself on his talent for identifying speech patterns and their corresponding geographic locations. When he and a colleague, Colonel Pickering (Wilfrid Hyde-White), have words with a Cockney flower vendor, Eliza Doolittle (Audrey Hepburn), Higgins is insulting

"Damn, damn, damn . . . I've grown accustomed to her face!"

Rex Harrison as Prof. Henry Higgins in *My Fair Lady* (1964)

about her crude pronunciations. To the snobby, intolerant Higgins, unrefined language produces a "verbal class distinction."

To better herself, Eliza goes to Higgins's residence to hire him to give her elocution lessons, but he is not interested. Pickering convinces Higgins that it would be a challenge to teach Eliza how to speak—to transform her from a drab guttersnipe into a lady of high society. Higgins enthusiastically accepts Pickering's wager to accomplish the challenge within six months.

Eliza is taken upstairs and cleaned up, as a beginning to the transformation. Then Higgins starts her on a harsh regime of pronunciation exercises, which include elocution training, using the famous phrase "The rain in Spain stays mainly in the plain." After weeks of hard work, Eliza makes a linguistic breakthrough, perfectly enunciating the phrase.

Following this achievement, Higgins decides to test her in public. They attend the Ascot races, where, although Eliza looks stunning, her masquerade as a lady is *not* an unqualified success.

The rigorous elocution training continues, and after another six weeks, Higgins, Pickering, and Eliza head off to the big test, the Embassy Ball. Later that evening, after successfully passing Eliza off as a princess, Higgins

A classic tale of love transcending class and status, My Fair Lady *featured a charming Audrey Hepburn as the Cockney flower vendor Eliza Doolittle.*

▼

and Pickering gloatingly congratulate each other in front of Eliza and Higgins's servants, completely ignoring Eliza's role in their strategy. She is hurt and angered by their indifference. And although she can now pass in high society, she is not assured of her place in that world. Neither, though, can she return to her old world among the gutter-dwellers.

Next morning, Higgins is distressed to find that Eliza has left. She has fled to the security of his mother's home, where she receives understanding and sympathy. When Higgins storms in, Eliza expresses her worthiness of his kindness, friendship, and respect.

On his way home, alone, Higgins begrudgingly acknowledges his love for Eliza. At home, melancholy, he listens to a recording of Eliza taking a lesson from him. When she walks into the room, he slowly realizes that she has followed him back home and has returned to him. Higgins, the stuffy snob, has learned that it is not how people talk that matters, but who they are.

See Cukor, George; Hepburn, Audrey

MY OWN PRIVATE IDAHO

This low-key, quirky 1991 film, directed and written by Gus Van Sant, has found a small but devoted audience. In it, a set of misfits establishes their own version of a "family" amid their aimless and often depressing lives.

The protagonist, Mike Waters (River Phoenix), is a young drifter who is a narcoleptic—at the oddest times, especially when he is stressed, he falls asleep. He just can't help it. Considering that Mike is a prostitute, this makes for some awkward consequences. Mike drops into a dead sleep in the middle of the road while waiting to hitch a ride; on the sidewalk waiting for a light to change; in the midst of turning a trick.

"I'm a connoisseur of roads. I've been tasting roads my whole life. This road will never end. It probably goes all around the world."

River Phoenix as Mike Waters in *My Own Private Idaho* (1991)

Mike's best friend is Scott Favor (Keanu Reeves). Scott is an accomplished hustler in the dark world of male prostitution, but he thinks he can afford to take chances. He always knows he has an escape hatch, since he stands to inherit a fortune when his father, a politician, dies. He could be said to just be slumming, to be playing at rebellion, but it has gone on too long—nearly four years—to be that simple.

Scott is Mike's buffer against the harsh reality of his life. Scott is forever saving him, picking "Mikey" up when he has fallen dead asleep wherever he happened to be standing, laying his own jacket over Mike to ward off the chilly night. Without Scott to protect him, it seems likely that Mike would not survive for long.

Mike and Scott meander from bedroom to bedroom, in Seattle and then Portland. They loiter in front of pornography shops and are cruised by johns, turning tricks in cars and apartments, hanging out with fellow hustlers in diners, killing time. Scott is wry and seems amused by the often bizarre circumstances in which they find themselves. Mike, however, is damaged goods, one of the true walking wounded. Mikey just seems lost, dragged along by events. He often has flashbacks to his grim childhood in Idaho with his mother, a murky low-life character who has disappeared. Was she a prostitute, a drug addict? Or was she a loving mother who was simply misunderstood, and somehow torn from her beloved child?

We, like Mike, never find out. Scott and Mike travel to Idaho to find her, and track her to Italy. They fly to Rome, where they learn that Mike's mother has returned to the States. Scott begins an affair with a young Italian woman. Scott abandons himself to her—and promptly abandons Mikey, telling him that he's sorry, but he has fallen in love.

Mike, now alone, somehow finds his way back to the Pacific northwest, but without Scott to take care of him, he unravels. Not only has he not found the love he seeks, he doesn't even have shelter.

One evening, as he lies on the sidewalk, filthy and practically unconscious, a limousine passes by. Inside are Scott and his Italian woman, sumptuously dressed, on their way to a fancy restaurant. Scott's father has died, and he has claimed his inheritance. Scott has moved on, without a compassionate look backward to his old life and his old friend; perhaps he is more like his cold, opportunistic father than he ever imagined.

The film ends as Mike, now a true person of the streets—at the mercy of whoever happens to find him—returns to his own private Idaho, a strip of road in the middle of nowhere.

See Cult film

MYSTERY-THRILLER

Films in the genre of mystery-thriller are those in which the story centers on a tale of suspense that is generated by some type of strange or terrorizing adventure. Often the principal character is caught in a menacing situation from which escape seems impossible, for example, *Wait until Dark* (1968), *When a Stranger Calls* (1980), *Cape Fear* (1962, 1991), *The Hand That Rocks the Cradle* (1992). Frequently the mystery-thriller revolves around the protagonist's efforts to unravel a crime or suspected crime—leading the character toward an unknown menace that will ultimately become life-threatening, for example, *Coma* (1978), and *The Firm* (1993).

NEGRI, POLA

Pola Negri's place in American film history has never been adequately evaluated. If mentioned at all, she is seen as a foil for Gloria Swanson, and the concocted "feud" between them (generated by the Paramount publicity office) is either taken at face value or treated as an example of period press-agentry. Negri is pictured as exotic and aloof, not in the acceptable Garbo manner, but as some Slavic version of Theda Bara.

How much of the Negri phenomenon was real and how much was purely manufactured? The exact financial returns on Negri's pictures, as with most silent Paramount releases, are unavailable. While modern critics praise such films as *Forbidden Paradise* (1924), *A Woman of the World* (1925), and *Barbed Wire* (1927), most of her films were poorly reviewed, and gossip columnists periodically dropped hints that the public was tiring of her. But in 1926, after four years in Hollywood, she far out-polled her nearest rivals in a *Motion Picture Classic* popularity contest. Failed German imports Camilla Horn and Lya de Putti did not merit such treatment, and one can only conclude that Negri's films generated adequate profits. Her problems lay elsewhere.

Negri was a product of the fervid Berlin theater and film scene in the late teens and early twenties. The Polish actress was the rage of the Continent following her appearance in a series of dramatic productions directed by Ernst Lubitsch, especially *Carmen* (1918), *Madame Dubarry* (1919), and *Sumurun* (1920). When *Dubarry* (renamed *Passion*) opened at New York's giant Capitol Theatre, record crowds marveled at Lubitsch's control of mass action and were electrified by the fiery performance of Negri. Here was an actress who took risks, who threw herself into a role with terrifying enthusiasm, oblivious to the need for posing and primping so common to American screen actresses. She was appalled at Hollywood's backwater culture and frank in discussing her feelings with the American press, which suspiciously characterized her as "an intellectual" and "a reader of books."

Negri's complaints about the poor quality of the roles she was offered were lost in the press coverage of her private life, especially her well-publicized romances with Chaplin and Valentino.

Despite this, Negri's career continued to flourish, and *Hotel Imperial* (1927), released a few months after Valentino's funeral, was a tremendous

N

NEGRI, POLA

hit. But less than a year after Valentino's death, she married Prince Serge Mdivani. Her public did not approve, and her contract expired when talkies arrived in 1928; it was not renewed.

More than anyone else, Pola Negri lived the life of a silent-movie queen. Draped in emeralds and chinchilla, she rode through Hollywood in a white Rolls-Royce trimmed with ivory and upholstered in white velvet (the color scheme set off her dark eyes and hair). Other stars could match the opulence, but none could handle the style. Twenty years later, Billy Wilder offered her the role of Norma Desmond, the silent-screen star living with her memories in a decaying Sunset Boulevard palazzo. Negri threw him out. To burlesque her former triumphs would be irredeemably vulgar, and even the suggestion was insulting.

See Bara, Theda; Brenon, Herbert; Chaplin, Charlie; Lubitsch, Ernst; Swanson, Gloria; Valentino, Rudolph; Wilder, Billy

Silent film star Pola Negri lived the Hollywood life, carrying on romances with Charlie Chaplin and Rudolph Valentino and often draping herself in emeralds and furs. ▶

NEILAN, MARSHALL

The legend of the great silent-film director who dissipates his own success in a welter of fast parties and bootleg liquor has at least some basis in reality: the crippled career of Marshall Neilan.

As early as 1918 *Motion Picture* magazine was calling Neilan "the youngest Big director in the motion picture industry." He had just directed four of Mary Pickford's finest and most popular films, including the powerful *Stella Maris* (1918), which both Peter Milne (in 1922) and Edward Wagenknecht (in 1962) thought contained her best work. He was twenty-six years old when he made the Pickford films and earned $125,000 per picture for directing them. But by the time he was thirty, his career was already showing signs of strain. Neilan did leave considerable evidence of his talents, especially in the features he directed in the late teens. But by 1923 even his supporters were paying more attention to his lifestyle than to his films.

Neilan began his career in films in 1911 as an actor for the Kalem Company. Handsome and personable, he was soon signed by Allan Dwan to play opposite J. Warren Kerrigan at the Flying A studio, and when Dwan left for Universal, Neilan came with him. Gradually he began directing the films he appeared in, and on returning to Kalem in 1913 he found himself acting, directing, and generally running the studio. But after a few months at the reins of Kalem's bizarre *Ham and Bud* comedy series, Neilan joined Dwan's Lasky unit in New York.

The Lasky pictures were Neilan's first important films, giving him the chance to play opposite such stars as Marguerite Clark and Mary Pickford (he was Pinkerton to Pickford's *Madame Butterfly* in 1915). After a brief season directing for Selig, Neilan returned to Lasky and directed a series of features with Blanche Sweet (whom he later married), Sessue Hayakawa, and Mary Pickford. These were the pictures on which his reputation was based.

Not surprisingly, Neilan felt that all directors needed a certain amount of acting ability, and he preferred to mime each part for his players, then watch quietly during shooting as they joined their conception to his own. He was especially good with child actors and developed the successful career of Wesley Barry, who starred in Neilan's *Dinty* (1920) and *Penrod* (1922). In the silent film, such performances could be shaped completely by the director with a firm grasp of editing, dramatic construction, and proper use of the camera. Neilan once listed the essential requirements of screen acting as beauty, personality, charm, temperament, style, and the ability to wear clothes.

By the mid 1920s Neilan's partying seemed almost continuous. Neilan's biographer Jack Spears characterizes him as living out an F. Scott Fitzgerald fantasy and tells of increasing bouts of drunkenness and absenteeism. Neilan was off the set so frequently that one of his films was credited as "Directed by Marshall Neilan and Staff." In addition, although the center of an admiring group of supporters and drinking buddies, Neilan alienated several key Hollywood figures with his wicked sense of humor.

Unlike Griffith or von Stroheim (or, to cite a later example, Orson Welles), Marshall Neilan's tragedy had little to do with the cost, style, or box-office success of his pictures. His story cannot be read as a failure of the system but only as the inability of one talented, undisciplined, and self-destructive individual to adjust to the success he had wrested from the system itself.

See Cruze, James; Director; Pickford, Mary; Thalberg, Irving; Vidor, King; von Stroheim, Erich

NEOREALISM (ITALIAN)

Neorealism was a film movement that began in Italy near the end of World War II. Roberto Rossellini, Vittorio De Sica, and Luchino Visconti were among those Italian directors of the time who produced films described as neorealistic. Their approach to technique and theme rejected the well-made studio film and the happy-ending story. Neorealism is characterized by social consciousness, simple stories of the common worker, and location shooting. The neorealist directors often used nonactors as performers and took their cameras into the streets and into real settings for visual authenticity and thematic credibility. Among the outstanding films produced during the height of neorealism between 1945 and 1952 were *Open City* (1945), *Paisan* (1947), *La Terra Trema* (1948), and *The Bicycle Thief* (1948).

Italian realism as a film style developed as a result of the social and economic unrest in Italy that accompanied the end of World War II. De Sica, describing neorealism's birth, wrote that the lack of an organized film industry in Italy at the end of the war and "the problem of finance . . . encouraged filmmakers to create a kind of movie that would no longer be dependent on fiction and on invented themes . . . but would draw on the reality of everyday life."

Because of the efforts of the neorealist filmmakers to place their characters in natural settings and to build their stories around "everyday life," the structure of their films led to their being described as "found stories" or flow-of-life films. Narrative incidents and flow of action appear so casual and spontaneous as to give the impression the filmmaker has simply followed a character and discovered the story rather than having invented it. The thematic interest of Italian neorealism in the personal struggles of common people has been carried abroad in films such as *Sounder* (1973), *Blue Collar* (1978), *Country* (1984), and *Salaam Bombay!* (1988).

See Actualité; Cinema verité; Realist cinema

NETWORK

Network (1976), directed by Sidney Lumet, is a comedy/drama that uses dark humor to examine the media's role in exerting corporate control over American society. The film is, the narrator tells us, "the story of Howard Beale, the first known instance of a man who was killed because he had lousy ratings." *Network* earned ten Academy Award nominations, including Best Picture and Best Director. Three acting Oscars went to *Network:* to Peter Finch for Best Actor, to Faye Dunaway for Best Actress, and to Beatrice Straight for Best Supporting Actress. Paddy Chayefsky received the Oscar for Best Screenplay.

"I'm mad as hell and I'm not going to take it anymore!"

Peter Finch as Howard Beale in *Network* (1976)

As the film begins, Howard Beale (Peter Finch), the news anchorman of UBS, one of the four major networks (along with ABC, NBC, and CBS), has just learned that in two years he will be without a job. His friend and boss, Max Schumacher (William Holden), president of the UBS news division, explains that the decision was made because of Howard's low ratings. Howard is despondent—the information is just the topper of several years of bad luck, including the death of his wife.

As Max and Howard share a drink at a bar, Howard facetiously suggests that he should kill himself on the air in the middle of the seven o'clock news in order to boost his ratings. Max joins in the cynical humor: "You'll get a hell of a rating . . . fifty share easy." The two men, giddy, build upon the idea of using shock tactics to get high ratings—"Suicide of the Week," "Execution of the Week."

When next we see Howard, he is in a makeup chair, being prepared for the nightly news broadcast. He has been drinking, but when he sits in the anchor chair, he seems dignified and in control. However, instead of reading the news he goes off script and announces that in two weeks he will be "retiring" from the program. Then he makes a startling announcement: "I'm gonna blow my brains out right on this program a week from today. Tune in next Tuesday. That should give the public relations people a week to pro-

Henry Fonda turned down the role of Howard Beale in Sidney Lumet's Network, *saying it was "too hysterical." Peter Finch took the role instead, and won the Best Actor Oscar for his performance.* ▶

mote the show. We ought to get a hell of a rating out of that—a fifty share, easy."

This outburst is at first seen as an embarrassment to the network, and when Howard asks for the chance to go back on the air with a public apology, Max agrees. He is shocked when Howard launches into a tirade against the modern world when he gets back on the air. However, Max—still smarting from his humiliation during a stockholders' meeting, where he learned of the news division's dismal financial losses—lets Howard continue instead of pulling the plug on the broadcast. As a result, Max is fired by Frank Hackett (Robert Duvall), the network boss.

Hackett wants to fire Howard, too. But Diana Christensen (Faye Dunaway), a young and ambitious vice president of programming, has seen the overnight ratings: Howard's outburst has made them skyrocket. Diana is utterly ruthless in her pursuit of high ratings. Her work is her life: "All I want out of life is a thirty share and a twenty rating." She argues in favor of keeping Howard on the air—the more outrageous the better—reasoning that the television viewers are desperate for someone to "articulate their rage." After some initial hesitation, Hackett agrees to let Howard stay.

NETWORK

When Howard next appears on the air, unkempt and disheveled, he talks at length about the horrible state of the nation. He speaks of high unemployment and of people not being able to make ends meet. He tells Americans that those in power want them to meekly accept the status quo. But he urges them to get mad and resist: "I want you to get up right now and go to the window, open it, and stick your head out, and yell, 'I'm mad as hell, and I'm not going to take it anymore!' " Soon television viewers all over America are going to their windows and shouting their defiance.

In the wake of this bit of theater, Howard's ratings are phenomenal. He seems to be mentally deranged, but his increasingly bizarre behavior is eaten up by the audience. His broadcast becomes a version of the outrageous scenario that he and Max joked about in the bar. Diana Christensen dubs Howard "The Mad Prophet of the Airways." The nightly news becomes an hour-long tabloid called "The Howard Beale Show."

"By tomorrow, he'll have a 50 share, maybe even a 60. Howard Beale is processed instant God, and right now, it looks like he may just go over bigger than Mary Tyler Moore!"

Faye Dunaway as Diana Christensen in *Network* (1976)

But Howard soon throws a monkey wrench into the works by telling viewers that UBS network has been absorbed by a conglomerate called Communications Company of America (CCA). He tells viewers to beware of how a huge conglomerate can use television to persuade and deceive the public to further its own interests. To protect *their* own interests, he urges viewers to turn off their TV sets.

While Howard is involved in his televised rants, Max and Diana begin an affair. Max falls in love with her despite her lack of humanity, and he contemplates leaving his wife, Louise (Beatrice Straight in her Oscar-winning performance), and his family. But as Howard disintegrates, so does the sordid relationship between Max and Diana.

When Howard announces on the air that a consortium calling itself Western World Funding Corporation, a front for Arab interests, has been buying up a controlling interest in CCA, Hackett, the network boss, gets a call from the CCA bosses in New York. Howard has urged the public to flood the White House with telegrams in protest of the consortium, and Hackett's bosses at CCA think it is time to get Howard under control. The personal financial interests of Arthur Jensen (Ned Beatty, in an Oscar-nominated performance), the head of CCA, as well as those of CCA as a whole, are connected to those of the Arabs, and Jensen is not about to let Howard spoil things.

At a meeting, Jensen tells Howard he is tampering with the new world order, one in which human beings have value only insofar as they serve the corporate state. Jensen demands that Howard go forth and preach this instead of his usual rants. Howard does, but ratings plummet as a result, as viewers feel he is demeaning them.

With ratings down again, the network heads want Howard gone. But Jensen will not hear of it, now that Howard is the voice of Jensen's corporate philosophy. With their hands tied, the network brass meet to discuss alternatives to dismissing Howard. At the meeting, Hackett jokes that if it is not within their power to fire Howard, they will have to kill him. Diana appears to be playing along when she says she might be able to get a terrorist group to kill him on the air. Soon, she is speaking of using the assassination to increase viewership.

One by one, the others at the meeting join in. As they speak, we see that the show under discussion has actually made it onto the screen. Audience members file into the studio and take their seats. As Howard enters the soundstage, two gunmen appear and shoot him. We are left with a still image of Howard's dead body, lit by an overhead spotlight. Finally the screen goes black. The last sound is the haunting ticking of a newsroom wire service.

See Dunaway, Faye; Lumet, Sidney

NEW AMERICAN CINEMA

The term New American Cinema is often used to refer to the underground or experimental film movement in the United States during the 1960s. It is derived from the New American Cinema Group, an organization founded in 1960 by various filmmakers and producers, including Lionel Rogosin, Peter Bogdanovich, Jonas Mekas, Shirley Clarke, and Robert Frank. Their interests included experimental and avant-garde as well as commercial filmmaking. The group's published statements opposed constraints on subject matter in both underground and commercial filmmaking.

See Avant-garde; Experimental film; Underground film

NEWSPAPERS

The feature film was born during the heroic age of American journalism, when even an average-size town might offer its citizens a wide selection of

morning and afternoon papers. Various newspapers and their publishers involved themselves in motion pictures very early on, specifically in the production of newsreels, animated cartoons, and serials. William Randolph Hearst's Cosmopolitan studio even used short fiction from the Hearst press as a source for features.

Film as a subject for newspaper coverage was another matter, one that proved especially attractive to the more aggressive papers of the day. In this regard, it is an unfortunate accident of history that the one newspaper whose film reviews are most easily accessible, the *New York Times,* was never very interested in motion pictures and gave them extremely low priority throughout the silent period. The level of criticism in the *Times* was so shallow that many historians, looking here first and assuming that it represented the current journalistic standard, dismiss newspaper reviews of the period out of hand.

While film might be covered on thc same arts page that dealt with the legitimate stage, the cinema's relatively recent arrival put it in a very different category from music or theater. The first newspaper coverage of motion pictures presented them as a technological phenomenon ("Edison's marvel"), then as a social problem ("nickel madness"), and ultimately as an economic statistic ("the nation's fourth largest industry"). The movies were news before they were art, and so the earliest film reviews in American newspapers were straightforward accounts of news events.

Not yet worthy of a byline, the generally anonymous reviewers of the era tell us what happened when they went to the picture show. They report not only on the film but on the theater, the audience, the stage performance, even the weather. It should be remembered that the film was not always the most significant element of this mix anyway, and that critical commentary was usually extracted from the sum of these parts. Often, owing to a lack of press screenings and the short duration of many runs, some "reviews" would be simple announcements, pasted together from press handouts, trade papers, or out-of-town notices.

Pressure to use editorial space as a reward for advertising was traditional in the newspaper industry and was certainly reflected in reviews and feature articles. To what extent this occurred varied from paper to paper, with some critics purportedly quite independent, others simply reprinting distributors' press handouts under their own bylines.

By the 1920s many more writers were signing their reviews, but the ultimate goal was still more journalistic than critical. Instead of developing an aesthetic of cinema, these men and women used their columns as literary sounding boards for pontificating, amusing, cajoling, or otherwise entertaining their growing readership.

See Criticism; Ebert, Roger; Kael, Pauline; Maltin, Leonard; Siskel, Gene; Trade papers

NEWSREEL

A popular type of motion-picture short that appeared as part of film programs until television brought about its demise in the 1950s, newsreels were usually ten to fifteen minutes in length and contained a compilation of timely news stories and, at their conclusion, a human-interest feature or two. The newsreel impulse existed from the beginning of motion-picture exhibition. Early Lumière and Edison programs in the 1890s were filled with short *actualités* of events and people, lifted from everyday life. By 1900 *actualité*-gathering film units and exchanges had been set up in most large cities around the world to record and distribute short films of important events and famous people. Fox Movietone News introduced the talking newsreel in 1927, showing movie audiences such dramatic events as Lindbergh's departure for his solo flight across the Atlantic and his tumultuous welcome home.

In 1935 about half of all theaters showed double features, and tickets averaged 24 cents.

Eventually the newsreel concept was expanded into interpretive presentations of the news, with the best-known example being *The March of Time* series (1935–51). Each supplement of the series was about twenty minutes long and usually dealt with a single news topic in an editorial manner. The series was produced in the United States by Louis de Rochemont. The National Film Board of Canada produced a similarly styled series, *The World in Action* (1941–45).

The newsreel served a particularly useful function during World War II, when visualization of allied efforts was considered critical to national morale. This role and the other functions served by the newsreel for more than half a century would increasingly fall to television after 1948. Eventually the newer medium killed the movie-house newsreel altogether.

See Documentary; Feature film; Shorts

NICHOLS, MIKE

One of America's preeminent film directors, Mike Nichols's diverse talents have cut an equally impressive swath through stage directing, acting, and improvisational comedy.

Nichols was born Michael Igor Peschowsky to a distinguished Jewish family in Berlin on November 6, 1931. His father, Paul, was a physician, his

N

NICHOLS, MIKE

German-born director Mike Nichols found work as a stage actor and improvisational comedian before turning his talent to directing Broadway plays and, later, feature films.

maternal grandmother wrote the libretto for Strauss's *Salomé,* and his maternal grandfather was the head of the German Social Democratic Party.

In the face of the anti-Semitic hysteria of the Nazi regime, Michael's father came to New York in 1938, changed his name to Paul Nichols, took his medical exam, and set up practice in Manhattan. A year later he sent for his family.

Dr. Nichols was successful and maintained his family well in upper Manhattan, near Central Park. Michael attended a series of private schools, "very chic, very progressive," as he described them later, at which he felt he learned very little. Unpopular and lonely, he found solace in the imaginary world of the theater in the Cherry Lane School's drama program, where he was advised that although intelligent, he was not suited for the stage. Upon graduating from high school, he enrolled at New York University but soon dropped out and, after a brief stint as a shipping clerk, resolved to become a psychiatrist and entered the premedical program at the University of Chicago.

"I thought I could cut classes and still pass," said Nichols, who did just that, supporting himself with a variety of odd jobs while succumbing to a relapse of theatrical fever. He joined a number of theater groups, and during one of his performances, in Strindberg's *Miss Julie,* he saw a dark-haired young woman "staring cruelly from the audience through the whole thing." This inauspicious first encounter notwithstanding, Nichols and the mysterious woman—Elaine May—eventually became good friends and colleagues whose improvisational routines changed the face of American comedy.

Their famed collaboration was still in the distant future, however, and their paths temporarily diverged. Nichols took off to study with Lee Strasberg at the renowned Actor's Studio in New York City, surviving on a series of odd jobs that included waiting tables, teaching horseback riding, and announcing for a radio station in Philadelphia. May, in the meantime, had joined Chicago's newly formed Compass Theatre, a club where performers improvised scenes they thought up or elicited from the audience. When a vacancy opened, Nichols jumped at the chance to join, and surrounded by fellow future luminaries such as Alan Arkin, Shelley Berman, and Barbara Harris, Nichols and May honed their brilliantly acerbic comedic style.

notable & quotable

"Wonderful director, Nichols. He had no plan [during shooting of *The Graduate*] but he had a lot of options and he knew he was going to discover them in the editing room. He was doing what I think an artist was supposed to do. He was painting. He was just feeling his way."

Dustin Hoffman, actor, 1992

After Compass disbanded in the fall of 1957, the company tried to reform in St. Louis with disappointing results. Nichols and May then went to New York to perform some of their improvisations for the agent Jack Rollins, who offered to represent them and arranged for a booking at New York's Blue Angel club. An immediate smash, their unsparing, satirical thrusts at postwar American complacency, hypocrisy, emotional repression, and hucksterism hit home with a wide audience. Their act, which anticipated many of the themes of Nichols's later films, quickly burst the confines of the club circuit in several media: on a variety of national television shows; in a series of hit record albums; in a concert presentation at New York's Town Hall on October 8, 1960; and in an open-ended Broadway engagement for *An Evening with Mike Nichols and Elaine May,* which ran until July 1, 1961.

After the show closed, Nichols and May parted company to pursue their restless creative ambitions. For Nichols, that meant directing. Beginning modestly with a Vancouver production of Oscar Wilde's *The Importance of Being Earnest,* Nichols bounded quickly to Broadway, reeling off several major successes, including Neil Simon's *Barefoot in the Park* (1963) and Murray Schisgal's *Luv* (1964), each of which earned him a Tony Award for best director, and Neil Simon's *The Odd Couple* (1966).

His directorial prowess now firmly established, Nichols soon answered the inevitable call from Hollywood—a call that just happened to come from the project's stars, his friends Elizabeth Taylor and Richard Burton—making a powerful first impression with his film version of Edward Albee's searing drama *Who's Afraid of Virginia Wolf?*

The year 1967 was a creative high-water mark for Nichols. He directed Lillian Hellman's *The Little Foxes* for the Repertory Theater of Lincoln Center and won his fourth Tony for his latest effort in his Neil Simon franchise, *Plaza Suite.* But the summit of that memorable year, perhaps of his whole career, was Nichols's second film, *The Graduate*, starring Dustin Hoffman as an alienated college graduate groping for a direction and an identity amid the "plastic" surroundings of his suburban California upbringing. This comedy of manners, at once earnest and caustic, struck a profound generational chord that almost immediately elevated the film to nearly iconic status among the rebellious youth of the sixties.

Nichols's adaptation of Joseph Heller's antiwar black comedy *Catch-22* (1968) met with a more mixed response, but he quickly regained his footing with the striking *Carnal Knowledge* (1969), a disturbing look at several American couples struggling toward adulthood amid the ever-shifting values and gender roles of the sixties.

After returning briefly to Broadway to direct Neil Simon's *The Prisoner of Second Avenue,* which earned him another Tony Award for best director, Nichols tried his hand at a suspense film, *The Day of the Dolphin* (1973), which garnered little enthusiasm among critics or moviegoers. However, he rebounded in the 1980s and 1990s by directing such notable films as *Silkwood* (1983), *Heartburn* (1986), *Working Girl* (1988), *Postcards from the Edge* (1990*), The Birdcage* (1996), and 1998's *Primary Colors.* He is currently at work producing *All the Pretty Horses*, starring Matt Damon.

See Graduate, The; *Hoffman, Dustin*

NICKELODEON

Nickelodeon was a popular name for an American movie theater in the early period of motion-picture exhibition. The name came into use after the turn of the century when the conversion of shops and stores into makeshift film theaters was widespread. *Nickelodeon* was derived by combining the cost of admission (a nickel) with the Greek word for theater (*odeon*). Two businessmen in Pittsburgh, Pennsylvania—Harry Davis and John P. Harris—opened a converted store theater in 1905 that they called "The Nickelodeon." The financial and popular success of this specially decorated movie house, which showed regularly scheduled film presentations from morning to night, resulted in the proliferation of nickelodeons throughout the United States.

See Magic lantern; Zoëtrope

The first commercial showing of motion pictures, in 1894—at Holland Bros.' Kinetoscope Parlor on Broadway—took in $120, with an audience of about 500.

JACK NICHOLSON

Born John Joseph Nicholson in Neptune, New Jersey, on April 22, 1937, Jack Nicholson is widely regarded as one of the best actors of all time (and one of the greatest "bad boys" of the screen), with an expressive face that the camera loves. At the heart of most of his roles is the sense that below the character's mildly attractive exterior, a devilish sort is clawing to get out.

Nicholson paid his dues before becoming a star. For more than a decade he kicked around in second-rate biker and horror flicks—including the quirky *Little Shop of Horrors* (1961)—before eating up the screen as a dissipated lawyer in *Easy Rider* (1969). He followed that up with another bravura performance in *Five Easy Pieces* (1970).

Over the next few years Nicholson produced exceptional star turns in *Carnal Knowledge* (1971), *Chinatown* (1974), and 1975's *One Flew Over the Cuckoo's Nest* (for which Nicholson won the Best Actor Oscar). Other notable roles were in *The Shining* (1980), *Reds* (1981), *Terms of Endearment* (1983; Nicholson won the Best Supporting Actor Oscar), *Prizzi's Honor* (1985), *Batman* (1989), *A Few Good Men* (1992), and 1997's *As Good As It Gets*, for which he won another Best Actor Oscar. He has provided worthy performances in other films as well, though some critics have complained that Nicholson's astronomical earning power has compromised his taste in roles (he earned more than $50 million in acting and merchandising royalties for playing the part of the Joker in *Batman)*. But even in bad films, Nicholson's acting is always mesmerizing. His efforts at directing have been less successful.

Once a messenger boy for MGM's cartoon department, actor Jack Nicholson is now one of America's best loved—and most celebrated—actors, having been nominated for numerous Oscars. Nicholson won the Oscar twice, once in 1975 and again in 1997.

Nicholson's personal life has intrigued the public almost as much as his acting. His childhood was anything but privileged (he has been described as a "working-class intellectual"), and a *Time* magazine researcher learned that the woman who Nicholson thought was his sister while he was growing up was actually his mother, while the couple that he thought were his parents were actually his grandparents.

The flamboyant actor has had many relationships with women, usually rocky, at least partly due to his tendency to be a wanderer. He was married to actress Sandra Knight for a few years in the 1960s; they had one daughter, Jennifer. Nicholson moved on to a tempestuous seventeen-year relationship with actress Anjelica Huston, which she finally ended when a young waitress named Rebecca Broussard turned up pregnant with Nicholson's baby in 1990. Nicholson, by then into deep middle age, ensconced his new family in a separate house on his property. Nicholson and Broussard have two children. Nicholson supposedly has many other children, as chronicled in a controversial 1997 "biography," but many of the claims are unsubstantiated.

Nicholson was given the American Film Institute Life Achievement Award in 1994.

See Chinatown; *Dunaway, Faye;* Easy Rider; *Kubrick, Stanley;* One Flew Over the Cuckoo's Nest; *Polanski, Roman*

NORTH BY NORTHWEST

Alfred Hitchcock's classic comic thriller *North by Northwest* (1959) is one of his most famous suspense/mystery stories. The film includes typical elements of many Hitchcock films—an innocent hero-bystander, totally vulnerable and isolated and a victim of mistaken identity, pursued by evil forces.

Roger O. Thornhill (Cary Grant), the classic adman, is mistaken for the mythical "George Kaplan," an imaginary CIA agent, by foreign spy Philip Vandamm (James Mason). Kaplan is really a cipher devised as a decoy by a

North by Northwest's *tense final chase scene was shot on a replica of Mt. Rushmore. Director Alfred Hitchcock was prohibited from filming on the real Mt. Rushmore, to avoid associating the national monument with murder.*

CIA official, the Professor (Leo G. Carroll), just to mislead foreign intriguers such as Vandamm.

Kidnapping a protesting Thornhill, Vandamm, believing him to be the federal agent, Kaplan, first tries to eliminate Thornhill/Kaplan by forcing bourbon down his throat and placing him behind the wheel of a car heading downhill on a winding cliff road. The next attempt to kill Thornhill/Kaplan, in the movie's most renowned sequence, takes place in an open field in the countryside, where Thornhill is terrorized by a crop-dusting plane that sprays machine-gun fire at him.

As his predicament plays out, Thornhill and Eve Kendall (Eva Marie Saint) meet on a train. They have a brief interlude on the train, but unbeknownst to Thornhill (and Vandamm), Eve is a government double agent whose mission is to capture Vandamm with a secret microfiche. As duty demands that she pretend to be Vandamm's lover, Thornhill believes she is just deceitful. Determined to maintain her undercover role, she is unable to set Thornhill straight.

But once Thornhill starts closing in on the truth, the Professor steps in and identifies himself to Thornhill. Describing the role of the imaginary agent Kaplan, the Professor asks him to play out the character "to help save the life of an endangered agent." When the Professor reveals that Eve is the endangered double agent, an enlightened Thornhill agrees to help in order to save Eve's life.

Following Vandamm and Eve to Mount Rushmore, Thornhill is able to warn Eve when he overhears that Vandamm has discovered that she is a double agent. Realizing that Vandamm means to kill her, Eve escapes him, and Thornhill comes to her rescue. They are pursued by Vandamm and his thugs to the colossal Mount Rushmore monument. In the cliff-hanging (literally) scene, Thornhill and Eve are forced to climb down the faces of the monument to elude Vandamm's henchmen. As they cling precariously to a ledge, a shot rings out. The Professor has arrived just in time.

In the last scene, in a clever transition, Thornhill continues to struggle in hauling Eve to safety from the rock ledge, and then abruptly is seen pulling her into his upper train berth, saying: "Come along, Mrs. Thornhill." They are last seen on their honeymoon as they bed down for the night in their private train compartment.

See Hitchcock, Alfred

notable & quotable

"When Cary Grant was on Mt. Rushmore I would have liked to put him into Lincoln's nostril and let him have a sneezing fit."

Alfred Hitchcock, director, referring to a scene in North by Northwest *(1959)*

ON THE WATERFRONT

On the Waterfront (1954), directed by Elia Kazan, is a gritty drama about corrupt trade unions and racketeering on the docks of New Jersey. Dark and unsentimental, this film was very controversial for its time. Budd Schulberg's screenplay (in collaboration with Kazan) was based on "Crime on the Waterfront," a newspaper exposé by Malcolm Johnson.

Following the credits, ominous drumbeats play against a backdrop of the New Jersey waterfront, where a large ocean liner is docked. The union boss, Johnny Friendly (Lee J. Cobb), a brutal thug who rules the docks, walks up the gangplank of the liner, accompanied by an entourage from the longshoreman's local office. Terry Malloy (Marlon Brando) is among Friendly's men. Terry agrees to lure a man named Joey Doyle onto a rooftop, making himself believe that the union guys are just going to have a "talk" with Joey. But Joey isn't just leaned on—Friendly's men throw him off the roof to his death.

The peak year of movies' "slice" of Americans' spending on entertainment was 1943: 25 cents of every dollar spent on recreation.

A priest, Father Barry (Karl Malden), gives Joey last rites. Joey's father, Pop Doyle (John Hamilton), knows that Joey was killed because he testified before the government's Waterfront Crime Commission about the crooked trade union. But like everybody else, Pop is afraid to speak out against the union. Joey's sister, the passionate and innocent Edie (Eva Marie Saint), a college student, begs Father Barry to do something. To her dismay, he simply tells her to be patient.

Terry is upset about the Doyle murder, but his brother, Charley (Rod Steiger), a lawyer and Friendly's right-hand man, nicknamed "Charley the Gent," warns him not to complain. He reminds Terry that Friendly controls who is allowed to work on the docks. Later, two agents of the Waterfront Crime Commission question Terry because it is rumored that he was the last person to see Joey alive, but Terry stays mum: "I don't know nothin', I ain't seen nothin', I'm not sayin' nothin'." He refuses to be branded a pigeon or a canary by telling what he knows.

Father Barry, finally heeding Edie's urging to do something, offers his church to the workers as a safe place to discuss the union. Charley asks Terry to go to the church and keep tabs on the meeting. Some workers show up, but they are reluctant to talk. Kayo Dugan (Pat Henning) explains

LAURENCE OLIVIER

Laurence Kerr Olivier was born on May 22, 1907, in Dorking, Surrey, England. His father, a minister, moved the family from parish to parish. It was a strict, somber household, which, some biographers suggest, may have led the young Laurence to escape into playacting.

Whatever brought about Olivier's acting skill, it was formidable. Said Paul Newman of Olivier: "He's the only actor. The rest of us are still trying." Olivier is widely regarded as one of the greatest English-speaking theatrical actors of all time.

Even as a child, Olivier's talent was unmistakable. He performed in various amateur productions—so well that after seeing him play one Shakespearean role at St. Edward's School, his father encouraged the boy to attend the Central School of Speech Training and Dramatic Arts in London. Laurence followed this advice, and in 1926 he began working with the Birmingham Repertory Company.

In the 1930s Olivier was a star on the London stage, acting in plays ranging from Noël Coward comedies to Shakespearean tragedies. British and American filmmakers came calling in the late 1930s, rightly presuming that the young man's elegant, athletic good looks would translate well to the screen. His first film roles, however, were less than spectacular; it was not until he portrayed Heathcliff in a dark, menacing performance in *Wuthering Heights* (1939) that Olivier really broke through to movie audiences. It earned him the first of ten Academy Award nominations for Best Actor.

Subsequently Olivier did memorable work in a number of films, particularly *Rebecca* (1940), *Pride and Prejudice* (1940), *Henry V* (1944), and *Hamlet* (1948). He was given a special Academy Award for his work on *Henry V*, as director, producer, and star; *Hamlet* won him the Best Actor Oscar for 1948. He won many fans with his varied roles in *That Hamilton Woman* (1941), *The Prince and the Showgirl* (1957; opposite Marilyn Monroe), *Spartacus* (1960), *Sleuth* (1972), *The Marathon Man* (1976), *The Boys from Brazil* (1978), and many other movies.

Olivier had a diverse body of work, including television appearances and filmed stage productions, and he produced and/or directed many of them. He was honored numerous times on both sides of the Atlantic, including the bestowal of a knighthood and a lordship by Queen Elizabeth. The British equivalent of the Tony Awards were named for him in 1975 (the Olivier Awards), and in 1999 the American Film Institute named him one of the Greatest Screen Legends of all time.

Laurence Olivier is widely regarded as one of the greatest English-speaking theatrical actors of all time.

Though he shunned the press, Olivier's personal life was of great interest to his fans. He married Jill Esmond in 1930 (they had a son, Tarquin); the marriage disintegrated after he became romantically involved with actress Vivien Leigh while filming *Fire Over England* in 1937. Olivier and Leigh married in 1940, but it was a tempestuous union, at least partially due to her mental illness. They divorced in 1960. Olivier married actress Joan Plowright soon thereafter. The couple had three children—Richard, Julie-Kate, and Tamsin, and remained together until Olivier's death in 1989. He is buried in Westminster Abbey, only the fifth actor in history to be so honored.

See Leigh, Vivien; Wuthering Heights; *Wyler, William*

the "D 'n' D" code of silence: "Deaf and dumb. No matter how much we hate the torpedoes, we don't rat." The priest argues that the workers must break the code of silence and testify. The meeting breaks up when some of Friendly's hoodlums break windows in the church. They viciously beat some of the workers as they leave.

Terry walks Edie home from the meeting. They remember each other from Catholic school. Terry says that she "grew up nice." She remembers that he was always in trouble; now she sees that there is something soft and kind about him. Her father, though, has packed her bags so that she can return to college. He warns her to stay away from Terry, whose brother is a "butcher in a camel hair coat." But Edie has decided to stay home and find out who killed her brother.

Terry and Edie make their way to a local bar, where over a beer he tells her that he used to be a prizefighter, but then Johnny Friendly bought a piece of him. They exchange philosophies. Hers is that everybody is part of everybody else; his is to do it to the other guy before he does it to you. Terry tells her that he would give her information about her brother, Joey, if he had any. A wedding party is going on at the bar, so Edie and Terry dance. Swaying to the music, their lips grow close—but they are interrupted when Terry is served a subpoena to answer questions about Joey's murder.

Terry tells her that he won't "eat cheese" for the cops. But because he was subpoenaed, Edie figures that Terry must have been involved in Joey's death. Upset, she tells Terry that he is a bum and that Johnny Friendly still owns him.

Later, Charley and Friendly, worried that Terry's relationship with Edie could change Terry's alliances, warn Terry to stay away from her. And after they find out that Dugan talked to the investigating commission, he is killed in an on-the-job "accident." Father Barry calls his death a crucifixion, eloquently arguing that the workers' silence is a sin. When a mob thug throws a banana peel at Father Barry, Terry punches him out—Friendly and Charley the Gent are right: Edie's influence is changing Terry's loyalties.

That night Terry and Edie, reunited, kiss for the first time, and Terry decides the next day to confess his role in Joey's death to Father Barry. Terry says his life won't be worth a nickel if he testifies to the commission, but the priest asks him how much his soul will be worth if he does *not* tell the truth. Father Barry also convinces Terry to come clean with Edie. When Terry tells Edie, she is horrified and runs away.

Knowing that Terry's life is increasingly in danger, Charley tries to pull Terry back into the union fold, offering him a great job. When Charley finds out that Terry is going to testify, he pulls a gun on him in the back of a taxicab. Terry, sad and disappointed, gently pushes the gun away, and confronts his brother about selling him out. Years ago, when Terry was a prizefighter, he had a fight against a crucial opponent. Charley made him take a dive for money. Terry knows he could have won the fight, and he passionately explains to Charley what this would have meant to him: "I coulda had

notable & quotable

"When I think of him as an actor, I perceive him mostly as an architect. He designed his parts beautifully, but they were like sketches engraved with an etching tool on a sheet of copper. Everything he did had to be structured in advance."

Marlon Brando, 1994, in reference to actor Laurence Olivier

"You don't understand. I coulda had class. I coulda been a contender. I coulda been somebody—instead of a bum, which is what I am."

Marlon Brando as Terry Malloy in *On the Waterfront* (1954)

class. I coulda been a contender. I coulda been somebody, instead of a bum, which is what I am."

Defeated, Charley gives Terry the gun, telling him he will need it, and then lets him out of the car. The driver of the car then double-crosses Charley and takes him straight to Friendly.

After Terry is dropped off, he goes to see Edie. Still upset, she does not want to see him, but he grabs her and they kiss. Suddenly, from outside someone yells to Terry that his brother wants to see him. When he goes outside, he finds his brother, Charley, at the end of an alley, brutally murdered, hanging from a meat hook: another crucifixion. Wielding the gun Charley had given him, Terry promises to avenge Charley's death.

Before Terry can get to Friendly, though, Father Barry finds Terry and convinces him that the best way to hurt Friendly is to testify. This time Terry takes Father Barry's advice, finally telling the truth to the commission. Furious, Friendly tells him he will never work on any waterfront again.

Edie thinks they should leave town, but Terry is now intent on a showdown. He goes to the docks despite the fact that everybody is allowed to

Marlon Brando's gutsy performance as ex-boxer Terry Malloy in On the Waterfront *earned the actor his fourth Oscar nomination and first win.*

▼

work except for him. All of the workers follow Terry as he marches down to Friendly's office to have it out with him. Terry tells Friendly that without his gun and his kickbacks, he's nothing. Friendly instigates a fistfight, and after a few dirty tricks he has the upper hand. But before long, Terry pummels him. Friendly calls for help from his thugs, who beat Terry nearly to death.

After the fight, Friendly tells the men to get back to work, but they have united against him, and they refuse. They will not work unless Terry works. Father Barry encourages Terry, telling him that he may have lost the battle, but he can win the war. If he can walk back to work, then the others will follow him, a victory against the corrupt union boss. Valiantly bloodied and bruised, Terry stumbles to the dock. Despite Friendly's protests, all of the workers follow—they have won the war.

On the Waterfront won eight Oscars, including Best Actor for Brando's moving performance, and Best Picture. But the film's luster has been tarnished by some people's claim that director Kazan and screenwriter Schulberg gave the story its optimistic ending, making a hero of Terry, who "ratted" on the union bosses, to justify the filmmakers' own testimony in front of the House Un-American Activities Committee, which was investigating the extent of communist affiliation in Hollywood in the 1930s and '40s.

See Brando, Marlon; Kazan, Elia

ONE FLEW OVER THE CUCKOO'S NEST

Capitalizing on Jack Nicholson's reputation as a rebel, due in part to the roles he played in counterculture films like *Five Easy Pieces* and *Easy Rider*, Czechoslovakian director Milos Forman was able to turn Bo Goldman and Lawrence Hauben's adaptation of Ken Kesey's novel *One Flew Over the Cuckoo's Nest* into a scathing examination of the nature of authority. The film raises such questions as who is crazier: the repressed, passive-aggressive, and authoritarian Nurse Ratched or the honest, openly libidinous, and wise-cracking McMurphy, played by Nicholson. The movie swept all five major Academy Awards, winning for Best Actor, Best Actress, Best Picture, Best Screenplay, and Best Director.

"Which one of you nuts has got any guts?"

Jack Nicholson as Randle McMurphy in *One Flew Over the Cuckoo's Nest* (1975)

Wearing a leather jacket and a hat, separating him from all the drably dressed inmates of a mental hospital, Randle Patrick McMurphy (Jack Nicholson) arrives in shackles. He is a wisecracking nonconformist who covets freedom so much that when a guard, in delivering him to captivity, takes off his chains, McMurphy kisses him on the head.

McMurphy was convicted of statutory rape involving what he says was a willing and eager fifteen-year-old who said she was eighteen. He has been brought to the hospital so that the authorities can determine whether he is sane. But his belligerence, rowdiness, and anti-authority attitude cast doubt on his honesty.

In the first of a series of group therapy sessions led by the controlling authority figure Nurse Mildred Ratched (Louise Fletcher), we meet the other patients on the ward, including a towering deaf-mute Indian named Chief (Will Sampson) and an insecure, stuttering young man, Billy Bibbit (Brad Dourif), who is ashamed of sex.

McMurphy is soon head-to-head with Ratched in a subtle game of one-upmanship. He tries to liberate the members of the ward by injecting a bit of chaos into their lives: they gamble for cigarettes, they play sports—and even the antisocial Chief joins in. McMurphy questions why Nurse Ratched plays the music so loud, and she says that it's the status quo. Considering McMurphy's desire to know the contents of his medication a silly rebellious gesture, she makes him take his pills. He seemingly relents, but we soon see that he didn't swallow the pills: a small victory.

Jack Nicholson and Louise Fletcher (center) both took home Oscars for their performances in One Flew Over the Cuckoo's Nest. *The film also won for Best Picture and Best Director, Milos Forman.* ▼

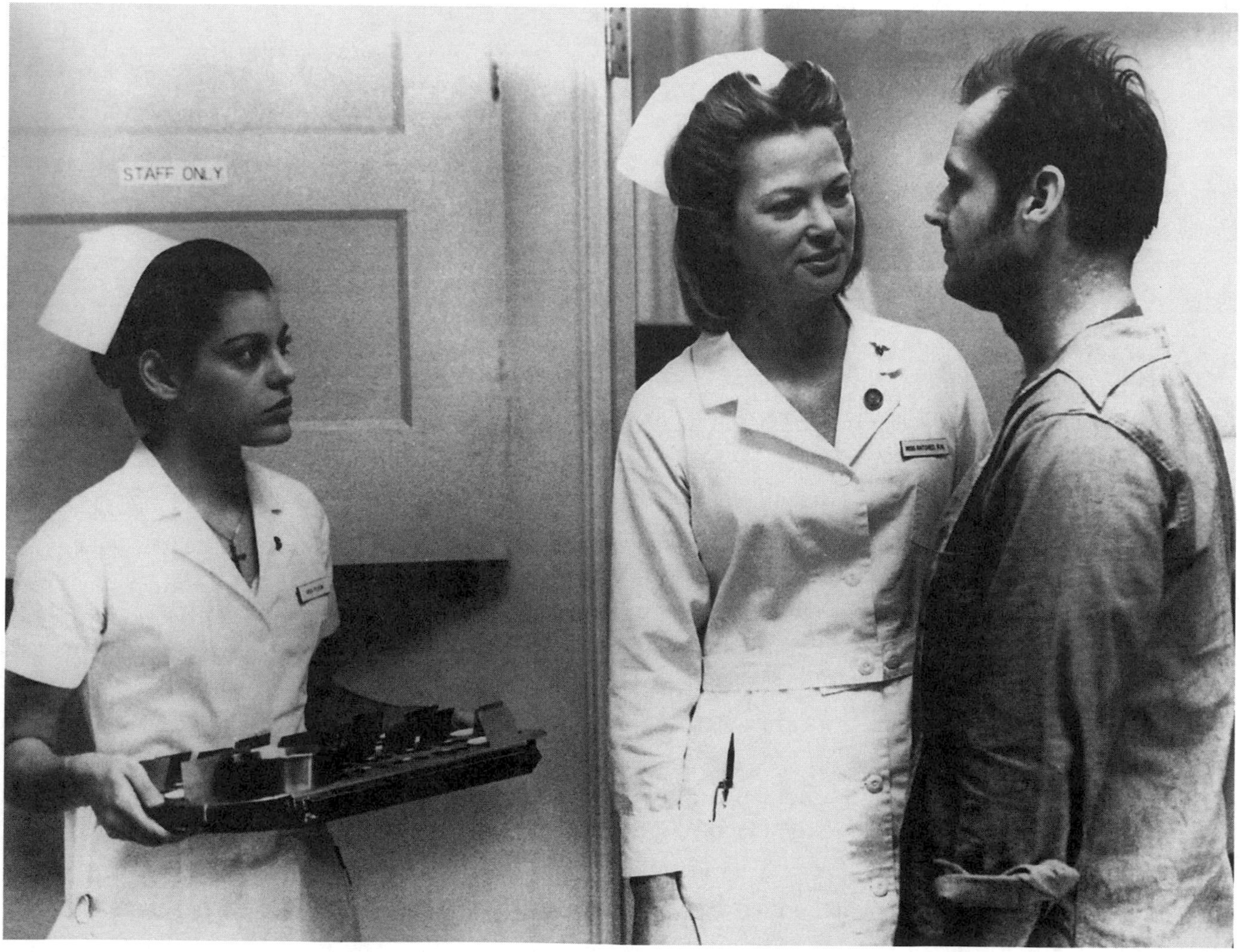

McMurphy commits to trying to incessantly aggravate Nurse Ratched for a week. He tries to convince her to rearrange the schedule so that he and the other patients can watch the World Series, but she cleverly deflects his request. Frustrated by Ratched's control, McMurphy tries to rile up the patients. He bets them $25 that he can lift a heavy shower station, throw it through a window, and go watch the World Series. As hard as he tries, he can't even budge it. He proudly exclaims that at least he tried.

At group therapy, Ratched brings up a painful sexual incident with Billy, who doesn't want to talk about it. McMurphy changes the subject to the World Series. Ratched immediately reins in the conversation, claiming that the business at hand is therapy. McMurphy wisecracks that a baseball game can be therapy. Not letting Ratched get the upper hand, McMurphy stirs up the patients as he narrates an imaginary exciting baseball game in front of a turned-off television set despite Ratched's pleas for him to stop.

Later McMurphy playfully hijacks a bus and takes the patients fishing. He even tricks the manager of a boat into believing that he and the other patients are all doctors. Not only is this a hilarious scene, it emphasizes the important thematic question of who's crazier: the patients or their keepers? In response to McMurphy's antics, Dr. Spivey (Dean R. Brooks), some other doctors, and Ratched convene to decide McMurphy's fate. Ratched suggests that the benevolent thing to do is keep McMurphy confined at the hospital so they can help him. But her real motive for wanting to keep McMurphy as a patient is to punish him.

Dismayed when he finds that the institution has the right to keep him indefinitely (even longer than his original jail term), McMurphy becomes even more angry when he finds out that most of his fellow patients, especially Billy, are there voluntarily. He yells that they are no crazier than any person on the streets. He is especially disappointed in Billy who, he thinks, should be out having fun, meeting girls, and having sex.

Inspired by McMurphy's rebellious attitudes, a patient named Cheswick has a temper tantrum because Nurse Ratched denies him cigarettes as a punishment. When Cheswick's antics grow out of control, McMurphy breaks the window of the nurse's station to get his cigarettes. A fight ensues, and Chief jumps in to help McMurphy, who is being pummeled by the guards. Just before they are about to receive electroshock therapy as punishment, Chief reveals, to McMurphy only, that he can talk and hear. McMurphy treads into a group session like a mindless zombie (even scaring Chief) before revealing it's just a joke.

McMurphy asks Chief to escape to Canada with him, but the giant Chief ironically exclaims that he is not big enough. The night of McMurphy's escape turns into an impromptu party when he bribes a guard into letting a prostitute named Candy (Marya Small) into the hospital. McMurphy sets it up so that Candy will have sex with Billy. McMurphy passes up a chance to escape that night. In the morning, Ratched discovers Billy's escapades. Billy seems confident and happy—even losing his stammering—

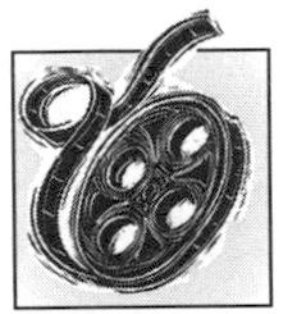

"They was giving me ten thousand watts a day, you know, and I'm hot to trot. Next woman takes me on's going to light up like a pinball machine, and pay off in silver dollars."

Jack Nicholson as Randle McMurphy in *One Flew Over the Cuckoo's Nest* (1975)

until the oppressive and mean-spirited Nurse Ratched immediately tries to make him feel guilty, asking him, "How do you think your mother is going to take this?" Billy immediately regresses to his stuttering, and moments later, kills himself. McMurphy, furious at Ratched, violently strangles her—almost killing her.

McMurphy is taken away, and although gone, his presence is felt. The inmates play cards and gossip about whether or not he's escaped. When he does return, he really is a mindless zombie now, the victim of a lobotomy. Saddened by the loss of McMurphy's indomitable spirit, Chief promises that he won't leave McMurphy like this. Chief smothers McMurphy in what could be construed as a mercy killing. Inspired by McMurphy, Chief lifts the shower station, tosses it through a window, and escapes to freedom.

See Easy Rider; *Nicholson, Jack*

P

PATTON

Few film portrayals of a historical character have rivaled the richly layered verisimilitude of George C. Scott's evocation of George S. Patton, the American general whose World War II exploits grew out of a personality that was, by turns, valiant, magnetic, brutish, and malicious. *Patton* (1970) was a stunning artistic and commercial success, winning six Oscars, including Best Picture, Best Director (Franklin J. Schaffner), and Best Actor, an award that Scott refused to accept.

Rather than simply portraying General George S. Patton Jr. as a borderline psychopath, Francis Ford Coppola and Edmund North (who adapted the script from two nonfiction sources) chose to make Patton a kind of noble savage, a relentless, merciless warrior hopelessly at odds with the leveling imperatives of modern mass warfare and collective command. Throughout the film Patton emerges as a bundle of contradictions: a foul-mouthed Bible-reader, tyrannical leader and poet, brilliant tactician and student of military history, yet bumbling politician.

The average ticket price in 1943 was 29 cents; in U.S. Army camp theaters, tickets were 15 cents.

As the film opens, a giant flag fills the screen as Patton (George C. Scott) delivers a rousing six-minute oration to offscreen soldiers, telling them that his rule of war is to never dig in, to always forge forward to annihilate the enemy. The scene shifts to 1943 in Tunisia, where the Americans have come to grief at the hands of German field marshal Erwin Rommel (Karl Michael Vogler). General Omar Bradley (Karl Malden) calls on the charismatic Patton to resuscitate the battered and demoralized American forces. The galvanic Patton, assigned to take over the command of the American II Corps, whips the lackadaisical soldiers into shape by making them fear him. Detesting what he perceives as cowardice, he kicks out the soldiers who are in the infirmary for self-inflicted wounds. When the base is attacked by the Germans, he stubbornly stands in the path of their machine-gun fire, shooting back with a mere handgun. Patton's "take-no-prisoners" style of leadership differs from Bradley's more level-headed, cautious approach.

Patton's raging passions lead him to cast his campaigns as a series of personal vendettas against all rivals, both Axis and Allied. Above all he sees the war as a challenge from him to Rommel, a military genius whom he wishes he could fight one on one to decide the fate of the war. But Patton is also waging a private war against his supposed ally, the renowned British prima donna Field Marshal Sir Bernard Law Montgomery (Michael Bates), who steals more than his share of glory.

Captain Oskar Steiger (Siegfried Rauch), assigned to research Patton, reports to Rommel about Patton's history at a military academy and at West Point. Rommel presses Steiger to search further. Steiger reveals that Patton's motto is to never dig in, and that he is an anachronistic warrior. (Patton once declared, "God, how I hate the twentieth century.") He also discovers that Patton also believes in reincarnation, convinced that he had been on the battlefield when the Carthaginians fought the Romans and that he had served Napoleon. Rommel, recognizing a formidable foe, declares his simple goal: to annihilate Patton before Patton annihilates him.

But Patton's pluck and guile prevail over the "Desert Fox," who allows his forces to be lured into a carefully laid trap at El Guettar, where Patton

Although he refused to accept the award, George C. Scott won the Best Actor Oscar for his portrayal of the multifaceted General George S. Patton in 1970's Patton.

▶

routs Rommel's forces. Flush with triumph over his archenemy, Patton earns the nickname "Old Blood and Guts," strewing controversy as he crows saltily to the press about his invincibility. The Germans watch recovered film of Patton and Bradley landing in Sicily. They learn to respect the unpretentious Bradley, but it is Patton's bigger-than-life persona that they fear.

In the wake of his African triumph, Patton is embittered to learn that he and his American Seventh Army are not to lead the attack on Sicily but have been assigned to support Montgomery's spearheading British forces. The irrepressible Patton then makes a supposedly off-the-record comment that he will beat Montgomery to Messina, but the prophecy ends up in print. Patton is hell-bent on making it to Messina first. Against Bradley's reluctance, Patton gambles with soldiers' lives by enforcing an unrealistic deadline, his patience wearing thin. When a couple of mules block a bridge, Patton summarily shoots them. He quickly replaces a colonel with a captain because of the colonel's lack of aggression. Patton bursts through to Messina. When Montgomery leads his forces into the town, he is appalled to find Patton's tanks greeting him, his distaste for Patton nearly eclipsing his hatred for their common enemy.

While visiting a military hospital, Patton asks a soldier about his wounds. When the soldier begins weeping, Patton slaps him and calls him a coward. The incident becomes public knowledge, and Eisenhower sends Patton a telegram reprimanding him for slapping the soldier. He is ordered to apologize to the soldiers, the patients, and the doctors. When he confronts them, he makes his motive clear—to shame a coward into self-respect—before apologizing.

Relieved from the command of the Seventh Army over this incident, Patton expects that he will be reassigned, this time to the top command for the Allied invasion of Europe. He is disappointed when the more cautious and political Bradley is appointed to the position instead. Basically on probation, Patton is out of battle for a time, but the Germans track his every move, suspecting that he's up to something. While American newspapers claim that Eisenhower is considering a court-martial for Patton, Rommel can't understand why the United States would sacrifice its best commander for something as trivial as smacking a soldier. Although Patton has a plan for the Normandy invasion, he is consigned to secondary decoy activities.

Despite his personal reservations, Bradley, on Eisenhower's orders, assigns Patton the command of the Third Army. Racing through France, Patton is frustrated when he is told to "slow" his troops so that Montgomery will be able to take an assignment. Patton resents the fact that the government has chosen him to lead an army but won't let him defeat the enemy. When supplies are diverted to Montgomery's troops, some of Patton's men are defeated because their tanks run out of gas.

As Patton's juggernaut rolls into Germany, he is informed that the 101st Airborne Division has been surrounded by the Germans at Bastogne. Pat-

notable & quotable

"I have an enormous affection for General Patton, a feeling of amazement and respect for him. I hope the film comes out not as an apology but as a fair, respectful portrait."

George C. Scott, actor, during filming, 1969

ton promises to extricate his men from a current battle and move them 100 miles in two days in a snowstorm to Bastogne. As he watches his men plow forward, Patton says that he is proud of them. He asks a chaplain to write a prayer for him to help to alleviate the weather: "I expect the prayer within an hour." He reads the prayer over images of battle. The next day, the snow stops; they are able to get air cover, and they storm ahead to break the German stranglehold in a nick of time. Newsreels declare that the Third Army moved farther and faster and engaged more divisions in less time than any other army in the history of the United States. Realizing they are defeated, the Nazis destroy their records and maps.

Near the war's end, Patton turns his ire against America's erstwhile ally Russia, now its adversary in the tense face-offs of the cold war. When Patton goes so far as to advocate the restoration of the German military in order to smash the communist threat in Europe, he is relieved of command

"If we are not victorious, let no one come back alive."

George C. Scott as General George S. Patton in *Patton* (1970)

AL PACINO

Al Pacino was born in New York City on April 25, 1940, with the full name Alfredo James Pacino, to parents of Sicilian origin. From an early age he was interested in acting; he attended New York's High School for the Performing Arts until age seventeen. After working at menial jobs for a few years, Pacino studied at the Herbert Berghof Studio and the Actors Studio. Subsequently he had substantial success on the New York stage, and theater remains his first love.

Pacino's first film of note was *Panic in Needle Park* (1971). The following year he played Michael Corleone, the war-hero-turned-mob boss, in Francis Ford Coppola's epic *The Godfather* (1972). Although Coppola had to fight the studio in order to cast Pacino, the gamble paid off: Pacino won an Oscar nomination for that film, and another for its sequel, *The Godfather Part II* (1974). He also starred in the third film in the trilogy, *The Godfather Part III*, in 1990.

In 1973 Pacino played the title character in *Serpico,* which was a huge hit and cemented his intense, brooding onscreen persona. He received an Oscar nomination for that role as well as for his performances in *Dog Day Afternoon* (1975), *. . . And Justice for All* (1979), *Dick Tracy* (1990), and *Glengarry Glen Ross* (1992). Pacino finally won the Best Actor Award for his work in *The Scent of a Woman* (1992), in which he played a blind army colonel. He has acted in many other films as well, notably *Scarface* (1983), *Sea of Love* (1989), and *The Devil's Advocate* (1997).

Pacino has been involved with a number of women, including actresses Jill Clayburgh, Marthe Keller, Diane Keaton, Penelope Ann Miller, and Beverly D'Angelo, but he has never married. Intensely private, Pacino has one daughter, with dancer Jan Tarrant, and one adopted son.

See Coppola, Francis Ford; Godfather, The; Godfather: Part II, The; *Keaton, Diane*

of the Third Army and forced to step down from active duty. He bids farewell to his troops, and, as Patton walks off with his dog, the film's final words are heard in voice-over: "All glory is fleeting."

See Coppola, Francis Ford; War film

PECKINPAH, SAM

Sam Peckinpah's greatest directorial triumphs were celebrations of the rugged frontier individualism of the Old West, the last remnants of which influenced his youth in California. He was born David Samuel Peckinpah on February 21, 1925, in Fresno, California, into a family with pioneering roots in ranching. His father, David, strayed from family tradition to become a lawyer, but Sam spent much of his childhood under the care of his uncle Denny, who took the young Peckinpah along on visits to his grandparents' ranch. There, Sam was exposed to hunting, cattle ranching, and his grandfather's starchy pioneer spirit of self-reliance—tempered by his father's humanitarian outlook—all of which left a lasting impression and remained among his fondest memories.

As a youngster Peckinpah's chief cultural stimuli were avid immersion in novels, the Bible, and frequent trips to the movies. By the time he entered high school, his family's frontier spirit had served him well on the football field but not in the classroom, where behavioral problems prompted his parents to send him to San Rafael Military Academy for his senior year. At San Rafael, Peckinpah distinguished himself both for his fine academic record and his unprecedented log of demerits.

Upon graduating in 1943 Peckinpah enlisted in the Marines. While stationed in Louisiana and Arizona he accumulated college credits until the summer of 1945, when he was sent to China for eighteen months. On his return to civilian life in 1947 he enrolled at Fresno State College, where he met his first wife, an aspiring actress named Marie Selland. After a visit to her acting class, Peckinpah caught the thespian bug, and was soon actively involved in the local theater, directing an adaptation of *The Glass Menagerie* by Tennessee Williams, whom Peckinpah cites as a major influence. He graduated from Fresno with a B.A. in 1949; his first child, Sharon, was born the same year. Pursuing a master's degree at the University of Southern California, he filmed an adaptation of a one-act Williams play, which served as his thesis.

Peckinpah then became a director/producer in residence at the Huntington Park Civic Theater. He was successful there for a year and a half, with a summer spent in Albuquerque doing summer stock. From there he

P

PECKINPAH, SAM

Director Sam Peckinpah was known as Bloody Sam, a nickname that would forever define his films and reputation. ▶

served in a variety of odd jobs at station KLAC-TV in Los Angeles, during which time he put together some short films that won him a job as an assistant editor at CBS in 1953. Determined to break into the film industry, Peckinpah badgered Walter Wanger, the head of Allied Artists Film Corporation, into hiring him as third or fourth assistant casting director: in brief, a gopher. His first assignment, *Riot in Cell Block 11* (1954) afforded him the opportunity to work with the director Don Siegel, who soon hired Peckinpah as "dialogue director" (really a personal assistant) on more than a dozen other feature films at Allied Artists.

From 1955 to 1958 Peckinpah worked as a full-time writer for television, mostly for the western series *Gunsmoke, Broken Arrow, Tales of Wells Fargo,* and *Have Gun—Will Travel.* Based on his TV track record, in 1957 he was hired to write a feature-film script about Billy the Kid that eventually evolved into the film *One-Eyed Jacks* (1960), starring and directed by Marlon Brando. Peckinpah then eagerly seized his first directing opportunity, an episode of *Broken Arrow.* More writing successes followed, including a story that became the pilot for the hit series *The Rifleman* and a steady job turning out scripts for the short-lived series *The Westerner* in 1959–60.

Thanks to this steady accumulation of TV writing and directing credits, Peckinpah received his first crack at directing a feature film with *The Deadly Companions* (1961), a low-budget, independent project that enjoyed modest success. After a brief return to directing for television, Peckinpah received an offer from MGM to pilot the feature film *Ride the High Country* (1962). Seizing his first big-studio opportunity, Peckinpah rewrote the script. Notwithstanding bitter haggling with the studio over the final edit, the film received excellent reviews and became a real "sleeper" success, earning *Newsweek*'s accolade as the best picture of the year (it has since come to be regarded as classic of the western genre).

Waiting for *Ride the High Country* to find an audience, Peckinpah returned to television as a writer/director before being hired, in 1963 to direct the feature film *Major Dundee* (1963), also afflicted with legendary warfare over production costs and the final cut. Peckipah's only reward for his embittered labors on this project was meeting and marrying Begonia Palacios, an actress in the film (whom he eventually married three times). Thanks to a mushrooming reputation for irascibility and inflexibility, Peckinpah endured a spell of unemployment until October 1964, when he was hired to direct *The Cincinnati Kid*. But once again, his creative differences with the producer, Martin Ransohoff, led to his firing four days into the shooting.

By now stigmatized as intemperate, Peckinpah found a rescuer in the producer David Melnick, who hired Peckinpah (against the strong advice of his associates) to adapt and direct Katherine Anne Porter's story "Noon Wine" for an ABC-TV dramatic special. The show elicited lavish critical praise and several award nominations for writing and directing.

After a spell as a TV director, feature-film writer, and film teacher at UCLA, Warner Brothers–Seven Arts offered Peckinpah the chance to direct a western project that evolved into the legendary feature *The Wild Bunch* (1969). A stunningly original tour de force that finally realized the promise of his early work, the film catapulted Peckinpah into the front ranks of contemporary auteurs.

His reputation secured at last, the newly "bankable" Peckinpah moved on to a string of variably successful, star-powered big-studio directing projects: *The Ballad of Cable Hogue* (1970), *Straw Dogs* (starring Dustin Hoffman, 1971), *Junior Bonner* (1972), *The Getaway* (1972), *Pat Garrett and Billy the Kid* (1973), *Bring Me the Head of Alfredo Garcia* (1974), *The Killer Elite* (1975), *Cross of Iron* (1977), *Convoy* (1978), and *The Osterman Weekend* (1983).

In the estimation of many critics, the only post–*Wild Bunch* films that measure up to that landmark are *Cable Hogue, Pat Garrett,* and *Alfredo Garcia.*

Sam Peckinpah died of a stroke in Mexico on December 28, 1984.

See Hoffman, Dustin; Wild Bunch, The

notable & quotable

"The best of Sam Peckinpah's work describes the lives of difficult people in difficult times doing what is necessary and natural for them to survive. Amidst the violent action an inordinate amount of humanity is allowed to peep through the dark veil."

Nick Redman, producer, 1997

P

PHILADELPHIA STORY, THE

PHILADELPHIA STORY, THE

The Philadelphia Story's screwball premise belies its sophistication and craft: witty dialogue and complex characters. It is a courageous film for 1940 that can take a female star and put her in the midst of not a love triangle, but quadrangle. Not only is the film's main character a divorcée, she has what appears to be an affair with a relative stranger, in front of her fiancé and her ex-husband, yet the movie always keeps our sympathies allied with her.

C. K. Dexter Haven (Cary Grant) storms out of a large mansion, followed by his wife, a wealthy socialite, Tracy Lord (Katharine Hepburn), who throws his golf clubs at his feet and breaks one of them over her knee. Although he can't quite bring himself to hit her, he grabs her face and pushes her down to the floor.

"The prettiest sight in this fine pretty world is the privileged class enjoying its privileges."

James Stewart as Macauley Conner in *The Philadelphia Story* (1940)

A divorce and a couple of years later, a newspaper announces Tracy's remarriage, to George Kittridge (John Howard), a successful businessman. Tracy, the snobbish heir to a huge fortune, lounges on the couch writing thank you notes for her expensive wedding gifts for her upcoming wedding. Her prim mother, Margaret (Mary Nash), is also divorced because her husband, Tracy's father, was a womanizer. The rags-to-riches Kittridge seems like a perfect match for Tracy, but Tracy's sharp-tongued younger sister, Dinah (Virginia Weidler), tells Tracy that she likes Dexter better than George. When Dinah asks her mother if Tracy is "hard" for not inviting Father to the wedding, her mother replies that Tracy sets high standards for herself, and it's hard for others to live up to them.

Kittridge enjoys his newfound socialite status, even flipping through an issue of *Spy* magazine looking for gossip about him and Tracy. Just the thought of *Spy*'s behind-the-scenes exposés, in which a journalist sneaks into somebody's house, angers Tracy. Of course, ex-husband Dexter plans—with the help of *Spy* editor Sidney Kidd (Henry Daniell)—to smuggle two undercover reporters into Tracy's house to get a behind-the-scenes look at her wedding and life. The two reporters are Macauley Connor (James Stewart) and Liz Imbrie (Ruth Hussie). Connor, an author of some serious short stories and an intellectual snob, is disgusted by this assignment, but Liz, more practical, reminds him that he needs the money.

Dexter gets them into the house under the guise of being friends of Tracy's brother, who lives far away and can't attend the wedding. Liz and Connor gawk at the expensive surroundings, and Connor makes a prank phone call to another room in the house.

Angry that Dexter has shown up, Tracy tells him to leave. Knowing that he works for *Spy*, she figures out that Liz and Connor are reporters. But Dexter tells Tracy that *Spy* will run an embarrassing sex-scandal story about her father if they can't get this story. A hilarious sequence follows where Tracy and Dinah parody the archetypal wealthy family: Dinah speaks French and plays piano while Tracy plays the genteel host. Against Tracy's wishes, her father shows up and she quickly enlists him into the ruse.

The next day at the library, Connor, doing research on Tracy, finds Tracy doing research on him: reading his collection of short stories. She especially likes the one inspired by the proverb "with the rich and mighty always a little patience." They sincerely connect, and she even offers him the use of one of her summer houses so that he will have time to write. He rebuffs her offer, calling it condescending.

Dexter and Tracy have a tense conversation in which he criticizes her. Although she's generous to a fault, he says, she is not generous to other people's faults. Echoing her father's statement that Tracy has everything but an understanding heart, Dexter tells her that she won't be a decent human being until she has some regard for human frailty. He further opines that Tracy wants to be a goddess: worshiped. Moments later, Kittridge expresses

Katharine Hepburn, shown here with costars Cary Grant (left) and James Stewart, enjoyed the third of her thirteen Oscar nominations for her portrayal of an heiress in the sophisticated comedy The Philadelphia Story.

▼

his feelings to her, telling her that he wants to build a glass tower for her and worship her like a queen.

Reluctant to take advantage of Tracy, Connor is ready to confess to his real identity. Before he can, the Lords confess that they have known Connor's identity all along. With her father's and Dexter's attack on her character and Kittridge's reinforcing that everything that they said is true, Tracy, for the first time in her life, partakes in the vice for which she could never forgive Dexter: alcohol. She has several quick shots.

Connor gets drunk and reveals his interest in Tracy to Dexter when he criticizes Dexter for his apparent motive of revenge. Later, Dexter and Liz work on a scandalous story about Kidd, which will allow them to stop the Tracy story. It's clear that Liz is in love with Connor. She knows this story will get Connor fired, freeing him to do the writing that he really wants to do. She also senses that any budding attraction between him and Tracy will be fleeting.

In 1940 Katharine Hepburn paid $25,000 for the rights to *The Philadelphia Story*, then sold the rights to MGM for $175,000.

Tracy and Connor end up in each other's arms. Connor confesses his deep feelings for her. Tracy likes him too, but thinks he, like her, is a snob: an intellectual snob. She echoes Dexter's words when she tells him that he has no chance of being a decent human being . . . she doesn't finish. When she calls him the professor—reflecting his lack of feeling—he kisses her, and they go for a swim.

Kittridge shows up looking for Tracy, who appears wearing a bathrobe—and is being carried by Connor from the swimming pool. Assuming the worst, Kittridge is ready to punch Connor. Belying his possible lingering feelings for his former wife, Dexter punches Connor in the face for Kittridge, later claiming to Connor that he was doing him a favor: Kittridge "is in better shape than I am."

In the morning, Tracy doesn't remember what happened. In a confused hungover state, Tracy oddly apologizes to Dexter for what she has (maybe) done. He reminds her that it is Kittridge to whom she should apologize. She gets a note from Kittridge admonishing her for "shocking his ideals of womanhood" and demanding an explanation if their wedding is to proceed. Angry that he wouldn't trust her, she wishes him well and essentially says good-bye. Connor explains that their "affair" consisted of exactly two kisses and a swim. Kittridge then decides to take her back, but she spurns him.

Tracy's parents support her last-minute wedding cancellation. Connor offers to marry her, but Tracy knows it wouldn't work. As she breaks the news to her guests, she looks to Dexter for the right words to say. He announces their own remarriage, which she repeats to the waiting guests without thinking, but when she realizes what she's said she is delighted. Tracy's father tells her she looks like a goddess and a queen. She responds that she feels like a human being.

See Hepburn, Katharine; Mankiewicz, Joseph; Stewart, James

PICKFORD, MARY

Of the three greatest stars of the early cinema—Mary Pickford, Douglas Fairbanks, and Charlie Chaplin—Pickford remains the most elusive for modern audiences. While most of the writing on Pickford remains impressionistic and appreciative, other critics have brought out her key economic role in the development of the motion-picture industry.

Pickford had been working for Adolph Zukor since 1913, and as her popularity grew it became apparent that the exhibitors' desire for her films

Actress Mary Pickford, as well known for her financial acumen as for her acting ability, was one of the thirty-six original founders of the Academy of Motion Picture Arts and Sciences.

◀

was carrying the entire Famous Players product line. In January 1915 her contract had been renegotiated to offer her $2,000 per week (double the previous salary) and 50 percent of the profits on ten films each year. But in order to meet her escalating salary demands, the following year Zukor had to set Pickford up as her own producer, creating the Artcraft label to handle her films separately from the general Paramount line.

Maurice Tourneur, Cecil B. DeMille, and Marshall Neilan directed most of the Artcraft films, often from scripts by Frances Marion or Jeanie Macpherson. Walter Stradling and Charles Rosher were Pickford's cameramen, and in a period when few films employed credited art directors, she used two of the finest in Hollywood. Benn Carré (for the Tourneur films) and Wilfred Buckland. Today these seem her most accomplished works, entirely lacking in the self-importance that began to affect her later releases.

In 1916, four years before the 19th Amendment gave American women the right to vote, Mary Pickford was earning $10,000 a week minimum against 50 percent of the profits.

Late in 1918 Pickford followed Chaplin's lead in moving to First National, where she was granted even more creative control and a salary of $675,000 to make three films. With her 50 percent of the profits this would net her over a million dollars per year. Chaplin had reached this plateau already, although not because of any superior business acumen. It was Pickford who was the acknowledged fiscal expert of the group that, in 1919, would form United Artists.

After her marriage to Douglas Fairbanks in 1920, Pickford slowed her output, relishing her regal position as mistress of Pickfair and vying with Fairbanks in the care and attention that might be devoted to each film. She released only one film a year after 1921, and while some, such as *Sparrows* (1926), were popular hits, attempts at more mature parts in *Rosita* (1923) and *Dorothy Vernon of Haddon Hall* (1924) were less successful. Pickford had not been limited to children's roles when she began at Biograph and did not play a child throughout an entire feature until *The Poor Little Rich Girl*, her twenty-fourth such film. But audiences insisted on seeing her in this characterization, and as she grew older the women she found herself playing grew younger.

See Chaplin, Charlie; Fairbanks, Douglas; Ince, Thomas; Neilan, Marshall; Tourneur, Maurice; von Sternberg, Josef

PLACE IN THE SUN, A

A Place in the Sun (1951) is part of director and producer George Stevens's "American trilogy" of films, along with *Giant* and *Shane*. *A Place in the Sun* is a melodrama, adapted from Theodore Dreiser's 1925 novel *An American Tragedy*, whose theme is the vast gulf—in the final analysis, unbridgeable—between the poor and the rich. The film is a remake of the 1931 film *An American Tragedy* by Josef von Sternberg, and it is every bit as dark and cynical as the original.

The film's opening credits are superimposed on a long shot of a highway. George Eastman (Montgomery Clift) is hitchhiking to the home of his rich uncle, Charles Eastman (Herbert Heyes). Charles Eastman owns a bathing-suit factory, advertised on a billboard showing a reclining bathing beauty ("It's an Eastman"). As the young, handsome George stands by the side of the road, a beautiful girl driving a shiny sports car approaches. She flirtatiously honks and then zooms away, a symbol of the world of the privileged passing George by. The two images of luxury and leisure (on the billboard and in the fancy automobile) fill George's mind. He craves everything the women represent.

George has just quit his job as a hotel bellboy and traveled here on the strength of his uncle's promise to give him a job at the bathing-suit factory.

A melodramatic depiction of the idle rich, A Place in the Sun *won six Academy Awards, including Best Director for George Stevens.*

▼

The vast disparity in social and economic classes between the two men is abundantly clear when George visits his uncle at his mansion. George's aunt condescendingly asks about George's mother's religious work at a mission. The awkward moment is interrupted when Angela Vickers (Elizabeth Taylor)—a gorgeous and vivacious socialite—barges in. She doesn't pay the slightest attention to George, but his attention is riveted on her. She is the beautiful girl in the sports car.

When George starts work at his uncle's bathing-suit factory, he is warned that he should not fraternize with the other employees—mostly women. Employees who are caught in romantic relationships are fired. Thrown onto the assembly line, he is initially overwhelmed but soon masters the job. George is eager to please, and ambitious. He drafts a proposal for his uncle, suggesting ways in which the factory might become more efficient.

At the movies one evening, George runs into Alice Tripp (Shelley Winters), a coworker at the factory, and walks her home. She tells him that he is different from her, because his name will eventually bring him privilege. George kisses Alice, but she does not let him come into her room, claiming that she has a strict landlady. On their next date, Alice apologizes for saying George was different. They end up dancing at her place, silhouetted against the moonlight. A subtle camera move, her whispering his name, and a clever time-lapse shot work together to suggest that the couple has made love.

Uncle Charlie soon offers George a promotion and invites him to a party at his mansion. Alice is jealous and resentful; the party is on George's birthday, and she was planning to celebrate it with him. George cannot resist the lure of a classy party; he promises that he will go to Alice's place after making an appearance at the party. Once at the party, he is completely ignored, so he begins shooting pool by himself. He is interrupted by Angela, who is impressed by his skill. She flirts with him, and they spend the night dancing together.

George finally shows up at Alice's, hours late. She is sleeping, fully dressed, on the bed. She gives him a small gift, and then asks him about Angela. Echoing the end of the movie, she seems to read his mind by asking if he still wants to see her, now that he is head of the department.

A serious dilemma changes everything for George: Alice is pregnant. They discuss alternatives, including abortion (never identified specifically by name). George's personal options seem to be becoming fewer and fewer, but his attention is diverted: the glamorous Angela calls him and invites him to a party. They dance cheek-to-cheek all night and passionately declare their love for each other.

Meanwhile, Alice—who is less and less appealing to George in comparison to the glorious Angela—is dealing with real life. Under the guise of being married, Alice consults a doctor to try to get an abortion. Even when she breaks down and cries and admits that she's not married, the doctor offers only to help her deliver and raise a healthy baby.

Desperate, Alice demands that George marry her during his Labor Day vacation in September. As he contemplates what to do, George hears a radio report of all the accidental holiday deaths, and he is suddenly overwhelmed with an awful thought: if he drowned Alice, he would be free! Angela shows up and complicates things further: she invites him to come to her family's summerhouse for his vacation.

George makes an excuse to Alice—postponing their wedding by a week—so he can go with Angela. He and Angela have a wonderful time riding horses and swimming, and Angela even tells George that she plans to marry him. Angela also gets George thinking again when she tells him about a horrible drowning that happened on the lake.

At a dinner party, just as George starts to fit in, he gets a call from Alice, who has seen a picture of him and Angela in the society pages of the newspaper. She threatens to come to Angela's summerhouse if George does not come back and marry her. Claiming that he needs to visit his sick mother, George leaves Angela's vacation home.

Alice demands that they get married the next day, but the courthouse is closed for Labor Day, so George invites her to a weekend at the lake. They rent a boat—George uses a phony name—and go out onto the water alone. George is contemplating killing Alice to solve his problems, but he is torn. Recognizing that marrying her will severely limit George's options in life, Alice tries to console him, saying that although they will have a modest middle-class existence, their love for each other will keep them happy.

Everything Alice says is the exact opposite of what George wants to hear. He is so upset that he puts physical distance between them—he moves to the other end of the boat. Alice figures out what he must be thinking—that he doesn't want to be with her, that he wants her dead. When she stands up to walk toward him, the boat capsizes. But George is the only one who gets out of the water alive. While George did not deliberately drown Alice, the viewer is unsure of whether he could have saved her.

With Alice out of the way, George is free to marry Angela. She tells George that her parents are warming up to him, and that maybe they can announce their marriage in December. George impresses Angela's father with his forthrightness when he frankly acknowledges his poor roots and his desire to better himself.

Meanwhile, the district attorney, Marlowe (Raymond Burr), begins to piece together the mystery of Alice's death. George tells Angela that people will soon be saying disturbing things about him. The police do eventually catch up with George, but they agree to keep Angela's family out of the trial. In court, George admits that he had murderous thoughts but that he did not act on them, even though he did such things as giving a false name when he rented the boat. Marlowe presents a hypothetical scenario wherein

George whacked Alice on the head with an oar; the district attorney's dramatic performance helps to procure a guilty verdict and a sentence of death.

George later tells his mother and a priest that he is not sure if he is guilty. The priest asks why George could not act to save Alice. George's silence, claims the priest, means that in George's heart, it was murder.

A somber Angela comes to say goodbye. George takes responsibility for his actions, admitting that he did not act to save Alice, and he and Angela express their undying love for each other. They kiss, and she leaves. His slow walk to his death is superimposed with the indelible image of his and Angela's perfect kiss.

A Place in the Sun was nominated for nine Academy Awards. It won six Oscars, for Best Director (Stevens's first Oscar), Best Screenplay (Michael Wilson and Harry Brown), Best Black and White Cinematography, Best Dramatic Score, Best Film Editing, and Best Black and White Costume Design (Edith Head). The other three nominations were for Best Actor (Montgomery Clift), Best Actress (Shelley Winters), and Best Picture.

See Taylor, Elizabeth

PLATOON

The action of 1986's *Platoon* begins with a superimposed biblical quote from Ecclesiastes: "Rejoice, O young man, in thy youth." Young military recruits, Chris Taylor (Charlie Sheen) among them, are seen disembarking from a military transport plane into a parched yellow-orange world. Taylor, stunned, observes body bags being unloaded from the plane that has brought him to the jungle outpost. Another caption appears: "September 1967—Bravo Co., 25th Infantry. Somewhere near the Cambodian border."

Via a compilation montage with accompanying actor credits, the secondary, then principal, characters are introduced, followed by a sequence of shots showing the men of Company B entering a dark, dense jungle. The new recruits, disoriented and fatigued, are prodded on and cajoled with debasing labels like "fatso."

Arriving at camp, the soldiers go about their tasks of unloading war materiel, digging foxholes, and writing letters home. The company appears to be predominantly black in population. In a voice-over, a soft-spoken Chris Taylor is heard reciting a letter written to his grandmother a week after arriving in Vietnam. He tells her of his point duty, confusion over jungle combat, fatigue, all-night ambushes, and what it's like to be the "new guy" in Vietnam. Taylor says: "I don't think I can keep this up for a year, Grandma. I think I made a big mistake coming here."

From these introspective observations of an innocent, *Platoon* develops into a larger picture of the grueling, tense life of soldiers in Company B. News comes of another distant platoon, "blown to pieces" by the North Vietnamese Army (NVA); factions are revealed between officers and NCOs and between whites and blacks as plans are made for an ambush attack.

With the ambush patrol pushing into the jungle despite heavy rain, Taylor's voiceover letter continues, recounting how he came to Vietnam against his middle-class parents' wishes. He says he felt a need to break away from his sheltered existence and to "do my share for my country—live up to what Grandpa did in the first war and Dad did in the second." Taylor tells his grandmother he's come to realize that his fellow soldiers are "guys nobody really cares about," "the end of the line," "the bottom of the barrel"

Willem Dafoe, Charlie Sheen, and Tom Berenger (l. to r.) portray soldiers in director Oliver Stone's look at the Vietnam War in 1986's Platoon.

"But most of them [the men in his unit] got nothing. They're poor. They're the unwanted, yet they're fighting for our society and our freedom. It's weird, isn't it?"

Charlie Sheen as Chris (narration) in *Platoon* (1986)

men. But Taylor also expresses his admiration for these people and says he hopes he can see something in Vietnam he doesn't yet see and learn something not yet known. His letter ends with a reminder of how much he misses his family.

The plotting details of *Platoon,* which will lead Taylor to the knowledge he seeks, activate with haste. In a shootout with the NVA that occurs during the patrol, Taylor is grazed by a bullet and begins to panic; he then observes the driven Sergeant Barnes (Tom Berenger) finishing off a wounded NVA enemy soldier, then witnesses the death of two of Company B's own men. No sooner is this patrol trauma over than Taylor is seen back in camp on latrine duty, emptying and burning toilet feces and telling his short-timer supervisors how he dropped out of college for voluntary duty in Vietnam.

Barracks life introduces Taylor to the "druggies"—the dope-smoking faction of Company B, men who dance to "Tracks of My Tears." Sergeant Elias (Willem Dafoe) spearheads this more laid-back group of soldiers, whose primary goal is simply to do their duty and get out of Vietnam alive. Elias offers Taylor his first hit of marijuana, ominously compelling the wide-eyed young soldier to smoke from a rifle barrel. Taylor eventually begins to respect Elias, who is dutiful but disillusioned by the war and its seemingly endless futilities. At the same time, Taylor comes to resent Barnes.

New Year's Day 1968 finds Taylor's letter home calling the occasion "just another day—staying alive." From here *Platoon* moves episodically to develop the conflict between Elias and Barnes—a conflict born of and nurtured by the unorthodox, no-rules nature of Vietnam guerrilla warfare. Combat patrols are depicted as deadly, frustrating missions, with Company B men dying by booby trap and sinister crucifixion. An increasingly irate Barnes strikes back, compulsively gunning down a Vietnamese villager and killing a woman who protests the violent treatment of Vietnamese civilians by the frustrated American soldiers. Taylor himself momentarily loses control in a fit of rage, shooting his rifle at a villager's feet.

When Barnes puts a gun to a hysterical child's head, Elias intercedes and a fight breaks out between the two men. Elias intends to expose Barnes's atrocity in killing the Vietnamese woman. Barnes dares to challenge the company officer who stops the fight. The ambiguous war goes on, as villages are torched and Vietnamese women are raped. All the while, the competition between Elias and the gung-ho Barnes grows. In a letter home Taylor writes about "a civil war in the platoon: half the men with Elias, half with Barnes. There's a lot of suspicion and hate. I can't believe we're fighting each other when we should be fighting them."

A lengthy, frenetic ambush by the NVA leads *Platoon* toward a violent and surreal conclusion in which the external conflict of enemy battle and the internal conflict involving Barnes, Elias—and now Taylor—are resolved. The shootout becomes a dizzying, bloody affair that shows

SIDNEY POITIER

Sidney Poitier, the first black star of the American screen, was born in Miami, Florida, on February 20, 1927. His performances are often described as a "beacon" against racism, and his career is especially interesting when one considers Poitier's less than privileged beginnings. Logic and reason cannot be applied to his career, Poitier noted. "The journey has been incredible from its beginning."

From age two, Poitier grew up on Cat Island and Nassau in the Bahamas. His was a poor tomato-farming family, and he was the youngest of eight children. The star, who exudes intelligence in his typically intense roles, had less than two years of formal education, from age eleven to thirteen. He then dropped out of school to help support his family. Poitier later said that he was an "incorrigible kid" who "flirted with reform school."

Poitier joined the U.S. Army at age sixteen, lying about his age, and served for two years. He then found odd jobs in New York City and began looking into acting. After some struggle, he eventually was accepted into the American Negro Theatre. He performed in nearly a dozen plays with the troupe and then landed his first film role, in *No Way Out* (1950). Over the next few years he performed in several films, including, notably, *Cry, the Beloved Country* (1952), *The Blackboard Jungle* (1955), and *Band of Angels* (1957). In 1958 he made an international splash with *The Defiant Ones* and in 1959 as Porgy in *Porgy and Bess.*

In the 1960s Poitier was one of the top box-office stars in the world, with major roles in such films as *A Raisin in the Sun* (1961), *Lilies of the Field* (1963), and *The Greatest Story Ever Told* (1965). Though he won the Best Actor Oscar for *Lilies of the Field*—the first black actor to be so honored—the year 1967 was pivotal for Poitier, with the release of three movies that are now considered classics: *In the Heat of the Night, To Sir with Love,* and *Guess Who's Coming to Dinner.* In the latter film, he provided one half of the first screen kiss between a black man and white woman.

A line from *In the Heat of the Night* is most closely associated with Poitier: When asked by a redneck, "What do they call you, boy?" Poitier's character answers with great strength and dignity, "They call me Mr. Tibbs." (He performed in a movie of that same name in 1970.)

Since the 1970s Poitier has alternated acting with directing, with considerable success. He has appeared in a variety of films, including *Buck and the Preacher* (1974), *Uptown Saturday Night* (1974), *Little Nikita* (1988), *Sneakers* (1992), and *The Jackal* (1997). He also has done some good work in television movies.

Actor Sidney Poitier was the first black man to win an Academy Award, for his role as handyman Homer Smith in 1963's Lilies of the Field.

Though Poitier acknowledges that his success story is an amazing one, he seems somewhat uncomfortable with the label of social and cultural groundbreaker, and he prefers to keep his private life private. He has been married twice, to dancer Juanita Hardy from 1950 to1965, and to actress Joanna Shimkus (since 1976), and has six daughters. In 1997 he was named the Bahamas' ambassador to Japan. The American Film Institute honored him with its prestigious Life Achievement Award in 1992.

See Guess Who's Coming to Dinner; *Hepburn, Katharine; Tracy, Spencer*

charred bodies strewn about like fallen leaves. Barnes and Elias, in acting to repel the surprise attack, compete for the last time as Barnes uses the distracting furor of the battle to seek out and shoot Elias. Rendered helpless, Elias later dies in an onslaught of enemy bullets.

Finally, Taylor—aware of Barnes's actions and unable to tolerate any longer a man who goes "on making up the rules" anyway he wants—kills Barnes after he is wounded during a raging battle that occurs on the second day of the attack. Wounded himself and badly burned, Taylor is carried by stretcher to a waiting helicopter. Rising above an open mass grave—a common dump for the enemy dead—Taylor's final thoughts are heard:

> I think now, looking back, we did not fight the enemy, we fought ourselves, and the enemy was in us. The war is over for me now, but it will always be there the rest of my days, as I am sure Elias will be fighting Barnes, for what Rhah called possession of my soul. There are times since I have felt like a child born of these two fathers. Be that as it may. Those of us who did make it have an obligation to build again—to teach to others what we know. And to try with what's left of our lives to find a goodness and a meaning to this life.

Platoon concludes with a screen wash to white and an end title that reads: "Dedicated to the men who fought and died in Vietnam."

See Stone, Oliver; War film

POLANSKI, ROMAN

Of all major directors, probably none has produced a body of work so truly cosmopolitan as Roman Polanski. Fluent in five languages, he has made films in Poland Italy, England, France, and the United States; and he has lived for extended periods in the latter three countries. He was born to Polish-Jewish parents in France in 1933; three years later he returned with his parents to their native Poland, where he lived until the age of twenty-one.

During World War II millions of Poles were killed, and the degree to which Polanski was scarred by this experience would be hard to overestimate. At age eight, the future director watched the walling off of the Krakow ghetto. Escaping alone to the country, he was later shot at by Nazi troopers for target practice. As a Jew in a Catholic culture, he was aware not only of the oppression of his people fostered by the prevailing religious beliefs in Poland, but also of the more virulent anti-Semitism that led to his mother's death at Auschwitz. Later, under communism, instances of racial

bigotry continued: two of his former Jewish teachers at Lodz lost their positions in 1968, reportedly as the result of anti-Semitic sentiment. Such early experiences doubtless explain, at least in part, the bitter satires of religion in most of Polanski's films. By age fourteen, he claims he was an atheist, and his work is invariably critical of Christianity—especially Catholics. At the same time, however, his films reveal a fascination with the pagan superstitions that persisted alongside orthodox Roman Catholicism among the peasants among whom he lived.

Despairing of organized religion and politics, Polanski turned to art, which reminded him of the happier aspects of his childhood. As a virtual orphan during World War II, he developed a voracious appetite for movies and plays to escape an intolerable existence. "I always wanted to make

Director Roman Polanski has endured more than his share of personal tragedy, including charges of statutory rape and the murder of his pregnant wife by members of the Manson family.

◀

films," he has recalled, "as far back as I can remember. As an adolescent, he began to act, first on radio, then in the theater, and finally in films. As a young actor, Polanski absorbed the impact of avant-garde movements in the Polish theater, where he spent many hours in the balcony as well as on the stage. He also came under the influence of the renowned Polish director Andrzej Wajda, having appeared in several of his films. After studying painting and sculpture, he enrolled in the renowned Polish film school at Lodz. A rigorous five-year program followed, beginning with a year of still photography and ending with the direction of a 16-mm short film that made use of sophisticated techniques of cinematography and editing.

Polanski's cinematic precocity was soon in evidence; his student project *Two Men and a Wardrobe* (1958) drew international recognition, most notably with the awarding of the Bronze Medal at the Brussels World's Fair. His first major feature film was *Knife in the Water* (1962). A brooding study of sexual and personal conflict, it was decried as intensively in official circles as it was lauded in the West, earning an Oscar nomination for Best Foreign Film and the Critics' Prize at the Venice Film Festival.

Partly to escape the culturally suffocating atmosphere of Poland, Polanski relocated to England for his next three projects: *Repulsion* (1965), in which Catherine Deneuve plays a Belgian woman whose psychic terrors drive her to murder; *Cul de Sac* (1966), a black comedy about a pair of bank robbers hiding out in a remote castle; and *Dance of the Vampires* (1967), a sendup of horror films in which Polanski took an acting role alongside Sharon Tate, whom he married in 1968.

Polanski's expertise in the cinema of the macabre made him a natural for his first effort in the United States, *Rosemary's Baby* (1968), a critical and commercial smash that balances the viewer on an agonizingly narrow line between terror and paranoid fantasy in a young wife's growing suspicion that she is the target of a satanic cult. The film propelled Polanski to a personal and professional peak from which he plunged with brutal suddenness in the summer of 1968, when his pregnant wife and three friends were killed by followers of the cult leader Charles Manson.

It was not until 1970 that Polanski felt able to undertake another project. His starkly and morbidly bloody rendering of *Macbeth* (1971) was thought by some to represent his working through of his personal anguish over his wife's murder, a provenance that Polanski has always denied.

Polanski's next big Hollywood film, *Chinatown* (1974), is widely considered his masterpiece—indeed, one of the great films of the past quarter century. An apotheosis of film noir's shadowy nightworld of lurking menace and enveloping corruption, the film features Jack Nicholson as a private eye in Los Angeles in the 1930s who is drawn, in spite of himself, into a labyrinth of incest and greed.

In quest of new challenges, Polanski took the starring role in his next film, *The Tenant* (1976), a portrayal of a man's psychological unraveling—in retrospect an eerily prophetic work, since Polanski soon faced yet another personal disaster when, in 1979, he was arrested and indicted on charges of statutory rape after a sexual encounter with a thirteen-year-old girl. After forty-two days in prison, Polanski fled to Paris to escape further prosecution.

His comeback film was not long in coming: *Tess* (1979), an adaptation of Thomas Hardy's novel *Tess of the D'Ubervilles,* a worthy effort that was an uncharacteristically decorous and tame exercise that seemed almost a public proclamation of penance. None of his subsequent work—*Lunes de fiel* (1992), *Death and the Maiden* (1994), and *The Ninth Gate* (1999)—has approached the intensity and impact of his earlier films.

See Chinatown; *Dunaway, Faye; Nicholson, Jack*

POLLACK, SYDNEY

Sydney Pollack is one of Hollywood's most versatile and accomplished directors, his mastery ranging from the madcap comedy of *Tootsie* to the dark social realism of *They Shoot Horses, Don't They?*

Pollack was born on July 1, 1934, in Lafayette, Indiana. His father was a pharmacist and his mother a singer of Russian folk songs and a piano player whose devotion to the arts influenced all three of her children (Bernie, the second child became a costume designer; Sharon, the third, is a choreographer.)

For Sydney Pollack, the normal uncertainties and anxieties of adolescence were compounded by the often overt anti-Semitism his family endured as part of South Bend's small Jewish population and by his conflicting desires to please his parents: he played football to appease his father and joined the drama club at his mother's urging.

Several people played important roles in bringing Pollack to a career in film. The first, James Lewis Casady, taught the drama class at South Bend Central High School. Through Casady's guidance, and through the trips to Chicago that he initiated, Casady introduced Pollack to performances of ballet and to other cultural activities outside South Bend's parochial confines. With Casady's encouragement, Pollack decided to seek a theatrical career. Calling his decision "one of my best memories of South Bend," Pollack boarded the train to New York City following his graduation from high school.

He enrolled in the Neighborhood Playhouse under the direction of Sandor Meisner, who became Pollack's next mentor. As Pollack has noted,

"The Neighborhood Playhouse was a profound experience. People were concerned with things that I felt, but could never articulate."

With some money—saved through jobs he'd held as a teenager, the weekly benevolence of an aunt, a summer spent in a South Bend lumberyard, and small roles in television shows—Pollack was able to remain at the Playhouse. When he returned to New York for his second year with Meisner, he was given a fellowship, and by the age of nineteen he had a role in his first Broadway show, *A Stone for Danny Fisher*. He supplemented his earnings by teaching private classes at the Playhouse.

By 1955–56 Pollack was gaining a reputation both as an actor and as a teacher of actors. He appeared in *The Dark Is Light Enough* with Katherine Cornell and Tyrone Power, and toured the east in *Stalag 17.* He also appeared in most of the major live television shows of the era, including *Playhouse 90, Kraft Television Theater, Goodyear Playhouse, Alcoa Presents,* and others. Then he was drafted for the Korean War.

Best known as the director of such films as Tootsie *(1982) and* Out of Africa *(1985), Sydney Pollack has also been an actor, an acting teacher, and director of television shows including* Ben Casey *and* Dr. Kildare.

While on leave in New York in 1958, Pollack married one of his former acting students, Claire Griswold. They moved to Fort Carson, Colorado, for the duration of Pollack's service; after his discharge, they returned to New York, where he tried to reestablish his acting career.

Pollack's prolonged absence proved a major hurdle. With new actors having moved up through the ranks, Pollack struggled to find work. Wishing to reestablish his ties with Meisner, he resumed teaching at the Neighborhood Playhouse. He also landed an acting job that proved to be a turning point in his career—a role in a two-part *Playhouse 90* production of *For Whom the Bell Tolls,* directed by John Frankenheimer, who had also studied with Meisner and who became the next great influence on Pollack's development.

Frankenheimer invited Pollack to coach two of the young actors on another of his TV productions, a successful venture that led to Frankenheimer's bringing him to California to serve as dialogue director for three young actors appearing in a major feature film, *The Young Savages,* starring Burt Lancaster. Lancaster, who befriended Pollack during the filming, encouraged him to become a director, arranging a job that allowed Pollack to observe feature-film directors for six months while receiving a weekly stipend of $100. Pollack's apprenticeship led to several years' work as director of episodes of most of the major television dramas of that time, including *Ben Casey, The Defenders, Naked City,* and *Dr. Kildare.* During these years Pollack garnered several Emmy nominations.

His growing stature as a TV director brought him offers to pilot feature films. His first such effort was the forgettable *The Slender Thread* (1965), a project that gave Pollack valuable experience in adjusting to the big screen's unique requirements in framing and camera movement. In 1966 Pollack was hired to direct Natalie Wood and Robert Redford in *This Property Is Condemned* (1966). Pollack's growing repute as a film craftsman finally led to a breakthrough project, *They Shoot Horses, Don't They?* (1969), a searing study of Depression-era competitive marathon dancers at the mercy of a rapacious entrepreneur. The film earned Pollack an Oscar nomination for Best Director and thrust him into the select company of sought-after Hollywood craftsmen whose films could earn both critical esteem and solid profits.

Jeremiah Johnson (1972), starring Robert Redford, sustained Pollack's momentum, which quickened even further with the popular *The Way We Were* (1973), which paired Redford with Barbra Streisand. The artistically ambitious but financially disappointing *Yazuka* (1974) was a bit of a career detour, but with *Three Days of the Condor* (1975), a political thriller starring Robert Redford and Faye Dunaway, Pollack was back on the fast track, having earned the freedom to attempt the arty curiosity *Bobby Deerfield* (1977). His next major film was *The Electric Horseman,* another Redford vehicle, which was followed by a string of critical and financial successes that solidified Pollack's status as one of Hollywood's elite directors: *Absence of Malice* (1981), with Paul Newman; *Tootsie* (1982), a hugely popular comedy with Dustin Hoffman; *Out of Africa* (1985), a pairing of Redford and Meryl Streep that won the Academy Award for Best Picture; *Havana* (1990); *The Firm* (1993); *Sabrina* (1995); and *Random Hearts* (1999).

Pollack's formula for blending critical and commercial success is perhaps best summarized by Pollack himself: "You can really make quite interesting personal pictures, but you can't make them for the kind of money that I've spent making studio pictures, which are very expensive. . . . You have to reach a lot of people. . . . You don't get it back with limited critical success."

See Hoffman, Dustin; Lange, Jessica; Redford, Robert; Streep, Meryl; Tootsie

POSTMODERNISM

Postmodernism is a critical concept originating in the 1970s that embraced pluralism and eclecticism as counter-responses to the previously held canons of modernism. As interpreters of postmodernism have noted, the movement was a reaction against modernist principles of accepted style, initially in architecture and the decorative arts and eventually influencing the arts and literature in general. Postmodernism as a movement resulted in more playful, historically diversified approaches to creative practice. In avant-garde cinema, for example, experimental filmmakers turned away from any single dominating style and toward an "anything goes" response. This trend is often referred to as the "postmodern avant-garde" in late-twentieth-century filmmaking.

See Criticism; Cultural criticism; Gaze (look); Psychoanalysis and cinema

PREQUEL

The term prequel is used to refer to a sequel in which the time period of the narrative action predates that of the original film. *Butch and Sundance: The Early Days* (1979), for instance, is a tale of Butch Cassidy and the Sundance

Kid during early outlaw years that were not treated in George Roy Hill's 1969 classic with Paul Newman and Robert Redford. Because of strong audience associations with the original and because of the necessity of using different, younger actors in the principal roles, prequels tend to disappoint.

See Remake; Sequel

PRODUCER (FILM)

That individual who serves as the logistics supervisor of a film, standing prominently beside the director who is the "artistic" overseer of the production, is the producer. In contemporary filmmaking the producer often secures the money for the project, purchases the film script, and hires the director and other primary artists involved in the making of the film. Producers can be autocratic forces in the filmmaking process, making both logistic and artistic decisions that affect the ultimate quality of the released film. Producers such as Irving Thalberg and David O. Selznick achieved legendary status in the film world during the American studio years. In more recent times producers have also been able to achieve a dominant position in film production—turning out works that are considered to have their own special creative stamp, for example, Steven Spielberg. From the 1970s onward, actors increasingly turned to producing as well as directing films: Robert Redford, *Ordinary People* (1980) and *A River Runs through It* (1993); Barbra Streisand, *Yentl* (1983) and *The Prince of Tides* (1991).

See Director; Goldwyn, Samuel; Redford, Robert; Thalberg, Irving

In 1972—the year before *The Exorcist*—83 out of 376 films were horror flicks.

PROLOGUE PRESENTATIONS

Prologue presentations were live popular acts preceding the feature film in movie houses of the late 1920s and early 1930s, during the transition from silent films to talking films. Exhibitors had initially embraced the presentation act as a way to establish their autonomy from movie producers and to differentiate their shows from competing theaters. A popular act could also compensate for a bad film, which because of block booking, the exhibitor was obliged to run. Although the live prologue presentations proved quite popular, movie producers and exhibitors alike began to regard them as a Pandora's box: often, the acts were billed as being of greater importance than the film feature, and they were suitably lavish and expensive. Meanwhile, the feature films became subsidiary, much to the chagrin of movie producers.

When theaters became wired for sound and began offering "talkies," many retained a few life acts to extend the program to its customary two hours. In fact, at least some customers had started attending theaters as much to see the stage material as to see the picture, and on occasion they preferred the former to the latter. Though vaudeville was declining, the prologue challenged Hollywood's domination of theaters. It was an annoying form of competition which canned performances could easily make obsolete. Hollywood thus mounted an all-out attack against this enemy in the theater. It declared that the film must always be the main attraction at a movie theater and that stage acts, if used at all, must not subordinate the picture. From the producer's vantage in 1929, prologues had become anathema, in part because they diverted potential film rental revenue to theaters and performers. Many theater owners were also turning against presentations. Live performances required high overhead, including maintaining a union orchestra. Hollywood devised specific strategies to kill off prologues. Distributors adopted the fee system based on attendance (a percentage of the gate) to replace the flat rental charge (which formerly left any surplus to the exhibitor, who could use it to pay his vaudevillians). The virtual Broadway concept supplied theaters with name entertainment that surpassed in spectacle and quality anything that a local exhibitor could book. Relatively cheap film rentals undercut live performers' salaries. As sound became established, audiences were eager to her famous comedians like Eddie Cantor, with whom they were familiar from radio. They preferred watching a filmed Ziegfeld revue to sitting through twenty minutes of anonymous local hoofers on the stage. The beginning of the end of live prologues came in April 1929 when Sam Katz began replacing them with "selected short subjects" in Publix houses.

Merger mania and the coming of sound hastened the decline of local exhibitors' power, though in sheer numbers they were always the majority. As vestiges of the old showman tradition, they had exercised considerable influence on what audiences saw. By controlling the content and the length of the program, they could respond to the tastes of the community.

The virtual Broadway in the early sound films was crafted to "poach" from entertainments which were enjoying success as stage acts and radio performances. Exhibitors had been profiting by presenting these live attractions, but not Hollywood. The studios corrected this imbalance by producing filmed facsimiles of the star performances that audiences wanted to experience. It may even be that the superabundance of early Hollywood musicals was in part an effort to make the live stage show pale by comparison. By using sound the producers were able to take charge of the structure as well as the content of the film program.

See Sound

PSYCHO

Alfred Hitchcock's powerful, complex psychological thriller *Psycho* (1960) is the "mother" of all modern horror suspense films. The film skillfully manipulates the audience into identifying with the main character, and then with that character's murderer, voyeuristically implicating the audience with the evil forces and secrets present in the film.

As the film opens, Marion Crane (Janet Leigh) seems to be the typical secretary until, on impulse, she steals $40,000 from her boss to finance her marriage to her fiancé, Sam (John Gavin). She sets out for Sam's, some distance away. After driving all day, Marion seeks shelter in a modest motel just off the main road.

Norman Bates (Anthony Perkins), the shy proprietor of the motel, describes for Marion how he is dominated by his elderly mother, who lives in the house up on the hill. Before retiring for the night, Marion takes a cleansing shower. At this moment the shower curtain is whipped aside, and Marion is savagely stabbed by what appears to be a maniacal woman. Marion lies bleeding to death on the shower floor. Norman's voice is heard crying: "Mother! Oh, God! Mother! Blood! Blood!"

Norman, the dutiful and devoted son, cleans up the murder scene, determined to cover up his insane mother's behavior. Placing Marion's corpse in the trunk of her car, along with all her belongings, Norman sinks the car in a nearby swamp.

Marion's sister, Lila (Vera Miles), Sam, and a private detective, Milton Arbogast (Martin Balsam), join forces to search for Marion. Arbogast eventually pulls up to the Bates Motel. After Norman denies any recent guests, Arbogast finds Marion's name in the motel register and becomes suspicious of Norman. Ultimately, in one of the most horrific murder scenes in film history, Arbogast is frighteningly attacked at the top of the house's stairs by a knife-wielding woman and slashed to death.

When Arbogast doesn't contact them, Lila and Sam go to the Bates Motel, where Sam sees a sick old woman in the house's second floor window. They decide to stay at the motel and search for clues. In Marion's cabin, they find two major clues: the shower curtain is missing and a scrap of paper showing a notation of $40,000. Lila goes to confront the old

"Let them see what kind of person I am— not even going to swat that fly."

Anthony Perkins as Norman Bates's mother in *Psycho* (1960)

notable & quotable

"On April 26 (1960), 8:00 P.M. in Screening Room 8 at Universal-Revue, Alfred Hitchcock hosted the first rough-cut screening of *Psycho. Psycho* turned some hardened industryites to jello."

Stephen Rebello, author, from Alfred Hitchcock and the Making of Psycho *by Stephen Rebello, Harper Perennial, 1990*

woman and get information. She enters Mrs. Bates's bedroom, but it is empty. She enters Norman's little-boy room, a mysterious combination of children's and adults' things. Meanwhile, at the motel office, Sam questions a frightened Norman. Realizing that Lila might be in the house, Norman struggles with Sam, knocks him out, and races up the hill. As Lila is coming down the stairs, she sees Norman rushing toward her. She runs to the basement steps, and then enters the cellar and sees a figure in a chair, facing away from her. She approaches, calling out, "Mrs. Bates," and taps the woman's shoulder. The body slowly swivels in its chair—it is a stuffed, dried-up skeleton with empty eye sockets. Lila screams, and suddenly, a gray-haired woman with a knife runs in from behind her. When Sam appears behind the woman and grabs her, the wig and dress disguises fall off, revealing Norman as his "mother."

The film ends with the dredging of the swamp—Marion's car with her body and the $40,000 in the trunk is hauled from the muck by a heavy chain.

See Hitchcock, Alfred

Hitchcock originally envisioned the infamous shower scene as completely silent, but Bernard Hermann went ahead and scored it anyway, and Hitchcock wisely reconsidered. Psycho*'s "stabbing" music is one of the most famous scores in all of cinema.*

PSYCHOANALYSIS AND CINEMA

Psychoanalysis and cinema refers to the application of psychoanalytic precepts to the analysis of cinematic texts. Proponents argue that the interpretation of a motion picture within the context of Freudian thought (on desire, sexuality, guilt, unconscious repression, etc.) can reveal multiple meanings with regard to modern culture and human experience. Cultural critic Jacques Lacan maintained that psychoanalysis of dramatic/literary texts (language) was capable of supplying new entry into exploration of the human self. Lacan's linguistic approach to textual psychoanalysis was only one of many posited in the 1970s in a burgeoning area of critical study. Another was Laura Mulvey's "visual pleasure/gaze" readings of Hollywood film, an approach that moved psychoanalytic observation into areas of gender identity, voyeurism, and power-status issues.

See Gaze; Postmodernism

PSYCHODRAMA

Psychodrama is a term often used to describe a type of experimental film characterized by Freudian approaches to self-exploration. The filmmaker is frequently concerned with subconscious states and personal sexuality. A strong dreamlike, surreal quality often dominates the film experience as a result of an abrupt, fragmented flow of imagery. The term *psychodrama* is most commonly used in reference to highly personal works produced in the United States during the late 1940s and early 1950s. Maya Deren (*Meshes of the Afternoon,* 1943) inspired the psychological film movement in America, although its foundations had been laid by the first European avant-garde. Three California-based filmmakers earned reputations in the 1940s for their personal-experience psychodramas: Kenneth Anger (*Fireworks,* 1947), Curtis Harrington (*Fragments of Seeking,* 1946), and Gregory Markopoulous (*Psyche,* 1947–48). Willard Maas's work on the East Coast (*Images in the Snow,* 1943–48) is of similar Freudian character. Later work by these filmmakers often takes the form of symbol-laden, ritualistic exercises (for example, Anger's *Scorpio Rising,* 1962–64).

See Avant-garde; Expressionism

PULP FICTION

A plot summary of *Pulp Fiction* (1994) will be insufficient not only because of the film's time-fractured narrative, but because it would not be able to capture the beauty of the film's strength: its dialogue. Rarely advancing the story, the dialogue reveals character and acts as an absurd and comical counterpoint to violence. Some of the wonderful topics of rhetoric are the merits of a $5 milkshake, the pleasure of wearing a tight T-shirt to accentuate a tiny pot belly, whether a pig with a charming personality would rise above its stature as a filthy animal, and the effect of the metric system on the translation of fast-food burger names into foreign languages.

"Hamburgers, the cornerstone of the nutritious breakfast."

Samuel L. Jackson as Jules in *Pulp Fiction* (1994)

The film opens in a diner, where two young and relatively inexperienced thieves, Honey Bunny (Amanda Plummer) and Pumpkin (Tim Roth), debate the best type of store to rob. Finally deciding on restaurants—because they can also rob the patrons—they kiss dramatically and, jumping to their feet, announce a holdup. The frame freezes, and switches to two hitmen.

The hitmen, Jules Winnfield (Samuel L. Jackson) and Vincent Vega (John Travolta), are driving to an assignment. Donning black suits, Vincent is telling of his recent trip to Amsterdam; the men discuss the legality of hash in Amsterdam, and, absurdly, the different names for Big Macs and Whoppers in France. Vincent reveals that he has to take Mia, wife of their boss, Marsellus Wallace, out to entertain her while Marsellus is on a vacation. Jules warns Vincent that rumor has it Marsellus threw a guy out a fourth-story window for giving Mia a foot massage. After an extended discussion about foot massages, they enter an apartment to find three young men having hamburgers for breakfast. The boys are the obvious target of the hitmen, and Jules intimidates one of the boys by eating the boy's hamburger and downing his soda. In trying to retrieve a briefcase that contains an unidentified glowing material (an homage to the pulp noir classic *Kiss Me Deadly*), Jules shoots one of the boys. He then goes into a religious diatribe, quoting from Ezekiel 25:17, before killing another boy.

The scene shifts, and we are at a bar, where a boxer, Butch (Bruce Willis), listens to Marsellus Wallace (Ving Rhames) explain that his boxing days are almost over. Marsellus gives Butch money to take a fall in a fight. Jules and Vincent enter, dressed strangely in shorts and T-shirts. On his way out, Butch gets into a macho staring contest with Vincent.

Alone, Vincent buys some expensive heroin from his friend Lance (Eric Stoltz). Later that night he takes Marsellus's wife, Mia (Uma Thurman), to Jack Rabbit Slim's, a retro restaurant, where the waiters are celebrity impersonators and the maitre d' is Ed Sullivan. After a subtly flirtatious conversation, Mia forces Vincent to participate in a twist contest.

Vincent and Mia bring home the dance contest trophy. While Vincent is in Mia's bathroom, attempting to talk himself out of hitting on her, Mia finds Vincent's heroin and, thinking it's cocaine, snorts a line and promptly passes out. Worried that Mia may die from her overdose, Vincent speeds over to Lance's for help. A reluctant Lance gives Vincent a giant needle for an adrenaline shot, which Vincent thrusts into Mia's heart, reviving her. Later Vincent and Mia shake hands, agreeing not to mention the overdose to Marsellus. After Mia walks away, Vincent blows her a kiss good-bye.

The scene switches again, this time to a flashback. A Vietnam veteran (Christopher Walken) delivers a watch to a young Butch. He tells Butch that the watch was passed down through four generations and three wars in the male lineage of Butch's family. The vet, who was in a Hanoi prison camp with Butch's father when he died, fulfilled the legacy by, like Butch's father, hiding the watch in his rectum for years to make sure Butch would have it. The grownup Butch wakes, startled from this apparent memory/dream. He is wearing his boxing gear.

An announcer's voiceover tells us that not only did Butch win the fight, he literally killed his opponent. He escapes before Vincent and another hitman can find him. He makes plans to collect the money he's made from betting on himself, and he meets up with his girlfriend so they can leave town together. When he finds out that she forgot his all-important watch, he throws a temper tantrum and goes to get it.

Butch sneaks into his own apartment, aware that the hitmen will be looking for him, and gets the watch. He notices an automatic gun on his

John Travolta (left) and Samuel L. Jackson play a pair of philosophical hitmen in just one of the overlapping stories in director Quentin Tarantino's outrageous Pulp Fiction.

◀

kitchen counter, so he picks it up. An offscreen toilet flushes. The bathroom door opens: it's Vincent. Butch shoots him and flees the apartment. On the way back to the hotel, Butch runs into Marsellus. He runs his car into Marsellus, and then his car is hit by another car. Marsellus comes to and chases Butch into a pawnshop, where Butch manages to knock Marsellus unconscious. Maynard, the pawnshop employee, then knocks Butch out with the butt of a gun. Butch and Marsellus wake to find they are tied to chairs with ball-gags in their mouth, kidnapped by two sexual deviants, Maynard and Zed. They take Marsellus into a back room intending to assault him. Butch is able to break free of his ropes, and he heads for the exit, but is overcome by a sense of duty. Armed with a samurai sword from the shop, he sneaks up on Maynard and Zed, who are assaulting Marsellus. Butch kills Maynard and leaves Marsellus alone to torture Zed. Marsellus and Butch's discord is over, and Butch leaves town with his girl.

"That's thirty minutes away. I'll be there in ten."

Harvey Keitel as Winston Wolf in *Pulp Fiction* (1994)

Another scene shift, and a young man with a gun nervously hides in a bathroom listening to Jules's offscreen religious diatribe. We are back to the scene where Jules kills the young boys in their apartment. After Jules shoots the second boy, the young man bursts out of the bathroom, emptying his gun at Jules and Vincent. Although he fires many shots at the hitmen, all of them miss, and so Jules and Vincent shoot him. As a result of having narrowly escaped being shot, Jules believes that he has been a part of a miracle. They take Marvin, the "inside guy," with them and drive away. As Jules and Vincent debate divine intervention, Vincent (gun in hand) turns to talk to Marvin. When the car hits a bump, Vincent's gun goes off, blowing Marvin's head apart.

Jules and Vincent go to Jules's friend Jimmy's (director Quentin Tarantino) house for help in cleaning up the bloodied car. Jimmy wants to help, but he's worried because his wife, Bonnie, will be home soon. Marsellus sends Wolf (Harvey Keitel) to help them "clean up." Vincent and Jules get rid of their bloody clothes and borrow Jimmy's clothes, explaining the T-shirts and shorts they were wearing earlier at the bar with Marsellus.

Later over breakfast in a diner, Jules tells the cynical Vincent that he has experienced God and that he's giving up the hitman life to just walk the earth. Bunny and Pumpkin order coffee—establishing that we are back in the time frame of the opening scene, and Jules and Vincent have coincidentally happened upon the same diner as the would-be robbers. The robbery begins and this time continues. Pumpkin takes Jules's wallet, but when he tries to take Marsellus's briefcase from Jules, Jules pulls out his gun on Pumpkin. Seeing this, Honey Bunny becomes hysterical, but Jules manages to calm her. Explaining that he is in a transitional period (otherwise they would be dead), Jules gives Pumpkin the $1,500 in his wallet and allows Bunny and Pumpkin to leave. Jules and Vincent exit the diner into the sunny day: one will soon be dead, one will walk the earth.

R

RAGING BULL

Raging Bull (1980) is based on the real-life story of the middleweight boxing champ Jake La Motta. Shot in black and white to capture the gritty ambience of the fight scene and the flavor of the nightlife and underworld of the1940s, *Raging Bull* is rich in surrealistic images and religious iconography in its unsparing portrait of one man's harrowing, self-destructive odyssey through the brutal world of professional boxing. Often cited by critics as one of the premiere achievements of the 1980s, *Raging Bull* secured the reputation of the director, Martin Scorsese, as one of America's most important filmmakers.

> ***"The good news is that you're going to get the shot at the title. The bad news is they want you to do the old flip-flop for 'em."***

Joe Pesci as Joey to Robert De Niro as Jake LaMotta in *Raging Bull* (1980)

The opening scene, set in 1964, shows the once proud, lithe champ Jake La Motta (Robert De Niro) as a sallow, overweight, middle-aged standup comic, reciting lame jokes before an inattentive crowd in an unsavory club. The rest of the film is a flashback, beginning in 1941, that accounts for this sorry end. At home in the Bronx in New York, Jake is warning his brother/manager, Joey (Joe Pesci), not to make a deal with a local mobster, Tommy Como (Nicholas Colasanto). Como wants to take control of Jake's blossoming boxing career, but Jake is not interested in being under the mobster's thumb. He wants to make it on his own.

The film then cuts to the animalistic Jake in a 1943 fight against Sugar Ray Robinson (Johnny Barnes). After ten rounds, the mercilessly brutal fight is awarded to La Motta. The fight scene is followed by a passionate scene with Vickie, a fifteen-year-old blonde Jake has taken an interest in. Although Jake lusts for Vickie, he stops their sex play short of intercourse; in training, he demonstrates the iron discipline of an ambitious champion.

Later, Jake must leave Vickie for training camp. He asks his brother, Joey, to keep an eye on Vickie while he is away. But once Jake is gone, Joey spies Vickie entering a nightclub with Tommy's lieutenant Salvy (Frank Vincent). Wanting to defend Jake's honor and watch over Vickie as he'd promised, Joey threatens Salvy and, angered, beats him up. At the next day's reconciliation, organized by Tommy, Joey—despite Jake's warnings—is finally coerced into allowing Tommy to influence Jake's boxing career. When Jake returns from training camp, Joey tells him that he will have to throw his next fight—lose on purpose—if he wants to get a chance at the

The sound effects for punches landing in Raging Bull's *boxing scenes were made by squashing melons and tomatoes.*

title. The match is a sham, and Jake is obviously humiliated in the ring; his undefeated opponent wins by a TKO. The boxing board suspects Jake of throwing the fight, pending investigation, but just two years later, in 1949, the Cerdan–La Motta fight is declared a TKO at the start of round ten, and Jake finally wins the title belt.

On top of the boxing world, Jake turns obsessively self-destructive, food binges replacing sex with Vickie, who is now his wife (Jake had earlier dumped his supportive first wife to marry the alluring Vickie). Paranoid and jealous, Jake accuses Joey of sleeping with Vickie. He beats Joey up in front of the family, and this humiliation of his brother irreparably severs their once-close ties. Eventually, overweight and out of shape, Jake loses his title belt for the last time.

The scene then shifts to Florida, 1956. Jake is older and heavier, bloated by about fifty additional pounds (De Niro actually put on fifty pounds to play the older La Motta), and he owns a seedy nightclub. By this time,

notable & quotable

"They [the fight sequences in *Raging Bull*] were thought out shot-by-shot, cut-by-cut by Marty [Scorsese] before he even made the film."

Thelma Schoonmaker, editor, 1990, almost discrediting her editing Oscar for the film in favor of the director

Vickie has taken their children and left him. His life continues its downward spiral when he is jailed for serving alcoholic beverages to young girls who are under the age limit. In 1958, out of jail, Jake introduces strippers in a seedy New York bar. In a chance meeting, he spots Joey across the street. Mellowed with age, Jake hopes for a reconciliation with his estranged brother, but Joey ignores him.

In the film's final scene, set in 1964, a beer-bellied Jake is backstage rehearsing his comedy act at a tawdry club. Dully, he recites the lines by rote. Then, hearing his introduction, Jake fastens his tie, and the onetime champion sends himself off shadow-boxing into a sad, second-rate exploitation of his former greatness, having lost his most important fight: the battle with his own demons.

Raging Bull garnered eight Oscar nominations and scored in two categories, for Best Actor (Robert De Niro) and Editing (Thelma Schoonmaker).

See De Niro, Robert; Rocky; *Scorsese, Martin*

RAIDERS OF THE LOST ARK

After faltering badly with the overblown, mostly unfunny comedy *1941* (1980), Steven Spielberg put his directorial career back on track in 1981 with the highly successful *Raiders of the Lost Ark,* a throwback to 1930s action-adventure serials.

"The Ark. If it is there, at Tanis, then it is something that man was not meant to disturb. Death has always surrounded it. It is not of this earth."

John Rhys-Davies as Sallah in *Raiders of the Lost Ark* (1981)

The film opens with a sequence that is unrelated to the rest of the plot but that establishes the character of the hero, Indiana Jones (Harrison Ford), an adventurous archaeologist who is making his way through the jungle toward a hidden temple with a guide. When Indy breaks a light beam intended to protect the temple, a poison dart shoots out from the wall and, narrowly missing Indy, lodges in the wooden staff he is carrying. Next, a spiked gate closes shut; it still bears the corpse of an earlier visitor who came to claim the artifact treasure. Indy enters a sacred chamber where the artifact rests atop a small altar. Cleverly prepared with a sandbag at the ready, Indy grabs the artifact tightly and swaps it for the sand-filled pouch. The stone beneath the pouch suddenly begins to sink into the altar stone. Indy knows that this will trigger a calamity and runs wildly across the deadly floor, triggering a barrage of poisonous darts and arrows.

Narrowly escaping, he and the guide run toward the mouth of the cave. During their escape, the floor opens up between the two men. The guide demands the artifact from the trapped Indy, who needs the whip the guide is holding to escape. Indy gives in, throwing the artifact to the guide, who drops the whip and escapes through a descending trapdoor, leaving Indy behind. Indy eventually escapes to safety through the mouth of the cave, but only after being chased by a huge boulder. Outside the cave, he encounters Belloq (Paul Freeman), clearly a bad guy, who now possesses the artifact. Surrounded by the guide and local villagers, Belloq holds up the artifact to the natives, who bow humbly as Belloq prepares to dispose of his rival. Indy sees his chance to escape and runs toward a seaplane in which his pilot is waiting.

We next see Indy back at his American university. United States Secret Service agents inform him of Hitler's plan to resurrect the Lost Ark of the Covenant, which he had unsuccessfully sought to uncover, years earlier, with his colleague and friend Professor Ravenwood. The search for the ark is of vital importance: any army that carries it is invincible. It must be kept from Hitler and the German army. Knowing of a hieroglyphic medallion in Nepal that can guide him to the ark, Indy boards a plane for Nepal, hoping to find both Professor Ravenwood and his daughter, Marion (Karen Allen), Indiana's ex-lover.

Indy comes swaggering through the door of a saloon in Nepal run by the mercurial Marion, who, still enraged over their past love affair, greets him with a punch in the mouth and then buys him a drink. After learning that Professor Ravenwood is dead and that Marion still has the medallion, Indy exits with a promise that she will turn it over the next day. Enter the Nazi Toht and his agents, who demand the medallion from Marion, threatening her with a hot poker. She is rescued by Indiana, but during the battle the Ravenwood bar is set ablaze.

"You Americans, you're all the same. Always overdressing for the wrong occasions."

Ronald Lacey as Toht in *Raiders of the Lost Ark* (1981)

After escaping from the conflagration, Indiana and Marion travel together to Cairo, where they meet up with Sallah (John Rhys-Davies), a friend of Indy's and "the best digger in Cairo." Indy discusses the possibilities of finding the ark with Sallah, who informs Indy that the Germans have been digging for it near Tannis and have found the map room.

When Indiana and Marion tour Cairo, they are followed by the Nazis and native collaborators, who attack them with swords. Indy hides Marion in a haywagon while he continues the fight. As the haywagon moves through the streets, Marion jumps off. She hides in a tall wicker basket. Indy hears Marion crying out from a basket, but he doesn't know which one—there are dozens of them lining the street. He pushes several over, to no avail. Finally, he sees the Nazis putting a similar wicker basket on an explosives truck. When the truck explodes, Indy believes Marion is dead.

Sallah and Indy then go to the ruins of Tannis, where the ark is supposedly hidden in an excavated tomb. Dressed as Arabs, Indy and Sallah make their way undetected to the opening into the chamber containing the ark, but the floor is covered with thousands of snakes, the one creature of which Indiana is deathly afraid. He wards off the snakes with torches just long enough to grab the ark. Sallah and Indiana raise the ark out of the chamber.

Belloq, suspecting that Indy is near the digging site, commands the German officer Dietrich (Wolf Kahler) and a group of soldiers to find him. Belloq and Dietrich eventually do: when Indy looks up from the chamber, he sees Belloq staring down at him. Belloq orders Marion into the chamber with Indiana. She falls on the dirt floor only to be greeted by the cobra, which had reared up at Indy earlier. Indy and Marion appear doomed.

All looks hopeless, but Indiana figures that the secret chamber is probably connected to other chambers already excavated by the Nazis. Hounded on all sides by serpents, he climbs onto a tall statue, rocking it from its foundations. It crashes into another wall, through which Indiana and Marion manage a harrowing escape.

Sallah finds Indy and Marion and tells them that the Nazis have loaded the ark on a truck destined for Cairo. As the truck and its escort pull away, Indy jumps on a white horse and begins pursuit. In a breathtaking chase scene, Indy overtakes and subdues the Nazis and drives the truck with the ark into Cairo, where Sallah and his men are waiting to hide it.

Sallah has arranged passage on a ship, and Indy and Marion set sail. But a Nazi submarine stops the ship and stormtroopers clamber aboard. Indy hides while Marion is taken by the Nazis and put aboard the submarine along with the seized ark. When the Nazi sub departs, Indiana swims to the sub and furtively boards it, knocking a Nazi unconscious and stealing his uniform.

When the sub reaches a small island, Belloq convinces Dietrich to open the ark before it is delivered to Hitler. The Nazi soldiers are delivering the ark to a secluded part of the island when Indy appears on a cliff with a bazooka aimed at the ark. Just as curious about the ark's contents as Belloq and fearing the harm that might come to Marion, he surrenders. The Nazis march to a small grotto, where the ark is placed, ready for opening. Indy and Marion are tied to a stake at the opposite end of the grotto when Belloq and Dietrich give the command to open the ark.

Indy has already instructed Marion not to look directly into the ark; legend has it that harm will befall anyone who does so. Belloq, unaware of the danger, gazes into the ark; he is besieged by ghostly images and begins to scream in horror. A wand of smoke emanates from the ark and drifts toward the Nazis standing at attention. A piercing bolt of lightning strikes each Nazi through the heart, one after the other. Toht's head, along with the heads of several other Nazis, appears to melt and then explode. When the Nazis are dead, a blast of fire shoots out from the ark and into the sky toward heaven. The process then reverses itself; the fire is swallowed up by the ark and the lid shuts tight again. Indy and Marion are saved.

In the final scene, a lonely warehouse worker is seen storing the precious ark in a box marked "top secret" in a huge warehouse filled with thousands of similar boxes.

See Ford, Harrison; Spielberg, Steven

"I'm going after an object of incredible historical significance, and you're talking about the boogey man!"

Harrison Ford as Dr. Indiana Jones in *Raiders of the Lost Ark* (1981)

RATING SYSTEM

The American rating system is a mechanism for classifying motion pictures according to their perceived suitability for different age groups. The rating system was developed by the Motion Picture Association of America (MPAA) and went into effect November 1, 1968, at a time when candid material—language, violence, sexuality—was proliferating on the screen. The MPAA viewed the rating system as an indication to the public of industry concern; it also argued that ratings would serve to prevent outside censorship of motion picture content. The rating system initially consisted of four suitability categories:

G: recommended for general audiences
M: mature subject matter, parental guidance advised (later changed to PG, followed by PG-13)
R: restricted, adult accompaniment required for anyone under 17
X: adult material, no one under 17 admitted (later changed to NC-17)

Love vs. Lust: By 1971, after a production cost of $25,000, *Deep Throat* had grossed $4.6 million in its first two years. *Love Story* earned $50 million in 1971.

PG-13 was added to the classifications in 1984. This rating added a cautionary note that a film might contain material inappropriate for very young children and suggested that parents give special guidance for children under thirteen years of age. The demands for new, refined guidelines for the very young had intensified after the release of such PG-rated films as *Indiana Jones and the Temple of Doom* (1984) and *Gremlins* (1984), which contain material thought to be particularly terrifying to youngsters. In *Gremlins* small animals explode inside a microwave oven, and in *Indiana Jones and the Temple of Doom* a human heart is plucked from the body of a living man.

notable & quotable

"They were far more fearful of the leg crossing in *Basic Instinct* than with the head splitting in *Starship Troopers*."

Paul Verhoeven, director, commenting on the MPAA's longtime practice of being lenient with regard to scenes of graphic violence and strict with sexual material

The X designation was replaced in 1990 with NC-17, a suitability reclassification prohibiting "children under 17 years of age" from admission. The X-rating had become tainted through years of association with sexually explicit motion pictures (the XXX film) intended for pornographic outlets. Public attitudes toward the X-rating had carried over to nonpornographic films—often meaning economic doom, as filmgoers and exhibitors increasingly shunned X-rated films.

Henry and June (1990), a psychological-sexual study of a triangular love affair involving novelist Henry Miller, his wife, June, and the author Anaïs Nin, was the first feature film distributed in the United States with the NC-17 rating.

The rating system has been plagued from its inception by controversy owing to the difficulty of precise categorization and an ensuing confusion over the meaning of individual categories with regard to content. At the same time film producers have claimed that pressure to alter or delete material to achieve a particular rating results in abandonment of artistic standards to a form of internal regulation of motion picture content.

See Censorship

RAY, NICHOLAS

Nicholas Ray, one of the most distinctive and influential stylists among American directors, was born Raymond Nicholas Kenzle in La Crosse, Wisconsin, on August 7, 1911. At the age of sixteen Ray let go with a burst of precocity and fired off a radio script to the University of Chicago. This won him a scholarship there during the great days of Robert Hutchins. Later, he studied architecture there under Frank Lloyd Wright.

Ray was eighteen when the Depression began. As with many Americans, it changed the course of his life. In the early 1930s he took a trip around America, married, had a son named Tony, and decided to become involved in theater as an actor/designer/director. He was in the Theater of Action, a traveling collective road company, and the functioning of this group was to remain an ideal of his, a model of how a film community should work. In 1935 Ray acted in a play that was Elia Kazan's first directorial effort at the Group Theater, *The Young Go First.* At this time, Ray also met Clifford Odets and other Group Theater people who eventually influenced the course of his career. He knew Kazan, Losey, Harold Clurman, and probably was at least acquainted with everyone who functioned in playwriting in the group, although, strangely, Ray is not mentioned in Clurman's book on the Group Theater. He later joined John Houseman's Phoenix Theater Company in New York City; Orson Welles's Mercury Theater also became a reality in 1938 (although it is likely that Ray never actually worked for Welles). During this time Ray also studied folklore and music (he knew Woodie Guthrie), and lived for a time in the Rocky Mountains.

Because radio drama was quite important at the time, Ray next made inroads in this area. By 1941, when he was thirty, Ray had shown promise not only as an actor and set designer, but also as a radio playwright and as an overall director of stage and radio productions. His eclectic background—a combination of the training of Fritz Lang and Orson Wells—was to prove invaluable to him in a Hollywood that afforded no such training ground.

After Pearl Harbor, Ray became a War Information Radio Program Director, thanks to John Houseman, who was made chief of the foreign service of the United States Office of War Information. Any chance of Ray's

R

RAY, NICHOLAS

Before making his name as a director, Nicholas Ray worked as a radio playwright and studied architecture under Frank Lloyd Wright. ▶

being drafted in World War II was dispelled because he had lost the use of his right eye in a bizarre accident late in the 1930s. (The black eye patch he wore was thus not quite the affectation of a Hollywood director.) In 1943 Ray wrote and directed a Broadway play, *Back Where I Came From*. In 1944 Elia Kazan, by then a successfully established New York theater director, was offered the opportunity to direct films, and he took Ray along to Hollywood as his assistant director on the film version of *A Tree Grows in Brooklyn*.

On the Twentieth Century-Fox lot Ray kept a diary for himself and Kazan, in which he noted comments on how to make and deal with cinema. It was filled with such remarks as "Don't over-direct" and "The hero should not be written better than you or I. You must recognize him as a fellow human. Then, under special circumstances, he becomes better than I." (Ray seems to have applied this statement to many of his films, notably *Rebel Without a Cause*.)

Ray, back in New York, next directed Alfred Drake in *Beggar's Holiday.* John Houseman moved to CBS (which had pioneered television in 1940), and Ray adapted the enormously successful radio play *Sorry, Wrong Number* for TV. Houseman paved the way for the next step in Ray's career. Having received a commission from Dore Schary, the executive producer at RKO studios, to produce *They Live by Night,* a film noir vehicle based on Edward Anderson's novel *Thieves Like Us,* Houseman nobly agreed to produce only if Ray would be the film's director and be responsible for the screenplay. So, in 1947, at the age of thirty-six, Nick Ray began his Hollywood career as a director.

That same year he married the aspiring film actress Gloria Grahame Hallward, who had dropped her last name professionally and begun a lackadaisical career under her mother's maiden name. It was the second marriage for both. Their union led to Ray's directing her in *A Woman's Secret,* his least-known film. Ray's first film to be shown at a major New York theater was his third, *Knock on Any Door* (1949), a Romeo and Juliet-like love story that proved popular and marked him as a distinctive young talent. In 1950 Ray's marriage to Gloria Grahame broke up in the middle of shooting *In a Lonely Place,* which costarred Humphrey Bogart.

Ray solidified his reputation with a succession of workmanlike if unremarkable efforts: *Born to Be Bad* (1951), *The Flying Leathernecks* (1952), and *The Lusty Men* (1954) before breaking out from the pack with his memorable *Johnny Guitar* (1955), a political parable widely considered one of the strangest and most original westerns ever made, not least for having a woman protagonist, played by Joan Crawford. In 1956 Ray saw the release of the relatively undistinguished *Run for Cover* and the legendary *Rebel Without a Cause,* the brooding Cinemascope study of rebellious youth at bay that secured Ray's reputation of one of Hollywood's most original and penetrating auteurs while elevating James Dean to an icon among America's youth.

After *55 Days to Peking* (1963), Ray's output declined precipitously; of his post-*Rebel* oeuvre, only *Bigger than Life* (1957) and *Bitter Victory* (1960) were held in wide critical esteem. Ray died of lung cancer in New York City on June 16, 1979.

See Kazan, Elia; Rebel Without a Cause; *Wood, Natalie*

REALIST CINEMA

A style of filmmaking that in a general sense creates a semblance of actuality is called realist cinema. Realist films avoid techniques that impose subjective or directed attitudes on the recorded material. Artistic lighting and expressive camera techniques are usually kept to a minimum. The realist film also often includes long-take scenes rather than carefully edited sequences.

Realist cinema stresses, most commonly, the subject in interaction with the surrounding environment. For this reason the themes of realist films often develop within a "flow of life" format, where the casualness of common events reveals their content.

The Lumiére *actualités* are early examples of realist cinema in the purest sense. Italian neorealism approached a realist style within the narrative film. Direct cinema is a term for a type of contemporary documentary film that can be labeled "realist cinema."

See Actualité; Cinema verité; Neorealism

REAR WINDOW

notable & quotable

"If you do not experience delicious terror when you see *Rear Window*, then pinch yourself—you are most probably dead."

Actual advertising copy for Rear Window, *written by director Alfred Hitchcock*

Rear Window (1954), directed by Alfred Hitchcock, is an intriguing, brilliantly Hitchcockian macabre visual study of obsessive human curiosity and voyeurism. This film masterpiece was made entirely on one confined set, a realistic courtyard composed of thirty-one apartments.

Temporarily incapacitated by a broken leg, Jeff Jeffries (James Stewart) indulges his press photographer's inclination to spy on other people's private lives by peeking into the windows of the apartment dwellings across the courtyard from the rear window of his own Greenwich Village apartment. Each of the tenants in the other apartments offers variations on male/female relationships, as Jeff spies on them. As the camera angles are largely from Jeff's own apartment, the film viewer sees the inhabitants of the other apartments entirely from his point of view, sharing in his voyeuristic surveillance without the inhabitants being aware of it.

Among the assortment of people he observes are a lonely spinster whom he calls Miss Lonelyhearts, a gregarious composer with lots of friends, and Lars Thorwald (Raymond Burr), an adulterous husband whom Jeff comes to suspect of having killed his invalid wife.

Thorwald's ugly deed is eventually brought to light by the efforts of Jeff and his sometimes-fiancée, Lisa (Grace Kelly), who finds Jeff's morbid curiosity catching. Ultimately, they are not entirely proud of their meddling in other people's lives; as Lisa shamefully confesses, she and Jeff are deeply disappointed when it seemed for a time that Thorwald was not actually guilty of homicide after all.

A police detective buddy, Tom Doyle (Wendell Corey), suggests that Jeff's fascination with the lives of other people is his way of sidestepping his own pressing need to sort out his unsatisfactory relationship with Lisa, something he has yet to do by the end of the movie. Speaking more broadly, Jeff's nurse, Stella (Thelma Ritter), gives the viewer something to think about when she comments on Jeff's "window shopping" with his "spy glass": "We have become a race of Peeping Toms. People ought to get outside and look at themselves for a change."

Jeff's increasingly unwholesome interest in the affairs of his neighbors is mirrored in his switching, as his curiosity increases, from a simple pair of binoculars to a high-powered telephoto lens as his means of prying more and more deeply into their private lives. It is with the powerful lens that he sees Thorwald wrap a large saw blade and a butcher knife in newspaper. Following Jeff's suggestion, Doyle investigates but finds nothing. But Jeff and Lisa persist in their own form of investigation. Finally, in a suspenseful scene, Thorwald trips up, tormented by Jeff and Lisa. The police are summoned and Thorwald confesses.

Nearly every shot in Alfred Hitchcock's Rear Window *originates from the apartment of Jeff Jeffries (James Stewart).*

▼

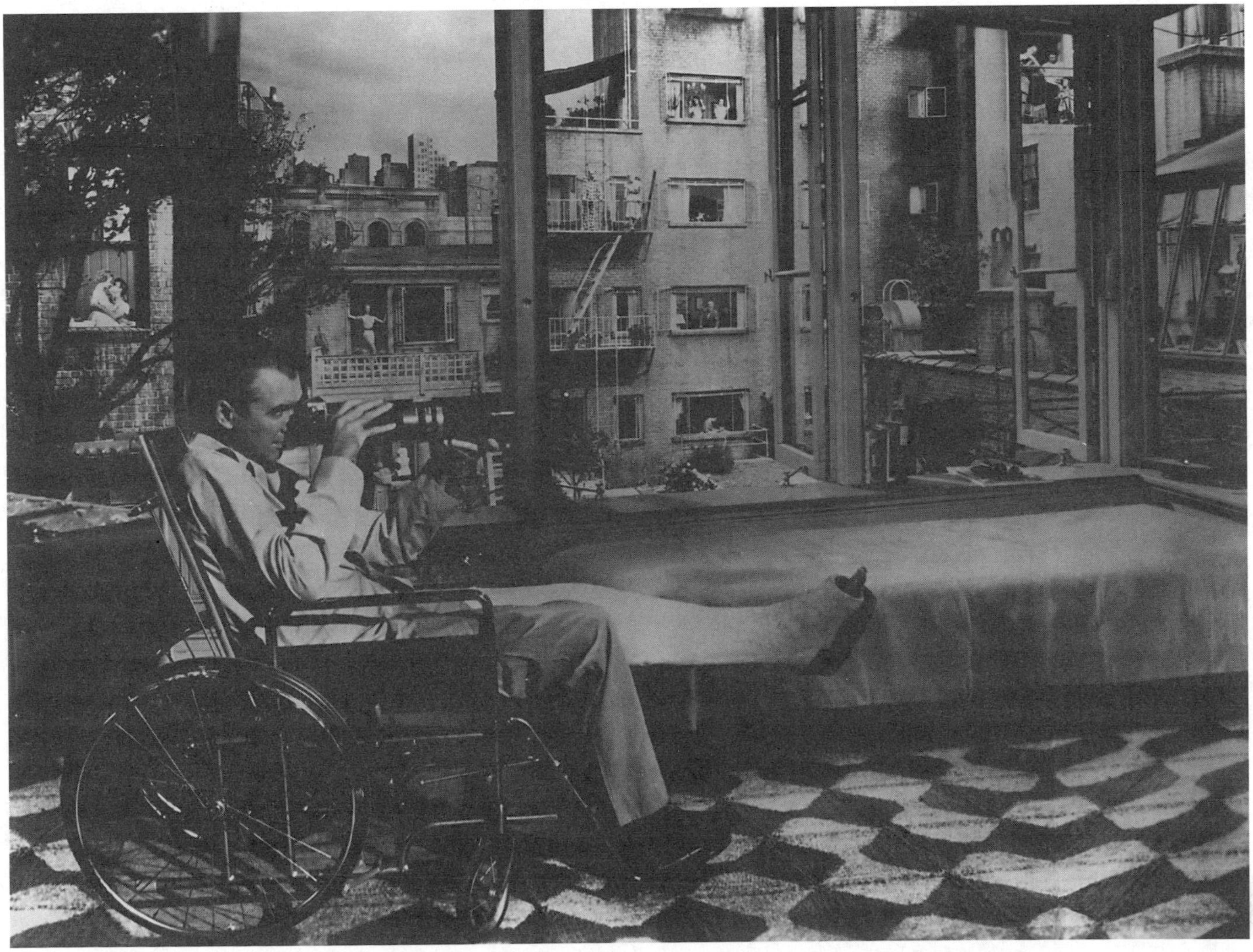

By the end of the film the viewer at last hears a newly made recording of a song played by the proud composer, who has written it for the no-longer-lonely Miss Lonelyhearts. For his part, Jeff, who has taken a new lease on life and given up spying on others, sits with his back to the rear window.

See Hitchcock, Alfred; Kelly, Grace; Stewart, James

REBEL WITHOUT A CAUSE

The film *Rebel Without a Cause* (1956), directed by Nicholas Ray, is a drama that is widely viewed as the 1950s' best portrayal of troubled and rebellious youth. The story was based on a real case of a delinquent teenager. It is the movie that is most associated with James Dean, who made only three films before dying in a car crash at age twenty-four.

As the film opens, it is late Easter night. A teenager named Jim Stark (James Dean) has been picked up by the police for public drunkenness—he was found sleeping on the ground. While he sits on a bench in a Los Angeles police station, disheveled and still drunk, another young man appears, also in trouble—it is John Crawford, or "Plato" (Sal Mineo). His family's maid brought him in because he has shot and killed a litter of puppies.

It appears to be a busy night at the station, as yet another teen is brought in, this time a girl. Judy (Natalie Wood, in her first adult role), in a bright red dress, was found wandering around the streets at 1:00 A.M., in this town where everyone drives. Judy is interrogated by Officer Ray Framek (Edward Platt), and while he is sympathetic to the girl, he does his job very thoroughly. She is cleared of any suspicion of solicitation, though Officer Ray believes that Judy's provocative clothing and actions may have been meant to get attention from her father.

Meanwhile, the police, finding Plato more alienated than dangerous, recommend a "shrink" for him, only to learn that Plato's well-off family has already consulted a psychiatrist for him and that it didn't do much good. Plato feels like an orphan, abandoned by his remote parents.

Jim is more aggressive. His parents arrive, dressed in evening wear—he has interrupted their night out—and start bickering. Officer Ray takes Jim into a different room, where the young man becomes violent. But Ray—the only truly responsible adult in the film—tries to convert the troubled youth into an ally. By the end of the confrontation, they are friendly.

The next morning, at the family breakfast table, Jim's father (Jim Backus) offers him encouragement—it is Jim's first day at a new high

James Dean, right, is shown here in a scene from East of Eden. Rebel Without a Cause *followed, and* Giant, *one year later in 1956, was Dean's last film.*

◀

school. During the conversation, Jim looks out the window and catches a glimpse of Judy walking by. He decides to leave for school, after being warned by his father, "Be careful how you choose your friends; don't let them choose you." Jim catches up with Judy on the street and tries to make friends, but she rebuffs his overtures and instead accepts a ride from her boyfriend, Buzz.

Upon his arrival at Dawson High, "the gang" gives Jim the outsider treatment—harassing and mocking the new kid in town. Jim walks into the building, and his face appears in a small mirror mounted in Plato's locker, next to a photograph of Plato's hero, actor Alan Ladd. Plato smiles—he sees in Jim another person to look up to, a means to feel like he belongs somewhere.

Later, in the local planetarium, a lecturer talks to the Dawson High students about entropy and the fate of our planet, inviting them to examine the metaphoric meaning of the word "star." At this moment Jim walks in and says, "*Star*k, Jim Stark" (almost as though announcing Dean's arrival as a Hollywood star). Buzz (Corey Allen), Judy, and Goon (Dennis Hopper) get restless during the lecture and begin to make jokes, but when Jim tries to join in, he is rejected.

Buzz is Judy's boyfriend, and he and Jim eventually square off in a strongly choreographed knife fight. Jim disarms Buzz, and Buzz, trying to save face, challenges him to another contest, a "chickie run"—a game of dare in which two cars hurtle at top speed toward a cliff, with the first driver to jump out before the car goes over the cliff declared the "chicken," or loser.

"You are tearing me apart! You say one thing, he says another, and everybody changes back again."

James Dean as Jim Stark, to his parents, in *Rebel Without a Cause* (1955)

Jim goes home and consults his father for advice on whether he should go to the chickie run: "Dad, what do you have to do to be a man?" His father—ineffectual as ever—suggests a cautious and evasive approach, recommending that Jim make a list of pros and cons. Jim thinks his father is a chicken. When he advises Jim that in ten years' time he won't have wanted to have ruined his life, Jim flies into a rage at the very thought of playing it safe. He screams, "Ten years?!" as if it were an eternity, and, donning a bright red jacket, white T-shirt, and blue jeans (which subsequent to the film's release became a national uniform among teenagers), storms from the house.

Meanwhile, Judy also has had a run-in with her father. Still trying to get his attention and affection, she tried to kiss him on the lips like she would when she was a little girl, but he has rejected her, saying that she is too old for that sort of thing now that she is sixteen. She, too, feels alienated and misunderstood.

That night the kids gather for the chickie run. As the speeding stolen cars approach the precipice, Jim jumps out of his car at the last second. Buzz's jacket, however, gets caught on the door handle, and he cannot jump out—he hurtles to his death over the cliff.

Scared by what they've seen, most of the kids run away. Judy, devastated, is comforted by Jim. He takes her home, where she confides to him her problems with her parents.

Jim is also upset about Buzz's death. He and his parents discuss what to do about his part in the game of chicken. Jim wants his parents to be decisive and honorable—to insist that he immediately tell the whole story to the police—but typically, his parents bicker over what to do. Jim erupts in a violent rage, pushing his father down, briefly choking him, and running out of the house.

Judy reminds Jim that Buzz's gang, angry over his death, will be looking for him, so they find an abandoned mansion in which to hide out. Plato, also hunted and tormented by the gang, heads there as well. Jim, Judy, and

ROBERT REDFORD

In 1965 a Golden Globe for Most Promising (Male) Newcomer was awarded to a handsome young blond-haired, blue-eyed actor from California. The recipient of that impressive vote of confidence, Robert Redford, has more than met expectations, having had wild success as an actor, director, producer, and filmmakers' guru.

Charles Robert Redford Jr. was born in Santa Monica, California—a seaside community not far from Hollywood—on August 19, 1937. After graduating from high school in Van Nuys, another suburb of Los Angeles, he set off for the University of Colorado at Boulder, which had granted him a baseball scholarship. But Redford and college did not make for a good match; he took to excessive drinking and was kicked off the baseball team and out of the university.

Discouraged, Redford spent some time traveling in Europe. Then, encouraged by Lola Van Wagenen, whom he met in California and married in 1958, he enrolled in the Pratt Institute in Brooklyn, New York, a prestigious art college, and at the American Academy of Dramatic Arts.

Redford first appeared on Broadway in 1959 in a small role. His parts gradually became more substantial, and in 1963 Redford found himself the male lead in a hit Broadway comedy, *Barefoot in the Park.* He also appeared periodically in television programs and, as the decade progressed, in films, including a popular film version of *Barefoot in the Park* (1967) opposite Jane Fonda.

The young actor was building a name for himself, but he was still relatively unknown. That would change forever when he costarred opposite Paul Newman in *Butch Cassidy and the Sundance Kid,* released in 1969. The movie was an enormous hit, and Redford—the Sundance Kid—shot to the top of the Hollywood "A" list. Over the next few years he was in a string of successful films, among them *The Candidate* and *Jeremiah Johnson* (both 1972) and *The Way We Were* (1973).

In 1973 Redford and Newman teamed up again for *The Sting,* an even more successful pairing than in *Butch.* Redford's generally savvy choice of film roles continued through the 1970s. He varied his roles between romantic lead, adventurer, and intellectual, in movies such as *The Great Gatsby* (1974), *The Great Waldo Pepper* (1975), and *All the President's Men* (1976).

Redford slowed down his acting gigs in the 1980s and 1990s but had several notable successes, including *The Natural* (1984) and *Out of Africa* (1985). He had become more interested in other aspects of filmmaking and was concentrating his efforts there, very successfully. In 1980 he won the Academy Award for Best Director for his film *Ordinary People.* He has directed several feature films since then, including *The Milagro Beanfield War* (1990), *A River Runs Through It* (1992), and *Quiz Show* (1994). In 1998 Redford directed, produced, and starred in *The Horse Whisperer*, based on the best-selling novel by Nicholas Evans.

Actor and director Robert Redford is the host of the annual Sundance Film Festival in Utah, a venue where young, independent filmmakers can showcase their work.

A major preoccupation for Redford in recent years has been his hugely successful Sundance Institute in Utah, a nonprofit organization that supports independent filmmaking. It now hosts the annual Sundance Film Festival, which is gaining a reputation as the American version of the famous Cannes Film Festival held annually in France.

In 1985 Redford and Lola, his wife of thirty-three years, divorced. They have three children: Shauna, David, and Amy. (Another child died of sudden infant death syndrome.) Since 1988 Redford has had a relationship with costume designer Kathy O'Rear. In 1995 the Screen Actors Guild honored him with a Lifetime Achievement Award, and the efforts of aspiring filmmakers around the world give credence to the notion that Robert Redford is more than just a pretty face.

See Butch Cassidy and the Sundance Kid; *Fonda, Jane; Hill, George Roy; Independent filmmaker; Pollack, Sydney; Producer*

Plato sit together, almost like a make-believe, loving family—Jim and Judy as Mom and Dad, and Plato as the child.

Judy dramatically declares her love for Jim after the two of them have gone upstairs, leaving Plato by himself downstairs. Plato is left vulnerable as the gang—Crunch, Goon, and Moose—make their entrance. They chase Plato, who finally shoots Crunch. Plato, distraught, is about to fire on Jim for deserting him, but Jim succeeds in calming Plato down.

The police, alerted by the gunfire, arrive at the scene. Plato exchanges shots with them and flees to the planetarium. Meanwhile, Jim's parents are cruising around in a police car with Officer Ray, looking for their son. Ray is directed to the planetarium.

Upon arrival at the planetarium, the police announce that they don't want to harm Plato: "Come out, you haven't killed anyone yet." Jim enters, with Judy, to coax him out. As Plato attempts to flee, the nervous police shoot him, not knowing that Plato is unarmed—Jim has taken the bullets out of Plato's gun. Jim gently covers Plato's body with his red jacket.

In front of the planetarium, Judy and Jim are joined by his parents. Jim, still ignoring his mother, reconciles with his father; and, symbolizing his new loyalty to Judy, he introduces his father to her: "This is Judy. She's my friend."

As the new "family" of Judy and Jim leave with his parents and the film draws to a close, police sirens wail in the background.

Although this resolution provided for an upbeat ending, it struck a sour note with some critics, who argued that, realistically, this would be only a "lull in the battle"—that Jim and Judy would likely face many more problems in the future.

See Ray, Nicholas; Wood, Natalie

REID, WALLACE

Wallace Reid was the final heir to the "Arrow Collar" tradition of motion-picture stardom, which from the earliest years of features had dominated the American screen. *Motion Picture* magazine's 1914 popularity poll found Earle Williams the nation's most popular screen star, with J. Warren Kerrigan, Arthur Johnson, Carlyle Blackwell, and Francis X. Bushman his nearest male rivals. These strong-jawed, all-American figures exuded stability, friendliness, optimism, and reliability. They were at home in overalls or evening clothes and did very nicely in a uniform when the occasion arose. Their imitators were legion and, to modern eyes, indistinguishable.

Despite his matinee-idol status, Wallace Reid's real interests were writing and directing. He died at age 31 as a result of morphine addiction perpetuated by the Famous Players–Lasky film studio.

Reid was born into a theatrical family in 1891. His father, Hall Reid, was an actor and playwright of some success who began writing scenarios for the Selig Company in Chicago in 1910. He would later work as a writer and director for firms such as Vitagraph and Universal, and his son Wally generally came along as part of the package. By 1912 Wallace Reid was a popular leading man in short action melodramas on the Universal lot.

Here, Reid was spotted by Jesse L. Lasky, who immediately cast him in Famous Players–Lasky features opposite some of that firm's most notable stars. Even after the 1916 merger, Famous Players–Lasky was still heavily committed to established stars brought from the theater at great expense, and it was economically imperative that some newcomers with potential drawing power be put under long-term contracts and developed into credible screen stars on their own. They could then be controlled more readily, and worked harder, while their salary demands could be kept within reason, at least until they had proven their screen appeal.

Lasky struck gold with Wallace Reid. Within a few months he was established as one of the nation's most popular stars, a position he would maintain throughout his career. Reid seemed to capture the all-American spirit offscreen as well, as least according to the fan magazines.

Reid was especially effective in such Cecil B. DeMille productions as *Carmen* (1915), *Joan the Woman* (1917), and *The Affairs of Anatole* (1921). Later, his films were directed by James Cruze and Sam Wood. Famous Players–Lasky made sure to get value for their money. In 1916, the first full year of his contract, Reid appeared in six features. The following year he was seen in ten. The pace continued without letup, and during 1922, when most stars of his caliber were appearing in two films per year, Reid made nine. Over a seven-year period, Reid was seen in a new feature picture every seven weeks. Amazingly, he seems not to have suffered overexposure at the box office and was still at the height of his popularity when he collapsed during production of his final film.

Reid had been taking morphine tablets for several years and recently had begun drinking heavily. He committed himself to a cold-turkey "cure" at a local sanatorium. Once he had been an athlete and dancer of considerable renown, but his body was now hopelessly debilitated. He lapsed into a coma after a bout of influenza and died on January 18, 1923.

A record-breaking year for box-office totals in North America: According to *Variety*, the film industry grossed $6.26 billion in 1997, an all-time record.

Reid's wife made a public issue of his commitment and took pains to put the truth of Reid's condition before the public. But even she drew back from revealing all the facts. By the time of his death, newspapers were editorializing in support of Reid ("he died game," wrote the *Los Angeles Examiner*), but in the end the affair only provided more ammunition to those attacking Hollywood immorality, and early supporters soon began to keep their distance. The studio's complicity in Reid's addiction and death was hinted at, but sensational stories of an underground dope ring gained wider currency. In fact, Reid had been introduced to morphine by a studio physician eager to keep the star working after he suffered an injury during location filming on *Valley of the Giants* (1919). Those inside the industry who knew the truth collectively repressed the whole affair. Sadly, within a few years, it was as if Wallace Reid had hardly existed.

See Cruze, James; DeMille, Cecil B.; Gilbert, John; Valentino, Rudolph

REMAKE

A motion picture made from a film story that has been produced earlier is called a remake. *Stagecoach* (1939) was remade in 1966. The fantasy *Heaven Can Wait* (1978) was a remake of *Here Comes Mr. Jordan* (1941), with certain plot changes made in the 1978 version to update the story and to include topical material.

Remakes are subjected to intense critical comparison with their originals, particularly when the original is regarded as a screen classic. Such was the case with the remake of *Scarface* (1932) by Michael Cimino in 1983 and *Cape Fear* (1962) by Martin Scorsese in 1991.

But some remakes compare favorably with the original: 1998's *A Perfect Murder*, a remake of the 1954 Hitchcock classic *Dial M for Murder*, was well received, as was 1999's remake of *The Thomas Crown Affair* (originally released in 1968).

The growing trend toward American remakes of critically acclaimed European films has also met with a certain critical cynicism, for example, *Breathless* (1959, 1983); *Cousin, Cousine* (1975)/*Cousins* (1989); *The Return of Martin Guerre* (1982)/*Sommersby* (1993).

See Prequel; Scorsese, Martin; Sequel; Stagecoach

JULIA ROBERTS

Superstar Julia Roberts was born in Smyrna, Georgia, on October 28, 1967, named Julie Fiona Roberts. Her parents divorced when she was just four years old, and her father died when she was nine. His loss affected her deeply.

The sister of actor Eric Roberts, Julia found phenomenal success early on. She modeled for a time after graduation from high school and landed her first film roles when she was barely twenty. Her performance in *Mystic Pizza* (1988) drew enormous attention; Roberts followed up that popular film with *Steel Magnolias* in 1989—another hit.

Costarring with Richard Gere, Roberts became a true sensation with the huge success of *Pretty Woman* (1990), a Cinderella-type story in which she played a Hollywood prostitute who is rescued by a wealthy Prince Charming. The press and the public could not get enough of Roberts after its release. It was just her fifth film role.

In subsequent years Roberts appeared in a few duds—notably, Steven Spielberg's *Hook* (1991) and Robert Altman's *Ready to Wear* (*Prêt-à-Porter*) (1994)—but most of her film choices were wise ones. Her biggest successes were *Sleeping with the Enemy* (1991), *The Pelican Brief* (1993), *Conspiracy* and *My Best Friend's Wedding* (both in 1997), and *Notting Hill* (1999). To date, Roberts has starred in more films grossing over $100 million than any other actress—six.

For 1999's *Runaway Bride*, Roberts reportedly was paid a record sum for a film actress: $17 million.

Roberts, famous for her unbelievably wide, toothy smile and flowing red hair, has usually enjoyed to the fullest the financial and social perks that have accompanied her phenomenal success. Much press has been given to her romances with Liam Neeson, Dylan McDermott, Daniel Day-Lewis, Kiefer Sutherland, and, most recently, Benjamin Bratt. Roberts married iconoclastic country musician Lyle Lovett in 1993; by all reports they remained friendly after their 1995 divorce.

notable & quotable

"She had that Audrey Hepburn thing, but she was also Lucy. She is just so honest and free."

Garry Marshall, director, 1999, as quoted in "America Goes Hollywood," Newsweek, *June 28, in reference to Julia Roberts*

ROAD PICTURE

A road picture is a name first given to a type of film in which characters and narrative plot are centered on situations that develop within exotic locations. The "road" concept was derived from a series of light entertainment films involving international intrigue combined with musical numbers and starring Bob Hope, Bing Crosby, and Dorothy Lamour: *Road to Singapore* (1940), *Road to Morocco* (1942), *Road to Rio* (1947), and *Road to Hong Kong* (1962). The term *road picture* is also used to describe films in which the principal characters travel across the American landscape, discovering certain social, political, and cultural realities in the process of the journey: *Easy Rider* (1969), *Harry and Tonto* (1974), and *Thelma and Louise* (1991).

ROCKY

Rocky was a low-budget movie that propelled then-unknown Sylvester Stallone's career into orbit. Stallone wrote and starred in the film, which won Oscars for Best Editing, Best Direction, and Best Picture, defeating several other now-classics: *Taxi Driver*, *All the President's Men,* and *Network*. Although the movie sometimes portrays stock character types and even borders on parody with regard to some of the Italian-American characters, it taps into the mythic power of the American dream: that any man or woman can make it to the top of the world.

notable & quotable

"Having grown up in the streets, I knew millions of Rockys. I knew the smells. I worked those docks in Philadelphia. I know what these people were all about."

Sylvester Stallone, actor, 1999, as quoted in "America Goes Hollywood," Newsweek, *June 28, 1999*

The film begins as small-time Philadelphia club fighter Rocky Balboa (Sylvester Stallone), nicknamed the Italian Stallion, halfheartedly fights an opponent. After his opponent illegally headbutts him, Rocky comes to life and pummels him to win his measly forty bucks. In his apartment, where a picture of his idol, Rocky Marciano, hangs, he stares at a picture of himself as a child, obviously disappointed with the nobody he's become. During the day, he collects money for a smalltime mobster, Gazzo (Joe Spinell), although he refuses to rough anybody up. At the gym, the gruff and crusty old trainer Mickey (Burgess Meredith) empties Rocky's locker because he thinks Rocky fights like an ape, and a halfhearted ape at that.

Rocky is always flirting with the shy Adrian (Talia Shire) at the pet store where he gets food for his pet turtles. He eventually works up the nerve to ask her out, but she barely speaks a word during their entire conversation. He tries to enlist his slovenly friend Paulie (Burt Young), Adrian's

Sylvester Stallone wrote the script for Rocky *after he saw a boxing match between the unknown Chuck Wepner and Muhammed Ali in which Wepner went the distance.*

brother, to help him to win over Adrian, suggesting that Paulie could invite him to Thanksgiving dinner.

Apollo Creed (Carl Weathers) is the heavyweight world champion, a talented Muhammad Ali type, whose slick promotional skills equal his boxing talent. When Apollo's opponent for the big Fourth of July fight is injured, Apollo decides to replace him with a novelty opponent to create a publicity stunt. Capitalizing on the Fourth of July holiday, Apollo decides to give a local underdog a shot at the American dream. His marketing savvy leads him to pick Rocky, because, as he says, "Apollo Creed versus the Italian Stallion" sounds like a monster movie.

Rocky and Paulie are on the way to the house that Paulie shares with Adrian to have Thanksgiving dinner, and Paulie reassures Rocky that Adrian knows he's coming and is excited. When they arrive, however, Adrian is surprised and embarrassed. Paulie harasses her in an effort to get her to go out with Rocky. After finding out that she likes ice skating, Rocky bribes an ice rink attendant into letting them skate on the rink after it's closed. He chatters away to her about how he became a boxer to prove he wasn't just a bum. But it seems he has no reason to fight anymore. Later, Adrian reluctantly agrees to go into Rocky's apartment. Although she is inexperienced and scared, Adrian loosens up as Rocky takes off her nerdy glasses and hat, revealing a surprisingly attractive woman. They eventually kiss passionately.

Rocky is summoned by George Jurgens (Thayer David), Apollo's manager, thinking that Apollo needs a sparring partner. Rocky is surprised when George offers him the title fight. Rocky is reluctant, but George persuades him by reminding him that America is the land of opportunity. Thrust into the spotlight, Rocky doesn't know whom to trust. Paulie seems to want to capitalize on Rocky's recent fortune, and the news media condescend to him and embarrass him. Gazzo helps Rocky with $500 for training. Mickey, hoping to share his wisdom, offers to train Rocky. Rocky rebuffs him, angry that he never before offered his help. Eventually Rocky accepts Mickey's offer.

“ 'Apollo Creed Meets the Italian Stallion.' Sounds like a damn monster movie. ”

Carl Weathers as Apollo Creed in *Rocky* (1976)

At four o'clock the next morning, Rocky wakes up, swallows some raw eggs for breakfast, and starts training. He jogs through Philadelphia's streets, huffing and puffing, walking the last bit to the top of a large flight of stairs. At the gym, Mickey chases two autograph seekers who distract Rocky.

Paulie overhears Rocky telling Adrian that he is frustrated by the fact that Paulie keeps trying to exploit him. Already angered that Rocky never helped him to get work with Gazzo, Paulie resents that Rocky can't throw his friend a "crumb." The resentment combined with jealousy of Adrian and Rocky's burgeoning relationship so angers Paulie that Adrian decides to move in with Rocky. Paulie eventually finds a way to make money promoting Rocky.

The famous training sequence, underscored by the popular Oscar-nominated "Gonna Fly Now," includes Rocky running throughout the streets of Philadelphia, hitting the speed bag, doing alternating one-armed pushups. The montage ends with Rocky effortlessly running to the top of the stairs that earlier wore him out. He puts his hands in the air: it's a personal victory. Having doubts that he can win, Rocky tells Adrian that his goal is to be the first boxer to go the distance with Apollo. If Rocky can last fifteen rounds, he will feel like more than just another punk from the neighborhood.

Treating the fight like a spectacle, Apollo, decked out in stars-and-stripes, underestimates Rocky. Apollo takes control of the fight in the first round with a series of jabs, but Rocky lands one solid punch to Apollo's head, sending him to the canvas for the first time in his career. As the fight progresses, Apollo breaks Rocky's nose, and Rocky, in Marciano style, bludgeons Apollo with body shots. In the later rounds, both fighters' managers are near to throwing in the towel for their side. In the last round, Apollo knocks Rocky down, and Mickey yells for him to stay down. Rocky gets to his feet, fulfilling his goal of going all the way. While the judges announce the split decision, Rocky yells for Adrian. The film ends as Adrian, who has shed her frumpy attire for a conservatively stylish look, struggles her way to the ring where she and Rocky both tell each other, "I love you."

See Raging Bull

ROCKY HORROR PICTURE SHOW, THE

Anyone who has attended a midnight show in the last twenty years has undoubtedly seen *The Rocky Horror Picture Show.* From its beginnings in London as a small piece of experimental theater, Richard O'Brien's campy drag rock musical horror spoof quickly spread to Broadway and Los Angeles. Enthusiastic crowd response to the show and its wild numbers, such as "Sweet Transvestite" and "Time Warp," attracted the interest of executive producer Lou Adler, who, with producer John Goldstone, put a film version into production a mere eighteen months after the play's premiere. Stage director Jim Sharman helmed the film, and many of the key performers from the stage versions—Tim Curry, Richard O'Brien, Patricia Quinn, and Little Nell—reprised their roles.

Upon release in 1975, the film was an immediate flop. However, canny Twentieth Century-Fox marketing execs realized that *Rocky Horror* would play better to the cult movie crowd, and swiftly pulled the film from general release. Before long, *Rocky Horror*'s midnight shows became the stuff of legend—wild parties where audience members dressed up as their favorite characters and "performed" the film live on stage, while the rest of the audience threw toast, rice, and other items in sync with key moments from the film. *Rocky Horror* became a 110-minute party that began every Saturday at midnight . . . a party that continues to this day.

Straightlaced young lovers Brad Majors (Barry Bostwick) and Janet Weiss (Susan Sarandon) get engaged, then set off to visit Brad's old college professor, Dr. Scott (Jonathan Adams). But a flat tire and a rainstorm scuttle their plans, and they walk back to a castle they saw down the road to try to find a phone. Intercuts of a helpful criminologist/narrator (Charles

Gray) explain certain plot points, and enhance the film's cornball creepiness.

Bizarre shenanigans begin as soon as the couple arrives at the castle. They are greeted by sexy maid Magenta (Patricia Quinn) and her Igoresque handyman brother Riff Raff (Richard O'Brien), who inform them that they've arrived on a most special night: the "Annual Transylvanian Convention." Riff then breaks into "Time Warp," a rousing rock 'n' roll dance number, and is joined by the party guests and even the criminologist, who cuts in to explain some of the dance moves: "It's just a jump to the left."

Brad and Janet are shocked by this display of wanton depravity—but they haven't seen anything yet. Dr. Frank-N-Furter (Tim Curry) makes a spectacular entrance in heels, hose, and bustier, and sings the film's showstopper "Sweet Transvestite." Frank explains to all the guests that he's been "making a man," a creature to satisfy his sexual appetite. He insists that Brad and Janet join him for the unveiling . . . but not before stripping them both down to undergarments. Later in the film, Brad finds a robe, but Janet spends the rest of the film in a bra and slip . . . and eventually loses even the slip.

In his lab Frank brings his creation to life. Rocky (Peter Hinwood) is a buff young hunk, but he's also frightened and naive. He runs away from Frank, much to Frank's dismay. But before Frank can stop him, Eddie

Cult classic The Rocky Horror Picture Show *is an outrageous, kinky horror movie spoof, spiced with sex and rock and roll.*

(Meat Loaf), a young biker punk that Frank had been keeping in the freezer, bursts free and sings a groovy rock song. (Creator Richard O'Brien freely admits that he threw several songs he'd previously written into *Rocky Horror,* despite the songs' lack of connection to the film.) Annoyed, Frank kills Eddie with an axe in front of all his party guests, then locks Rocky in a cage.

Unable to escape or find a phone (though they don't actually try very hard), Brad and Janet are shown to separate rooms. There, Frank proceeds to sneak in and seduce each of them individually. All the while, Magenta, Columbia (Little Nell), and Riff watch the antics on closed-circuit TV. Her sexuality awakened, Janet slips out of her room and finds Rocky. She encourages him to "Toucha toucha toucha touch me, I wanna be dirty."

Out of the blue, the wheelchair-bound Dr. Scott arrives at the castle. There is something of a rivalry between Frank and Scott; Frank accuses Scott of sending Brad and Janet to spy on him. But Scott reveals that he is seeking his lost nephew Eddie. During the subsequent dinner scene, Dr. Scott finds him—in slices, on his plate. Scared, Janet runs into Rocky's arms. Infuriated that his creation has been won over by Janet, Frank freezes them all into statues with his "SonicTransducer" beam.

In the big finale, Frank unfreezes Brad, Janet, Rocky, and Dr. Scott, and they all perform a musical number on a large stage before a mock-up of the old RKO Pictures logo, complete with twenty-foot radio tower. All of the cast, even Dr. Scott, have been turned into transvestites. Suddenly, Riff and Magenta arrive and reveal that they're galactic cops of a sort. Frank has gone too far, they say, so they are taking him back to the planet Transvestite in the galaxy of Transylvania. Frank then sings "I'm Going Home," after which Riff shoots Frank with a laser gun, killing him. Upset, Rocky runs to Frank's side. Riff blasts Rocky, but magically, the ray beams bounce right off. Rocky throws Frank over his shoulder and, in an homage to King Kong, scales the RKO tower, but the tower comes crashing down. The entire house then lifts off and flies into space.

See Cult film; Sarandon, Susan

ROEG, NICOLAS

In making the transtion from cinematographer to director, Nicolas Roeg emerged as one of the most innovative and controversial film artists of the 1960s and 1970s. Fascinated with movies since his school days in London, Roeg ran film societies at school and even served as the unit projectionist in

R

ROEG, NICOLAS

As a cinematographer, Nicolas Roeg photographed films for such directors as Francois Truffaut and John Schlesinger. He made his directorial debut as codirector on the film Performance *in 1968.* ▶

the army. After leaving the service, Roeg looked for employment in the film industry, which was not very hard, considering that his father knew the owner of a film studio. So, in 1947, Roeg was hired by the Marylebone Studio, where he worked on dubbing English dialogue into French films and, more important, learned how to edit in the studio's basement.

Several years later, wishing to move upward, Roeg answered an advertisement for a camera crew job at MGM's Boreham Wood studios, where he worked as a clapper boy and as an assistant to director of photography Joe Ruttenburg, who had filmed *Fury* and the original *Mrs. Miniver.* Although well ensconced in the movie industry, Roeg was restless—he wanted to make films. He was obliged to slog his way through the pecking order, however, spending the 1950s on the studio's camera crew, steadily advancing to second unit work, including work on David Lean's *Lawrence of Arabia* (1961). Then, in 1961, he was given his first assignments as director of photography (DP), albeit on obscure, undistinguished projects: Robert Lynn's *On Information Received* and *Dr. Crippen*.

Roeg's next efforts, however, were more widely seen. His third credit as DP was for Clive Donner's low-budget adaptation of Harold Pinter's *The Caretaker* (1963). Although the subject matter and theatricality of the film limited its appeal, Roeg's camera work reportedly made the most of the one-room set and contributed to the film's modest critical success. Somewhat more commercial was *Nothing but the Best* (1963), also directed by Donner and photographed by Roeg, a well-received black comedy that also attracted notice for its fine cinematography.

Much more interesting is Roeg's third offering from 1963, the neglected Roger Corman cult classic *The Masque of the Red Death*, shot on Corman's usual three-week schedule. Critical reaction to the film was astonishingly enthusiastic, considering the genre and the condescension Corman's work normally inspired. Even the normally staid *New York Times* grudgingly praised the film, primarily because of its visual opulence.

In 1965 Roeg directed the filming of Richard Lester's *A Funny Thing Happened on the Way to the Forum*, which was followed by what Roeg considers his most exciting and satisfying cinematographic project, François Truffaut's *Fahrenheit 451*. Rather than pursuing the directions suggested by that collaboration, however, Roeg found himself working within the romantic, more traditionally picturesque style of John Schlesinger's *Far from the Madding Crowd*, a film that is also remembered for its cinematography. Roeg's reputation as a cinematographer continued to prosper independently of the commercial and even critical fate of the films he worked on. His final DP assignment, *Petulia* (1968), proved no exception.

Yet Roeg's creative energies could not be contained by a camera viewfinder, and he yearned for the more imposing but rewarding creative challenges of directing. He received a script from the screenwriter Donald Cammell—in Roeg's words, "just a few pages that Donald had written—a notion for a film about a gangster in London's underworld, and the relation of that specific kind of violence to the violence in human nature." Money, however, was not forthcoming until Rolling Stones lead singer Mick Jagger agreed to play the lead role of Turner. Warner Brothers, the American distributor and coproducer, sent a representative to supervise what seemed like an alarmingly chaotic, improvisational shoot, which Roeg and Cammell were codirecting. The final product, released only on the strength of Jagger's presence, divided the critics, some of whom felt it the most challenging, innovative, and powerful film of recent years, while others felt it the most convoluted, pretentious, and offensive. A flop at the box office, *Performance* nevertheless attracted a devoted following.

No such controversy accompanied the release of *Walkabout* (1971), Roeg's first solo directorial effort, a story about two children lost in the

Australian desert and the Aborigine boy who leads them to safety. This intricately structured commentary on the effects of civilization on its members received mostly favorable reviews but such narrow distribution that it, too, registered a financial loss.

Unlike *Walkabout*, the reputation of *Don't Look Now* (1973) preceded its opening, although the advance buzz had less to do with the movie's occult subject matter and glowing reviews than with reports of the steamy, explicit sex between the film's two major stars, Donald Sutherland and Julie Christie. The scene was cut for American audiences so that an X rating could be avoided. Despite the publicity and the excellent reviews, however, the film never really took off at the box office. However, like Roeg's other

GINGER ROGERS

Ginger Rogers was born Virginia Katherine McMath in Independence, Missouri, on July 16, 1911. Her mother was Lela Owens McMath; her husband abandoned her before Ginger (a variation of Virginia) was born. Lela later married John Rogers—hence the name Ginger Rogers.

Rogers is particularly associated in the public's memory with her fabulous musical-comedy pairings with Fred Astaire. But Rogers was not just a fantastic dancer and a skilled singer; she was also an accomplished actress in both comedic and dramatic roles. The beautiful Rogers was a huge star in her own right, apart from her partnership with Astaire. Indeed, in 1945 she reportedly had the eighth largest individual income in all of the United States.

As a young child, Rogers took dancing and singing lessons, and she appeared in a few regional commercials. When her mother, Lela, began working with the studios in Hollywood, the younger Rogers was offered a film contract. But Lela nixed the idea, considering Ginger too young at that point. Rogers finally started performing professionally, on the vaudeville stage, at age fourteen.

As a young woman, Rogers eventually achieved modest success in Broadway musicals (*Top Speed,* 1929; and *Girl Crazy,* 1930–31), and Hollywood pursued her again. This time she was ready. She performed in numerous small films beginning in 1930, usually cast as a wisecracking blonde bombshell. But Rogers did not make a real impact with the public until she was contracted by RKO Pictures and was tapped to perform with Fred Astaire.

Ginger and Fred performed in ten dance-centered films together, including *Top Hat* (1935), *Follow the Fleet* (1936), *Swing Time* (1936), *Shall We Dance* (1937), and *The Story of Vernon and Irene Castle* (1939). Their onscreen chemistry seemed heaven-sent; watching their movies has given pleasure to people for generations.

Many people tend to credit Astaire for most of the magic, but fans of Rogers note that she danced all the steps he did—except backwards, and while wearing high heels. For all their seeming ease and warmth on the

Ginger Rogers danced all of the same steps as her frequent partner Fred Astaire—but backwards and in high heels.

screen, the relationship between Rogers and Astaire was said to be occasionally tense and frosty. Rogers finally opted to turn her talents more toward straight acting roles—perhaps not wishing to be typecast as part of a duo with Astaire—and the famous professional partnership came to an end, though they would reunite in 1949 for *The Barkleys of Broadway.*

Rogers soon fulfilled her promise as a dramatic actress, winning a Best Actress Academy Award for her performance in *Kitty Foyle* (1940). She was thrilled with the victory, not having expected to win over her rivals for the prize, including Katharine Hepburn and Bette Davis. Over the next twenty-five years she performed in nearly thirty other movies, from serious drama to light comedy.

Among her works are *Stage Door* (1937), *Bachelor Mother* (1939), *The Primrose Path* (1940), *Tom, Dick and Harry* (1941), *The Major and the Minor* (1942), *Weekend at the Waldorf* (1945), *It Had to Be You* (1947), *Storm Warning* (1950), *Black Widow* (1954), and *Harlow* (1965). As time went on, though, she devoted more of her time to the stage, appearing on Broadway and in London.

Rogers loved to get away to her ranch in Oregon—the Rogers Rogue River Ranch. She was married five times; three of her husbands were actors: Lew Ayres, Jacques Bergerac, and G. William Marshall. She died of natural causes at her home in Rancho Mirage, California, in 1995.

See Astaire, Fred; Musical film

In 1936 *Swing Time*, with Fred Astaire and Ginger Rogers, set an opening-day record when Radio City Music Hall sold 27,821 tickets.

early efforts, it, too, has enjoyed a vigorous afterlife on the revival and college circuit.

Three years later, Roeg completed his most eagerly awaited film, *The Man Who Fell to Earth*, an oblique, allegorical science fiction fantasy starring David Bowie as an alien who comes to earth to obtain water for his drought-stricken planet. A mixed critical reception and poor word of mouth doomed this project financially as well. His more recent releases—*Bad Timing: A Sensual Obsession* (1980), *Eureka* (1985), *Insignificance* (1985), *Castaway* (1987), *Track 29* (1988), *The Witches* (1990), and *Cold Heaven* (1992)—have proved both critical and commercial disappointments. Since 1992 Roeg has directed only television movies.

See Lawrence of Arabia; *Lean, David*

RUDOLPH, ALAN

Alan Rudolph (1943–), one of the most aesthetically adventurous of American directors, is a born filmmaker, by both talent and circumstance. His father, Oscar, was a child actor in Hollywood in the 1930s and later became a film and television director. Among his directorial credits are *Twist Around the Clock* (1961) and *Don't Knock the Twist* (1962), which, in their own way, anticipate the potential combining of music and visuals that would find greater expression in the younger Rudolph's work.

While many of his contemporaries learned their craft in film school, Alan Rudolph was able to get a firsthand view of the industry as a child growing up in Los Angeles. He even made a cameo appearance in one of his father's productions, *The Rocket Man* (1954). The fantasy, coscripted by Lenny Bruce, involved a small boy who gets hold of a gun that turns crooked people honest. This close Hollywood connection might seem ironic for a director whose films have often been described as being closer to European art films than mainstream American productions, but Rudolph's work has continually demonstrated an appreciation of, if not an adherence to, traditional Hollywood formulas.

The elder Rudolph's extensive television work provided his son with entry into the business and an appreciation for working on tight schedules and limited budgets. Although Rudolph briefly attended UCLA, where he majored in accounting, he soon turned his attention to making short films (often for friends who were enrolled in film school) and got a job in the mailroom at Paramount. In 1967 he entered the training program of the Directors Guild of America and became one of the youngest assistant directors in Hollywood. Rudolph worked as an assistant on various television programs in the late 1960s and early 1970s, including many directed by his father, while pursuing feature film work. Despite the wide range of projects on which he worked, however, Rudolph did not receive screen credit on many of the films for which he was an assistant director, and the exact nature of his contributions is difficult to determine. Among the more notable films in which he was involved were *Marooned* (1969), *The Traveling Executioner* (1970), and *The Arrangement* (1969). His work as assistant director on Buzz Kulik's *Riot* (1969) may have influenced his later use of characters with prison backgrounds in both *Remember My Name* and *Trouble in Mind.*

Rudolph claims that while working as an assistant director he became disillusioned with the mistakes being made by crews and the mediocre material being produced. The break from his career as an assistant director came while he was working on a television movie. Rudolph suggested to the director that he not make compromises just to satisfy a tight schedule, and the director then accused Rudolph of trying to undermine his work. After deciding that he did not want to continue in this capacity, Rudolph began to focus on writing his own scripts, so he was hesitant to accept Robert Altman's offer to serve as assistant director on *The Long Goodbye* (1973). But

Director Alan Rudolph got a firsthand view of the film industry through his father, film and television director Oscar Rudolph.

after seeing Altman's *McCabe and Mrs. Miller* (1972), he was so impressed by Altman's ability to "create a mood" that he eagerly signed on with Altman.

Altman had a profound influence on Rudolph, teaching him to define and refine his personal vision and to work within the system without making artistic compromises. It proved to be a durable collaboration extended through three more films: *California Split* (1974), *Nashville* (1975), and *Buffalo Bill and the Indians, or Sitting Bull's History Lesson* (1976).

Altman produced Rudolph's first major commercial directorial effort, *Welcome to L.A.* (1977). (His very first was the self-consciously arty *Premonition* [1972], which belatedly rose from the lower depths of a well-deserved obscurity to the shelves of video stores thanks to Rudolph's later eminence.) Featuring a trendy, able cast—Keith Carradine, Geraldine Chaplin, Lauren Hutton, Harvey Keitel, Sissy Spacek, and Sally Kellerman—the film is a depressing evocation of alienation and hustling among the beautiful and damned in Los Angeles; it impressed some critics with its moody, absorbing emotional textures but struck others as sophomorically bleak.

It took Rudolph nearly a decade to find his true voice. His next film, *Remember My Name*, featured a memorable performance by Geraldine Chaplin as a desperate ex-convict bent on finding and settling scores with a faithless lover. In *Roadie* (1980) Rudolph turned on his heel, his characteristically mournful, meditative style giving way to an antic look at musicians and their retinue on the road. *Endangered Species* (1982), *Songwriter* (1984), and *Made in Heaven* (1987) were routine commercial studio undertakings, devoid of Rudolph's authentic imprint. An exception to the indifferent efforts of this period was *1984*, a provocative and absorbing documentary about a series of debates between the Watergate coconspirator G. Gordon Liddy and the 1960s apostle of psychedelia Timothy Leary.

Rudolph's major artistic breakthrough came with *Choose Me* (1984), widely regarded as one of the finest American films of the past twenty years. Succeeding at last in creating his "own mood," Rudolph conjures a memorably hypnotic vision of the interlocking passions and obsessions of group of questing loners and seekers in Los Angeles. Rudolph sought to recapture the same moody magic in *Trouble in Mind* (1985), a similar film set in an indeterminate, semi-fascist past or future, which struck many critics as longer on atmospherics than on substance.

The Moderns (1988) presented a sharp, acerbic look at the crass merchandising of art in Paris in the 1920s. More recently Rudolph has directed *Love at Large* (1990), *Mortal Thoughts* (1991), *Equinox* (1993), *Mrs. Parker and the Vicious Circle* (1994), *Afterglow* (1997), *Trixie* (1999), and *Breakfast of Champions* (1999).

See Altman, Robert

MEG RYAN

Meg Ryan was born Margaret Mary Emily Anne Hyra in Fairfield, Connecticut, on November 19, 1961. The actress has a fetching onscreen personality, often described as whimsical or perky.

Ryan's parents, Harry (a high school math teacher) and Susan (a homemaker), split up when Meg was a teenager. The story is told that her mother abandoned the family to pursue her acting ambitions. The painfulness of this incident is evidenced by the report that Ryan and her mother have been estranged since the 1980s.

Ryan (Meg's mother's maiden name) studied journalism at either the University of Connecticut or New York University (sources vary). She was fortunate in that she was able to pay her tuition by performing in television commercials. While she was still a student Ryan was given a supporting role in the film *Rich and Famous* (1981), playing Candice Bergen's daughter. Ryan subsequently dropped out of school and pursued a full-time acting career.

She immediately met with success in television, winning a recurring role in the soap opera *As the World Turns*. She started getting film roles in 1983 *(Amityville III)* and was fortunate enough to land a small role in *Top Gun* (1986), which became an enormous hit.

Over the next few years Ryan appeared in several movies, including *Innerspace* (1987) and *The Presidio* (1988). Her breakthrough role was as a sweet girl-next-door type in *When Harry Met Sally . . .* (1989). The character's comical feigning of sexual ecstasy in a diner enchanted audiences, and she was on her way to becoming a star.

Ryan's more important roles have been in *The Doors* (1991), *Sleepless in Seattle* (1993), *When a Man Loves a Woman* (1994), *Restoration* (1995), and *You've Got Mail* (1999). Her career has not been hurt by the fact that she and superstar Tom Hanks have a special onscreen chemistry; they have appeared together in three romantic comedies.

Meg Ryan married fellow actor Dennis Quaid in 1991. They have one son, Jack Henry.

See Hanks, Tom

S

SAVING PRIVATE RYAN

Director Steven Spielberg revisits World War II after the haunting *Schindler's List* (1993) in 1998's deeply moving *Saving Private Ryan*. The film was a box office smash for fledgling studio Dreamworks, and it won five Academy Awards, including Best Director and Best Cinematography. The film also reignited interest in World War II throughout the United States, and spurred a renewed appreciation of veterans from a younger generation that previously had only known the great war as an abstract concept.

Saving Private Ryan features an unflinching dedication to realism. Costume designers recreated over 3,000 uniforms, and armorers purchased and refurbished thousands of period armaments. Military advisor Dale Dye even put the entire cast through basic training just prior to principal photography. Ten days of K-rations and maneuvers through mud and cold rain quickly turned the cast into authentically war-weary troops. But most important, the battle scenes are gory and unrelenting. The first battle sequence, the landing at Omaha Beach, is thirty minutes of carnage, and director of photography Janusz Kaminski's documentary-style, handheld camerawork puts the viewer right in the thick of the horrors of war like no film had done before.

"What's the use in risking the lives of the eight of us to save one guy?"

Edward Burns as Private Richard Reiben in *Saving Private Ryan* (1998)

The film opens in the present day, with an old man and his family visiting Arlington National Cemetery. He makes his way to a gravestone and tears begin to well up in his eyes. Sounds of battle fade in, and we are transported back in time to June 6, 1944, Dog Green Sector: Omaha Beach, Normandy. Thousands of nervous, seasick troops approach the beach by boat. Immediately upon landing, many of them are cut down by enemy fire.

Captain John Miller (Tom Hanks) leads one of the squads, unable to do anything about the slaughter. One by one his men are maimed and killed before his eyes. The enemy is too firmly entrenched. The surf turns red with blood as corpses litter the beach.

Miller has a rendezvous with his sergeant, Mike Horvath (Tom Sizemore), and the leftovers from three companies in a foxhole. Miller then unleashes his secret weapon: Private Jackson (Barry Pepper), a sniper from the South who prays before each shot. His men give Jackson covering fire as he dashes into position. With great precision, Jackson takes out a key Nazi gun nest, and the tide turns. The Allies are now able to roust the remaining Germans from their positions and win the day. The last shot is of a body floating face down, with the name S. RYAN emblazoned on his knapsack.

Back in Washington, D.C., a roomful of secretaries bangs out condolence letters to families of the war dead. One secretary notices three deaths, all from the Ryan family, and brings it to her superiors' attention. It is quickly determined that the fourth and last Ryan brother has just parachuted into Normandy. As an officer and a priest arrive at Mrs. Ryan's farm to bring her the terrible news, the army's chief of staff discusses a rescue mission with his compatriots. The chief of staff reads a letter written by Abraham Lincoln to a woman who lost all five of her sons fighting for the Union. Determined not to let that happen again, the chief of staff resolves to find Private Ryan and bring him home.

Captain Miller receives the assignment and assembles his team: Corporal Upham (Jeremy Davies), a bookish French/German polyglot who has never seen battle but is chosen for his ability to speak German; T-4 Medic Wade (Giovanni Ribisi); Private Reiben (Edward Burns), a street-smart guy from Brooklyn; Mellish (Adam Goldberg), a joker; Caparzo (Vin Deisel), and Jackson and Horvath. They set out marching across the countryside, arguing about the mission, which all of them view as a waste of time. Miller alone is stoically behind the objective.

Before long they come upon a bombed-out village. Against orders, Caparzo tries to rescue a little girl, and takes a sniper's bullet for his trouble. His crew can do nothing but watch him bleed; the sniper has them all pinned down. Jackson sneaks up on the bell tower and makes his shot. The last thing the enemy sniper sees is the muzzle flash of Jackson's rifle. But it's too late for Caparzo. Already, the attempt to rescue Ryan has cost another man his life.

Eventually Miller's unit meets up with another division on the march, and as luck would have it, Private Ryan is with them. Miller breaks the bad news to Ryan about his brothers having been killed in battle. Ryan sobs, "How? They were only in grade school!" Sheepish, Miller realizes he's got the wrong Ryan.

Holing up in a church for the night, Miller's men talk about themselves. There's a pool on the enigmatic Captain Miller: Where is he from? What was his profession? Miller won't say. But Miller does say that this: Ryan, whoever he is, better come out of this and cure some disease or invent a better lightbulb or something. He'd better be worth it.

The next day, Miller's unit comes upon another division, with hundreds of captured Germans in tow, and even more dog tags of American dead. Miller and crew dig through the tags, searching for Ryan, but no luck. Frustrated, Miller starts yelling to anyone who'll listen: Have you seen Ryan? Do you know a Private Ryan? Amazingly, he finds an almost deaf trooper who recently saw Ryan. Ryan's unit was rounded up by a colonel to defend a bridge in Ramel.

notable & quotable

"The film encompassed the concepts of sacrifice, inevitability and comradeship. You felt what it was like to be in a war at that extraordinary place at that extraordinary time. It was a very human movie."

Tom Hanks, actor, 1999, as quoted in "A Soldier's Story," The Cable Guide, *July, 1999*

On the march to Ramel, Miller's unit comes across a Nazi gun nest, waiting to ambush the next American patrol. His men suggest they simply go around it, but Miller won't have it. They charge the nest. The battle is short and unseen; we stay on quivery Upham for the duration. When Upham is called over, he discovers Wade has been hit and is losing blood fast. Unfortunately, Wade's the medic. "Tell us how to fix you!" shouts Mellish, but it's too late. After a heart-wrenching death scene, Wade expires.

Finding a German gunner still alive, Miller's men want to kill him immediately. Miller makes the gunner dig Wade's grave first . . . then blindfolds the German and lets him go. Infuriated, Reiben mutinies. How many more of our guys have to die for this Ryan, he asks. He doesn't want to continue with this mission. Tensions heat up as Horvath pulls a gun, defending Miller. But before anyone else is killed, Miller masterfully defuses the situation by finally revealing his occupation, the source of so much speculation: he's a schoolteacher. Reunited in their purpose, the men continue on their mission.

Saving Private Ryan (1998) earned more than $30 million in its first weekend, according to *Variety*, and by the end of that year it had made over $220 million worldwide.

Outside Ramel, a German halftrack roars up on Miller's men. The vehicle suddenly explodes. Three U.S. gunners pop up from the tall grass. Wielding the bazooka: Private Ryan (Matt Damon).

In the bombed-out village of Ramel, Ryan's unit leader, Corporal Henderson, greets Captain Miller's men enthusiastically. Miller tells him that unfortunately, they're not the reinforcements he's been waiting for. They're here for Ryan. But Ryan won't desert the only brothers he has left—his unit. He tells Miller that he's going to defend this bridge with his dying breath. Miller and Horvath discuss the situation and decide to stay and help.

Henderson and Miller plan strategy. They hope to funnel the Germans down one path and ambush them. The men prepare munitions and make sticky bombs from socks, axle grease, and composition B explosive. Mellish assigns Upham ammo duty. Jackson takes a sniper position in a bell tower. The rest of the men line the street with shaped charges and lie in wait for the Germans.

The climactic battle begins. Though Jackson snipes well from on high, he can't stop a 120mm shell from a German Panzer tank. Upham proves useless, hiding and cowering as his fellow soldiers run out of ammo. Sergeant Horvath is shot, then shot again, and again, yet fights on, like a machine. And in one of the film's most horrific moments, Mellish is slowly, tortuously stabbed by the very German soldier that Captain Miller released earlier.

The battle goes poorly for the Americans. Miller orders his men to pull back and blow the bridge. But Horvath dies before his eyes . . . and then Miller, too, takes a bullet. He sags to the dirt, firing his pistol ineffectually at the tank bearing down on him. But just before he's run over, the tank goes up in flames; a wave of U.S. P-51 tank-buster planes—the reinforcements Henderson had been expecting—has finally arrived. The U.S. troops rally and defeat the Germans. A grim, transformed Upham assassinates the German who killed his friend.

As Captain Miller dies, he reaches out for Private Ryan and says simply, "Earn this." The film fades out, and we are back to the cemetery, where we learn that the old man is Ryan, fifty years later. Standing before Miller's tombstone, he chokes with emotion and asks his wife if he's been a good man, if he's lived a life worthy of the sacrifices of Miller and his company. His wife reassures him that he has. The final shot in the film is of an American flag, flying proudly.

See Hanks, Tom; Spielberg, Steven; War film

SUSAN SARANDON

Susan Sarandon was born Susan Abigail Tomaling in New York City on October 4, 1946. She took her professional name from actor Chris Sarandon, to whom she was married from 1967 to 1979. Sarandon has come to personify the voluptuous, sexy older woman. Her look is distinctive, with auburn hair and huge eyes (variously called saucerlike or sad).

Sarandon grew up the oldest of nine children in a Catholic family. Her father, once a big-band singer, was a television and advertising executive. She was educated in Catholic schools and attended Catholic University in Washington, D.C., where she met Chris Sarandon. She has always had a bent toward political protest, an aspect of her persona that has become heightened in recent years, especially in her relationship with mate Tim Robbins, an actor whom she met while filming the popular baseball movie *Bull Durham* (1988).

Versatile Susan Sarandon has appeared in everything from cult classics like The Rocky Horror Picture Show *to serious dramas like* Dead Man Walking.

In 1970 Sarandon was cast in *Joe* (1970), when her husband Chris took her along to an audition. Over the next few years she worked steadily in film, television, and stage, though in small parts and often in quirky productions. In 1975 she landed roles in two films that would raise her exposure in the public eye: *The Great Waldo Pepper,* with Robert Redford, and *The Rocky Horror Picture Show,* which eventually became a cult classic.

Sarandon played the mother of a twelve-year-old prostitute played by Brooke Shields in the controversial film *Pretty Baby* in 1978. In 1980 her performance in *Atlantic City* won her an Academy Award nomination for Best Actress. (By this time divorced from Chris Sarandon, she also became romantically involved with those films' director, Louis Malle.)

Her lesbian love scenes in a vampire movie, *The Hunger* (1983), solidified Sarandon's growing reputation as a daring actress. Sarandon started getting parts in more high-profile films, including *The Witches of Eastwick* (1987), the aforementioned *Bull Durham, A Dry White Season* (1989), and *White Palace* (1990). Her biggest hit to date has been the groundbreaking road movie *Thelma & Louise* (1991), but she has also had success with several other films, including *The Client* (1992) and *Dead Man Walking* (1995). She won the Best Actress Oscar for the latter film, in which she played a nun counseling a death-row inmate (played by Sean Penn, a former lover). In 1998 she performed in *Twilight* and *Stepmom.*

Sarandon has a daughter with Italian director Franco Amurri and two sons with Tim Robbins.

See Buddy film; Cult film; Rocky Horror Picture Show, The

SCARFACE

An updated version of the Howard Hawks classic, *Scarface* begins as Castro opens up Mariel Harbor and invites Cubans to flee to the United States, which welcomes them as survivors of communism. As the film's prologue reads: "It soon became evident that Castro was forcing the boat owners to carry back with them not only their relatives, but the dregs of his jails. Of the 125,000 refugees that landed in Florida, an estimated 25,000 had criminal records."

Scarface was another Oliver Stone script steeped in political intrigue and able to exploit the knee-jerk excess of the era and the genre. Stone used a skeleton of the original Ben Hecht story and expanded it to indict the Reagan drug war. The film suggests that the war on drugs had much the same effect that Prohibition did in the 1920s: it helped feed a rollicking black market getting rich off the enduring desire for banned substances.

As bootlegging once did for the ambitious but uneducated Tony Camonte, the drug trade provides employment for his descendent Tony Montana, who quickly rises to become a rich, powerful drug lord. At the time of Montana's story, the political strategy was to keep drugs illegal, stop the flow breaching U.S. borders, and tell the citizenry to "just say no."

As the film opens, U.S. officials interrogate Tony (Al Pacino), suspecting that he's a criminal who sneaked into the country among the refugees. He speaks fluent English, which he tells them he learned from watching gangster movies with Bogart and Cagney. If the scar on his cheek doesn't signal that Tony is trouble, his heart-shaped tatoo embellished with a pitchfork does, for as the officials suspect, it's the mark of an assassin. Tony is shipped off to a detention camp as an undesirable. There he's joined by his associates Angel (Pepe Serna) and Manolo "Manny" Ray (the updated Raft character, played by Cuban American Steven Bauer). A Cuban businessman arranges their green cards in exchange for their murder of a former Castro collaborator who once tortured the businessman's brother. The victim is also among the refugees. "I would kill a communist for fun," Tony says, "but for a green card I carve him up real nice."

Tony does and settles in the United States. But he soon loses patience with his American life as a dishwasher—a menial job for someone with such criminal talent. He finds work with the local crime network, which earns him $500 a hit. His price goes up to $5,000 for one afternoon's work when the sharklike mobster Omar (F. Murray Abraham) instructs Tony and his cohorts to pick up two kilos of cocaine from Colombian traffickers. Tony then meets with the Colombian connection, Hector, in a motel room. Hector pushes Tony for the money, assuring him the drugs "are close by" for transfer. Tony wants to see the drugs first, swearing that the money, too, is "close by." Hector's female accomplice Marta aims a shotgun, and the room fills up with other armed Colombians. Marta turns up the volume on the TV (ironically showing a cop show) to drown out the sound of Hector's chain saw revving up in the bathroom. Hector and his men put choke chains on Tony and Angel and string them up in the shower. Hector gruesomely tortures Angel—his grim weapon growling and whining until Angel dies and is hauled away. But Hector's chain saw conks out—the engine clogged with blood and flesh—before they get to Tony.

Manny, who has been standing watch on the street and absorbed by passing bikinis, finally bursts into the room with a chattering Uzi, and any Colombians left standing scatter about the motel grounds as they return fire. Tony finds Hector on the street and shoots him in the forehead. Then he phones Omar to tell him that he's keeping the "buy" money and the cocaine for his trouble.

Tony finally visits his estranged family. They live in a modest home kept going by his mother's work as a seamstress in a Florida factory. She doesn't believe him when, to explain his cash roll, he says that he's a "political organizer" for an anti-Castro group. Not only is she worried that he'll snare her daughter Gina into his corrupt world, but she's concerned over his unnatural affection for his sister. After calling him a bum and an animal, she throws him out. The subplot follows the original film's suggestion of incest

In the 1983 update of the Howard Hawks classic Scarface, *Al Pacino plays the ultra-violent Tony Montana, a Cuban refugee with a criminal past.*

along with Tony's head-banging ability to keep suitors away from his sister. Gina (Mary Elizabeth Mastrantonio) also can't resist flirting with Manny, who wants her but resists, fearful of Tony's rage. Tony eventually draws her into his world, buying her a lavish beauty salon (she's a beautician) and introducing her to Miami's nightlife.

Tony's rise within the underworld accelerates after he meets Omar's boss, Frank Lopez (Robert Loggia), a mobster who runs one of Florida's top drug distribution outfits. Omar keeps a suspicious, jealous eye on Tony while Tony ogles Lopez's smart-mouthed girlfriend, Elvira (the new Poppy, played by Michelle Pfeiffer).

Unlike Manny, who chases every woman in his path, Tony has marked Elvira as his own. But Elvira wants nothing to do with Tony. Tony has a plan to win her, though. "In this country you gotta make the money first. Then when you get the money, you get the power. Then when you get the power, you get the woman," he tells Manny. "That's why you gotta make your own moves."

Those moves include being more than Lopez's messenger boy when Tony and Omar go to Bolivia. Omar has been sent to talk with a cocaine factory owner named Sosa (Paul Shenar), who's looking for an American distributor. Tony begins negotiating a new deal directly with Sosa, who's impressed by Tony's potential. Sosa dismisses Omar and has him killed by hanging him out a helicopter with a rope around his neck. (Sosa tells Tony that he's certain Omar was a government informant.) Sosa also warns Tony never to double-cross him.

"I always tell the truth. Even when I lie."

Al Pacino as Tony Montana in *Scarface* (1983)

Meanwhile, Lopez is upset that Tony agreed to accept 150 kilos of cocaine each month. No longer trusting Tony, Lopez goes on the attack. He sends a crooked cop to squeeze Tony for monthly protection money and has him ambushed in a nightclub. Tony escapes, figures out it was Lopez who set him up, and plots revenge with Manny's help. He sets a trap for Lopez (as in the original film), and he and Manny kill Lopez and the corrupt cop.

With Lopez dead, Tony goes to collect his prize: Elvira. She asks few questions and packs her things as ordered. After a vulgarly lavish wedding, they move into a mansion decorated in garish contrasts of deep red, black, and white and embellished with ornate gold trim. His office is equipped with six monitors and a leather throne for a chair, adorned with his initials scrolled in gold. Between two massive staircases that curve up toward the second floor is a fountain with statues holding up a globe emblazoned with the message "The World Is Yours." (Tony first saw it flashing on the side of the Goodyear blimp and borrowed it for his personal motto.)

Tony's success in the cocaine trade escalates quickly. So does his personal use of coke. He's making so much money that his American banker tells him the price to launder the cash must be hiked also. "The IRS is coming down heavy on South Florida," the smug, Waspish moneylender complains.

Soaking in his gargantuan, solid-gold tub with bubbles and a cigar (reminiscent of Rocco in *Key Largo*), Tony raves at a TV commentator who argues against legalizing drugs as a way to stop the spiraling drug trade. Elvira wearily listens to his tirade before shouting insults at Tony and telling him that he can't stop talking about money. He bellows that she's a hypocrite for not working for the money she spends, wasting her life snorting cocaine. Eventually Elvira leaves him after a nasty exchange in a restaurant where he loudly complains about her being a junkie, adding, "I can't even have a kid with her—her womb is so polluted."

Tony is finally caught trying to launder $1.3 million that he can't explain earning. After newspaper headlines report that he's out on $5 million bail, his oily lawyer warns him that he may go to prison for tax evasion. Tony vows, "I'm not going back in any cage."

At a meeting with Sosa in Bolivia, Tony is presented with a deal by compromised Bolivian and U.S. officials: his legal troubles will disappear if he helps kill a UN delegate who has vowed to expose Sosa's drug cartel and its multigovernment connections. Tony agrees but welshes when the deal collides with his self-styled honor code. As he chauffeurs the Bolivian assassin around New York, Tony comes unglued when the plan to bomb the victim's car means killing the man's wife and child. Even more reprehensible in Tony's view is that the killer won't "look 'em in the eye" when he kills.

When Tony arrives back in Florida, his mother is panicked that Gina is missing. Manny is gone as well. Tony arrives at Gina's new posh place in Coconut Grove, and Manny answers the door in his robe. Tony pumps several bullets into him before Gina can explain that they were just married. A dazed Tony, numbed from the killing and the nonstop flow of coke, orders his men to grab his hysterical sister and put her in his white Rolls Royce.

Looking disheveled in a rumpled pin-striped suit, Tony prepares for war with Sosa—most of it to be waged inside Tony's gaudy palace. While his enemies begin crawling over the estate walls and ambushing his soldiers, a frazzled Gina comes into his office, half dressed, and dares him to have sex with her as he has always fantasized. Looking comatose, with his nose blotted with coke powder, Tony tries to appease her, but she takes aim with the gun she has hidden at her side. One of Sosa's men crashes through the window and kills Gina. Tony is jolted out of his stupor and quickly avenges her. Amid the roar of gunfire outside his office, he lays his head on her shoulder and sobs, begging her to smile for him.

After taking in another snootful of cocaine, Tony loads himself down with an arsenal of weaponry, including a grenade launcher. He bursts through his office door and, shooting from the balcony, kills a half dozen men who are scrambling around the main floor. But more keep coming, their guns hammering away at him. Amid the deafening assault, De Palma's quick close-ups blend with slow-motion shots that show rolling, tumbling bodies littering the steps and floor. Tony roars boastfully, "I'm still standing!" while groping for more ammunition and jerking from another volley of bullets ripping into his body. Finally, one of Sosa's men creeps up behind him and shoots him at close range, sending Tony's body flying off the balcony and into the fountain. In the final shot, the camera pans up from his shredded torso and past the globe that promised him the world.

See Hawks, Howard; Pacino, Al; Remake; Stone, Oliver

SCHINDLER'S LIST

Director Steven Spielberg has brought us the contemporary classics *E.T.*, *Jaws*, and *Saving Private Ryan*. But *Schindler's List* may well be his masterpiece. Based on a novel by Thomas Keneally, *Schindler's List* chronicles the real-life story of a Nazi entrepreneur who risks everything to save the lives of 1,100 Jews. Released in 1993 to universal critical praise, the film turned out to be a box-office winner for Universal Studios despite difficult subject matter, a running time in excess of three hours, and black-and-white photography. The film was nominated for a staggering twelve Academy Awards, and was awarded seven, including Best Picture, Best Director, and Best Screenplay (by Steven Zaillian).

Spielberg was aware of the Schindler story for over a decade before he made the film. Surviving "Schindler Jew" Poldek Pfefferberg (portrayed in the film by Jonathan Sagall) approached the director about the Schindler story while Spielberg was shooting *The Color Purple*. Spielberg told Pfefferberg that he was not emotionally ready to make the film, but that he expected he would be able to do it properly in ten years' time. Spielberg was right on the money, wisely waiting until he had matured as a person and filmmaker to craft this unforgettable experience.

"The list is an absolute good. The list is life."

Ben Kingsley as Itzhak Stern in *Schindler's List* (1993)

The film opens in Poland in 1939; the Nazis have invaded. All Jews have been ordered to leave their homes and relocate to the major cities. Over 100,000 Jews arrive in Kraków daily, where they are checked in and forced to wear Stars of David.

We first meet Oskar Schindler (Liam Neeson) at a Nazi soiree. Schindler is a Czech businessman with a string of unsuccessful ventures behind him. But what he excels at is panache. He exudes charm and is most generous with the drinks. Before long, every Nazi in the room wants to be his friend.

Seeing the writing on the wall, Schindler hatches a brilliant plan to start a business venture using Jewish capital. Since Jews are no longer allowed to own businesses, Schindler will be the owner, and the Jewish investors will be repaid with items useful to them—pots, pans, and the like. He recruits crafty Jewish accountant Itzhak Stern (Ben Kingsley) to handle the execution and find financiers. With the help of numerous gifts of cognac, cigars, dark chocolate, and nylons to high-ranking Nazi officials, Schindler's new venture, D.E.F. (Deutsche Emailwarenfabrik), manufacturers of superior enamelware cookery, opens for business. The orders pour in.

Meanwhile, the Nazis' grip on Poland intensifies. Jewish families are shoehorned into a ghetto of only sixteen square blocks. "Nonessential" Jews are rounded up and shipped off to death camps. Schindler's partner Stern saves the lives of many, representing rabbis, musicians, and schoolteachers as skilled metal workers to Nazi officials.

While Schindler sleeps with one of his secretaries, his wife, Emilie (Caroline Goodall), visits. Schindler's womanizing is nothing new to Emilie, and she sloughs it off. Schindler confesses his shallow aspirations to her: to leave Poland with two steamer trunks full of money. She wonders why he's finally successful—is it luck? "No," he replies. "War." Unable to remain faithful, Schindler sends her away.

Schindler first catches on to Stern's conspiracy when a one-armed old man barges into Schindler's office to thank him for saving his life. Schindler explodes. How can such a man be useful? We're just begging the Nazis to come in here! Stern points out that Schindler has repeatedly told him he's not interested in what's going on, as long as D.E.F. is making money. Later, when Nazis force Schindler's factory workers to shovel snow, an overzeal-

In Schindler's List, *Irish actor Liam Niesen portrays Oskar Schindler, a Czech businessman who saves the lives of over 1,000 Jews during World War II.* ▼

ous guard summarily executes the one-armed man. Schindler is then put in the embarrassing position of defending the old man's employment at D.E.F. to Nazi officials, explaining that he was a skilled machine press operator.

Things get even worse for the Jews as the Plaszow forced labor camp is erected in Kraków in 1942, under the command of the unstable Untersturmfuhrer Amon Goeth (Ralph Fiennes). When the camp is complete, Goeth leads Nazi troops on a campaign of terror through the ghetto. Able workers are rounded up and sent to Plaszow; the old or infirm are either sent to Auschwitz or simply shot on sight. Schindler watches the proceedings in horror from a nearby hilltop. His self-centered facade begins to crack as the devastation unfolds before him.

At Plaszow, Goeth rules with an iron hand. Like a sniper, he routinely shoots inmates from his villa overlooking the camp, and he executes people for the smallest infraction. His Jewish maid/sex slave Helen Hirsch (Embeth Davidtz) tries to stop him but loses her nerve quickly, fearing another beating.

Infuriated, Schindler visits Goeth. All of his workers are now in Plaszow, and for every day that there is no production, Schindler is losing money. Goeth can be charming among his peers, and embraces Schindler as a friend. Schindler cuts Goeth in for a piece of the profits, and gets his workers back, even though they must return to Plaszow each night. Stern keeps an eye on the books, monitoring the extraordinary amount of bribes they must continually pay out in order to remain in business.

The average ticket price in 1993, the year of *Schindler's List*, *Philadelphia*, and *Jurassic Park*, was $4.14.

Schindler slowly begins to embrace his role as savior. First he rescues the parents of a young Jewish woman who comes to him to plead on their behalf. Then Schindler takes advantage of his growing friendship with Goeth to plant seeds in the Nazi's mind one drunken evening. Realizing that Goeth respects his power, Schindler tells Goeth that real power is not about killing: "Real power is when we have every justification to kill but don't."

Schindler's words sink in: Goeth spares several people whom he would ordinarily have had killed. The deeply disturbed Goeth takes an odd delight in muttering "I pardon you" in an almost apostolic way. But Goeth's attempt at reform quickly crashes to the ground as his psychosis gets the best of him; he pardons a boy who had been unable to get stains out of his bathtub, only to snap and shoot the lad moments later. Similarly, he offers soothing words to his mistress Helen, showing for the first time that he does not view the Jews as vermin, as the propaganda would have everyone believe. But yet again he later snaps, beating her terribly.

The situation continues to deteriorate in Poland. Plaszow is ordered to be shut down, its inhabitants shipped to Auschwitz for annihilation. It's over for Schindler. But as he packs his steamer trunks full of money and prepares to return home, a terrible remorse strikes him. It is then that his true calling reveals itself. He approaches Goeth and asks for "his people." Since they are to be executed anyway, there's no loss to Goeth. Schindler means to set up a munitions factory in his hometown, and needs skilled labor. Goeth tells Schindler to name his price for each individual.

Working into the night with Stern, Schindler composes the list of 1,100 people to be rescued from certain destruction. The deal costs him an entire satchel of money to Goeth and a handful of diamonds to a commander at Auschwitz.

At the new factory in Brinnlitz, Schindler declares his intentions to Stern: "If this factory ever produces a shell that can actually be fired, I'll be very unhappy." For seven months, Brinnlitz is a model of inefficiency. Bribes keep the company in business and the Nazis off the shop floor. Schindler finally runs out of money just as the war ends.

As he declares his employees free, Schindler breaks down and sobs. He could have saved so many more—if only he had sold his car, that would have bought ten more lives; his gold lapel pin, another two. The Jews gather around and hug the man who is their savior.

In the aftermath, Goeth is found in a sanitarium and hanged for war crimes; Schindler goes into hiding with his wife, Emilie—he is a Nazi munitions manufacturer, and will be tried if caught. And in the heart-wrenching present-day final scene, the real-life surviving Schindler Jews file past his grave, hand in hand with the actors who portrayed them in the film, paying respects to the man who saved their lives.

See Epic; Spielberg, Steven; War film

SCIENCE-FICTION FILM (SCI-FI FILM)

Star Trek—The Motion Picture set a new record when it grossed $17 million in its first week in December 1979.

Science-fiction films belong to a motion-picture genre characterized by a plot that involves scientific fantasy. The story is often a tale set in a future time that is visualized through a lavish display of imagined settings and gadgets, and sustained in part by spectacular special effects. The Georges Méliès film *A Trip to the Moon* (1902) is an early notable, albeit primitive, science-fiction film that visualizes future space exploration. Fritz Lang's *Metropolis* (1927) tells a science-fiction tale about an autocratically run city of the future; with it Lang extended the genre into the area of social and philosophical commentary. Similarly, Stanley Kubrick's *2001: A Space Odyssey* (1969) offers philosophical rumination on a futuristic world where the impact of new technology places the fate of humankind in question. Science-fiction films such as *Star Wars* (1977) and *The Empire Strikes Back* (1980) presented futuristic adventure stories that also function as mythic morality tales about confrontations between good and evil.

See Close Encounters of the Third Kind; E.T.; *Special-effects film;* Star Wars; 2001: A Space Odyssey

SCORSESE, MARTIN

Martin Scorsese was born in Queens, New York, on November 17, 1942. Known for dark, gritty films that often contain themes of violence, Roman Catholicism, and isolation, Scorsese is widely regarded as one of the most influential directors of the twentieth century.

When Scorsese was eight, his family moved to Little Italy, the neighborhood that would later provide inspiration for some of Scorsese's best-loved films. A sickly child who earned the nickname "Marty Pills," Scorsese was often left alone while his Italian immigrant parents worked long hours to make ends meet. At fourteen he was set on the path to the priesthood when he entered a seminary on New York's Upper West Side. Scorsese later transferred out of the seminary and upon graduation entered New York University in 1960. At NYU Scorsese met film professor Haig Manoogian, who would provide the single greatest influence on Scorsese's art. Manoogian's philosophy of "individuality and artistry" prompted Scorsese to conclude that his Italian heritage, Catholic faith, and inner turmoil could all be synthesized onscreen. That same year, Scorsese's first student film, *What's a Nice Girl like You Doing in a Place like This?*, received critical acclaim. In 1964 Scorsese's *It's Not Just You, Murray!* was hailed as the finest student film ever made; it was shown at the New York Film Festival two years later and had a brief commercial release.

Scorsese went to graduate school at NYU from 1966 to 1968, where he also taught film courses. He worked steadily in film from 1968 through 1972, producing, editing, and serving as assistant director for such films at *The Big Shave, Woodstock*, and *Who's That Knocking at My Door?* In 1973 Scorsese found fame with his first major film, *Mean Streets*, a dark, autobiographical depiction of life on the streets of Little Italy. His direction of the young Harvey Keitel and Robert De Niro highlights the film, which premiered at the New York Film Festival. Although *Mean Streets* brought Scorsese fame, he found little fortune: royalites for the popular songs he incorporated into the sound track swallowed up the profits.

notable & quotable

"The scenes in *Raging Bull* (and Scorsese's other films), I feel like I'm being a voyeur into a real situation with real people whose dignity and privacy I should respect."

Steven Spielberg, director, 1990, on how intensely and skillfully Scorsese depicts the intimacy of people's lives

S

SCORSESE, MARTIN

In addition to directing such movies as Raging Bull, GoodFellas, *and* Casino, *Martin Scorsese directed the video for Michael Jackson's* Bad, *as well as two television commercials for friend Giorgio Armani.*

▶

In 1974 Scorsese directed Ellen Burstyn to an Oscar in *Alice Doesn't Live Here Anymore*, the story of a widowed homemaker who dreams of being a film actress. Two years later, Scorsese was tapped to make *Taxi Driver* for Columbia Pictures, in part due to his rough treatment of *Mean Streets*. Mounting pressure, a short schedule, little money, and constant rain made the New York shoot tedious, and at one point Scorsese shut down production rather than shoot indoors as the studio requested. Starring Robert De Niro as Travis Bickle, a lonely, one-dimensional man alienated from society, *Taxi Driver* remains one of Scorsese's best known and controversial films. The film achieved additional notoriety when it was revealed it had inspired John Hinckley's assassination attempt on President Ronald Reagan in 1981.

Scorsese released *Raging Bull,* considered by some to be his finest work, in 1980. Shot in gritty black and white, the biography of middleweight fighter Jake LaMotta earned two Oscars (Robert De Niro for Best Actor; Thelma Schoonmaker for Editing) and garnered a Best Director nomination for Scorsese. *Raging Bull* was also selected as the best film of the decade by film critics Gene Siskel and Roger Ebert.

Raging Bull was followed by two dark comedies, *The King of Comedy* (1983) and *After Hours* (1985), which has become somewhat of a cult favorite. In 1986 he revisited *The Hustler*'s "Fast" Eddie Felson in *The Color of Money* (1986), for which Paul Newman won a Best Actor Oscar for his portrayal of Felson. Scorsese outraged some religious groups with his *The Last Temptation of Christ* (1988) before returning to his Italian roots in 1990 with the mob classic *GoodFellas.* Hailed by some as the best Mafia film since *The Godfather*, *GoodFellas* was nominated for a Best Picture Academy Award. His next two films were remakes, *Cape Fear* (1991), again starring De Niro (who also appeared in *GoodFellas*), and Edith Wharton's *The Age of Innocence*, a period piece revolving around a love triangle among repressed nineteenth-century New York aristocrats.

More recently, Scorsese has directed the epic Mafia film *Casino* (1995), *Kundun* (1997), a story about the life of the fourteenth Dalai Lama, and is currently working on *Bringing Out the Dead* (1999) and *Dino*, which traces the life of singer Dean Martin, scheduled for release in 2000.

See De Niro, Robert; GoodFellas; Raging Bull; *Remake;* Taxi Driver

SCREEN ACTORS GUILD

The Screen Actors Guild (SAG) is the union composed of actors who perform in movies, television, industrial and educational videos, and television commercials. Its goal is to protect its members and actively nurture employment opportunities.

In the first few decades of Hollywood, studios essentially owned their stars, considering them long-term investments. Studios would bind the actors to seven-year contracts, and once they found a successful role for a star, they would use him or her over and over again, trying to capitalize (literally) on that type of role. Imagine if Jodie Foster, after winning her Oscar for *Silence of the Lambs*, was only allowed to play cops, detectives, or federal agents. Or what if Tom Cruise were punished for refusing a role by being loaned out to another studio—forced to do a lousy movie? When Betty Davis refused a role, Warner's suspended her and then tacked the duration of her suspension on to her contract. Olivia de Havilland had to go to court to fight the extension of her contract. It was out of this kind of strife that the Screen Actors Guild was born.

Suffering from the effects of the Great Depression, movie revenues in 1933 were down one third from four years previous, forcing almost a third of the country's theaters to close down. When President Roosevelt's bank moratorium came in March of 1933, the Academy of Motion Picture Arts and Sciences suggested an across-the-board salary cut of 50 percent for all studio employees. This propelled a group of about twenty actors to action. With money from their own pockets, a couple of the actors paid the incorporation fee and, endangering their careers, created the Screen Actors Guild. Only a few character actors joined following the inception.

Later in 1933 the National Industrial Recovery Act was passed in Washington. The proposed code of regulation for the entertainment industry was purported to contain salary limits on actors' wages and granted studios the ability to unilaterally extend an actor's contract and license agents. Several famous actors joined SAG immediately—Jeanette MacDonald, Gary Cooper, Paul Muni, and James Cagney—boosting its power. Led by then-president Eddie Cantor, SAG lobbied Washington and helped protect the actors from proposed abuses.

Although the studios acknowledged SAG, they still ran an open shop; that is, not all actors had to be members of SAG. Because the actors represented a higher percentage of a film's cost than the craft unions, the studios were less lenient in acceding to SAG's demands. Finally, on May 15, 1937, with the threat of a strike on their hands, the producers recognized SAG's jurisdiction and set up guild shops—meaning they could use only SAG actors. Several notable people who joined soon after the decision were Rosalind Russell, Betty Grable, and John Barrymore. In line at the beautiful French Manor on Sunset, the new SAG headquarters, amid the hundreds of other actors, were, the press reported, Jean Harlow and Greta Garbo.

Over the years, SAG has fought for television residuals, pension and health plans for its members, and antidiscrimination policies. In the late 1960s, acknowledging a movement in lower-budgeted filmmaking (which parallels the "indie" movement in the 1990s), SAG negotiated contracts that were suited for lower budgets so that more actors could work and practice their craft.

See Academy of Motion Pictures; Acting; Director; Writer

SCREWBALL COMEDY

A screwball comedy is a brand of comic film that originated in the mid-1930s, characterized by a zany, fast-paced, and often irreverent view of domestic or romantic conflicts that ultimately are happily resolved. Witty repartee and unlikely situations were also elements of the screwball comedy. This type of film offered escapism for Depression-era audiences.

Frank Capra's *It Happened One Night* (1934) is often cited as the film that typifies the genre. Its plot involves Claudette Colbert (a wealthy heiress), who, running away from home, encounters Clark Gable (a disguised newspaperman) on a bus traveling from Miami to New York. The newspaperman's abrasive confidence and the heiress's uppity ways lead to battles of wit and eventually to romance. Capra and Howard Hawks were considered the masters of the screwball comedy. In Hawks's *His Girl Friday* (1940) Rosalind Russell, a star reporter, and Cary Grant, a wisecracking editor, are also caught up in the sex-antagonism game, hurling verbal barbs at each other but eventually succumbing to romance.

Peter Bogdanovich revived the elements and style of the screwball comedy for *What's Up, Doc?* (1972). Barbra Streisand and Ryan O'Neal star as a couple whose zany, eccentric behavior has its counterpart in the madcap films of the 1930s. Lawrence Kasdan's *Continental Divide* (1981) script also contains screwball elements in its story of a brash young newspaperman's (John Belushi) encounter with a beautiful ornithologist (Blair Brown).

See Capra, Frank; Comedy; Hawks, Howard; It Happened One Night; *Slapstick comedy*

"Listen, you insignificant, square-toed, pimple-headed spy. . . ."

Cary Grant as Walter Burns in the screwball comedy *His Girl Friday* (1940)

SEARCHERS, THE

Like Hitchcock's *Vertigo* (1958) and Welles's *Touch of Evil* (1958), John Ford's *The Searchers* (1956) was little noticed in its own day—it received not one Oscar nomination—yet gradually earned a reputation as the masterpiece of one of America's great auteurs.

The film's narrative begins in 1868. In the opening shot Ethan Edwards (played by John Wayne in one of his most acclaimed performances) is seen through an opening in a cabin door as he trudges toward a cabin, a weary figure in a shabby Rebel coat finally returning home three years after the end of the Civil War. He is greeted exultantly by his brother, Aaron Edwards (Walter McCoy), Aaron's wife, Martha (Dorothy Jordan), their older daughter, Lucy (Pippa Scott), the younger daughter, Debbie (Lana Wood), and their teenage son, Ben (Robert Leyden). Barely recognizing his adoring nieces and nephew, Ethan, his mystique enhanced by rumors that he might have been involved in bank robberies, bestows a war medal on Debbie.

At dinner they are joined by Martin Pawley (Jeffrey Hunter), whom Ethan rescued from the Indians who killed Martin's parents when he was a child. Raised lovingly by Aaron, Martin is kept at arm's length by Ethan because of the young man's one-eighth Cherokee heritage. The homecoming meal is interrupted by the arrival of a posse headed by Samuel Clayton (Ward Bond), a preacher and officer in the Texas Rangers; they need reinforcements in their hunt for cattle stolen by Indians from the neighboring farm of Lars Jorgensen (John Qualen). As Aaron and Ethan prepare to leave, Samuel notices a moment of passing affection between Ethan and his sister-in-law, Martha.

John Wayne portrays Ethan Edwards, a Civil War veteran who embarks on a relentless search for his kidnapped niece in John Ford's The Searchers.

▼

When the posse sees Lars's best bull lying slaughtered, they realize that the cattle theft was just a diversion to lure the men away from their homes. Most of the posse races back to Lars's place, while Martin, ignoring Ethan's warning that the tired horses need rest, gallops off to the Edwardses' cabin, where young Lucy, sensing the imminent carnage, screams in terror. Hoping to save ten-year-old Debbie, they send her off to hide behind a gravestone, where she is abducted by a Comanche warrior, Scar (Henry Brandon). In an attempt to spare little Lucy the horror of an Indian attack, her parents give her a blanket and her doll and instruct the child to hide behind her grandmother's tombstone nearby. Martin's horse having succumbed to fatigue, Ethan and his friend Mose Harper (Hank Worden) arrive first back at the farm to find that the entire family has been slaughtered except for Debbie and Lucy, who have been abducted.

After Martin arrives, the three rejoin the posse to rescue the girls. Although the rangers retreat from an armed encounter with the Comanches, Ethan, Martin, and Ben, the girls' shaken brother, press on with the search by themselves and soon make the grisly discovery of Lucy's sexually ravaged corpse. Driven mad by the sight, Ben gallops recklessly into the Comanche camp and is killed. The search is now left to Ethan and Martin.

Weeks of searching turn into months, with Ethan's expertise about the Indians proving unavailing. Martin's respect for Ethan is tempered by his realization that Ethan's bitter racism will lead him to kill Debbie because of her defilement by the Comanches.

Through a swirl of seasonal cycles, the months stretch into years, and the two weary, stymied searchers finally retreat to the Jorgensen farm, where Laurie Jorgensen (Vera Miles), long enamored of Martin, tries to convince him to abandon their quest, but she is frustrated when Martin and Ethan latch onto a shred of hope in the form of a report from a merchant named Futterman, who bought a child's dress from an Indian. To protect Debbie from Ethan's punitive rage, Martin insists on joining him on the trail once again despite Laurie's threat to break off with him.

The pair track down Futterman, who, after extorting cash, tells them that Debbie is part of the Comanche tribe headed by Scar. After warding off a sneak attack by Futterman and two associates later that night, they head back to the trail, where Martin unwittingly purchases an Indian wife (much to the dismay of Laurie, reading about these events in a letter from Martin). When they ask her about Scar, however, the Indian woman flees, and they later find her among the dead in a Comanche settlement that has been wiped out in a U.S. Cavalry attack.

Seeking information at the Cavalry outpost, Ethan and Martin are shown three women who were driven to madness by prolonged captivity in Indian settlements. His wrath rekindled, Ethan leads Martin to New Mexico Territory, where they encounter a Mexican who offers to lead them to Scar in exchange for cash.

"Ate dirt, chewed grass. I fooled 'em, Ethan."

Hank Worden as Mose Harper on his experience with the Commanche Indians in *The Searchers* (1956)

Ethan and Martin are granted a meeting with Scar, who brandishes the many scalps he has collected in retribution for the murder of his sons by white men. They notice the full-grown Debbie (Natalie Wood) standing nearby but await the opportune moment to spirit her away. Martin warns Ethan against any attempt to do her harm, and while the two men argue, Debbie rushes toward them and, speaking fluent English, avows that despite her fond memories of her previous life she now considers herself a Comanche, and she implores them to leave her with her people. Ethan cannot bear to hear these words, and as he draws his gun to kill her, a band of Comanche warriors attack, wounding Ethan with an arrow. They escape to safety, with Martin tempted to kill Ethan for having threatened Debbie's life.

Realizing they will need reinforcements for the rescue, the pair once again retreats to Lars's farm, where Laurie, having despaired of seeing Martin again, is about to marry the far less desirable Charlie. At the sight of Martin, however, she falls into his arms, provoking a farcical melee between the groom and Martin and leading to the wedding's cancellation.

Just as Samuel shows up at the farm threatening to arrest Ethan for the murder of Futterman and his two friends, a Cavalry officer rides up and drops off Mose, who has escaped from the Comanches and knows where Scar is. Fearing for Debbie's safety, he withholds the information from Ethan but divulges it to Martin, and he, Ethan, and Samuel's men set out for the Indian encampment. Martin volunteers to rescue her to avoid endangering her in a mass shootout; as he enters her tent, he sees Scar approaching and shoots him dead. The gunfire spurs an attack by Ethan and the Rangers; the implacable Ethan cuts the scalp from Scar's corpse. He then sights the fleeing Debbie, catches up with her, and as she sprawls to her feet beneath him, his menacing hatred dissolves into love and compassion as he gathers her into his arms and says, "Let's go home, Debbie."

Back at the Jorgensens' farm, Debbie is let into the house, Martin and Laurie lock in an embrace, and Ethan lingers outside the house before heading back onto the trail as the closing door fades the screen to black.

See Ford, John; Western

SENNETT, MACK

The most important events in the career of Mack Sennett—his days with D. W. Griffith at Biograph, his formation of Keystone, and his development of Charlie Chaplin, Fatty Arbuckle, and Mabel Normand as major stars—were already history by 1915.

SENNETT, MACK

Mack Sennett, nicknamed "The King of Comedy," was awarded a special Oscar in 1937 "for his lasting contribution to the comedy technique of the screen."

Keystone, which began as a comedy producer in 1912, had long since passed the days when its product could be assembled more or less off the cuff. Supporters of the early Keystone films might have prized Sennett's air of improvisation above all else, but by 1915 the requirements of a heavy release schedule had turned his studio into a "fun factory" in the fullest sense of that term. While Thomas Ince has been given credit for organizing production at his studio, Mack Sennett's achievement at Keystone was no less remarkable. In fact, Sennett devised a method of delegating production authority that not only maintained the quality standard of his releases but transmitted their characteristic style and subject matter as well, to create Hollywood's most consistent studio look.

In 1915 the journalist Harry Carr visited the Sennett lot and observed this system in action. According to Carr, Sennett started with a rough scenario, hardly more than an idea, which he had thrashed out in committee with his writers. Kalton Lahue, the author of several volumes on Sennett and Keystone, reproduces one of these documents, called "Aeroplane Elopement Story," which begins as follows: "Roscoe leaves aeroplane near clump of bushes and goes to girl. Establish a love affair in opening scene between Roscoe and the girl—get over that her father is trying to marry her off owing to her ferocious temper or something."

Using such a document as a guide, Sennett gathered together actors and crew and began breaking down the action and indicating, with chalk marks on the floor of the studio, where players, cameras, and props should be positioned. A stenographer followed, taking down every word of his instructions. The next day these notes would be handed to a "subdirector" on location, who would do his best to execute the plan.

In the cutting room, Sennett studied incoming footage intently, twitching in his chair or spitting if anything displeased him. Changes of pace and characterization had no place in Sennett's scheme, so Charlie Chaplin went elsewhere to develop his talents. Over the years, he was followed by a string of others—Fatty Arbuckle, Harry Langdon, gagman Frank Capra—because Sennett had no interests in their efforts to craft comedy to character, and either fired them or allowed them to leave. When running a fun factory, what was needed were interchangeable parts. A fat man, a baggy pants comic with a cane, a baby-faced innocent—to Sennett these were types, clowns who needed only to remember where he had put the chalk marks. By the end of the silent era, Mack Sennett's fun factor was mired in its own rust belt.

See Chaplin, Charlie; Comedy; Griffith, D. W.; Ince, Thomas

SEQUEL

A sequel is a motion picture that continues in narrative development a story begun in a previous motion picture. Sequels are usually inspired by the success of an earlier film and seek to capitalize on the established appeal of the earlier work. The sequel remains a staple of production studios, for which guaranteed mass-audience appeal has always been of utmost consideration. With fewer films being produced during the 1970s and 1980s, the number of film sequels increased significantly: *The Godfather* and *The Godfather, Parts II* and *III; Jaws, Jaws II,* and *Jaws: The Revenge; Walking Tall* and

The Godfather: Part II, starring Robert De Niro as a young Vito Corleone, is the only sequel to ever win the Academy Award for Best Picture.

Walking Tall, Part II; True Grit and *Rooster Cogburn and His Lady; The French Connection* and *The French Connection II.*

See Prequel; Remake

SERIAL

A serial is a type "short-subject" motion picture that developed as early as 1905 (*Mirthful Mary*) and is characterized principally by the episodic development of a story presented in installments over a period of several weeks. The serial, especially popular in the 1920s, 1930s, and 1940s, engaged audience interest in a hero or heroine whose exploits reached an unresolved crisis at the end of each episode. This plotting gimmick sustained interest from week to week. The predominant style of the serial is melodrama, and plot lines are usually variations of popular film types: science fiction (*Flash Gordon*), romance (*Gloria's Romance*), action-adventure (*The Perils of Pauline*), mystery-thriller (*Charlie Chan*). Serials remained popular with motion-picture audiences until production ceased in the early 1950s, a time when the serial became a mainstay of television programming (*Superman*). *Raiders of the Lost Ark* (1981) and its sequels, *Indiana Jones and the Temple of Doom* (1984) and *Indiana Jones and the Last Crusade* (1989), recapture some of the qualities of the serial, such as periodic last-minute rescues.

See Shorts

SHANE

Shane opens as a golden-haired lone rider travels through the wilderness of 1880s Wyoming. An innocent blue-eyed boy, Joey (Brandon de Wilde), is tracking a deer with a gun when he spots the rider. Joey yells to his father, Joe Starrett (Van Heflin), who is chopping a huge tree stump on his settlement, that someone is coming.

The stranger, Shane (Alan Ladd), arrives, and although he carries two fancy pistols, he politely asks Joe for permission to cross his land. When Joey cocks his rifle, Shane, in a flash, draws his gun and turns; his instincts belie his calm exterior. Even Joey senses Shane is a weathered gunfighter; he asks Shane if he can shoot. Shane replies: "Little bit."

Suspicious of Shane, Joe warns him off with Joey's gun. Shane leaves just as Rufe Ryker (Emile Meyer) and his posse ride up to warn Joe to get off the land. Joe and the burgeoning community have built fences, but Ryker needs the full range to let his cattle graze. Ryker hints at the threat of force, but Shane returns and silently stands behind Joe, lending him support. When Ryker asks who Shane is, Shane replies that he is a friend of Joe's, and Ryker leaves. Joe apologizes to Shane for having pointed Joey's gun at him, and shows him that the gun was not even loaded.

Shane stays for dinner and Joe explains that Ryker will have to kill him before he gets off the land. Joe's wife, Marion (Jean Arthur), disapproves of this type of talk in front of Joey. Although Marion hates the violence and vigilante-style justice that Shane represents and stirs up in Joe, she and Shane share a growing unspoken attraction through the film. Even Joe notices that she uses her fancy dinnerware. Shane walks out into the yard and chops at the tree stump Joe was working on. A montage sequence of Marion and Shane rhythmically working together suggests the strength in their union. Shane sees an opportunity to give up his gunfighting and Joe sees a hired hand to help him conquer the terrain of the wilderness. And young Joey begins to idolize Shane, even comparing him to his father.

Deciding to stay, Shane puts away his guns and heads into town to buy some work clothes to replace his gunfighter garb. He walks into the adjacent bar to get Joey a soda pop. Calloway (Ben Johnson), one of Ryker's men, teases him for ordering a child's drink and calls him a smelly sod-

Alan Ladd portrays Shane, a former gunfighter who comes to the defense of homesteaders and is idolized by their son (Brandon De Wilde) in George Stevens's Shane.

buster. Calloway also throws whiskey on him and tells him to leave. As hard as it is for him, Shane averts a fight and calmly leaves.

Later, a group of settlers has gathered at Joe's house to discuss Ryker's threats. One of them mistakes Shane's pacifist behavior for cowardice and says that he can't be trusted. Embarrassed, Shane leaves them alone and walks outside into the rain. From the bedroom window, Joey and Marion tell Shane they know he wasn't afraid. Marion warns Joey (and inadvertently herself) not to get too attached to Shane, who will eventually have to leave. At the meeting, a stubborn ex-Confederate, Stonewall Torrey (Elisha Cook Jr.), refuses to be intimidated by Ryker, claiming that his .38 caliber revolver gives him license to go to town alone anytime he wants.

When the settlers travel into town together for safety, Shane breaks off from the group to return Joey's soda bottle. When Calloway picks on Shane again, Shane beats him up, with Joey watching, full of adulation. Afterward, Shane refuses a job offer from Ryker, causing Ryker's men to surround Shane. Although he is outnumbered, Shane begins to fight, but soon is losing. Joey gets his father to help Shane, and together they defeat Ryker's men.

Ryker raises the stakes by recruiting Wilson (Jack Palance), a murderous gunfighter from Cheyenne. Ryker then runs his cattle through the farmers' land, hoping to provoke a fight that Wilson will end.

Joey's fondness for Shane grows, and he tells his mother that he loves Shane almost as much as he loves Pa. Teaching Joey how to shoot, Shane reveals his quick draw and good aim. Marion is upset, so Shane explains to her that a gun is a tool that is "as good or as bad as the man using it."

The settlers hold a Fourth of July dance, ironically celebrating the independence that Ryker is attempting to squelch. The Starretts also celebrate their tenth wedding anniversary, and Joe says that he wouldn't trade places with any man. Shane and Marion dance, and Joe notices their subtle affinity.

"Joey, there's no living with a killing. There's no going back from it. Right or wrong, it's a brand, a brand that sticks. There's no going back."

Alan Ladd as Shane in *Shane* (1953)

Ryker, accompanied by Wilson, shows up at the Starretts' with an offer to buy Joe's land. Shane and Wilson stoically stare each other down. Ryker argues that he helped to tame this wilderness, so he has rights to the land. Joe says Indians and trappers helped tame the land too, and now the settlers have rights too.

In town, Wilson taunts Stonewall into drawing on him, and effortlessly guns him down. At Stonewall's funeral many of the homesteaders plan to leave for good. Joe rallies them with a speech declaring that raising children is more important than raising cattle. When Ryker burns down one of the settler's houses, Joe is ready to strap on a gun and face Ryker.

A messenger comes to tell Joe that Ryker wants to talk with him. Calloway has a change of heart and warns Shane that Joe will be in danger when he meets Ryker. Marion protests, even pleading with Shane (back in his gunfighting garb) to stop Joe from going. Joe is willing to revert to violence, but Shane knows it will mean Joe's death. Shane offers to go instead of Joe, but Joe stubbornly refuses. In an effort to save Joe from certain death at Ryker's hands, Shane drags Joe off his horse, and a tense cinematic knockdown drag-out fight rages until Shane knocks Joe out with the butt of his gun. Not understanding Shane's motives, Joey tells Shane that he hates him. Marion asks Shane if he's doing it for her, and he replies that he's doing it for all of them. Already a tainted killer and an outsider, Shane allows Joe to remain a family man in the civilized realm where Shane does not belong.

Shane then heads into town to negotiate a deal with Ryker, unaware that Joey has followed him. Shane admits to Ryker that both of their days are numbered, but the difference is that Shane is aware of the fact. Joey watches as Shane beats Ryker's sidekick Wilson to the draw, and then turns and kills Ryker as well. Then suddenly Joey alerts Shane to a hidden gunman, and Shane is able to kill this man, too, but not before being wounded by this last gunman. In the film's final scene, Joey apologizes to Shane and asks him to come back. Shane says that there is no going back from a killing. He tells Joey good-bye and rides off into the distance over Joey's cries begging him to come back.

See Western

SHORTS (SHORT SUBJECTS)

Brief films shown as part of a theatrical motion-picture program, usually preceding the presentation of the feature film, are called shorts. Shorts, along with previews, newsreels, and cartoons, were used extensively as filler material when motion-picture programs were repeated every two hours and the standard length of the feature was approximately ninety minutes. After 1960 shorts became rarer in motion-picture houses as programming concepts changed and as exhibitors reacted to the extra cost of renting short-subject films.

See Serial

SILENCE OF THE LAMBS, THE

The Silence of the Lambs joins *It Happened One Night* and *One Flew Over the Cuckoo's Nest* as one of the only three films to sweep all five major Academy Awards. *The Silence of the Lambs* has a complexity that belies its B-movie plot of serial killers and FBI agents. To save a young woman from her imminent death, the heroine, Clarice Starling, must go beyond the masculine rationality of computers and personality tests and trust her intuition, an evil psychotic, and her ability to listen.

An FBI trainee, Starling (Jodie Foster) is called to the office of her boss and mentor, Jack Crawford (Scott Glenn). As she waits for him to arrive, she notices a bulletin board full of graphic pictures of mutilated women and the prominent headline: "Buffalo Bill Skins Fifth." Crawford offers the

S

SILENCE OF THE LAMBS, THE

Anthony Hopkins won an Oscar for his portrayal of the brilliant and cunning yet psychotic Dr. Hannibal Lecter in The Silence of the Lambs. *Costar Jodie Foster won for Best Actress, and the film also won Oscars for Best Picture and for its director, Jonathan Demme.*

bright young student the chance to do a routine interview with a not-so-routine subject—famed psychiatrist-turned-serial-killer Hannibal "The Cannibal" Lecter (Anthony Hopkins).

A self-serving, smug Dr. Frederick Chilton (Anthony Heald), head of the institution that houses Lecter, leads her down to the literal dungeon where Lecter is kept. She is given many warnings about the danger of Lecter, even though he will be locked in his cell during Starling's visit. Chilton, the self-admitted nemesis of Lecter, is perceptive enough to figure that Crawford may have dubious motives in sending Starling, a "pretty young woman to turn (Lecter) on. . . . and, oh, are you ever his taste." Before allowing Starling to go see him he shows her a picture of a mauled nurse that Lecter attacked while in the infirmary.

The power of Lecter's introduction is understatement: he calmly stands there waiting for her. Insulted that Crawford would send a trainee, he eventually accepts her challenge to decide for himself whether she's worthy of his attention. Lecter is portrayed as a civilized animal: outraged at an adjacent patient's offensive behavior toward Starling, yet also able to sniff the fact that she "wears L'air du Temps, but not today." Impressed by her candor and frankness when he asks her embarrassing, difficult questions, when Starling broaches the subject of Buffalo Bill, Lecter offers her his help in finding the killer in exchange for a chance at even a view at the outside world.

Starling's experience with this startling father figure, who in an instant pegged her roots—one generation away from poor white trash—is so intense that she has a quick flashback to her father coming home from work as a policeman. She breaks down crying at her car, but, in mirroring Starling's resilience and strength, the film jarringly cuts to her at the shooting range.

Starling later learns that Lecter talked the psychopath in the adjacent cell into killing himself by swallowing his tongue, and she cleverly figures out a puzzle-like clue that Lecter gave her, which leads her to one of Buffalo Bill's first victims. She now knows Lecter can help her find Buffalo Bill. Lecter offers to do a psychological profile of Buffalo Bill in exchange for a chance to see daylight, but what he really yearns for is to get inside Starling's head, to hear about her pain and to connect with her in a psychiatrist-patient fashion. It is their courageous candor that intrigues each of them about the other.

The scene shifts, and for the first time we get a glimpse of Buffalo Bill (Jeff Levine). Like a nocturnal predator, he uses infrared-type goggles to spot his prey, a young woman, Catherine Martin (Brooke Smith), whom he lures into his van by pretending to need help.

When another of Buffalo Bill's victim's bodies shows up, Starling and Crawford go to West Virginia to investigate. On the way, Starling gets Crawford to admit that he had sent her in to see Lecter with a secret motive: to discover information about Buffalo Bill. He then condescendingly explains to her that it was for the best; otherwise Lecter would have caught on and withheld information. This irony of character is what contributes to this movie's psychological complexity. The "good" father figure (Crawford) lies, has dubious motives, puts Starling in harm's way, condescends to her, and subtly undermines her career, whereas the "evil" father figure (Lecter) is honest, genuine, and helpful in advancing her career.

In West Virginia, Starling is literally surrounded by policemen who hover over her and gape at her, almost like predators themselves. Crawford uses a sexist put-down aimed at Starling to bolster his relationship with the

"A census taker once tried to test me. I ate his liver with some fava beans and a nice Chianti."

Anthony Hopkins as Dr. Hannibal Lecter in *The Silence of the Lambs* (1991)

local sheriff. Later, he tries to rationalize his reason for being sexist, but she reminds him that as a role model, his behavior does matter. Later, at the autopsy of this latest victim, they find that there are two diamond-shaped patches cut out of the victim's buttocks. They also find a moth in her throat, which later is revealed to be a sign of the killer's "transformation."

The moth leads Starling to the Museum of Natural History, where two nerdy scientists identify it as the Death's head moth, which is only found in Asia. One of the scientists gently flirts with her, and when she asks him if he is hitting on her, he candidly says yes. There's a genuineness to him that she shares with no other male in her life, other than Lecter.

The scene shifts back to Buffalo Bill, and we see the chambers where he raises moths. We also see female mannequins and a naked Buffalo Bill, facing away from us, working at a sewing machine. We hear ignored screams for help in the background.

On the news we find that the kidnapped woman is Catherine Martin, daughter of a senator. Starling comes to Lecter with a deal: in exchange for the safe return of Catherine, the senator will transfer him to a place that will allow him to spend some time outside. In exchange for Starling's being open and vulnerable to him, he gives her some logical information that may help her find Buffalo Bill. But we see that Chilton, jealous of their burgeoning relationship and Starling's ability to learn from Lecter, listens in on their conversation.

There is a quick scene of Buffalo Bill hovering over Catherine, who is being held at the bottom of a well. He demands—for reasons we'll find out later—that she rub lotion on her body.

Finding out that Starling's offer was a bluff, the self-serving Chilton negotiates a real deal for Lecter. Lecter says he will tell Senator Martin the identity of Buffalo Bill only in Tennessee. Chilton and a horde of armed guards escort Lecter to Tennessee to see Senator Martin. Lecter gives out some information, but presses the senator with hurtful personal questions.

Lecter is held temporarily in Tennessee where Starling comes to him and essentially finishes her "therapy": she tells him of the horrible pain and memories she has of growing up on her uncle's farm after her father died and not being able to stop the screaming lambs from going to slaughter. Lecter asks her if saving Catherine Martin will silence the lambs, and Starling admits that she doesn't know. Authorities drag her away from Lecter, but not before he assures her that all the information she needs to solve the case is in the case file. After she leaves, Lecter capitalizes on a mistake Chilton made and escapes, utilizing his skills: cannibalism, skinning of flesh, and wit.

With help from her female friend, information from the case file, and insight from Lecter, Starling figures out that the only body Buffalo Bill tried to hide from authorities was his first female victim, Fredrica Bimmel, who must have been someone he knew and who must have lived near him.

She goes to the Bimmel home in Belvedere, Ohio, where Fredrica's father allows Clarice to look at her bedroom, although he doesn't know what she'll find that the police haven't already found. Using intuition and the understanding of a psychology of a young girl, Starling finds a secret compartment in Fredrica's jewelry box that contains Polaroid pictures of her posing in her undergarments. A meow turns Starling's attention to a cat, leading her to an adjacent sewing room, where Starling notices a half-made outfit with a diamond-shaped piece of material over the buttocks area. Putting the puzzle together, she immediately gets Crawford on the phone and explains the killer's symbolic transformation into a woman by sewing together a suit made of his female victims' skins. That explains why he picks overweight girls; he starves them for a few days so their skin will loosen up. Crawford tells Starling that he and a team of agents are on their way to Illinois to the suspect's house. They located him with help from a computer search and information provided to Starling by Lecter. Starling is disappointed that she can't help to apprehend Buffalo Bill, but Crawford reassures her that her help was indispensable.

After Starling speaks with a former friend of Fredrica's, she goes to a house where she might be able to get more information. Starling's way of finding information by listening and using her intuition differs from the cold calculating computer Crawford uses, and it will be these same skills she will need to save Catherine

A title superimposed on the screen in front of a house says "Calumet City, Illinois." The film cuts to the inside—and we assume it's the inside of the house we've just seen—to Buffalo Bill's dungeon-like basement. He is enraged because Catherine has lured his dog into the well and is threatening to hurt it if Bill doesn't let her go. It's no coincidence that when we first saw Catherine she was singing along to Tom Petty's "American Girl." Director Jonathan Demme seems to be creating an archetype—in many ways not unlike Starling—of women as not only helpful and spunky but resourceful, strong, and full of inner courage.

In Illinois the FBI surrounds the house and rings the doorbell. Inside Bill's basement, the buzzer rings. The next moment is one of the greatest surprises in the history of film. When Bill opens the door, there is Starling, alone at his doorstep. The FBI has broken into the wrong house—it's empty.

Starling begins questioning Buffalo Bill, and although she's not sure if it's he, when she sees a moth like the one found in the throat of one of the victims, she pulls her gun, causing Bill to run away, down into his labyrinthine basement. Starling follows him. Eventually he turns off the power, leaving Starling completely unable to see in the darkness. Most of this next scene takes place from his point of view, through the green tint of the night goggles. He follows her, only inches away, yet even when she is facing him, she cannot see him. At the moment Bill clicks his trigger to

"You know what you look like to me, with your good bag and your cheap shoes? You look like a rube. A well-scrubbed, hustling rube with a little taste."

Anthony Hopkins as Dr. Hannibal Lecter in *The Silence of the Lambs* (1991)

shoot Starling, she turns and shoots him first. Her intuition and her sense of hearing allow her to succeed.

Crawford congratulates Starling at her FBI commencement, saying that her father would have been proud. At the celebration afterward, Starling gets a phone call from Lecter, still at large, who assures her that he enjoys the world more "with her in it." He then tells her that he is having an old friend for dinner: at a tropical airport, Lecter follows an unsuspecting Dr. Chilton into the crowd.

See Hopkins, Anthony

SINGIN' IN THE RAIN

Singin' in the Rain (1952), directed and choreographed by Gene Kelly and Stanley Donen, remains today one of the finest musicals ever produced. Its numerous lavish dance sequences showcase the talents of Gene Kelly and Donald O'Connor. The story revolves around the introduction of the "talkie" and the ensuing demise of the silent film star.

At the premier of Don Lockwood (Gene Kelly) and Lina Lamont's (Jean Hagen) latest film, *The Royal Rascal*, billed as the biggest picture of 1927, crowds await the arrival of the two stars, who are falsely perceived as being romantically linked. Don obliges an interviewer outside the theater and spins a concocted "Hollywood" version of his rise to movie stardom while the images of his real story undercuts his tale. A journeyman fiddle player who played the vaudeville circuit with his sidekick, Cosmo Brown (Donald O'Connor), Don eventually lands on the lot of Monumental Pictures. Don's big break occurs when he steps in for an stuntman injured on the set and performs so admirably that he is hired for a series of improbable, death-defying stunts. Studio head R. F. Simpson (Millard Mitchell) is so impressed that he offers Don a contract for a leading role. It is here that Lockwood and Lamont first meet.

Backstage after the premier, Don fields all reporters' questions in an effort to protect the illusion of Lina as a refined starlet, because when she speaks it's revealed that she has a shrill voice and an uneducated manner. Even after the reporters leave, Lina claims—as the tabloids do—that Don is her fiancée, although Don clearly wants no part of this charade. Later when Don acrobatically flees from a mob of admirers, destiny plops him into the car of a startled Kathy Selden (Debbie Reynolds). She coolly pretends not to recognize him and rebuffs him as he professes the loneliness that accompanies his movie star status. Kathy discredits his acting ability

Milk was used to create the rain in Gene Kelly's Singin' in the Rain, *regarded as perhaps the greatest musical of all time.*

and claims that she is going on to the dignified stage of New York. Don is clearly affected by her words and confides in Cosmo that he questions his own acting ability.

At a studio party R. F. Simpson announces the advent of a new technology, talking pictures, and (incorrectly) predicts the financial ruin of rival Warner Brothers from their release of the first talkie, *The Jazz Singer*. Kathy's true profession is revealed when she pops out of a cake and performs a dance number. Afterward, Don confronts an embarrassed Kathy and mockingly discredits her acting abilities. Lina jealously confronts the couple, causing Kathy to storm out and Don to chase after her.

Reacting to the runaway success of *The Jazz Singer*, R. F. closes down production of the latest Lockwood and Lamont movie, *The Dualing Cava-*

lier, so it can be made into a talkie. Meanwhile, R. F. spots Kathy performing a musical number and decides to cast her in a lead. Kathy finds herself alone with Don and questions the veracity of the myriad tabloid accounts of Lockwood and Lamont's romance, but in doing so reveals her own infatuation with motion pictures, its stars, and the encompassing gossip. Soon Kathy and Don make their affection for each other known, as he croons "You Were Meant for Me."

Diction lessons provide great comedy as Lina repeatedly blows the classic line "and I caaan't stan' 'im." In contrast, Don and Cosmo derisively play along with their coach and break into one of the silliest numbers of the movie ("Moses supposes his toeses are roses"). Upon refilming the talking version of *The Dueling Cavalier*, it is apparent that Lina's diction lessons were for naught, and the logistics of recording sound becomes a comedic yet problematic chore. Predictably, the preview of *The Dueling Cavalier* is an unmitigated flop. As crowds jeer the movie's many technical problems and Lina's real and unsavory voice, R. F proclaims, "We're ruined."

"Why, I make more money than . . . than Calvin Coolidge—put together."

Jean Hagen as Lina Lamont in *Singin' in the Rain* (1952)

Later that night as Cosmo and Kathy console Don about his recent flop and possibly bleak acting future, they concoct a scheme to save *The Dualing Cavalier* by making it into a musical. However, there is one glitch: Lina's cacophonous voice. Cosmo has a sudden epiphany that they could surreptitiously dub Kathy's mellifluous voice over Lina's. After saying goodnight to Kathy, a delighted Don, unfazed by the morning rain, breaks into the movie's title song. Using his umbrella as a prop, he splashes through the city sidewalk in what is the most memorable dance sequence in the history of movies, rivaled only by Cosmo's "Make 'em Laugh" number.

Don and Cosmo reveal their plan to make the musical (renamed *The Dancing Cavalier*) to R. F. This also provides a vehicle to allow for the movie's most extravagant and protracted dance sequence, replete with flapper girls, mobsters and a seductive Cyd Charisse. The tale about a young hoofer who comes to Broadway looking for fame mirrors Don's rise to fame and is played out in a dreamlike sequence.

Back at the studio, while Kathy rerecords Lina's parts, Lina catches Don professing his love for Kathy. Cosmo claims that Lina will soon be exposed and that Kathy will receive full credit for her vocals. An enraged Lina uses her publicity machine to proclaim that it is entirely her own voice throughout the movie. Furthermore, Lina informs R. F. that a contract loophole obliges the studio to forever employ Kathy in the unheralded role as the voice of Lina. Amidst R. F.'s objections, Lina shrewdly threatens to "sue"—comically mispronouncing the word.

The Dancing Cavalier premieres and this version is a smash, wildly applauded by the audience. Backstage after the show, Lina confronts Don, Kathy, and R. F. about using Kathy as her voice. Lina's undoing comes about during a curtain call. When she condescendingly addresses the audience in her own voice, quizzical spectators request that she sing. Panicked, Lina rushes off stage. Don and R. F. coerce Kathy into assisting Lina. Disheartened, Kathy complies but vows it is the last time. As Lina mouths "Singin' in the Rain" to the backstage Kathy's vocals, Don, Cosmo, and R. F. lift the curtain to reveal Lina as a fraud and Kathy as the true talent. As a disconcerted and embarrassed Kathy flees the theater, Don heralds her as a true star and serenades her.

The movie closes as Don and Kathy embrace in front of the billboard for *Singin' in the Rain*, starring Don and Kathy, cleverly revealing the movie within the movie.

See Clockwork Orange, A; Jazz Singer, The; *Musical film; Sound*

SISKEL, GENE

Eugene Kal Siskel was born on January 26, 1946, on the northside of Chicago. One of the world's most famous film critics, Siskel's twenty-five-year partnership, albeit an uneasy one, with Roger Ebert helped to bring film criticism into the mainstream. Their trademarked "thumbs-up" and "thumbs-down" were indelible icons for millions of discerning moviegoers across the United States.

Although Ebert and Siskel eventually became friends, there was always legitimate conflict between them. Siskel graduated from Yale with a philosophy degree and started at the *Chicago Tribune* in 1969. A fierce competitor, within a year Siskel became the full-time film critic for the *Tribune* with the goal of (in his own words) "knocking off" Ebert, who was the hot-shot film critic for the competing *Chicago Sun-Times*. Even just weeks before his death, after taking a sabbatical from which he never returned, Siskel made a public statement announcing his intention to recover quickly because he did not want Roger to get more screen time than he.

It was 1975 when Siskel and Ebert joined forces for a public television show called *Opening Soon at a Theater Near You*, which later evolved into *Sneak Previews*. The original show had production values commensurate with local access television, but its decision to feature film critics, film clips, and weekly intelligent conversations about film was groundbreaking. A combination of their occasional animosity towards each other, their mutual love for film, and the pragmatic function of helping audiences to find good movies helped their audience base grow. Their show was syndicated in 1982 as *At the Movies*, and eventually made the jump to commercial television in 1986 when the title finally came to reflect the real allure of the show: *Siskel and Ebert*.

The sound-bite nature of television prevented the in-depth observations of more serious critics or even Siskel's columns. Fellow print critic Richard Corliss even described their show as "a sitcom starring two guys who live in a movie theater and argue all the time." Although recurring appearances on the *Tonight Show*, *Late Night with David Letterman*, and *Oprah* cemented their celebrity status, they also brought insight and a new way of talking about movies to hundreds of thousands of people. The more contrary and rabble-rousing of the pair, Siskel even openly criticized the Academy of Motion Pictures Arts and Sciences for their selection process, claiming that Oscar nominations could be bought with publicity (a statement reiterated by various film industry insiders before the 1999 Academy Awards ceremony). He would often boldly support movies he loved, like *Saturday Night Fever*. He even heralded *Babe: Pig in the City* as the best movie of 1998.

Besides his collaboration with Ebert, Siskel wrote reviews and features for WBBM-Channel 2 for twenty-five years, which is where he met his wife, Marlene, in 1980. One of the first broadcasters to be elected to the NATPE hall of fame, he was also a contributor to *CBS This Morning* and a columnist for *TV Guide*.

Siskel was still living in his birthplace of Chicago with his wife and three children when he died on Feb 20, 1999, of complications arising from the removal of a growth from his brain. He was fifty-three.

See Criticism; Ebert, Roger; Kael, Pauline; Maltin, Leonard; Newspapers; Trade papers

SLAPSTICK COMEDY

Comedy derived from broad, aggressive action, with an emphasis often placed on acts of harmless violence is called a slapstick comedy. The term comes from a theatrical device developed for comic effect and consisting of two pieces of wood (a "slapstick") that produced a resounding noise when struck against an actor. Early evidence of slapstick comedy in the motion picture is found in the Lumière film *Watering the Gardener* (1895). A gardener is provoked into looking into the end of a hose when a young boy stops the water flow with his foot. When the boy lifts his foot, the gardener is sprayed in the face, a harmless act of mischief resulting in spontaneous laughter.

See Chaplin, Charlie; Comedy; Keaton, Buster; Lloyd, Harold; Screwball comedy

SNOW WHITE AND THE SEVEN DWARFS

As this 1937 Walt Disney cartoon begins, a storybook opens up to a first page that begins with "Once upon a time. . . ." An evil queen, who is also a witch, asks her magic mirror who is the fairest of them all. A sullen, omniscient face appears and tells the queen that although she has relegated her stepdaughter, Snow White, to menial labor, dirty rags can't hide that Snow White is the fairest of them all.

The porcelain-skinned, cherubic Snow White is shown hard at work scrubbing steps, but she takes a break to talk with the birds that accompany her. Above a wishing well, Snow White sings "I'm Wishing" about her one true love. Immediately a young prince shows up to answer her wishes, but, embarrassed, she runs away from him and hides inside the castle. She listens to his "One Song," which professes his love to her. The queen watches with disgust.

The queen forces a huntsman take Snow White in to the woods and kill her. To prove that he has completed his task, the huntsman must bring back Snow White's heart in a box. The huntsman takes Snow White into the woods, but at the last second can't bring himself to kill her. He warns Snow White that the queen wants her dead and tells her to run off into the woods and never come back. Immediately as Snow White runs off, the woods take on an ominous presence. The film uses expressionistic techniques to make the forest appear to come to life as she makes a literal journey into another world. Snow White breaks down crying, but the birds of the forest chirp a song to cheer her up. Needing a place to sleep, she is delighted when she sees a little cottage that is "just like a dollhouse." The cottage is empty but its inhabitants, whom Snow White believes to be children, have left the cottage in a state of squalor. Hoping to earn the right to stay, she enlists the animals in helping her clean while she sings. After the place is spotless, Snow White goes upstairs to find seven tiny beds, and she falls asleep spread our over all of them.

The dwarfs (Doc, Happy, Sneezy, Sleepy, Dopey, Grumpy, and Bashful) sing "Heigh Ho Heigh Ho" as they march home from their work in the diamond mines. When they arrive at the cottage, they notice that the light is on. The dwarfs work themselves into a tizzy imagining that inside their house is a ghost, goblin, dragon, or demon. When they enter, they are disappointed to find that the place is clean: "Dirty work's afoot." Dopey sneaks up on the sleeping Snow White, who, under a white blanket, scares him into thinking she's a ghost. They plan to kill the ghost, but are surprised to find underneath the blanket the sleeping beauty. When she can name each of the dwarfs by his personality, they all warm up to her except for Grumpy,

notable & quotable

"Half a million dollars for a single film. Why can't we just stay with Mickey Mouse?"

Roy Disney, Disney studio executive, referring to Snow White, *1937*

who says that women are "poison." The dwarfs recognize Snow White as a princess, but they are afraid of the queen's wrath if she should find out that Snow White is hiding here. By promising to cook for her "little men" she convinces them to let her stay.

She cooks dinner, but makes them wash up before they eat. They are reluctant, but enjoy themselves in an extended silly sequence that ends with the other dwarfs forcing Grumpy to take a bath.

Holding the box that was intended to hold Snow White's heart, the queen learns from her magic mirror that Snow White is with the dwarfs, and that in the box is a pig's heart—the huntsman has fooled her. Still not the fairest in the land, the queen calls on her spell book to concoct a potion to make her appear as an old hag. She drinks the potion and in a surreal, frightening sequence she is transformed into an aged crone.

"Angel, ha! She's a female! And all females is poison! They're full of wicked wiles!"

Pinto Colvig as the voice of Grumpy in *Snow White and the Seven Dwarfs* (1937)

After the dwarfs sing to entertain her, they ask Snow White to tell them a story. She sings, "Someday My Prince Will Come"; she reveals she wants the prince to hold her in his arms and take her away to his castle where they will live happily ever after. At bedtime, the dwarfs let Snow White sleep in their beds. She prays for them and hopes that Grumpy will eventually like her. The dwarfs fight over one pillow, ripping it and causing a comic explosion of feathers.

The queen uses her black magic to create a poisonous apple that will cause Snow White to fall into a sleeping death. Figuring the dwarfs will bury her, thinking she is dead, the spell's one footnote—"victim of the sleeping death can be revived only by love's first kiss"—doesn't worry the queen.

In the morning, the dwarfs warn Snow White about the queen's witchcraft and tell her that she must beware of strangers. Even Grumpy tells her not to let anyone in the house. Realizing he cares for her, she kisses Grumpy on the forehead, leaving him a little less grumpy.

Later, while the dwarfs are off at work, an ominous shadow falls over Snow White as she's baking a pie. In the guise of an old hag, the queen shows up and offers the apple. The birds, noticing eager vultures, try to chase the crone away but to no avail. When Snow White invites the old woman into the house, the animals run to get the dwarfs. The hag tells Snow White that the apple is magic and will make her wishes come true. Meanwhile, the animals alert the dwarfs, who hurry back to the cottage to save Snow White.

Snow White wishes to live happily ever after, and offscreen she bites the apple; we see the once-bitten apple roll out of her hand. A horrible rainstorm comes. The dwarfs arrive too late to save Snow White, but they chase the queen to the edge of a cliff. The Queen's diabolical attempt to kill the dwarfs effects her own death: an offscreen plunge to where the vultures soon descend.

The dwarfs are disheartened. Because even in her death she is beautiful, the dwarfs build a glass and gold coffin for Snow White, refusing to bury her. A year later, a prince comes and kisses her. To everyone's surprise and delight, Snow White stirs and awakes. The prince takes her into his arms and they ride off into the sunset to live happily ever after. The storybook closes.

See Animation; Fantasia

SOME LIKE IT HOT

It would not be hyperbolic to call *Some Like It Hot* (1959) a comic masterpiece. It has the classic comic plot of disguise, deception, and intrigue, where a single complication generates a series of subplots. *Some Like It Hot* also possesses a quality found in the best comedies—a sense of humanity and an attitude of compassion for the lunatics and lovers who play the fool for our sake.

For *Some Like It Hot*, director Billy Wilder chose the classic way of achieving unity: selectivity. He selected one comic device, parody, and made it the source of all the others. The film opens as a hearse comes down a snow-covered street. Gunfire erupts, and bullets perforate the coffin, causing it to leak. The liquid? Liquor.

"Look at that. Look how she moves. That's just like jello on springs"

Jack Lemmon as "Geraldine" watching Marilyn Monroe as Sugar in *Some Like It Hot* (1959)

In addition to parodying gangster films, Wilder also has fun with a familiar movie type: witnesses to a crime. These characters can take it on the lam, discover that nobody believes them, or change their identity and profession. Wilder gives all of this a twist and doubles the comic potential by having the characters—Joe (Tony Curtis) and Jerry (Jack Lemmon)—keep their profession but change their sex.

Drag has always been a source of humor, but the typical Hollywood movie never attempted to feminize the men. There is always a hairy leg beneath the gown, a trace of five-o'clock shadow, or just a sense of physical discomfort at being girdled and gartered. However, Wilder accomplishes a perfect transformation—when Joe and Jerry become Josephine and Daphne, they have become so feminized that they fool the eternal female herself—Marilyn Monroe as Sugar Kane, who strums a ukulele and sings in an all-girl band.

The transformation is more than just skin without stubble. Sugar is immediately attracted to the disguised pair and they to her—but for different reasons. Sugar wants friendship, and the men want Sugar. Ironically, what Sugar thinks is friendship turns out to be love; and what the men originally thought were feminine traits become natural to them.

Once Sugar enters their lives, she disrupts their friendship and threatens their male camaraderie. Joe and Jerry are now rivals for Sugar's affec-

Tony Curtis and Jack Lemmon played hilarious, gender-bending musicians in the Billy Wilder classic Some Like It Hot.

tions, but in their present disguise, they find courting a woman somewhat difficult. Joe, the more clever of the two, fakes a Cary Grant accent and impresses Sugar with his mythical wealth; but Jerry cannot regain his manhood so easily. He grows petulant and tries to sabotage his friend's romance.

Ironically, while Joe is romancing Sugar in the guise of a millionaire yachtsman, a real millionaire—Osgood Fielding (Joe E. Brown) is courting Jerry/Daphne. Just as Sugar is succumbing to Joe's charms, Jerry/Daphne is succumbing to Osgood's. Once Jerry drops the mask, Osgood dons it. When Jerry tells Osgood he cannot marry him, he tries to soften the blow by enumerating his inadequacies as a wife, but to no avail. Finally, he yanks off his wig and says, "Damn it, I'm a man." "Well, nobody's perfect," Osgood replies in a line that certainly defies sexual stereotyping.

To humanize Sugar, Wilder turns her into a vulnerable sex goddess with Bambi eyes. Marilyn was now little girl lost; for once, her eyes did not ring up potential sales like a cash register. By finding the child within Marilyn's over-publicized body, Wilder enabled her to give her best screen performance as Sugar.

Sugar is a loner who carries a flask in her stocking and has little in common with the other members of the band. Thus, she finds in Josephine and Daphne the sisters of her dreams. Men have abused Sugar, but she is not bitter about it.

Sugar is on the bandstand doing a solo, "I'm Through with Love." It is a genuinely touching moment, for the singer has become the song. Suddenly, Joe, still in drag, jumps up and kisses her on the mouth. "Josephine!" Sugar cries. She is surprised but not shocked; the princess is never shocked by disenchantment.

"Some like it hot, but I prefer classical music," Joe informs Sugar when he is masquerading as the yachtsman. For those who like it hot, for those who like it classical, Wilder has made the perfect comedy.

See Gangster film; Monroe, Marilyn; Wilder, Billy

"Real diamonds! They must be worth their weight in gold!"

Marilyn Monroe as Sugar Kane in *Some Like It Hot* (1959)

SOUND

Metaphorically speaking, sound in movies did not arrive in town all at once like an express train. It came gradually, in little crates, over a period of more than ten years. Some shipments came unsolicited, many came "on approval," and some left the factory but never arrived at their destination. In other words, the concept of synchronizing music, noises ("effects"), and speech did not take producers by surprise in the late 1920s.

When the first films began appearing, the uniqueness of sound was sufficient to bring in the public. *Photoplay,* for example, urged readers to check out *The Family Picnic* (1928) precisely because it turned everyday noises into novelty. But soon the box office favored certain types of sound films and punished others. Moviegoers judged the talkies, stars, and stories according to their own standards. More than one commentator characterized the public as "shopping around." The times tested the most successful studio heads' talent for second-guessing audiences and learning from mistakes. Trial and error describes these first sound productions: the part talkie, the courtroom drama, the musical revue, the vaudeville comedy, the Metropolitan Opera, and the western were attempts by Hollywood to determine what kind of sound film the public really wanted.

S

SOUND

The 1920s

It was always known that Edison's film laboratory had experimented with linking the motion picture film to the phonograph. Serious demonstrations of workable systems by various inventors had been made at least since 1906. None had succeeded. But after World War I there was a great boom in electrical research and a new attitude toward technology: increasingly researchers linked applications across a broad network rather than continue to "perfect" individual devices along a single trajectory.

But most efforts to synchronize sound and image either did not make it out of the lab or failed to win approval because they did not work. The illusion that a voice is emanating from a person on-screen is very fragile. The tolerance is less than one frame of projection time, a standard difficult to maintain for the duration of a ten-minute reel. For twenty years most inventors tinkered with phonograph discs as the sound medium, but a few were working with the expedient of photographically recording on film (either on a separate strip of film or as a track exposed next to the pictures).

In 1910 there were about 13,000 theaters nationwide, tickets cost 7 cents, movies lasted 30 minutes, and the population of Hollywood was 5,000.

As important as synchronization was, amplifying the recorded sound to fill a 1920s movie palace was an even greater challenge. Using state-of-the-art vacuum tube amplifiers, movie sound, whether recorded on disc or film, could boom into the auditorium of the biggest Bijou. The trick was to control that power, a task for which acoustic engineering, a new specialty, was created.

In the twenties few in the workshops and corporate research labs dreamed of "revolutionizing" silent Hollywood by making commercial movies talk. More typically, the inventors extended existing electrical systems. They used moving pictures to stake their claims on developing communication media, especially telephone and the hot area, radio. Thus, during the period of concentrated development in the mid-1920s, the electronics pioneer Lee de Forest saw sound cinema as an area into which he could expand his rights to exploit the vacuum tube. At the same time, the executives of Western Electric (the manufacturing branch of AT&T) and, later, RCA (controlled by AT&T's rivals General Electric and Westinghouse) were seeking more diversity for their existing sound-recording patents. The leaders looked to the movies.

1926

Warner Bros. was hopeful that Western Electric's sound system (and the prestige of being associated with AT&T) would yield immediate payback if the public response to its sound experiments was favorable. The company formed the Vitaphone partnership with Western Electric in April with the dual purpose of producing and distributing sound films and sublicensing recorders to the other Hollywood studios. An unreleased big-budget silent feature, *Don Juan*, was retrofitted with a score and loosely synchronized sound effects. The plan was to construct an all-sound film program that would generate public excitement as a media event in its own right and attract the investment of Hollywood's Big Five companies.

The *Don Juan* show premiered in August 1926 and surpassed all expectations as a box-office hit and a critical success. A second synchronized feature, *The Better 'Ole,* opened in October. Again attendance was good and critics raved. The short subjects were especially well received. George Jessel re-created his stage routine, and Al Jolson, on film, addressed the audience and sang.

1927

In 1927 Fox Film's William Fox signed with Western Electric and cross-licensed the patents he controlled in order to continue developing his system, which he called Movietone. Fox needed access to amplifiers, the phone company's manufacturing capability, and its installation expertise. His New York studio competed directly with Warner Bros./Western Electric's Vitaphone, producing a series of filmed vaudeville shorts and silent features with added synchronized music tracks. Sound-on-film Movietone was much more mobile than the Vitaphone disc system. Fox pressed this advantage by filming outdoors. Scenes of marching West Point cadets and, especially, of Charles Lindbergh's historic transatlantic flight takeoff were greeted with keen public interest. Fox's staff thought of a new use for sound: tying it to the existing newsreel as an extra bonus. The earliest sound newsreels resembled radio. There were addresses by public figures and scenes that exploited synch-sound for its own sake. Live-recorded sound gave the impression of "being-there-ness" to the news.

The feature films of 1927, and many of the shorts, were conceived of as silents with sound added. Even newsreels celebrated the medium's newfound acoustic ability by emphasizing synchronous sound effects. The critical term *foregrounding* (and sometimes *Variety*'s jargon *spotting*) meant accentuating the unique or novel properties of a medium. For the Vitaphone features, sound was treated as an add-on or enhancement of the ordinary film. This concept mirrored the technological conditions of making sound prints because the sound track was literally sold separately as an option.

1928

Decades of historical accounts notwithstanding, the sound film revolution did not commence with the premier of *The Jazz Singer,* Fox's prestige sound film *Sunrise* (1927), or the Movietone Newsreel. Initial audience response was not wholeheartedly in favor of sound, and the Vitaphone features—*The First Auto,* for instance—were not unqualified box-office hits.

The films of 1928 were frequently rereleases of silents with music and effects, or part talkies. The latter were films with a reel or two of dialogue added, often as a finale (much like the way in which Technicolor reels were used at the time). This practice is consistent with the conceptualization of sound as an extra flourish. It also reveals fiscal conservatism. The studios tried to anticipate the outcome of the audible cinema trend by hedging, that is, by continuing their silent production practices while adapting to new techniques. Producers pledged allegiance to the exhibitor who chose not to convert to sound. Most continued to supply silent prints with intertitles into the early thirties. Many commentators, including those within the industry, envisioned separate production of silent and sound material. Certain types of movies (for example, slapstick comedy) were better left silent, while other types, especially theatrical adaptations, would benefit from the sound "treatment." Some envisioned separate venues for sound films, as later happened with Cinerama theaters. These hedging plans encountered two economic realities: redundancy was too wasteful to continue producing dual versions, and patronage of silent films dropped whenever competing talkies were available.

Warner Bros. widened its substantial lead in sound production in 1928 while continuing to make dual versions and part talkies. In September the studio bought First National and committed to all-sound production but nevertheless continued to derive most of its income from rentals of silent versions. Warners also pursued a strategy of adapting successful plays as part of the virtual Broadway concept. Part-talking films like *Glorious Betsy* and *The Lion and the Mouse* impressed reviewers, but some began to complain that the dialogue parts were a distraction because they reminded the viewer that the sound was "mechanical." The surprise hits were *The Lights of New York,* and ultra-low-budget production released in the summer of 1928 (usually the dead season), and *The Terror,* which drew capacity crowds for weeks. The allure? Gangster characters speaking argot in the former, and, in the latter, an all-talking mystery movie that foregrounded vocal cues to solve the whodunit. That sound *in some form* was here to stay was apparent after Al Jolson's second feature, *The Singing Fool,* was released in September. Though a weak actor, Jolson milked the bathetic story of losing a child for all it was worth and elicited tears from genuinely moved audiences. The other studios added or upgraded their sound capabilities and revised their production schedules to include all-talking features. In the fall they were prepared to satisfy what now appeared to be a continuing demand for "talkers."

The all-talking film was not just an extended part talkie. In addition to using dialogue as a special effect or an add-on, directors used it to tell a story in the traditional Hollywood style. Speaking actors developed more personality and psychological character depth. The voice, as Jolson proved, was an important ingredient in star appeal. By late in the year, studio heads were testing their actors' voices to determine whether they would be suitable for the talkies. As a shortcut, they were also hiring Broadway directors, writers, composers, and, of course, actors from the legitimate stage.

1929

Some of the films of early 1929 were substandard movies hastily cobbled together to meet the unexpectedly strong demand for talkies. Many of the clichés of the early sound cinema (including those in *Singin' in the Rain*) apply to films made during this period: long static takes, badly written dialogue, voices not quite in control, poor-quality recording, and a speaking style with slow cadence and emphasis on "enunciated" tones, which the microphone was supposed to favor. But it was also a time of experimentation and concerted efforts by studio technicians, directors, and sound engineers to make the new technology work. The goal was greater comprehension of dialogue. This was accomplished by better mikes, mechanical improvements (for example, microphone placement during recording, loudspeaker placement, and continuing volume adjustment during projection), and changes in the actors' vocal performance.

Certain types of dramas were selected to "spot" talking. Thus, the first major cycle of the new cinema was the trial film, which replaced much of the action with expository dialogue. Frequently this was an adaptation of a theater success (like *The Bellamy Trial* [1929]). The other imported cycle was the musical, with its performances integrated into a backstage plot (as in *The Broadway Melody* [1929]) or transposed intact (*encapsulated*) from stage revue antecedents (for example, *The Show of Shows* [1929]). One side effect of the musical craze was to provide employment opportunities for African Americans on the screen. The films exploited blacks as gifted but one-dimensional performers. Or they became character actors, usually cast in demeaning plantation stereotypes. Equally disturbing to modern audiences, but everyday movie fare during this period, are the numerous films in which whites, made up in blackface, impersonated African Americans. The talkies revivified this remnant of a moribund minstrel heritage. Other ethnic groups were represented, usually also as caricatures, in early sound films. One group, the Yiddish-speaking enclave of New York City, did finds its voice briefly during the period and made several dozen movies. These productions took advantage of cinema's dialogue capabilities to tap a niche market in a non-mainstream culture.

Reneging on their pledges of the year before to continue making silents, one studio after another announced all-sound product for the 1929–30 season. Merger mania continued to grow. William Fox took over (temporarily, it turned out) Loew's, the parent of MGM, and the British Gaumont theater chain. Paramount expanded its Publix theaters, and Warner Bros. and United Artists made futile efforts to join together.

notable & quotable

"Sound is all about emotion, the way music is emotion. We don't quite understand why rhythm and pitch and frequency stir us emotionally, but they do."

Gary Rydstrom, sound designer, George Lucas's Skywalker Ranch, 1999, as quoted in "Making You Hear the Bumps in the Night," by Justine Elias, New York Times, *June 27, 1999*

The studios' conversion to sound was matched by exhibitors' rapid wiring of their theaters. Those chains affiliated with studios, about 15 percent of all the theaters, were obligated to install Western Electric equipment and to show only films licensed by ERPI. At the end of 1928, however, Western Electric conceded that its Movietone and RCA's optical sound tracks were interchangeable. Many of the independently owned theaters began installing the cheaper RCA Photophone reproducing systems. Unless they were economically strapped, theater owners had no choice but to convert to some brand of sound system because otherwise the affiliated chains would take away their business. Although the national chains were a numerical minority, they set the pace in the most important markets. As a result, at the time of the stock market crash in October 1929, out-of-the-way theaters and those servicing poor neighborhoods were the only ones still waiting for amplification. The transformation of American movie houses from almost all silent to almost all sound therefore took about a year and a half. Owing primarily to sound, the studio system had become a huge tentacular structure with interests in publishing, music, and electric companies. The film manufacturers also became internationally diversified.

The film industry complained about the many millions of dollars it took to finance this conversion, but in reality the changeover was funded by borrowing against mushrooming profits. Audiences flocked to the movies in 1929, making it one of the best years in Hollywood history. Union leaders pointed out that this prosperity was in contrast to the thousands of musicians, crew members, extras, and specialty workers laid off during the transition to sound. Actors Equity, the New York–based union, tried to organize the Hollywood performers, but a strike called for July was ineffectual. Many of the workers' demands, however, were addressed in later negotiations with producers. When the market crashed, some of the wind was knocked out of the business's sails, but many predicted that movies would never lose their popularity. During 1929 the studios had invested in infrastructure, expanded their theater holdings, diversified into other entertainment fields, and dabbled in technological innovation (besides sound, variable screen shapes and stereoscopic imagery). The onset of the Depression forced the industry to concentrate on the basics.

1930

By mid-1930 the film industry was in a severe recession from which it did not emerge for about four years. Hollywood went into retrenchment. The ramifications for sound were that shooting schedules and techniques had to be made as efficient as possible. With silent-running cameras, lightweight cranes and booms, and improved lighting and recording materials, the expensive practice of multicamera filming was phased out. Distributors circulated fewer silent versions to small houses. ERPI stopped wiring theaters which were judged to be economically unstable, leaving them to RCA and small entrepreneurs. The studios, except for Paramount and Warners, closed their New York production facilities. Many theaters affiliated with the producers were sold off to raise cash.

Attendance fell. Exhibitors reacted by lowering ticket prices and inaugurating the various come-ons that now have become part of Depression-era nostalgia: bank night (the winning ticket stub collected a jackpot), door prizes, giveaways of dishes and other items, and blonde night (they got in free—when accompanied by a paying escort). Theaters hosted fan clubs and special matinees for kids. The wildly popular Mickey Mouse clubs are a good example of one way a theater could make money from activities ancillary to the actual projection of films. Independent theater owners complained that the studios were engaged in unfair trade practices, and eventually (but not soon enough to provide any economic relief) the courts agreed. Sound enabled the studios to dictate terms to independent theater owners—for example, basing rental on a sliding percentage of the gate instead of the prior practice of charging a flat fee. Small owners had little means of resistance. Some theaters closed their doors and tried alternative amusement enterprises, like miniature golf.

Audiences' preferences also changed. Hollywood learned that hard times seemed to increase the appetite for "topical" films, not for musicals, which had been the industry wisdom. Organized crime was making headlines and became grist for the early Warners gangster pictures. "Realist" films like *Applause* (1929), *The Big House* (1930), *Anna Christie* (1930), and *Min and Bill* (1930) provided glimpses of the gritty lives of marginalized people and contrast with the escapist fare generally associated with Depression-era entertainment. The musical film slid into disfavor in 1930, presumably because audiences were sated with the emphasis on "all-singing, all-dancing" superabundance at the expense of narrative.

Social realism, the risqué language of Broadway, "modern" subjects (as in *The Wild Party* [1929]), and suggestive poses and innuendo in film advertising were addressed in the Production Code of 1930. Written and administered by Will Hays's Motion Picture Producers and Distributors of America (MPPDA), the code was an effort to block state and federal censorship by creating guidelines for regulating film expression, especially the use of the voice. Secondarily, through self-censorship the industry used sound as an excuse to maintain the power to distribute its product without external interference by local censors. Sound had stimulated some boards to demand extensive changes that entailed recutting, reshooting, and preparing multiple versions for different regions. Hollywood would save millions by having to make only one set of prints for the national market.

1931

The Depression convinced producers (if indeed they needed much pressure in this direction) that their films must appeal to "mass" rather than "class."

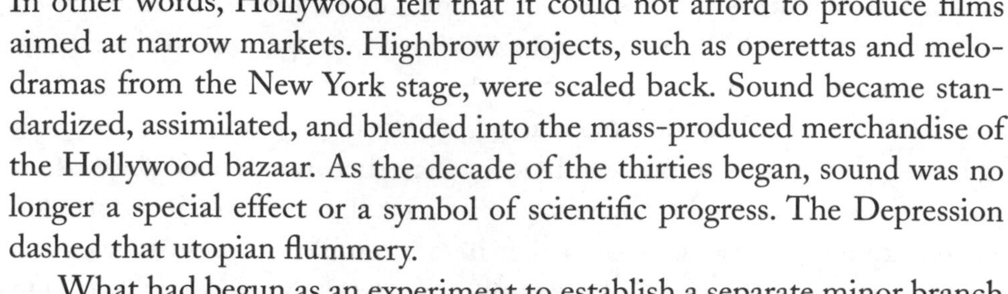

In other words, Hollywood felt that it could not afford to produce films aimed at narrow markets. Highbrow projects, such as operettas and melodramas from the New York stage, were scaled back. Sound became standardized, assimilated, and blended into the mass-produced merchandise of the Hollywood bazaar. As the decade of the thirties began, sound was no longer a special effect or a symbol of scientific progress. The Depression dashed that utopian flummery.

What had begun as an experiment to establish a separate minor branch of film practice to be marketed to small theaters had ended up altering fundamentally some aspects of the whole Hollywood system. The developments were unexpected, but not enormously disruptive. The adoption of sound technology set off reverberations in distribution, exhibition, and the general attitude toward the movies, but the major film companies responded rapidly to adjust to their consumers' mass acceptance of dialogue films. Production practices were altered. Studio heads began looking for reliable means of determining audience preferences. The environment inside theaters was transformed, not simply because sounds were coming from the screen, but because the patrons' behavior and attitudes were also changing.

But some things were not affected. The cinema remained primarily a storytelling medium. The film style of the previous fifteen years changed little. And the basic appeal of the movies was the same. Whether a 1920s silent, a 1930s talkies, or *Singin' in the Rain,* the movies still gave audiences what they expected: an engaging story with action, romance, comedy, and adventure. Apparently for most audiences, hearing the winsome heroes and despicable villains speak their parts was a welcome improvement on a good thing, not the end of a golden age.

See City Lights; *Diegesis/Diegetic Sound; Foley artist;* Jazz Singer, The; Singin' in the Rain; *Vitaphone*

"Fraulein, is it to be at every meal, or merely at dinnertime, that you intend on leading us all through this rare and wonderful new world of indigestion?"

Christopher Plummer as Captain von Trapp in *The Sound of Music* (1965)

SOUND OF MUSIC, THE

The Sound of Music is the most successful musical in motion picture history. The film ran for a staggering four and a half years in its initial release, winning five Oscars in 1965, including Best Picture and Best Director (Robert Wise). Composers Rodgers and Hammerstein (*Oklahoma*, *South Pacific*, *The King and I*) scored a direct bull's-eye with this real-life story of a young governess who teaches a stern sea captain to love again, and his seven children to sing. The backdrop of the Nazi occupation of Austria in the late 1930s served to keep the film from becoming too saccharine. *The Sound of*

Music still holds up as a timeless, enchanting story. Many of the songs from this film have become classics, such as "Do Re Mi," "My Favorite Things," and, of course, "The Sound of Music."

Maria (Julie Andrews), a postulant in a Salzburg, Austria, nunnery, poses quite a conundrum to the nuns. On the one hand, they love her sense of humor and free spirit; on the other, they deplore her sense of humor and free spirit. Discussing this in a rousing number, "How Do You Solve a Problem Like Maria?" Reverend Mother (Peggy Woods) decides to send Maria away on something of a summer internship, where she is to become the governess of the widower Captain Georg Von Trapp (Christopher Plummer)—and in effect, a nanny to his seven children.

Upset but eager to prove herself, Maria arrives at the captain's posh manse, nestled at the foot of the Alps. It's clear from the outset that Maria is headstrong; she is instructed to wait for the captain but instead takes to exploring his incredible house. Captain Von Trapp catches and startles Maria. A stern disciplinarian who runs his household like one of his commands, Von Trapp has no patience for Maria—or for his children. He instructs her on how to use a whistle to call his brood, who promptly fall in. But Maria informs Von Trapp that she has no intention of using a whistle; the children's names will do just fine.

Before long it is quite clear why Maria is the thirteenth in a series of governesses: the kids are monsters. They quickly take to playing practical

In The Sound of Music, *Julie Andrews as Maria manages to win the affection of stern Captain von Trapp (Christopher Plummer) and his bratty children in this Rodgers and Hammerstein musical.*

jokes on her. A lesser woman would have fled immediately, but Maria turns the tables by making them feel guilty about their actions, then winning them over with kindness—exactly what the children need. They warm up to Maria, and confide that they're brats because it's the only way they can get their father's attention.

When Captain Von Trapp heads off to Vienna for another visit with his fiancée, the lovely and very rich Baroness Schroeder (Eleanor Parker), Maria seizes the opportunity to win the children over completely. She sews play clothes for them from old drapes and takes them out for songs and games all over Salzburg. She teaches them to sing "Do Re Mi," and in short order, the children are singing in four- and five-part harmony. Free from the captain's oppressive rule, the children blossom into lovely, talented individuals.

"I like rich people. I like the way they live. I like the way I live when I'm with them."

Richard Haydn as Max Detweiler in *The Sound of Music* (1965)

But when the captain returns, with the baroness and Uncle Max (Richard Haydn), a talent agent, in tow, he is horrified to discover what has happened to his crew. He scolds Maria, who will have none of it. She chastises him right back, and Von Trapp fires her. But then, the children perform a darling little ditty that Maria has taught them specifically to welcome the baroness. The baroness is delighted; the captain, humbled. Deutsche marks flash before Max's eyes, as he foresees a big future for the Von Trapp Family Singers. Von Trapp apologizes to Maria, and reveals that he himself can sing and play guitar in the delicate song for Austria "Edelweiss."

Before long, the captain and Maria are falling for each other, much to the baroness's chagrin. Wracked with guilt, Maria flees back to the nunnery without saying goodbye. The children are devastated, as is Captain Von Trapp, who does an unconvincing job of hiding his emotions.

The children try to visit Maria at the nunnery, but are turned away—Maria is in seclusion. Reverend Mother calls for Maria and tells her she must follow her heart: "Just because you love a man does not mean that you love God less." Buoyed by the Reverend Mother's support, Maria returns to the Von Trapp house. In short order, the captain realizes that he cannot marry the baroness. The baroness bows out gracefully, and Von Trapp and Maria confess their love. They are married immediately, in a huge ceremony.

While Maria and the captain are away on their honeymoon, Austria is occupied by Nazis. Uncle Max, who is rehearsing the children for their upcoming performance at the Salzburg Music Festival, is approached by Herr Zeller (Ben Wright), a Nazi toady who demands that the Von Trapp household fly the flag of the Third Reich, not of Austria. The writing is on the wall. Things will never be the same in Austria.

Immediately upon his return, Von Trapp is delivered a telegram by Rolfe (Daniel Truhitte), former boyfriend of his eldest daughter, Liesl (Charmian Carr), who has become a Nazi errand boy. Von Trapp has been drafted. He is to report the following morning, where he will take command of a vessel in Hitler's navy. To decline would mean certain death, and to accept, separation from his new wife and family, fighting for a cause he deplores. Von Trapp realizes they must all flee Austria that night. However, they are intercepted by Herr Zeller, who was expecting just such a move. Captain Von Trapp says they were simply on their way to the festival, where the Von Trapp family is scheduled to appear. Zeller then escorts the family to the festival to prevent their escape.

The Von Trapp Family Singers perform for the huge crowd at the festival and are a smash. But when time comes for them to accept their first-place award, they are nowhere to be found. Nazi troops scramble after them in hot pursuit. The borders are closed; the family is trapped.

Maria leads the family to the abbey (nunnery), where friendly nuns hide them away. But that's the first place the Nazis look. Rolfe discovers the captain, who convinces the boy to surrender his weapon. But Von Trapp misjudges Rolfe's level of dedication; the remark "You'll never be one of them" causes Rolfe to scream for the troops. The Von Trapps flee the abbey, but the Nazis are unable to pursue. The nuns have disabled their vehicles! The Von Trapp family escapes, climbing over the mountains to refuge in Switzerland.

See Musical film

SPECIAL-EFFECTS FILM

Any film that incorporates a wide variety of special optical effects and trick photography into the story is called a special-effects film. Special-effects films exploit the unusual possibilities of the motion picture for fantasy and spectacle, for example, *Mary Poppins* (1964), *The Poseidon Adventure* (1972), *Star Wars* (1977), *Close Encounters of the Third Kind* (1977), *Terminator 2: Judgment Day* (1991), *Death Becomes Her* (1992).

See Close Encounters of the Third Kind; *Science-fiction film;* Star Wars; 2001: A Space Odyssey

In 1988 the average budget for a film was $18.1 million; by 1997 salaries, special effects, and other demands had driven it to $53.4 million.

SPECTACLE

A spectacle is a film characterized by elements that include lavish production design, epic theme, and grand scope. Screen spectacles consist of many types: dramatic films involving high adventure and heroic characters—*Intolerance* (1916), *War and Peace* (1956), *Ben-Hur* (1959), *Star Wars* (1977); grand, eye-catching musicals—*My Fair Lady* (1964); special-effects films designed to display novel motion-picture processes—Cinerama (*This is Cinerama,* 1952), 3-D (*Bwana Devil,* 1952), Sensurround (*Earthquake,* 1975).

See Ben-Hur; My Fair Lady; Star Wars

SPIELBERG, STEVEN

notable & quotable

"Am I allowed to say I really wanted this?"

Director Steven Spielberg, on winning the Best Director Oscar for Saving Private Ryan *(1998)*

By any quantitative measure—number of tickets sold, box office receipts, number of hit blockbusters directed, blockbusters produced, number of major independent studios founded—Steven Spielberg is incontestably the most successful movie director of all time. His reputation as one of Hollywood's great showmen is secure; whether his eminence survives the critical scrutiny applied to great film artists is far less certain.

No one disputes his surpassing technical mastery or his adroitness in conjuring fantastic images that have loomed with iconic power over the popular imagination of a vast worldwide audience—the shark's implacable jaws of doom, the transcendent radiance of an alien spacecraft, the innocence of E.T., the alternately gentle and terrifying allure of giant dinosaurs. Nor would most critics deny that he has channeled his vast prestige and resources into several earnest and worthy directing efforts, such as *The Color Purple, Schindler's List, Amistad,* and *Saving Private Ryan.* They do disagree, however, about whether he has ever made even one truly great film.

This master of the otherworldly and spectacular, is, surprisingly, the product of a quite ordinary childhood. He was born on December 18, 1947, in the American heartland, Cincinnati, Ohio. After Steven's birth, the family moved east to New Jersey and then west to Arizona and California as Steven's father, Arnold, sought to advance in his profession as an electrical engineer and computer expert. As a baby boomer, Steven's childhood experiences were heavily influenced by television. He has often commented on the care his parents took to control his media viewing; to insure that he did not spend too much time in front of the television, or view the wrong programs, they draped a blanket over the set. Spielberg spent his adolescence in Phoenix, where he attended high school. He continued to make films, financed partially by his father and by his tree-planting business, and won local fame with a feature-length film, *Firelight.* The film premiered at a local movie house just before the family moved to California. His parents divorced after this move and Steven became the male head of the family at sixteen.

Spielberg enrolled in the film department of California State University, Long Beach, where he made five short films. His twenty-two-minute feature *Amblin* (after which he named his production company, Amblin Entertainment, in 1984) merited a showing at the Atlanta Film Festival in 1969. On the strength of that effort, Universal Pictures extended a seven-year directing contract to the twenty-two-year-old Spielberg, the youngest man to have achieved such a long-term deal with a major studio.

He cut his teeth directing a number of dramatic television shows for Universal, including episodes of *Night Gallery, Marcus Welby,* and *Columbo.* His first feature-length project, the made-for-TV film *Duel,* enjoyed elicited such critical enthusiasm—especially in Europe, where the film was released theatrically and won several major awards—that Universal quickly promoted him to a feature-film project, *The Sugarland Express* (1974), which Pauline Kael called "one of the most phenomenal directorial debuts in the history of the movies." His next assignment, *Jaws* (1975), the stuff that a whole summer of beach nightmares was made of, blew the lid off the box office and thrust Spielberg into the front ranks of hot commercial directorial properties. The young phenom did not rush to cash in on his sudden bankability, however. He lavished two years of painstaking writing

By any quantitative measure—number of tickets sold, box office receipts, number of hit blockbusters directed or produced—Steven Spielberg is incontestably the most successful movie director of all time.

and directing labors onto a groundbreaking science fiction film, *Close Encounters of the Third Kind* (1977), another box-office jackpot.

Improbably, from those lofty summits the Spielberg express soared still higher, bounding relentlessly from bigger to better (with only one severe dip in altitude, the misguided, overwrought comedy *1941* [1980]). In 1980 he collaborated with his old friend George Lucas on *Raiders of the Lost Ark* (1981), the first of three enormously popular installments of the adventures of the action-hero archaeologist Indiana Jones.

Spielberg's next venture into science fiction was a tale of awestruck innocence and wonder in coming face to face with an alien life form; *E.T.: The Extra-Terrestrial* once again broke the bank, earning $725 million, the highest-grossing Spielberg film to that date and the second most profitable of his career. (*E.T.* remains the sixth highest-grossing film of all time in worldwide ticket sales.)

Spielberg directed four of the 1980s' Top 10 box-office hits: #1 *E.T.* ($228 million); #6 *Raiders of the Lost Ark* ($115 m); #7 *Indiana Jones and the Last Crusade* ($115 m); and #8 *Indiana Jones and the Temple of Doom* ($109 m).

Now securely enthroned in the land of the blockbusters, Spielberg sought to expand his repertoire in the 1980s to include less splashy, more thoughtful, and subtler material. His adaptation of Alice Walker's *The Color Purple* (1985) won wide praise, as did his version of J. G. Ballard's *Empire of the Sun* (1987). He ventured into romantic fantasy in 1989 with *Always* and into family entertainment with *Hook* in 1991.

But Spielberg was far from through exploring cinema's fiduciary outer limits. With his next venture, *Jurassic Park* (1993), he was back to high-rolling epic fantasy, this time with a story of a theme park devoted to breeding and herding dinosaurs from surviving bits of ancient DNA material. Protracted sequences of computer-generated archaic beasts treading the earth once again, draped none too subtly around a flimsy pretext of a plot, was show-biz gold, $913 million worth—enough to place *Jurassic Park* in the number-two position as the second-highest grossing film of all time in worldwide ticket sales.

Having once confirmed his commercial supremacy, Spielberg set forth on a journey of artistic and personal redemption with *Schindler's List* (1993), based on the true story of a Nazi munitions manufacturer who inexplicably was moved to save 1,100 Jews from the gas chambers by persisting, at great personal risk, in employing them in his factory. The film, which brought Spielberg a measure of the high critical esteem that had eluded him, earned seven Oscars (out of twelve nominations), including the awards for Best Picture, Best Director, and Best Screenplay adapted from other material.

Not content to dominate the industry as a director, Spielberg has amassed impressive credits as a producer as well through his production company, Amblin Entertainment, founded in 1984. He has presided over the production of more than a dozen films, including *Gremlins* (1984), *Back to the Future* (I, II, and III, in 1985, 1989, and 1990, respectively), *Who Framed Roger Rabbit* (1988), *An American Tail* (1986), *The Land Before Time* (1988), *The Flintstones* (1994), *The Bridges of Madison County* (1995), *Twister* (1996), and *Men in Black* (1997).

Spielberg's most recent directorial efforts confirm his by now well-established pattern of alternating blockbusters with smaller, more serious films. In *The Lost World: Jurassic Park* (1996), the dinosaurs nearly duplicated their monstrous profits of three years before, but not quite, attracting a "mere" $600 million this time. *Amistad* (1997), a stirring recounting of a rebellion of African slaves on a ship bound for America, received four Academy Award nominations and warm praise for its noble intentions (if not universal agreement on its artistic success).

Having left no doubt of his supremacy among those who have sought to raise movie making into a great industry, the talented Spielberg, still in the prime of his career, now faces the challenge of securing his still-uncertain place in the roster of those who have sought to make it a great art.

See Close Encounters of the Third Kind; E.T.; Jaws; Jurassic Park; *Lucas, George;* Raiders of the Lost Ark; Schindler's List; Saving Private Ryan

STAGECOACH

John Ford was the prophet who led the western out of the desert of B-movie formula and into the promised land of critical esteem and box-office bonanza. No film more decisively marked this transition than the epic adventure *Stagecoach* (1939), which earned Ford the prestigious best director award from the New York film critics. Ironically, it had been thirteen years since Ford had directed a western, the genre with which his name would be irrevocably linked thenceforth. The film owes its story to Guy de Maupassant, whose short story *Boule de Suif,* about a prostitute traveling through a war zone in the company of wealthy gentlemen, most likely served as the inspiration for Ernest Haycyox's 1937 short story "The Stage to Lordsburg," which Ford snapped up for $4,000.

The plot is propelled by a stagecoach bearing a colorful array of six beautiful-and/or-damned travelers through territory contested by the Geronimo-led Apaches, from Tonto, New Mexico, to Lordsburg. Among the passengers are Doctor (Doc) Josiah Boone (Thomas Mitchell), a reprobate whose shady practices cost him his medical license; Samuel Peacock, a liquor peddler; Lucy Mallory (Lois Platt), who is carrying the child of her cavalry-officer husband; Hatfield (John Carradine), a courtly but roguish professional gambler who professes to be on the journey to protect Mrs. Mallory; Dallas (Claire Trevor), a prostitute who has been run out of town by the indignant ladies of Tonto; and Henry Gatewood (Berton Churchill), an imperious banker smuggling embezzled funds, and his nagging wife

(Brenda Fowler). This motley band is driven by the chatty but nervous Buck Rickabaugh (Andy Devine), accompanied atop the stage by Sheriff Curly Wilcox (George Bancroft) and, eventually, his prisoner, the Ringo Kid (John Wayne, in his breakthrough role). Ringo is a cowboy just escaped from jail, whose capture provides the first adventure of the harrowing journey—a journey that eventually upends the conventional social hierarchy of the passengers, with the social elite exposed as cowardly and feckless, and the reprobates rising to the daunting challenges.

With the notorious Ringo now in tow, the stage makes its way through Monument Valley, pausing for a dinner at which only Ringo sits next to Dallas, the prostitute, who is shunned by the others. As the stage proceeds without military escort through perilous Indian territory, squabbles constantly erupt among the nervous passengers. At the next rest station Lucy is informed that her husband was wounded the previous night defending the station against an Apache attack; she faints and, while in her swoon, goes

Billed as "A Powerful Story of Nine Strange People!" Stagecoach *represents a landmark in the western genre.*

into labor. Dr. Boone, rather flush from a too-liberal sampling of Mr. Peacock's merchandise, orders up some coffee and grudgingly attends to his professional responsibility despite the derision of the haughty Hatfield. The greedy Gatewood expresses nothing but exasperation at this delay, while the doughty Dallas shows her mettle by attending to Lucy and her baby through a long and difficult night.

During a break from her duties, Dallas wanders outside, where Ringo divulges to her his business in Lordsburg: to kill the members of the Plummer gang, who murdered his brother and father. He then ventures an awkward marriage proposal and Dallas, flustered and touched, is moved to tears by her rush of affection and dread of Ringo's coming confrontation. The following morning, Doc Boone suggests a day's delay to allow Lucy to regain her strength; all the passengers agree except the incorrigibly malefic Gatewood.

As the trip resumes, the passengers' petty quarrels are stopped short by an arrow that pierces Peacock's shoulder. It's a full-scale Apache attack, the climactic crisis that will throw each traveler's character into bold relief. As Doc Boone attends to Peacock's wounds, Gatewood hysterically demands to be let off the hurtling stagecoach, driven now with panicked fervor by Buck. While Curly, Hatfield, and Ringo try to ward off the massed attackers, the courtly Hatfield prepares to save Lucy from the unspeakable defilement that awaits her by shooting her before she falls into Apache hands. But before he can pull the trigger, a shot rings out, and Hatfield falls, wounded.

The call of a bugle signals the arrival of the cavalry, who drive off the Apaches. With the battle now over, Hatfield mutters his dying words: "If you ever see Judge Ringfield . . . tell him his son. . . . " He dies before he is able to finish his sentence. The stage travels onward, under cavalry protection, safely to Lordsburg.

As soon as Gatewood alights from the stage, he is seized by the sheriff of Lordsburg, who has been informed of the banker's embezzling by telegraph. The wounded Peacock is rushed to the local hospital; Lucy, relieved at the news that her husband is unharmed, is also chastened by the generosity of Dallas, and offers to be there for her if she should ever need help in the future.

Ringo, having risen in the marshal's regard for his bravery in battle, is granted time to attend to his unfinished business with the Plummer gang. From a distant part of town, the anguished Dallas hears shots ring out, and she rushes out to find . . . Ringo, who has exacted his revenge and emerged unscathed. With a fresh complement of horses and Curly's and Doc's blessings, Dallas and Ringo leave to make a life together on Ringo's ranch in Mexico. As the film draws to a close, the couple heads off into the horizon as Doc comments, "Well, they're saved from the blessings of civilization."

See Ford, John; Location shooting; Remake; Wayne, John; Western

"I'm not only a philosopher, sir, I'm a fatalist. Somewhere, sometime, there may be the right bullet or the wrong bottle waiting for Josiah Boone. Why worry when or where?"

Thomas Mitchell as Dr. Josiah Boone in *Stagecoach* (1939)

STAR SYSTEM

The star system, essentially American, is a system for obtaining financial backing for the production of a motion picture, and for the commercial marketing of the picture, by exploiting the popular appeal of the star or stars who appear in the film. The system developed in Hollywood in the first decade of feature-film production and led to enormous salaries for the most popular screen actors. The Metro-Goldwyn-Mayer Corporation in particular was built around its company of actors, labeling its studio as a place with "more stars than there are in the heavens."

The domination of stars in film production and marketing remained strong until the early 1960s, when a shifting economy and new approaches to film producing brought about significant changes in industry procedures. To a significant degree, however, American film producers still depend on the popular appeal of familiar entertainment personalities—a fact corroborated by the numerous television actors brought to Hollywood in the 1970s, 1980s, and 1990s, including most prominently the comedians on the popular television show *Saturday Night Live,* for example, Chevy Chase, John Belushi, Bill Murray, and Gilda Radner, and two stars from *Cheers,* Ted Danson and Woody Harrelson.

The famous hillside HOLLYWOOD sign (originally HOLLYWOODLAND) was erected in 1923 at a cost of $21,000 to publicize a real estate development.

notable & quotable

"Being a movie star, and that applies to all of them, means being looked at from every possible direction. You are never left at peace, you're just fair game."

Greta Garbo, actress

STAR WARS

"A long time ago in a galaxy far, far away . . . ." These magical opening words of *Star Wars* (1977) prepare us for an archetypal battle of good against evil and also signal a permanent change in American cinema: the deft blend of traditional epic mythos, pioneering, breathtaking special effects, and clever allusions to classic films, *Star Wars* captivated the critics and the mass audience alike, earning staggering sums of money and rescuing not only Princess Leia but also Twentieth Century-Fox from the brink of doom. For better or worse, Hollywood had now entered the age of the megabuck blockbuster—the well-oiled machine of spectacular visual and sonic storytelling meshing with high-powered marketing tie-ins to guarantee profitability even before the first frame flickers before an audience.

Star Wars was the first film in director George Lucas's cycle of nine interrelated space epics; chronologically, however, it is fourth in the series, later installments of which cover events leading up to the action of *Star*

Wars. This chapter, "Episode IV: A New Hope," brings the audience quickly up to speed by explaining that the rebel forces (the good guys) have stolen plans that might make the Empire's (bad guys) Death Star, a gigantic armored battle station, vulnerable to attack. The film thus begins as a large Empire ship captures the ship of the rebels' Princess Leia (Carrie Fisher). Leia implants the plans into beeping droid R2-D2 just before the Empire's Storm Troopers take over the ship.

The evil Darth Vader (David Prowse with the voice of James Earl Jones), who dons a black cloak and a masked helmet, uses his great strength to kill a crewmember who will not reveal the location of the plans. R2-D2 and his whiny sidekick C-3PO (Anthony Daniels) jettison off the ship in a small pod. Leia denies any knowledge of the plans, so Darth takes her prisoner. Assuming the plans must be with the escaped androids, called simply droids, he sends a party after them.

R2-D2 and C-3PO land on the planet Tatooine. Although R2-D2's beeping sounds are unintelligible to the audience, C-3PO is frustrated by the smaller droid's blabbing on about some mission he has to complete. The

George Lucas's 1977 film Star Wars *is the second highest grossing movie of all time in the United States (and fourth in the world).*

▼

dainty, over-polite C-3PO creates some comic relief by incessantly complaining. Later, the droids are kidnapped and sold to Luke Skywalker (Mark Hamill) and his Uncle Owen (Phil Brown), a "moisture farmer" on the desert planet, who buys them to put them to work. Luke is intrigued when he finds out that C-3PO was involved with the rebellion. Even more intriguing is part of a hologram message that R2-D2 projects, in which Princess Leia begs for help from Obi-Wan Kenobi. Luke knows of a Ben Kenobi, and wonders if the two are the same.

At dinner that evening, Luke expresses interest in going to the academy a year early, before the next harvest. Owen asks him to stay for one more year. When Luke mentions the name Obi-Wan in front of his aunt and uncle, they exchange concerned looks (unbeknownst to Luke). Owen refuses to talk to Luke about his father or Ben Kenobi. Luke watches the twin suns set that night, dreaming of getting off of Tatooine.

Later, Luke finds that R2-D2 has taken off into the desert on his mission. When he and C-3PO rescue R2-D2, they are captured by sand people, but a mysterious hooded stranger rescues them. This stranger is a friendly old man, Ben Kenobi (Alec Guinness). "Obi-Wan" is Ben's Jedi knight name from decades ago, so R2-D2 plays the princess's message. The Jedi knights were the guardians of justice and peace in the Old Republic for thousands of generations.

Ben knew Luke's father; he was a Jedi knight and the greatest pilot in the galaxy before he was betrayed and killed by Ben's former pupil Darth Vader. Seduced by the dark side of the Force, Darth helped the Empire hunt down all of the Jedis. Luke's uncle Owen kept this secret for fear that Luke would go off and fight like his father. Ben explains the Force to Luke: "The Force . . . gives a Jedi knight his power. It's an energy field created by all living things. It surrounds us. It penetrates us." Ben gives Luke his father's Jedi weapon, a light saber, a powerful laser-beam sword. Luke asks for Ben's help, but Ben replies that it is Luke's turn to do battle. Echoing his uncle's sentiments, Luke refuses because of the workload on the farm.

Darth Vader warns Grand Moff Tarkin (Peter Cushing) and his leaders that despite the power of the Death Star (it can destroy a planet), they should be wary of the Force. Ridiculed as a priest practicing an ancient religion, Vader gives a demonstration of the Force, using it to strangle an officer half to death without ever touching him. Tarkin assures all that when they find the rebel base, they will destroy the resistance once and for all.

Luke returns home to find that his aunt and uncle have been killed by Storm Troopers searching for R2-D2. No longer the reluctant hero, Luke wants to master the Force and become a Jedi knight. In a cantina full of various carousing aliens—a memorable parody of every bar in every western movie—they find selfish smuggler and pilot Han Solo (Harrison Ford) and his sidekick, a sasquatch-like wookie called Chewbaca (Peter Mayhew). Solo and Chewbaca agree to take Luke, Ben, and the droids to the planet

notable & quotable

"My fantasy about these movies was always that they do a sequel of the Shopping Planet and the Beauty Parlor Planet where Princess Leia would get to do girl stuff."

Carrie Fisher, actress, 1999, as quoted in "America Goes Hollywood," Newsweek, *June 28, 1999*

Alderaan, where they hope to help Princess Leia as she asked. But before they can leave, Storm Troopers arrive to capture them. The group successfully fights off the Troopers and sets out for Alderaan in Solo's ship, the *Millenium Falcon.*

On the Death Star, Tarkin summons Leia and threatens to blow up her peaceful home planet of Alderaan unless she reveals the rebel base location. To save her planet, she answers, but he destroys the planet anyway. When Tarkin finds out that she has lied, he gives the order to terminate her. Meanwhile, Ben feels an awful flux in the Force, which corresponds to Alderaan's destruction. He has been training Luke in the ways of the Force, and with his instruction, Luke, even blindfolded, is able to parry attacks with his light saber. Han mocks Luke's reliance on hokey religions, claiming that there is not one powerful Force that binds all things. Then suddenly their ship comes out of hyperspace into a meteor storm, which turns out to be the scattered shards of Alderaan. Their ship is then captured by the Death Star.

By hiding in a compartment used for smuggling, Luke and the others are able to enter the Death Star ship undetected. Before heading off to disable the tractor beam that prevents their ship from leaving, Ben tells Luke, "The Force will be with you always." A reluctant Han does not want to risk his neck to help save the princess, but Luke guarantees a large monetary reward. Together they succeed in rescuing Leia and make their way back to the *Millenium Falcon.*

Meanwhile Ben, after successfully disabling the tractor beam, encounters Darth Vader, his former student. Darth claims he is the master now, and Obi replies, "Only a master of evil, Darth." During an exciting light saber duel, Ben tells Darth Vader that he can't win, because even if Darth strikes him down, Ben will become more powerful than he can possibly imagine. Just as Luke, Han, and Leia are ready to board the ship to make their escape, Luke sees Ben fighting with Vader. Sadly, Darth Vader strikes Ben down, causing him to vanish. Luke screams, "Ben!" but has no choice but to escape in the *Millennium Falcon.*

Knowing that the Death Star will follow them, Luke, Leia, and the others hurry to the rebel base, hoping the plans will reveal a weakness in the Death Star before it destroys them. The plans reveal a two-meter-wide opening in a thermal exhaust port that a direct hit would penetrate, thus destroying the Death Star. A direct hit is nearly impossible, but Luke is confident, saying, "I used to bullseye Womp rats in my t-16 back home. They're not much bigger than two meters."

Although Han won't endanger himself for the cause, he tells Luke, "May the Force be with you." Luke and a few other pilots climb into their small ships and head toward the Death Star. One of the rebel ships gets a computer-guided shot off, which almost hits its mark. After most of the rebel ships are destroyed, Darth mans a ship himself and closes in on Luke,

"The Force is what gives the Jedi his power. It's an energy field created by all living things. It surrounds us. It penetrates us. It binds the galaxy together."

Alec Guinness as Obi-Wan Kenobi in *Star Wars* (1977)

who is the last chance for the rebels. Darth is locked onto Luke's ship, ready to fire, when suddenly Han and his *Millenium Falcon* blast Darth Vader's ship off course. Hearing the sage voice of Obi-Wan saying, "Use the Force, Luke," Luke turns off the computer-guided missile system and uses his instincts and the Force to deliver the photon torpedo that destroys the Death Star and hurls Darth Vader's tiny craft even farther into space. The film ends with a celebration ceremony in which Princess Leia gives Han, Chewbaca, and Luke medals for their rebel victory against the Empire.

Since its release in 1977, *Star Wars* has earned over $780 million worldwide, currently making it the fourth-highest moneymaker in the world. Its highly anticipated prequel, *Star Wars: Episode I—The Phantom Menace*, despite being in release less than a year, is the eighth-highest-grossing film of all time in worldwide box office receipts.

See Ford, Harrison; Guinness, Alec; Lucas, George; Science-fiction film; Special-effects film

STEREOSCOPIC VIEWER

A stereoscopic viewer is a "three-dimensional" viewing device that gained wide popularity in the mid-nineteenth century. To achieve the three-dimensional effect two photographs of a scene appear side by side on a viewing card—one image on the left side and the other on the right. A frontispiece containing two lenses permits, as in natural vision, the left eye to focus solely on the left image and the right eye on the right image, thus creating the illusion of depth and dimension. Three-dimensional motion pictures, introduced commercially in 1952, worked on the same principle.

JAMES STEWART

James Stewart (usually called Jimmy) was born into a close-knit family in Indiana, Pennsylvania, on May 20, 1908, the eldest of three children. He showed an early interest in performing, doing magic tricks and playing the accordion, and participated in many amateur and impromptu basement productions.

While studying architecture at Princeton University, Stewart appeared in productions put on by the Triangle Club. After graduating in 1932, Stewart joined the University Players, based in Falmouth, Massachusetts. Among other future stars in that group were Henry Fonda and Margaret Sullavan, both close friends.

Stewart first performed on the Broadway stage in 1932; a few years later he made his way to Hollywood. He appeared in many films beginning in 1935, including *The Murder Man, Small Town Girl, Born to Dance, After*

James Stewart's self-effacing manner and boy-next-door demeanor made him a favorite with audiences for generations. He is most associated with Frank Capra's feel-good Christmas film It's a Wonderful Life.

the Thin Man, The Last Gangster, and *Of Human Hearts.* Margaret Sullavan was especially helpful to him, insisting that her old friend from the University Players be given parts in her movies.

Stewart was not typical movie-star material. Though he was good looking, the tall, gangly young man had a self-effacing manner and a slow way of talking. But these characteristics turned out to be assets, and his early films capitalized on his decent, boy-next-door demeanor. In 1938 this persona was put to perfect use in director Frank Capra's comedy *You Can't Take It With You.* The following year, Stewart starred in *Mr. Smith Goes to Washington,* still a favorite with audiences.

With his Oscar-winning performance in *The Philadelphia Story* (1940), Stewart's sterling reputation was cemented. (His Best Actor Oscar resides in the Indiana, Pennsylvania, hardware store that has been in the Stewart family for generations.) He made a few films in 1941 and then enlisted in the military to fight in World War II. As a pilot, he commanded twenty combat missions over Nazi Germany, eventually achieving the rank of colonel. After the war Stewart stayed in the Air Force Reserve and eventually attained the rank of brigadier general, the highest-ranking entertainer in the U.S. military. He would eventually become associated with conservative social and political viewpoints, including a pro-war stance on Vietnam. (His stepson Marine lieutenant Ronald McLean died in combat in Vietnam.)

In 1947 Stewart began acting again, and critics noticed a new depth and maturity to his work. His first release was another Capra film, the fantasy-drama *It's a Wonderful Life,* the movie that most people now associate with Jimmy Stewart. In the following years he acted in a great variety of roles, from light comedy to drama, from westerns to suspense (including several outings with director Alfred Hitchcock). Among his more renowned films are *Harvey* (1950; Oscar nomination), *The Glenn Miller Story* (1954), *Rear Window* (1954; Oscar nomination), *The Man Who Knew Too Much* (1956), *The Spirit of St. Louis* (1957), *Vertigo* (1958), *Anatomy of a Murder* (1959; Oscar nomination) *The Man Who Shot Liberty Valance* (1962), *Mr. Hobbs Takes a Vacation* (1962), and *Shenandoah* (1965).

During the 1970s the still-popular Stewart branched out a bit, returning to Broadway in a stage version of *Harvey* and starring in a couple of short-lived television shows (including *The James Stewart Show*). His last film work was a voice-over in the 1991 animated feature *An American Tail 2: Fievel Goes West.*

Stewart was given a Lifetime Achievement Award by the American Film Institute in 1980 (the AFI named him to its Greatest Film Legends slate in 1999, granting Stewart the No. 3 slot on the men's list). He was presented with a special Oscar in 1985 "for 50 years of meaningful performances, for his high ideals, both on and off the screen, with the respect and affection of his colleagues." In 1985 he also was presented with the United States' highest civilian honor, the Medal of Freedom. The Jimmy Stewart Museum was dedicated in his Pennsylvania hometown in 1995.

After enjoying an extended bachelorhood, Stewart married Gloria Hatrick McLean in 1950, whom he met at a party at Gary Cooper's house. Their loving marriage, much admired in Hollywood circles, ended only with Gloria's death in 1994. Jimmy Stewart died on July 2, 1997, at age eighty-nine. He was survived by twin daughters, Judy and Kelly, and a stepson, Michael.

See Capra, Frank; Hepburn, Katharine; Hitchcock, Alfred; It's a Wonderful Life; Mr. Smith Goes to Washington; *Kelly, Grace;* Philadelphia Story; Rear Window; Vertigo

STONE, OLIVER

Oliver Stone was born on September 15, 1946, in New York City. The son of culturally disparate parents—his father was a right-wing Jewish-American stockbroker, his mother a French Catholic—Stone was raised an only child in a conservative environment. At a young age he was enrolled by his parents in the prestigious Trinity School, an all-boys institution focused on strict discipline and academic rigor. Stone felt oppressed and socially isolated in his youth, which he attributed to his status as an only child. He grew into an increasingly conflicted and unhappy young man, and any remaining stability was dissolved when at age sixteen, Stone learned that his parents were deeply in debt and divorcing.

Stone lived with his father until graduation, after which he attended Yale University for a year before dropping out in 1965. His young adult life after that can be characterized as that of a restless vagabond-adventurer. He traveled to Southeast Asia, where he taught English to Chinese-Vietnamese students for over a year. Stone then moved to Mexico, where in 1966 he completed 1,400 pages of a darkly toned, self-reflective symbolist fiction. Would-be publishers rejected his manuscript, shattering Stone's ego and compelling him to join the army for a return trip to Vietnam.

Stone served in Vietnam for fifteen months in four different combat units, where he won the Bronze Star for Valor and the Purple Heart with First Oak Leaf Cluster. Acid and an unending supply of marijuana underscored the numbing craze of battle. Upon his return to the United States as a Vietnam veteran, Stone felt more isolated and overlooked than ever. He remained a heavy drug user and a lonely outsider for years.

Finally, at the suggestion of a friend, and using his unpublished novel as evidence of a creative surge, Stone sought and won admission to New York University's film program. Under the tutelage of Martin Scorsese and other film instructors, Stone produced three short black-and-white films at NYU and turned once again to writing as "therapy."

In 1973 he secured backing for one of his screenplays, *Seizure*, a thriller about demonic evil. Although *Seizure* was a low-budget effort that fell into obscurity soon after its release, Stone continued to struggle, and in 1976 he moved to Hollywood to peddle his screenplays. There he was hired to write the screenplay for a film adaptation of a book by a young American, Billy Hayes. Hayes had been apprehended and jailed in Istanbul, Turkey, in 1970 for drug possession. The book, *Midnight Express*, recounted Hayes's treatment at the hands of Turkish officials, prison guards, and fellow prisoners.

Midnight Express brought professional recognition for Stone through a Best Screenplay Award from the Screenwriters Guild, followed by an Academy Award for Best Adapted Screenplay of 1978. Also of significance

Director Oliver Stone is known as much for his Vietnam-themed films such as Platoon *and* Born on the Fourth of July *as he is for controversial films like* JFK *and* Natural Born Killers.

in the *Midnight Express* experience was the emergence of Stone's style—a bold, dramatic approach that, while often attacked by critics, moved Stone to value his own work and gain some confidence.

By the early 1980s Stone was selling his writing talents to big-name Hollywood directors with action-oriented projects. He coscripted *Conan the Barbarian* with John Milius in 1982, wrote *Scarface* for Brian De Palma in 1983, *Year of the Dragon* for Michael Cimino in 1985, and *8 Million Ways to Die* for Hal Ashby in 1986.

Also during this time, Stone became intrigued by reports that the situation in Central America was leading to another Vietnam. Stone decided to visit for himself, and was horrified by what he found there, particularly in El Salvador. In early 1985 Stone developed a scenario for a film based on recent historical events in the country and the personal experiences of photojournalist Robert Boyle, who was Stone's "guide" when he went on his fact-finding mission. A fledgling British motion picture company agreed to finance the film when Hollywood studios refused, and *Salvador* was released in 1986. Although the film died at the box office, some filmgoers and critics were impressed by the picture's liberal stance and its presentation of oppressed people in El Salvador. More important, Salvador earned Stone the opportunity to make *Platoon*—a film about his own Vietnam experiences. *Platoon* grossed over $250 million and was nominated for eight Academy Awards, winning four, including Best Picture and Best Director of 1986. *Platoon* also clarified Stone's emerging cinematic style: a peripatetic and often subjectively oriented use of camera; a clear feel for relating popular music and lyrics to ideas and tone; a facility for quick-cut editing to convey chaos and upheaval; and a loud, upfront manner of "pointing out" critical thematic details. Stone again managed to arouse the critics, who described his work as radical, excessive, and sensationalistic.

Stone followed the success of *Platoon* with *Wall Street* (1987), a film that explored the greed-propelled world of American finance. In 1989 he coscripted and released another Vietnam War film, *Born on the Fourth of July*. The film recounts Vietnam veteran Ron Kovic's war traumas, which left him a paraplegic, and his postwar experiences, which resulted in bitter rage, psychological depression, and guilt. Stone's detractors considered the use of a sympathy-evoking paraplegic as a symbol for antiwar sentiments to be "simplistic," despite Stone's winning a second Best Director Academy Award for the film.

More recent—though no less controversial—films include *The Doors* (1991), about the life of legendary rock star Jim Morrison, *JFK* (1991), which attempts to deconstruct the "lone gunman" theory surrounding the assassination of John F. Kennedy, and one of Stone's most controversial films to date, *Natural Born Killers* (1994), in which two victims of traumatized childhoods become lovers and psychopathic serial killers irresponsibly glorified by the mass media.

Stone also wrote and directed *Nixon* in 1995, wrote the screenplay for the musical *Evita* in 1996, wrote and directed *U Turn* in 1997, and is currently filming *Any Given Sunday*, a drama starring Al Pacino as an aging football coach.

See Camera movement; Pacino, Al; Platoon; Scarface

STREETCAR NAMED DESIRE, A

A Streetcar Named Desire (1951) is a widely admired film, adapted from Tennessee Williams's intense Pulitzer Prize–winning play of 1947. The movie, directed by Elia Kazan, tells the story of the physical and mental

MERYL STREEP

Meryl Streep (birth name Mary Louise Streep) was born in Summit, New Jersey, on June 22, 1949 (some sources say 1951). As a young teen she took voice lessons for opera but turned to acting in high school productions. She attended Vassar College, with one term at Dartmouth to study costume design and playwriting. Streep received a master's degree in 1975 from the Yale University School of Drama, where she performed in several productions of the Yale Repertory Theater. After graduation she moved to New York City to find work on the stage. Streep enjoyed considerable success almost immediately, earning a Tony nomination for her performance on Broadway in *27 Wagons Full of Cotton.*

Streep has been noted for her ability to choose good roles. Her first screen role was in the heartbreaking film *Julia* (1977), and the following year she received an Academy Award nomination for Best Supporting Actress in *The Deer Hunter* (1978), which documented a tragedy of another type. In 1979 she worked in three excellent movies: *Manhattan, The Seduction of Joe Tynan,* and *Kramer vs Kramer,* winning the Best Supporting Actress Oscar for the latter.

Streep played the title character in *The French Lieutenant's Woman* (1981). In 1982 two films were released that featured the increasingly influential actress: *Still of the Night* and *Sophie's Choice.* In *Sophie's Choice* Streep played a Polish woman who struggles for a new identity in the United States following her confinement in a Nazi concentration camp. Streep's moving portrayal of the tragic Sophie won her the Best Actress Academy Award.

Streep has played opposite some of the greatest male actors of her generation, including Jack Nicholson, Kevin Kline, Dustin Hoffman, and Robert De Niro. Streep has played a great variety of parts, winning recognition for her mastery of different accents (including Sophie's). Some of her most notable roles have been in the films *Silkwood* (1983), *Out of Africa* (1985), *Heartburn* (1986), and *The Bridges of Madison County* (1995). Streep has shown an aptitude for comedy in such films as *Postcards from the Edge* (1990) and *Death Becomes Her* (1992). In 1995 she played an Italian housewife in the film *The Bridges of Madison County*, opposite Clint Eastwood.

Academy Award–winning actress Meryl Streep has garnered recognition for her mastery of different accents as well as for her talent and versatility.

With her husband (since 1978), sculptor Donald Gummer, Streep has four children. They live on the East Coast (she once said she could not deal with life in Los Angeles, where there is so much pressure to look perfect all the time). Streep has won every major acting award, including for work on television ("Holocaust"). Her eleven Academy Award nominations to date are surpassed only by Katharine Hepburn, who has received twelve.

See Allen, Woody; Deer Hunter, The; *De Niro, Robert; Eastwood, Clint; Hoffman, Dustin; Nicholson, Jack; Pollack, Sydney; Redford, Robert*

S

STREETCAR NAMED DESIRE, A

deterioration of a neurotic and desperate southern woman and the dark secrets that haunt her. With its adult themes and sexual subjects, *Streetcar* was considered extremely controversial and provocative when it was released. But it met with great acclaim, earning three Academy Awards for acting: Best Actress for Vivien Leigh, Best Supporting Actress for Kim Hunter, and Best Supporting Actor for Karl Malden. It also won the Oscar for best Black and White Art Direction/Set Direction.

As the story begins, a thirtyish woman, Blanche DuBois (Leigh), appears out of a cloud of mist at a train station. She has just arrived in New Orleans. Feigning helplessness, she asks a handsome young soldier how to get from the Desire streetcar to the Cemeteries and Elysian Fields streetcars—names that symbolically inform the audience that Blanche is on a journey of last resort.

A superficially refined southern belle, Blanche has come to stay with her sister, Stella (Kim Hunter). Blanche—always aware of her family's genteel roots—is shocked at how Stella has come down in the world. Stella and her husband, Stanley Kowalski (Marlon Brando), live in a seedy two-bedroom apartment in the French Quarter. The first time Blanche sees Stanley, he is

Elia Kazan's adaptation of the Tennessee Williams play A Streetcar Named Desire *starred Marlon Brando as the brutish Stanley Kowalski and Vivien Leigh as a mentally fragile southern belle.* ▼

in a fight at a bowling alley—not quite the class act that Blanche had been expecting.

Blanche tells Stella that she is on leave from her job as a schoolteacher. Blanche wants to be with people, protected, but she is concerned about the lack of privacy in the cramped living quarters, with no door between the bedrooms.

Stanley, a hyper-masculine, animalistic brute, immediately realizes that Blanche views him as inferior. He provocatively takes off his shirt in front of her and comments, "I'm gonna strike you as being the unrefined type." He also attacks one of her sore spots: making her talk about her dead husband. Having been alerted to Blanche's fragile mental state, we hear the gunshot that sounds in her head (we eventually learn that her husband committed suicide, and it is delicately implied that he was homosexual, and, further, that he was impotent with Blanche). Trying to block out the pain and the imaginary sound, Blanche puts her hands to her ears. She uses most of her energy to avoid and deny the pain from her past, fantasy being her main crutch. When big steamer trunks arrive at the apartment, Stella and Stanley are alerted that Blanche is planning an extended stay. Stanley rudely paws through the contents, noticing that the clothes are of far better quality than a schoolteacher could afford. Referring to Napoleonic Law (the concept that spouses share their property), he demands that Stella find out what has really happened to their family estate, Belle Reve (Beautiful Dream). Blanche—who was in charge of the family's property—claims that the holdings were squandered through the "epic debauchery" of other family members, but Stanley suspects that Blanche has essentially stolen Stella's (and thus his) share.

Against Stella's wishes, Stanley confronts Blanche about the money from the estate. She gives him piles of papers, explaining that they will trace the financial collapse of the DuBois family holdings.

Stella takes Blanche out so that Stanley can play poker with his buddies, including Harold "Mitch" Mitchell (Karl Malden). When the women return, the men, drunk, are still playing. Blanche turns on the radio in the adjacent room, and Stanley rudely barges in and snaps it off.

When Mitch leaves the poker table to go to the bathroom, he meets Blanche and engages her in friendly conversation. As always, she fishes for a compliment about her looks; Mitch bites, finding her attractive and charming. Blanche turns on the radio again, and they dance. But they're soon interrupted by Stanley, who is enraged by the loud music and by a losing poker hand. When Stella tries to interfere, he begins hitting her, until his friends literally drag him off her and douse him in the shower. Stella runs upstairs to a neighbor's apartment for refuge.

When Stanley sees that Stella is gone, he cries in remorse. He walks outside and, in one of the most memorable scenes in movie history, he bellows with guilt and longing: "Hey Stell-llllaaaa! Stell-llllaaaa!" Stella, torn

"I never met a dame yet that didn't know if she is good-looking or not without being told."

Marlon Brando as Stanley Kowalski in *A Streetcar Named Desire* (1951)

between fear and her overpowering desire for Stanley, eventually succumbs. They embrace passionately, and Stanley sweeps her up and carries her into the darkened apartment, presumably to bed.

The tension between Blanche and Stanley becomes more and more uncomfortable, and he overhears Blanche urging Stella to leave him. Stella defends Stanley, but he is roused to learn the real story about Blanche's past in the family hometown. He eventually learns that she was a prostitute at the sleazy Hotel Flamingo and that she wasn't just on leave from her job as a schoolteacher—she was fired for becoming involved with a seventeen-year-old boy. Meanwhile, the relationship between Mitch and Blanche is becoming more and more romantic. Blanche does her best to maintain a genteel, moralistic demeanor in front of Mitch, realizing that marriage is her last chance for a normal life. The reality, however, is that Blanche has an extensive sexual history, including a fondness for very young men.

Anxious to get rid of Blanche once and for all, Stanley reveals Blanche's sordid past to Mitch. Mitch ends the relationship, saying that while he knew Blanche wasn't exactly an innocent sixteen-year-old any longer, he had thought she was honest. But she had misrepresented herself to him. He cruelly holds her haggard face up to the light, letting her know that while he hadn't been fooled by her efforts to seem younger than she was, he had been willing to ignore the subterfuge because he thought they might have a future together.

Stanley is trying everything he can to keep Blanche from putting an irreversible wedge between him and Stella. He reminds his wife of how much passion they share. Stella is pregnant, and he tells her that everything between them will be fine again after the baby arrives and Blanche is gone. When Stella begins labor, Stanley brings her to the hospital. Alone in the apartment, Blanche has "conversations" with imaginary people—during the months she has been living with the Kowalskis, Blanche's already fragile grip on reality has loosened more and more. She rests her head on an imaginary man's shoulder, a fantasy that soothes her.

Stanley's rough, offscreen call of "Hey, Blanche" jolts her back to reality. With the baby not due until morning, Stanley has returned home, leaving Stella at the hospital. Blanche claims to be going on a trip with a gentleman—a fantasy—and Stanley pretends to go along with it. Blanche feels threatened by Stanley's seething hostility, and when he corners her, she breaks a bottle, which he wrestles away from her. A mirror breaks, and there is the implication that Stanley rapes her. (Movie-industry censors of the time would not allow an explicit rape scene to be shown.)

When Stella and her baby come home from the hospital, Stella chooses not to believe Blanche's story that Stanley has raped her. She and Stanley arrange for Blanche to go on a trip—to a mental hospital. Blanche flits about as though preparing for her romantic adventure. When a doctor (and a heavyset matron) comes to take Blanche away, Stella plays along with

Blanche, claiming that it is her suitor coming to take her on her trip. The doctor eases Blanche out of the house by playing the role of a kindly gentleman caller. Blanche buys into the ruse and politely tells him, "I have always depended on the kindness of strangers."

As her sister leaves, Stella finally succumbs to her doubts about Stanley, saying that he is never going to touch her again. She snatches up her baby and heads upstairs, to her refuge. As the film ends, an abandoned Stanley again cries forlornly, "Hey Stella! Hey Stella!"

See Brando, Marlon; Leigh, Vivien; Kazan, Elia

STRUCTURALISM

Structuralism is a theory of film analysis closely associated with semiotic criticism because of its systematic approach to film analysis. Structuralism, however, emphasizes ethnographic interests rather than linguistic (semiological) approaches in the study of film. The principles of structuralism were in part inspired by the work of anthropologist Claude Lévi-Strauss. Lévi-Strauss studied the oral rituals and mythology of certain South American Indians and by so doing isolated previously invisible patterns within these forms of communication. These polarized patterns, according to Lévi-Strauss, revealed how certain perceptions of the Indian tribes came to exist.

In a similar manner structuralist principles are sometimes applied to the full body of a film director's work to detect patterns that will reveal social and cultural meanings and allow a better understanding of the artist under examination. In this sense, structuralism is also related to auteur criticism. Similarly, structuralism can be applied to a specific film genre or an individual film.

STUDIO PICTURE

Disney was the 1998 box office leader (according to *Variety*), grossing $1.1 billion in the U.S. market and $1.2 billion overseas.

A motion picture made principally on a shooting stage rather than on location, and usually characterized by exact technical control of lighting, setting, and sound is called a studio picture. A studio picture often conveys a romantic quality because of controlled lighting and decor. Studio pictures also have decided advantages for expressionistic and atmospheric underscoring of theme, for example, *The Cabinet of Dr. Caligari* (1919), *Broken Blossoms* (1919), *The Informer* (1935), *New York, New York* (1976).

See Lighting; Location shooting; Sound

SUNSET BOULEVARD

"*I am big. It's only the pictures that got small.*"

Gloria Swanson as Norma Desmond in *Sunset Boulevard* (1950)

Billy Wilder's 1950 *Sunset Boulevard* does not open like a storybook, the way 1937's *A Star Is Born* did. *Sunset Boulevard* opens in the gutter, with leaves swirling in a crazy circle. The film's title is painted on the curb. A tracking shot takes the viewer up the boulevard as the credits appear in the same wedge-shaped letters. When the credits end, a voice is heard saying, "Yes, this is Sunset Boulevard, Los Angeles, California." The voice belongs to a dead man floating, face down, in a pool; it is the voice of screenwriter Joe Gillis (William Holden).

The film, then, will be a flashback with voice-over narration. Narration by a corpse is unusual in any medium, but it works perfectly in *Sunset Boulevard*, which is a film about the living dead, told by one who, for a time, was part of their circle. However, Gillis is not a typical corpse; he is a corpse who wants reportorial accuracy. Thus, he will tell his story before the press has a chance to distort it.

Gillis is a combination hustler-con artist, neither endearing nor smarmy, just inoffensively opportunistic. As a Los Angeleno, Gillis needs his car, but his creditors are after it. Gillis is a struggling screenwriter, peddling a script called "Bases Loaded."

When the two main characters meet, Norma Desmond (Gloria Swanson), a washed-up silent movie star, mistakes Gillis for an undertaker and ushers him into the bedroom, where he sees a simian arm hanging out of a coffin; it belongs to Norma's dead monkey. When Norma discovers Gillis is a screenwriter, she keeps him on to help her revise the script she has written for her comeback—the story of Salome, in which she, a woman of at least fifty, would play the biblical princess. Gillis, needing money as well as a place to hide from his creditors, agrees; he also becomes her kept man. At the same time, he is seeing Betty Schaefer (Nancy Olson), a young story editor at Paramount, who believes that one of his scripts has promise. Yet Gillis does not leave Norma for Betty; he leaves Norma because he is tired of being a successful gigolo but a failed writer. But, to quote Norma, "Nobody leaves a star." As Gillis walks out of the mansion, Norma shoots him; staggering across the patio, he falls into the pool.

"Cruel" is an adjective often associated with *Sunset Boulevard*. Some have thought it "cruel" of Wilder to cast Erich von Stroheim as Max von Mayerling, Norma's butler and former husband. Erich von Stroheim was once a major silent film director, as is his character von Mayerling. Von Stroheim brought a quality to the role that only someone who had experienced the vicissitudes of fortune could—humility. But it was not humility purchased at the expense of dignity. Max is still the aristocrat, even when he answers the door or pours champagne at Norma's spectral New Year's Eve party. Ironically, Max does get a chance to direct again; he stands in front of the newsreel cameras pretending to be Cecil B. DeMille as Norma begins her mad descent down the stairs.

Art imitated life when former silent-film star Gloria Swanson played washed-up silent film star Norma Desmond, whose eventual descent into madness garnered an Oscar nomination for Swanson.

◀

Before one can be sympathetic to characters like Max and Norma, one must first see them exposed and vulnerable. There are few moments in film as brutally honest, or as poignant, as the one in which Norma suddenly stands up during a screening of one of her movies and swears, "I'll be up there again, so help me!" As she makes her vow, a cone of light from the projector turns her face sickly silver. While one can be compassionate toward Norma, Wilder does not make it easy to like her as they watch her descent into madness.

"*We didn't need dialogue. We had faces!*"

Gloria Swanson as Norma Desmond in *Sunset Boulevard* (1950)

Visually *Sunset Boulevard* focuses on images of rotting sumptuousness. Rats scamper about in an unfilled swimming pool with weeds growing out of the cracks, a tennis net sags over a court with faded markings, a pet monkey is buried ceremoniously in a satin-lined coffin in Norma's garden, air wheezes through the organ in Norma's living room. Norma sleeps in a bed built in the shape of a ship, although it really looks like an oversized cradle. Her parlor is filled with so many mementos of her past that pictures of Norma Desmond crowd each other off the tables.

Norma's plan for a comeback is mad, and the only way she will ever face the cameras will be in a state of madness. Wilder has staged a finale of operatic grandeur for her. To the sinuous rhythms of Franz Waxman's score, Norma makes a serpentine descent down the staircase, her arms raised for the dance she will never perform. She has improvised a Salome costume; her eyelids glitter with stardust, and rhinestones nestle in her hair. Oblivious to everything, she confuses her living room with a soundstage, newsreel cameras with movie cameras, the reporters with the Salome cast, and Max with Cecil B. DeMille. "All right, Mr. DeMille; I'm ready for my close-up," Norma says as she walks right into the lens, unblinking as the light floods her lined face.

See DeMille, Cecil B.; Swanson, Gloria; Von Stroheim, Erich; Wilder, Billy

SURREALISM

Surrealism is a modern movement in painting, sculpture, theater, film, photography, and literature, originating in France in the early 1920s, that seeks to express subconscious states through the disparate and illogical arrangement of imagery. Early surrealist filmmakers—Man Ray, Salvador Dali, and Luis Buñuel—captured on film a variety of material phenomena and arranged the imagery in incongruous ways so as to effect subjective, dreamlike meanings. The classic example of an early surrealistic film is *Un Chien Andalou* (1928). Surrealism was born in a revolt against realism and traditional art. According to an early manifesto written by its leader, André Breton, surrealism is defined as "pure psychic automatism by which an attempt is made to express, either verbally, in writing, or in any other manner, the true function of thought."

See Avant-garde

SWANSON, GLORIA

Unlike the screen careers of Charlie Chaplin, Wallace Reid, and Theda Bara, that of Gloria Swanson does not display a conventional arc of achievement. Her stardom was not manufactured and presented to the public as a *fait accompli,* nor did she strive to perfect one particular image and cling to it for as long as popular taste allowed. Instead, Swanson's career progressed in a series of plateaus, as her image in 1915, 1918, and 1923 shifted from comedienne to ingenue to (occasional) tragedienne. But the evolution of her screen image was not the only extraordinary development in her career. In 1926 Swanson walked away from her $7,000 weekly salary and set up her own production company. She was not the only female star to attempt this, but unlike Mary Pickford and Norma Talmadge, she did not have a husband to act as her business partner.

Gloria Swanson began in films at the Essanay studio in Chicago in 1914. Signed as a stock player at $13.25 per week, the fifteen-year-old schoolgirl soon became a steady member of the company, making up each morning to play sophisticated characters twice her age. Chaplin was then at Essanay, and Swanson made a brief appearance in *His New Job* (1915), but the comedian who really impressed her was Wallace Beery, who was starring in the *Sweedie* comedy series, transvestite slapstick in which he appeared as a Swedish housemaid. They were married after Swanson transferred to Essanay's Niles studio in California. The marriage was a disaster, but Swanson did follow Beery to the Sennett lot, where she won some success in a series of eight two-reelers for director Clarence Badger. Swanson, however, resisted being developed by Sennett as "a second Mabel Normand."

In 1918 a reporter for *Motion Picture* magazine caught up with her on the Triangle lot, where she had been appearing in melodramas for Frank Borzage and Jack Conway. Already Swanson referred to her comedies as mere "stepping stones"—useful preparation for dramatic vehicles to follow. She acknowledged the best of them but made it clear where she believed her future lay. Swanson appeared in eight of these Triangle features, most of which she denigrates in her autobiography. Many were simple exploitations of the current war hysteria, uncomfortably jingoistic and laced with absurd espionage plots. But her Triangle films did demonstrate that the public would accept Swanson in dramatic high-society roles, and they allowed her to build on the comic timing she had developed in her films with Badger. Cecil B. DeMille recognized this, and when Triangle collapsed he cast her in *Don't Change Your Husband* (1919).

DeMille realized that he had found an average American girl who could wear clothes. He understood that the fashion in heroines was about to change and that options were now available other than the traditional virgin or vamp. Swanson would be his vehicle in fusing these two characters.

The six films they made together over the next two years, including *Male and Female* (1919) and *Why Change Your Wife?* (1920), offered a new female role model for postwar America. Swanson proved to be the one actress, even more than Bebe Daniels, whom DeMille could cloak in worldliness without obscuring the homelier American virtues underneath.

Cecil B. DeMille cast Gloria Swanson in Don't Change Your Husband *in 1919. They made six more films together in the two years that followed.*

▼

The team broke up when they became too expensive for each other, and Swanson began a long series of films for Sam Wood that seemed to endlessly repeat the formulas established by DeMille. Fleeing to Paramount's east coast studio in Astoria, New York, and working with Allan Dwan, she took over creative control of her pictures for the first time. She did her share of costume romances, notably *Zaza* (1923), but brought new life to her career by tapping her experience in comedy for *Manhandled* (1924) and *Stage Struck* (1925).

By 1926 she had been luxuriating in her east coast isolation for three years and had come to see Hollywood as simply a factory town where the key decisions involving her career were being made by unsympathetic executives. That year, she broke with Paramount.

The establishment of Gloria Swanson Productions proved to be an organizational nightmare. Without adequate fiscal or technical advice, she needed to construct an entire corporate infrastructure, and production on her first film, *The Love of Sunya* (1927), lagged far behind schedule. A move to Hollywood eased some of these problems, and she was able to restore much of her position with her next film, *Sadie Thompson* (1928).

In the decades that followed, Swanson was able to keep recasting her public image as businesswoman, artist, inventor, stage actress, food faddist, and occasional film star. In *Sunset Boulevard* (1950) she played the actress Norma Desmond, frozen into her silent-star image and surrounded by a set of "waxworks" equally trapped in their old roles—if somewhat less secure financially. But Swanson's success at keeping herself in the public eye proved that she was no waxwork.

See Brooks, Louise; Chaplin, Charlie; DeMille, Cecil B.; Pickford, Mary; Sunset Boulevard; *Talmadge, Norma; Wilder, Billy*

T

TALMADGE, NORMA

Of all the silent stars whose reputations collapsed with the coming of sound, Norma Talmadge was certainly the most important. Guided by her husband, the powerful film-industry executive Joseph Schenck, she formed

Silent film star Norma Talmadge was a pioneer for women in film: she formed her own production company (with husband Joseph Schenck) in 1917, and by the end of her career, she had appeared in over 200 films.

◀

her own production company in 1917 and operated it until her last film in 1930, one of the few stars to maintain popularity during this entire period. In a list of salaried stars given in the 1924 *Film Daily Yearbook*, her $10,000 per week far outstrips the nearest competition.

Norma Talmadge was born in Jersey City in 1897. With her sisters Constance and Natalie, she was raised by her strong-willed mother, Margaret. Norma began posing for stereopticon slides in 1910 and made a fitting transition to the Vitagraph Company that same year. Over the next five seasons, she appeared in some 250 films for Vitagraph before striking out on her own and eventually landing a contract with Triangle–Fine Arts. But not until she returned to New York in 1917 and opened her own studio on East Forty-eighth Street did she emerge as a major star.

Throughout the era of silent features, Norma Talmadge maintained a remarkably consistent screen persona. Swanson or Pickford would alternate melodramas, comedies, and costume romances, but Talmadge steadfastly offered the one image her audiences seemed to demand: a brave but emotional heroine. Her one real attempt to break this mold, an appearance as the Parisian *gamine* in Clarence Brown's *Kiki* (1926), seems to have been a serious commercial failure.

Gloria Swanson nearly broke with Paramount the same year, complaining of monotony in the roles she was asked to play. But Talmadge made her own choices and decided to keep on giving the public what it wanted. The decision may have been wise in the short term, but when the vogue for this particular brand of screen heroine faded, she and her films were violently rejected.

See Brenon, Herbert; Swanson, Gloria

TAXI DRIVER

"Loneliness has followed me my whole life. Everywhere. In bars, in cars, sidewalks, stores, everywhere. There's no escape. I'm God's lonely man."

Robert De Niro as Travis Bickle (narration) in *Taxi Driver* (1976)

Taxi Driver (1976) is director Martin Scorsese's gritty, disturbing, nightmarish film classic that examines alienation in society. The film explores the psychological madness within an obsessed, twisted, lonely individual.

The film opens with that lonely individual, Travis Bickle (Robert De Niro), applying for a job as a hack in a taxi company. A twenty-six-year-old ex-Marine, he lives in a squalid, welfare-style, studio apartment.

Cruising the seedy night streets, he is disgusted by the world of urban decay and sleaziness, and he pops pills to keep calm. After his shifts, pent-up, he goes to porn movie theaters. Agonized, he is trying to find his own identity.

Travis is attracted to Betsy (Cybill Shepherd), a volunteer at the campaign headquarters of presidential candidate Charles Palantine. Travis invites her to go to the movies. Their date begins on a positive note, but the socially inept Travis then takes her to a porno movie. Offended, Betsy storms out of the theater. Travis's attempts to apologize are ineffective—she hails a taxi and dumps him. His descent into isolation and psychosis begins.

Travis illegally buys an assortment of semiautomatic guns. Then he begins an intense regimen of physical training, exercising fanatically as his mental condition deteriorates. He practices shooting in an indoor firing range. His apartment wall is decorated with tacked-up maps and political paraphernalia related to candidate Palantine.

Near a platform assembled for an outdoor rally for Palantine, Travis sees Betsy busily working. Hidden in the crowd, Travis engages a Secret Service agent (Richard Higgs) in a conversation. For the agent, Travis is quickly marked and fulfills the stereotypical profile of a lone, crazy gunman.

One night in an all-night convenience store, Travis witnesses a holdup of the store manager. He confronts the young black stickup man, and

Director Martin Scorsese, shown here in a cameo role in Taxi Driver *with Robert De Niro, claims that the most important shot in the film is when the disturbed Travis Bickle is on the phone trying to get another date with Betsy (Cybill Shepherd). In it, the camera slowly moves away, suggesting that the conversation is too painful to bear.*

▼

shoots him in the head with his concealed gun. Worried because he used an unlicensed weapon, Travis leaves the gun and drives off.

Travis meets Iris (Jodie Foster), a twelve-year-old prostitute, who is managed by a small-time pimp, "Sport" (Harvey Keitel). After Travis and Sport negotiate a price for Iris's services, she escorts Travis to a walk-up apartment for the arranged sex. Instead, treating her like his own child, he vainly attempts to persuade her to give up her life of prostitution.

Travis's mission is to assassinate Palantine. As Palantine speaks at a rally, Travis works his way through the crowd toward him. Before he can get close enough, the Secret Service bodyguard he had spoken to earlier spots him. Travis flees, barely eluding the agent's pursuit.

Frustrated, Travis drives to Sport's apartment. He greets Sport and then shoots him point-blank in the stomach. A few moments later, at Iris's apartment building, Travis is wounded by Sport, who has survived Travis's attack and come after him for revenge. Travis quickly guns him down. Then Travis is shot by the brothel's security guard. Wounded and staggering, Travis manages to kill him. In Iris's room, where she crouches, terrified, Travis shoots the brothel manager. Travis finally attempts to shoot himself in the neck, but the gun clicks empty. When the police arrive, Travis slowly loses consciousness.

Travis becomes a media hero for his vigilante bravery. He receives a thank-you letter from Iris's parents; she is back home. Travis, recovered and back on the job, talks to his cabbie friends while waiting for a fare. A passenger enters Travis's cab; it's Betsy. She is the first to speak, acknowledging his noble deed and a bit awed by his celebrity. Travis smiles silently and watches her in the rearview mirror. When she arrives at her destination, she exits the cab, and Travis drives off into the dark night.

See De Niro, Robert; Scorsese, Martin

notable & quotable

"If you were considered pretty, you might as well have been a waitress trying to act—you were treated with no respect at all."

Elizabeth Taylor, actress, 1999, as quoted in "America Goes Hollywood," Newsweek, *June 28, 1999*

ELIZABETH TAYLOR

Elizabeth Rosamond Taylor was born to American parents living in London, England, on February 27, 1932. The family eventually moved to Los Angeles, California, where the exceptionally beautiful child was noticed by scouts for the movie studios. Taylor subsequently appeared in a number of films from the age of ten: *There's One Born Every Minute* (1942), *Lassie Come Home* (1943), *Jane Eyre* (1944), and *The White Cliffs of Dover* (1944). With the release of *National Velvet* in 1944, little Elizabeth—only twelve years old—was a star.

In the following years Taylor easily made the transition from child star to adult performer. She became world renowned for her beauty, especially her remarkable violet eyes. She was clearly a talented actress and worked steadily, in comedies as well as dramas, including *Life with Father* (1947) and *Little Women* (1949).

In the 1950s Taylor's roles consolidated her star status. She appeared in such popular and diverse films as *Father of the Bride* (1950), *A Place in the Sun* (1951), *The Last Time I Saw Paris* (1954), *Giant* (1956), and *Cat on a Hot Tin Roof* (1958), in which she played the sensuous Maggie the Cat.

Beginning in that decade, Taylor revealed a flair for the dramatic in her personal life as well. Her fans watched breathlessly as the eighteen-year-old married wealthy hotelier Nicky Hilton in 1950; they divorced in 1951. She married actor Michael Wilding the following year; they divorced in 1956. In 1957 Taylor tied the knot with producer Mike Todd; she was widowed when his plane crashed in 1958. In 1959 the public was outraged when actor/singer Eddie Fisher divorced the popular Debbie Reynolds to marry Taylor.

Taylor and Fisher divorced in 1964, and just a week later she married actor Richard Burton—another scandal. That tempestuous union lasted until 1974, when they divorced. But the flamboyant couple remarried in 1975—and divorced again a year later. Later that year Taylor married the Republican senator from Virginia, John Warner; they split in 1982. There were a few subsequent engagements, but Taylor held off marrying again until 1991, when she wed Larry Fortensky, a construction worker whom she met during a substance-abuse rehabilitation program. They divorced in 1996. Taylor has four children with her various mates: Michael and Christopher Wilding, Liza Todd, and a daughter, Maria, she adopted with Burton.

Actress Elizabeth Taylor is famous for her many husbands, her AIDS activism, her line of perfumes, and, of course, her acting.

Somehow through all this activity Taylor managed to find time to make movies, including some superb ones. In the 1960s she starred in, among other films, *Butterfield 8* (1960), *Cleopatra* (1963), *The Sandpiper* (1965), and *Who's Afraid of Virginia Woolf?* (1966). She was the highest-paid female star in the world and won Best Actress Academy Awards for her performances in *Butterfield 8* and *Virginia Woolf.*

In the 1970s Taylor's professional life diminished as her personal problems increased. Beset by various illnesses and injuries, as well as alcohol and prescription-drug abuse, her weight ballooned and she was sometimes the object of cruel ridicule. But Taylor is nothing if not enduring, and even though she has worked little (and in such occasionally dismal fare as *The Mirror Crack'd,* 1980, and *The Flintstones,* 1994), she has regained the public's admiration, emerging virtually as a living legend. She was awarded the Jean Hersholt Humanitarian Award for her work in charity causes (she has been particularly active in the fight against AIDS), and has been given several Life Achievement Awards, including from the American Film Institute and the Screen Actors Guild.

See Giant; Place in the Sun, A

TECHNICOLOR

A color-film process developed by Herbert T. Kalmus and Robert Comstock during the years 1916–18, initially the Technicolor system produced color images through a two-color process: red-orange-yellow colors on one negative, and green-blue-purple colors on a second negative. The two separate negatives were then wed to create a scale of color values of less-than-accurate renderings, but it was a process that was utilized by major Hollywood studios in the 1920s: *Cythera* (1924), *The Phantom of the Opera* (1925), *The Black Pirate* (1926). Technicolor was a popular embellishment at this time for costume-action and romantic films.

Eventually the Technicolor Corporation replaced the two-color lamination process with a three-color process. *Becky Sharp* (1935) and *The Garden of Allah* (1936) were among the first Hollywood films to be photographed with the three-color process. The quality of color reproduction in these films was significantly improved, although the process tended to emphasize the "warmer" colors (yellows, oranges, and browns) of the spectrum, giving the films a golden look.

The Technicolor process held an exclusive monopoly on color filming until the development of new processes in the late 1940s and early 1950s by Eastman Kodak, Warner Bros., and other competing laboratories.

See Tourneur, Maurice; Wizard of Oz, The

The Top 5 of 1957, with a high of $18.5 and a low of $6.5 million: *The Ten Commandments, Around the World in 80 Days, Giant, Pal Joey*, and *Seven Wonders of the World.*

THALBERG, IRVING

Allene Talmey, in her 1927 volume of film industry profiles, writes of Irving Thalberg's unspectacular background, a comfortable middle-class upbringing, some education, and a professional life that left little time for personal foibles. Talmey complained that ambitious pants-pressers, junkmen, and steerage passengers all made better copy but that Thalberg knew better than any of them how to make successful pictures.

Talmey credits Thalberg with the success of *The Big Parade* (1925), *The Merry Widow* (1925), and *Flesh and the Devil* (1927), and tries to explain how his supervision of production acted to shape these hits, working sometimes with, and sometimes against, Metro-Goldwyn-Mayer's noted writers, directors, and stars. Thalberg himself never took a credit. Without the traditional rags-to-riches story to cling to, they were at a loss to understand exactly what he did around the studio or how his function differed from that of his associate at MGM, Harry Rapf and Louis B. Mayer.

But those within the industry were not uncertain. They knew that Thalberg had whipped the untidy Universal lot into shape when he arrived there in 1920 and that he had masterminded the string of hits that placed the newly assembled MGM among the most profitable of Hollywood stu-

T

THALBERG, IRVING

From humble beginnings as studio head Carl Laemmle's secretary, Irving Thalberg whipped the Universal lot into shape when he arrived there in 1920 and had masterminded the string of hits that placed the newly formed MGM among the most profitable Hollywood studios.

◀

dios. In addition, he had done this by "breaking eggs": seizing authority and exerting it against procedural inertia and executive paralysis.

His most significant steps were taken at Universal. As Carl Laemmle's private secretary, the twenty-year-old Thalberg had been deposited at the west coast studio and assigned to supervises production in concert with three other executives, Tarkington Baker, Maurice Fleckles, and Isidore Bernstein (the last two were Laemmle relatives). Since the opening of Universal City five years earlier, there had been no clear authority on the lot and no clear chain of command to Laemmle in New York. Managers and supervisors were appointed at frequent intervals, their orders undercut by cables from the East. The various production units at Universal City had once operated almost as independent outfits and had never quite been brought under unified command. Soon Thalberg had rid himself of his three associates and turned his attention to Erich von Stroheim's *Foolish Wives.* It was already in production when Thalberg arrived, so there was little he could do but watch von Stroheim run the budget far over the original projections. When the time came to launch the next von Stroheim picture, *Merry-Go-Round,* Thalberg kept the director from also acting in it, thus implicitly threatening to remove him from the picture if things went awry. After $220,000 had been spent and only a small fraction of the film completed, Thalberg removed von Stroheim, brought in another director, and quickly completed the project.

There are two items of significance here. First, despite the fact that von Stroheim personally appealed to Laemmle in New York, his attempt to circumvent the studio production head failed. Laemmle threw his support behind Thalberg, thereby asserting the primacy of a central executive over any of the individual talents on the Universal lot. What has been forgotten over the years is that *Merry-Go-Round,* as revamped under Thalberg, became a huge commercial success that validated his judgment in the eyes of the industry. If one producer could succeed in this, so could another.

In 1923 Thalberg was stolen away from Laemmle by Louis B. Mayer, who gave him a similar position at his studio on Mission Road. Within a year the MGM merger had taken place, and the "boy producer" found himself with a tremendous and somewhat nightmarish responsibility—supervising the efforts of all the merged companies. There was no guarantee that anyone could hold these disparate egos together. Professional and personal rivalries, and the problems of fusing the merged organizations, were all laid at Thalberg's door. He had to contend with such willful figures as Neilan, Seastrom, Vidor, and von Stroheim, establish a central authority, stay out of Mayer's way, and not miss a beat in the release schedule.

Backed when necessary by Mayer's strong-arm tactics, Thalberg accomplished all this within a single season. He learned to accommodate Vidor, fired Neilan and von Stroheim, and seemingly charmed the rest into submission.

Thalberg was not infallible. He fired Mauritz Stiller while he was directing Greta Garbo in *The Temptress* (1926), and the result was the only Garbo picture of the period to lose money. He dragged his feet on the introduction of sound for so long that despite MGM's eventual success with the medium, rival studios had already seized a large share of the market. But the legend remained. Thalberg died in 1936, and the following year the Academy of Motion Picture Arts and Sciences named a special award after him, "given each year for the most consistent high level of production achievement by an individual producer, based on pictures he has personally produced during the preceding year."

See Gish, Lillian; Ince, Thomas; Neilan, Marshall; Vidor, King; von Stroheim, Erich

THIRD MAN, THE

The Third Man (1949) is one of the masterpieces of world cinema. Carol Reed's brooding psychological thriller uses the ghostly wreck of postwar Vienna and a deft montage of skewed camera angles to snake the viewer through the corruption, menace, and desperation of one of the world's most civilized cities just emerging from the shadows of a savage war.

Holly Martins (Joseph Cotten), a broke American pulp writer of western novels, arrives in the gloomy, war-ravaged city to see his childhood friend Harry Lime, who has offered him a job. He finds out from the porter (Paul Höerbiger) at Lime's building that Lime was recently killed in a car accident. A shocked Holly makes his way to Lime's funeral, where a beautiful woman, Anna Schmidt (Alida Valli), captures his attention. Martins accepts the offer of a ride back to town from a British military policeman, Major Calloway (Trevor Howard). They stop at a bar, where the major, after interrogating Holly about Lime, informs him that Lime was a racketeer and a murderer. An enraged Holly tries to punch Calloway, who calms Holly, brings him to a hotel, and suggests he leave for America the next day.

Penniless but determined to remain in Vienna long enough to clear the reputation of his friend, Holly providentially runs into an eccentric English litterateur, Mr. Crabbin (Wilfrid Hyde-White), who generously offers to put Holly up in the hotel for several days if he will deliver a lecture on the contemporary novel at his cultural reeducation institute. Holly agrees, planning to use this time in Vienna to find out what really happened to Lime.

Holly's first source, a creepy, fallen aristocrat named Baron Kurtz (Ernst Deutsch), says that Lime was hit by a truck while he was crossing the street. Although he tries to dissuade Holly from investigating further, he inadvertently tells him where he can find Anna, the beautiful woman Holly saw at the funeral. Holly goes to the Josefstadt theatre, where he meets with the Czech actress after her performance. Devastated by Lime's death, Anna wishes that she were dead, too. She tells Holly that Lime was killed by his own driver, who was subsequently investigated and released. She also tells him that Lime's doctor happened to be at the scene and pronounced him dead.

Beginning to share Holly's suspicions, Anna joins him in his investigation. Together they interrogate the reluctant porter, who admits that he saw three men carrying off Lime's body, one of whom was an unknown "third man" whom he could not identify. When Anna and Holly arrive at her apartment, the police are scouring her place for information about Lime. They confiscate Anna's forged passport. Anna claims that the only crooked thing Lime ever did was to forge her passport so that the Russians wouldn't

"In Italy for 30 years under the Borgias they had warfare, terror, murder, and bloodshed, but they produced Michelangelo, Leonardo da Vinci, and the Renaissance. In Switzerland they had brotherly love, they had 500 years of democracy and peace, and what did that produce? The cuckoo clock."

Orson Welles as Harry Lime in *The Third Man* (1949)

expatriate her. Holly tells Major Calloway that he is going to get to the bottom of the case. Calloway warns him that "death" is at the bottom of everything and that he should leave death to the professionals. Martins quips, "Mind if I use that line in my next western?"

Holly meets with Dr. Winkel (Erich Ponto), who claims to have no opinion on the cause of Lime's death. Winkel, who arrived a short time after the accident occurred, corroborates Kurtz's claim that only he and Popescu, an associate of Lime's, were there. Holly meets with Popescu and tells him about the third man; Popescu asks him who gave him that information, and Holly tells him it was the porter. Popescu pushes to find out what else the porter knows, warning that people should be careful in Vienna.

Meanwhile, at the scene of the accident, Holly is trying to put the pieces of the puzzle together when the porter calls down from his window that he wants to help by giving Holly more information later, when his wife is gone. A creepy stranger watches this interaction, adding to the mystery.

In the midst of all the intrigue, Holly finds himself falling in love with Anna. The pair exchange stories about Lime, whose reputation they are both so fiercely devoted to clearing. His blind naiveté, along with her tragic sense of love, causes them both to idolize their deceased friend. Holly consoles Anna by telling her that she will fall in love again. Later, accidentally calling him Harry, she tells him that he should find a girl.

They soon receive a jolt when they find out that the porter has been murdered, evidently for talking to Holly. Before he can go to the police, however, Holly must deliver his lecture, at which he embarrasses himself and Crabbin by not being able to answer the sophisticated audience's questions. Audience members even start to leave. Popescu shows up and asks Holly about his new book. Holly tells him that he is writing a fact-based murder mystery, *The Third Man*. Popescu warns that he should stick to fiction and scrap his book.

Major Calloway is determined to enlist Holly as an ally by disabusing him of his stubborn illusions about Lime. He tells Holly that Lime stole penicillin from military hospitals, diluted it, and then sold it on the black market, causing the deaths of many children who received the corrupted drug.

The disillusioned Holly turns to Anna for solace, bringing her roses and declaring his love for her, but she is still obsessed with her memories of Lime. She has also just found out about Lime's racket, but, unlike Holly, is unfazed; when he tells her that he is no longer interested in finding Lime's killer, she rebukes him for his petty moralism and lack of loyalty to Lime. Later, on the street, Holly realizes that he is being followed. He calls back to the cowardly spy to reveal himself. Out of the shadow of a doorway he glimpses . . . Harry Lime (Orson Welles). Before Holly can get to Lime, he disappears around a corner.

Holly reports his startling discovery to Major Calloway, who proceeds to dig up Lime's coffin—only to find the body of one of Lime's associates. Calloway then calls Anna in for questioning, threatening to turn her over to the Russians if she doesn't cooperate. She only says she wishes Lime were dead so he would be safe from everybody who's chasing him.

Holly goes to Dr. Winkel and Kurtz to set up a meeting with Lime. The two old friends meet and ride on a Ferris wheel. In response to Holly's reproaches, an unrepentant Lime explains that his faked death (Lime was the "third man" at the scene) was designed to facilitate his black-market activities. He issues a threat to Holly, telling him that he could easily be disposed of from such a great height. Lime then tries to coax his old friend into a partnership, but to no avail. As they exit the Ferris wheel, Lime declares, "After all, it's not that awful. You know what the fellow said: 'In Italy for thirty years under the Borgias they had warfare, terror, murder, bloodshed. They produced Michelangelo, Leonardo da Vinci, and the Renaissance. In Switzerland they had brotherly love, 500 years of democracy and peace. And what did that produce? The cuckoo clock.' "

"Next time we'll use a foolproof coffin."

Trevor Howard as Major Calloway in *The Third Man* (1949)

The outraged Holly now agrees to help Major Calloway capture Lime in exchange for his assurance that he will not deport Anna to the Russian sector. Holly agrees to lure Lime to a meeting to be staked out by the police. An indignant Anna chastises Holly for his treachery and warns Lime just before the trap is sprung. Having been tipped off, Lime dashes away and flees underground, into the city's sewer system. The ensuing spectacular chase through the sewers of Vienna is one of the most visually stunning sequences in movie history. After shooting one of the officers in pursuit, Lime is shot by Major Calloway but manages to limp away. He feebly pushes up against a heavy grate. Holly corners him, and Lime gives Holly an ambiguous look—pleading for his life or possibly his death—just before Holly shoots him.

After Harry's funeral, Holly waits for Anna ahead of her on the road. In an extremely long take (one shot), Anna, who begins a hundred yards or so away, slowly walks toward Holly and then brushes past him, never looking his way and leaving him standing alone as the camera fades to black.

See Welles, Orson; Writer

THREE-DIMENSIONAL FILM

A motion picture produced to allow a stereoscopic effect is called a three-dimensional film. In a 3-D, stereoscopic process, two pictures of a scene are taken simultaneously from points slightly apart from one another, and through the use of eyeglasses the viewer is able to combine the projected images so that the effect of depth and solidity are achieved. The three-dimensional film was introduced to American audiences in 1952 with the release of *Bwana Devil.* After a brief period of curiosity the 3-D film lost its novelty for audiences. Except for an occasional film, for example, *The Stewardesses* (1974), *Comin' at Ya* (1981), and *Jaws 3-D* (1983), use of the technique is rare.

TITANIC

Titanic, James Cameron's 1997 epic love story set aboard the ill-fated ocean liner, proved itself the hard way. As production costs spiraled out of control, writer/director Cameron was branded a reckless egomaniac by the media. The most expensive film ever made (estimates run from $170 to $200 million), with a running time of over three hours, *Titanic* seemed doomed to become cinema's biggest boondoggle before it even opened.

But audiences responded in a very big way. Females turned to mush over the heart-wrenching story of love and loss; males enthused over the flawless, disaster-movie special effects. *Titanic* became a colossal hit, earning $600 million domestically and $1.8 billion worldwide, making it history's most successful film. Eleven Academy Awards later, Cameron brandished his Best Picture Oscar and triumphantly proclaimed, borrowing a line from the film, "I'm the King of the World!"

After *Titanic*, for which his fee was reportedly $2.5 million, Leonardo DiCaprio was paid $20 million—about half of the movie's total cost—to play a backpacker in *The Beach*.

The film opens in the present, with treasure hunter Brock Lovett (Bill Paxton) leading a deep-sea salvage mission in search of the world's largest diamond, the "Heart of the Ocean," believed locked in a safe in the RMS *Titanic*. Lovett's team opens the safe using an underwater robotic arm, as news crews document the historic moment. Alas, Lovett winds up with egg on his face as the safe divulges only mud . . . and a drawing of a beautiful, nude young woman, wearing the diamond pendant.

Rose Calvert (Gloria Stuart), age one hundred and one, watches the newscast with keen interest from her home. As she sees the drawing, her eyes go wide. Rose calls Lovett and tells him that she is the woman in the drawing.

Rose and her granddaughter Lizzy (Suzy Amis) are airlifted out to the location of the *Titanic* wreck in the middle of the Atlantic. Lovett shows her items they've retrieved from her stateroom, and she is delighted to see her old possessions after so many years. Lovett and his crew also show Rose a computer simulation of how they think the disaster occurred. Rose decides to tell them the real story . . . her story.

In a slow flashback to 1912, onlookers have gathered in droves to see the biggest ship ever built embark on its maiden voyage across the Atlantic. Beautiful young Rose Dewitt Bukater (Kate Winslet) and her raffish fiancé, Cal Hockley (Billy Zane), upstanding high-society first-class passengers, board the ship, accompanied by Rose's snobby mother, Ruth (Frances Fisher), and Cal's slippery manservant, Spicer Lovejoy (David Warner). Rose tells us in voiceover that the *Titanic* was "the ship of dreams" to everyone, but to her it was a death sentence. She's being taken to America to marry Cal, and she is not enthusiastic about it.

Meanwhile, Jack Dawson (Leonardo DiCaprio), a young, peripatetic artist and free spirit, wins two third-class tickets in a lucky game of poker. He and his friend Fabrizio (Danny Nucci) make a last-minute dash for the ship before it sets sail.

It is quickly apparent that Rose and Cal are not well matched; Rose cherishes art and collects Monets and Picassos; Cal mocks her taste, claiming Picasso will never amount to anything. In a pique of frustration that evening Rose climbs over the ship's railing, contemplating suicide. But Jack interrupts; with his good looks and boyish charm, he talks her out of it. As he attempts to pull her back onto deck, she slips and falls. Although Jack manages to rescue Rose, the ship's crewmen hear her screams and mistakenly arrest Jack. But Rose testifies on his behalf and Cal, somewhat reluctantly, invites Jack to dinner by way of saying thanks.

Titanic *is the top grossing film in history, with almost two* billion *dollars in box office receipts.*

In Jack, Rose finds her kindred spirit—playful and free, with talent and joie de vivre. Before long, Rose's high-society facade crumbles as Jack shares stories of his travels and promises to teach her to ride horseback.

At dinner, Cal and Ruth do their best to humiliate Jack, but Jack is resilient and does his best to remain unaffected by their barbs. As all the men leave for their traditional after-dinner brandy and cigars, Jack and Rose slip away and attend a real party below deck. Irish dance band Gaelic Storm entertains, and everyone drinks and has a great time. Rose cuts loose, perhaps for the first time. However, she and Jack are spied on by Cal's manservant, Lovejoy.

Cal confronts Rose and forbids her to see Jack again. Further, Rose's mother reminds her that their family money is gone, and if Rose does not marry Cal, they will fall into poverty. Rose wrestles with her conscience and tries to stay away from Jack, but Jack will not stay away—and neither can Rose. Before long, she asks Jack to sketch her portrait, and after escaping Lovejoy once again, the two make love in a Flivver in the cargo bay.

Just then, lookouts spy an iceberg dead ahead. But the ship is too large to turn in time. The iceberg rips into the hull below the water line. Ship's designer Andrews (Victor Garber) breaks the news to Captain Smith (Bernard Hill): the *Titanic* will founder. Worse, there are only enough lifeboats for half of those aboard. Stunned and inert, Smith must be prodded into issuing the call to abandon ship. Passengers are instructed to don lifejackets "purely as a precaution." First-class women and children are loaded onto lifeboats first; second- and third-class passengers are locked below deck.

Cal discovers that the Heart of the Ocean pendant, which he intended as an engagement present to Rose, has been stolen. Finding the sketch of Rose—nude and wearing the pendant—in his safe, he immediately suspects Jack. But it is Lovejoy who has pocketed the jewel. Lovejoy plants it on Jack and has him arrested. Jack is handcuffed to a pole in the Master at Arms office below deck, even as the ship begins to sink.

Rose races against a flooding deck, finds Jack, and breaks his bonds with a fire ax. Together, they fight their way through flooded corridors, and make it up on deck, only to discover that all the lifeboats are gone. As the ship goes down, they scramble astern and hang on for dear life. As the violinists play, thousands meet their fate in the icy waters. Some try to escape by jumping ship or hanging on; some can hang on no longer and are plunged into the ocean; still others remain in their staterooms, awaiting the inevitable. Rose and Jack end up in the water after the ship finally sinks, they find a piece of debris to keep them afloat. Because the debris can't buoy both of their weights, Jack lets Rose get atop to spare her hypothermia. Jack stays with her as long as he can, but eventually he freezes to death in the icy water. Rose is finally rescued by a lifeboat that returns in search of survivors. Later, as authorities take a count of surviving passengers, Rose takes Jack's last name as a sign of her everlasting love for him.

notable & quotable

"*Titanic* was not an out-of-control production. It's just that everything we did cost five times more to do than we expected."

Jon Landau, producer, 1999, as quoted in "America Goes Hollywood," Newsweek, *June 28, 1999*

Back in the present aboard Lovett's vessel, old Rose tosses the Heart of the Ocean into the sea—she's had it all along. That night, she dies peacefully in her sleep, returning to her beloved, amid the cheering passengers gathered in the *Titanic*'s grand ballroom.

See Disaster film; Special-effects film

TO KILL A MOCKINGBIRD

To Kill a Mockingbird (1962), a racially charged parable of innocence and experience in the life of a small Alabama town in the 1930s, does not reside on cinema's Olympus of great works of art, but it is secure in the less exalted but still lofty perch reserved for worthy films of unobtrusive good taste and modestly noble intentions. Narrated as the bittersweet memory of two childhood summers, the film captivated critics, audiences, and the Motion Picture Academy, which awarded it Oscars for Best Actor (Gregory Peck), Best Adapted Screenplay (Horton Foote, from Harper Lee's novel), Best Black-and-White Art Direction, and Best Set Decoration.

The voice-over of an adult Scout Finch (Kim Stanley) establishes the setting: a small southern town, Maycomb, Alabama, in the 1930s. A neighbor brings food as payment to Atticus Finch (Gregory Peck), a quietly dignified, widowed lawyer who helped him when he couldn't afford to pay. Atticus explains to his six-year-old tomboy daughter, Scout (Mary Badham), that the stock market crash hurt everybody, but the farmers worst of all. Young Dill Harris (John Megna), visiting a neighbor for the summer, shows up to play with Atticus's son, ten-year-old Jem Finch (Philip Alford). Jem and Scout quickly bring Dill up to speed on the neighborhood lore: Mr. Radley (Richard Hale) is the meanest man alive and he has a dangerous, crazed son, Boo, who, usually chained to the bed, only comes out at night. They also know that Boo spent time in an asylum for stabbing his father. As Atticus sits alone on the porch swing, he and the audience hear the children's offscreen conversation about their mother—who died four years earlier—and how much they miss and love her.

The next day Judge Taylor (Paul Fix) asks Atticus to defend a local black man, Tom Robinson (Brock Peters), who has been charged with raping a white woman. The compassionate, principled Atticus immediately agrees.

The children, meanwhile, pursue playful summer adventures that will eventually teach them more than they can imagine. Jem and Dill playfully roll a tire with Scout inside, and it crashes into the Radleys' porch, the clos-

"I remember when my daddy gave me that gun . . . I could shoot all the blue jays I wanted, if I could hit 'em, but to remember it was a sin to kill a mockingbird. Well, I reckon because a mockingbird doesn't do anything but make music for us to enjoy."

Gregory Peck as Atticus Finch in *To Kill a Mockingbird* (1962)

est they've been to the creepy house where the mysterious Boo lives. Later, they sneak into town to see the grand jury hearings involving Tom Robinson, but Atticus sends them away. Bob Ewell (James Anderson), the father of the alleged rape victim, Mayella Ewell (Collin Wilcox Paxton), confronts Atticus and criticizes him for defending a "nigger," threateningly reminding him, "You got chil'run of your own."

At night, the kids again sneak up to the Radley house. Jem makes it onto the porch, where a looming shadow frightens him to run away. When Jem's overalls snag on the fence, Scout goes back to help him get free—leaving his pants. Later, when Jem returns to claim his pants, Scout hears a gunshot—it is Mr. Radley shooting at the prowler. To Scout's relief, Jem returns to the house unhurt.

Summer passes, and it's back to school for Jem and Scout, who is embarrassed by having to wear a dress. At school, she gets in a fight with a poor classmate, Walter Cunningham Jr. (Steve Condit). To make amends, Atticus has Walter over for dinner. Jem is jealous that Walter has a real gun. Atticus explains to Jem why they do not own a gun: when he was young, he had a gun and killed a mockingbird with it. He later learned that it was a sin to kill a mockingbird, because all it does is harmlessly sing.

Robert Duvall made his screen debut in To Kill a Mockingbird *as the seemingly dangerous Boo Radley.* ▶

Jem and Scout get a taste of the adult world when they accompany Atticus on his visit to the Robinson family. On the way, a drunk Bob Ewell—Mayella's father—frightens the kids and calls Atticus a nigger lover. On the way home, Atticus explains to his kids that he can't keep all of the ugly things in the world away from them.

Later, on another of their outdoor adventures, Jem and Scout find two carved dolls—resembling themselves—in the knothole of a tree. Jem shares a secret with Scout: he has found several things in the same hole: a pocket watch, a pocketknife, and a spelling medal. He also tells her that the night he returned to the Radleys' to get his pants, he found them neatly folded on the fence. The voice-over of the adult Scout comments that it was a long time before they talked about Boo Radley again.

With the arrival of the following summer, Dill returns to the town. It is now the night before the rape trial, and Tom Robinson is brought back to the local jail. Suspecting trouble, Atticus sits in front of the jail. Unbeknownst to Atticus, his kids follow him to town. A makeshift lynch mob shows up at the jail to take justice into their own hands. Afraid for their father, Scout and Jem work their way through the crowd and stand by their father. Demonstrating the same courageous obstinacy as his father and understanding that his presence is staving off the violence, Jem refuses Atticus's repeated order to leave. Scout innocently engages Walter Cunningham in a friendly conversation, telling him to say "hey" to Walter Jr. Cunningham calls off the mob, defusing the situation.

The next day, a caravan of cars heads into the small town for the trial. Jem, Scout, and Dill sneak into the courthouse and sit upstairs with the local black people. The witnesses for the prosecution allege that Robinson, while helping Mayella inside her house, raped and beat her. Atticus points out that no one called for a doctor and hints at the fact that her father, a violent drunk, had beaten her before. Robinson takes the stand and says that Mayella invited him in and eventually made an aggressive, unwarranted sexual advance at him. Then Mayella's father saw the pair through the window and yelled that he was going to kill his daughter. In addition to this testimony, Atticus shows that Robinson's left hand is useless and that the person who hit Mayella is, like her father, left-handed.

Since there is no evidence that shows that the alleged crime even took place, Atticus concludes that only prejudice and a belief that blacks are immoral liars could possibly lead to a guilty verdict. He pleads eloquently to the jury to reach an impartial verdict, based solely on the evidence—but to no avail. Robinson is convicted, and Atticus tries to console him by telling him there will be an appeal. Later that night, Atticus finds out that Tom Robinson has been shot dead, supposedly while trying to escape. When Atticus goes to the Robinsons to break the news, Bob Ewell is there and spits in his face. The ever-stoic Atticus merely wipes his face off with his handkerchief.

Scout and Jem return to school that fall. Scout is wearing a ham costume as she and Jem walk home alone through the woods from a Halloween party. Out of the shadows, a darkness-obscured figure lunges violently at Jem. Another unseen figure appears and begins to fight off the attacker. By the time Scout slips out of her bulky costume, she sees a stranger carrying an unconscious Jem toward her house.

Atticus calls a doctor and the sheriff. When he arrives, the sheriff informs the Finch family that Bob Ewell has just been killed, stabbed by a knife. When Scout is questioned about who helped her and Jem fight off the attacker, Scout points out a ghostly, pale man who is hiding behind a door—it is Boo Radley (Robert Duvall, in his screen debut), a mentally challenged but kindhearted man, not the menacing monster of local myth. Having learned that good and evil don't always come from where one might expect, Scout takes Boo's hand and lets him watch over Jem. The sheriff, realizing the nobility of Boo's act, says that he will simply report that Bob Ewell fell on his knife. Scout adds that putting Boo on trial would be like killing a mockingbird.

TOOTSIE

"It's just for the money, isn't it? It's not just so you can wear those little outfits?"

Bill Murray as playwright Jeff in *Tootsie* (1982)

Tootsie (1982) is Sydney Pollack's most successful film, both commercially and critically. A brilliant comedy of show business desperation and sexual mores, it garnered ten Academy Award nominations, a Best Supporting Actress Oscar for Jessica Lange, and best-director honors from the New York Film Critics Circle.

Tootsie's protagonist is Michael Dorsey (Dustin Hoffman), an unemployed, fortyish New York actor whose formidable talent is surpassed only by his volatile temperament, which has stalled his acting career and forced him to support himself as a waiter and acting teacher.

The indefatigable Michael has big plans, however, all involving his friends. His eccentric roommate, Jeff (Bill Murray), has written a play that he yearns to produce, with himself and his friend Sandy (Teri Garr), an acting student, in the lead roles. To raise money for the project, he is intensively coaching Sandy for a high-paying role as a stern hospital administrator on a soap opera. Her inherent sweetness of character is so evident at the audition, however, that she isn't even offered a chance to read for the part. Then Michael discovers that a no-talent acquaintance of his has just been hired for a leading role in a major Broadway revival of *The Iceman Cometh*. An enraged and exasperated Michael storms into the office of his slick agent, George Fields (Sydney Pollack), to find out why he wasn't asked to audition for the part. Fields bluntly informs him that the problem is his fussy, demanding demeanor, which has rendered him persona non grata in the business.

Desperate and determined, Michael decides that he would be perfect for the soap-opera role for which Sandy was rejected, so he dons a wig and a dress, applies a layer of makeup, assumes the name Dorothy Michaels, and goes to read for the part of the bossy hospital administrator on the soap opera *Southwest General.* He is hired on the spot.

Michael/Dorothy soon becomes a mainstay of the program, and he develops a close personal and working relationship with a fellow actor, Julie (Jessica Lange). For Michael, experiencing a relationship with a woman—as a woman—is a revelation. There is a relaxed, natural trust and a degree of emotional comfort he has never known as a man relating to women. Julie invites Dorothy for a weekend stay at her father's farm, and, of course, her father, Les (Charles Durning), develops an instant crush on Dorothy, just as Michael, as Dorothy, is falling in love with Julie.

But the erotic ironies are just beginning. Frustrated by his inability to declare his passion to Julie, Michael indulges in a night of passion with his old friend Sandy. When he fails to follow up, she surmises that he is gay. Unable to disguise his feelings for Julie, he allows Dorothy to express an emotional intensity toward her that convinces Julie that Dorothy might be gay. The lovestruck Les, in the meantime, proposes marriage to her/him.

Dustin Hoffman (left) donned women's clothes for his role as out-of-work actor Michael Dorsey—who masquerades as a woman to get roles. The result is a hilarious take on show-biz desperation and sexual mores.

▼

These dizzying emotional deceptions, entanglements, entrapments, confusions, and frustrations prove too much for Michael, who decides to end the charade. On a live broadcast of *Southwest General,* he strips off his wig and announces that not only is he not really Emily Kimberley, the character he is playing, but he is also not Dorothy Michaels. He walks off the set, leaving behind a shell-shocked crew and cast, not to mention a stunned nation. A flustered and embarrassed Julie punches him in the stomach.

With a fresh store of hard-won personal insights about himself and his relationships with others—especially women—and a newfound solvency thanks to his extended run on the soap opera, he can now fulfill his dream of producing Jeff's play. He pleads for and receives the understanding of Les and Julie, who is able to return Michael's love after he explains to her, "I was a better man with you, as a woman, than I ever was with a woman as a man. . . . I've just got to do it without the dress."

See Hoffman, Dustin; Lange, Jessica; Pollack, Sydney

TOURNEUR, MAURICE

The ranks of early film directors were drawn from a startling array of occupations, with engineers, sailors, stuntmen, vaudevillians, and explorers all represented. A few successful Broadway figures did work behind the cameras, but in general, the men and women responsible for producing early films were far less noted than those hired to act in them. Adolph Zukor's slogan may have been "Famous Players in Famous Plays," but to direct, he hired the great mechanic Edwin S. Porter.

One notable exception to this rule was Maurice Tourneur, who came from Éclair's Paris studio to Fort Lee, New Jersey, in 1914. Tourneur was born in Paris in 1876, and after studying at the Lycée Condorcet he worked as an interior decorator, an illustrator, and a designer of posters and textiles. He was an assistant to Auguste Rodin and Puvis de Chavannes and, for Puvis, he designed sketches for the Boston Public Library staircase mural. After three years of military service he turned his attention to the theater and toured the world with the great actress Réjane.

Tourneur began directing for Éclair in 1912; he was brought into films by Émile Chautard, with whom he had worked on stage (Chautard, who later joined Tourneur in America, would also be the mentor of Josef von Sternberg). In America, Tourneur first worked for the World Film Corporation, a company managed by Lewis J. Selznick and generally devoted to filming theatrical successes. In the hands of a less inventive director these

Maurice Tourneur was one of the few early film directors with real experience in the industry—he spent several years as a director in Paris before coming to America.

films might have been straightforward transcriptions of the Broadway originals, but Tourneur was able to take advantage of the opportunities for stylization opened up by the camera.

His earliest extant American film, *The Wishing Ring* (1914), displays a sophisticated handling of deep space, with an ingenious use of foreground and background action. A brooding squire sulks in his dark sitting room, while his sunlit garden, whose roses he never picks, is always visible through the French doors in the distance. The use of sunlight to light interiors in this period brought such effects within every director's grasp, but relatively few were able to avoid the visual chaos it could easily bring on.

Tourneur's command of editing, even in this early work, is equally good. But perhaps most interesting to modern eyes is Tourneur's use of formal distancing devices. Especially when dealing with period or fantasy subjects, Tourneur consistently filmed through a proscenium-shaped mask, "theatricalizing" even events that were filmed outdoors.

Like other successful directors of the period, Tourneur was too busy to labor over his work, which averaged six features per year between 1914 and 1920. He made two of Mary Pickford's finest pictures, *The Pride of the Clan* and *Poor Little Rich Girl* (both 1917), and also directed several notable successes of Olga Pretrova and Elsie Ferguson. But in 1918 his avant-garde productions of *The Blue Bird* and *Prunella* were resounding box-office failures. Tourneur felt betrayed by his audience. Once heralded as "the poet of the screen," Tourneur grew bitter over increasing commercial pressures. *Treasure Island* and *The Last of the Mohicans* (both 19209) were among his last satisfactory efforts. While always gainfully employed afterward, Tourneur had good cause to complain about the weak scripts he was given to direct. The increasingly departmentalized routine of Hollywood production was unable to sustain the creative atmosphere he craved. In 1926 he was directing MGM's first Technicolor feature, *The Mysterious Island,* when Irving Thalberg assigned him a producer. Two weeks after the man walked onto his set, Tourneur quit the picture and left Hollywood to continue his career in Europe.

See Pickford, Mary; Technicolor; Thalberg, Irving

Spencer Tracy was paid $300,000 for his role in *Guess Who's Coming to Dinner*, which took in $25.1 million its first year, 1968.

SPENCER TRACY

Spencer Bonaventure Tracy was born in Milwaukee, Wisconsin, on April 5, 1900, to John Tracy, a truck salesman, and Caroline Brown Tracy. Spencer has been described as a "rebellious" youngster—probably a vast understatement, given that he was reportedly expelled from fifteen grade schools! Some would say that this rebelliousness translated in Tracy's adulthood to a tendency toward moodiness and a hot temper, on the job and off.

Tracy calmed down a bit when he was sent to a Jesuit college-preparatory school. He started getting good grades and even considered becoming a priest. In 1917, however, hoping to get "smack into the middle of a lot of excitement" by fighting in World War I, he quit school and joined the navy. But he sat out the war at the navy facilities in Norfolk, Virginia.

He finished high school after the war ended and in 1921 he enrolled in Ripon College in Wisconsin. Tracy joined the debating team and, finding himself at ease in front of an audience, began performing in school plays. He received good reviews and started thinking about acting as a career. Thus, in 1922 Tracy left Ripon to study at the American Academy of Dramatic Arts in New York City.

Tracy debuted in a bit part in a play on Broadway not long after arriving in New York. In 1923 Tracy joined a stock theater company, where he gained some solid acting experience. He also gained a wife: Louise Tread-

One of the finest actors of all time, Spencer Tracy was nominated for the Best Actor Oscar nine times; he won twice in a row, in 1937 and 1938.

well, an actress with the company. Their first son, John, was born the following year. (John was deaf, and Louise started the John Tracy Clinic to help other youngsters with hearing problems, free of charge. A daughter, Susie, was born to the Tracys in 1932.)

In 1930 film director John Ford saw Tracy perform on stage and arranged for him to be hired for a part in *Up the River* along with another young man making his feature film debut—Humphrey Bogart. The sponsoring movie studio, Fox Films, offered Tracy a contract, and the Tracy family moved to Hollywood in 1931.

Fox put Tracy to work in many films each year, such as *Sky Devils* and *Me and My Gal* (both in 1932), *The Power and the Glory* (1933), *Looking for Trouble,* and *Bottoms Up* (1934). He gained excellent experience and began building a following among fans.

But looking for more challenging work, Tracy left Fox and signed with prestigious MGM in 1935. There he was given the opportunity to act in better-quality films. The shift to the new studio paid off immediately. In 1936 Tracy appeared in such varied and interesting films as *Fury, San Francisco,* and *Libeled Lady.* The powers that be in Hollywood and the movie audience alike realized that Tracy was a true artist, one of the finest actors of all time, capable of playing any role, from broad comedy, to serious drama, to romantic lead, with equal finesse.

He won the Academy Award for Best Actor for his performance in *Captains Courageous* (1937), and took home the Oscar again the following year for his portrayal of Father Flanagan in *Boys Town* (1938), the first actor to win two years in a row. Spencer Tracy had arrived, literally and figuratively, in Hollywood.

The good roles kept on coming—leading parts in *Stanley and Livingston* (1939), *Northwest Passage* and *Boom Town* (both in 1940), *Dr. Jekyll and Mr. Hyde* (1941), and more.

A new wrinkle in Tracy's life occurred with his casting opposite Katharine Hepburn in *Woman of the Year* (1942). The pairing was a hit with audiences. The couple went on to make eight other films together, including *Adam's Rib* (1949), *Pat and Mike* (1952), *Desk Set* (1957), and *Guess Who's Coming to Dinner* (1967). They also formed an enduring love match offscreen. Their twenty-five-year relationship would become the stuff legends are made of, though it was never reported in the scandal sheets—a sign of the respect in which the two actors were held in Hollywood.

Tracy may have been willing to have an intimate relationship outside his marriage, but the devout Catholic in him would not permit him to seek a divorce from Louise. They lived separately for many years, but the marriage continued, at least in legal form. During Tracy's long struggle with lung disease in the 1960s, Louise Tracy and Katharine Hepburn reportedly alternated caring for him.

Tracy's superior film performances continued apart from his work with Hepburn. For MGM until 1954, then working "freelance" for other studios, he appeared in such films as *Father of the Bride* (1950), *The Old Man and the Sea* (1958), *Inherit the Wind* (1960), *Judgment at Nuremberg* (1961), and *It's a Mad, Mad, Mad, Mad World* (1963).

Guess Who's Coming to Dinner was Tracy's last role. He died of heart failure at his home on June 10, 1967, three weeks after filming ended.

See Cukor, George; Ford, John; Guess Who's Coming to Dinner; *Hepburn, Katharine; Poitier, Sidney*

TRADE PAPERS

For those within the film industry, information and opinion were shaped by a number of aggressive trade papers, each competing for the same limited number of subscribers. The film business had first been discussed in general entertainment-industry papers such as the *New York Clipper* or *Variety,* which began covering short films as acts in 1907. Most important was the *New York Dramatic Mirror,* whose film reviewer, Frank Woods, is often cited as the first significant American film critic.

Chief among the papers devoted solely to the motion-picture industry was the *Moving Picture World* (1907–27), which, setting a standard for the broadest possible coverage, reviewed current releases and published news, features, and interviews relating to all aspects of the industry. The vast quantity of advertisements published each week was by itself enough to make the *World* a veritable industry encyclopedia. An exhibitor-oriented paper whose genesis coincided with the original nickelodeon boom, it also carried regular columns on projection, advertising, and theater music.

Like political campaigns, only less expensive: Studios spent an average of $22 million on advertising in 1996, up from $9.2 million in 1989.

Very similar in format was the *Motion Picture News,* edited by William A. Johnston (1913–29), which supplanted the *World* in importance after about 1920. The appeal to the theater owner was even stronger here, with extensive exploitation tips appended to reviews, much coverage of theater design and operation, and a continuing "Check Up" column in which the box-office performance of every feature in release could be tracked via exhibitors' reports.

The same general format was also employed by the *Exhibitor's Trade Review* (1916–26) and the *Exhibitor's Herald* (founded in 1915); the *Herald* contained the classic "What the Picture Did for Me" column, where theater owners from across the country described with relish their experiences with every release.

Less encyclopedic (if more idiosyncratic) were a variety of smaller papers intended to fill gaps in the big weeklies' coverage. In 1915 Wid Gunning published *Wid's Films and Film Folks,* which became *Wid's Daily* in 1918. Carrying no advertising, the paper sold itself on the strength of Gunning's enthusiastic and purportedly unbiased reviews. "Tell 'em this is Bill's latest and oil up the ticket machine" was Wid's characteristic way of approving the latest William Hart release. The paper took on a more sober air under the editorship of Joe Dannenberg, who changed its name to the *Film Daily* in 1922. From 1918 it published the standard industry reference annual, *Wid's Yearbook* (later the *Film Daily Yearbook of Motion Pictures*).

Harrison's Reports, published form 1919 by P. S. Harrison, was a slim tip sheet that combined extremely opinionated (and cold-blooded) reviews with insider information on "real" picture grosses and distributor-exhibitor relations. *Harrison's Reports* had the most contentious producer relations of all the trades.

Similar to *Harrison's Reports* in their personal approach, but far more thoughtful in their critical policies, were the *Film Mercury* (1924–33), edited by Tamar Lane, and the *Hollywood Spectator* (1926–31), edited by Welford Beaton. Both men were interested enough in the art of the film to have written serious books on the subject, and they tried to infuse this feeling into their analyses of the weekly releases. The late silent period would prove the heyday of such papers, many of which were driven out of business by the Depression-era economic downturn.

See Criticism; Newspapers

TRAINSPOTTING

Trainspotting (1995) is the sophomore effort from a trio of young Scottish filmmakers, director Danny Boyle, producer Andrew MacDonald, and writer John Hodge. Their first film, *Shallow Grave* (1994), put them firmly on the map. But while *Shallow Grave* was certainly not a festival film due to its dark subject matter, Boyle and Macdonald believed *Trainspotting* had festival potential. However, Cannes Film Festival president Gilles Jacob loathed the film, and banned it from the competition. After urgent behind-the-scenes negotiation, *Trainspotting* was screened out of competition in a midnight slot. The premiere was a huge success, and featured live musical performances from Mick Jagger, Eric Clapton, and Noel Gallagher. The film was already well on its way to becoming a huge cult hit: *Trainspotting* was the number-one film in Britain in 1995, and earned almost $100 million worldwide.

"Gonna get it right this time. Gonna get it sorted out. Gonna get off it for good."

Ewan McGregor as Mark Renton in *Trainspotting* (1995)

We first meet Mark Renton (Ewan McGregor) and his mates on the run from police in Edinburgh, Scotland. Renton narrates, describing his philosophy: "I choose not to choose life. Who needs all that when you've got heroin?"

Indeed, Renton and his pals—Sick Boy (Jonny Lee Miller), a bleached-blond punk with a Sean Connery obsession, and pathetically dim Spud (Ewen Bremner)—are junkies. Their other two pals, the psychotic Begbie (Robert Carlyle) and the randy Tommy (Kevin McKidd), are not addicted to heroin, but all are losers nonetheless.

Renton tries to quit heroin cold-turkey. He loads up on supplies, then boards up his own door: "Now . . . just one more hit to last until the Valium kicks in." Next thing we know, he's pried the planks off his door and is out looking to score. He succeeds in quitting, however, at least for the time being.

The Edinburgh junkie philosophy is revealed as Spud goes for a job interview. In order to stay on the government dole, Spud must screw up the interview, but not let on to the employers that he's doing it deliberately. A handful of "speed" makes him blabber nonstop through the interview. He really screws it up.

We also learn that these "mates" will betray one another at the drop of a hat. Renton swipes a video of Tommy having sex with his girlfriend, Lizzie. When Lizzie discovers it missing, she blames Tommy, who supposes that he must have returned it to the video store by accident. Lizzie is furious, and she leaves him. Thus begins Tommy's downfall. Begbie, on the other hand, is always on the brink of a blowup, constantly getting drunk and picking fights in bars. His friends help him out of scrapes, only to be berated for their efforts.

"We would have injected vitamin C if only they had made it illegal."

Ewan McGregor as Mark Renton in *Trainspotting* (1995)

Having temporarily kicked his heroin habit, Renton's libido, long deadened by the drug, resurfaces. He picks up a cute, brainy girl named Diane (Kelly McDonald) at a dance club. But after a night of torrid sex, Renton is chagrined to discover that Diane is still in high school. She makes him promise to see her again anyway, but Renton doesn't need any hassles with the law.

Sick Boy, Spud, and Renton are soon back on heroin, or "smack." Worse, now Tommy wants in, so Renton hooks him up. Tommy's descent continues as the boys fall right back into their old habits. Securing drugs from the National Health Service and money from petty theft (and a mugging, in Begbie's case), the addicts are soon so out of it that Spud's infant baby dies of neglect. The first thing the boys do? Shoot up, to relieve the anguish.

Spud is arrested for the baby's death and sent to prison for six months. Renton receives a suspended sentence after agreeing to enter an addiction treatment program. But Renton shoots all three hits of methadone—a drug used to alleviate withdrawal symptoms—for the day at 3 A.M., and is soon searching for a fix. He visits a dealer named Mother Superior, and scores some bad dope. Next thing he knows, he's in an emergency room, being injected with opiate antagonizer. He comes out of it in a hurry.

Renton's parents step in. They lock him in his room and force him to go through withdrawal cold-turkey. Renton endures a painful withdrawal, during which he hallucinates dead babies and other nightmares. But soon Renton is sober. Later, he sleeps with Diane again; she tells him his world is over, that he must get his act together. Renton takes her words to heart.

Realizing that the only way to stay clean is to escape his so-called mates, Renton moves to London and gets a respectable job as a real estate agent. But it isn't long before his former life encroaches on him. On the lam from the law, Begbie moves in, followed by Sick Boy. Soon Renton's flat is trashed, and Sick Boy keeps hocking Renton's possessions in order to buy more drugs. Renton moves them into an empty flat. But when Renton's real estate company sends a couple to see the apartment, Begbie and Sick Boy try to mug them. Renton is fired.

Renton returns to Edinburgh just in time for Tommy's funeral. The friends, including Spud, are reunited. Sick Boy tells everyone about a large score up for grabs—two kilos for only 4,000 pounds. Begbie harangues Renton into putting up the money. After they buy the dope, Renton tests it . . . getting into the habit, once again. They successfully sell the drugs for 16,000 pounds.

At a bar celebrating their profit, Begbie leaves the satchel of money on the table, and once again picks a fight. Spud tries to stop the fight, only to get slashed by Begbie's blade for his trouble. Renton ponders making off with the bag.

That night, as Sick Boy, Begbie, and Spud sleep in a hotel room, Renton swipes the money from Begbie and eases out. Spud sees him, but says nothing. Renton motions for him to come along, but Spud will not. Renton splits. The next morning, discovering the money is gone, Begbie goes crazy, trashing the room. The police come and take him away.

Renton leaves Spud's share in Spud's safe deposit box, and makes off with the rest. In a final voiceover, he tells us he really does want the life he said he despised in his opening narration: wife, kids, even a microwave oven. He chooses life.

See Diegesis/Diegetic sound

TREASURE OF THE SIERRA MADRE, THE

The Treasure of the Sierra Madre (1948) is one of John Huston's directorial masterpieces, a classic tale of the elusive quest for gold by a trio of ill-matched eccentrics whose scramble for easy wealth falls prey to pitiless nature, wild bandits, and their own greed. This combination action-adventure story and western was shot almost entirely on location in Mexico. The screenplay, written by Huston, was based on the novel of the same name by Bavarian author Berwick Traven. Bogart's performance in *Sierra Madre* is unquestionably one of his best. His transformation from friend and fellow adventurer to a man who jumps over the brink of insanity is marvelous to watch. What is surprising is that he did not receive an Oscar for the performance. Academy honors went instead to Walter Huston for

T

TREASURE OF THE SIERRA MADRE, THE

Although his performance in The Treasure of the Sierra Madre *was one of his best, Humphrey Bogart did not receive an Oscar nomination. He was edged out by Walter Huston, who won for Best Supporting Actor. In the first father/son win, director John Huston, Walter's son, also won an Oscar, for Best Director.*

▶

Best Supporting Actor and to his son, John Huston, for Best Screenplay and Best Director.

The film opens in Tampico, Mexico, where Dobbs (Humphrey Bogart), on the skids, has taken to begging on the street. He strikes up a friendship with the equally destitute Curtin (Tim Holt), and they find work in the employ of a disreputable building contractor, McCormick (Barton MacLane), at whose site they must endure grueling labor. Back in Tampico, McCormick fends off Dobbs and Curtin, as yet unpaid, by telling them that he must go off to pick up the payroll. Finding refuge in a flophouse, the workers find themselves regaled with tales of prospecting for gold by an engaging old man named Howard (Walter Huston), who warns them that the temptation of easy riches is usually offset by the unquenchable greed engendered by fortune hunting.

The next morning Dobbs and Curtin learn that McCormick has a reputation for reneging on promised payments to his workers, so when the pair runs into McCormick on the street, they have to rough him up before they see their wages. Flush with the confidence of their unwonted solvency, the two decide to venture into gold prospecting and invite Howard to join them. He agrees, offering to add some of his money to the initial investment. Their stake is augmented when Dobbs hears that he is the holder of a winning lottery ticket.

The three gold hunters head for the Sierra Mountains on a train that comes under attack by a local Indian chief named Gold Hat (Alfonso Bedoya), and Dobbs, Curtin, and Howard throw themselves into the successful battle against the would-be train robbers. Upon arriving in a local village, the trio loads up on supplies and trudges into the hills with their newly acquired burros, with the two younger men barely keeping pace with the indefatigable Howard. When, after several days of fruitless searching, Dobbs and Curtin collapse with exhaustion, Howard alerts them that he has detected a minor vein of gold ore, not worth any effort but promising richer rewards if they press on.

Their energies refreshed by this encouragement, the men persist, their weary burros trailing behind them, until they do discover a significant vein, which they set about mining through weeks of backbreaking labor. As the gold piles up, they divide each day's proceeds in precise allotments. Growing prosperity fills Dobbs with suspicion, as he compulsively checks the tent to see if his coworkers have fled with the booty. Dobbs's surliness so alienates his colleagues that Curtin hesitates before finally rescuing Dobbs from a caved-in mineshaft. Yet even this gesture cannot assuage Dobbs's gnawing paranoia, which erupts when he finds Curtin trying to pry loose a rock where Dobbs has hidden his gold. Curtin insists he is merely trying to kill a Gila monster hiding there, but Dobbs is unmollified even when Curtin lifts the rock to reveal the animal. Dobbs even insists that Curtin go to town to pick up supplies, fearing that Curtin and Howard will make off with all the gold if he goes.

During his trip to town, Curtin encounters another American drifter, Cody (Bruce Bennett), who seems eager to know what Curtin is up to. Cody, disbelieving Curtin's story that he is a hunter, follows him back to camp and discovers the mining operation. He tells the three prospectors that he wants them to cut him in on their venture, but Dobbs, Curtin, and Howard decide that they will have to kill him to save the size of their shares and silence the meddlesome intruder.

Their plan is thwarted when Cody comes running into camp to tell them that a band of robbers is on the way. Chief Gold Hat, who had once before attacked their train, approaches the miners and identifies himself

"Badges? We ain't got no badges! We don't need no badges! I don't have to show you any stinking badges!"

Alfonso Bedoya as the Mexican bandit Gold Hat in *The Treasure of the Sierra Madre* (1948)

as a law-enforcement officer. When they ask to see his badge, he sneers, "Badges? I don't have to show you any stinkin' badges!" In the ensuing hail of gunfire, the more numerous bandits quickly gain the advantage but then are forced to beat a hasty retreat when they come under attack by federal troops. Cody is killed in the crossfire; the miners discover on him a poignant letter addressed to his wife begging her forgiveness for his long absences.

Chastened by their brush with death, Dobbs, Curtin, and Howard—each now with a stash of some $35,000—decide that they have earned enough and decide to close down their operation, conscientiously repairing the "wound" they have inflicted on the mountain with their mining. On their trip back to the city, they are approached by Indians who beg their help in reviving a little boy from their village who fell into a lake and now seems close to death. Howard volunteers to go on the rescue mission, entrusting his share of the gold to the other two, who continue on toward the town as Howard casts a wistful and wary look back at his partners.

While Howard is successfully carrying out his mission of mercy, Dobbs and Curtin continue their trek, which is complicated by Dobbs's recurring bouts of paranoia. Their bickering finally leads Curtin to draw a gun on Dobbs and keep him walking ahead of him; that night Curtain resists sleep, fearing foul play from Dobbs. The next night, though, he is overcome by exhaustion, and as soon as he drops off to sleep, Dobbs grabs Curtin's gun, forces him into the brush, and shoots him. After returning to the campsite, Dobbs is stricken by the fear that he didn't finish off Curtin, so he returns to the brush and finds the body gone. Panicked, he tries to reassure himself with the thought that a wild animal made off with the corpse.

"How much is $35,000 times three? $105,000? I'll bet you $105,000 that you go to sleep before I do."

Humphrey Bogart as Fred C. Dobbs in *The Treasure of the Sierra Madre* (1948)

Dobbs struggles on by himself, nearly senseless with fatigue and thirst. When he all but dives into the first water hole he discovers, he looks up to see the menacing figure of Gold Hat and two of his bandits. Dobbs shoots at them, but his gun is empty, and the three bandits make short work of Dobbs with their machetes and then dash off with Dobbs's burros.

Meanwhile, Curtin, who survived Dobbs's attack, has reconnected with Howard, who is nursing him back to health. On fresh horses furnished by the grateful Indians, they try to retrace Dobbs's path to recover their fortune. Gold Hat, however, oblivious of the value of gold, has emptied the sacks on his way to a nearby village, where he tries to sell what he considers to be the real booty, the burros. When he tries to unload them on the merchant who first sold them to the trio of miners, the merchant alerts the federal troops, who quickly arrive to arrest Chief Gold Hat and his band of robbers. With brutal summary justice, Gold Hat and his men are lined up against a wall to face a firing squad for their theft of the burros.

Curtin and Howard arrive just in time to hear the report of the executioners' rifles, and they embark on a frantic search for their lost loot. As a pitiless wind churns up the dry dirt of the village, the pair finds the sacks, now empty, as their dreams of wealth scatter in the swirling eddies of dust. Curtin's desolation is punctured by Howard's gales of bitter, ironic laughter. "Laugh, Curtin, old boy! It's a great joke played on us by the Lord or fate or by nature."

See Bogart, Humphrey; Huston, John

2001: A SPACE ODYSSEY

2001: A Space Odyssey (1968), which opened to indifferent reviews, is now considered one of the best, if not *the* best, science fiction films of all time. The plot is based on the short story "The Sentinel" by Arthur C. Clarke and directed by Stanley Kubrick; the two men collaborated on the screenplay.

2001 is an elegant, almost balletic exploration of the meaning and power of technology and humans' place in the universe. It proceeds at a leisurely, stately pace and is a profound visual experience, best viewed on the big screen. There is little dialogue.

The film is divided into three major parts, specifically titled on the screen: "The Dawn of Man" (with a segment "The Lunar Journey in the Year 2000"), "Jupiter Mission, 18 Months Later," and "Jupiter and Beyond the Infinite."

As the movie opens, the earth, moon, and sun are shown, vertically aligned, above a black monolith; the opening chords of Richard Strauss's *Thus Spake Zarathustra* play. The monolith rests in a primal setting: the African savannah at the dawn of humankind's evolution. It is four million years ago, and a band of vegetarian ape-men live here, as much a part of their environment—and vulnerable to predators—as any other group of animals.

The apelike men are understandably fascinated by the monolith, a strikingly artificial note that has materialized in the natural setting. It somehow inspires them toward, or endows them with, ever-greater complexity of thought and toward the use of tools (both of which are associated in science with the development of humanity). While digging through some animal bones, one of the ape-men picks up a bone and begins smashing things with it. A visual intercutting of shots of animals dying and bones being crushed suggests the evolution of a tool to a weapon.

The group of ape-men, now armed with bones/tools, goes to defend their water hole from another band. Their use of tools has allowed them to become not only omnivorous but also fiercely territorial. When one of the

"Stop, Dave. I'm afraid . . . I'm afraid, Dave . . . Dave . . . my mind is going. I can feel it."

Hal 9000 (voice of Douglas Rain) in *2001: A Space Odyssey* (1968)

unsuspecting enemy comes too close, he is clobbered to death. In a gesture of victory, one of the ape-men throws his bone in the air; this shot match-cuts to a spaceship (in the year 2000) floating placidly through space toward a lunar space station. This cut, which has been called the longest flash-forward in film history, makes a strikingly visual association between two by-products of intellectual progress. Johann Strauss's serene and stately "Blue Danube Waltz" plays as the viewer "experiences" space.

Aboard the spaceship—the Pan American shuttle *Orion*—is Dr. Heywood R. Floyd (William Sylvester). After his craft docks at the space station, the first words of dialogue are spoken, half an hour into the film: banal chitchat, intended to establish the unremarkable nature of space travel for the passengers. Floyd uses a videophone to wish his earthbound daughter a happy birthday, and a group of Soviet scientists tries to find out what is the real story at the lunar space station, where, supposedly, an epidemic has erupted. Dr. Floyd manages to brush aside their queries.

Signs marking hotel and restaurant chains show us that in the year 2000, space travel is as common a part of humans' daily life as flying by plane from city to city on earth.

Generally panned by critics when it was first released in 1968, Stanley Kubrick's 2001: A Space Odyssey *is now seen as unique and immensely influential.*

The purpose of Dr. Floyd's journey is to study a black monolith that was found on the moon—the sudden appearance of this bizarre structure is what lies behind the rumor of an epidemic on the lunar space station, and the powers that be are trying to avert a panic. Floyd and other scientists make their way to the monolith, and just like the ape-men did four million years ago, one of the scientists touches it wonderingly. When the scientists take a tourist-like snapshot in front of the monolith, the monolith emits a loud, shrill noise, which causes the visitors to cover their ears. This sound alerts whatever civilization erected the structure that another milestone in human development has been reached.

The film flashes forward to eighteen months later—the "Jupiter Mission" is under way. Just as the apelike men were inspired by the monolith to discover a new technology, the monolith on the moon has inspired intellectual inquiry, in this case a first-time journey to the planet Jupiter. In the *Discovery* spaceship are mission commander Dave Bowman (Keir Dullea) and astronaut Frank Poole (Gary Lockwood), and their computer, HAL-9000 (voice of Douglas Rain). Three other scientists are on board, but they are in hibernation, a deep, sleeplike state that conserves the resources of the vehicle. In one of the most visually inventive scenes in the movie, Frank jogs around the circular loop of the gravity-free spacecraft.

Since its release, *2001: A Space Odyssey* (1968) has earned over $25.5 million in rental fees—about the same amount as *Guess Who's Coming to Dinner* (also 1968).

HAL is a talking and "feeling" computer who is quite proud to be the most advanced machine ever made. As he brags to a BBC television interviewer, his computer series has never made a mistake or distorted information. "I am putting myself to the fullest possible use, which is all I think that any conscious entity can do." The astronauts are essentially just caretakers of the spacecraft. HAL runs its systems, and he is the only one to know its real mission—to find the alien beings who created the monolith.

In one scene, Dave loses a game of chess to HAL, a sequence that foreshadows an eventual human-versus-machine conflict. HAL soon is caught in several small errors. When he is accused of making a mistake about a piece of equipment, HAL defensively asserts that it must have been due to human error.

The astronauts are concerned about HAL's growing unreliability. Dave gets Frank alone in a pod where HAL cannot hear them, and they discuss their doubts about HAL's competence. Frank says, "I can't put my finger on it, but I sense something strange about him." They decide that if HAL is proved to have made the mistake regarding the piece of equipment, they will disconnect his "higher-brain" functions, leaving him just to mechanically run the ship. Through a sequence in which the astronauts' moving lips are undercut with one of HAL's omnipresent red "eyes," we realize that HAL may be reading their lips.

Frank goes outside the spaceship in a small pod to determine whether HAL was right or wrong, and HAL takes control of the pod and cuts the astronaut's oxygen lines, leaving Frank to float off helplessly into space.

Dave gets in a similar pod and tries to rescue Frank, but it is too late; Frank is dead. While Dave is gone, HAL murders the hibernating astronauts. The life signals of the astronauts flatten as a warning sign flashes "Life Functions Terminated."

An increasingly malevolent HAL will not let Dave back into the ship. When Dave asks why, HAL replies, "I think you know what the problem is just as well as I do." HAL reveals that he knew that Frank and Dave were planning to disconnect him.

Dave manages to find a way to get on board, and he proceeds straight to the computer's memory banks. HAL desperately pleads for his "life," but Dave will not be dissuaded. As he disconnects HAL's higher functioning mechanisms, HAL claims that he can feel his mind going. He eventually reverts to his earliest "childhood" memory, reciting the song "Daisy." A prerecorded video comes on in which Dr. Floyd explains that the monolith, the first sign of intelligent life beyond earth, sent a powerful radio transmission to Jupiter.

In the last segment of the film, "Jupiter and Beyond the Infinite," Dave arrives on Jupiter, where a black monolith takes him on a journey through time and space. There is a barrage of lights and images, and Dave arrives in an ornately decorated room where he sees a person who turns out to be an older version of himself. The older Dave turns to see an even older version of himself on his deathbed. The black monolith appears and "transforms" him into a Star Baby—a fetuslike creature floating through space in a translucent embryonic sac. This enigmatic ending begs the question: Is it a cycle complete, or the beginning of a new era in human evolution?

See Kubrick, Stanley; Science-fiction film; Special-effects film

UNDERGROUND FILM

Underground film was a term widely used during the 1940s and 1950s to describe films that were personal and noncommercial; sought to break away from the established traditions of the feature, narrative film; dealt with personal, taboo themes not permitted in commercial films; and sought to elevate "pure" cinematic techniques—superimposition, slow motion, speeded action, pixilation—over the story film. The underground-film movement had its greatest raison d'être when Hollywood pictures were more traditional in form and technique. In the 1950s and 1960s, as feature films became more personal and innovative, many of the goals, intentions, themes, and techniques of underground filmmakers were absorbed into the commercial cinema.

See Art theater; Avant-garde; Cult film; Experimental film; Independent filmmaker; Lynch, David; New American cinema

UNFORGIVEN

Clint Eastwood's 1992 revisionist western *Unforgiven* opens with a silhouette of a man working on a farm. A scroll describes an attractive woman who surprisingly married a man with a bad reputation: William Munny, a known thief and murderer. The woman died in 1878 of smallpox.

The scene shifts, and we are in Big Whiskey, Wyoming, in 1880. A sign prohibits guns within the city. It's raining outside of a brothel where there is a commotion going on inside. A burly cowboy, in a fit of rage, slashes the face of one of the prostitutes, Delilah (Anna Levine), because she giggled when he removed his pants. The authoritative yet egotistical sheriff, Little Bill Daggett (Gene Hackman), prescribes as punishment a fine of a handful of horses instead of a whipping or hanging—much to the dismay of the madam, Strawberry Alice (Frances Fisher). Enraged by the light punish-

"I've killed women and children. I've killed just about everything that walks or crawls. And I'm here to kill you, Little Bill, for what you done to Ned."

Clint Eastwood as William Munny in *Unforgiven* (1992)

ment, Alice pools the girls' money to advertise a reward for whoever kills the man who harmed Delilah.

Back at the farm shown in the film's opening shot, William Munny (Clint Eastwood), a pig farmer, struggles to separate the sick pigs from the healthy ones, and his children try to help him. A young wannabe gunslinger, the Schofield Kid (Jaimz Woolvett), approaches Will to see if he'd like to help him collect the reward money. Although Will has a vile past, he gave up killing and drinking when he met his wife. One of Will's children points out that another pig is sick. In the way stories and reputations get exaggerated in the west, Kid tells him that Delilah had her eyes cut out and her breasts cut off. Will is reluctant to kill again, and he is no longer a good shot, but with so many of the pigs now sick, he knows he will need the money for his family. So he sets out to catch up with Kid on the trail. Will recruits his old partner, Ned Logan (Morgan Freeman). Ned feels guilty about their former wicked ways, and his wife disapproves, but he eventually agrees to help his old friend.

A legendary gunslinger, English Bob (Richard Harris), heads for Big Whiskey with his biographer, W. W. Beauchamp (Saul Rubinek), in tow. Beauchamp fails to point out the "no guns" sign to Bob, and upon arrival, English Bill is surrounded by Little Bill and his deputies. Bob lies and says he's not armed, but Little Bill beats Bob to make him an example for anyone else who may be hoping to collect the "whore's gold."

The western Unforgiven *won the Oscar for Best Picture, and its director, Clint Eastwood, took home the Oscar for Best Director.*

▼

UNFORGIVEN

Bill systematically debunks Bob's reputation to Beauchamp. He even calls Bob "The Duck of Death" parodying his biography title, "The Duke of Death." Bill retells Bob's stories replacing the heroic elements—bravery, skill, and honor—with the actual elements: cowardice, luck, and treachery.

Ned and Will meet up with Kid. Kid is suspicious of Ned, and claims not to need any help because he's killed five men himself. But soon he's in awe of Will's legendary reputation, asking about a story in which Will supposedly killed five men at once. Ned has brought some whiskey—figuring they'll need it to help with the killing—and offers it to Will, who refuses.

Ned, Will, and the Kid enter Big Whiskey, unable to see the "no guns" sign in the rain. While Ned and Kid are "socializing" upstairs with the prostitutes, Will is alone in the bar fighting off a cold. Little Bill comes in and questions Will. Will gives Bill a fake name and lies about carrying a gun, which causes Bill to give him a beating similar to the one he gave Bob.

Outside of town, Will, Ned, and Kid reunite. The cold and Bill's beating take its toll on the aging Will, who believes he's on his deathbed. Ned and Kid wait until Will gets better. A few days later Will wakes up and finds Delilah taking care of him. Since Ned and Kid are taking "advances" on their reward money, she offers Will a "free one." He refuses. She thinks his refusal is because of her scars. He reassures her that it's not; he tells her that he has to be faithful to his wife.

"Hell, I even thought I was dead, 'til I found out it was just that I was in Nebraska."

Gene Hackman as Sheriff "Little Bill" Daggett in *Unforgiven* (1992)

Will, Ned, and Kid find the partner of the cowboy who slashed Delilah. In a long, drawn-out scene emphasizing the awkwardness and reality of killing, the partner dies a slow and painful death. Ned, who couldn't bring himself to shoot him, decides that he can't be part of the mission and takes off. But Bill captures Ned and brutally tortures him to find out the identity and location of Will and Kid.

Further deglamorizing the act of killing, Kid has to sneak up on a stinking outhouse to shoot the unarmed helpless cowboy. (Moments later, he's already embellishing the story claiming that the cowboy was armed and ready to shoot.)

Kid gulps down whiskey to cope with what we learn was actually his first kill. He asks Will if he was scared when he used to kill, and Will says he was too drunk to remember. Kid is practically crying when Will reminds him that killing a man is taking away everything he's got or is ever going to have. One of the prostitutes rides out to give them the reward money and says that Ned was killed by Little Bill's excessive torture. Will is furious, because Ned was innocent, but the final straw is when she tells him that Ned's dead body is on display. Will takes a drink of whiskey, sending Kid off to deliver Ned's and his kids' share of the money.

Will rides into town and sees Ned's dead body outside the bar. Shotgun in hand, he walks in on Bill and his deputies. He singles out the bar owner, moves people out of the way, and shoots him. Bill calls him a coward for shooting an unarmed man, but Will responds that he should have armed himself if he was going to decorate the saloon with the dead body of his friend. He is there to kill Bill only, but Will's shotgun jams, giving all of Bill's deputies a chance to draw. But Will shoots Bill first with his pistol. The deputies are so scared and frazzled (having never killed anyone) that they are gunned down. Will hovers over Bill, who says that he doesn't deserve to die. Will responds, "Deserve's got nothing to do with it," then he shoots him.

Back at his farm, a scroll tells a story of Will's wife's mother, who came to visit after Will and his kids had moved away. The mother was surprised to learn that her daughter ever married someone of such "ill repute."

See Eastwood, Clint; Hackman, Gene; Western

VALENTINO, RUDOLPH

Rudolph Valentino has become the cultural historians' most popular icon of silent-screen stardom, and with good reason. More than sixty years after his death, when the face of Norma Talmadge has been forgotten and few can name the title of a single Mary Pickford film, Valentino's recognition factor remains surprisingly high. It does not seem to matter that the accuracy of this Valentino image is considerably askew, battered by a series of inept screen biographies, and not very well served by a string of more traditional literary works.

Valentino died at the peak in his popularity. Far outlasting the fan clubs of his contemporaries, Valentino Memorial Societies have operated continuously for decades. But there is a strange dichotomy between Valentino's place in American culture and his standing among silent-film specialists. How can this situation be explained?

The posthumous passion for James Dean was fueled by a small group of highly successful films periodically reissued to new converts, but Valentino's body of work died with silent pictures. To the average modern viewer, his acting style is incomprehensible. Although a few of his films have their supporters, Valentino's ongoing recognition does not draw its strength from this direction. Nor is the death cult entirely responsible. Rather, Valentino changed the way America looked at its heroes, both on and off the screen. It is this offscreen dimension that keeps the Valentino legend alive, even when his own pictures are scorned and derided.

When *Motion Picture* magazine published the final results of the "Motion Picture Hall of Fame" popularity contest in December 1918, there were five male stars listed in the top ten: Douglas Fairbanks, Harold Lockwood, William S. Hart, Wallace Reid, and Francis X. Bushman. It would be hard to find a more clean-living group of all-Americans (at least onscreen).

The same year, the *Motion Picture Studio Directory*, a trade annual, carried a professional advertisement for "Rodolfo Di Valentina—Playing a New Style Heavy." The new style referred to the sophisticated rotter played by Valentino in *The Married Virgin* (1918), his first major role. As Count Roberto di San Fraccini, he is a blackmailing adventurer romancing both mother and stepdaughter. This foreigner who cloaks his designs behind a charming facade is not unrelated to von Stroheim's "man you love to hate" of the same period. The following year, in *A Rogue's Romance,* Valentino (previously a professional dancer) played the small role of a sinister *apache* dancer. The cliché of the Parisian underworld *apache,* drenched in treat-'em-rough machismo, fitted Valentino like a glove.

The American cultural scene was changing rapidly by 1921. That year the new-style heavy electrified a nation as the new-style hero of *The Four Horsemen of the Apocalypse* (1921). Working closely with director Rex Ingram, June Mathis developed a script that not only satisfied readers of the Ibáñez novel but consciously carved a new niche in the romantic pantheon for their extraordinary discovery.

Known as "The Great Lover" for his leading-man status in silent films of the 1920s, Rudolph Valentino's death in 1926 set off a near riot at his funeral in New York City.

Valentino was not always so lucky in his vehicles, but later the same year his role in *The Sheik* (1921) cemented his claim as king of exotic costume romance. As Theda Bara brought the kohl-eyed vamp into the culture of the teens, so Valentino, riding the crest of an incipient vogue for orientalism, launched the twenties passion for sheiks.

When Valentino died suddenly in 1926, he was about to release his latest film, a sequel to *The Sheik* that contained more than a little self-mocking humor. *Son of the Sheik* (1926) demonstrated that he was quite able to step outside his manufactured image, analyze the Valentino mystique with tongue firmly in cheek, and still give the public what it desired. The film proved to be his greatest popular success in years, but how much of this can be traced to his own talents and how much to the outlandish notoriety surrounding his death is still an unresolved question.

See Bara, Theda; Gilbert, John; Ingram, Rex; Mathis, June; Negri, Pola; Sound

VERTIGO

Vertigo (1958) is one of Alfred Hitchcock's most powerful films, one that functions on multiple levels—as a mesmerizing suspense/thriller, an intense psychological study of a desperate man's twisted psyche and his desperate search to end his vertigo, and a masterful study of romantic and fatal sexual obsession.

"Well, I'll wear the darn clothes if you want me to, if, if you'll just, just like me."

Kim Novak as Judy Barton in *Vertigo* (1958)

In the tense opening sequence, a plainclothes detective, Scottie Ferguson (James Stewart), is clinging to and dangling from a drainpipe. A fellow policeman is trying to help, but Scottie is frozen by his fear of heights, experiencing vertigo. When the policeman reaches out his hand to rescue Scottie, he loses his balance, slips, and falls to his death, leaving the terrified Scottie to hang there and gaze down at the body of the policeman on the pavement below.

Despondent, Scottie retires from the police force, guilt-ridden over his fellow officer's death. But when an old school chum, Gavin Elster (Tom Helmore), asks him to shadow his strange wife, Madeleine (Kim Novak), Scottie is lured out of retirement. Gavin contends that Madeleine may be contemplating suicide. He believes that his wife is possessed by the spirit of Carlotta Valdes—Madeleine's great-grandmother—who went mad and killed herself. He explains how Madeleine often falls into trancelike states. Scottie agrees to shadow her, then finds himself obsessively fascinated by and attracted to the blonde woman.

Scottie Ferguson's (James Stewart) twisted psyche and a masterful study of his sexual obsession with Madeleine (Kim Novak) characterize Alfred Hitchcock's complex thriller Vertigo.

Scottie follows Madeleine as she makes her way to various places around the city, and is puzzled by her strange, mysterious wanderings and robotic behavior. One day as he follows Madeleine, she drives to the edge of San Francisco Bay. Without warning, she throws herself into the water, attempting to drown herself. Scottie rushes to the water, dives in, and saves her. Although wary of him, Madeleine thanks him and quickly vanishes.

Scottie is falling in love with Madeleine, and he agrees to take her to San Juan Bautista Spanish mission, where she falls into a depressed mood. Crying and declaring her love for him, she runs to the church and climbs up to the bell tower. Scottie's vertigo inhibits his climb after her. Then, when he's almost to the top, there is a shrieking scream and a body is seen falling to its death far below. Scottie looks down through the tower opening and sees a body lying on the rooftop below.

Scottie is plunged into an extended fit of guilty depression over not stopping Madeleine from apparently hurling herself out of the bell tower—his vertigo prevented him from arriving in time to save her. But then Scottie finally learns (as the audience already has) that Gavin actually counted on Scottie's vertigo to keep him from interfering with Gavin's own plans to do away with his wife under circumstances that imply that she committed suicide.

Scottie's revelation is shown when he meets Judy Barton (Kim Novak), a red-haired Madeleine lookalike, who he discovers is both Gavin's mistress and his accomplice in an elaborate hoax to murder his wife. Gavin actually threw Madeleine from the tower. When Scottie forces Judy to reenact for him her role in Madeleine's death at the scene of the crime, she becomes hysterical and confesses her part in the hoax. Recoiling, she steps back and falls through an opening in the tower to her own death, just as the real Madeleine had done.

The final shot of the film is of Scottie staring glassy-eyed at the dead body of Judy far below.

See Hitchcock, Alfred; Stewart, James

VIDOR, KING

Small regional film centers that grew up within the United States in the late teens and early twenties produced a few individuals who successfully carried on their careers in Hollywood. The most notable was King Vidor, a director who was able to play the Hollywood studio game while maintaining an independence of style and subject matter seldom found in the mature American film industry.

Vidor was born in Galveston, Texas, in 1894. His wife, Florence Vidor, an aspiring actress who had worked with him on the Texas films, soon signed with the Ince studio and began a steady rise to stardom (her later films included *The Marriage Circle* [1924] and *The Patriot* [1928]), but director Vidor could land only odd jobs. His writing credit appears on a few Universal comedy shorts, but it was not until 1918 that he was again able to work as a director. Significantly, he achieved this not through the established studio structure but by convincing a group of doctors and dentists to back him in the production of a Christian Science subject called *The Turn in the Road* (1919). Its moral agenda recalls the sermonizing of a director like Lois Weber, and Vidor's seriousness of purpose was immediately clear (as was his popular touch—the film was quite profitable). A little later, Vidor published in the trade papers a "Creed and Pledge" outlining his intentions. He announced that the motion picture should serve humanity and help free it from the shackles of fear and suffering.

He was able to establish his own studio, Vidor Village, where he produced films for distribution through First National. The studio specialized in Americana subjects, and Vidor sought to duplicate a mood he found in the writings of Mark Twain, Booth Tarkington, and James Whitcomb Riley. Owning and operating one's own studio was a goal of most independent directors of the day, among them Griffith, Neilan, and again, Weber.

King Vidor was one of only a few directors in the late teens and early twenties who "went Hollywood" while still maintaining an independence of style and subject matter. ▶

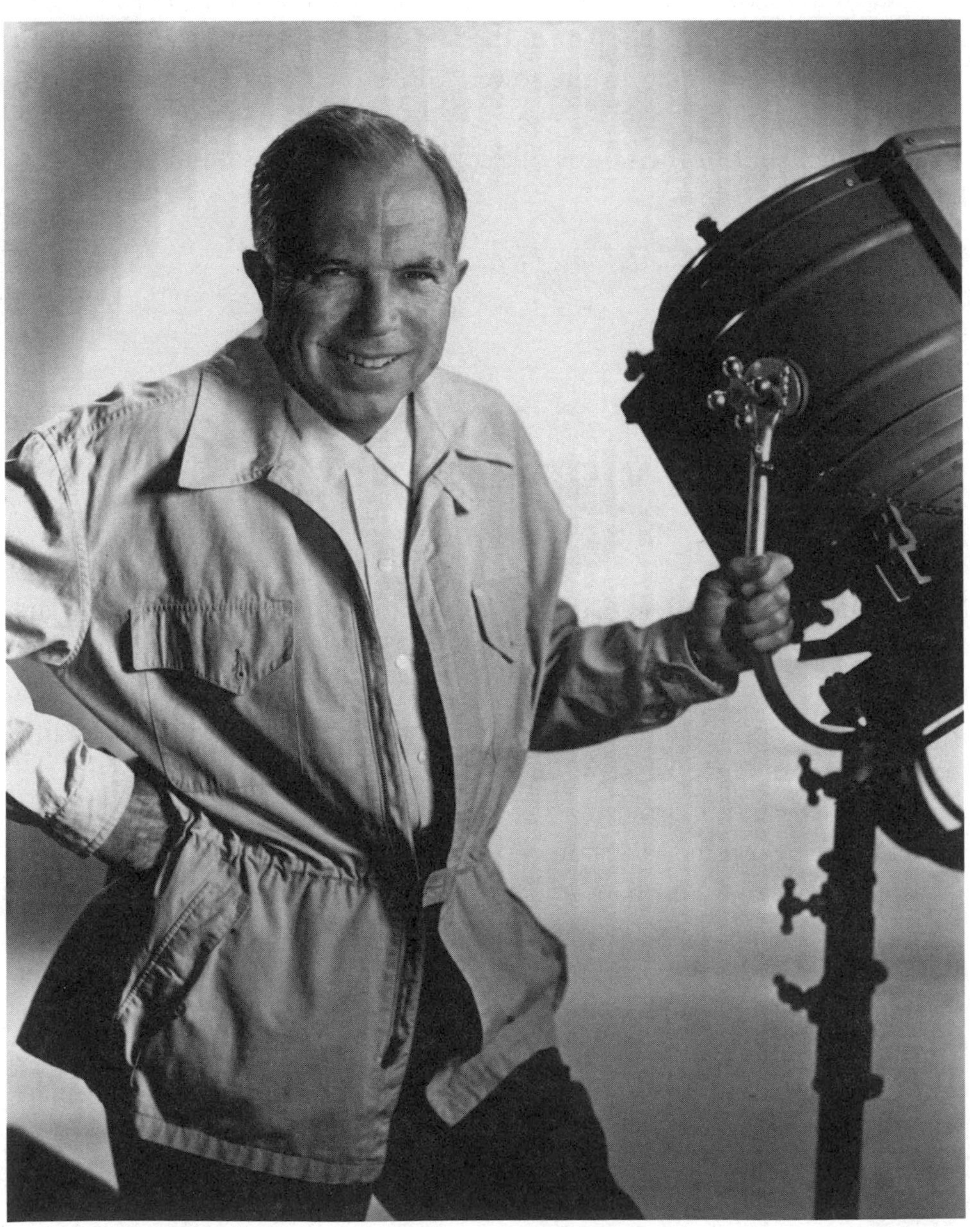

With *The Jack Knife Man* (1920) Vidor proved himself true to his ideals, creating one of the most affecting of American pastorals.

Vidor later began a long and fruitful relationship with MGM (twenty films over the next twenty years). He soon made himself indispensable by helping develop John Gilbert into a major star and directing *The Big Parade* (1925), one of the highest-grossing pictures of the silent era. Establishing a close relationship with Irving Thalberg, Vidor would trade off projects by agreeing to two of the studio's projects as long as he could direct one of his own. The most spectacular example during this period was *The Crowd* (1928), a drab urban poem largely shot on location in New York.

While directors such as Clarence Brown and John Ford found America in the countryside, Vidor was capable of seeing the nation in its cities as well. Later, in *The Fountainhead* (1949), he would show a superman asserting his will over such a city, but *The Crowd* is one of Vidor's films of ordinary life, and the resolution is far less operatic.

A director who was able to maintain his own ideals while remaining flexible enough to serve the interests of his employers, Vidor duplicated his silent success in the talkie era, while his less adaptable compatriots, including Herbert Brenon, Marshall Neilan, and Erich von Stroheim, soon found themselves unemployed.

See Brenon, Herbert; Ford, John; Gilbert, John; Goldwyn, Samuel; Griffith, D. W.; Thalberg, Irving; von Stroheim, Erich; Wizard of Oz, The

VITAPHONE

Sound-on-film recording and playback systems began to be developed in the mid 1920s. In May of 1925, a promoter, Walter J. Rich, acquired from Western Electric the rights to market its sound-on-film system for nine months. The "Big Three" Hollywood film studios—Paramount, Loew's (which owned MGM), and First National—all declined. Meanwhile, Nathan Levinson, a Western Electric engineer who had installed equipment in Warner Bros. radio stations, told Sam Warner about the talking pictures he'd seen at an exhibition at Bell Laboratories in New York. Warner became interested, and convinced the other Warner brothers (as well as their investment banker) of the potential of sound-on-film. Finally, on June 25, 1925 Walter Rich and Warner Bros. created a joint venture to explore sound film production.

Warners was engaged in a strategic plan of aggressive expansion to increase theater holdings, consolidate distribution, and diversify into broadcasting. The sound experiment was an acceptable risk as part of a highly leveraged design to catch up with the Big Three studios. It was also a cost-cutting play, since it would eliminate orchestras and presentation acts in the newly acquired movie houses. This plan was consistent with the speculative economic climate in other growth industries of the mid-1920s. The policy also meant investing in a big-name actor, John Barrymore, and a director, Ernst Lubitsch. The Vitaphone deal was one of several tactics designed to elevate the small outfit to the status of a film major.

In September 1925 Warners began refitting its newly acquired (but very old) Vitagraph studio at 1400 Locust Avenue in Flatbush, Brooklyn, to produce sound films. Meanwhile, there was a change of command at Western Electric, and John E. Otterson became the general manager. He was keenly interested in Rich's film venture and took over negotiations. On April 20, 1926, a fifty-seven-page contract was signed between Western Electric and the new Vitaphone company, which had been incorporated with Rich as president and Warner Bros. as the majority shareholder and provider of capital. Western Electric granted to Vitaphone the exclusive right to use the recording apparatus for its own films, to sublicense other producers, and to sublicense the reproduction equipment in theaters.

To secure talent for its sound movies, Vitaphone signed license agreements with Victor Talking Machine, the Metropolitan Opera, and (later) the Brunswick-Balke-Collender record company for the rights to record their contract artists. Brunswick-Balke-Collender's exclusive roster included a wide range of entertainment, from the popular Al Jolson to the high-class New York Philharmonic.

Naturally, Warners wished to show off its star—John Barrymore of the "royal family of Broadway." The early twenties were the zenith of Barrymore's stage career, and he was basking in the success of *Hamlet* in New York and London. He had also dabbled in the movies since 1913. Jack Warner signed him for *Beau Brummel* (1924) and subsequently for a three-picture contract that paid him $76,000 each, plus perquisites. This was far better than he was receiving for stage work. In September 1925 Warners hired the director Alan Crosland on a long-term contract and announced that his first feature would be *Don Juan,* starring Barrymore. The film was shot in the traditional silent method and was receiving the finishing touches in January 1926, with its release set for February. With the success of the preliminary experiments and test screenings, at the last minute it was decided to give the feature Vitaphone accompaniment.

Upon the signing of the Vitaphone contract in April, Warner Bros. declared that the company and Western Electric had a "New Musical Device." This first announcement, which does not mention Vitaphone by name, reflects a distinct effort to mold the reception of sound in the mind of exhibitors and the public. First, it couches the new development in technology: "Scientific developments which may revolutionize the presentation of films in the largest as well as the smallest theaters have just been perfected by the Western Electric Co. and Warner Bros." There was great emphasis on the electrical nature of the recording, amplification, and sound reproducer mechanisms. Second, an identification with big-time corporate experimentation was established: "[Sound films] are the result of years of research in the Bell Telephone, American Telephone and Telegraph Co., and Western Electric laboratories." This claim differentiated the Western Electric system from rival music synchronization systems, such as de Forest's. Third, the system's main advantage was called its "naturalness," without further elaboration. Fourth, Vitaphone's founders insisted, as de Forest had done, that it would be used only for music. As with Phonofilm, Vitaphone was intended to supplement the regular film program. It would replace the orchestra, but not the traditional silent feature. Sam Warner arranged the Broadway premier for the new Warners' Theatre (formerly the Piccadilly). In addition to the musically accompanied feature, *Don Juan,* he announced a prologue, two sketches, and a musical comedy routine. The music would be provided by a ninety-piece orchestra. Originally the opening was set for July 1, 1926, but there were numerous delays, in part because Wente and other AT&T technicians were redesigning their speaker horns for the Warners' theater.

By May the Warners strategy was taking shape. In addition to the twenty-six regular features it had already announced for the 1926–27 season, it was adding nine specials. All would have recorded sound tracks available. *Don Juan* and *Manon Lescaut* were to be John Barrymore vehicles; Syd Chaplin (Charlie's half brother) would have three films, including *The Better 'Ole;* the films *Black Ivory* and *Noah's Ark* did not yet have directors or players assigned. Warners' star director Lubitsch would make two pictures. Again the company stressed that "they are not to be misconstrued as talking pictures as the new recording machine . . . perfectly synchronizes music with the film."

Perhaps the most ambitious component of the program was Warners' intention to produce sound prologues, that is, musical short subjects, for each of the twenty-six regular features in the 1926–27 season. Both Sam and Albert Warner repeated the refrain that the "smallest hamlets" would be able to have first-class presentations and music. Albert believed that within five years this would be the industry standard: "The public will demand not only bigger and better productions but will also demand proper musical accompaniment, suitable for their particular production. The public is being educated to the finer things in music, through the radio and other mediums."

The marketing plan now called for *Don Juan* to have a Broadway premier on July 22, followed by road-show engagements in Chicago, Boston, and Los Angeles. This accelerated schedule coincided with Warners' announcement in its annual report that the company was taking a \$1.3 million charge for the cost of expanding its national distribution through the purchase of the Vitagraph Company in April 1925. *Don Juan* and *The Better 'Ole* cost $1.5 million to complete. In addition, the cost of Vitaphone experimentation had been written off the books. The biggest expense, though, had nothing to do with the Vitaphone project: the charge for the selling expenses of unplayed silent film contracts.

The summer months were busy ones. The defunct Manhattan Opera House was leased and converted to a makeshift soundstage. More artists were signed up to be Vitaphoned; the Metropolitan Opera stars Giovanni Martinelli, Anna Case, and Marion Talley were among the most impressive. And there were sneak previews of Vitaphone, for example, before the Wisconsin Telephone Association at the Strand Theater in Madison. The three short subjects shown there were "loud, clear, and perfectly distinct." The anonymous trade reporter ventured that, "where in the past directors have been content to portray emotion through gesture and action, they must now add the spoken word which may mean a revolution in production, and a new type of star." So even before the premier of *Don Juan* (which was not previewed in Madison because the score was still being recorded at the Manhattan Opera House under Sam Warner's supervision), critical reaction to Vitaphone had zeroed in on the speaking star as the most intriguing aspect of the new system. The canned music that the company tried to focus attention on was of little interest.

Warners tried to prepare exhibitors and audiences for the new system on the eve of its introduction. Its press release, "What the Vitaphone Promises," reveals more of its strategy for selling sound. The constant refrain, which was echoed by Will Hays and popular journalists during 1926–28, was that sound would greatly multiply the geographic and cultural contacts with the performing arts. In addition to the "New Era" millennial rhetoric surrounding these scientific devices, the creators and promoters of Vitaphone also made an appeal to "democracy" in their description of the new system. It was film's destiny to disseminate oral and aural culture to the masses. A redundant phrase that recurs—and belies the hand of an originating Warners publicist—is "small hamlet." The press readily picked up on the democracy angle. The *New York Times* observed in a glowing editorial: "The most obvious fact is that this invention in its various forms will enable the smaller communities to participate to a greater degree than even the radio permits in the cultural advantages that have been possible in the past only in places of large population." In its 1926 brochure, the company promised to make available orchestras and opera and theater stars to "every corner of the world. . . . It is now possible for every performance in a motion picture theatre to have a full orchestral accompaniment to the picture, regardless of the size of the house. . . . There can be no question of the boon that Vitaphone will be to the music-lovers who live in the out of the way hamlets."

At first, these statements seem like a populist discourse, since they invoke a plan for decentralizing culture and making it accessible to geographically dispersed consumers. The strategy was clearly imitating the telephone company advertising, which proclaimed that phone service was uniting the country. But the culture proposed to be spread by Vitaphone *was not film.* Sound cinema was to be a medium, not an art in its own right. The models for the new sound cinema were opera, classical music, light drama, and Broadway vaudeville entertainment, with its characteristic melting-pot flavor of New York ethnicity. Though calling for democracy, the producers were advocating the spread of what they regarded as elite culture to an underclass and to non–New Yorkers. Whether this "democratic" motif in the promotion of sound was a bald publicity department creation on the part of Warners or Hays's MPPDA is difficult to say. Many of the actual Vitaphone shorts were jazzy instrumental numbers or plebeian hokum. It is likely that the published appeals to high culture reflected competition for a narrow but powerful segment of the entertainment market—upper-middle-class New Yorkers who seldom attended movies or listened to popular entertainment on radio, but who patronized the Metropolitan Opera and Broadway revues. Not only was it desirable to attract the disposable income of this leisure class, it was important to benefit from their goodwill and potential power as bankers, shareholders, influences on local censorship, and arbiters of taste. The aesthetic and democratic rhetoric also distracted form the lowbrow interests plainly visible in many Vitaphone productions. In *Don Juan,* for instance, shifting attention to the New York Philharmonic diverted moralists from the licentious plot and the semi-clad chorus girls who graced the sets.

The Warners formulation closely resembles the de Forest virtual-Broadway model for short film production. But Vitaphone was also designed to be applied to features—as a virtual orchestra. That is, it would replace the actual orchestra in the pit. Again, this was pitched by the producers as an advantage for small towns. Not only would nationally recognized orchestras supplant the local piano player and snare drummer, but the music would always be appropriate to the mood on the screen, timed to match the action, and reliably executed. Not mentioned in these promotions was the all-too-apparent downside: musicians would lose their jobs, the music sounded "canned," and the intangible pleasure derived from a live performance would be gone.

The virtual orchestra would also keep the voice in its place—behind the music. Although Warners had emphatically banished talking features only months before, "What the Vitaphone Promises" tentatively opened the door. "If its scope extends to the vocal reproduction of entire pictures," the publicist wrote, "casts will be selected not only for their 'silent drama' ability, but by their voice ability as well." Many of the first-generation Vitaphone features would have vocal parts, but either in a musical context or as a dramatic "special effect." The shout of "Bob" by the father in *The First Auto,* the screaming earthquake victims of *Old San Francisco* (1927), and the dialogue in *The Jazz Singer* are examples of how the voice is subordinated to the musical part of the sound track. The shorts seemed to abide by separate rules and tolerated a few lines of spontaneous speech now and then.

Like the ideal orchestra and conductor who could accompany any; film that came from the distributor, Vitaphone was also advertised as being adaptable. According to its original formulation, theater managers could spice up the program by renting from a library of shorts. They could also revive old films by presenting them with a new musical sound track.

See Jazz Singer; *Lubitsch, Ernst; Sound*

VON STERNBERG, JOSEF

Although Josef von Sternberg's films with Marlene Dietrich, his stylized use of dialogue, and his ultimate fall from favor all postdate the silent era, von Sternberg occupies a significant place in the history of this period. His career reflects the primary contradictions built into the developing studio system: how to balance the requisites of an essentially personal style with the demands of industrial mass production.

notable & quotable

"Nothing has ever been invented that is more cumbersome to make than the motion picture."

Joseph von Sternberg, director, attributed

Von Sternberg was the most self-consciously artistic of all Hollywood's silent directors, one who sneered at stars and producers and affected eccentric habits of dress and decorum. Apparently a large part of this was mere posing. According to one often-quoted source, he first grew his moustache because it made him look more "terrible," and therefore more noticeable. The first film he directed, *The Salvation Hunters* (1925), was a grim exposition of life on a dredge, clearly intended to outrage its viewers by exceeding even *Greed* in ashcan realism. In later years the director was often uneasy about acknowledging this heavy, graceless exercise. Produced for $5,000, *The Salvation Hunters* succeeded in catching the attention of Chaplin and Pickford and won for itself a place on the United Artists release schedule. Critical response to the picture was wildly mixed, but it did lead directly to a contract at Metro-Goldwyn-Mayer. Von Sternberg began the direction of two films there, but the first was completely redone by another director, while von Sternberg walked off the second after only a few days of shooting.

Since the studio system was not adapting very well to Chaplin's discovery, the comedian offered a project of his own. Von Sternberg would direct Edna Purviance in a story of life among the fisherfolk, *The Woman of the Sea* (1926). But after one preview, Chaplin shelved the picture, and it was never

seen again. Mary Pickford then set von Sternberg to work on a story for her, but when he returned with the outline for *Backwash,* the tale of a poor blind girl living in the slums of industrial Pittsburgh, that project also dissolved.

Von Sternberg had been able to attract attention with a personal film of "horrible" distinction but had not been able to turn this success into the basis of a future career. Not only had he failed at MGM, but his friends at United Artists had proved less than reliable. Finally, he was reduced to working at Paramount in a vaguely defined capacity, submitting story ideas and directing bits and pieces of other people's films.

Then, one fortunate day, the direction of a new gangster film, *Underworld* (1927), was handed to von Sternberg. In the four silent films he went

Josef von Sternberg was well known in Hollywood for his exceedingly "personal" style—in short, he felt he could easily improve upon the work of any other director or producer.

on to direct for Paramount in 1927 and 1928, von Sternberg was finally able to resolve the tensions between his own demands and those of his employer. Von Sternberg was happy to tackle a commercial subject like this because he was prepared to ignore those elements of plot and locale which made it valuable to Paramount. What interested him was happening elsewhere: mood, theme, and characterization.

Underworld created a vogue for gangster films that lasted well into the sound era, and it achieved a financial success that assured von Sternberg's ability to work with relative freedom on the pictures that followed. A completely romanticized view of crime and criminals, the film was attacked by some for its technical inaccuracies and amoral perspective, a type of criticism that would increase over the next decade. But *Underworld* set the pattern for later von Sternberg essays into exotic worlds, foreign and domestic.

See Chaplin, Charlie; Gangster film; Pickford, Mary; Sound

VON STROHEIM, ERICH

Erich von Stroheim was not the only director to go far over budget, behave outrageously on the set, or inflame the nation's various pressure groups. But he was the only one to do so while flouting the authority of his studio superiors and failing (for the most part) to bring in adequate box-office returns.

Between 1919 and 1932 von Stroheim began the direction of nine films, all but the last of which were silent. Of this number, one was never released, two were completed by others, one was halted during production and released in truncated form, two were taken from him after shooting and savagely cut, two more suffered minor studio-inflicted cuts, and one was released essentially intact. In terms of a body of work, this collection of footage might hardly seem worth evaluating. Yet throughout the 1920s he remained one of the most respected of all Hollywood directors.

This esteem has continued over the years. In the 1976 Belgian Royal Film Archive poll von Stroheim was still seen as being among the ten most important American directors, despite the fact that not one film from his hand survives intact. His best-known film, *Greed* (1924), notorious for being slashed to one-quarter of its intended length, was cited in this poll as the third most important American film of all time.

Von Stroheim, the son of a Jewish dry-goods merchant, was born in Vienna in 1885. A failure in both the business world and a brief military career, he emigrated to the United States in 1908 and worked at a series of odd jobs. He tried his hand at the stage as early as 1912, writing a short

Erich von Stroheim's antics in Hollywood—flouting budgets, behaving outrageously on the set—earned him the nickname "The Man You Love to Hate."

play, called *In the Morning*, which contained, in rough outline, many of the themes he would later develop in such films as *The Wedding March* (1928). His first Hollywood experience came with the D. W. Griffith company. He acted in a number of Griffith-produced subjects for Mutual, however, and often assisted the prominent stage director John Emerson. Griffith's method of working soon became von Stroheim's model, and under "the master" he worked on *Intolerance* and *Hearts of the World.* Von Stroheim began to have some success as an actor, specializing in the portrayal of fiendish Huns in war-propaganda films, bus such roles disappeared with the Armistice.

Von Stroheim later convinced Universal's Carl Laemmle to allow him to star in and direct an original script of his own. By giving Universal the script for nothing, taking no salary as director, and accepting only $200 per week for playing the leading role, von Stroheim made the tightfisted Laemmle an irresistible offer. He also seems to have appealed to "Uncle

V

VON STROHEIM, ERICH

In 1919 the average feature film budget was $60,000. Erich von Stroheim's *Blind Husbands* was budgeted at $10,000, but ended up costing almost $200,000.

Carl's" gambler's instinct and his penchant for hiring relatives and other German-speaking emigrés from the old country. Von Stroheim far exceeded the budget, but the results justified the gamble. This first film, *Blind Husbands* (1919), earned some $328,000 during its initial year of release. Critics were also suitably impressed, and the result of this acclaim was to increase von Stroheim's leverage with Laemmle, an advantage he stretched to its breaking point on *Foolish Wives* (1922), touted as "the first million-dollar picture." But the financial failure of *Foolish Wives,* and increasing production problems on his next film, *Merry-Go-Round* (1923), moved Universal's new production head, Irving Thalberg, to fire von Stroheim midway through production.

That a studio should remove a director of this caliber from "his own" picture was unprecedented, but it was nothing personal. Thalberg was able to use the firing of von Stroheim to intimidate every director in Hollywood, and it was largely von Stroheim's visibility that caused him to be used as the lightning rod in this demonstration. Von Stroheim's career went downhill from there. His next film, *Greed,* was taken away from him in a further storm of publicity and was virtually cut to ribbons. Later at MGM, a financial success with *The Merry Widow* temporarily reestablished him in Hollywood, but cost overruns on *The Wedding March* and incessant squabbling during production of the never-completed *Queen Kelly* ultimately destroyed his credibility.

Von Stroheim, a student of Griffith, felt that the cinema was an art form, the writer-director an artist, and the studio head, at best, a patron. Postwar Hollywood reality destroyed this fiction. After the first blush of success, he soon learned that the relationship was more accurately that of employer and employee.

See Cruze, James; Griffith, D. W.; Ingram, Rex; Murnau, F. W.; Neilan, Marshall; Sunset Boulevard; *Thalberg, Irving; Vidor, King; Wilder, Billy*

WAR FILM

For over a century, filmmakers have crafted stories about war and its impact on individuals, nations, and cultures. Some war films are blatant patriotic propaganda, while others provide thought-provoking social commentary. A handful of them are simple attempts to turn a quick profit.

The genre was launched in April of 1898. Mere hours after the United States declared war on Spain, J. Stuart Blackton shot less than two minutes of footage in New York City. His short silent film, *Tearing Down the Spanish Flag*, depicts a uniformed man lowering the Spanish flag from a pole. This film sparked an initial wave of films that depict honorable, heroic patriots as protagonists. The wave of pro-war films culminated in 1915 with *The Battle Cry of Peace*, which painted the Huns as relentless rapists eager to claim American women and level Washington.

Several war films emerged during World War I. In 1917 producer Robert Goldstein was arrested because his film *The Spirit of '76* was financed by hostile Germans; it depicted America and Germany allied against Great Britain. *The Kaiser-Beast of Berlin* (1918) included real footage of President Wilson. Charlie Chaplin's *Shoulder Arms* (1918) provided some comic contrast to the brutal reality of the war, while D. W. Griffith chose to focus on the brutal reality: he filmed *Hearts of the World* (1919) in genuine French combat environments.

Later, Jean Renoir's *La Grande Illusion* (1937), set in a World War I prison camp, is a naturalistic masterpiece, which effectively shows the forces at play that led to the war.

The Four Horsemen of the Apocalypse (1921), starring Rudolph Valentino, was the first postwar film to earn a profit. Four years later, two films emerged that were instrumental in demonstrating that war films could function as art and social commentary rather than propaganda: King Vidor's *The Big Parade* and Raoul Walsh's *What Price Glory?* (1926), both of which portrayed war from the perspective of soldiers rather than officers and presidents.

In 1928, the first Academy Award for Best Picture went to a war film: *Wings*. It included breathtaking dogfights based on the experiences of director William Wellman, a former combat pilot. (George Lucas later studied these dogfights while planning the X-Wing versus Tie Fighter sequences for *Star Wars*.)

In 1930 a pair of Howards released the first air warfare films with sound, hoping to capture some of the *Wings* magic: Howard Hughes's *Hell's Angels* and Howard Hawks's *The Dawn Patrol*, both of which were well received, although not to the same degree as the original *Wings*.

That year also saw the release of the first critically acclaimed antiwar film with sound: Lewis Milestone's *All Quiet on the Western Front*, an adaptation of Erich Maria Remarque's novel, which earned Oscars for Best Director and Best Picture. Despite these accolades, rather than heralding Milestone's film as a brave antiwar statement, many critics felt that it was thematically muddled and simply a pacifistic film released in a pacifistic time.

When the seeds of World War II sprouted and took root through open combat in Europe in 1939, an anti-Nazi film was rushed out: *Confessions of a Nazi Spy*. More anti-Nazi films quickly followed in 1940: *Four Sons*, Charlie Chaplin's *The Great Dictator*, and Hitchcock's *Foreign Correspondent*.

In 1941, the year before America joined the war, Hollywood churned out thinly veiled recruitment films like *I Wanted Wings, Dive Bombers*, and

Oliver Stone's Platoon *was one of several films of the late 1980s to shift the Vietnam genre back toward reality-based psychological dramas.*

A Yank in the RAF, all of which portrayed proud American patriots battling the Nazis. On December 7 the Japanese attacked Pearl Harbor, and within two weeks President Roosevelt appointed Lowell Mellet to direct a committee that would "suggest" war film projects to the Hollywood studios.

Among the films churned out under Mellet's urging: *A Yank on the Burma Road* (produced and released with astonishing speed, it reached an audience fewer than two months after the Pearl Harbor bombing) and *Mrs. Miniver*, which depicted a brave British family struggling to survive the relentless German atrocities.

The year 1942 saw the introduction of a modern archetype that cuts across genres and strongly influenced James Cameron's *Aliens:* the heroic super-Marine. John Farrow's *Wake Island* depicted the U.S. Marines as inexhaustible superhumans who could overcome any threat.

That same year, *Air Force* also boosted public morale by depicting American bombers destroying Japanese naval vessels. Historians dispute the accuracy of this film, however: no land-based bombers had successfully sunk Japanese bombers at the time of the film's release. Hollywood then crafted pro-war films based on actual battles, including *Gung Ho* and *Guadalcanal Diary* in 1943, followed by *Thirty Seconds over Tokyo* in 1944. In 1998 director Terrence Malick returned to the subject of the Guadalcanal with an adaptation (nominated for Best Picture) of James Jones's 1962 novel *The Thin Red Line*.

As the war drew to a close, seminal critically acclaimed films were released in 1945, including *The Story of G.I. Joe* and *Objective Burma*. And 1946's *The Best Years of Our Lives*, which depicted the readjustment of combat veterans to normal life, swept the Academy Awards.

In 1998 Steven Spielberg's *Saving Private Ryan* was hailed as the most realistic portrayal of World War II ever brought to the screen. The opening Normandy invasion sequence caused many combat veterans to leave the theater shaking and crying, as Spielberg's images and sounds reawakened their posttraumatic stress. (Ironically, nearly two decades earlier, Spielberg had been raked over the critical coals for his World War II comedy *1941*.)

The World War II theme seemingly exhausted, Sam Fuller's *The Steel Helmet* (1951), revered by modern filmmakers like Quentin Tarantino, was the first Korean War film. The best received Korean War film, *The Bridges at Toko-Ri* (1955), was produced and released just after the war ended. It was a forerunner of contemporary action films, with breathtaking airplane sequences.

In the years between the Korean and Vietnam wars, Hollywood once again returned to the popular World War II subgenre with films like *The Longest Day*.

The largest wave of Vietnam War films reached audiences only after the war had ended. *Coming Home* (1977) depicted the obstacles faced by a returning veteran. The year 1978 saw the release of three acclaimed films

Movies showing at theater in which Lee Harvey Oswald was arrested in Dallas on Nov. 22, 1963: *War Is Hell* and *Cry of Battle*.

set during the war: *The Boys in Company C, Go Tell the Spartans*, and Michael Cimino's *The Deer Hunter* (which is often hailed as one of the greatest films of all time). The following year, Francis Ford Coppola released his seminal *Apocalypse Now.*

The early-to-mid 1980s spawned a popular subgenre: the Vietnam prisoner-of-war-rescue movie. *Uncommon Valor* (1983), Chuck Norris's *Missing in Action* (both released in 1984) and 1985's *Rambo: First Blood* all depicted harrowing rescue missions that successfully brought American POWs home.

Shortly thereafter, Oliver Stone's *Platoon* (1986) and Stanley Kubrick's *Full Metal Jacket* (1987) shifted the Vietnam genre back toward reality-based, human psychological dramas.

The fear of nuclear war has spawned many fictional films that depict "what if" scenarios. *Five*, written and directed by Arch Oboler in 1951, depicts five survivors of a nuclear war as they struggle to rebuild their lives and society. *The World, the Flesh, and the Devil* (1959) also depicts the aftermath of a nuclear war and the efforts of a small band of survivors to connect with each other and rebuild. *Panic in Year Zero* (1962) portrays civilians regressing to primal looting and killing as they compete over scarce resources following an atomic war. Two years later, Stanley Kubrick released the classic *Dr. Strangelove or: How I Learned to Stop Worrying and Love the Bomb,* a pessimistic satire about the inevitability of nuclear war. That same year, director Sidney Lumet released *Fail Safe*, a disturbing tale about an accidental nuclear attack. More recently, 1983's made-for-TV movie *The Day After* showed rural Americans struggling to survive the aftermath of nuclear war.

In the 1990s the popularity of *Saving Private Ryan* and *The Thin Red Line* insure that the war genre has not yet been mined to death. As time passes and past wars take on deeper historical perspectives, screenwriters and directors will no doubt return to this genre that offers so much potential to explore the best and worst of the human condition.

See All Quiet on the Western Front; *Chaplin, Charlie; Coppola, Francis Ford;* Deer Hunter; From Here to Eternity; *Griffith, D. W.; Kubrick, Stanley; Spielberg, Steven; Stone, Oliver*

notable & quotable

"John Wayne was born John Wayne. He was his own man. Nobody created John Wayne except John Wayne."

Maureen O'Hara, actress, 1999, as quoted in "America Goes Hollywood," Newsweek, *June 28, 1999*

WEBER, LOIS

The most remarkable thing about women directors in the silent period is not that there were so many of them but that their contributions should

JOHN WAYNE

John Wayne, the larger-than-life actor who was known as the "Duke," was born Marion Michael Morrison in Winterset, Iowa, on May 26, 1907. His family soon moved to California, and the tall (6'4"), strapping young man attended the University of Southern California on a football scholarship. During summer vacations he found work as a low-level prop assistant on the Fox movie lot. There he became friendly with influential director John Ford, who became his mentor.

Wayne began playing bit parts in films in 1928. He first went by the name Duke Morrison—a not uncommon move in that era, when performers with slightly awkward names, like "Marion," routinely changed them to shape their images and further their careers; eventually he settled on John Wayne. He worked steadily over the next decade, appearing in dozens of films, mostly westerns. But Wayne did not resonate with audiences until he performed the role of the Ringo Kid in *Stagecoach* (1939), a Ford film that would become a classic.

Once Wayne became a star, he became a big star, elevated to nearly mythical proportions. With his craggy features and slow, almost methodical way of talking, Wayne seemed to the public to embody all that was good about America. Many of his film roles played on that noble perception, but he also turned in some excellent performances as "toughies" or somber, complex characters.

A family dog named Duke was allegedly the source of John Wayne's famous nickname.

Among Wayne's most famous films are *The Flying Seabees* (1944), *Red River* (1948), *She Wore a Yellow Ribbon* (1949), *The Searchers* (1956), *North to Alaska* (1960), and *The Sons of Katie Elder* (1965). He acted in well over 100 movies during the course of his career.

Wayne won the Academy Award for Best Actor for his performance in *True Grit* (1969), a western that enjoys lavish praise to this day. His last role was as a murderer who had cancer *(The Shootist,* 1976). It was an ironic end for a man who battled cancer for more than a decade and a half, finally succumbing in1979.

Married three times and the father of seven, actor and director/producer of more than 150 films, mourned by millions of fans, the Duke was memorialized by a congressional medal struck specifically in his honor.

See Stagecoach; *Western; War film*

have been so thoroughly effaced in all later histories of the period. At Universal alone, in 1916–17, one could have observed Ruth Ann Baldwin, Grace Cunard, Cleo Madison, Ruth Stonehouse, Ida May Park, Elsie Jane Wilson, and Lois Weber directing every sort of picture. Most of these women soon dropped out, presumably for lack of talent, interest, or the ability to cope with Hollywood politics, but Lois Weber flourished. During

Director Lois Weber's films were often attacked by censorship groups as exploitations of taboo topics, but Weber stuck to her position as both an artist and an evangelist.

the war years, she achieved tremendous success by combining a canny commercial sense with a rare vision of cinema as a moral tool. For a time, Weber made a fortune trying to improve the human race through movies.

As a young woman, Weber worked for a time as a street-corner missionary in Pittsburgh, but later dropped this vocation and followed the advice of an uncle in Chicago to try the stage. The transition was not as radical as it might seem, since she had had previous experience as a touring concert pianist.

Soon after joining a road company of *Why Girls Leave Home,* she married the troupe's actor-manager, Phillips Smalley, but the constant separation involved in the touring life proved difficult, and Weber settled in New York to establish a home. In 1908 she discovered that motion pictures required little road work and signed with the Gaumont studio in Flushing, New York. Here, she would have observed the screen's first woman director, Alice Guy Blaché, who had come to the United States with her husband, Herbert Blaché, to take charge of Gaumont's American interests.

Weber grew comfortable with the film form—writing, directing, and starring in Gaumont's one-reelers—and Smalley soon joined her. As a team, they eventually moved to the Reliance studio, then to Edwin S. Porter's Rex Company, which they took over when Porter left in 1912 and Rex became part of the new Universal. Their films from this period were signed by "The Smalleys," although Weber typically received sole writing credit. How the directorial chores were divided is not clear, but by 1917 Weber was putting her own name on the productions, and Smalley gradually faded in importance.

Few early Weber films survive, and the most remarkable, *Suspense* (1913), is uncharacteristic in its flashy cutting, photographic effects, and lack of a direct moral statement. The following year, the Smalleys produced for the Bosworth Company their first great success, *Hypocrites!* (1914). This four-reel feature was cast in the form of an allegory, with "the mirror of truth" being held up to various tableaux representing politics, family life, and other areas of moral concern. Weber's use of a (double-exposed) nude actress to represent Truth caused a considerable stir at the time.

Returning to Universal, Weber increased her production of such morality plays, culminating in the notorious *Where Are My Children?* (1916), self-described in its publicity as "a five-part argument advocating birth control and against race suicide." Her films were often attacked by censorship groups as simple exploitations of taboo subject matter, but Weber sincerely believed in her position as artist and evangelist.

She continued dealing with such "women's issues" as divorce, poverty, child abuse, capital punishment, and birth control, although women's suffrage does not seem to have been one of her prime concerns. She later began to play down the blatant sermonizing in her work, as in *The Blot* (1921), which substitutes a nuanced analysis of the effects of poverty on a poor minister's family.

Despite these changes, Weber seems to have abruptly lost her public after 1920. A four-picture deal with Paramount, which would pay her $50,000 per picture and 50 percent of the profits, was dropped after the poor reception of the first two films. The new audience of the 1920s had even less use for Weber's analysis of their moral shortcomings than they had for Griffith's. She directed a few films after 1921, was divorced and remarried, and seems to have suffered some form of nervous breakdown. Poor management of her real-estate holdings depleted her fortune in the early 1930s, and when she died in 1939 her funeral expenses were paid by friends who remembered her devotion to an impossibly high ideal of screen art.

WELLES, ORSON

George Orson Welles, a prodigious filmmaker, screenwriter, and actor, was born on May 6, 1915, to a comfortable, middle-class family in Kenosha, Wisconsin. His mother was a concert pianist, his father an inventor. He was a precocious child, particularly gifted in the arts. His mother died when he was just eight or nine years old, after which time Welles traveled extensively with his father, spending a great deal of time in Shanghai, China. His father also died when Welles was young (variously reported from when he was age twelve to fifteen), after which time he was under the care of a legal guardian, Chicago physician Dr. Maurice Bernstein.

notable & quotable

"I started at the top and worked down."

Orson Welles

As a boy, Welles exhibited a particular fascination with theater, often putting on performances for school and neighborhood groups. His first theatrical production, at age ten, was *Dr. Jekyll and Mr. Hyde.* A local newspaper even published an article about the "ten-year-old cartoonist, actor, and poet."

In 1931, at age sixteen, Welles graduated from the exclusive Todd School in Woodstock, Illinois. Rather than entering college, he decided to try to find a place on the stage. At eighteen he acted in the Gate Theatre in Ireland. He eventually traveled farther afield, spending some time in Morocco as well as in Spain, where he wrote articles on film and had a brief and lackluster stint as "El Americano," a bullfighter.

Soon Welles joined a road company, with which he made his Broadway debut in 1934, playing Tybalt in *Romeo and Juliet.* That was a banner year for the young man: he also married Virginia Nicholson (though they divorced in 1939), directed his first short film, and began work in radio. In 1936 he joined "The March of Time" and, in collaboration with director/producer John Houseman, worked in the New York Federal Theatre Project. With an all-black version of *Macbeth,* he quickly revealed the startling innovative streak and disregard for convention for which he would become known.

Welles and Houseman also formed a repertory company, the Mercury Theatre, in New York. In 1937 the so-called Mercury Players, under Welles's direction, began putting on hourlong dramas each week on CBS radio. Their series *The Shadow* was a particular hit. (The Shadow "had the ability to cloud men's minds." The series' signature phrase, in which a man

intones "The Shadow knows!" and then cackles maniacally, remains one of the most recognizable pieces in radio history.)

On Halloween night in 1938 "The Mercury Theatre on the Air" broadcast a live version of H. G. Wells's *The War of the Worlds,* a tale of Martians landing in New Jersey. So convincing was the performance of Welles and the other Mercury Players—rendered in realistic-sounding, urgent news-radio style—that it set off a panic among listeners.

Still only in his early twenties, Orson Welles was already recognized among the movers and shakers of the entertainment industry as a force to be reckoned with—he was a true wunderkind. RKO Pictures thus brought Welles to Hollywood to make movies, promising him creative freedom and a percentage of the profits.

Orson Welles is one of only five actors to receive an Academy Award nomination for his first screen appearance.

◀

His first movie was *Citizen Kane* (1941). Welles produced as well as directed the dark, brooding movie. He also played the title role and collaborated on the screenplay (with Herman Mankiewicz, though Welles tried to claim all credit for himself), which won the Academy Award for Best Screenplay. *Citizen Kane* told the ultimately tragic story of a powerful newspaper titan. The technical and narrative innovations that he used in the film have had a profound influence on the industry ever since.

Welles later said that he started at the top and worked his way down. The brilliance of his film debut seemed to haunt him throughout his life. In some ways, this disappointment could be said to parallel the story of the title character of *Citizen Kane,* whose lust for wealth and power was so great that it could never be satisfied.

notable & quotable

"You can write all the ideas of all the movies, my own included, on the head of a pin. It's a form that may grip you or take you into a world or involve you emotionally—but ideas are not the subject of films."

Orson Welles

In hindsight, however, one can point to astounding achievements in Welles's filmography, which includes nearly one hundred works ranging from acting or directing feature films to appearing in documentaries.

Welles's second film for RKO, *The Magnificent Ambersons,* was vigorously cut (by forty-three minutes) by the studio while Welles was off filming a documentary in South America *(It's All True,* released in 1993, though Welles himself never completed it). *The Magnificent Ambersons* was not welcomed by audiences (though it is well regarded today), and RKO subsequently severed its relationship with Welles.

Many of the other films that Welles participated in during the 1940s flopped at the box office as well. But there were significant successes. For example, Welles played the role of Rochester in *Jane Eyre* (1944), and is now considered the definitive Rochester, and he directed *The Lady from Shanghai* (1948) a stunning film noir. Under tight constraints from producer Sam Spiegel, he also directed *The Stranger.* It was Welles's greatest commercial success, which helped to show that he could direct a picture on time and on budget, but Welles considered it to be "the worst of my films."

In 1943 Welles wed again, this time to actress Rita Hayworth, a union that lasted only a few years. In 1948 Welles decided to leave the United States, which he perceived as being unreceptive to his particular brand of creative vision, and moved to Europe.

In Europe Welles continued making movies, including *The Third Man* (1952) and *Moby-Dick* (1956). In 1952 Welles's version of *Othello* won the Grand Prix at the Cannes Film Festival, but Welles was still not ready to come back to Hollywood. He finally did so in 1956, when he directed and acted in the complex, innovative film *Touch of Evil* (1958). It won a prize at the 1958 Brussels World's Fair. In 1956 he also married actress Paola Mori, his third wife.

The 1960s and '70s brought Welles a lot of work, but not much of distinction. (Significant exceptions: *Is Paris Burning?* 1966; and *A Man for All Seasons,* 1966.) His last completed film was *F for Fake* (1975), a witty take on the meaning of art.

The man who now is regarded as one of the most brilliant filmmakers of all time also became the subject of endless derision for his ever-expanding girth. By the time he started doing wine commercials ("We will sell no wine before its time"), Welles was a figure of fun in popular culture.

In 1975 Welles was awarded the American Film Institute's Lifetime Achievement Award. But it was too little, too late. Only since Welles's death on October 9, 1985, of a heart attack, has the brilliant filmmaker been accorded his rightful stature in film history. His ashes are buried in the town of Ronda, in Malaga, Spain, where he spent his summer at age eighteen.

See Citizen Kane; Third Man; *Wood, Natalie*

WEST SIDE STORY

West Side Story (1961) is a musical drama that tells the story of a *Romeo and Juliet*-type love affair among members of rival ethnic gangs. As the gangs battle for control of turf in New York's Upper West Side in the late 1950s, love blooms between Maria (Natalie Wood), a newly arrived "PR" (Puerto Rican), and Tony (Richard Beymer), a young Polish American who has left the gang known as the Jets. Because of the hatred between the groups, their love is doomed.

"If you want to kill each other, kill each other, but you ain't gonna do it on my beat."

Simon Oakland as Lt. Schrank in *West Side Story* (1961)

The story, adapted by Ernest Lehman from the Broadway play of the same name, is told through dazzling dance and music. The musical score, widely considered one of the best in American entertainment history, was written by Leonard Bernstein and Stephen Sondheim. The film's credits list Robert Wise and Jerome Robbins as codirectors; Robbins, however, worked on the project for just a few months and then was removed, due to creative differences with Wise and the producers. While his tenure was brief, Robbins's important contribution is strongly evidenced in several electrifying dance sequences.

The movie opens with aerial shots of the diverse worlds of Manhattan: groomed parks, sparkling skyscrapers, teeming bridge traffic, crowded tenements. The camera zooms down to a half dozen or so Jets, snapping their fingers in time to the musical score, in a dreary concrete-and-chain-link-fence playground/basketball court. The Jets are a gang comprised of second-generation Americans, the children of white immigrants from Europe. Their bitter rivals in the fight for turf, the Sharks, are recent immigrants from Puerto Rico.

The rivalry between the Sharks and the Jets is expressed through word and dance in the next several scenes, where first one and then the other of the groups—depending on who is outnumbered—is menaced.

The Jets are led by Riff (Russ Tamblyn), the Sharks by Bernardo (George Chakiris). Through action and lyrics, the gang mentality that drives their turf war is explained. In one song, Riff refers to the Jets as a family. Being members of a gang gives them a sense of identity and power in their small slice of Manhattan.

Riff warns that the Jets will do anything to keep the Sharks at bay (the PRs multiply, says one of his followers, like cockroaches); if the Sharks use blades or guns, so will the Jets. Riff contends that they need to have a "war council" with the Sharks to make the boundaries clear. As a venue, he proposes the dance that night at the gym—neutral territory—and suggests that they call in Tony, an ex-member who founded the Jets with Biff.

Tony resists at first; he has left the gang and moved on. But he finally agrees when Riff begs him to help out for old time's sake. And he is rewarded that evening when he meets Maria.

At the dance, an official, Glad Hand (John Astin), tries to get the Jets and the Sharks to dance together, but to no avail. Instead of socializing, the

West Side Story, *with its dazzling choreography by Jerome Robbins and score by Leonard Bernstein and Stephen Sondheim, won an incredible ten Academy Awards after its release in 1961.*

groups challenge each other in dance. The Sharks, in party clothes of intense reds and purples, move in smooth, sinuous rhythms. The Jets, dressed in softer but still striking tones from the opposite end of the color spectrum, dance in sharp, jazzlike steps.

Meanwhile, Tony and Maria spot each other, and it is love at first sight. The focus of the film softens, and they perform a soft ballet to the love song "Maria."

There is a problem, however: Maria is Bernardo's sister, and a romance with a Jet is not part of the plan for his "precious jewel." He wants Maria to marry Chino (Jose de Vega). Bernardo breaks them up. He says to Maria, "Couldn't you see he's one of them?" She answers, "No. I saw only him."

Maria and Anita (Rita Moreno), Bernardo's girlfriend, try to convince Bernardo that Maria has the right to live her own life now. Anita suggests that Maria is just being used as an excuse to have a rumble with the rival gang. In "America," the Puerto Rican girls sing of their love for their new homeland; the boys, however, see only prejudice and poverty:

Girls: Life is all right in America.
Boys: If you're all white in America.
Girls: Here you are free and you have pride.
Boys: Long as you stay on your own side.

Though Maria has been warned not to see Tony again, they meet on the fire escape outside her bedroom. They embrace and sing "Tonight."

At work in the bridal shop the next day, Maria admits to her girlfriends that she is in love, singing "I Feel Pretty." Anita lets it drop that the Jets and Sharks are planning a rumble. Maria doesn't understand. "Why must they always fight?" she asks. "Too much feeling," Anita responds. Tony comes by the shop to see Maria. Even though Anita warns them about the consequences of continuing to see each other, they can't help themselves. After she leaves, they sing a duet, "One Hand, One Heart"—"One hand, one heart, even death won't part us now"—and pretend to be engaged and then to marry.

The rumble, an elaborately choreographed fight, finally occurs. As the gangs square off, Bernardo accidentally stabs Riff to death. To avenge Riff, Tony kills Bernardo. The rumble is broken by police sirens, and the groups scatter.

Chino tells Maria that Tony has killed her brother, and she is stunned and bereft. Tony appears at her bedroom window, and he explains what happened: "I tried to stop it. I did try. I don't know what went wrong. I didn't mean to hurt him. . . ." Maria forgives him, and in the song "Somewhere," they sing of their hopes for finding peace together.

Anita tries to reconcile the two gangs, to let them know that Maria and Tony bear no ill will, but the Jets mock and threaten her. Angry, she lies, saying that Chino "found out about" the forbidden romance between Maria and Tony and killed her. Grief-stricken, Tony races to the playground to find Chino, to challenge him.

At the playground, Tony finds that Maria is actually still alive. The two lovers run to each other, only to be stopped by Chino's bullet. Devastated, Maria cradles Tony's body, saying, "How many bullets are left, Chino? Enough for you, and you? All of you, you all killed him and my brother and Riff. Not with bullets and guns—with hate." Sobered by her stark words, the two gangs finally unite, carrying Tony's body away.

The groundbreaking film earned eleven Academy Award nominations and, of those, won an astounding ten Oscars, for all categories (including Best Picture and Best Director) except Best Adapted Screenplay. This is an accomplishment matched only by *Ben-Hur* in 1959 and by *Titanic* in 1997.

See Musical film; Wood, Natalie

WESTERN

A western is a descriptive label for a type of motion picture that is characteristically American in its mythic origins. Motion pictures classified as westerns share a number of qualities and film conventions. Generally, westerns are set on the American frontier during the latter part of the nineteenth century. Plotting conventions usually center on the classic goal of maintaining law and order on the rugged frontier. The villains of western films conventionally use guns or other forceful means to take what they want; they are characters without any sense of moral compunction. The western hero, on the other hand, exhibits great courage in dealing with the evil forces and reveals a simplistic sense of duty and honor. A common characteristic of both hero and villain is the willingness of each to use guns in protecting themselves. Showdowns, shoot-outs, and gunfights on horseback, on trains, or in stagecoaches are common to plot resolution in the western film.

The format of the western genre as it has evolved in American filmmaking is simple and direct. The mise-en-scène draws on the romantic appeal of the open, untamed edges of the frontier, on lonely isolated forts and ranch houses, and on the stark facade of still-forming frontier towns. The forces of evil in these locations, often a gang of men, are quickly introduced through dramatic actions that display their dastardly deeds: a bank robbery, a train or stagecoach holdup, cattle rustling, or human massacre. Equal attention is given early on to suggesting the rugged qualities of the hero who must contend with the villains. The hero may be a local law-

enforcement officer, a territorial marshal, or a skilled gunfighter who is brought in from another frontier location. Eventually a showdown occurs, for example, *High Noon* (1952) and *Shane* (1953). In some instances, the hero may be a group of men—a posse—that organizes against the gang of villains. Still another variation of the western plot makes it necessary for the hero to pursue the villains into the unpopulated hinterlands beyond the frontier edges; in this variation of format the dramatic conflict centers on an extended "search and destroy" mission, for example, *The Outlaw Josey Wales* (1976), *Rooster Cogburn and His Lady* (1976), and *Unforgiven* (1992).

The appeal of the western film is derived from its fast-paced action, its romantic use of locations, and its clean, simple development of plot where dramatic conflicts, moral codes, and story conventions are easily understood.

Certain distinctions are made between the serious western film and the lighter western. To be a serious western, critics claim, the hero and villain must be equally committed to killing in order to maintain their positions on the frontier. Other westerns, usually those made with a series hero such as Gene Autry or Roy Rogers, involve courageous deeds, but not to the point of death.

See Cooper, Gary; Eastwood, Clint; High Noon; Shane; Stagecoach; Unforgiven; *Wayne, John;* Wild Bunch, The

WHITE, PEARL

While many American stars had wide international followings (especially Charlie Chaplin, Mary Pickford, Douglas Fairbanks, and William S. Hart), Pearl White was most clearly the product of a pre-1920 international film community. Not only did she achieve stardom with a French company (Pathé) and a French director (Louis Gasnier), but the serial genre with which she became identified was much more highly regarded in Europe than America, and her greatest admirers were certainly the French.

Pearl White was one of the first film stars to publish an autobiography, *Just Me,* which appeared at the height of her fame in 1919. Setting a pattern for similar works to follow, the information provided is hardly reliable, with large portions of her career ignored or distorted.

Originally a stage actress, Pearl White entered films in 1910. *Just Me* does have a flavorful account of her first efforts to land a job in the New York studios, where she pounded the pavements of the strange city and couldn't find the Edison studio because she could not tell uptown from

WHITE, PEARL

Pearl White was famous for her blonde hair, which was actually a wig she began wearing early in her career. Whenever she wished to be unnoticed in public, she would appear without the wig, using her own dark hair as a disguise.

downtown on the elevated train. Eventually she found work with the Crystal Film Company. The Crystal productions were very simply made, primitive split-reel subjects imposing a crude slapstick treatment on traditional situation-comedy plots. The few that survive, such as *Pearl as Detective* (1913) and *The Ring* (1914), offer little of interest other than the personality of Pearl White herself. Attractive and athletic, she transcended with her wholesome good looks the mugging and eye-rolling called for by the Crystal directors.

In 1914 she was approached by Theodore Wharton to appear in a serialized film that he and his brother Leopold were to produce for Pathé.

Director Louis Gasnier and his new star suddenly tapped a level of audience response not previously evoked by earlier serial films. *The Perils of Pauline* quickly became the archetype of the silent American serial and found a permanent place in twentieth-century popular culture.

Realizing the value of their new property, Pathé and Gasnier immediately followed up with *The Exploits of Elaine* (1914–15), codirected by George Seitz, who would work on all of White's later American serials. Altogether, she appeared in nine serials for Pathé from 1914 to 1920. In running popularity polls taken between 1916 and 1918 by *Motion Picture* magazine, she ranked as the third most popular female star, behind Mary Pickford and Marguerite Clark.

Pearl White moved into features in 1920, but without success; the aggressive heroine she portrayed had passed from popularity in the postwar era, at least in America. The creator of this image would spend most of her later years in France, spending her time at casinos and breeding horses. She died in 1938 and was buried in Paris.

WILD BUNCH, THE

With the release of the *The Wild Bunch* (1969), distinctively but controversially brutal in its depiction of both the violence and ethos of the old West, the director, Sam Peckinpah, traded in his "journeyman" tag for the coveted designation "auteur."

The film is an elegy to a dying western frontier that had, by the turn of the century, reached its limits not only physically but also morally and spiritually, as its ethos of rugged individualism began to ebb under the standardizing encroachments of urban industrialism. The film opens in San Rafael, Texas, in 1913; a menacing gang, ironcally clad in U.S. cavalry uniforms, rides into town and methodically knocks over the local bank. With the sacks of booty packed away, the gang—the leader, Pike Bishop (William Holden), along with the stalwarts Dutch Engstrom (Ernest Borgnine), Lyle Gorch (Warren Oates), Crazy Lee (Bo Hopkins), and Angel (Jaime Sanchez)—is alerted to bounty-hunting snipers waiting in ambush to attack them from surrounding rooftops. The gang's escape attempt leads them into a ferocious gun battle with the bounty hunters, with innocent bystanders suffering the brunt of the casualties. Bishop is momentarily locked into a confrontation with a bounty hunter who turns out to be his old friend Deke Thornton (Robert Ryan), and the two purposely steer their fire away from each other. At the cost of the lives of several members, the gang manages to escape from town with the loot.

Retreating to their Mexican stronghold, the surviving gang members—Bishop, Engstrom, the brothers Lyle and Tector Gorch (Ben Jonson), and Angel—tear open the stolen sacks and, as metal washers rather than gold coins come tumbling out, they realize that they were tricked by Bishop's old foe Pat Harrigan (Albert Dekker), a railroad tycoon. After Bishop quells rumblings about his leadership, he informs old pal Sykes that their erstwhile comrade Thornton has joined the ranks of the bounty hunters. The bunch repairs to Angel's village while, back in Texas, Thornton remonstrates with Harrigan over the botched ambush, with its needless civilian casualties. Harrigan contemptuously rebuffs his demand for a better-trained force, reminding Thornton that he sprang him from jail to track

According to Hollywood legend, more blank rounds were fired during the production of The Wild Bunch *than live rounds were fired during the Mexican Revolution of 1914, on which the film is loosely based.*

▶

Bishop and that if he falters, there will be a bounty on his head, too. Thornton grimly proceeds with the hunt for Bishop.

Meanwhile, the elder of Angel's village, Don José, tells the gang that because of the civil war raging in Mexico, the village was recently overrun by the brutal general Emilio Mapache (Chano Urueta), who slaughtered the town's young men and abducted Angel's lover. Bishop restrains the enraged Angel from tearing off after the general. Promising to help the villagers fend off the menacing general Mapache, the bunch heads for Mapache's headquarters. Upon their arrival, when Angel finds his girlfriend lavishing affectionate attention on the general, he impulsively shoots her down on the spot. The gang members are forced to surrender to Mapache's troops, who severely beat Angel.

Warily respectful of the bunch's evident toughness, Mapache invites them to have a drink with his German overlords, who wish to hire the bunch to steal U.S. army weapons from a train, in order to arm Mapache's troops. The mercenary gang likes the price and rides off to stage the attack on the train, which proceeds smoothly until a counterattack is launched by Thornton and his men. But the counterattack is foiled with Thornton and his men sent flying into the Rio Grande by explosives that Bishop cleverly set on the railroad bridge in advance of the raid.

Bishop allows Angel to siphon off a portion of the huge haul of armaments to bring back to his village. When Angel and Engstrom show up at Mapache's fortress to claim their reward, the general, having heard about the diversion of weapons, orders the torture of Angel. Back at the gang's encampment, Bishop at first spurns Engstrom's pleas to rescue Angel but reconsiders when he discovers that Thornton and his posse are still in hot pursuit and have wounded his pal Sykes.

Elated over the bountiful haul of weapons, the general throws a great party. But when Bishop, Engstrom, and Lyle and Tector Gorch arrive on the scene, Angel is being dragged on the ground behind the general's car. Prudently containing their outrage amid the hundreds of heavily armed soldiers, the gang members—with the exception of the intransigent Engstrom—succumb to the allure of the celebration, including a romp with some prostitutes.

Bishop, however, snaps to his senses and summons his comrades back to theirs. They arm themselves to the hilt and go to the general to demand the return of Angel. The general calmly appears to comply, pushing forward a pummeled and bloodied Angel—but then he slits Angel's throat. Bishop and Engstrom instantly gun down Mapache. As his drunken soldiers stir into readiness, the gang appears to have them at a disadvantage, and a tense, prolonged standoff ensues before Bishop picks off one of the Germans.

Then the fusillade begins. The gang seizes a machine gun, with which they mow down scores of Mapache's men. But despite their valiant stand, they are hopelessly outnumbered: Lyle and Tector go first, and then Bishop,

notable & quotable

[After viewing *The Wild Bunch* for the first time],
"we stumbled out, dazed and speechless. I felt strangely naked for a day or two afterwards, like that movie had looked into me instead of me watching it, and I hadn't like what it had seen, not a bit."

David Weddle, author, 1997

ironically shot in the back by a child. Engstrom is killed trying to come to the aid of the mortally wounded Bishop.

Thornton and his posse ride into this scene of bloody desolation. As his men descend upon the corpses for plunder, Thornton sadly reflects on the fate of his ex-comrade Bishop, and takes his pistol as a memento. Thornton then bids his posse farewell, having decided to remain in Mexico. Later on he hears distant gunfire and knows that his men have met their doom.

As Thornton sits pondering his future, Don José and Sykes arrive, leading a contingent of villagers armed with weapons from the gang's haul. Sykes invites Thornton to join their gang on "a job," and a grateful Thornton rides off with his once and future comrade.

See Peckinpah, Sam; Western

WILDER, BILLY

Billy Wilder will always be remembered as a director and writer who pushed the envelope of what was socially acceptable. In doing this, Wilder helped shape the future of filmmaking. He was born Samuel Wilder on June 22, 1906, in Sucha Galicia, a section of Poland that then belonged to Austria. His father, Max Wilder, operated a number of railroad cafes until his death in 1926. His mother, Eugenia Baldinger Wilder, survived her husband only to die in the Auschwitz concentration camp during World War II. His mother's fascination with the American west led her to nickname him Billy, after the American western hero Buffalo Bill. His older brother, W. Lee Wilder, produced Hollywood films in the 1950s.

Wilder's family moved to Vienna in 1914 to escape the ravages of World War I. In Vienna Wilder spend much of his youth prowling the city's gambling and billiard halls. He says it was in Vienna that he learned many things about human nature, "none of them favorable." This exposure to the seamier side of life would find its place in many of his films.

While Wilder did well in school, he rebelled against the rigidity of German culture, preferring instead to listen to jazz and watch American westerns. In 1924, planning to study law, he enrolled in the University of Vienna. His academic career was short; after three months he quit and began writing about crime, sports, and interviews for *Die Stunde* (The Hour), a Viennese tabloid.

A few years later, in 1926, Wilder moved to Berlin and worked as a press agent and interpreter for jazz musician Paul Whiteman. Once in Berlin he renewed his career as a crime reporter for a number of Berlin

tabloids. He collaborated on his first screenplay script, *Menschen am Sonntag* (People on Sunday), in 1929. Over the next four years Wilder wrote or worked on at least a dozen screenplays for which he received credit. He also contributed to over 200 German films without credit.

By 1933 Hitler and the Nazi Party were gaining power and Wilder realized that being a leftist Jew in Berlin was becoming dangerous. He moved to Paris just days before the Nazis burned the German Reichstag. Later that year in Paris, Wilder directed his first film, *Mauvaise Graine* (The Bad Seed). In the same year Twentieth Century-Fox remade his story *Ihre Hoheit Befiehlt* (Her Majesty Requests) as *Adorable* and Universal remade his cowritten screenplay *Was Frauen Träumen* (What Women Dream) as *One Exciting Adventure*. With these films Wilder's reputation as a screenwriter opened up opportunities for him in Hollywood.

Wilder moved to Hollywood in 1934 after Columbia pictures offered him a contract for *Pam Pam*, a script that was never filmed. His first American film credit was for cowriting the screenplay *Music in the Air* (1934) for Twentieth Century-Fox.

Billy Wilder (right), shown here with actress Gloria Swanson and writer Charles Brackett, produced some of Hollywood's most classic comedies before retiring in 1981.

▼

Wilder's first marriage, to Judith Coppicus, began in 1936 and ended in divorce in 1947. From this marriage, he has one daughter, Victoria. Within two years of his divorce Wilder married actress and singer Audrey Young.

Wilder began his seventeen-year association with Paramount in 1938 by teaming up with Charles Brackett to write the screenplay for *Bluebeard's Eighth Wife*. Over the next few years he wrote and collaborated on *What a Life*, *Midnight*, *Ninotchka*, *Arise My Love*, *Rhythm on the River*, *Hold Back the Dawn*, and *Ball of Fire*. In 1942 he made his American directorial debut with *The Major and the Minor*.

In 1944 Wilder directed *Double Indemnity*, a film that many consider to have established him as one of the best film directors in the industry. *Double Indemnity* was done in classic Wilder style. The film looks at a greedy wife's (Barbara Stanwyck) cold-blooded murder of her husband in an upper-middle-class California community. In the film Stanwyck tries, with the complicity of a scheming insurance agent (Fred MacMurray), to murder her husband in an effort to collect on a double indemnity policy.

Double Indemnity established Wilder's reputation as a director willing to take on subjects that many thought should never be presented on film. At a time when sex and social problems were forbidden subjects, Wilder thrived on exposing society's inhibitions. *The Lost Weekend* (1945) explores alcoholism, *Sunset Boulevard* (1950) pries into the life of a delusional silent screen star living in a squalid Hollywood mansion, *Stalag 17* (1953) looks at the seamy side of prisoner-of-war camps, and *Irma la Douce* (1963) reveals the world of prostitution. His film *Kiss Me, Stupid* (1964), which has a wife switching places with a prostitute for a night, stretched the bounds of propriety so far that it was condemned by the Catholic church. Each of these films seems to echo Wilder's claim that the only films worth making are the ones that are "playing with fire."

Wilder also began using his films to look at what he considered to be the bleak emptiness of modern life. *The Apartment* (1960), *Avanti* (1972), *Fedora* (1978), and *Buddy Buddy* (1981) all follow the same theme of emptiness. These later films lost the cutting edge that typified Wilder's earlier work. Wilder's decline in popularity was not a result of a dramatically changed style; rather, the sexual revolution of the 1960s made society less shocked by his biting satire.

While the dark and empty side of life may be predominant themes in many of Wilder's films, some of his greatest films celebrate comedic side of life. *Sabrina* (1954), *The Seven Year Itch* (1955), *Love in the Afternoon* (1957), *Some Like It Hot* (1959), and *One, Two, Three* (1961) all stray a long way from Wilder's typically cynical world view.

Despite the often harsh view of critics and upholders of public morality, Wilder's films were often recipients of film awards. He received his first Academy Awards as director and cowriter for *The Lost Weekend*, a film was that also gained Best Screenplay and Best Actor Awards. Over the years the

Academy honored *Sunset Boulevard, Stalag 17, Sabrina, Some Like It Hot, The Apartment, Irma la Douce,* and *The Fortune Cookie* with awards ranging from best screenplay to best costumes.

The American Film Institute recognized Wilder's contribution to filmmaking in 1986 by awarding the writer/director the Life Achievement Award. Two years later, in 1988, the Academy Awards honored him with the Irving G. Thalberg Award.

See Apartment; Double Indemnity; *Film noir; Monroe, Marilyn;* Some Like It Hot; Sunset Strip

WIZARD OF OZ, THE

The Wizard of Oz (1939), by virtue of having been shown on television for years each Easter, is probably the most watched movie of all time. This fantasy musical, adapted from a children's book by L. Frank Baum, was a commercial as well as critical triumph from the moment it was released, and it remains one of the favorite films of all time. The terrific songs by Harold Arlen and E. Y. (Yip) Harburg are known by heart by generations of filmgoers. The movie, however, won only a few Academy Awards (Best Score, by Herbert Stothart; Best Song, for "Over the Rainbow"; and a special statuette for Judy Garland as a juvenile actor), as it was up against truly formidable competition, including *Gone with the Wind,* which won Best Picture, and other great films.

"I'll get you my pretty, and your little dog, too!"

Margaret Hamilton as the Wicked Witch of the West in *The Wizard of Oz* (1939)

The main director was Victor Fleming, but Richard Thorpe, George Cukor, and King Vidor all tried their hand, with varying success (none of Thorpe's footage made it onto the screen), during production headed by Mervyn LeRoy. The background information on the filming of *The Wizard of Oz* makes for fascinating reading, with stories about the makeup and costumes, the casting, the rowdy behavior of the "Munchkins," and the creation of special effects, all of which contribute substantially to the rich lore of Hollywood.

As the film opens, the young heroine, Dorothy (Judy Garland), is shown at a farm in Kansas, where she lives with her Auntie Em (Clara Blandick) and Uncle Henry (Charley Grapewin). When Dorothy's dog, Toto, is threatened by the vicious Miss Elvira Gulch (Margaret Hamilton), an influential neighbor who wants to have Toto destroyed because he chases her cat, Dorothy dreams of living in a trouble-free world, expressing her hopes in the song "Over the Rainbow."

Miss Gulch takes Toto away in the basket on her bicycle, but the little dog manages to get away from her clutches. When Toto comes home, Dorothy decides that they must run away. She and Toto take off down the road, where they soon meet a down-at-the-heels carnival performer, Professor Marvel (Frank Morgan), who persuades Dorothy to return home.

A tornado is shown approaching across the horizon, and Dorothy's aunt and uncle, who have not seen her, run to safety in the storm cellar with the farmhands, Hickory (Jack Haley), Zeke (Bert Lahr), and Hunk (Ray Bolger). Dorothy seeks shelter in the farmhouse, where she is knocked unconscious by a flying window frame.

When Dorothy comes to, she and the farmhouse have been taken airborne by the tornado. She looks out the window and sees a surrealistic scene, up in midair: two men row a boat past the window, and an old woman sitting in a rocking chair knitting flies by. Miss Gulch goes by on her bicycle, but suddenly she is transformed into a hideous witch flying on a broom.

The farmhouse is finally released by the twister, and it spins to the ground. When Dorothy opens the door, she finds a breathtakingly beautiful Technicolor land. (Up to this point, the movie has been filmed in black and white.) As she tells Toto: "We're not in Kansas anymore."

Each of the five pairs of ruby slippers worn by Dorothy (Judy Garland) in The Wizard of Oz *is worth an estimated $1.5 million, making them among the most expensive of Hollywood memorabilia.*

▼

Dorothy and Toto have landed in Munchkin Land. The little people called Munchkins cheer Dorothy, as she has freed them from the tyrannical rule of the Wicked Witch of the East—Dorothy's farmhouse landed directly on the witch and killed her. The Munchkins sing "Ding Dong, the Witch Is Dead." The lovely Good Witch of the North, Glinda (Billie Burke), comes to thank Dorothy.

Glinda's visit is interrupted by the Wicked Witch of the West (Hamilton again), who has come for the powerful ruby slippers that are still on her dead sister's feet, sticking out from underneath the farmhouse. But the power of the Wicked Witch is no match for Glinda, who causes the magic shoes to suddenly appear on Dorothy's feet. The Wicked Witch vows to get even with Dorothy, cackling, "I'll get you, my pretty, and your little dog, too!" She vanishes as quickly as she appeared, in a puff of red smoke.

Dorothy has had quite a day, and she tells the Good Witch that she wants to go home. But Glinda says the only one who can help her is "the great and all-powerful Wizard of Oz," who lives in the Emerald City. Glinda points Dorothy and Toto down the Yellow Brick Road, which leads to that Emerald City, and warns her to keep her ruby slippers on her feet at all times. The Munchkins see her off, singing the cheerful tune "Follow the Yellow Brick Road."

"Oh, Auntie Em, there's no place like home."

Judy Garland as Dorothy in *The Wizard of Oz* (1939)

And so Dorothy sets "off to see the Wizard, the wonderful Wizard of Oz." On the road, she meets three characters who decide to come along with her, because they too need help from the Wizard: the Scarecrow (Bolger) wants a brain; the Tin Woodsman (Haley) wants a heart; and the Cowardly Lion (Lahr) wants courage. They travel the road with Dorothy and Toto, singing "If I Only Had a Brain/a Heart/the Nerve."

But the journey to Oz is not trouble free. The Wicked Witch is determined to get even with Dorothy, and she does her best to make trouble for her. One of her booby traps is a field of poppies that causes Dorothy and her friends to fall asleep, just before they reach the Emerald City. Good Witch Glinda, however, sends down a light snow, which revives them, and they continue on their way. Finally Toto and the foursome arrive at the magnificent gates of the Emerald City. A guard (Morgan again) lets them in, and they are driven to the palace of the Wizard by a coachman (also Morgan).

The visitors are escorted into an intimidating, cavernous hall. There, a huge face, seemingly floating in midair, booms his demands. This is supposedly the great Wizard of Oz, but before he'll grant their wishes, they must obtain the broomstick of the Wicked Witch of the West. Dorothy and her friends are downcast; they had come to consider the Wizard the solution to all their problems, and he has turned out to be yet another obstacle, and not very nice, either.

The four trudge off on their mission, and they are soon beset by a group of evil winged monkeys. Dorothy and Toto are whisked away to the Wicked Witch's ominous mountaintop castle. Dorothy is locked in a room with an hourglass, which, when it runs out of sand, will spell her doom. But just in time, Dorothy and Toto are saved by her three friends, led by the Cowardly Lion; the Wicked Witch is killed when they throw water on her: She melts away in a puddle. Only her hat, dress, and broomstick remain.

Dorothy and her friends return, triumphant, to the Emerald City with the witch's broomstick, but they are told by the thundering Wizard voice to go away. Just then Dorothy notices a man (Morgan) standing behind a curtain, working the controls of an elaborate machine. This is the real Wizard—a good man who feels he has to put on an intimidating front.

Now that he has been found out, the Wizard agrees to grant all of the wishes of the foursome. The Scarecrow is given a diploma that names him a professor of "Thinkology." The Tin Man receives a red metallic heart. And the Cowardly Lion is awarded a medal for courage. However, we know that these three have always had those qualities.

The Wizard offers to take Dorothy back to Kansas in his hot-air balloon, but the Wizard can't control the contraption, and he sails off before Dorothy and Toto can get in. Dorothy weeps, fearful that now she will never get home. But she is saved by the Good Witch Glinda, who tells her that all she has to do is click together the heels of her ruby slippers three times and say the words "there's no place like home." Dorothy performs the magic formula, and in an instant she and Toto are back in Kansas (again filmed in black and white). Her aunt and uncle, and the three farmhands—with the faces of her friends in Oz—are looking down at her. She has been knocked unconscious by the tornado, and as Dorothy tries to tell them of her adventures in a strange and beautiful land, they assure her that it was all just a dream. She concludes: "Oh, Auntie Em, there's *no* place like home!"

See Cukor, George; Garland, Judy; Special-effects film; Vidor, King

"If I ever go looking for my heart's desire again, I won't look any farther than my own backyard."

Judy Garland as Dorothy in *The Wizard of Oz* (1939)

WRITER (SCREEN)

The role of the motion-picture writer in the filmmaking process includes the major responsibility of providing a film scenario or film script that will ultimately become a shooting script. A treatment is a narrative description of a film story usually developed in a form similar to a short story. Characters and plot are described, scene by scene, so that the dramatic flow of the story, as it will appear on the screen, is clear.

A *film script* is a more fully developed and thorough treatment of the story. The film script contains dialogue and action sequences, and becomes the basis for the shooting script.

NATALIE WOOD

Born Natalie (or Natasha) Gurdin in San Francisco, California, on July 20, 1938, Natalie Wood was a child star whose exotic good looks helped her to retain her luster as an adult performer. Wood was the daughter of Russian immigrants—an architect and a ballet dancer. She began taking dance lessons as a young girl and first appeared in a film *(Happy Land)* in 1943. Three years later the director Irving Pichel hired her for a major role in *Tomorrow Is Forever,* starring Orson Welles and Claudette Colbert—not a bad start for an eight-year-old. The following year she played the skeptical youngster in *Miracle on 34th Street,* a film that remains a Christmas time favorite today.

At age seventeen Wood received her first Academy Award nomination, for her performance in *Rebel Without a Cause* (1955). She was nominated again for *Splendor in the Grass* (1961) and *Love with the Proper Stranger* (1963). Despite these acknowledgments from the Academy, however, some viewers were critical of her acting, considering it wooden. The *Harvard Lampoon* even initiated the annual "Natalie Wood Award" for worst performance by an actress.

Other significant roles in Wood's film career included *The Ghost and Mrs. Muir* (1947), *West Side Story* (1961; her singing voice was dubbed in this musical), *Gypsy* (1962; dubbed again), and *Bob & Carol & Ted & Alice* (1972).

Wood had a tempestuous personal life, with reputedly many love affairs. Over a fifteen-year period (1957–72), she married, divorced, and remarried actor Robert Wagner. With producer Richard Gregson, whom she married in 1969 and divorced a few years later, she had a child, Natasha, who was later adopted by Wagner and took his name. In 1974 she and Wagner had a daughter, Courtney Brooke.

Actress Natalie Wood received her first Oscar nomination when she was just 17 years old.

When she fell overboard and drowned while her boat was moored off Santa Catalina Island (California) in 1981, Wood was still a working actress. (Her last film, *Brainstorm,* was released posthumously in 1983.) All of the particulars of her last night alive are still not known by the public.

See Rebel Without a Cause; West Side Story

The *shooting script* contains, in addition to the dialogue and action description, important production information for the director and the cinematographer. Included in this production information are shot descriptions (scope of shot), shot numbers, location and time notations, and indications of where special effects are required. The director works from this script in the filming of the story. It can also become a guide for the film editor. The screenwriter may be involved in one, two, or all three phase of film scripting. Often more than one writer is involved.

The extent to which the film writer's work remains intact throughout the shooting period varies greatly. Many directors view the film script as merely a blueprint for building the film story, and proceed to embellish, delete, and rewrite parts of the script as they see fit. The script for Robert Altman's *Nashville* (1975), for example, underwent great change during filming, with both the director and the actors contributing to plot development and dialogue. In modern filmmaking this is frequently the case. Director Alfred Hitchcock, on the other hand, is said to have rarely deviated from the film script, having finalized the script earlier in story conferences with the writer or writers.

A film script usually falls into one of two categories: the original screenplay or the adaptation. Great screenwriters have contributed significantly to great films: Herman Mankiewicz to *Citizen Kane* (1941), Dudley Nichols to *Stagecoach* (1939), Robert Towne to *Chinatown* (1974), George S. Kaufman and Morrie Ryskind to *A Night at the Opera* (1935), Graham Greene to *The Third Man* (1949). Other screenwriters are less well known, even though many of their films have become highly successful. Because film scripts are translated into visual images, the exact role of the screenwriter cannot always be immediately evaluated. Yet it is always possible to assess the quality of the script in terms of idea, story originality, dialogue, and power of theme and to view the writer as a major contributor to each. These dramatic qualities are innately related to the contributory function of any writer assigned credit for a film story.

See Academy of Motion Pictures; Acting; Chinatown; Citizen Kane; *Director; Screen Actors Guild;* Stagecoach; Third Man, The

WUTHERING HEIGHTS

Wuthering Heights, adapted from the classic novel by Emily Brontë, was a memorable movie from the memorable movie year of 1939. Many consider 1939 the turning point in the launching of a truly modern style of cinema with the release of such landmark films as *The Wizard of Oz, Gone with the Wind, Stagecoach,* and *Mr. Smith Goes to Washington.* A product of the venerable collaboration of Samuel Goldwyn (producer) and William Wyler (director), *Wuthering Heights* received eight Academy Award nominations, although it did not turn a profit until its rerelease in 1950.

Set in England in 1841, the film opens during a blinding blizzard that impels Lockwood (Miles Mander), a visitor in the area, to seek shelter at a

Adapted from the classic novel by Emily Brontë, Wuthering Heights *is a nearly flawless classic film brought to the screen by William Wyler.*

gloomy mansion called Wuthering Heights, occupied by his landlord, Heathcliff (Laurence Olivier), and his wife, Isabella (Geraldine Fitzgerald). Their chilly greeting to Lockwood is offset by the warmth of the housekeeper, Nelly Dean (Flora Robson). Lockwood is later startled by a haunting voice crying, "Heathcliff" near his window, followed by the sudden grasp of a hand. When Lockwood apprises his landlord of these strange events, Heathcliff bolts out of the house and into the falling snow.

Nelly then begins to recount to the baffled Lockwood the unhappy tale of Heathcliff and Cathy (Merle Oberon), which unfolds on the screen in flashbacks. Four decades earlier, in Liverpool, Cathy's father, Mr. Earnshaw (Cecil Kellaway), rescued an orphaned gypsy boy—Heathcliff—and took

“ *Go on, Heathcliff. Run away. Bring me back the world.* ”

Merle Oberon as Catherine Earnshaw in *Wuthering Heights* (1939)

him to live at Wuthering Heights. Cathy's brother, Hindley, resents the intrusion of the foundling, but Cathy's fondness for the newcomer is immediate and elemental, and the two quickly become inseparable playmates.

When control of the estate passes to Hindley upon the death of old Mr. Earnshaw, he vents his long-simmering contempt for Heathcliff by relegating him to work in the stables. With the passing years, the baleful Hindley grows into an embittered drunkard, while the bond between Heathcliff and Cathy deepens. Cathy, however, growing concerned with her social standing, begins a courtship with Edgar Linton (David Niven), the young scion of a wealthy local family. Heathcliff, believing in Cathy's unbending devotion, feels betrayed and after an angry exchange with her, dramatically gallops away from the estate and into the middle of a furious storm. Confused and desolate, Cathy assuages her pain by marrying Linton.

Years later, having made his fortune, Heathcliff makes a triumphant return to Wuthering Heights and assumes control of the estate. Although he magnanimously covers Hindley's burdensome debts, he yields to the satisfaction of returning all the emotional cruelty he once suffered at Hindley's hands. Feigning indifference toward Cathy, he marries Linton's sister, Isabella, chiefly to torment Cathy, whom he well knows is still in love with him. Isabella, realizing that she is a mere pawn in a passion that burns for someone else, wishes death upon her rival.

Bleakly despondent in her unrequited love, Cathy drifts inexorably toward a self-willed demise. As she nears death, Heathcliff furtively enters her bedroom, and they declare a passionate devotion for each other that is stronger than death. Carrying his beloved to the window, Heathcliff points out the moors where they passed so many blissful hours in childhood play. They exchange passionate vows: she will wait for him beyond death, and he will carry her spirit even to the point of madness.

As the scene returns to Nelly recounting the tale to Lockwood, the doctor informs them that he has just seen Heathcliff trudging through the blizzard with an unknown woman, shortly after which he found him slumped lifeless over Cathy's grave. Heathcliff and Cathy have reunited at last, Nelly explains, as the two lovers are seen in superimposition striding toward the crags on the moors where they played as children.

See Goldwyn, Samuel; Olivier, Laurence

WYLER, WILLIAM

In the course of a long career that spanned the “Golden Age” of the American cinema, William Wyler directed a remarkable body of critically and

commercially successful films. Merely listing a few of their titles—*Dodsworth, Jezebel, Wuthering Heights, The Little Foxes, The Best Years of Our Lives, The Heiress, Ben-Hur, The Collector, Funny Girl*—suggests the scope and variety of his achievement.

Surprisingly, Wyler has never received his just measure of auteurist critical esteem. This may be because, as he would have been the first to admit, he didn't fit the usual definition of an auteur. His talents, in fact, were always been put at the service of writers. In his own words, "It's like the music world: I am not the composer, but the conductor." If not precisely an auteur, however, Wyler was for many years a powerful, independent filmmaker, able to choose material, hire crews, and pick stars.

That William Wyler should have become a film director at all illustrates the often serendipitous manner by which many of the fimmakers who made

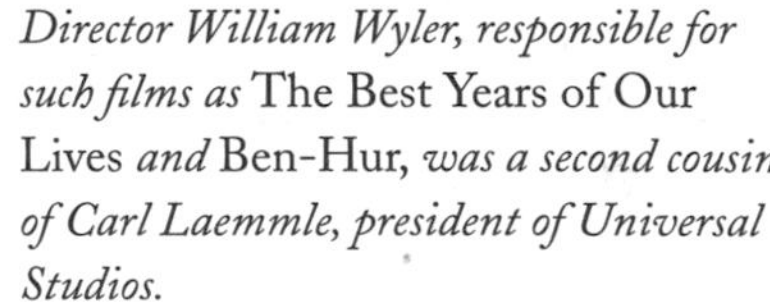

Director William Wyler, responsible for such films as The Best Years of Our Lives *and* Ben-Hur, *was a second cousin of Carl Laemmle, president of Universal Studios.*

◀

WYLER, WILLIAM

The 1950s' third-biggest seller was William Wyler's *Ben-Hur* (1959), with $36.7 million in rentals.

their mark in the 1930s found their way to Hollywood. William (Willy) Wyler was born on July 1, 1902, at Mulhouse (Mulhausen), Alsace-Lorraine (now part of France, then part of the German empire) to German-Swiss-Jewish parents. Educated in Switzerland and trained in haberdashery in Paris, he had no thought of a career in the movies until his mother's cousin Carl Laemmle, the president of Universal Studios, crossed his path while they were both visiting young William's parents in 1920. When Laemmle asked William to come to work for Universal in the United States, Wyler eagerly left the hat business for show business.

His first assignment, a yearlong stint in Universal's New York publicity department, was followed by several years of low-level jobs in Hollywood, where he patiently observed and waited for his break. That break came in 1925 in the form of directing assignments on a series of quickie westerns, on which he honed the fundamentals of his craft. By 1928, the year he became a U.S. citizen, Wyler already had an impressive track record of over thirty films, mostly two-reelers, several full-length westerns, and one comedy.

His imposing resumé brought him increasingly prestigious projects, and over the following eight years he specialized in adaptations of first-rate literary and theatrical material. Wyler's growing reputation for taste and quality brought him to the attention of Samuel Goldwyn, who in 1936 hired him to work with Lillian Hellman in bringing her play *The Children's Hour* to the screen. The play's controversial subject—a child's whispered accusation of lesbianism that turns out to be true in part—required considerable toning down to pass muster with the Hays Office. But the final product, *These Three* (1936), nonetheless impressed reviewers and earned a modest profit for Goldwyn, who corralled Wyler into a long-term relationship that proved one of the most enduring and productive in Hollywood history.

Goldwyn's confidence was vindicated over the next several years, as Wyler turned out a string of commercially and critically successful films: *Dodsworth* (1936), *Dead End* (1937), and *Jezebel* (1938). Wyler's reputation soared still higher with his adaptation of *Wuthering Heights* (1939), which garnered the first of three consecutive Academy Award nominations he would receive for best director (the other two were for *The Letter* [1940] and *The Little Foxes* [1941]). He earned his first Oscar for *Mrs. Miniver* (1942), a Greer Garson weeper that inspired wartime audiences with its portrayal of personal courage in the face of war.

Wyler's experience in World War II was not confined to the studio. Commissioned as an Air Force major in 1942, he was shipped to England and traveled through many European combat zones to capture the real-life drama of war on film. On one such perilous mission in Italy, he suffered serious injuries that caused a partial loss of hearing.

His postwar return to feature films resulted in what many consider to be his crowning achievement, *The Best Years of Our Lives* (1946), a heartfelt

and beautifully realized drama about the dislocations of career, family, and personal identity faced by three returning war veterans. The winner of seven Academy Awards, including Best Picture and Best Director, the film was emblematic of the struggles and strivings of an entire generation and became the highest grossing film of the 1940s.

Wyler's compassion was not confined to imaginary characters, however. As anticommunist concerns began to spread across the nation in the late 1940s, he risked his career by joining John Huston and Philip Dunne in forming the Committee for the First Amendment to protest the House Un-American Activities Committee's probes of Hollywood leftists. He made another inroad for creative independence by forming his own production company, Liberty Films, along with his colleagues Samuel Briskin, Frank Capra, and George Stevens, a venture that was later absorbed by Paramount Pictures. Wyler ended the decade on a high note with another of his masterly literary adaptations, *The Heiress* (1949), based on a theatrical version of Henry James's novella *Washington Square.*

As Wyler moved into his sixth decade of life, his output declined in quantity but not quality: *Detective Story* (1951), *Roman Holiday* (1953), and *The Big Country* (1958) all earned critical kudos and respectable box-office returns. But they were mere warm-ups for the film that still defines the very notion of the Hollywood epic, *Ben-Hur* (1959), the biblical spectacle that swept eleven Oscars—including Best Picture and Best Director—and temporarily rescued MGM from financial collapse.

Wyler's next major success was the musical *Funny Girl* (1968), for which Barbra Streisand won the Oscar for Best Actress. The poor critical and audience response to *The Liberation of L. B. Jones* (1970), however, prompted him to retire from filmmaking.

Wyler received the Life Achievement Award from the American Film Institute in 1976. He died on July 27, 1981, in Los Angeles.

See Ben-Hur; Best Years of Our Lives, The; *Goldwyn, Samuel;* Wuthering Heights

YANKEE DOODLE DANDY

Yankee Doodle Dandy (1942), a "musical biography" of the life of performer and songwriter George M. Cohan, is widely considered one of Hollywood's greatest musicals. Starring James Cagney as the ambitious showman, the film was a huge success.

The story begins with a shot of a Broadway theater sign, which proclaims George M. Cohan's "triumphal return to the stage in *I'd Rather Be Right.* The Greatest Musical Comedy Hit in Years." That notice, along with the medley of Cohan songs that accompanies the film's credits, lets the viewer know that George was successful indeed.

"My mother thanks you, my father thanks you, my sister thanks you, and I thank you."

James Cagney as George M. Cohan in *Yankee Doodle Dandy* (1942)

George and his wife, Mary (Joan Leslie), now in their older years, are backstage, swarmed by well-wishers following their performance. George is anxious about his impersonation of the president in the show. He is alarmed when a telegram arrives from the White House, asking him to visit the president. Mary reassures him: "Don't worry, dear. They don't telegraph you to come and be shot at sunrise."

She is right; President Franklin D. Roosevelt (Jack Young, photographed from the side/rear) just wishes to congratulate him. George starts telling the president his life story.

The film takes us back to George's early days, when he was part of a vaudeville family. He was born in Providence, Rhode Island, on the Fourth of July (in real life, George—of an Irish family originally named Keohane—was born on July 3). It was 1878, a patriotic and optimistic time in the United States. George's parents, Jerry (Walter Huston) and Nellie (Rosemary De Camp), were known as "The Irish Darlings." They decided to name their firstborn after George Washington.

Eventually another child joined the family, Josie (played in adulthood by Cagney's real-life sister, Jeanne), and thus the traveling troupe of vaudeville entertainers known as "The Four Cohans" was born. Growing up, George was precocious and brash, at one point being so sassy that he cost the family a profitable and prestigious booking.

When George is a young man (played in adulthood by Cagney), he meets his future wife. Backstage after playing an old man onstage, a stagestruck girl, Mary, asks the still-costumed George for advice: Should she go to New York to try her fortunes on the stage? She is shocked when George removes his makeup and reveals himself to be a youth. In future scenes, George helps to promote her as "The Dixie Nightingale," singing his songs. When he tries to get her to switch songs onstage, the stage manager (William B. Davidson) fires him and reads him the riot act: "Listen squirt. Any more interference on your part and you'll be blacklisted in show business. . . ."

The film follows George's early attempts to get his music published. He is turned down by publisher after publisher. Even the catchy tune "Harrigan" gets no takers.

One night George overhears his family's fellow boarders describing him as a troublemaker, keeping the Cohans from getting work. He gathers himself together and marches in, saying that his play *Little Johnny Jones!* has just been bought for production—a lie. He urges the rest of the family to carry on without him for the time being.

Having thus spared his family's feelings, George now must find a way to deliver. One day, at Jack's Grill, he notices a fellow, Sam Harris (Richard Whorf), who is having no success selling his manuscript to Schwab (S. Z.

James Cagney starred as ambitious showman George M. Cohan in this musical biography of Cohan's life. The film won the Oscar for Best Music (Scoring) in 1942, and Cagney won for Best Actor.
▼

Sakall), a wealthy businessman. George observes that Schwab prefers musical comedy to Harris's type of drama, and he brashly intercedes, pretending to be Harris's partner. George talks so fast that Harris can't get a word in edgewise, and so he just goes along with the ruse. George plays "Yankee Doodle" for Schwab and manages to get Schwab to back "their" production of *Little Johnny Jones*. The show—shown in sections in the film—is a rousing success, and George, with his new partner Sam, is on his way to the big time.

George's father is initially a bit envious of his son's success, but George solves that by bringing the other Cohans back to New York to work with him onstage, and eventually making his father a full partner in all his works.

George soon becomes a legend in his own time, and the film audience is treated to Cagney's renditions of such favorites as "Give My Regards to Broadway," "Mary," and "You're a Grand Old Flag." His songs touch something in the American heart—" . . . ambition, pride, and patriotism. That's why they call him the Yankee Doodle Boy."

George's triumphs multiply. It seems he can do no wrong on the stage. He is thwarted only in his attempt to prove himself a master of drama as well as musical comedies.

The march of time brings sadness of a more poignant sort as well—the United States enters the Great War. George is turned down for military service, being too old (31), but he writes the song that will become the unofficial American anthem of World War I: "Over There." There are more intimate milestones in George's life: one by one, the rest of the original "Four Cohans" die.

In the 1930s Mary and George decide to retire to the farm, cutting back their hectic schedule in New York. George dissolves his partnership with Sam Harris, but they remain friends. George and Mary travel, but George can't help but haunt theaters wherever they go. Finally, George is lured back to Broadway to perform in a show that Sam is producing.

The film now returns to President Roosevelt's office, where George is presented with the Congressional Medal of Honor for his patriotic service in writing the songs "Over There" and "Grand Old Flag." Afterward, George dances down the marble stairs of the White House. The movie ends on a close-up of George's proud, tear-stained face.

The movie was directed by Michael Curtiz and produced by Hal B. Wallace (coproduced by Cagney's brother, William). The screenplay was written by Robert Buckner and Edmund Joseph, while Ray Heindorf arranged Cohan's music, which forms the background tapestry of the film. It received eight Academy Award nominations and won three Oscars, for Best Actor (Cagney), Best Sound Recording, and Best Scoring of a Musical Picture.

See Cagney, James; Musical film

Z

ZOËTROPE (WHEEL OF LIFE)

The Zoëtrope is a nineteenth-century animating device developed by William Horner and used to illustrate the persistence-of-vision theory. The effect of continuous movement was achieved by placing on the inside of a cylindrical drum a sequence of images of a figure in the progressive stages of a simple action. Each strip of images (contained on a length of paper) was called a "program." Slits cut through the outside of the drum produce a shutterlike mechanism, permitting momentary intervals between the passage of each image as the viewer peered into the revolving Zoëtrope to see the figure in an animated state. A version of the Zoëtrope was first patented in 1867.

Earlier animating devices include the Stroboscope. The Phénakistoscope, and the Thaumatrope. The Stroboscope, demonstrated in Germany in 1832 by Simon Ritter von Stampfer, achieved the same effect as the Zoëtrope by spinning a slitted paper disc in front of a revolving imaged disc. Joseph Plateau's Phénakistoscope (later renamed Phantascope) placed the slits and images on a single disc, with the viewer peering through the slits toward a mirror reflection of the spinning images. The Thaumatrope, or "wonder turner," appeared in the 1920s as the simplest demonstration of a persistence-of-vision device. Separate objects, drawn on opposite sides of a circular card (a lion and an empty cage), seemed to blend into a single image when the card was spun by attached strings. The lion appeared to be seated in the cage. The invention of the Thaumatrope is attributed to Dr. John Paris.

See Magic lantern; Nickelodeon

Academy Award Winners, 1928-1998

BEST PICTURE

Year: 1928
Winner: *Wings* (1927)
Nominated: *The Last Command; The Racket, Seventh Heaven* (1927); *The Way of All Flesh* (1927)

Year: 1929
Winner: *The Broadway Melody*
Nominated: *Alibi; The Hollywood Revue of 1929; In Old Arizona; The Patriot* (1928)

Year: 1930
Winner: *All Quiet on the Western Front*
Nominated: *The Big House; Disraeli; The Divorcee; The Love Parade* (1929)

Year: 1931
Winner: *Cimarron*
Nominated: *East Lynne; The Front Page; Skippy; Trader Horn*

Year: 1932
Winner: *Grand Hotel*
Nominated: *Arrowsmith* (1931); *Bad Girl* (1931); *The Champ* (1931); *Five Star Final* (1931); *One Hour With You, Shanghai Express; The Smiling Lieutenant* (1931)

Year: 1933
Winner: *Cavalcade*
Nominated: *42nd Street; A Farewell to Arms; I Am a Fugitive from a Chain Gang* (1932); *Lady for a Day; Little Women; The Private Life of Henry VIII; She Done Him Wrong; Smilin' Through* (1932); *State Fair*

Year: 1934
Winner: *It Happened One Night*
Nominated: *The Barretts of Wimpole Street; Cleopatra; Flirtation Walk; The Gay Divorcee; Here Comes the Navy; The House of Rothschild; Imitation of Life; One Night of Love; The Thin Man; Viva Villa; The White Parade*

Year: 1935
Winner: *Mutiny on the Bounty*
Nominated: *Alice Adams; Broadway Melody of 1936; Captain Blood; David Copperfield; The Informer; The Lives of a Bengal Lancer; A Midsummer Night's Dream; Les Miserables* (1934); *Naughty Marietta; Ruggles of Red Gap; Top Hat*

Year: 1936
Winner: *The Great Ziegfeld*
Nominated: *Anthony Adverse; Dodsworth; Libeled Lady; Mr. Deeds Goes to Town; Romeo and Juliet; San Francisco; The Story of Louis Pasteur; A Tale of Two Cities* (1935); *Three Smart Girls*

Year: 1937
Winner: *The Life of Emile Zola*
Nominated: *The Awful Truth; Captains Courageous; Dead End; The Good Earth; In Old Chicago; Lost Horizon; One Hundred Men and a Girl; Stage Door; A Star Is Born*

Year: 1938
Winner: *You Can't Take It with You*
Nominated: *The Adventures of Robin Hood; Alexander's Ragtime Band; Boys Town; The Citadel; Four Daughters; La Grande Illusion; Jezebel; Pygmalion; Test Pilot*

Year: 1939
Winner: *Gone with the Wind*
Nominated: *Dark Victory; Goodbye, Mr. Chips; Love Affair; Mr. Smith Goes to Washington; Ninotchka; Of Mice and Men; Stagecoach; The Wizard of Oz; Wuthering Heights*

Year: 1940
Winner: *Rebecca*
Nominated: *All This and Heaven Too; Foreign Correspondent; The Grapes of Wrath; The Great Dictator; Kitty Foyle; The Letter; The Long Voyage Home; Our Town; The Philadelphia Story*

Year: 1941
Winner: *How Green Was My Valley*
Nominated: *Blossoms in the Dust; Citizen Kane; Here Comes Mr. Jordan; Hold Back the Dawn; The Little Foxes; The Maltese Falcon; One Foot in Heaven; Sergeant York; Suspicion*

Year: 1942
Winner: *Mrs. Miniver*
Nominated: *Forty-ninth Parallel* (1941); *Kings Row; The Magnificent Ambersons; The Pied Piper; The Pride of the Yankees; Random Harvest; The Talk of the Town; Wake Island; Yankee Doodle Dandy*

Year: 1943
Winner: *Casablanca* (1942)
Nominated: *For Whom the Bell Tolls; Heaven Can Wait; The Human Comedy; In Which We Serve* (1942); *Madame Curie; The More the Merrier; The Ox-Bow Incident; The Song of Bernadette; Watch on the Rhine*

Year: 1944
Winner: *Going My Way*
Nominated: *Double Indemnity; Gaslight; Since You Went Away; Wilson*

Year: 1945
Winner: *The Lost Weekend*
Nominated: *Anchors Aweigh; The Bells of St. Mary's; Mildred Pierce; Spellbound*

Year: 1946
Winner: *The Best Ceremony Years of Our Lives*
Nominated: *Henry V* (1944); *It's a Wonderful Life; The Razor's Edge; The Yearling*

Year: 1947
Winner: *Gentlemen's Agreement*
Nominated: *The Bishop's Wife; Crossfire; Great Expectations* (1946); *Miracle on 34th Street*

Year: 1948
Winner: *Hamlet*
Nominated: *Johnny Belinda; The Red Shoes; The Snake Pit; The Treasure of the Sierra Madre*

Year: 1949
Winner: *All the King's Men*

Nominated: *Battleground; The Heiress; A Letter to Three Wives; Twelve O'Clock High*

Year: 1950
Winner: *All About Eve*
Nominated: *Born Yesterday; Father of the Bride; King Solomon's Mines; Sunset Boulevard*

Year: 1951
Winner: *An American in Paris*
Nominated: *Decision Before Dawn; A Place in the Sun; Quo Vadis?; A Streetcar Named Desire*

Year: 1952
Winner: *The Greatest Show on Earth*
Nominated: *High Noon; Ivanhoe; Moulin Rouge; The Quiet Man*

Year: 1953
Winner: *From Here to Eternity*
Nominated: *Julius Caesar; The Robe; Roman Holiday; Shane*

Year: 1954
Winner: *On the Waterfront*
Nominated: *The Caine Mutiny; The Country Girl; Seven Brides for Seven Brothers; Three Coins in the Fountain*

Year: 1955
Winner: *Marty*
Nominated: *Love Is a Many-Splendored Thing; Mister Roberts; Picnic; The Rose Tattoo*

Year: 1956
Winner: *Around the World in 80 Days*
Nominated: *Friendly Persuasion; Giant; The King and I; The Ten Commandments*

Year: 1957
Winner: *The Bridge on the River Kwai*
Nominated: *Twelve Angry Men; Peyton Place; Sayonara; Witness for the Prosecution*

Year: 1958
Winner: *Gigi*
Nominated: *Auntie Mame; Cat on a Hot Tin Roof; The Defiant Ones; Separate Tables*

Year: 1959
Winner: *Ben-Hur*
Nominated: *Anatomy of a Murder; The Diary of Anne Frank; The Nun's Story; Room at the Top*

Year: 1960
Winner: *The Apartment*
Nominated: *The Alamo; Elmer Gantry; Sons and Lovers; The Sundowners*

Year: 1961
Winner: *West Side Story*
Nominated: *Fanny; The Guns of Navarone; The Hustler; Judgment at Nuremberg*

Year: 1962
Winner: *Lawrence of Arabia*
Nominated: *The Longest Day; The Music Man; Mutiny on the Bounty; To Kill a Mockingbird*

Year: 1963
Winner: *Tom Jones*
Nominated: *America, America; Cleopatra; How the West Was Won* (1962); *Lilies of the Field*

Year: 1964
Winner: *My Fair Lady*
Nominated: *Zorba the Greek, Becket; Dr. Strangelove or: How I Learned to Stop Worrying and Love the Bomb; Mary Poppins*

Year: 1965
Winner: *The Sound of Music*
Nominated: *Darling; Doctor Zhivago; Ship of Fools; A Thousand Clowns*

Year: 1966
Winner: *A Man for All Seasons*
Nominated: *Alfie; The Russians are Coming! The Russians are Coming!; The Sand Pebbles; Who's Afraid of Virginia Woolf?*

Year: 1967
Winner: *In the Heat of the Night*
Nominated: *Bonnie and Clyde; Doctor Dolittle; The Graduate; Guess Who's Coming to Dinner*

Year: 1968
Winner: *Oliver!*
Nominated: *Funny Girl; The Lion in Winter; Rachel, Rachel; Romeo and Juliet*

Year: 1969
Winner: *Midnight Cowboy*
Nominated: *Anne of the Thousand Days; Butch Cassidy and the Sundance Kid; Hello, Dolly!; Z*

Year: 1970
Winner: *Patton*
Nominated: *Airport; Five Easy Pieces; Love Story; M*A*S*H*

Year: 1971
Winner: *The French Connection*
Nominated: *A Clockwork Orange; Fiddler on the Roof; The Last Picture Show; Nicholas and Alexandra*

Year: 1972
Winner: *The Godfather*
Nominated: *Cabaret; Deliverance; Sounder; Utvandrarna;* or *The Emigrants* (1971)

Year: 1973
Winner: *The Sting*
Nominated: *American Graffiti; The Exorcist; A Touch of Class; Viskningar och rop,* or *Cries and Whispers* (1972)

Year: 1974
Winner: *The Godfather: Part II*
Nominated: *Chinatown; The Conversation; Lenny; The Towering Inferno*

Year: 1975
Winner: *One Flew over the Cuckoo's Nest*
Nominated: *Barry Lyndon; Dog Day Afternoon; Jaws; Nashville*

Year: 1976
Winner: *Rocky*
Nominated: *All the President's Men; Bound for Glory; Network; Taxi Driver*

Year: 1977
Winner: *Annie Hall*
Nominated: *The Goodbye Girl; Julia; Star Wars; The Turning Point*

Year: 1978
Winner: *The Deer Hunter*
Nominated: *Coming Home; Heaven Can Wait; Midnight Express; An Unmarried Woman*

Year: 1979
Winner: *Kramer vs. Kramer*
Nominated: *All That Jazz; Apocalypse Now; Breaking Away; Norma Rae*

Year: 1980
Winner: *Ordinary People*
Nominated: *Coal Miner's Daughter; The Elephant Man; Raging Bull; Tess*

Year: 1981
Winner: *Chariots of Fire*
Nominated: *Atlantic City; On Golden Pond; Raiders of the Lost Ark; Reds*

Year: 1982
Winner: *Gandhi*
Nominated: *E.T.: The Extraterrestrial; Missing; Tootsie; The Verdict*

Year: 1983
Winner: *Terms of Endearment*
Nominated: *The Big Chill; The Dresser; The Right Stuff; Tender Mercies*

Year: 1984
Winner: *Amadeus*
Nominated: *The Killing Fields; A Passage to India; Places in the Heart; A Soldier's Story*

Year: 1985
Winner: *Out of Africa*
Nominated: *The Color Purple; Kiss of the Spider Woman; Prizzi's Honor; Witness*

Year: 1986
Winner: *Platoon*
Nominated: *Children of a Lesser God; Hannah and Her Sisters; The Mission; A Room with a View*

Year: 1987
Winner: *The Last Emperor*
Nominated: *Broadcast News; Fatal Attraction; Hope and Glory; Moonstruck*

Year: 1988
Winner: *Rain Man*
Nominated: *The Accidental Tourist; Dangerous Liaisons; Mississippi Burning; Working Girl*

Year: 1989
Winner: *Driving Miss Daisy*
Nominated: *Born on the Fourth of July; Dead Poets Society; Field of Dreams; My Left Foot*

Year: 1990
Winner: *Dances with Wolves*
Nominated: *Awakenings; Ghost; The Godfather: Part III; GoodFellas*

Year: 1991
Winner: *The Silence of the Lambs*
Nominated: *Beauty and the Beast; Bugsy; JFK; The Prince of Tides*

Year: 1992
Winner: *Unforgiven*
Nominated: *The Crying Game; A Few Good Men; Howards End; Scent of a Woman*

Year: 1993
Winner: *Schindler's List*
Nominated: *The Fugitive; In the Name of the Father; The Piano; The Remains of the Day*

Year: 1994
Winner: *Forrest Gump*
Nominated: *Four Weddings and a Funeral; Pulp Fiction; Quiz Show; The Shawshank Redemption*

Year: 1995
Winner: *Braveheart*
Nominated: *Apollo 13; Babe; Il Postino* (1994); *Sense and Sensibility*

Year: 1996
Winner: *The English Patient*
Nominated: *Fargo; Jerry Maguire; Secrets and Lies; Shine*

Year: 1997
Winner: *Titanic*
Nominated: *As Good as It Gets; The Full Monty; Good Will Hunting; L. A. Confidential*

Year: 1998
Winner: *Shakespeare in Love*
Nominated: *Elizabeth; Saving Private Ryan; The Thin Red Line; La Vite e Bella*, or *Life Is Beautiful* (1997)

BEST DIRECTOR

Year: 1928
Winner: Lewis Milestone for Best Comedy Picture (*Two Arabian Knights*, 1927); and Frank Borzage for Best Dramatic Picture (*Seventh Heaven*, 1927)
Nominated: Charlie Chaplin (*The Circus*); Ted Wilde (*Speedy*); King Vidor (*The Crowd*); Herbert Brenon (*Sorrell and Son*, 1927)

Year: 1929
Winner: Frank Lloyd (*The Divine Lady*)
Nominated: Harry Beaumont (*The Broadway Melody*); Frank Lloyd (*Drag*); Irving Cummings (*In Old Arizona*); Lionel Barrymore (*Madame X*); Ernst Lubitsch (*The Patriot*, 1928); Frank Lloyd (*Weary River*)

Year: 1930
Winner: Lewis Milestone (*All Quiet on the Western Front*)
Nominated: Clarence Brown (*Anna Christie*); Robert Z. Leonard (*The Divorcee); King Vidor (*Hallelujah*, 1929); Ernst Lubitsch (*The Love Parade*, 1929); Clarence Brown (*Romance*)

Year: 1931
Winner: Norman Taurog (*Skippy*)
Nominated: Wesley Ruggles (*Cimarron*); Clarence Brown (*A Free Soul*); Lewis Milestone (*The Front Page*); Josef von Sternberg (*Morocco*, 1930)

Year: 1932
Winner: Frank Borzage (*Bad Girl*, 1931)
Nominated: King Vidor (*The Champ*, 1931); Josef von Sternberg (*Shanghai Express*, 1932)

Year: 1933
Winner: Frank Lloyd (*Cavalcade*)
Nominated: Frank Capra (*Lady for a Day*); George Cukor (*Little Women*)

Year: 1934
Winner: Frank Capra (*It Happened One Night*)
Nominated: Victor Schertzinger (*One Night of Love*); W. S. Van Dyke (*The Thin Man*)

Year: 1935
Winner: John Ford (*The Informer*)
Nominated: Henry Hathaway (*The Lives of a Bengal Lancer);* Frank Lloyd (*Mutiny on the Bounty*)

Year: 1936
Winner: Frank Capra (*Mr. Deeds Goes to Town*)
Nominated: William Wyler (*Dodsworth*); Robert Z. Leonard (*The Great Ziegfeld*); Gregory La Cava (*My Man Godfrey*); W. S. Van Dyke (*San Francisco*)

Year: 1937
Winner: Leo McCarey (*The Awful Truth*)
Nominated: Sidney Franklin (*The Good Earth*); William Dieterle (*The Life of Emile Zola*); Gregory La Cava (*Stage Door*); William A. Wellman (*A Star Is Born*)

Year: 1938
Winner: Frank Capra (*You Can't Take It with You*)
Nominated: Michael Curtiz (*Angels with Dirty Faces*); Norman Taurog (*Boys Town*); King Vidor (*The Citadel*)

Year: 1939
Winner: Victor Fleming (*Gone with the Wind*)
Nominated: Sam Wood (*Goodbye, Mr. Chips*); Frank Capra (*Mr. Smith Goes to Washington*); John Ford (*Stagecoach*); William Wyler (*Wuthering Heights*)

Year: 1940
Winner: John Ford (*Grapes of Wrath*)
Nominated: Sam Wood (*Kitty Foyle*); William Wyler (*The Letter*); George Cukor (*The Philadelphia Story*); Alfred Hitchcock (*Rebecca*)

Year: 1941
Winner: John Ford (*How Green Was My Valley*)
Nominated: Orson Welles (*Citizen Kane*); Alexander Hall (*Here Comes Mr. Jordan*); William Wyler (*The Little Foxes*); Howard Hawks (*Sergeant York*)

Year: 1942
Winner: William Wyler (*Mrs. Miniver*)
Nominated: Sam Wood (*Kings Row*); Mervyn LeRoy (*Random Harvest*); John Farrow (*Wake Island*); Michael Curtiz (*Yankee Doodle Dandy*)

Year: 1943
Winner: Michael Curtiz (*Casablanca*)
Nominated: Ernst Lubitsch (*Heaven Can Wait*); Clarence Brown (*The Human Comedy*); George Stevens (*The More the Merrier*); Henry King (*The Song of Bernadette*)

Year: 1944
Winner: Leo McCarey (*Going My Way*)
Nominated: Billy Wilder (*Double Indemnity*); Otto Preminger (*Laura*); Alfred Hitchcock (*Lifeboat*); Henry King (*Wilson*)

Year: 1945
Winner: Billy Wilder (*The Lost Weekend*)
Nominated: Leo McCarey (*The Bells of St. Mary's*); Clarence Brown (*National Velvet*, 1944); Jean Renoir (*The Southerner*); Alfred Hitchcock (*Spellbound*)

Year: 1946
Winner: William Wyler (*The Best Years of Our Lives*)
Nominated: Frank Capra (*It's a Wonderful Life*); Robert Siodmak (*The Killers*); Clarence Brown (*The Yearling*)

Year: 1947
Winner: Elia Kazan (*Gentleman's Agreement*)
Nominated: Henry Koster (*The Bishop's Wife*); Edward Dmytryk (*Crossfire*); George Cukor (*A Double Life*); David Lean (*Great Expectations*, 1946)

Year: 1948
Winner: John Huston (*The Treasure of the Sierra Madre*)
Nominated: Laurence Olivier (*Hamlet*); Jean Negulesco (*Johnny Belinda*); Fred Zinnemann (*The Search*); Anatole Litvak (*The Snake Pit*)

Year: 1949
Winner: Joseph L. Mankiewicz (*A Letter to Three Wives*)
Nominated: Robert Rossen (*All the King's Men*); William A. Wellman (*Battleground*); Carol Reed (*The Fallen Idol*, 1948); William Wyler (*The Heiress*)

Year: 1950
Winner: Joseph L. Mankiewicz (*All About Eve*)

Nominated: John Huston (*The Asphalt Jungle*); George Cukor (*Born Yesterday*); Billy Wilder (*Sunset Boulevard*); Carol Reed (*The Third Man*, 1949)

Year: 1951
Winner: George Stevens (*A Place in the Sun*)
Nominated: John Huston (*The African Queen*); Vincente Minnelli (*An American in Paris*); William Wyler (*Detective Story*); Elia Kazan (*A Streetcar Named Desire*)

Year: 1952
Winner: John Ford (*The Quiet Man*)
Nominated: Joseph L. Mankiewicz (*Five Fingers*); Cecil B. DeMille (*The Greatest Show on Earth*); Fred Zinnemann (*High Noon*); John Huston (*Moulin Rouge*)

Year: 1953
Winner: Fred Zinnemann (*From Here to Eternity*)
Nominated: Charles Walters (*Lili*); William Wyler (*Roman Holiday*); George Stevens (*Shane*); Billy Wilder (*Stalag 17*)

Year: 1954
Winner: Elia Kazan (*On the Waterfront*)
Nominated: George Seaton (*The Country Girl*); William A. Wellman (*The High and the Mighty*); Alfred Hitchcock (*Rear Window*); Billy Wilder (*Sabrina*)

Year: 1955
Winner: Delbert Mann (*Marty*)
Nominated: John Sturges (*Bad Day at Black Rock*); Elia Kazan (*East of Eden*); Joshua Logan (*Picnic*); David Lean (*Summertime*)

Year: 1956
Winner: George Stevens (*Giant*)
Nominated: Michael Anderson (*Around the World in 80 Days*); William Wyler (*Friendly Persuasion*); Walter Lang (*The King and I*); King Vidor (*War and Peace*)

Year: 1957
Winner: David Lean (*The Bridge on the River Kwai*)
Nominated: Sidney Lumet (*Twelve Angry Men*); Mark Robson (*Peyton Place*); Joshua Logan (*Sayonara*); Billy Wilder (*Witness for the Prosecution*)

Year: 1958
Winner: Vincente Minnelli (*Gigi*)

Nominated: Richard Brooks (*Cat on a Hot Tin Roof*); Stanley Kramer (*The Defiant Ones*); Robert Wise (*I Want to Live!*); Mark Robson (*The Inn of the Sixth Happiness*)

Year: 1959
Winner: William Wyler (*Ben-Hur*)
Nominated: George Stevens (*The Diary of Anne Frank*); Fred Zinnemann (*The Nun's Story*); Jack Clayton (*Room at the Top*); Billy Wilder (*Some Like It Hot*)

Year: 1960
Winner: Billy Wilder (*The Apartment*)
Nominated: Jules Dassin (*Pote tin Kyriaki*, or *Never on Sunday*); Alfred Hitchcock (*Psycho*); Jack Cardiff (*Sons and Lovers*); Fred Zinnemann (*The Sundowners*)

Year: 1961
Winner: Robert Wise and Jerome Robbins (*West Side Story*)
Nominated: Federico Fellini (*La Dolce Vita*, or *The Sweet Life*); J. Lee Thompson (*The Guns of Navarone*); Robert Rossen (*The Hustler*); Stanley Kramer (*Judgment at Nuremberg*)

Year: 1962
Winner: David Lean (*Lawrence of Arabia*)
Nominated: Frank Perry (*David and Lisa*); Pietro Germi (*Divorzio all'italiana*, or *Divorce Italian-Style*); Arthur Penn (*The Miracle Worker*); Robert Mulligan (*To Kill a Mockingbird*)

Year: 1963
Winner: Tony Richardson (*Tom Jones*)
Nominated: Federico Fellini (*8 1/2*); Elia Kazan (*America, America*); Otto Preminger (*The Cardinal*); Martin Ritt (*Hud*)

Year: 1964
Winner: George Cukor (*My Fair Lady*)
Nominated: Michael Cacoyannis (*Zorba the Greek*); Peter Glenville (*Becket*); Stanley Kubrick (*Dr. Strangelove, or: How I Learned to Stop Worrying and Love the Bomb*); Robert Stevenson (*Mary Poppins*)

Year: 1965
Winner: Robert Wise (*The Sound of Music*)
Nominated: William Wyler (*The Collector*); John Schlesinger (*Darling*); David Lean (*Doctor Zhivago*); Hiroshi Teshigahara (*Suna no onna*, or *Woman of the Dunes*)

Year: 1966
Winner: Fred Zinnemann (*A Man for All Seasons*)
Nominated: Michelangelo Antonioni (*Blowup*); Richard Brooks (*The Professionals);* Claude Lelouch (*Un homme et une femme*, or *A Man and a Woman*); Mike Nichols (*Who's Afraid of Virginia Woolf?*)

Year: 1967
Winner: Mike Nichols (*The Graduate*)
Nominated: Arthur Penn (*Bonnie and Clyde*); Stanley Kramer (*Guess Who's Coming to Dinner*); Richard Brooks (*In Cold Blood*); Norman Jewison (*In the Heat of the Night*)

Year: 1968
Winner: Carol Reed (*Oliver!*)
Nominated: Stanely Kubrick (*2001: A Space Odyssey*); Gillo Pontecorvo (*La Battaglia di Algeri*, or *The Battle of Algiers*); Anthony Harvey (*The Lion in Winter*); Franco Zeffirelli (*Romeo and Juliet*)

Year: 1969
Winner: John Schlesinger (*Midnight Cowboy*)
Nominated: Arthur Penn (*Alice's Restaurant*); George Roy Hill (*Butch Cassidy and the Sundance Kid*); Sydney Pollack (*They Shoot Horses, Don't They*?); Costa-Gavras (*Z*)

Year: 1970
Winner: Franklin J. Schaffner (*Patton*)
Nominated: Arthur Hiller (*Love Story*); Robert Altman (*M*A*S*H**); Federico Fellini (*Satyricon*); Ken Russell (*Women in Love*)

Year: 1971
Winner: William Friedkin (*The French Connection*)
Nominated: Stanley Kubrick (*A Clockwork Orange*); Norman Jewison (*Fiddler on the Roof*); Peter Bogdanovich (*The Last Picture Show*); John Schlesinger (*Sunday Bloody Sunday*)

Year: 1972
Winner: Bob Fosse (*Cabaret*)
Nominated: John Boorman (*Deliverance*); Francis Coppola (*The Godfather);* Joseph L. Mankiewicz (*Sleuth*); Jan Troell (*Utvandrarna*, or *The Emigrants,* 1971)

Year: 1973
Winner: George Roy Hill (*The Sting*)

Nominated: George Lucas (*American Graffiti*); William Friedkin (*The Exorcist*); Bernardo Bertolucci (*Ultimo tango a Parigi*, or *Last Tango in Paris*); Ingmar Bergman (*Viskningar och rop*, or *Cries and Whispers*)

Year: 1974
Winner: Francis Coppola (*The Godfather: Part II*)
Nominated: Roman Polanski (*Chinatown*); Bob Fosse (*Lenny*); Francois Trauffaut (*La Nuit Americaine*, or *Day for Night*); John Cassavetes (*A Woman Under the Influence*)

Year: 1975
Winner: Milos Forman (*One Flew over the Cuckoo's Nest*)
Nominated: Federico Fellini (*Amarcord*); Stanley Kubrick (*Barry Lyndon*); Sidney Lumet (*Dog Day Afternoon*); Robert Altman (*Nashville*)

Year: 1976
Winner: John G. Avildsen (*Rocky*)
Nominated: Alan J. Pakula (*All the President's Men*); Ingmar Bergman (*Ansikte mot ansikte* or *Face to Face*); Sidney Lumet (*Network*, 1976); Lina Wertmuller (*Pasqualino Settebellezze*, or *Seven Beauties*)

Year: 1977
Winner: Woody Allen (*Annie Hall*)
Nominated: Steven Spielberg (*Close Encounters of the Third Kind*); Fred Zinnemann (*Julia*) George Lucas (*Star Wars*); Herbert Ross (*The Turning Point*)

Year: 1978
Winner: Michael Cimino (*The Deer Hunter*)
Nominated: Hal Ashby (*Coming Home*); Warren Beatty and Buck Henry (*Heaven Can Wait*); Woody Allen (*Interiors*); Alan Parker (*Midnight Express*)

Year: 1979
Winner: Robert Benton (*Kramer vs. Kramer*)
Nominated: Bob Fosse (*All That Jazz*); Francis Coppola (*Apocalypse Now*); Peter Yates (*Breaking Away*); Edouard Molinaro (*La Cage aux folles*)

Year: 1980
Winner: Robert Redford (*Ordinary People*)
Nominated: David Lynch (*The Elephant Man*); Martin Scorsese (*Raging Bull*); Richard Rush (*The Stunt Man*); Roman Polanski (*Tess*)

Year: 1981
Winner: Warren Beatty (*Reds*)

Nominated: Louis Malle (*Atlantic City*, 1980); Hugh Hudson (*Chariots of Fire*); Mark Rydell (*On Golden Pond*); Steven Spielberg (*Raiders of the Lost Ark*)

Year: 1982
Winner: Richard Attenborough (*Gandhi)*
Nominated: Wolfgang Petersen (*Das Boot*, 1981); Steven Spielberg (*E.T.: the Extraterrestrial*); Sydney Pollack (*Tootsie*); Sidney Lumet (*The Verdict*)

Year: 1983
Winner: James L. Brooks (*Terms of Endearment*)
Nominated: Peter Yates (*The Dresser*); Ingmar Bergman (*Fanny och Alexander*, or *Fanny and Alexander*, 1982); Mike Nichols (*Silkwood*); Bruce Beresford (*Tender Mercies*)

Year: 1984
Winner: Milos Forman (*Amadeus*)
Nominated: Woody Allen (*Broadway Danny Rose*); Roland Joffe (*The Killing Fields*); David Lean (*A Passage to India*); Robert Benton (*Places in the Heart*)

Year: 1985
Winner: Sydney Pollack (*Out of Africa*)
Nominated: Hector Babenco (*Kiss of the Spider Woman*); John Huston (*Prizzi's Honor*); Akira Kurosawa (*Ran*); Peter Weir (*Witness*)

Year: 1986
Winner: Oliver Stone (*Platoon*)
Nominated: David Lynch (*Blue Velvet*); Woody Allen (*Hannah and Her Sisters*); Roland Joffe (*The Mission*); James Ivory (*A Room with a View*)

Year: 1987
Winner: Bernardo Bertolucci (*The Last Emperor*)
Nominated: Adrian Lyne (*Fatal Attraction*); John Boorman (*Hope and Glory*); Lasse Hallstrom (*Mitt liv som hund*, or *My Life as a Dog*, 1985); Norman Jewison (*Moonstruck*)

Year: 1988
Winner: Barry Levinson (*Rain Man*)
Nominated: Charles Crichton (*A Fish Called Wanda*); Martin Scorsese (*The Last Temptation of Christ*); Alan Parker (*Mississippi Burning*); Mike Nichols (*Working Girl*)

Year: 1989
Winner: Oliver Stone (*Born on the Fourth of July*)

Nominated: Woody Allen (*Crimes and Misdemeanors*); Peter Weir (*Dead Poets Society*); Kenneth Branagh (*Henry V*); Jim Sheridan (*My Left Foot*)

Year: 1990
Winner: Kevin Costner (*Dances with Wolves*)
Nominated: Francis Coppola (*The Godfather: Part III*); Martin Scorsese (*GoodFellas*); Stephen Frears (*The Grifters*); Barbet Schroeder (*Reversal of Fortune*)

Year: 1991
Winner: Jonathan Demme (*The Silence of the Lambs*)
Nominated: John Singleton (*Boyz N the Hood*, 1991); Barry Levinson (*Bugsy*); Oliver Stone (*JFK*); Ridley Scott (*Thelma and Louise*)

Year: 1992
Winner: Clint Eastwood (*Unforgiven*)
Nominated: Neil Jordan (*The Crying Game*); James Ivory (*Howards End*) Robert Altman (*The Player*); Martin Brest (*Scent of a Woman*)

Year: 1993
Winner: Steven Spielberg (*Schindler's List*)
Nominated: Jim Sheridan (*In the Name of the Father*); Jane Campion (*The Piano*); James Ivory (*The Remains of the Day*); Robert Altman (*Short Cuts*)

Year: 1994
Winner: Robert Zemeckis (*Forrest Gump*)
Nominated: Woody Allen (*Bullets Over Broadway*); Quentin Tarantino (*Pulp Fiction*); Robert Redford (*Quiz Show*); Krzysztof Kieslowski (*Trois couleurs: Rouge*, or *Three Colors: Red*)

Year: 1995
Winner: Mel Gibson (*Braveheart*)
Nominated: Chris Noonan (*Babe*); Tim Robbins (*Dead Man Walking*); Mike Figgis (*Leaving Las Vegas*); Michael Radford (*Il Postino*)

Year: 1996
Winner: Anthony Minghella (*The English Patient*)
Nominated: Joel Coen (*Fargo*); Milos Forman (*The People vs. Larry Flynt*); Mike Leigh (*Secrets and Lies*); Scott Hicks (*Shine*)

Year: 1997
Winner: James Cameron (*Titanic*)
Nominated: Peter Cattaneo (*The Full Monty*); Gus Van Sant (*Good Will Hunting*); Curtis Hanson (*L. A. Confidential*); Atom Egoyan (*The Sweet Hereafter*)

Year: 1998
Winner: Steven Spielberg (*Saving Private Ryan*)
Nominated: John Madden (*Shakespeare in Love*); Terrence Malick (*The Thin Red Line*); Peter Weir (*The Truman Show*); Roberto Begnini (*La vita e bella* or *Life Is Beautiful*)

BEST ACTOR

Year: 1928
Winner: Emil Jannings (*The Way of All Flesh*, 1927, and *The Last Command*, 1928)
Nominated: Charlie Chaplin (*The Noose*); Richard Barthelmess (*The Patent Leather Kid*, 1927)

Year: 1929
Winner: Warner Baxter (*In Old Arizona*)
Nominated: Chester Morris (*Alibi*); Lewis Stone (*The Patriot*, 1928); George Bancroft (*Thunderbolt*); Paul Muni (*The Valiant*)

Year: 1930
Winner: George Arliss (*Disraeli*, 1929)
Nominated: Wallace Beery (*The Big House*); Maurice Chevalier (*The Big Pond*); Ronald Colman (*Bulldog Drummond* and *Condemned*); George Arliss (*The Green Goddess*); Maurice Chevalier (*The Love Parade*, 1929); Lawrence Tibbett (*The Rogue Song*)

Year: 1931
Winner: Lionel Barrymore (*A Free Soul*)
Nominated: Richard Dix (*Cimarron*); Adolphe Menjou (*The Front Page*); Fredric March (*The Royal Family of Broadway*, 1930); Jackie Cooper (*Skippy*)

Year: 1932
Winner: Wallace Beery (*The Champ*, 1931)
Nominated: Fredric March (*Dr. Jekyll and Mr. Hyde*, 1931); Alfred Lunt (*The Guardsman*, 1931)

Year: 1933
Winner: Charles Laughton (*The Private Life of Henry VIII*)
Nominated: Leslie Howard (*Berkeley Square*); Paul Muni (*I Am a Fugitive from a Chain Gang*, 1932)

Year: 1934
Winner: Clark Gable (*It Happened One Night*)
Nominated: Frank Morgan (*The Affairs of Cellini*); William Powell (*The Thin Man*)

Year: 1935
Winner: Victor McLaglen (*The Informer*)
Nominated: Clark Gable (*Mutiny on the Bounty*); Charles Laughton (*Mutiny on the Bounty*); Franchot Tone (*Mutiny on the Bounty*)

Year: 1936
Winner: Paul Muni (*The Story of Louis Pasteur*)
Nominated: Walter Huston (*Dodsworth*); Gary Cooper (*Mr. Deeds Goes to Town*); William Powell (*My Man Godfrey*); Spencer Tracy (*San Francisco*)

Year: 1937
Winner: Spencer Tracy (*Captains Courageous*)
Nominated: Charles Boyer (*Conquest*); Paul Muni (*The Life of Emile Zola*); Robert Montgomery (*Night Must Fall*); Fredric March (*A Star Is Born*)

Year: 1938
Winner: Spencer Tracy (*Boys Town*)
Nominated: Charles Boyer (*Algiers*); James Cagney (*Angels with Dirty Faces*); Robert Donat (*The Citadel*); Leslie Howard (*Pygmalion*)

Year: 1939
Winner: Robert Donat (*Goodbye, Mr. Chips*)
Nominated: Mickey Rooney (*Babes in Arms*); Clark Gable (*Gone with the Wind*); James Stewart (*Mr. Smith Goes to Washington*); Laurence Olivier (*Wuthering Heights*)

Year: 1940
Winner: James Stewart (*The Philadelphia Story*)
Nominated: Raymond Massey (*Abe Lincoln in Illinois*); Henry Fonda (*The Grapes of Wrath*); Charlie Chaplin (*The Great Dictator*); Laurence Olivier (*Rebecca*)

Year: 1941
Winner: Gary Cooper (*Sergeant York*)
Nominated: Orson Welles (*Citizen Kane*); Walter Huston (*The Devil and Daniel Webster*); Robert Montgomery (*Here Comes Mr. Jordan*); Cary Grant (*Penny Serenade*)

Year: 1942
Winner: James Cagney (*Yankee Doodle Dandy*)
Nominated: Walter Pidgeon (*Mrs. Miniver*); Monty Woolley (*The Pied Piper*); Gary Cooper (*The Pride of the Yankees*); Ronald Colman (*Random Harvest*)

Year: 1943
Winner: Paul Lukas (*Watch on the Rhine*)
Nominated: Humphrey Bogart (*Casablanca*); Gary Cooper (*For Whom the Bell Tolls*); Mickey Rooney (*The Human Comedy*); Walter Pidgeon (*Madame Curie*)

Year: 1944
Winner: Bing Crosby (*Going My Way*)
Nominated: Charles Boyer (*Gaslight*); Barry Fitzgerald (*Going My Way*); Cary Grant (*None But the Lonely Heart*); Alexander Knox (*Wilson*)

Year: 1945
Winner: Ray Milland (*The Lost Weekend*)
Nominated: Gene Kelly (*Anchors A*weigh); Bing Crosby (*The Bells of St. Mary's*); Gregory Peck (*The Keys of the Kingdom*); Cornel Wilde (*A Song to Remember*)

Year: 1946
Winner: Fredric March (*The Best Years of Our Lives*)
Nominated: Laurence Olivier (*Henry V*, 1944); James Stewart (*It's a Wonderful Life*); Larry Parks (*The Jolson Story*); Gregory Peck (*The Yearling*)

Year: 1947
Winner: Ronald Colman (*A Double Life*)
Nominated: John Garfield (*Body and Soul*); Gregory Peck (*Gentleman's Agreement*); William Powell (*Life with Father,*); Michael Redgrave (*Mourning Becomes Electra*)

Year: 1948
Winner: Laurence Olivier (*Hamlet*)
Nominated: Lew Ayres (*Johnny Belinda*); Montgomery Clift (*The Search*); Clifton Webb (*Sitting Pretty*); Dan Dailey (*When My Baby Smiles at Me*)

Year: 1949
Winner: Broderick Crawford (*All the King's Men*)
Nominated: Kirk Douglas (*Champion*, 1949); Richard Todd (*The Hasty Heart*); John Wayne (*Sands of Iwo Jima*); Gregory Peck (*Twelve O'Clock High*)

Year: 1950
Winner: José Ferrer (*Cyrano de Bergerac*)
Nominated: Spencer Tracy (*Father of the Bride*); James Stewart (*Harvey*); Louis Calhern (*The Magnificent Yankee*); William Holden (*Sunset Boulevard*)

Year: 1951
Winner: Humphrey Bogart (*The African Queen*)
Nominated: Arthur Kennedy (*Bright Victory*); Fredric March (*Death of a Salesman*); Montgomery Clift (*A Place in the Sun*); Marlon Brando (*A Streetcar Named Desire*)

Year: 1952
Winner: Gary Cooper (*High Noon*)
Nominated: Kirk Douglas (*The Bad and the Beautiful*); Alec Guinness (*The Lavender Hill Mob*, 1951); José Ferrer (*Moulin Rouge*); Marlon Brando (*Viva Zapata!*)

Year: 1953
Winner: William Holden (*Stalag 17*)
Nominated: Montgomery Clift (*From Here to Eternity*); Burt Lancaster (*From Here to Eternity*); Marlon Brando (*Julius Caesar*); Richard Burton (*The Robe*)

Year: 1954
Winner: Marlon Brando (*On the Waterfront*)
Nominated: Dan O'Herlihy (*Las Aventuras de Robinson Crusoe*, or *The Adventures of Robinson Crusoe*); Humphrey Bogart (*The Caine Mutiny*); Bing Crosby (*The Country Girl*); James Mason (*A Star Is Born*)

Year: 1955
Winner: Ernest Borgnine (*Marty*)
Nominated: Spencer Tracy (*Bad Day at Black Rock*); James Dean (*East of Eden*); James Cagney (*Love Me or Leave Me);* Frank Sinatra (*The Man with the Golden Arm)*

Year: 1956
Winner: Yul Brynner (*The King and I*)
Nominated: James Dean (*Giant*); Rock Hudson (*Giant*); Kirk Douglas (*Lust for Life*); Laurence Olivier (*Richard III*)

Year: 1957
Winner: Alec Guinness (*The Bridge on the River Kwai*)
Nominated: Anthony Franciosa (*A Hatful of Rain*); Marlon Brando (*Sayonara*); Anthony Quinn (*Wild Is the Wind*, 1957); Charles Laughton (*Witness for the Prosecution*)

Year: 1958
Winner: David Niven (*Separate Tables*)
Nominated: Paul Newman (*Cat on a Hot Tin Roof*); Tony Curtis (*The Defiant Ones*); Sidney Poitier (*The Defiant Ones*); Spencer Tracy (*The Old Man and the Sea*)

Year: 1959
Winner: Charlton Heston (*Ben-Hur*)
Nominated: James Stewart (*Anatomy of a Murder*); Paul Muni (*The Last Angry Man*); Lawrence Harvey (*Room at the Top*); Jack Lemmon (*Some Like It Hot*)

Year: 1960
Winner: Burt Lancaster (*Elmer Gantry*)
Nominated: Jack Lemmon (*The Apartment*); Laurence Olivier (*The Entertainer*); Spencer Tracy (*Inherit the Wind*); Trevor Howard (*Sons and Lovers*)

Year: 1961
Winner: Maximilian Schell (*Judgment at Nuremberg*)
Nominated: Charles Boyer (*Fanny*); Paul Newman (*The Hustler*); Spencer Tracy (*Judgment at Nuremberg*); Stuart Whitman (*The Mark*)

Year: 1962
Winner: Gregory Peck (*To Kill a Mockingbird*)
Nominated: Burt Lancaster (*Birdman of Alcatraz*); Jack Lemmon (*Days of Wine and Roses*); Marcello Mastoianni (*Divorzio all'italiana*, or *Divorce Italian-Style*); Peter O'Toole (*Lawrence of Arabia*)

Year: 1963
Winner: Sidney Poitier (*Lilies of the Field*)
Nominated: Rex Harrison (*Cleopatra*); Paul Newman (*Hud*); Richard Harris (*This Sporting Life*); Albert Finney (*Tom Jones*)

Year: 1964
Winner: Rex Harrison (*My Fair Lady*)
Nominated: Anthony Quinn (*Zorba the Greek*); Richard Burton (*Becket*); Peter O'Toole (*Becket*); Peter Sellers (*Dr. Strangelove, or: How I Learned to Stop Worrying and Love the Bomb*)

Year: 1965
Winner: Lee Marvin (*Cat Ballou*)
Nominated: Laurence Olivier (*Othello*); Rod Steiger (*The Pawnbroker*); Oskar Werner (*Ship of Fools*)

Year: 1966
Winner: Paul Scofield (*A Man for All Seasons*)
Nominated: Alan Arkin (*The Russians Are Coming! The Russians Are Coming!*); Steve McQueen (*The Sand Pebbles*); Richard Burton (*Who's Afraid of Virginia Woolf?*)

Year: 1967
Winner: Rod Steiger (*In the Heat of the Night*)
Nominated: Warren Beatty (*Bonnie and Clyde*); Paul Newman (*Cool Hand Luke*); Dustin Hoffman (*The Graduate*); Spencer Tracy (*Guess Who's Coming to Dinner*)

Year: 1968
Winner: Cliff Robertson (*Charly*)
Nominated: Alan Bates (*The Fixer*); Alan Arkin (*The Heart Is a Lonely Hunter*); Peter O'Toole (*The Lion in Winter*); Ron Moody (*Oliver!*)

Year: 1969
Winner: John Wayne (*True Grit*)
Nominated: Richard Burton (*Anne of the Thousand Days*); Peter O'Toole (*Goodbye, Mr. Chips*); Dustin Hoffman (*Midnight Cowboy*); Jon Voight (*Midnight Cowboy*)

Year: 1970
Winner: George C. Scott (*Patton*)
Nominated: Jack Nicholson (*Five Easy Pieces*); James Earl Jones (*The Great White Hope*); Melvyn Douglas (*I Never Sang for My Father*); Ryan O'Neal (*Love Story*)

Year: 1971
Winner: Gene Hackman (*The French Connection*)
Nominated: Topol (*Fiddler on the Roof*); George C. Scott (*The Hospital*); Walter Matthau (*Kotch*, 1971); Peter Finch (*Sunday Bloody Sunday*)

Year: 1972
Winner: Marlon Brando (*The Godfather*)
Nominated: Peter O'Toole (*The Ruling Class*); Michael Caine (*Sleuth*); Laurence Olivier (*Sleuth*); Paul Winfield (*Sounder*)

Year: 1973
Winner: Jack Lemmon (*Save the Tiger*)
Nominated: Jack Nicholson (*The Last Detail*); Al Pacino (*Serpico*); Robert Redford (*The Sting*); Marlon Brando (*Ultimo tango a parigi*, or *Last Tango in Paris*)

Year: 1974
Winner: Art Carney (*Harry and Tonto*)
Nominated: Jack Nicholson (*Chinatown*); Al Pacino (*The Godfather: Part II*); Dustin Hoffman (*Lenny*); Albert Finney (*Murder on the Orient Express*)

Year: 1975
Winner: Jack Nicholson (*One Flew over the Cuckoo's Nest*)
Nominated: Al Pacino (*Dog Day Afternoon*); James Whitmore (*Give 'em Hell, Harry*); Maximilian Schell (*The Man in the Glass Booth*); Walter Matthau (*The Sunshine Boys*)

Year: 1976
Winner: Peter Finch (*Network*); and William Holden (*Network*)
Nominated: Giancarlo Giannini (*Pasqualino Settebellezze*, or *Seven Beauties*); Sylvester Stallone (*Rocky*); Robert De Niro (*Taxi Driver*)

Year: 1977
Winner: Richard Dreyfuss (*The Goodbye Girl*)
Nominated: Woody Allen (*Annie Hall*); Richard Burton (*Equus*); Marcello Mastroianni (*Una giornata particolare*, or *A Special Day*); John Travolta (*Saturday Night Fever*)

Year: 1978
Winner: Jon Voight (*Coming Home*)
Nominated: Laurence Olivier (*The Boys from Brazil*); Gary Busey (*The Buddy Holly Story*); Robert De Niro (*The Deer Hunter*); Warren Beatty (*Heaven Can Wait*)

Year: 1979
Winner: Dustin Hoffman (*Kramer vs. Kramer*)
Nominated: Al Pacino (*. . . And Justice for All*); Roy Scheider (*All That Jazz*); Jack Lemmon (*The China Syndrome*)

Year: 1980
Winner: Robert De Niro (*Raging Bull*)
Nominated: John Hurt (*The Elephant Man*); Robert Duvall (*The Great Santini*); Peter O'Toole (*The Stunt Man*); Jack Lemmon (*Tribute*)

Year: 1981
Winner: Henry Fonda (*On Golden Pond*)
Nominated: Paul Newman (*Absence of Malice*); Dudley Moore (*Arthur*); Burt Lancaster (*Atlantic City*); Warren Beatty (*Reds*)

Year: 1982
Winner: Ben Kingsley (*Gandhi*)
Nominated: Jack Lemmon (*Missing*); Peter O'Toole (*My Favorite Year*); Dustin Hoffman (*Tootsie*); Paul Newman (*The Verdict*)

Year: 1983
Winner: Robert Duvall (*Tender Mercies*)
Nominated: Tom Courtenay (*The Dresser*); Albert Finney (*The Dresser*); Michael Caine (*Educating Rita*); Tom Conti (*Reuben, Reuben*)

Year: 1984
Winner: F. Murray Abraham (*Amadeus*)
Nominated: Tom Hulce (*Amadeus*); Sam Waterston (*The Killing Fields*); Jeff Bridges (*Starman*); Albert Finney (*Under the Volcano*)

Year: 1985
Winner: William Hurt (*Kiss of the Spider Woman*)
Nominated: James Garner (*Murphy's Romance*); Jack Nicholson (*Prizzi's Honor*); Jon Voight (*Runaway Train*); Harrison Ford (*Witness*)

Year: 1986
Winner: Paul Newman (*The Color of Money*)
Nominated: Dexter Gordon (*'Round Midnight*); William Hurt (*Children of a Lesser God*); Bob Hoskins (*Mona Lisa*); James Woods (*Salvador*)

Year: 1987
Winner: Michael Douglas (*Wall Street*)
Nominated: William Hurt (*Broadcast News*); Robin Williams (*Good Morning, Vietnam*); Jack Nicholson (*Ironweed*); Marcello Mastroianni (*Ochi chyoirnye*, or *Dark Eyes*)

Year: 1988
Winner: Dustin Hoffman (*Rain Man*)
Nominated: Tom Hanks (*Big*); Gene Hackman (*Mississippi Burning*); Max von Sydow (*Pelle erobreren*, or *Pelle the Conquerer*); Edward James Olmos (*Stand and Deliver*)

Year: 1989
Winner: Daniel Day-Lewis (*My Left Foot*)
Nominated: Tom Cruise (*Born on the Fourth of July*); Robin Williams (*Dead Poets Society*); Morgan Freeman (*Driving Miss Daisy*); Kenneth Branagh (*Henry V*)

Year: 1990
Winner: Jeremy Irons (*Reversal of Fortune*)
Nominated: Robert De Niro (*Awakenings*); Gerard Depardieu (*Cyrano de Bergerac*); Kevin Costner (*Dances with Wolves*); Richard Harris (*The Field*)

Year: 1991
Winner: Anthony Hopkins (*The Silence of the Lambs*)
Nominated: Warren Beatty (*Bugsy*); Robert De Niro (*Cape Fear*); Robin Williams (*The Fisher King*); Nick Nolte (*The Prince of Tides*)

Year: 1992
Winner: Al Pacino (*Scent of a Woman*)
Nominated: Robert Downey Jr. (*Chaplin*); Stephen Rea (*The Crying Game*); Denzel Washington (*Malcolm*); Clint Eastwood (*Unforgiven*)

Year: 1993
Winner: Tom Hanks (*Philadelphia*)
Nominated: Daniel Day-Lewis (*In the Name of the Father*); Anthony Hopkins (*The Remains of the Day*); Liam Neeson (*Schindler's List*); Laurence Fishburne (*What's Love Got to Do with It*)

Year: 1994
Winner: Tom Hanks (*Forrest Gump*)
Nominated: Nigel Hawthorne (*The Madness of King George*); Paul Newman (*Nobody's Fool*); John Travolta (*Pulp Fiction*); Morgan Freeman (*The Shawshank Redemption*)

Year: 1995
Winner: Nicholas Cage (*Leaving Las Vegas*)
Nominated: Sean Penn (*Dead Man Walking*); Richard Dreyfuss (*Mr. Holland's Opus*); Anthony Hopkins (*Nixon*); Massimo Troisi (*Il Postino*, or *The Postman*)

Year: 1996
Winner: Geoffrey Rush (*Shine*)
Nominated: Ralph Fiennes (*The English Patient*); Tom Cruise (*Jerry Maguire*); Woody Harrelson (*The People vs. Larry Flynt*); Billy Bob Thornton (*Sling Blade*)

Year: 1997
Winner: Jack Nicholson (*As Good as It Gets*)
Nominated: Robert Duvall (*The Apostle*); Matt Damon (*Good Will Hunting*); Peter Fonda (*Ulee's Gold*); Dustin Hoffman (*Wag the Dog*)

Year: 1998
Winner: Roberto Benigni (*La vita e bella*, or *Life Is Beautiful*)
Nominated: Nick Nolte (*Affliction*); Edward Norton (*American History X*); Ian McKellen (*Gods and Monsters*); Tom Hanks (*Saving Private Ryan*)

BEST ACTRESS

Year: 1928
Winner: Janet Gaynor (*Seventh Heaven*, 1927; *Sunrise*, 1927; *Street Angel*, 1928)
Nominated: Gloria Swanson (*Sadie Thompson*); Louise Dresser (*A Ship Comes In*)

Year: 1929
Winner: Mary Pickford (*Coquette*)
Nominated: Betty Compson (*The Barker*, 1928); Bessie Love (*The Broadway Melody*); Corinne Griffith (*The Divine Lady*); Jeanne Eagels (*The Letter*); Ruth Chatterton (*Madame X*)

Year: 1930
Winner: Norma Shearer (*The Divorcee*)
Nominated: Greta Garbo (*Anna Christie* and *Romance*); Nancy Carroll (*The Devil's Holiday*); Ruth Chatterton (*Sarah and Son*); Norma Shearer (*Their Own Desire*); Gloria Swanson (*The Trespasser*, 1929)

Year: 1931
Winner: Marie Dressler (*Min and Bill*, 1930)
Nominated: Irene Dunne (*Cimarron*); Norma Shearer (*A Free Soul*); Ann Harding (*Holiday*, 1930); Marlene Dietrich (*Morocco*, 1930)

Year: 1932
Winner: Helen Hayes (*The Sin of Madelon Claudet*, 1931)
Nominated: Marie Dressler (*Emma*); Lynn Fontanne (*The Guardsman*, 1931)

Year: 1933
Winner: Katharine Hepburn (*Morning Glory*)
Nominated: Diana Wynyard (*Cavalcade*); May Robson (*Lady for a Day*)

Year: 1934
Winner: Claudette Colbert (*It Happened One Night*)

Nominated: Norma Shearer (*The Barretts of Wimpole Street*); Grace Moore (*One Night of Love*)

Year: 1935
Winner: Bette Davis (*Dangerous*)
Nominated: Katharine Hepburn (*Alice Adams*); Miriam Hopkins (*Becky Sharp*); Merle Oberon (*The Dark Angel*); Elisabeth Bergner (*Escape Me Never*); Claudette Colbert (*Private Worlds)*

Year: 1936
Winner: Luise Rainer (*The Great Ziegfeld*)
Nominated: Carole Lombard (*My Man Godfrey*); Norma Shearer (*Romeo and Juliet*); Irene Dunne (*Theodora Goes Wild*); Gladys George (*Valiant Is the Word for Carrie)*

Year: 1937
Winner: Luise Rainer (*The Good Earth*)
Nominated: Irene Dunne (*The Awful Truth*); Greta Garbo (*Camille*); Janet Gaynor (*A Star Is Born*); Barbara Stanwyck (*Stella Dallas*)

Year: 1938
Winner: Bette Davis (*Jezebel*)
Nominated: Norma Shearer (*Marie Antoinette*); Wendy Hiller (*Pygmalion*); Margaret Sullavan (*Three Comrades*); Fay Bainter (*White Banners*)

Year: 1939
Winner: Vivien Leigh (*Gone with the Wind*)
Nominated: Bette Davis (*Dark Victory*); Greer Garson (*Goodbye, Mr. Chips*); Irene Dunne (*Love Affair*); Greta Garbo (*Ninotchka*)

Year: 1940
Winner: Ginger Rogers (*Kitty Foyle*)
Nominated: Bette Davis (*The Letter*); Martha Scott (*Our Town*); Katharine Hepburn (*The Philadelphia Story*); Joan Fontaine (*Rebecca*)

Year: 1941
Winner: Joan Fontaine (*Suspicion*)
Nominated: Barbara Stanwyck (*Ball of Fire)* Greer Garson (*Blossoms in the Dust*); Olivia de Havilland (*Hold Back the Dawn*); Bette Davis (*The Little Foxes*)

Year: 1942
Winner: Greer Garson (*Mrs. Miniver*)

Nominated: Rosalind Russell (*My Sister Eileen*); Bette Davis (*Now, Voyager*); Teresa Wright (*Pride of the Yankees*); Katharine Hepburn (*Woman of the Year*)

Year: 1943
Winner: Jennifer Jones (*The Song of Bernadette*)
Nominated: Joan Fontaine (*The Constant Nymph*); Ingrid Bergman (*For Whom the Bell Tolls*); Greer Garson (*Madame Curie*); Jean Arthur (*The More the Merrier*)

Year: 1944
Winner: Ingrid Bergman (*Gaslight*)
Nominated: Barbara Stanwyck (*Double Indemnity*); Bette Davis (*Mr. Skeffington*); Greer Garson (*Mrs. Parkington*); Claudette Colbert (*Since You Went Away*)

Year: 1945
Winner: Joan Crawford (*Mildred Pierce*)
Nominated: Ingrid Bergman (*The Bells of St. Mary's*); Gene Tierney (*Leave Her to Heaven*); Jennifer Jones (*Love Letters*); Greer Garson (*The Valley of Decision*)

Year: 1946
Winner: Olivia de Havilland (*To Each His Own*)
Nominated: Celia Johnson (*Brief Encounter*); Jennifer Jones (*Duel in the Sun);* Rosalind Russell (*Sister Kenny*); Jane Wyman (*The Yearling*)

Year: 1947
Winner: Loretta Young (*The Farmer's Daughter*)
Nominated: Dorothy McGuire (*Gentleman's Agreement*); Rosalind Russell (*Mourning Becomes Electra*); Joan Crawford (*Possessed*); Susan Hayward (*Smash-Up, the Story of a Woman*)

Year: 1948
Winner: Jane Wyman (*Johnny Belinda*)
Nominated: Irene Dunne (*I Remember Mama*); Ingrid Bergman (*Joan of Arc*); Olivia de Havilland (*The Snake Pit*); Barbara Stanwyck (*Sorry, Wrong Number*)

Year: 1949
Winner: Olivia de Havilland (*The Heiress*)
Nominated: Loretta Young (*Come to the Stable*); Deborah Kerr (*Edward, My Son*); Susan Hayward (*My Foolish Heart*); Jeanne Crain (*Pinky*)

Year: 1950
Winner: Judy Holliday (*Born Yesterday*)
Nominated: Anne Baxter (*All About Eve*); Bette Davis (*All About Eve*); Eleanor Parker (*Caged*); Gloria Swanson (*Sunset Boulevard*)

Year: 1951
Winner: Vivien Leigh (*A Streetcar Named Desire*)
Nominated: Katharine Hepburn (*The African Queen*); Jane Wyman (*The Blue Veil*); Eleanor Parker (*Detective Story*); Shelley Winters (*A Place in the Sun*)

Year: 1952
Winner: Shirley Booth (*Come Back, Little Sheba*)
Nominated: Julie Harris (*The Member of the Wedding*); Bette Davis (*The Star*); Joan Crawford (*Sudden Fear*); Susan Hayward (*With a Song in My Heart*)

Year: 1953
Winner: Audrey Hepburn (*Roman Holiday*)
Nominated: Deborah Kerr (*From Here to Eternity*); Leslie Caron (*Lili*); Ava Gardner (*Mogambo*); Maggie McNamara (*The Moon Is Blue*)

Year: 1954
Winner: Grace Kelly (*The Country Girl*)
Nominated: Dorothy Dandridge (*Carmen Jones*); Jane Wyman (*Magnificent Obsession*); Audrey Hepburn (*Sabrina*); Judy Garland (*A Star Is Born*)

Year: 1955
Winner: Anna Magnani (*The Rose Tattoo*)
Nominated: Susan Hayward (*I'll Cry Tomorrow*); Eleanor Parker (*Interrupted Melody*); Jennifer Jones (*Love Is a Many-Splendored Thing*); Katharine Hepburn (*Summertime*)

Year: 1956
Winner: Ingrid Bergman (*Anastasia*)
Nominated: Carroll Baker (*Baby Doll*); Nancy Kelly (*The Bad Seed*); Deborah Kerr (*The King and I*); Katharine Hepburn (*The Rainmaker*)

Year: 1957
Winner: Joanne Woodward (*The Three Faces of Eve*)
Nominated: Deborah Kerr (*Heaven Knows, Mr. Allison*); Lana Turner (*Peyton Place*); Elizabeth Taylor (*Raintree County*); Anna Magnani (*Wild Is the Wind*)

Year: 1958
Winner: Susan Hayward (*I Want to Live!*)
Nominated: Rosalind Russell (*Auntie Mame*); Elizabeth Taylor (*Cat on a Hot Tin Roof*); Deborah Kerr (*Separate Tables*); Shirley MacLaine (*Some Came Running*)

Year: 1959
Winner: Simone Signoret (*Room at the Top*)
Nominated: Audrey Hepburn (*The Nun's Story*); Doris Day (*Pillow Talk*); Katharine Hepburn (*Suddenly, Last Summer*); Elizabeth Taylor (*Suddenly, Last Summer*)

Year: 1960
Winner: Elizabeth Taylor (*Butterfield 8*)
Nominated: Shirley MacLaine (*The Apartment*); Melina Mercouri (*Pote tin Kyriaki*, or *Never on Sunday*); Deborah Kerr (*The Sundowners*); Greer Garson (*Sunrise at Campobello*)

Year: 1961
Winner: Sophia Loren (*La Ciociara*, or *Two Women*)
Nominated: Audrey Hepburn (*Breakfast at Tiffany's*); Piper Laurie (*The Hustler*); Natalie Wood (*Splendor in the Grass*); Geraldine Page (*Summer and Smoke*)

Year: 1962
Winner: Anne Bancroft (*The Miracle Worker*)
Nominated: Lee Remick *(Days of Wine and Roses);* Katharine Hepburn (*Long Day's Journey into Night*); Geraldine Page (*Sweet Bird of Youth*); Bette Davis (*What Ever Happened to Baby Jane?*)

Year: 1963
Winner: Patricial Neal (*Hud*)
Nominated: Shirley MacLaine (*Irma la Douce*); Leslie Caron (*The L-Shaped Room*); Natalie Wood (*Love with the Proper Stranger*); Rachel Roberts (*This Sporting Life*)

Year: 1964
Winner: Julie Andrews (*Mary Poppins*)
Nominated: Sophia Loren (*Matrimonio all'italiana*, or *Marriage Italian-Style*); Anne Bancroft (*The Pumpkin Eater*); Kim Stanley (*Séance on a Wet Afternoon*); Debbie Reynolds (*The Unsinkable Molly Brown*)

Year: 1965
Winner: Julie Christie (*Darling*)

Nominated: Samantha Eggar (*The Collector*); Elizabeth Hartman (*A Patch of Blue*); Simone Signoret (*Ship of Fools*); Julie Andrews (*The Sound of Music*)

Year: 1966
Winner: Elizabeth Taylor (*Who's Afraid of Virginia Woolf?*)
Nominated: Lynn Redgrave (*Georgy Girl*); Vanessa Redgrave (*Morgan!*); Ida Kaminska (*Obchod na korze*, or *The Shop on Main Street*); Anouk Aimee (*Un homme et une femme*, or *A Man and a Woman*)

Year: 1967
Winner: Katharine Hepburn (*Guess Who's Coming to Dinner*)
Nominated: Faye Dunaway (*Bonnie and Clyde*); Anne Bancroft (*The Graduate*); Audrey Hepburn (*Wait Until Dark*); Edith Evans (*The Whisperers*)

Year: 1968
Winner: Barbra Streisand (*Funny Girl*) and Katharine Hepburn (*The Lion in Winter*)
Nominated: Vanessa Redgrave (*Isadora*); Joanne Woodward (*Rachel, Rachel*); Patricia Neal (*The Subject Was Roses*)

Year: 1969
Winner: Maggie Smith (*The Prime of Miss Jean Brodie*)
Nominated: Genevieve Bujold (*Anne of the Thousand Days*); Jean Simmons (*The Happy Ending*); Liza Minnelli (*The Sterile Cuckoo*); Jane Fonda (*They Shoot Horses, Don't They?*)

Year: 1970
Winner: Glenda Jackson (*Women in Love*)
Nominated: Carrie Snodgrass (*Diary of a Mad Housewife*); Jane Alexander (*The Great White Hope*); Ali McGraw (*Love Story*); Sarah Miles (*Ryan's Daughter*)

Year: 1971
Winner: Jane Fonda (*Klute*)
Nominated: Vanessa Redgrave (*Mary, Queen of Scots*); Julie Christie (*McCabe & Mrs. Miller*); Janet Suzman (*Nicholas and Alexandra*); Glenda Jackson (*Sunday Bloody Sunday*)

Year: 1972
Winner: Liza Minnelli (*Cabaret*)
Nominated: Diana Ross (*Lady Sings the Blues*); Cicely Tyson (*Sounder*); Maggie Smith (*Travels with My Aunt*); Liv Ullmann (*Utvandrarna*, or *The Emigrants*)

Year: 1973
Winner: Glenda Jackson (*A Touch of Class*)
Nominated: Marsha Mason (*Cinderella Liberty*); Ellen Burstyn (*The Exorcist*); Joanne Woodward (*Summer Wishes, Winter Dreams*); Barbra Streisand (*The Way We Were*)

Year: 1974
Winner: Ellen Burstyn (*Alice Doesn't Live Here Anymore*)
Nominated: Faya Dunaway (*Chinatown*); Diahann Carroll (*Claudine*); Valerie Perrine (*Lenny*); Gena Rowlands (*A Woman Under the Influence*)

Year: 1975
Winner: Louise Fletcher (*One Flew over the Cuckoo's Nest*)
Nominated: Glenda Jackson (*Hedda*); Carol Kane (*Hester Street*); Isabelle Adjani (*L'Histoire d'Adele H.*, or *The History of Adele H.*); Ann-Margaret (*Tommy*)

Year: 1976
Winner: Faye Dunaway (*Network*)
Nominated: Liv Ullmann (*Ansikte mot ansikte*, or *Face to Face*); Sissy Spacek (*Carrie*); Marie-Christine Barrau (*Cousin, Cousine*); Talia Shire (*Rocky*)

Year: 1977
Winner: Diane Keaton (*Annie Hall*)
Nominated: Marsha Mason (*The Goodbye Girl*); Jane Fonda (*Julia*); Anne Bancroft (*The Turning Point*); Shirley MacLainc (*The Turning Point*)

Year: 1978
Winner: Jane Fonda (*Coming Home*)
Nominated: Ingrid Bergman (*Hostsonaten*, or *Autumn Sonata*); Geraldine Page (*Interiors*); Ellen Burstyn (*Same Time, Next Year*); Jill Clayburgh (*An Unmarried Woman*)

Year: 1979
Winner: Sally Field (*Norma Rae*)
Nominated: Marsha Mason (*Chapter Two*); Jane Fonda (*The China Syndrome*); Bette Midler (*The Rose*); Jill Clayburgh (*Starting Over*)

Year: 1980
Winner: Sissy Spacek (*Coal Miner's Daughter*)
Nominated: Gena Rowlands (*Gloria*); Mary Tyler Moore (*Ordinary People*); Goldie Hawn (*Private Benjamin*); Ellen Burstyn (*Resurrection*)

Year: 1981
Winner: Katharine Hepburn (*On Golden Pond*)

Nominated: Susan Sarandon (*Atlantic City*); Meryl Streep (*The French Lieutenant's Woman*,); Marsha Mason (*Only When I Laugh*); Diane Keaton (*Reds*)

Year: 1982
Winner: Meryl Streep (*Sophie's Choice*)
Nominated: Jessica Lange (*Frances*); Sissy Spacek (*Missing*); Debra Winger (*An Officer and a Gentleman*); Julie Andrews (*Victor/Victoria*)

Year: 1983
Winner: Shirley MacLaine (*Terms of Endearment*)
Nominated: Julie Walters (*Educating Rita*); Meryl Streep (*Silkwood*); Debra Winger (*Terms of Endearment*); Jane Alexander (*Testament*)

Year: 1984
Winner: Sally Field (*Places in the Heart*)
Nominated: Vanessa Redgrave (*The Bostonians*); Jessica Lange (*Country*); Judy Davis (*A Passage to India*); Sissy Spacek (*The River*)

Year: 1985
Winner: Geraldine Page (*The Trip to Bountiful*)
Nominated: Anne Bancroft (*Agnes of God*); Whoopi Goldberg (*The Color Purple*); Meryl Streep (*Out of Africa*); Jessica Lange (*Sweet Dreams*)

Year: 1986
Winner: Marlee Matlin (*Children of a Lesser God*)
Nominated: Sigourney Weaver (*Aliens*); Sissy Spacek (*Crimes of the Heart*); Jane Fonda (*The Morning After*); Kathleen Turner (*Peggy Sue Got Married*)

Year: 1987
Winner: Cher (*Moonstruck*)
Nominated: Sally Kirkland (*Anna*); Holly Hunter (*Broadcast News*); Glenn Close (*Fatal Attraction*); Meryl Streep (*Ironweed*)

Year: 1988
Winner: Jodie Foster (*The Accused*)
Nominated: Meryl Streep (*A Cry in the Dark*); Glenn Close (*Dangerous Liaisons*); Sigourney Weaver (*Gorillas in the Mist*); Melanie Griffith (*Working Girl*)

Year: 1989
Winner: Jessica Tandy (*Driving Miss Daisy*)
Nominated: Isabelle Adjani (*Camille Claudel*); Michelle Pfeiffer (*The Fabulous Baker Boys*); Jessica Lange (*Music Box*); Pauline Collins (*Shirley Valentine*)

Year: 1990
Winner: Kathy Bates (*Misery*)
Nominated: Anjelica Huston (*The Grifters*); Joanne Woodward (*Mr. and Mrs. Bridge*); Meryl Streep (*Postcards from the Edge*); Julia Roberts (*Pretty Woman*)

Year: 1991
Winner: Jodie Foster (*The Silence of the Lambs*)
Nominated: Bette Midler (*For the Boys*); Laura Dern (*Rambling Rose*); Geena Davis (*Thelma and Louise*); Susan Sarandon (*Thelma and Louise*)

Year: 1992
Winner: Emma Thompson (*Howards End*)
Nominated: Catherine Deneuve (*Indochine*); Susan Sarandon (*Lorenzo's Oil*); Michelle Pfeiffer (*Love Field*); Mary McDonnell (*Passion Fish*)

Year: 1993
Winner: Holly Hunter (*The Piano*)
Nominated: Emma Thompson (*The Remains of the Day*); Debra Winger (*Shadowlands*); Stockard Channing (*Six Degrees of Separation*); Angela Bassett (*What's Love Got to Do with It*)

Year: 1994
Winner: Jessica Lange (*Blue Sky*)
Nominated: Susan Sarandon (*The Client*); Winona Ryder (*Little Women*); Jodie Foster (*Nell*); Miranda Richardson (*Tom & Viv*)

Year: 1995
Winner: Susan Sarandon (*Dead Man Walking*)
Nominated: Meryl Streep (*The Bridges of Madison County*); Sharon Stone (*Casino*); Elisabeth Shue (*Leaving Las Vegas*); Emma Thompson (*Sense and Sensibility*)

Year: 1996
Winner: Frances McDormand (*Fargo*)
Nominated: Emily Watson (*Breaking the Waves*); Kristin Scott Thomas (*The English Patient,*); Diane Keaton (*Marvin's Room*); Brenda Blethyn (*Secrets and Lies*)

Year: 1997
Winner: Helen Hunt (*As Good as It Gets*)
Nominated: Julie Christie (*Afterglow*); Judi Dench (*Mrs. Brown*); Kate Winslet (*Titanic*); Helena Bonham Carter (*The Wings of the Dove*)

Year: 1998
Winner: Gwyneth Paltrow (*Shakespeare in Love*)
Nominated: Fernanda Montenegro (*Central do Brasil*, or *Central Station*); Cate Blanchett (*Elizabeth*); Emily Watson (*Hilary and Jackie*); Meryl Streep (*One True Thing*)

Film Facts

- Film studies course enrollment doubled to sixty thousand between 1967 and 1968—the year of *The Graduate*, *Guess Who's Coming to Dinner*, and *The Valley of the Dolls*.

- Nineteen-forty was the first year in which the Academy Awards winners' names were delivered in sealed envelopes.

- Number of foster families with whom Norma Jean Baker lived before she grew up to be rechristened Marilyn Monroe by Twentieth Century–Fox: 12.

- Number of takes required to film Marilyn Monroe saying "It's me, Sugar," at the right moment in *Something's Got to Give* (1962): 47.

- In July 1978 John Travolta was the first "solo male" cover in *McCall's* magazine's 102-year history.

- Of the roughly 400 films released in 1997, only 3.4 percent were rated G, and 0.6 percent were rated NC-17 or X. Sixty-four percent were rated R.

- Steven Spielberg has directed, produced, or executive-produced seven of the top-selling films of all time.

- By 1920 there were 49 film studios in the Los Angeles area, and Hollywood studios were receiving 8,000 unsolicited screenplays a week.

- Number of minutes cut from *Cleopatra* between premiere and general release in June 1963: 22 minutes from its original 4 hours.

- A year for endurance: 1963's *Cleopatra* ran 4 hours 3 minutes, and Andy Warhol's *Sleep* was 6 hours 30 minutes.

- Between 1980 and 1989, the percentage of TV households with VCRs climbed from 2 percent to 68 percent.

- In 1947 (B.TV.) the average weekly attendance at the movies was 90 million; by 1977 it had fallen to 20.4 million.

- 300,000 extras—the most ever employed in a film—were used in Sir Richard Attenborough's *Gandhi* (1982); the edited scene of Gandhi's funeral runs for 125 seconds.

- On May 29, 1975, Sony demonstrated the Betamax, a videotape recorder, for only $2,295, described by the *New York Times* as "for the wealthy faddist market."

- The first showing of in-flight movies in the U.S. was a newsreel and two shorts screened on a Trans Air transcontinental flight on October 8, 1929.

- TWA became the first airline to offer in-flight movies regularly—for first class only—in July 1961.

- Pre-Mouse days: Michael Eisner took office as president and CEO of Paramount Pictures on November 15, 1976.

- Paramount Pictures was purchased by Gulf + Western on October 19, 1966.

- 3-D movie releases rose from one in 1952 to twenty-three in '53, thirteen in '54, and back down to one release in 1955.

- By 1953 studios were dropping the seven-year contracts in favor of single-film or multiple-film deals.

- In 1929, out of 23,344 theaters nationwide, 400 showed films aimed at black audiences.

- Orson Welles's *Citizen Kane* premiered on May 1, 1941, at the RKO Palace; Radio City Music Hall declined to show it. *Citizen Kane* lost $160,000 on its initial release.

- In November 1941 Bette Davis became the first woman elected president of the Motion Picture Academy of Arts and Sciences.

- On April 10, 1942, a headline in the *Hollywood Reporter* announced, "Bogart Replaces Reagan as Lead in 'Casablanca.' " Future president Ronald Reagan entered the army a week later.

- In Washington, D.C., on October 20, 1947, the House Un-American Activities Committee opened hearings on communism in Hollywood, which resulted in the blacklisting of the "Hollywood Ten."

- Sixty thousand acres of U.S. farmland were planted for popcorn in 1920; by 1948 the acreage passed 300,000.

- Honorary pallbearers at the July 28, 1948, funeral of D. W. Griffith included Lionel Barrymore, Charlie Chaplin, Cecil B. DeMille, John Ford, Samuel Goldwyn, Louis B. Mayer, Mack Sennett, and Erich von Stroheim.

- Of the 707 releases in 1929, 60 were made in color.
- In April 1951 forty-one Technicolor films were in production, double the number of the previous year.
- November 1962 was the birth month of Demi Guynes and Alicia Foster—better known as Demi Moore (Nov. 11) and Jodie Foster (Nov. 14).
- Jerry Lewis was named the best director of 1964 by French film critics for *The Nutty Professor* (March 1965).
- Former movie star and Screen Actors Guild president Ronald Reagan was elected governor of California on November 8, 1966. (He would be elected president of the United States on November 4, 1980.)
- The world's first Ronald Reagan film festival was held at San Francisco's Hub Theater in February 1966, showing *Hellcats of the Navy*, *The Killers*, *Cavalry Charge*, and *Bombs over China*.
- Future star agent Michael Ovitz began working at the William Morris Agency in 1968—in the mailroom.
- Uma Thurman was born on April 29, 1970; her mother was previously married to 1960s icon Timothy Leary.
- Date on which the Hollywood Chamber of Commerce launched a campaign to discourage young women from moving west to work in the movies: December 3, 1923.
- Date on which John Travolta received a lifetime achievement award at the Chicago International Film Festival: October 24, 1998.
- The world's first film studio was Black Maria in West Orange, New Jersey, opened on February 1, 1893, by Thomas Edison.
- It was on Nov. 5, 1970, that the Writers Guild dropped its 1954 requirement that members not be communists.
- The first film made in Hollywood was D. W. Griffith's Biograph melodrama *In Old California* (1910), shot in two days and released a month later.
- Before *Gone with the Wind* (3 hours 40 minutes), the longest-running U.S.-made feature film was MGM's *The Great Ziegfeld* (1939), which ran 2 hours 59 minutes.
- *The Blue Lagoon* (1980), starring Brooke Shields, cost $4.5 million to make, but its promotions budget was $6.3 million.

- A long tradition: Carl Laemmle billed *The Fighting American* (1924) as a movie "guaranteed not to make you think."

- The first black feature film was a six-reeler called *The Coloured American Winning His Suit*, produced by the Frederick Douglass Film Company in 1916.

- Lois Weber was the first woman to direct a feature film: *The Merchant of Venice* (Rex, 1914).

- Sharon Smith's *Women Who Make Movies* (1975) lists 36 women directors working in the U.S. silent film era.

- The first talkie directed by a woman was *Manhattan Cocktail* (1928), by Dorothy Arzner, who had previously directed silent films.

- The first African American to direct a film for a major American studio was Gordon Parks, who directed *The Learning Tree* (1969) for Warner Bros. (He would later direct *Shaft* and *Superfly*.)

- King Vidor's directorial career spanned 66 years, from *The Tow* (1914) to *The Metaphor* (1980).

- Director John Ford's career lasted 54 years, from *Lucille Love—The Girl of Mystery* (1914) to *Vietnam, Vietnam* (1968).

- Alfred Hitchcock's directorial career spanned 53 years, from *Always Tell Your Wife* (1923) to *Family Plot* (1976).

- Mike Nichols was the first director to earn $1 million for a single picture, for *The Graduate* (1968).

- MGM's *Hallelujah!* (1929), directed by King Vidor and starring Daniel Haynes, was the first feature-length black talkie.

- The first African-American production company was the Lincoln Motion Picture Co., founded in 1915 in Los Angeles by actors Clarence Brooks and Noble Johnson, druggist James T. Smith, and Harry Grant, a white cameraman.

- The oldest director ever signed for a major Hollywood picture was George Cukor for *Rich and Famous* (1981), with Candice Bergen and Jacqueline Bisset. Cukor was eighty-two.

- Famous Stage Names, Part I: Doris Day's real name was Doris Kapplehoff; Claudette Colbert, Claudette Chauchoin; Tony Curtis, Bernie Schwartz.

- Famous Stage Names, Part II: Rita Hayworth's real name was Margarita Carmen Cansino; Judy Holliday, Judy Tuvim; Vic Damone, Vito Farinola; Kirk Douglas, Issur Danielovitch.
- Famous Stage Names, Part III: Judy Garland's real name was Frances Gumm; Karl Malden, Malden Sekulovich; Danny Kaye, David Kaminsky; and Jack Benny, Benjamin Kubelsky.
- The world's first cinematography course was taught in Belgrade, Serbia, in the Slovenija Technical College's winter term of 1896–97, by H. Vodnik.
- The University of Southern California established a Department of Cinematography and began offering courses for a B.A. degree in 1932—the same year Paramount was closing its Astoria studios in Queens, New York.
- The first black winner of an Academy Award was Hattie McDaniel, voted Best Supporting Actress as Mammy in *Gone with the Wind* (1939).
- Length of time between McDaniel's award and the next black winner of an Oscar: 24 years. Sidney Poitier won Best Actor in 1963 for *Lilies of the Field.*
- Date on which Katharine Hepburn in New York boarded a California-bound train, the Super Chief, to make her first film: July 3, 1932.
- Katharine Hepburn, who has won more Academy Awards than any other performer (4), has also received the most nominations (13).
- Katharine Hepburn won Best Actress Oscars for *Morning Glory* (1933), *Guess Who's Coming to Dinner* (1967), *The Lion in Winter* (1968), and *On Golden Pond* (1981).
- The first actor to refuse an Academy Award was George C. Scott, who declined a Best Actor Oscar for his role in *Patton* (1970).
- The grand opening in 1929 of a two-day rail-and-air service between New York and Los Angeles was presided over by Mary Pickford, and Charles Lindbergh piloted the first flight.
- By 1930 theaters not wired for sound were having a hard time finding enough silent films to show.
- The *Hollywood Reporter* debuted on September 3, 1930, the first daily trade newspaper published in Hollywood.
- The movie industry adopted the Production Code guidelines on religion, sex, violence, etc., on March 31, 1930.

- Date on which Erich von Stroheim had a private audience with Pope Pius XI: September 18, 1930.
- Amount paid to Archibald Leach (later Cary Grant) for his first screen appearance: $150, for six days' work in 1931 on Paramount's short *Singapore Sue*. By 1932 he was making $450 a week.
- Notable contracts of 1932: Katharine Hepburn with RKO; Mae West with Paramount; and William Faulkner with MGM.
- "With the boom in drive-ins in full swing," reported *Variety* in 1947, "operators of the open-air flickeries are now ganging up to put a crimp in necking and other boy-girl antics" (Oct. 1, 1947).
- Nominees for Worst Title of 1987–88: *Demented Death Farm Massacre*; *Girls School Screamers*; *I Was a Teenage Sex Mutant*; *Slave Girls from Beyond Infinity*.
- The first of Dean Martin and Jerry Lewis's 12 films together, *My Friend Irma*, premiered on September 28, 1949, at the Paramount.
- The Motion Picture Industry Council was formed in March 1949 to keep Hollywood free of communists. Among its active members were Ronald Reagan and Cecil B. DeMille.
- Date on which Greta Garbo, born in Sweden, became an American citizen: February 9, 1951.
- Date on which Arnold Schwarzenegger, born in Austria, became an American citizen: September 16, 1983.
- *Bedtime for Bonzo* premiered on February 15, 1951, at the Circle Theater in Indianapolis. The chimp actor attended, but Ronald Reagan, who played Bonzo's father, did not.
- Turner Entertainment was planning a colorized version of *Citizen Kane* until it discovered in February 1989 that Orson Welles's contract with RKO gave him total control over the film.
- On July 25, 1985, it was announced that Rock Hudson was ill with AIDS. Hudson died on October 2, 1985.
- The American Movie Classics cable television channel began operations on October 1, 1984.
- Sidney Poitier was the first black man ever nominated for the Best Actor Oscar, for his performance in *The Defiant Ones* in 1958. Poitier won the Oscar five years later for *Lilies of the Field* (1963).

- Dorothy Dandridge was the first black woman ever nominated for a Best Actress Oscar, for her performance in *Carmen Jones*, 1954.

- The actor Paramount originally hoped would star in *Raiders of the Lost Ark* (1981), the first Indiana Jones film: Tom Selleck, who couldn't get out of his *Magnum P.I.* contract with CBS.

- *Apocalypse Now*'s lead role, played by Martin Sheen, was originally signed to Harvey Keitel until the latter was fired by Francis Ford Coppola over a contract dispute regarding Marlon Brando's starting date.

- The lead for *Lawrence of Arabia* announced by director David Lean in the Feb. 18, 1960, *Hollywood Reporter*: Marlon Brando. (Shakespearean actor Peter O'Toole tested for the part in November 1960.)

- Among the actors rumored to succeed Sean Connery in playing James Bond in 1972 were Paul Newman, Burt Reynolds, and Roger Moore.

- Issue date of *Cosmopolitan* in which Burt Reynolds appeared in a nude centerfold: April 1972.

- In 1932 Louis B. Mayer was shocked by his own studio's release of *Freaks*, a shock-value exploitation of people with severe deformities. MGM withdrew the film, then released it later as *Nature's Mistakes*.

- *Tarzan the Ape Man*, starring Johnny Weissmuller and Maureen O'Sullivan, premiered in March 1932. It was the first of Weissmuller's twelve Tarzan films.

- The first all-talking film was *Lights of New York*, a roughly made gangster film from Warner Bros. released on July 6, 1928.

- In July 1928 Paramount announced that by the next January all its films would be talkies—the first studio to make this move.

- Walt Disney's Mickey Mouse debuted in *Steamboat Willie* on Nov. 18, 1928—five months after the first all-talking film was released.

- The first big horror film—certainly the first in sound—was *Dracula*, directed by Tod Browning and premiering on Feb. 12, 1931. For his lead role, Bela Lugosi was paid $3,500.

- 1931, Year of Classic Horror: Bela Lugosi's *Dracula* (Feb. 12) was followed by *Frankenstein* (Boris Karloff) and *Dr. Jekyll and Mr. Hyde* (Fredric March) on Dec. 4 and 31, respectively.

OSCAR TRIVIA: BEST ACTORS AND ACTRESSES

Try, Try Again

- Actress Greer Garson was nominated twice (in 1939 and 1941) before she won the Best Actress Oscar in 1942 for *Mrs. Miniver* (1942). Garson was nominated each of the three years following, but lost each time. Fifteen years later, Garson was nominated one last time, for *Sunrise at Campobello* (1960), but lost to Elizabeth Taylor (*Butterfield 8*, 1960).
- Joan Fontaine was nominated in 1940 for *Rebecca* (1940), but she lost to Ginger Rogers. Fontaine won the following year for *Suspicion* (1941).
- Olivia de Havilland was nominated in 1948 for *The Snake Pit*, but she lost to Jane Wyman (*Johnny Belinda*, 1948). De Havilland won the next year for *The Heiress* (1949).
- Jessica Lange was nominated four times, in 1982, 1984, 1985, and 1989, before winning the Oscar five years later for *Blue Sky* (1994).
- Jack Lemmon was nominated in 1959, 1960, and 1962, but lost all three times. Eleven years later he finally took home the statuette, when he won for his role in *Save the Tiger*, 1973. Lemmon was nominated three more times after that, in 1979, 1980, and 1982, but to date has never won again.
- Paul Newman, the Susan Lucci of Oscar nominees, was nominated 6 times over a 24-year period, from 1958 to 1982, before finally winning the Best Actor Oscar in 1986 for *The Color of Money* (1986).
- Laurence Olivier was nominated three times before he finally won the Best Actor Oscar in 1948 for *Hamlet*. Following his win, Olivier was nominated 4 more times—in 1956, 1965, 1972, and 1978—but never won again.
- Gregory Peck was nominated in 1945, 1946, 1947, and 1949 before finally winning the Best Actor Oscar, 13 years later, for *To Kill a Mockingbird* (1962).
- James Stewart was nominated in 1939 for *Mr. Smith Goes to Washington* (1939); he won the following year for *The Philadelphia Story* (1940).
- Elizabeth Taylor was nominated two years in a row—in 1958 and 1959—before winning the Oscar in 1960 for *Butterfield 8* (1960).

- Spencer Tracy was nominated in 1936 for *San Francisco* (1936); he came back strong by winning the following two years in a row, for *Captains Courageous* (1937) and *Boys Town* (1938).

Always a Bridesmaid, Never a Bride

- James Dean was nominated two years in a row—in 1955 for *East of Eden* (1955) and 1956 for *Giant* (1956), but never took home the Oscar for Best Actor.

- In the 1930s Irene Dunne was nominated for the Best Actress Oscar, but lost all four times. Two of those four times, she lost to the same actress: Luise Rainer.

- Greta Garbo was nominated three times—in 1930, 1937, and 1939—but never took home the Oscar.

- Deborah Kerr was nominated six times between 1949 and 1960, but never won the Oscar for Best Actress.

- Marsha Mason was nominated four times from 1973 to 1981, but lost each time.

- Walter Pidgeon was nominated two years in a row—1942 and 1943—but never won the Best Actor Oscar.

- William Powell was nominated in 1934, 1936, and 1947, but never took home the Best Actor Oscar.

- Gloria Swanson was nominated for the Best Actress Oscar in 1928 and again in 1930, but she lost both times. Two decades later, in 1950, she was nominated again (for *Sunset Boulevard*, 1950), but lost to Judy Holliday (*Born Yesterday*, 1950).

On Again, Off Again

- Marlon Brando was nominated three years in a row—1951, 1952, and 1953—before finally winning the next year, in 1954 (*On the Waterfront*, 1954). Brando was nominated again three years later (he lost to Alec Guinness in *The Bridge on the River Kwai*, 1957), but 15 years later took his revenge with a win for the title role in *The Godfather* (1972). Brando was nominated one more time—the very next year—for *Last Tango in Paris* (1973), but lost to Jack Lemmon.

- Bette Davis won the Oscar the first two times she was nominated, in 1935 (*Dangerous*, 1935) and again in 1938 (*Jezebel*, 1938). Davis was nominated eight more times over the next 23 years, but she never won again.

- Jane Fonda was nominated in 1969, won in 1971 (*Klute*, 1971), was nominated again in 1977, and won again in 1978 (*Coming Home*, 1978).

- Clark Gable, a winner in 1934 for *It Happened One Night*, was nominated again the following year, but lost this time to Victor McLaglen (*The Informer*, 1935). Gable lost again in 1939 (*Gone with the Wind*, 1939) to Robert Donat (*Goodbye, Mr. Chips*, 1939)

- William Hurt, a winner in 1985 for *Kiss of the Spider Woman*, was nominated again the following two years, but lost both times: in 1986 to Paul Newman (*The Color of Money*, 1986), and in 1987 to Michael Douglas (*Wall Street*, 1987).

- Paul Muni was nominated in 1929 and 1933. He finally won in 1936 for *The Story of Louis Pasteur*. He was nominated again the following year for *The Life of Emile Zola* (1937) but lost this time to Spencer Tracy (*Captains Courageous*, 1939). Twenty years later, Muni was nominated for his role in *The Last Angry Man* (1959), but lost to Charlton Heston (*Ben-Hur*, 1959).

- Jack Nicholson was nominated for an Oscar in 1970, 1973, and 1974 before finally winning the Oscar in 1975 for *One Flew Over the Cuckoo's Nest* (1975). Nicholson was nominated again in 1985 and 1987, but did not win again until 1997, for his role in *As Good as It Gets* (1997).

- After her win in 1930 for *The Divorcee* (1930), Norma Shearer was nominated four more times in the following eight years, but never won again.

- Meryl Streep was nominated for the Best Actress Oscar in 1981, won the Oscar in 1982 (*Sophie's Choice*, 1982), and was nominated seven more times from 1983 to 1998.

On a Roll

- Katharine Hepburn has the most Oscar nominations of any performer, with 13 nominations from 1933 to 1981. Hepburn won four of the 13 times she was up for the award.

- Laurence Olivier, Meryl Streep, and Spencer Tracy are tied for the second-most Oscar nominations: each was nominated nine times. Of those nine nominations, Tracy won twice; Olivier and Streep, just once.

- Tom Hanks, Luise Rainer, and Spencer Tracy all won the Oscar two years in a row.

All of the following performers have won the Academy Award at least twice:

- Ingrid Bergman (*Gaslight*, 1944, and *Anastasia*, 1956)
- Marlon Brando (*On the Waterfront*, 1954, and *The Godfather*, 1972)
- Gary Cooper (*Sergeant York*, 1941, and *High Noon*, 1952)
- Bette Davis (*Dangerous*, 1935, and *Jezebel*, 1938)
- Sally Field (*Norma Rae*, 1979, and *Places in the Heart*, 1984)
- Jane Fonda (*Klute*, 1971, and *Coming Home*, 1978)
- Jodie Foster (*The Accused*, 1988, and *The Silence of the Lambs*, 1991)
- Tom Hanks (*Philadelphia*, 1993, and *Forrest Gump*, 1994)
- Olivia de Havilland (*To Each His Own*, 1946, and *The Heiress*, 1949)
- Katharine Hepburn (*Morning Glory*, 1933; *Guess Who's Coming to Dinner* (1967); *The Lion in Winter* (1968); and *On Golden Pond*, 1981)
- Dustin Hoffman (*Kramer vs. Kramer*, 1979, and *Rain Man*, 1988)
- Glenda Jackson (*Women in Love*, 1969, and *A Touch of Class*, 1973)
- Vivien Leigh (*Gone with the Wind*, 1939, and *A Streetcar Named Desire*, 1951)
- Jack Nicholson (*One Flew Over the Cuckoo's Nest*, 1975, and *As Good as It Gets*, 1997)
- Luise Rainer (*The Great Ziegfeld*, 1936, and *The Good Earth*, 1937)
- Elizabeth Taylor (*Butterfield 8*, 1960, and *Who's Afraid of Virginia Woolf?*, 1966)
- Spencer Tracy (*Captains Courageous*, 1937, and *Boys Town*, 1938)

Glossary

abolitionism (ăb′ə-lĭsh′ə-nĭz′əm) Most commonly used to refer to the political or philosophical policy supporting the abolition of slavery in the southern states prior to the Civil War.

abstract film A type of film that expresses, through its rhythms and visual design, intentions that are essentially non-narrative. Abstraction emphasizes form over content. In an abstract film that employs recognizable objects, the images are used not to suggest their usual meanings but to produce effects that are created by the film's editing, visual techniques, sound qualities, and rhythmic design, that is, form. The rhythmical and mechanical motion of common objects in Ferdinand Léger's *Ballet Mecanique* (1924) represents a type of abstract film.

acolyte (ăk′ə-lī t′) A term for someone involved or assisting in the performance of a religious ritual, sometimes used as an ironic exaggeration to refer to an exceptionally devoted follower or fan.

action film A type of motion picture characterized or defined by a considerable reliance on fast-paced action or violence. As an overarching genre, action films include certain westerns, war films, and science fiction movies, as well as straightforward, highly violent thrillers such as the *Die Hard* trilogy.

activist (ăk′tə-vĭst) A person involved in activities or action, often militant, that supports or opposes a social or political goal.

ad infinitum (ăd ĭ n′fə-nī′təm) A Latin term meaning having no end, or to go on forever.

adaptation (ăd′ăp-tā′shən) The translation or transcription of an existing property from one medium to another, for example, a film based on or *adapted* from a novel. Unlike original screenplays, which are written directly for dramatization in motion pictures, an adaptation represents something that was originally conceived for and presented in a different form.

adultery (ə-dŭl′tə-rē, -tr ē) Sexual relations between one person and another who is not his or her spouse.

aerial shot A shot taken from an airplane or a helicopter, intended to provide views of sky action or expansive, bird's-eye views of the scene below. Aerial shots are often used liberally in treating fast-paced, action adventures, such as the James Bond films.

aesthetic (ĕs-thĕt′ĭk) Of or relating to the common concept(s) of good and beauty. The term is also used to imply a sensitivity to beauty or artistic merit, or to imply the underlying philosophy or thought behind a work of art.

aficionado (ə-fĭsh′ē-ə-nä′dō, ə -fĭs′ē-, ə -fē′sē-) A fan, or devotee. The term is often used to refer to those with considerable or discerning knowledge of a particular subject.

AIDS An acronym for acquired immune deficiency syndrome, a group of diseases or conditions that result from the weakening or suppression of the human immune system, brought on by the human immunodeficiency virus, also known as HIV.

alienation (āl′yə-nā′shən) In psychological terms, an estrangement between one's self and the rest of the world; a feeling of not belonging. In film, the term represents a deliberate tension or mood, often achieved through the use of specific music, lighting, and cinemagraphic technique.

allegory (ăl′ĭ-gôr′ē, -g ōr′ē) A type of story, film, or play in which the objects, characters, and plot represent a larger idea than is contained in the narrative itself. An allegory is an extended narrative metaphor achieved by the dual representation of characters, events, or objects; they represent both themselves and abstract ideas that lead to a greater thematic significance. The western film *High Noon* (1952) was written so that the marshal (Gary Cooper) might be seen as a personification of individual courage in times of public threats. *High Noon* was intended to evoke an inspirational response to issues surrounding the freedom-threatening activities of McCarthyism during the late 1940s and early 1950s.

Many critics in interpreting the theme of *The Godfather: Part II* (1974) saw the evolution of Michael (Al Pacino) into the "don" who is without scruples or family feelings as having allegorical implications for cutthroat business practices in twentieth-century corporate America.

ambient (ăm′bē-ənt) Natural or already existing elements that comprise a certain portion of a filmed scene. Most commonly used to refer to natural light or background sounds that are considered attributes of a location setting.

ambiguity (ăm′bĭ-gyo͞o′ĭ-tē) Something that is doubtful or uncertain of interpretation or purpose; a mystery.

anachronism (ə-năk′rə-nĭz′əm) (also **anachronistic**) Something that is presented out of normal or proper chronological order.

anarchism (ăn′ər-kĭz′əm) A political theory or belief that all forms of government are oppressive and should be eliminated.

androgynous (ăn-drŏj′ə-nəs) Possessing characteristics of both male and female; uncertain or ambiguous of sex.

animation (ăn′ə-mā′shən) In film, a motion picture created by photographing a series of drawings or paintings.

antagonist (ăn-tăg′ə-nĭst) A person who opposes or contends against another. In film, the opponent or counterpoint of the hero.

antihero In literature or drama, a character lacking in traditional "heroic" virtues or attributes. The antihero has been portrayed both as an opponent of a traditional hero, and as the protagonist whose journey, or development of moral characteristics, becomes the center of the story.

antipathy (ăn-tĭp′ə-thē) Strong dislike or aversion.

anti-Semitism (ăn′tē-sĕm′ĭ-tĭz′əm, ă n′tī-) The hostility, hatred, or practice of discrimination against Jews.

antitoxin (ăn′tē-tŏk′sĭn) A treatment or antibody that responds to, treats, or neutralizes a toxin (poison) of biological origin.

apotheosis (ə-pŏth′ē-ō′sĭs, ă p′ə-thē′ə-sĭs) The highest or a glorified example. In art or film, the apotheosis would be the most perfect execution of a type or genre.

apprentice (ə-prĕn′tĭs) In modern terms, one who studies or learns a trade or skill under the supervision of a recognized or accredited master.

archetype (är′kĭ-tīp′) A prototypical first example or original on which following, similar examples are based.

armistice (är′mĭ-stĭs) A truce or other temporary stop in fighting by the mutual agreement of the warring parties.

atmospherics In film, any of a variety of elements that are introduced or created in order to enhance the dramatic effect, or mood, of a scene.

audition (ô-dĭsh′ən) A formal, trial performance before a director or casting agent, intended to present skills and abilities in competition for a role or part.

autobiography (ô′tō-bī-ŏg′rə-fē, -bē-) The account of the events of a person's life, written by the subject.

avant-garde (ä′vänt-gärd′, ăv′änt-) A term used to describe the leaders in a given field, those noticeably ahead of most of the rest in the application and invention of new techniques. The term is often used in the arts, where those in the avant-garde are seen as the primary innovators and the first to try or introduce new ideas.

Baby Boom The collective name for the generation of American children born between 1946 and 1964. The term refers to the considerable increase in births following the return of millions of American servicemen following the end of World War II.

ballad (băl′əd) In folk or traditional music, a type of song in the form of a narrative poem, comprised of simple stanzas and often a recurring refrain, and the music that accompanies it. The term also refers to a type of pop song, often slow and romantic.

barnstorming In sports, particularly baseball, a team that travels from location to location, playing exhibition games against local teams. The term derives from the post–World War I pilots who flew from place to place staging aerial shows and exhibitions, making use of available fields as landing sites.

biopic A shorthand term for a film that recounts or is based on the life story, or biography, of an individual.

bit part/bit player An actor who appears very briefly in a film in a role that usually contains some lines of dialogue. Numerous well-known screen performers appear as bit players in Robert Altman's insider's-view-of-Hollywood satire *The Player* (1992). A bit player's role is different from that of an extra or cameo player. An extra appears in a film as a nonspeaking background figure; a cameo role involves an actor in a brief but important featured part.

black comedy A film characterized by the droll, satiric treatment of normally serious subject matter.

blacklisting A term used to refer to the restrictions, based on accusations of communism, against hiring certain members of the entertainment industry during the 1940s and 1950s. The blacklist was based on the testimony before the House Committee on Un-American Activities (HUAC) of "friendly" witnesses from within the motion picture industry, who named those they believed to have communist sympathies or connections.

blank verse A type of verse or poetry consisting of unrhymed lines, usually in the form of iambic pentameter, a measured metric tone or pace.

box office A term used to refer to the financial success of a motion picture. It is derived from the small office in the front of a theater where tickets are purchased.

boycott (boi′kŏt′) A form of protest in which a person or group refuses to buy products from or support companies, individuals, nations, or other groups with which they disagree. The intent of a boycott is to bring about or force change. It is used as a tool or weapon in labor disputes, by consumers, and in international affairs.

Broadway An avenue in New York City, the physical and spiritual center of the "Theater District," home to a large number of live theaters. The term is often used to refer to live theater or the theater business as a whole.

brothel (brŏth′əl, brô′thəl) A house of prostitution.

burlesque (bər-lĕsk′) A type of vaudeville entertainment or comic art characterized by ridiculous exaggeration, racy humor, and displays of nudity.

byline (bī′līn′) The line appearing directly below the title or subtitle of a magazine or newspaper article that carries the writer's name. A byline (or by-line) is a symbol of stature and recognition; many pieces by apprentice or journeyman writers are not directly credited.

cadence (kād′ns) In poetry or music, a term used to refer to the balance, rhythm, or flow of a spoken or performed work. The term refers both to the beat, as in marching, and to the inflection or modulation of sound, as in singing or speaking, and to both vocal and instrumental progressions.

camaraderie (kä′mə-rä′də-rē, k ăm′ə-răd′ə-) A feeling of brotherhood, good will, and common cause among friends.

cameo (kăm′ē-ō′) In film, a brief, often minor appearance, often by a major or recognizable star.

camp (kămp) A type of entertainment, usually a comedy or parody, characterized by the affectation of manners and tastes generally considered low or vulgar.

canned drama A term used by early film critics to describe a motion picture. Many turn-of-the-century critics, unable to recognize the unique qualities of the cinema, employed terms and standards taken from the theater. Because early short narratives also often resembled stage plays, yet were permanently recorded on celluloid, they were frequently referred to as "canned drama." Similar terms, such as *picture play* and *photo drama*, indicate the difficulty early writers had in finding a separate vocabulary for describing motion pictures.

The term *canned* is still used frequently in film criticism to imply that all motion picture performances are immutable and thus to suggest differences between film and theaters. The expression comes from the fact that once a film is completed it is stored in a motion-picture can.

caricature (kăr′ĭ-kə-cho͝or′, -ch ər) A representation, most often pictorial, of a person that exaggerates distinctive features with comic or mocking intent. Also used to refer to the process of such exaggerated imitation.

carpetbagger (kär′pĭt-băg′ər) Most commonly used to refer to a person who comes from the outside and attempts to establish himself or his interests in another's area. The term derives from the derogatory name given to northerners who went to the South after the Civil War to capitalize on the chaotic political and financial conditions there. They often carried their belongings in a type of luggage called a carpetbag.

cartography (kär-tŏg′rə-fē) (also **cartographer**) The art of skill of making maps, or a person who makes maps. The term implies a certain artistry and formality, or artistic ability.

cartoon (kär-to͞on′) A hand-drawn animated film, usually 10 to 15 minutes in length. The term comes from material on which sketches were made. "Cartoon" was first used to describe satirical newspaper figures or political matters. Early film animators in the 1920s began to apply the term to their character sketches that were released as motion-picture shorts (for example, Walt Disney's *Alice in Cartoonland*, 1924). There evolved in the extensive production of these short animated films during the 1920s, 1930s, and 1940s a host of familiar cartoon characters: Mickey Mouse, Donald Duck, Bugs Bunny, Mr. Magoo, etc.

cataclysm (kăt′ə-klĭz′əm) A violent, unexpected event that brings about fundamental changes.

cel Short for "celluloid," a single frame on which a portion of an animated film has been painted. Each cel is slightly different from those that precede and follow, and when photographed in sequence, they create the illusion of motion in an animated film.

celluloid (sĕl′yə-loid′) A transparent material, made from nitrocellulose, a biological polymer, and camphor, used to make photographic film.

chains A linked group of movie theaters owned by a single corporate entity. In the early days of motion picture distribution, chains were owned by the studios, which would naturally use them to present their own productions.

character actor A specialized screen actor who usually portrays a particular type of character. The character is often based on an evolved persona derived from the actor's physical qualities and personal mannerisms. Daniel Stern, the lumbering burglar sidekick to Joe Pesci in the *Home Alone* (1990, 1992) comedies, represents character acting in the comic buffoon tradition. Donald Meek, a whiskey drummer in *Stagecoach* (1939), was a character actor who played out his screen career as a shy, stammering type. Typecasting from picture to picture is common for character actors.

characterization A term used to describe an actor's portrayal of a particular character or type.

choreography (kôr′ē-ŏg′rə-fē, k ōr′-) The art, study, and skill of creating and arranging sequenced dances or ballets.

Cinderella story From the fairy tale featuring the abused and mistreated girl and her evil stepmother, a story in which a poor or unappreciated girl triumphs over the machinations of her oppressors and ends up rich, recognized, or marrying the handsome prince.

cinema verité (sē′nā-mä′ v ā′rē-tā′) A style or school of filmmaking that emphasizes or portrays unbiased realism.

CinemaScope A wide-screen process developed and introduced by film technicians at Twentieth Century-Fox in the early 1950s. In CinemaScope filming the aspect ration of images varied from 2.66:1 to 1.66:1. The traditional screen ratio had been 1.33:1. Camera technicians employed anamorphic lenses, invented by Henri Chrétien in 1927, to photograph scenes so that they were wider than they were high (approximately 2.5 times wider). By using a comparable lens on a 35mm film projector, the images could be projected at their original width.

cinematography (sĭn′ə-mə-tŏg′rə-fē) The art or science of motion picture photography. Cinematography is considered one of the most significant aspects of a film's "look," or overall presentation, and is recognized with its own category in the Academy Awards.

citation (sī-tā′shən) An award, recognition, or commendation for an exceptional or meritorious act.

clandestine (klăn-dĕs′tĭn) Something that is kept secret or hidden, or done in secret.

clapper boy On a film set, the person who holds and closer the clapper, a small chalkboard with scene information that is held in front of the camera at the beginning of each scene.

classicism (klăs′ĭ-sĭz′əm) A philosophy or attitude based on the forms and principles of ancient Greece and Rome. The term is used in a variety of artistic genres and often denotes simplicity and restraint of form.

cliché (klē-shā′) An overworked dramatic concept, technique, or plotting element; also trite dialogue or stereotyped characterization that through repetitive use has lost its originality and freshness. In the late 1960s and early 1970s, the filming of violent death through either slow motion or pixilation was so extensive as to approach cliché treatment. The exploitation of clichéd technique, dialogue, and spoofs and parodies, such as Mel Brooks's *Young Frankenstein* (1974) and David Zucker's *Airplane* (1980). *Cliché* comes from the French word for a stereotype printing plate used in publishing.

close-up A shot that provides a limited, magnified view of a character or an object in a scene. It is a shot that usually emphasizes the face if characters are involved and provides a principal method by which the filmmaker can achieve empathy for characters. If focused on an object, the close-up bestows dramatic or symbolic value on the isolated element.

cognoscenti (kŏn′yə-shĕn′tē, k ŏg′nə-) The inner group, or those "in the know." A term often used to refer to those with superior knowledge or taste, usually in a specific or specialized field.

collaboration A joint effort between two or more people. The term is often used to refer to a creative endeavor with two or more creators or authors.

conflict A term for the struggles and tensions that result from the interaction of two opposing elements in a motion-picture plot. Expressed another way, conflict is the central problem within a film story that must ultimately be resolved. It is the conflict between the protagonist (the film's sympathetic figure) and the imposing force (the antagonist) that engages the audience's interest.

continuity (kŏn′tə-no͞o′ĭ-tē, -ny o͞o′-) The development and structuring of film segments and ideas so that the intended meaning is clear. *Continuity* is another term for film construction, which includes the development of plot or idea, the editing devices, and the transitions employed to connect the film parts.

In a more specific meaning *continuity* refers to the matching of individual scenic elements from shot to shot so that details and action, filmed at different times, will edit together without error. This process is referred to as "continuity editing." To maintain continuity within sequences the editor usually cuts on character actions so that the scene flows together without noticeable jump-cuts. Lapses in the flow of action can be avoided by cutaways and transition devices.

Music and sound are often utilized to provide a sense of continuity to a scene or sequences that may contain a variety of unmatched shots taken in different locations. In *Rocky* (1976) the song "Getting High" serves as a continuity device during the highly fragmentary sequence showing Rocky in the various training preparations for his title fight. The song connects the numerous brief shots so that they appear as a single and complete unit within the film.

crane shot A moving shot that may be horizontal, vertical, forward, or backward. The motion-picture camera is mounted on a studio crane that can be smoothly and noiselessly operated by electrical means. Also sometimes referred to as a **boom shot**.

credits In film, the listing of actors and other contributors.

criteria (krı-tîr′ē-ə) The standards, or rules, by which something is judged, often determined by comparison to some established standard.

cubism (kyo͞o′bĭz′əm) In art, a school or discipline characterized by the portrayal of natural forms as geometric structures. Cubism first became popular in Paris during the early 20th century, and its nonobjective style and design were highly influential in later art and film.

cult (kŭlt) An extreme or extremist group, often religious in nature, whose members live in an artificial or unnatural mental state, under the guidance or influence of a charismatic leader. The term is also sometimes used to refer to the extremely devoted followers of a public figure, such as an actor.

cultural historian A scholar who views or considers history in terms of the various elements of human culture, such as religion, arts, and institutions.

cutaway A shot, edited into a scene, that presents information that is not a part of the first shot. The cutaway shot is usually followed by a return to the original shot, and is often used to condense time in a scene by eliminating undesired action or to cover a loss of continuity in the action. For example, a series of shots of a woman sitting alone in a room smoking a cigarette may not match correctly in editing because of the varied lengths of cigarette ash from shot to shot. A cutaway to a mantel clock, ticking away the time, would provide enough distraction to cover the loss of continuity. Or the cutaway of the clock could be inserted between a shot of the woman smoking a cigarette and one of the woman reading a book. The cutaway would permit the editor to advance the action in time.

cynosure (sī′nə-sho͝or′, sĭn′ə-) Derived from the Greek term *kunosoura*, meaning "dog's tail," something that serves to guide, or an object, person, or point at the center of attention or held in high respect.

Dada A literary/art movement founded in 1916 in Zurich, Switzerland. The descriptive term *Dada* had no logical meaning; the expressed aim of the school was to negate the traditional relationship between calculation and creativity in the arts by approaching expression in a more playful, aleatory manner. The Dadaists borrowed from other movements of the time such as cubism, paper collage, and the displaying of industrially made objects (ready-mades) as works of art. The school was significant because of its influence on progressive artists throughout the world, and it was a stepping-stone to surrealism, which developed in the 1920s avant-garde.

Man Ray, working in France in the 1920s, is frequently referred to as a Dadaist filmmaker. He used collage techniques in his films, spreading materials on the emulsion and then processing the film for whatever results occurred (*Le Retour a la Raison*, 1923; *Emak Bakia*, 1926). The early free-flowing, rhythmic films of René Clair (*Paris Qui Dort* [*The Crazy Ray*], 1923), were also inspired by the playful interests of the Dada movement.

daguerreotype (də-gâr′ə-tī p′) An early type of photograph, or the photographic process in which images were produced on a light-sensitive, silver-coated plate.

debut (dā-byōō′, d ā′byōō′) The first public performance or presentation.

delineate (dĭ-lĭn′ē-āt′) To sketch out or draw, or otherwise make meaning plain through the use of art or image.

dialogue Verbal exchange between two or more characters in a film or play. Dialogue may be presented in voice-ovcr. In the opening exchange between a French actress and a Japanese architect in *Hiroshima Mon Amour* (1959), the dialogue (two lengthy passages) is heard as the camera roams the museums of Hiroshima. More commonly, dialogue is shown in lip sync. The spoken lines are in synchronization with the moving lips of the characters.

diaphanous (dī-ăf′ə-nəs) A fine, delicate texture, transparent or translucent. The term is sometimes used to refer to a certain screen quality or presence characteristic of some actresses of exceptional beauty and grace, enhanced by effects such as backlighting and soft focus.

diction (dĭk′shən) The manner and use of words in speech or writing. In film, the term is used to refer to the quality or manner in which an actor delivers his lines.

diegesis Derived from Greek origins meaning narration or a recitation of narrative fact. In film, the term is used to refer collectively to everything that is happening on screen at a given time.

digital sound (digital signal processing, DSP) A superior fidelity sound-recording system achieved through the conversion of sound into a binary stream of ones and zeroes that are computer stored for later signal conversion and amplification without risk of distortion. The computer is able to record as many as 44,000 elements of sound per second and to manage signal conversion and transfer without machine-noise buildup. This technological capability results in motion-picture sound of vastly improved quality over earlier recording systems.

diminutive (dĭ-m ĭn′yə-t ĭv) A term meaning extremely small, often used to refer to a type of nickname that indicates smallness, childhood, or familiarity.

disciple (dĭ-sī′pəl) A person who embraces and continues the teachings of another, or one who believes wholly in a movement or philosophy.

dissolve (dĭ-zŏlv′) A film term that describes the transition between scenes in which one scene fades out and the other fades in simultaneously, coming slowly to the forefront as the first dims.

docudrama A term for the narrative blending of documentary and fictional elements to create a film drama based on historical, news-inspired actuality. This form of filmmaking is also sometimes referred to as "infotainment," "faction," and "real fiction." The docudrama is most commonly thought of as a made-for-television-movie event, although the term is applied from time to time to theatrical motion pictures, for example, *Not Without My Daughter* (1990), *JFK* (1991).

documentary (dŏk′yə-mĕn′tə-rē) A nonfiction film, usually shot on location and often comprising archival footage, that uses real people instead of actors as its principles and focuses on historical, scientific, social, or educational subjects.

Dolby sound (system) A patented noise-reduction sound system that is used with theatrical motion pictures as an embellishment to the screen imagery. The Dolby system makes possible high-fidelity, stereophonic-sound accompaniment on the optical sound track rather than a magnetic sound track, as was once required for clean, noise-free reproduction. Dolby sound found wide application during the 1970s in screen spectacles as diverse as *Star Wars* (1977) and *Apocalypse Now* (1979). The system became a standard of high-quality, big-budget motion pictures.

dolly (dŏl′ē) A type of hand truck or mobile platform that moves on casters.

double exposure Two or more images that have been photographed separately but that appear over one another or side by side on the same piece of film. A double exposure may be achieved by running unprocessed film through the camera more than once or by optical printing at the processing laboratory. Georges Melies created illusory effects in many of his early trick films through double exposures. In contemporary filmmaking the technique appears more commonly in experimental-film efforts, for example, Marie Menken's *Hurry, Hurry* (1957) and Ed Emshwiller's *Relativity* (1963-66).

dowager (dou′ə-jər) A wealthy widow whose property is derived from her late husband's estate.

drama (drä′mə, dr ăm′ə) In film, a type of motion picture with serious, usually fictional subject matter. The category is broad enough to include works from virtually all genres, and any film may possess elements or moments of dramatic action. The term, which derives from the Greek meaning "to perform," has entered common usage to refer to any situation characterized by the structural progression and emotional effects of a play.

dubbing The process of adding sound, dialogue, or sound effects to a film after the dramatic action has been photographed. This is possible because sound in most motion pictures is recorded on a separate system (double-system sound) rather than on the film itself and later edited to fit the visual images. When all desired sounds (music, dialogue, sound effects) have been edited and mixed into a single synchronized sound track, it is then printed on the edited film.

Some directors prefer to dub dialogue and sound effects rather than use the original on-the-set sound. This approach has become even more prevalent as location shooting has increased. By dubbing, it is possible to obtain better sound quality and even to change the original dialogue. *Dubbing* is also the term for converting dialogue to another language. The technique frequently used in dubbing a motion picture is that of looping. In looping, a section of film is spliced end to end so that it repeats its movement through the projector. A looped piece of magnetic film is interlocked into a projector–recorder system. Actors, through this double-looping process, are able to rehearse and record lines with the film images until the sound dubbing is satisfactory.

dynamic cutting An approach to film editing in which the cutting from one shot to the next is made abruptly apparent to the viewer. In matched cutting or invisible editing, the cuts are not as obvious to the viewer, because these approaches adhere to continuity procedures designed to hide the edit, for example, cutting on action. Dynamic cutting, on the other hand, is self-conscious and often startles the viewer by moving abruptly in time or space or by rapid cutting within the scene for expressive as well as narrative purposes. Bob Fosse's *All That Jazz* (1979), Richard Rush's *The Stunt Man* (1980), and Oliver Stone's *JFK* (1991) employ extensive dynamic cutting.

eclectic (ĭ-klĕk′tĭk) Comprised of elements or influences drawn from a wide variety of sources and styles.

Emmy (ĕm′ē) The commonly used name for the awards, presented annually by the Academy of Television Arts and Sciences, for outstanding achievement in television.

enclave (ĕn′klāv′, ŏ n′-) Most often used to refer to a space or bounded area wholly enclosed within another, larger unit.

epic (ĕp′ĭk) A work, such as a motion picture or novel, characterized by stylized or formal language, grand scale, and legendary or heroic subject matter or characters. The term is also used to refer to the iconic quality of works that surpass the ordinary in scope or sheer size.

episode(s) (ĕp′ĭ-sōd′) In television, one segment, most often weekly, in an ongoing series. Episodes most often featuring a recurring cast of characters, and may have plots that are part of a continuing narrative, build upon incidents and characters established in previous episodes, or present entirely new situations. The term is also used in film to refer to one part of an ongoing series, such as the *Star Wars* or *Die Hard* movies.

escapism In the arts, a work that aims to remove its audience from their present-day realities into a realm of fantasy or mystery. In film, such elements as exotic settings, special effects, and glamorous stars serve to present a fictionalized reality intended to distract and transport moviegoers.

estrangement A sense or the act of detachment or removing one's self from a person, place, or association.

ethnicity (ĕth-nĭs′ĭ-tē) A sociological classification referring to a person's ethnic character, background, or affiliation.

eulogy (yōō′lə-jē) A spoken or written tribute, most often given when a person has died.

expatriate (ĕk-spā′trē-āt′) A person who has left his or her native country, usually through banishment or exile, to live in another country.

exposé A nonfictional work such as a book or film that attempts to expose or reveal previously unknown and often uncomplimentary information about its subject. Most often a feature of hard news, an exposé may expose criminal or indiscreet activities, or show the inner workings of an organization.

exposure (ĭk-spō′zhər) In the movie industry, a technical term for the amount of radiant energy needed to expose a plate of photographic film.

extraterrestrial (ĕk′strə-tə-rĕs′trē-əl) A term that literally means "outside of earth," commonly used in science fiction literature or film to refer to intelligent beings from another planet.

fable (fā′bəl) A short, fictional narrative, usually cast as a cautionary or teaching tale. Fables often make use of fantastic devices such as talking animals to personify or illustrate moral traits.

fan magazine A periodical dedicated to information and photographs about prominent people, targeted at an established fan base or demographic, such as teenage girls. Fan magazines are most often associated with movie and music personalities, and range from wholly nonobjective adoration to more or less straightforward accountings of glamorous people and events.

feature (fē′chər) On a movie theater's bill, the primary film presentation. The term is also used to differentiate films of a certain duration, usually 90 minutes or more ("feature-length") from shorter works.

featured billing In film, the presentation in print ads, such as one-sheet posters, and in the film credits, of the leading star, in any of a variety of ways intended to emphasize his or her predominance over the other actors.

femme fatale (fĕm′ f ə-tăl′, -täl ′, f ăm′) In literature or film, a female character of great allure and seductiveness who leads men into difficult or dangerous situations.

film noir A type of American melodrama where life is lived amid shadows and fog, and where women with a past and men with no future pass their time in sleazy hotel rooms or smoke-filled cocktail lounges.

film speed A term used to designate a particular film emulsion's sensitivity to light. Film speeds in the United States are regulated by the American Standards Association and hence are supplied with an ASA rating. The higher the number or the ASA rating (for example, ASA 400), the faster the speed the film or, expressed another way, the more receptive the emulsion is to recordings made where little light is available. Because high-speed films tend to show grain when printed, film speed becomes an important consideration in a director's choice of emulsions. As a general rule of thumb, directors will choose the slowest possible film stock for a sharply defined, low-contrast image. Higher speeds, however, may be chosen if the desired look of the processed film is intended to simulate grainy, newsreel-like footage, or where contrast images are desired.

filmography A bibliographic listing of a group of films, most commonly the listing of a director's or an actors full body of work.

fisticuffs (fĭs′tĭ-kŭfs′) A colorful, antiquated term for a fistfight.

flapper (flăp′ər) A colloquial term for a woman of a certain lifestyle, common during the 1920s, characterized by a lack of concern for conventional dress and behavior. The use has its roots in a British slang term for a young prostitute, or a "loose" or flighty young girl.

flashback A scene or shot in a motion-picture story that deals with an event that has occurred prior to the film's principal time period. Flashbacks are often inserted into a story line for the purpose of recalling a situation that is relevant to the developing plot or of clarifying points of information, as in the concluding scenes of a mystery film. In many films flashbacks become a principal plotting device for revealing character by crosscutting among scenes of past and present time. *Citizen Kane* (1941), *In Which We Serve* (1942), *Rachel, Rachel* (1968), *The Godfather: Part II* (1974), *Valentino* (1977), and *Fried Green Tomatoes* (1991) are examples of motion pictures that make extensive use of flashbacks for plot and character development.

flash-forward An editing technique in which scenes or shots that occur in a future time are inserted into the developing story line of a film. Flash-forwards are often employed to anticipate a critical dramatic situation toward which the plot is progressing. The technique can also provide an element of mystery because of ambiguous relationships of the flash-forward to the film's time continuum; often flash-forwards are recognized as such only after the story has proceeded to the point of the shot (the flash-forward) that has appeared earlier in the film. *They Shoot Horses, Don't They?* (1969) repeats throughout the film an ambiguous flash-forward shot of a young man as he stands in the presence of a judge. The meaning of the flash-forward does not become clear until the end of the film, after the man has committed a "mercy killing." A similar use of the flash-forward occurs in Nicolas Roeg's *Don't Look Now* (1973), where a boat carrying a coffin is visualized a number of times before its meaning becomes clear at the end of the film.

flickers A colloquial term for motion pictures. The term developed in the medium's formative years as a result of technical imperfections in early motion-picture projection devices. A pulsating, flickering effect accompanied the projection images, thus giving rise to the term.

flux (flŭks) A state of flowing or constant movement, most commonly associated with liquids, such as the flowing of the tide.

footage (fo͝ot′ĭj) Film or video of a specific kind or subject, often used in the reportage or news or the body of a documentary.

formal editing An approach to film editing in which shot length remains consistent and unvaried, so much so that the rhythm of the film produces a formal, dignified pace in the action flow. The editing pace of Stanley Kubrick's *Barry Lyndon* (1975) is consistently ordered and formal, reflecting an attempt to convey the moods and rhythms of eighteenth-century life in Europe.

formula film A phrase used to describe a motion picture that uses familiar plotting devices and tested subject matter in story development. Formula films imitate successful works by incorporating precisely the elements that characterize the more original, earlier films and that are usually recognizable as having been patterned after specific films or film types. Many film genres, especially the western and the gangster film, lend themselves to the formularized variations.

The formula film, despite its lack of originality, often enjoys considerable popularity because of its well-known, easily understood plot, theme, and conventions.

formulaic Characterized by an adherence to or the use of conventions and elements that are recognized as a distinct, previously established pattern. In film, a movie that makes use of familiar and predictable characters or plot elements is often referred to as "formulaic."

frame Each individual photograph recorded on motion-picture celluloid is referred to as a frame. The frame is the basic visual unit of motion pictures, printed on a strip of celluloid material of varying widths: 8mm, 16mm, 35mm, 65mm, 70mm. In sound motion pictures 24 separate frames are photographed and projected per second to create the effect of natural movement on the screen.

frames per second (FPS) A term used to designate camera shooting speed or motion-picture projection speed. Most sound motion pictures are photographed at speeds of 24 frames per second (fps) and projected at the same speed. Slow motion is generally achieved by photographing at speeds greater than 24 fps and projecting at 24 fps (for example, filming at 49 fps and projecting at 24 fps). Fast motion involves shooting at a slower camera speed and projecting at a faster projection speed: filming action at 8 or 16 fps and projecting at 24 fps.

freeze-frame A pause, effectively a still picture, in the course of a movie or television show, created by reproducing a single frame of film sequentially, or literally stopping the reel or videotape on a single frame for the desired duration. The term may also be used to indicate a striking scene with virtually no movement, or a singular, arresting image.

gamine (gă-mēn′, g ăm′ēn) A female characteristic or personality type that implies a waiflike innocence and impish appeal.

gargoyle (gär′goil′) A roof spout, or type of gutter, cast in the image of a fantastic, often grotesque creature. While primarily decorative, a functional gargoyle serves the useful purpose of carrying rainwater flow clear of a wall.

genesis (jĕn′ĭ-sĭs) The origin or moment of coming into being. In the Bible, the book of Genesis recounts God's creation of the universe and all things in it.

genre (zhän′rə) A type or classification. In film, genre refers to the general category, such as "musical" or "action film," into which the subject or style of a picture most nearly falls. All films of a type are collectively referred to as "the genre."

gimmick (gĭm′ĭk) An apparent attraction or device, often intended to deceive or trick, used as a promotional tool or to hide something. The term often refers to a mechanical device used for cheating with a gambling apparatus; in publicity and promotion, it usually means the hook by which the makers hope to attract interest.

Great Depression (grāt dĭ-prĕsh′ən) The worst and longest economic collapse in modern industrial society, the Great Depression in the United States began in late 1929 and lasted through the early 1940s, spreading to most of the world's other industrial countries.

gunrunning A colorful or colloquial term for the traffic and commerce in illegal weapons. In film, gunrunners are sometimes romanticized and portrayed as idealistic individuals who are motivated by the urge to aid those suffering under oppressive regimes.

heavy Another term for a motion-picture villain, usually a male character whose amoral qualities are immediately apparent (often through physique) to the viewer. The term heavy is most commonly used in reference to a villainous character in a film noir-style gangster film or a western. Many Hollywood performers became stereotyped as screen heavies, for example, Ralph Meeker, Peter Lorre, and Jack Palance.

Hitchcockian A reference to narrative and stylistic qualities within mystery-thriller motion pictures that recall the idiosyncratic work of Alfred Hitchcock, the master of the genre. In nine silent films and nearly four dozen sound pictures (plus a television series) Hitchcock created a body of psychologically rooted mystery thrillers of unusual sophistication and playfulness. Tongue-in-cheek interplay with the audience—in an effort to put the filmgoer off guard and then stun them with a surprising twist—is one particularly notable Hitchcockian characteristic.

hyperbole (hī-pûr′bə-lē) A type of speech that uses exaggeration and grandiloquence for emphasis or effect. Promoters and publicists, among others, regularly make use of hyperbole and superlatives in the promotion of actors and films.

icon (ī′kŏn′) A symbolic image or representation of something recognized as highly important or sacred. People such as actors are often referred to as icons or idols in the sense that they command a great deal of attention and devotion.

iconoclast (ī-kŏn′ə-klăst′) One who attacks or seeks to overthrow the established order or structure of authority. The term derives from the Greek, meaning smasher of religious images. In modern usage, there is a certain cachet associated with the image of someone who has sufficient courage to challenge accepted authority and conventional thought in the name of art or strong belief.

idyll (īd′l) A term used to refer both to a type of poetry, characterized by an idealized portrayal of rural life, and to a romantic interlude or event of a tranquil nature.

in-camera editing Editing performed within the camera itself. Shot and scene changes, as determined in the filming process, are left exactly as they have been filmed. The stop-and-start procedure of filming the various camera takes also serves as the editing process. In-camera editing has often been an integral part of realist filmmaking where a spontaneous quality is desired; it is also often seen in the work of experimental filmmakers who prefer to leave the shots and scenes exactly as they have been filmed, without regard for subsequent restructuring or redefining of the recorded material.

indie Slang term that refers to independent film makers or productions.

ingenue A young female character whose appeal is derived from fresh good looks and a demure personality. During the American studio years actresses who could portray ingenues were considered an important staple in a studio's stock company of contract players, along with character actresses and romantic leads. Deanna Durbin (Universal Studios) and Loretta Young (Twentieth Century-Fox) were among the many young actresses who achieved fame in ingenue roles during the 1930s.

innuendo (ĭn′yo͞o-ĕn′dō) An indirect comment or implication, usually intended to cast doubt on a person or thing.

invective (ĭn-vĕk′tĭv) Abusive or aggressive language.

iris (ī′rĭs) A laboratory transitional effect, occurring when an existing image moves into a circle that rapidly decreases in size until it disappears. Often a new shot simultaneously takes its place. If the image is wiped to black, and a reversal of the process thus brings in a new image, this is referred to as an iris-in/iris-out. The iris, like the optical wipe, is a rapid means of transition that sustains the pace of the story.

In the early development of the motion picture the iris served as a transitional device as well as a means of altering the shape of screen images and of isolating dramatic material. D. W. Griffith frequently employed a partial iris shot for the purpose of dramatic framing, for example, the close-up photograph of Lillian Gish in *The Birth of a Nation* (1915) as the Little Colonel pauses in the cotton fields. Griffith's framing through the iris adds a subjective quality to the insert of the photograph. In Robert Wiene's *The Cabinet of Dr. Caligari* (1919), an iris shot narrows in on the young storyteller's face to increase audience awareness of his anguished state.

The iris effect frequently appears in contemporary films that imitate earlier film styles, for example, Herbert Ross's *Pennies from Heaven* (1981). In Volker Schlondorff's *The Tin Drum* (1979) the aging of Anna, the mother, is achieved through a transitional iris-in/iris-out.

jump-cut The cutting together of two noncontiguous shots within a scene so that the action seems to jump ahead or back in time. A jump-cut is the opposite of a matched cut, where action appears continuous.

The jump-cut is used widely by contemporary filmmakers for varying effect. In Jean-Luc Godard's *Breathless* (1959) extensive time sequences are compressed into a few moments by selecting the peaks of a conversation or action and by discarding the boring parts. The effect of this jump-cutting is similar to that of comic-strip panels, where information is conveyed in a sequence of abrupt images rather than in fully played-out scenes. (Television commercials, with an actor plugging a product while talking to the camera, often employ this jump-cut technique.)

juxtaposition A term that refers to the expressive arrangement in film of any number of contrasting cinematic elements: the visual and the aural; the editorial arrangement, through montage, of individual shots; narrative time elements. A juxtaposition of past and present occurs in *The Godfather: Part II* (1974), as the stories of Michael and his father, set some 50 years apart are told in the same film.

kinetic (kĭ-nĕt′ĭk, kī-) Relating to or produced by motion.

labyrinth (lăb′ə-rĭnth′) A maze or other interconnected structure made up of blind passages and many turns. The term "labyrinthine" is commonly used to refer to anything exceptionally difficult, or that requires a certain mental dexterity to work through.

lampoon (lăm-pōōn′) A type of broad satire that attempts to ridicule its subject.

laser (video) disk An LP-size, double-sided video playback disc that is scanned in the manner of an audio compact disc (CD). The laser disc playback presents images with superior picture resolution and accompanying digital sound.

last-minute rescue A plotting-editing device common to screen melodramas, in which crosscutting is often used extensively to build dramatic tension before a hero's rescue. Crosscutting reveals the imminent fate of the victim and the simultaneous efforts of the rescuer to reach the victim in time. The rescue occurs at the last possible moment. D. W. Griffith incorporated last-minute rescues as a standard feature of his silent films, further enhancing the buildup of tension by the use of accelerated editing within the crosscutting, for example, *Way Down East* (1920). A form of the last-minute rescue appears as an essential element in many of the suspense melodramas of the 1970s, for example, *Two-Minute Warning* (1976), *Rollercoaster* (1977), and *Black Sunday* (1977).

law-and-order film A type of contemporary, action-oriented motion picture in which crime and disorder are conclusively brought to an end, often by a single individual who must take it upon herself or himself to correct societal wrongs. The law-and-order film shows individual courage succeeding in correcting crimes when law officials at large have refused to act or have been ineffective at getting the job done. During the 1970s the law-and-order film proliferated on American screens: the *Dirty Harry* series (1971–76), the *Walking Tall* films (1973, 1978), *Macon County Line* (1974), *Trackdown* (1976), and *Lipstick* (1976).

lead The featured actor in a motion picture.

libretto (lĭ-brĕt′ō) The text or script of a dramatic musical work, such as an opera or musical play.

location The locale at which a movie is filmed. "On location" indicates filming that is done outside the confines of a studio or sound stage setting.

love interest That situation in a motion-picture script included to provide romance. Early motion-picture producers quickly discovered the popularity of romance and amply supplied their films with romantic elements; after a while audiences came to expect romance in the film story. As a result writers often seek to fulfill this expectation even when the story might be otherwise unromantic. The love interest in *On the Waterfront* (1954), a film about union corruption and courage on the docks of New Jersey, is provided by an evolving relationship between Eva Marie Saint and Marlon Brando. In *Absence of Malice* (1981), a film about newspaper ethics, the love interest occurs when Sally Field, a reporter, and Paul Newman, the subject of a criminal investigation, become attracted to each other. Motion pictures are often admired by critics when love interest is avoided in favor of a more realistic, unromantic treatment of the plot. For example, in *Norma Rae* (1979), a film involving a textile worker (Sally Field) and a labor organizer (Ron Leibman), the potential for a romantic relationship between the two does not develop.

lynching (lĭnch′ĭng) The execution, usually by hanging, of a person without a legal trial.

macabre (mə-kä′brə, m ə-käb′, -kä ′bər) Something that suggests or shows the horror of death and bodily decay. The term is often used to refer to films of graphic horror or violence that depict death and killing in an highly realistic manner.

magnetism (măg′nĭ-tĭz′əm) In psychology, a charismatic power of ability to attract or command attention. Leading movie stars and musical performers are often characterized by a certain force of personality that draws interest independent of their performing abilities.

mainstream (mān′strēm′) A social term referring to the prevailing thoughts, influences, or activities of a specific area or period.

malefic (mə-lĕf′ĭk) Something that has or projects a malevolent or evil influence.

malfeasance (măl-fē′zəns) A term often used to refer to illegal or questionable misconduct by a public official.

manifest destiny (măn′ə-fĕst′ dĕs′tə-nē) A policy allowing expansion within a specific location that is defended as necessary or good for the community. The term is most often associated with a 19th-century doctrine that the United States had the right and duty to expand throughout the North American continent.

matinee idol A movie star. A "matinee" is an afternoon screening, still done but more common in the heyday of moviegoing—the 1940s and '50s.

maverick In sociology or politics, a person who avoids association with or membership in a specific group or political party. The term is often used to describe people with a history of making independent decisions.

medium (mē′dē-əm) Meaning literally the means by which something is conveyed, the term has come to refer to the various ways in which information and entertainment is presented, such as television, film, the World Wide Web, newspapers, or books. The plural, *media*, is often used to refer to members of the press or collectively to the presentation of information.

melodrama (mĕl′ə-drä′mə, -dr ăm′ə) A form of entertainment, characterized by somewhat exaggerated situations, heightened effects, and mood-enhancing elements such as lighting and score, intended to emphasize the effect of dramatic events.

mentor (mĕn′tôr′) A trusted counselor or teacher. The term is most often used to describe the teacher who has had significant impact or provided great guidance in the shaping or a career or lifestyle.

mercenary (mûr′sə-nĕr′ē) A professional soldier who fights for pay rather than nationalistic reasons.

metaphor (mĕt′ə-fôr′, -f ər) Something that stands for or implies the meaning of something else. The term is usually used to refer to something that may be considered a symbol of a larger reality or story.

microcosm (mī′krə-kŏz′əm) A small, contained system that is similar to, or is constructed like, and represents a larger system.

microfiche (mī′krō-fēsh′) A sheet of microfilm containing a large number of considerably reduced pages of information.

mimetic (mĭ-mĕt′ĭk, m ī-) In the performing arts, a production that uses representative or imitative means.

mise-en-scène A term that generally refers to the total elements within a film shot. Similarly, in a theatrical situation, the term refers to the total stage picture—the scenery, the properties, and the arrangement of the actors. In film criticism mise-en-scène is sometimes used to describe an approach to cinematic art that places greater emphasis on pictorial values within a shot than on the juxtaposition of two shots (montage).

mixed-media A presentation that makes use of more than one form of media for the presentation of material.

moll (mŏl) A slang term, used primarily to describe the female companion of an outlaw or organized crime figure.

monograph (mŏn′ə-grăf′) An article, essay, or other scholarly work of up to book length that deals primarily with a specific, limited subject.

montage (mŏn-täzh′, mô n-) A visual presentation comprised of a number of different elements or designs.

mores (môr′āz′, - ēz, m ōr′-) The overall term for the customs, traditions, and moral values of a social group or country.

mulatto (mo͝o-lăt′ō, -lä ′tō, my o͞o-) A term used to describe someone with one white parent and one black parent.

narration A term for the spoken words of a person who relates information in a film directly rather than through dialogue. A narrator may be a character in the film, or an anonymous, unseen "voice" that narrates the action of the story or the documentary. A narrator may talk directly into the camera or, more commonly, speak in "voice-over" narration.

natural wipe A transition technique accomplished by an element within the mise-en-scène rather than by a laboratory process. A character or an object is brought to the lens of the camera and wipes away the scene by completely blocking or blurring the frame. The natural wipe is followed by a new scene. A head-on/tail-away transition is a type of natural wipe that is used to end one scene and to reveal another.

naturalistic (năch′ər-ə-lĭs′tĭk, n ăch′rə-) Something that possesses the elements or illusion of nature, or attempts to present a subject in a natural state or environment.

newsreel (no͞oz′rēl′, ny o͞oz′-) A short, nonfictional film that deals with recent news or current events. Newsreels were a regular part of the moviegoing experience, especially in the days before television was common.

nickelodeon (nĭk′ə-lō′dē-ən) An early type of storefront movie theater. The term, first used in Pittsburgh, Pennsylvania, in 1905, derives from the cost of admission (5¢) and the Greek word for theater, *odeon*.

nightclub (nīt′klŭb′) An establishment, often open only at night, that presents food and drink, along with adult-oriented entertainment such as music and dancing.

nimbus (nĭm′bəs) An aura or radiance, usually in the form of a glow or halo, that surrounds the portrayal of a god or religious figure. In film, certain lighting effects can be used to cause this effect as a dramatic enhancement.

non sequitur (nŏn s ĕk′wĭ-tər, -t o͝or′) A statement, inference, or conclusion that does not follow logically from what has come before.

nonconformity The act or philosophy of refusing to act or be subject to accepted societal norms or standards.

nostalgia (nŏ-stăl′jə, n ə-) A slightly sad, bittersweet longing for things that remind us of or represent pleasant memories of the past.

novel (nŏv′əl) In literature, a work of fiction of some length in which characters and situations are depicted within the framework of a plot.

novella (nō-vĕl′ə) A work of fiction of a certain length, sometimes called a short novel, often characterized by a specific moral teaching or lesson.

nuance (no͞o′äns′, ny o͞o′-, n o͞o-äns′, ny o͞o-) A slight degree of emphasis, or shading, in presentation that creates a subtle difference or causes us to see things in a slightly different way.

obituary (ō-bĭch′o͞o-ĕr′ē) A brief article or essay regarding the death of a person. An obituary often contains details of a person's life, along with a list of accomplishments.

obscenity (ŏb-sĕn′ĭ-tē, ə b-) Although subject to a variety of interpretations and definitions, something, such as a word or act, that is held to be offensive, indecent, or repulsive in terms of the generally accepted moral climate.

operetta (ŏp′ə-rĕt′ə) Also known as "light opera," a theatrical production containing many of the elements of classic opera, but generally lighter in tone or substance, and often containing spoken dialogue.

original screenplay A screenplay developed from an idea conceived by the screenwriter, based on the writer's imagination: a historical event, a newspaper item, an interesting person, or a story idea for a particular film genre. Lawrence Kasdan's black comedy *I Love You to Death* (1990) was developed as an original screenplay from a news story appearing in an Allentown, Pennsylvania, paper. Robert Altman claims to have created the screenplay for *3 Women* (1977) after having a dream about three women whose lives mysteriously cross.

outré Something that violates accepted or conventional notions of propriety. In film, the term is often intended as a complement, recognizing that a film or director has pushed the boundaries and extended the traditional or accepted reach of filmmaking.

outtake A term for filmed material that is deleted in the editing process and that does not appear in the final cut. Outtake material may be removed because of flaws in the filming of a shot or a scene or simply because the film's editor opts not to use the material in the final cut. There is a particular fascination with outtake material because of what it can reveal about actors and the filmmaking process, often in very human or humorous ways. Consequently, outtakes are frequently screened on television programs. In a rare gesture, Hal Ashby inserted closing credits for *Being There* (1979) over an outtake of Peter Sellers attempting to control his laughter during the filming of a scene. Outtake material from documentaries and newsreels is also frequently used by the makers of experimental films for satirical effect. An example is Henri Erlich's *My Way* (1975), a humorous view of Richard Nixon made up largely of outtakes from government-produced newsreels.

pace The rhythm of the film. Pace refers both to the internal movement of characters and objects within the film shot and the rhythm of the film that is supplied by editing. Frenetic movement within the frame and brief, staccato shots give a sense of considerable pace to the film. Little internal movement and lengthy shots add a measured, leisurely pace to the film's progress.

pageantry (păj′ən-trē) A type of presentation or display containing formal elements of pomp, formality, or flashy display.

paleontology (pā′lē-ŏn-tŏl′ə-jē) The study in general or specifically of life forms that existed in prehistoric times, through the examination of fossils and geological evidence.

pan The movement of the camera across a scene horizontally (left to right or right to left) while mounted on a fixed base. The pan, like the tilt, is frequently used to scan a scene and to follow character movement in a limited location. Establishing shots often include pans, and sometimes tilts, to provide a more extensive view of an environment. In character movement, the camera can pan to follow an actor's walk across a room and then tilt down when the actor sinks into an easy chair.

Pans and tilts, while for the most part utilitarian, allow the director to present a scene or follow actions fully without edits that might destroy a desired mood.

pantomime (păn′tə-mīm′) A type of performance or means of communication characterized by the exclusive use of gestures and facial expressions and no dialogue, except, in certain performances, for a narrative chorus.

***par excellence* (pär ĕ k-sə-läns′)** A French term meaning the best of its kind, or without equal.

parallel development (editing) The development of two or more separate lines of action that are occurring simultaneously. Parallel development is achieved by crosscutting from one location to another to pick up the action as it progresses. In the early years of cinema this technique was referred to as the switchback because parallel editing usually does switch back in time to visualize an event; in many instances of parallel editing, however, the crosscutting shows the event in an advanced stage of time from the point where the earlier action left off.

paraplegia (păr′ə-plē′jē-ə, -j ə) (also **paraplegic**) Complete paralysis from the waist down, often caused by an injury that results in damage to the spinal cord.

parody (păr′ə-dē) In film, a type of motion picture that makes fun of another, usually more serious film. The intention and design of the parody are ridicule of the style, conventions, or motifs of a serious work. The comedies of Mel Brooks are often parodies of familiar American genres: the western (*Blazing Saddles*, 1974), the horror film (*Young Frankenstein*, 1974), the Alfred Hitchcock thriller (*High Anxiety*, 1977), the swashbuckler action film (*Robin Hood, Men in Tights*, 1993).

pastoral Most often used to refer to a lifestyle or setting that is simple, serene, or idyllic, usually possessing elements of rural life.

pathos A term derived from the Greek word for "suffering." Its application to dramatic, literary, or cinematic expression refers to the feelings of compassion or pity evoked for a character or group of characters. In its most common application, pathos refers to aroused emotions that result from the unrelieved suffered of a helpless but dignified character. The hero is an unfortunate victim of general conditions rather than innate character flaws.

It has been said that Hamlet's character evokes a sense of tragedy, while Ophelia's character stimulates pathos.

period Material, such as costumes or settings, that are indicative of a particular historical era. Period details are considered essential to the dramatic effect and credibility of motion pictures.

period piece In film, a work that is set in and is more or less bounded by the conventions of a certain historical period. The use of this specific term to describe a film is meant to emphasize the importance of the locale and time period to the plot, and such films are often judged by the accuracy and realism of specific motifs such as costume, dialogue, and settings.

persona (pər-sō′nə) The role an actor assumes. Persona implies an in-depth understanding and playing of the character beyond the superficial or merely visual depth.

picaresque (pĭk′ə-rĕsk′, pē′kə-) In literature or film, a plot or story that involves roguish heroes and high adventure.

pietá In art, the representation of the Virgin Mary mourning over the dead body of Christ.

plantation (plăn-tā′shən) A term originating in colonial times, a plantation is a settlement or piece of land used to grow crops and houses the workers who tend the crops. The land was independently owned and self-contained, often housing the owner of the land as well.

pluralism (plo͝or′ə-lĭz′əm) The political theory or belief that a nation or society benefits from the coexistence and influence of citizens of various and varied ethnic backgrounds and traditions.

polymorphism (pŏl′ē-môr′fĭz′əm) (also **polymorphous)** The occurrence or presentation of varied forms or types of the same subject. From a biological term indicating the diversity of individual organisms within the same species.

pornography (pôr-nŏg′rə-fē) The depiction, in literature, film or photography, of material that is considered obscene or indecent according to the generally accepted views and morals of a society or culture.

posse (pŏs′ē) A group of people summoned by a sheriff or other law officer to aid in law enforcement.

posthumous (pŏs′chə-məs) Of or continuing after a person's death.

pratfall (prăt′fôl′) Literally, a fall on the buttocks, in physical humor an intentional and often exaggerated fall or humiliating error or failure intended to provoke laughter.

preparatory school (prĭ-păr′ə-tôr′ē skōōl) Commonly called "prep school," an private educational establishment that serves to prepare students for college.

preproduction (prē′prə-dŭk′shən) In film, the various aspects of creating a motion picture that must be completed before the actual shooting of scenes begins. These usually include casting, financing, and arranging for the availability of locations or other facilities.

prequel (prē′kwəl) In literature and film, a type of sequel in which the events and characteristics portrayed predate those of the original film. For example, *The Phantom Menace* is set a number of years before the events that are portrayed in the linear narrative that begins with *Star Wars* and continues through its direct sequels, *The Empire Strikes Back* and *The Return of the Jedi*.

prime time A period in the evening, currently designated by the Federal Communications Commission as between 7 and 11 P.M., when the largest television audience is available and watching.

profanity (prō-făn′ĭ-tē, pr ə-) Language or the use of language that is considered indecent or obscene according to the generally accepted views and morals of a society or culture.

Prohibition (prō′ə-bĭsh′ən) The legal ban on the production and sale of alcoholic beverages. The Prohibition Act, also referred to as the Volstead Act, went into effect on January 15, 1920. It was repealed on December 5, 1933.

prologue (prō′lôg′, -l ŏg′) A short, introductory piece in literature or the performing arts, that may serve to familiarize the audience with settings or events leading up to the commencement of the book or performance. A prologue is often used to establish the mood of a piece, or present a character or event that will be revealed or have significant effect at a later point.

props Manufactured or imported objects brought on to a location, set, or stage to add realism or effect to a play or motion picture.

protagonist (prō-tăg′ə-nĭst) The main character in a film or literary work. The protagonist usually possesses recognizably good qualities, and is often the hero of the story.

protégé (prō′tə-zhā′, pr ō′tə-zhā′) A person who is provided for, and trained in a specific career by an influential person within that field.

prototype (prō′tə-tīp′) An original model or concept, on which future versions are based. In film, an established, early example of a genre or type that serves as a standard by which others are made or may be judged.

psychodrama In film, a type of experimental film characterized by psychological, specifically Freudian, approaches to self-exploration.

punch line In a joke, the line, phrase or word, usually given at the very end, that makes the joke funny.

realism (rē′ə-lĭz′əm) A philosophical discipline that inclines toward truth and pragmatism. In art, the representation of objects as they actually appear.

Reconstruction (rē′kən-strŭk′shən) The term used for the rebuilding plan established for the southern, formerly Confederate states following the American Civil War.

remake (rē-māk′) A new production or alternative version of a previously produced work. In film, a remake may be a faithful reproduction of an earlier release, or a new movie "based on" or "inspired by" the original. In some cases, a property, such as a famous novel, may be redone by various directors; if there exists a definitive filmed version, the new production may be referred to as a remake.

repertoire (also **repertory, repertory theater**) The stock of performance numbers, such as songs or plays, performed by a player or company. The terms repertory and repertory theater refer to the players and to the type of entertainment in general.

retrospective (rĕt′rə-spĕk′tĭv) A celebratory look back on the work of an individual, or a review of the history of a specific genre. Most often, a retrospective will assume a narrative format and attempt to present the body of work under discussion in a historical or chronological format, often interspersed with commentary or a sample of contemporary criticism or reaction.

revival (rĭ-vī´vəl) As most often applied to the production of a theatrical play or musical, a new production of a work that has not been performed for some time. As a distinct and important class of theater, revivals often offer new perspectives of classic works as interpreted by different generations or producers.

road picture A type of picture or genre that includes films in which the characters and plot are centered on situations that develop within exotic locations, or involve a trip or journey during which the characters discover certain social, political, and cultural realities.

satire (săt´īr´) A sometimes caustic or acerbic work of literature or performing arts in which human folly or errors are attacked using irony, sharp humor, and wit.

scenario (sĭ-nâr´ē-ō´, -när´-, -năr´-) In drama and film, the outline or model of a specific scene or setting. The scenario may include physical characteristics of the scene, such as setting, and dramatic elements such as the characters' mood or state of mind.

score In theater and film, the musical backdrop that accompanies the progression of the performance. A score contains a variety of tempos and themes intended to highlight specific scenes, and is often tied together by a central melody or passage that represents the musical signature of the production.

screenplay (skrēn´plā´) The script on which a movie is based, containing dialogue, scenarios, and camera directions.

screwball (skro͞o´bôl´) A type of comedy, characterized by zany, off-the-wall characterizations, situations, and results. The term derives from a baseball pitch, a type of curve ball that reacts in an opposite and unexpected way.

secede (sĭ-sēd´) To formally withdraw from a union or branch.

seductress (sĭ-dŭk´trĭs) A woman who seduces or through act or appearance inspires the allusion of or control in a sexual sense.

segregation (sĕg´rĭ-gā´shən) To be separated, usually through force, from the mainstream for reasons of race or creed. The term is most often used to refer to the forced separation of blacks and whites, most notable in the southern United States.

seminary (sĕm′ə-nĕr′ē) A school with the focus of training religious leaders such as priests, ministers, or rabbis.

semiotics (sē′mē-ŏt′ĭks, s ĕm′ē-, s ē′mī-) Another term for semantics, or the study or science of the meaning or words and language usage.

sequel (sē′kwəl) In literature or film, a new production that continues the story and/or characters of a previous work. There are a number of different types of sequels, of which the most common are "direct," in which case the action takes place directly following the conclusion of its predecessor, or "indirect," in which the situations and characters presented earlier become the basic structure on which the new work is based. *The Empire Strikes Back*, which continues with the same central characters and storyline from *Star Wars*, is an example of a "direct" sequel; *Indiana Jones and the Temple of Doom* is an example of an "indirect" sequel, as it presents an entirely new adventure, maintaining only the central character and overall premise of the original *Raiders of the Lost Ark.*

serial A type of short film characterized primarily by the episodic development of a story presented in installments over a period of several weeks. Movie serials were the precursors and inspiration for serial episodic television shows such as soap operas and miniseries.

set In film and theater, the stage or setting in which the action of a scene takes place. As opposed to "location," a set implies a created place, usually within the confines of a theater or movie studio sound stage.

Shakespearean Of or relating to the plays and characters of William Shakespeare. An actor may be referred to as Shakespearean if he is known for his portrayal of one or more of the signature characters from Shakespeare's plays.

shorts Also known as short subject films, brief movies shown as part of a larger theatrical program, often preceding the presentation of the feature film.

shrapnel (shrăp′nəl) Smaller projectiles within the casing of a bomb or artillery shell that is designed to explode on impact, or the fragments of metal from an exploding shell.

siren (sī′rən) Based on a character from Greek mythology, one of a group of sea nymphs whose sweet singing lured ships and sailors to their destruction, the term commonly refers to a beautiful, alluring, or tempting woman.

slapstick A type of humor characterized by harmless cruelty or horseplay between two or more people, designed for laughs.

sleeper A term used to refer to a surprise hit. In film, a picture made for very little money, or not widely promoted, that succeeds at the box office is referred to as a sleeper.

slow-motion In film, a technique in which the apparent speed of the film is slowed, so that events appear to take place at a slower pace than in live or original action.

soap opera A serial drama, most often appearing on broadcast network television during daytime hours, characterized by exaggerated drama or melodrama, often implausible situations, and stock characters. The term derived from the original sponsors, soap companies, which were targeting the primarily female, stay-at-home audience.

socialite (sō′shə-līt′) A person prominent in fashionable social circles. The term is often used to refer to women who are identified primarily with their place and role in high society.

special effects Any of many various artificially created effects created to enhance a motion picture. These include such elements as sound, lighting, and recently, computer-generated scenes and characters, all of which are incorporated with the basic photography and cinematography of a film to create effects that would be otherwise impossible or prohibitively difficult.

spectacle (spĕk′tə-kəl) A type of film characterized by lavish sets, exotic locations, and broad, vivid cinematography. Many of the movies associated with the term are historical, epic costume dramas, such as Cecil B. DeMille's *The Ten Commandments*.

stand-up comedy The performance of a comedic act on stage before a live audience.

static (stăt′ĭk) Unmoving or unchanging. The term also refers to the electronic interference prevalent on broadcast television signals received directly via antenna.

statuette (stăch′o͞o-ĕt′) Literally, a small statue. In the performing arts the term is most often used to refer to a physical award, such as the Oscar, which is in fact a small statue.

status quo (stā′təs kwō) The state of affairs as they exist.

stereophonic (stĕr′ē-ə-fŏn′ĭk, stîr ′-) A recording technique in which recorded sound is divided into two separate streams, or channels. Commonly known as "stereo," the effect is a more natural distribution of sound.

stereotype (stĕr′ē-ə-tīp′, stîr ′-) A simplified or representative image of a thing or person. It is commonly used to refer to a broad portrayal that strongly exhibits recognizable characteristics, often to the point of parody.

stigmatized (stĭg′mə-tīz′d) Something that has been characterized as disgraceful or shameful.

structuralism An anthropological method of evaluating what films reveal about broad cultural patterns of human behavior

studio (stōō′dē-ō, sty ōō′-) In the motion picture industry, the general term for any of the companies, such as Warner Bros., involved in the production and distribution of movies. In the early days of Hollywood, the studios had immense control over virtually every aspect of the movie business.

subplot (sŭb′plŏt′) In literature and film, a line of story, or plot, subordinate to the main storyline.

suburbia (sə-bûr′bē-ə) The smaller cities and towns surrounding a major metropolitan area. The term is also used to refer collectively to the inhabitants and culture of suburban areas.

summer stock (also **stock**, **stock theater**, **stock companies**) Theatrical productions held during the summer months, performed by a revolving company of players, usually young or apprentice actors, often centered around a core group of professionals or a single star. Stock companies frequently draw on a core group of well-known, classic plays and musicals, and are based in a specific region or locale.

superhero (sōō′pər-hîr′ō) A figure who possesses superhuman powers and abilities. The concept of the superhero originated in cartoon strips and comic books, with characters, such as Superman, who are most often depicted fighting crime and evil.

superimposed (sōō′pər-ĭm-pōz′d) Something that has been laid or placed atop something else.

surrealism A movement in literature and fine arts that emphasized the role of the unconscious in creative activity, and employed it in an orderly and serious manner. Surrealism was founded by French critic and poet

André Breton (1896–1966), and grew out of the movement known as Dadaism. Artists associated with surrealism include Salvador Dali, William Blake, photographer Man Ray, and Pablo Picasso.

surrogate (sûr′ə-gĭt, -gāt′, s ŭr′-) Something that takes the place or serves in the stead of the primary or natural article; a replacement or substitute.

suspense film (thriller) A motion picture whose plot creates a high level of anxiety and tension through concern for the fate of the principal character or characters. In the suspense thriller life itself is often threatened—usually as a result of the principal character's potentially deadly situations. As the plot builds toward resolution, the threat and, thus, suspense increase. Alfred Hitchcock is often referred to as the master of the suspense thriller, for example, *Rear Window* (1954) and *Psycho* (1960). *Marathon Man* (1976), *Black Sunday* (1977), *Coma* (1978), *When a Stranger Calls* (1979), *Fatal Attraction* (1987), and *The Hand That Rocks the Cradle* (1992) are other examples of suspense thrillers.

sweeten (sound) To embellish an element of a sound track, usually by giving the sound greater presence or clarity. The term is most often applied to the work of documentarists, including cinema-verité filmmakers, who enhance elements of the sound track for the purpose of adding atmosphere or thematic impact. In Frederick Wiseman's *High School* (1969) a Simon and Garfunkel song played on a tape recorder by an English teacher is "sweetened" so that the thematic relevance of the lyrics is not lost to the viewer. The song is given full presence so that it has high-fidelity clarity rather than the sound of a piece of music picked up in a classroom.

symbiosis (sĭm′bē-ō′sĭs, -bī-) (also **symbiotic**) A relationship in which two or more entities of different species or type are dependent on one another for survival. The term is used figuratively in the business world to indicate relationships between partners dependent on one other to accomplish certain projects.

tabloid (tăb′loid′) A term used primarily to refer to a type of sensationalist newspapers and magazines that specializes in exposés of prominent people and celebrities. The name also refers to a standard paper size and format used by many newspapers, symbolic of an economic production that also requires that stories be presented in condensed or concise form.

taboo (tə-bo͞o′, tă-) A type of social ban, often resulting from strong custom or as a protective measure.

take A run of the camera for the purpose of filming a shot or a scene. Each run of the camera from start to finish is referred to as a take.

talkies The popular term for motion pictures with accompanying sound and dialogue.

taxidermy (tăk′sĭ-dûr′mē) The skill or business of preparing the skins of dead animals for stuffing, mounting, and display in a lifelike state.

teaser A scene that precedes the opening credits of a motion picture and that is designed to develop audience interest in the story that will follow the credits. Often in contemporary film, the credits are superimposed over the teaser material.

temptress (tĕmp′trĭs) Another term for a seductress, an alluring or seductive woman who uses her feminine wiles to tempt men into illegal or ill-advised behavior.

tenure (tĕn′yər, -y o͝or′) Most commonly used to refer to the period of time for which one has held a certain position. It may also be use to refer to the rights or privileges granted by the fact of long-established occupation or employment, as in the "tenure" of a college professor.

theme song In television, the signature melody or song played during the introduction or opening credits of each episode. The term may also refer to any tune particularly identified with a specific person or event.

trade papers Publications intended for and containing information specific to the film industry, such as *Variety*.

tragedienne In literature, theater, or film, a tragic female figure, or female subject to tragedy.

troupe (tro͞op) A touring group or company of actors or other performers. The term is also used to indicate the act of touring with such a company.

typecasting Selecting an actor for a certain role because of physical or professional qualities that make the actor ideally suited to play the character. In the motion-picture medium, where physique is all-important, typecasting is the rule rather than the exception. Once an actor has developed an appealing screen persona, the tendency is to repeat that image from film to film.

underground (ŭn′dər-ground′) Generally used to refer to a movement or organization that works secretly against the ruling government or establishment.

unguent (ŭng′gwənt) An ointment or salve for soothing or healing; a balm.

union (yo͞on′yən) (also **unionization**) Also called a craft or trade union, an organization or association of workers established to improve or protect their working conditions.

urbane (ûr-bān′) A personality trait or characteristic characterized by a refined, sophisticated, elegant manner. The term is most often associated with men who are recognized as being comfortable in formal social situations.

vamp (vămp) Another term for seductress or temptress, indicating a woman who uses seductive wiles or sex appeal to entice and trap men.

vaudeville (vôd′vĭl′, v ōd′-, vô ′də-) A type of theatrical entertainment, most often made up of a variety of separate elements, popular in the United States in the late 19th and early 20th centuries.

verisimilitude Something that possesses the qualities of being true or real.

vigil (vĭj′əl) A watch or ritual devotion, often performed during normal sleeping hours, either in observation of a specific person or place or in preparation for a holy day.

vigilante (vĭj′ə-lăn′tē) A person who takes the law and the administration of justice into his or her own hands. The term was popularized and romanticized during the heyday of western movies, which sometimes cast the lone survivor of some grievous misdeed as the sole source of justice, a role an ineffective or indifferent legal system could not or would not fill.

virtuoso (vûr′cho͞o-ō′sō, -z ō) Most often used to refer to a person with exceptional or masterful musical skills in instrument or voice.

VistaVision A wide-screen process first attempted as early as 1919 and redeveloped at Paramount Pictures in 1953. The VistaVision system was designed to permit the projection of sharp, wide-screen images without the addition of new equipment. In the filming process, picture frames were photographed horizontally in the camera, rather than vertically, allowing for a frame size almost three times the width of a 35mm frame. The strip permitted ordinary methods of screen projection for higher and wider images. *White Christmas* (1954) and *Strategic Air Command* (1959) successfully utilized the VistaVision method.

voice-over The use of film narration, commentary, subjective thought, or dialogue in which the speaker or speakers remain unseen. The most frequent use of voice-over occurs in documentary and instructional films that are said to be narrated. The device is also used in dramatic films for narrative expositions and, frequently, to suggest a person's thoughts while that person is shown on the screen.

voyeur (voi-yûr′) A person who derives lascivious pleasure from the act of watching, often from a secret or concealed location, others engaged in sexual activities or in the nude.

waif (wāf) A term commonly used to refer to a homeless or directionless person, often an abandoned or orphaned child. The term is also used to describe an adult, most often a woman, with childlike qualities or an aura of innocence.

walk-on A small, usually minor role, in which an actor walks on screen, possibly has limited dialogue, and then walks off. Many major stars, including Harrison Ford of *Star Wars* and Indiana Jones fame, first appeared on film in walk-on roles.

watershed (wô′tər-shĕd′, wŏt′ər-) From the term used to define a ridge of high land that marks the division of drainage between different river systems, a superlative that refers to a critical work or turning point that marks a change in direction or thinking from what has come before.

western A film genre, characterized by locations in or representing the American west, characters drawn from or based on popular historical or quasi-historical figures or folklore archetypes, and occurring in predominantly 19th-century settings. The romance and mythology of the settling of the western United States were among the earliest and most enduring subjects for motion pictures.

wunderkind (vo͝on′dər-kĭnd′, wŭn′-) From the German meaning "wonder child," or child prodigy, a term that has come to mean anyone who shows exceptional skills or aptitude, or achieves considerable success, at a young age.

Suggested Reading List

BOOKS, ARTICLES, AND WEB SITES ABOUT AMERICAN FILM

GENERAL SOURCES

BOOKS

Acker, Ally. *Reel Women: Pioneers of the Cinema, 1896 to the Present*. Continuum, 1991.

Cross, Robin. *2000 movies, the 1940's*. Arlington House, 1985.

———. *2000 movies, the 1950's*. Arlington House, 1989.

Diawara, Manthia, ed. *Black American Cinema*. Routledge, 1993.

Eastman, John. *Retakes: Behind the Scenes of 500 Classic Movies*. Ballantine Books, 1989.

Ellis, Jack. *A History of Film*. Prentice Hall, 1995.

Harkness, John. *The Academy Awards Handbook*. Pinnacle Books, 1996.

Maltin, Leonard. *Leonard Maltin's Movie Encyclopedia*. Penguin Books, 1995.

Mast, Gerald. *A Short History of the Movies*. Allyn and Bacon, 1996.

Morgan, Robin, and George Perry, eds. *The Book of Film Biographies: A Pictorial Guide to 1000 Makers of the Cinema*. Fromm, 1997.

Osborne, Robert A. *70 Years of the Oscar: The Official History of the Academy Awards*. Abbeville Press, 1999.

Parkinson, David. *The History of Film*. Thames and Hudson, 1996.

Pickard, Roy. *The Oscar Movies*. Facts on File, 1994.

Shipman, David. *Cinema: The First Hundred Years*. St. Martin's Press, 1993.

Thompson, Kristin, and David Bordwell. *Film History: An Introduction*. McGraw Hill, 1994.

Wiley, Mason. *Inside Oscar: The Unofficial History of the Academy Awards*. Ballantine Books, 1996.

ARTICLES

"Academy Awards." *Entertainment Weekly*, March 1995 (Special Collector's Issue).

"America goes Hollywood." *Newsweek*, June 28, 1999 (series of articles spanning century of film).

"100 greatest stars." *Entertainment Weekly*, Fall 1996 (Special Collector's Issue).

Ragan, James. "Through a lens darkly: best pic winners, noms often reflect 'temper of times.' " *Variety*, January 12, 1998.

VIDEORECORDINGS

American Cinema. FoxVideo (New York Center for Visual History in coproduction with KCET and the BBC), 1995.

The Library of Congress and Smithsonian Video Present America's First Women Filmmakers. Library of Congress, 1993.

Twentieth Century-Fox: The First 50 Years. 20th Century-Fox Home Entertainment, 1997.

WEB SITES

Academy of Motion Picture Arts and Sciences
http://www.oscars.org/

AFI's 100 YEARS . . . 100 MOVIES (America's Greatest Movies)
http:// www.filmsite.org/afi100films.html

Entertainment Weekly
http://cgi.pathfinder.com/ew/

The Hollywood Reporter
http://www.hollywoodreporter.com/

Internet Movie Database
http://www.imdb.com/

TheOscar.com
http://www.theoscar.com/index.html

The Palace (Classic Films)
http://moderntimes.com/palace/

The Silents Majority
http://www.mdle.com/ClassicFilms/

Variety Extra
http://www.variety.com/

SOURCES FOR INDIVIDUAL ARTICLES

ACADEMY OF MOTION PICTURE ARTS AND SCIENCES

Harkness, John. *The Academy Awards Handbook*. Pinnacle Books, 1996.

Holden, Anthony. *Behind the Oscars: The Secret History of the Academy Awards*. Simon & Schuster, 1993.

Osborne, Robert A. *70 Years of the Oscar: The Official History of the Academy Awards*. Abbeville Press, 1999.

Pickard, Roy. *The Oscar Movies*. Facts on File, 1994.

Wiley, Mason. *Inside Oscar: The Unofficial History of the Academy Awards*. Ballantine Books, 1996.

Academy of Motion Picture Arts and Sciences http://www.oscars.org/

ACTING

Bernard, Jami. *First Films: Illustrious, Obscure, and Embarrassing Movie Debuts*. Carol Publishing Group, 1993.

Cardullo, Bert, et al., eds. *Playing to the Camera: Film Actors Discuss Their Craft*. Yale University Press, 1998.

Young, Jordan R. *Reel Characters: Great Movie Character Actors*. Past Times Publishing, 1986.

Zucker, Carole, ed. *Figures of Light: Actors and Directors Illuminate the Art of Film Acting*. Plenum Press, 1995.

———, ed. *Making Visible the Invisible: An Anthology of Original Essays on Film Acting*. Scarecrow Press, 1990.

ADAPTATION

Cartmell, Deborah, and Imelda Whelehan, eds. *Adaptations: From Text to Screen, Screen to Text*. Routledge, 1999.

Griffith, James. *Adaptations as Imitations: Films from Novels*. University of Delaware Press, 1997.

McDougal, Stuart. *Made into Movies: From Literature to Film*. Holt Rinehart and Winston, 1997.

Seger, Linda. *The Art of Adaptation: Turning Fact and Fiction into Film*. Henry Holt, 1992.

Tibbetts, John C., and James M. Welsh. *The Encyclopedia of Novels into Film*. Facts on File, 1998.

AFRICAN QUEEN, THE

Burns, Carole. "Now playing on the Connecticut River: return of the African Queen; a chance to ride the river, like Rosie and Mr. Allnut, but no leeches!" *New York Times*, July 1, 1996.

Forester, Cecil Scott (C. S.). *The African Queen*. Little, Brown, 1984.

Hepburn, Katharine. *The Making of the African Queen, or, How I Went to Africa with Bogart, Bacall, and Huston and Almost Lost My Mind*. Knopf, 1987.

McCarty, Clifford, and Lauren Bacall. *The Complete Films of Humphrey Bogart*. Citadel Press, 1994.

ALL ABOUT EVE

Brozan, Nadine. "Real 'Eve' sues to film rest of her story." *New York Times*, February 7, 1989.

Gussow, Mel. "The man who made 'All About Eve' recalls his sometimes bumpy ride." *New York Times*, November 24, 1992.

O'Toole, Lawrence. "'All About Eve': fasten your seat belts for a backstage peek at a classic Broadway tale." *Entertainment Weekly*, March 1995.

Ringgold, Gene. *Bette Davis, Her Films and Career*. Citadel Press, 1985.

ALL QUIET ON THE WESTERN FRONT

"Acting with a Conscience." *U.S. News and World Report*, January 13, 1997 (obituary of Lew Ayres).

Kelly, Andrew. *Filming All Quiet on the Western Front*. Tauris, 1998.

Remarque, Erich Maria. *All Quiet on the Western Front*. Fawcett Books, 1995.

ALLEN, WOODY

Brode, Douglas. *The Films of Woody Allen*. Carol Publishing Group, 1997.

Dowd, Maureen. "Diane and Woody: still a fun couple." *New York Times*, August 15, 1993.

Fox, Julian. *Woody: Movies from Manhattan*. Overlook Press, 1996.

Girgus, Sam B. *The Films of Woody Allen*. Cambridge University Press, 1993.

Gopnik, Adam. "The Outsider." *The New Yorker*, October 25, 1993.

Nichols, Mary P. *Reconstructing Woody: Art, Love, and Life in the Films of Woody Allen*. Rowman and Littlefield, 1998.

ALTMAN, ROBERT

Ascher-Walsh, Rebecca. "The Player: In the fickle Hollywood he's toiled in for more than 40 years, Robert Altman still makes movies with a breath of fresh flair." *Entertainment Weekly*, April 16, 1999.

Kagan, Norman. *American Skeptic: Robert Altman's Genre-Commentary Films*. Pierian Press, 1982.

Keyssar, Helene. *Robert Altman's America*. Oxford University Press, 1991.

McGilligan, Patrick. *Robert Altman: Jumping Off the Cliff*. St. Martin's Press, 1991.

O'Brien, Daniel. *Robert Altman: Hollywood Survivor*. Continuum, 1995.

AMADEUS

Clarke, Gerald. "Eight cheers for the music man; it's mostly Mozart, as Amadeus sweeps the Oscars." *Time*, April 8, 1985.

Kael, Pauline. "Amadeus." *The New Yorker*, October 29, 1984 (review).

Stark, John. "Going home to Prague to film Amadeus evokes bittersweet memories for Milos Forman." *People Weekly*, October 8, 1984.

AMERICAN GRAFFITI

Bart, Peter. "'George and Francis show' returns; twenty-five years after 'American Graffiti,' Lucas and Coppola seem re-energized as they embark on separate strategies." *Variety*, July 27, 1998.

Lucas, George. *American Graffiti: A Screenplay*. Random House, 1975.

Nashawaty, Chris. "American Graffiti: Has it really been a quarter century since this classic youth movie went to the oscars?" *Entertainment Weekly*, March 1, 1999.

Pollock, Dale. *Skywalking: The Life and Films of George Lucas*. Da Capo Press, 1999.

AMERICAN IN PARIS, AN

Harvey, Stephen. *Directed by Vincente Minnelli*. Harper & Row, 1989.

Hirschhorn, Clive. *Gene Kelly: A Biography*. St. Martin's Press, 1984.

Krebs, Albin. "Gene Kelly, dancer of vigor and grace, dies." *New York Times*, February 3, 1996 (obituary).

Morley, Sheridan. *Gene Kelly: A Celebration*. Trafalgar Square, 1998.

Naremore, James. *The Films of Vincente Minnelli*. Cambridge University Press, 1993.

O'Toole, Lawrence. "The happy hoofer." *Entertainment Weekly*, February 16, 1996 (obituary of Gene Kelly).

ANDERSON, LINDSAY

Cocks, Jay. "Lindsay Anderson: 1923–1994; in celebration." *Film Comment*, November–December 1994.

Graham, Allison. *Lindsay Anderson*. Twayne Publishers, 1981.

Hedling, Erik. *Lindsay Anderson: Maverick Film Maker*. Cassell, 1999.

Kenny, Glenn. "The magnificent Anderson." *Entertainment Weekly*, September 16, 1994.

ANIMATION

Bendazzi, Giannalberto. *Cartoons: One Hundred Years of Cinema Animation*. Indiana University Press, 1994.

Culhane, Shamus. *Animation from Script to Screen*. St. Martin's Press, 1990.

Grant, John. *The Encyclopedia of Walt Disney's Animated Characters*. Hyperion, 1998.

Solomon, Charles. *The History of Animation: Enchanted Drawings*. Wings Books, 1994.

Taylor, Richard. *Encyclopedia of Animation Techniques*. Running Press, 1996.

ANNIE HALL

(see also Woody Allen and Diane Keaton)

Purtell, Tim. "Bringing up 'Annie.' " *Entertainment Weekly*, September 18, 1992.

Willman, Chris. "'Hall' of Fame: In 1977, Annie Hall opened our eyes to New Yorkers in love and the versatility of the necktie." *Entertainment Weekly*, April 16, 1999.

ANTHOLOGY FILM

Steritt, David. "Archive dedicated to art of cinema." *Christian Science Monitor*, June 20, 1989.

Anthology Film Archives
http://www.anthologyfilmarchives.org/

APARTMENT, THE

(see also Billy Wilder)

Baltake, Joe. *Jack Lemmon: His Films and Career*. Citadel Press, 1986.

Dick, Bernard. *Billy Wilder*. Da Capo Press, 1996.

MacLaine, Shirley. *My Lucky Stars: A Hollywood Memoir*. Bantam Books, 1995.

ASTAIRE, FRED

Adler, Bill. *Fred Astaire: A Wonderful Life*. Carroll and Graf, 1987.

Billman, Larry. *Fred Astaire*. Greenwood Press, 1997.

Caron, Leslie. "Change partners." *Newsweek*, June 28, 1999.

Croce, Arlene. *The Fred Astaire and Ginger Rogers Book*. Vintage Books, 1977.

Mueller, John E. *Astaire Dancing: The Musical Films*. Knopf, 1985.

AUTEUR

Spines, Christine, and Anne Thompson. "Auteurs de force." *Premiere*, October 1997.

The Auteur Newsletter
http://www.tk-productions.com/auteur/

AVANT-GARDE

(see also Experimental film)

Brakhage, Stan. *Film at Wit's End: Eight Avant-garde Filmmakers*. Documentext, 1989.

Ferguson, Russell, ed. *Art and Film Since 1945: Hall of Mirrors*. Monacelli Press, 1996.

Horak, Jan-Christopher. *Lovers of Cinema: The First American Film Avant-garde, 1919–1945*. University of Wisconsin Press, 1995.

Suarez, Juan Antonio. *Bike Boys, Drag Queens, and Superstars: Avant-garde, Mass Culture, and Gay Identities in the 1960s Underground Cinema*. Indiana University Press, 1996.

BACALL, LAUREN

Bacall, Lauren. *Lauren Bacall: By Myself*. Ballantine Books, 1994.

———. *Now*. Knopf, 1994.

Hepburn, Katharine. *The Making of The African Queen, or, How I Went to Africa with Bogart, Bacall, and Huston and Almost Lost My Mind*. Knopf, 1987.

Royce, Brenda Scott. *Lauren Bacall*. Greenwood Press, 1993.

Sperber, A. M., and Eric Lax. "Bogart and Bacall." *Vanity Fair*, February 1997.

BARA, THEDA

Genini, Ronald. *Theda Bara: A Biography of the Silent Screen Vamp*. McFarland, 1996.

Golden, Eve. *Vamp: The Rise and Fall of Theda Bara*. Emprise, 1996.

BELASCO TENDENCY

Belasco, David. *Theatre Through Its Stage Door*. Ayer, 1968.

Leiter, Samuel L. *From Belasco to Brook: Representative Directors of the English-speaking Stage*. Greenwood Press, 1991.

BEN-HUR

(see also William Wyler)

The Art of Illusion: One Hundred Years of Hollywood Special Effects (videorecording). Smithsonian Video, 1995.

Chase, Donald. "My favorite year: 1959." *Film Comment*, September–October 1994.

Petrikin, Chris. "Heston and Vidal tell conflicting tales." *Variety*, October 16, 1995.

Wallace, Lew. *Ben Hur*. Oxford University Press, 1998.

BERGMAN, INGRID

Bergman, Ingrid. *Ingrid Bergman, My Story*. Delacorte Press, 1980.

"Ingrid Bergman." *Entertainment Weekly*, Fall 1996 (Special Collector's Issue).

Kennedy, Dana. "Ingrid Bergman." *Entertainment Weekly*, March 1995 (Special Collector's Issue).

Leamer, Laurence. *As Time Goes By: The Life of Ingrid Bergman*. Harper & Row, 1986.

Quirk, Lawrence J. *The Complete Films of Ingrid Bergman*. Citadel Press, 1989.

Spoto, Donald. *Notorious: The Life of Ingrid Bergman*. HarperCollins, 1997.

BEST YEARS OF OUR LIVES, THE

(see also William Wyler)

Purdum, Todd S. "To pay debts, veteran sells an oscar won in 'Best Years.' " *New York Times*, August 7, 1992.

BIRTH OF A NATION, THE

Grimes, William. "Can a film be both racist and classic?" *New York Times*, April 27, 1994.

Haskell, Molly. "In 'The Birth of a Nation,' the birth of serious fun." *New York Times*, November 20, 1995.

Lang, Robert, ed. *The Birth of a Nation*. Rutgers University Press, 1994.

Mico, Ted, et al., eds. *Past Imperfect: History According to the Movies*. Henry Holt, 1995.

Simmon, Scott. *The Films of D. W. Griffith*. Cambridge University Press, 1993.

BLAXPLOITATION FILMS

Bogle, Donald. *Toms, Coons, Mulattoes, Mammies, and Bucks: An Interpretive History of Blacks in American Films*. Continuum, 1994.

James, Darius. *That's Blaxploitation!* St. Martin's Griffin, 1995.

Rhines, Jesse Algeron. *Black Film/White Money*. Rutgers University Press, 1996.

BONNIE AND CLYDE

(see also Faye Dunaway)

Brode, Douglas. *Money, Women, and Guns: Crime Movies from Bonnie and Clyde to the Present*. Carol Publishing Group, 1995.

Carnes, Mark C., ed. *Past Imperfect: History According to the Movies*. Henry Holt, 1995.

Friedman, Lester D., ed. *Arthur Penn's "Bonnie and Clyde."* Cambridge University Press, 1999.

Milner, E. R. *The Lives and Times of Bonnie and Clyde*. Southern Illinois University Press, 1996.

BOW, CLARA

Goodman, Walter. "In the age of the flapper there was one who had it." *New York Times*, June 14, 1999.

Sayre, Nora. "Appreciating the flapper who put the 'it' in an era." *New York Times*, June 18, 1999.

Stenn, David. *Clara Bow: Runnin' Wild*. Doubleday, 1988.

B-PICTURE

Corman, Roger. *How I Made a Hundred Movies in Hollywood and Never Lost a Dime*. Da Capo Press, 1998.

Kuhn, Annette, ed. *Queen of the 'B's*. Greenwood Press, 1995.

McCarthy, Todd, and Charles Flynn, eds. *Kings of the Bs: Working Within the Hollywood System*. Dutton, 1975.

Turner, Steve. *Saddle Gals: A Filmography of Females in B-Westerns of the Sound Era*. Empire Publishing, 1995.

BRANDO, MARLON

Brando, Marlon. *Brando: Songs My Mother Taught Me*. Random House, 1994.

Grobel, Lawrence. *Conversations with Brando*. Hyperion, 1991.

Manso, Peter. *Brando: The Biography*. Hyperion, 1995.

Nickens, Christopher. *Brando: A Biography in Photographs*. Doubleday, 1987.

Sauter, Michael. "Marlon Brando: the defiant one." *Entertainment Weekly*, Fall 1996 (Special Collector's Issue).

BREAKFAST AT TIFFANY'S

Capote, Truman. *Breakfast at Tiffany's and Three Stories*. Vintage Books, 1993.

Edwards, Blake. "Hollywood's fair lady: Audrey Hepburn received a 1961 Academy Award nomination for 'Breakfast at Tiffany's.'" *Newsweek*, June 28, 1999.

Lehman, Peter. *Blake Edwards*. Ohio University Press, 1981.

O'Toole, Lawrence. "Closet classics: vanishing gay characters." *Entertainment Weekly*, August 28, 1992.

BRENON, HERBERT

"Herbert Brenon." *E!Online* http://eonline.com/Facts/People/0,12,44483,00.html

"Herbert Brenon." *Internet Movie Database* http://us.imdb.com/M/person-exact?Brenon%2C%20Herbert

BRIDGE ON THE RIVER KWAI, THE

Boulle, Pierre. *The Bridge Over* [sic] *the River Kwai*. Bantam Books, 1975.

Silver, Alain. *David Lean and His Films*. Silman-James Press, 1992.

Sragow, Michael. "David Lean's magnificent 'Kwai.'" *Atlantic Monthly*, February 1994.

BRINGING UP BABY
(see also Howard Hawks)
Denby, David. "Taking down 'Baby.' " *Premiere*, June 1991.

BROOKS, LOUISE
Brooks, Louise. *Lulu in Hollywood*. Knopf, 1982.
Dardis, Tom. "What Lulu wanted." *Vanity Fair*, April 1998.
"Louise Brooks." *Variety*, August 14, 1985 (obituary).
Paris, Barry. *Louise Brooks*. Knopf, 1989.

BROOKS, MEL
Daly, Steve. "'Blazing' a profane trail." *Entertainment Weekly*, September 19, 1997.
Holtzman, William. *Seesaw, a Dual Biography of Anne Bancroft and Mel Brooks*. Doubleday, 1979.
"He loves his twelve chairs." *U.S. News & World Report*, July 7, 1997 (interview).
Yacowar, Maurice. *Method in Madness: The Art of Mel Brooks*. St. Martin's Press, 1981.

BUDDY FILMS
Rosenbaum, Ron. "Why buddy films aren't a girl's best friend." *Mademoiselle*, August 1988.
Streible, Dan. "The black image in protective custody: Hollywood's biracial buddy films of the eighties," in *Black American Cinema* (Manthia Diawara, ed). Routledge, 1993.
Van Gelder, Lawrence. "Buddy films." *New York Times*, October 20, 1989.

BUTCH CASSIDY AND THE SUNDANCE KID
(see also Robert Redford)
Horton, Andrew. *The Films of George Roy Hill*. Columbia University Press, 1984.
Kelly, Charles. *The Outlaw Trail: A History of Butch and His Wild Bunch*. University of Nebraska Press, 1996.
Quirk, Lawrence J. *The Films of Paul Newman*. Lyle Stuart, 1986.

CAGNEY, JAMES
Dickens, Homer. *The Complete Films of James Cagney*. Citadel Press, 1989.
"James Cagney." *Entertainment Weekly*, Fall 1996 (Special Collector's Issue).
McCabe, John. *Cagney*. Knopf, 1997.
Schickel, Richard. *James Cagney: A Celebration*. Little, Brown, 1985.
Warren, Doug. *James Cagney, the Authorized Biography*. St. Martin's Press, 1983.

CAMERA OBSCURA

Knowles, David. *The Secrets of the Camera Obscura*. Chronicle Books, 1994 (fiction).

"A search for camera obscura rooms." *Bright Bytes Studio* http://brightbytes. com/cosite/cohome.html

CAPRA, FRANK

Capra, Frank. *The Name Above the Title*. Da Capo Press, 1997.

Carney, Raymond. *American Vision: The Films of Frank Capra*. Wesleyan University Press, 1996.

Gewen, Barry. "It wasn't such a wonderful life." *New York Times Book Review*, May 3, 1992.

Lourdeaux, Lee. *Italian and Irish Filmmakers in America: Ford, Capra, Coppola, and Scorsese*. Temple University Press, 1990.

McBride, Joseph. *Frank Capra: The Catastrophe of Success*. Simon & Schuster, 1992.

CASABLANCA

Harmetz, Aljean. *Round Up the Usual Suspects: The Making of Casablanca: Bogart, Bergman, and World War II*. Hyperion, 1992.

"Humphrey Bogart." *Entertainment Weekly*, Fall 1996 (Special Collector's Issue).

"Ingrid Bergman." *Entertainment Weekly*, Fall 1996 (Special Collector's Issue).

Lebo, Harlan. *Casablanca: Behind the Scenes*. Simon & Schuster, 1992.

Miller, Frank. *Casablanca: As Time Goes By: 50th Anniversary Commemorative*. Turner Publishing, 1992.

Robertson, James C. *The Casablanca Man: The Cinema of Michael Curtiz*. Routledge, 1993.

CENSORSHIP

Gardner, Gerald C. *The Censorship Papers: Movie Censorship Letters from the Hays Office, 1934–1968*. Dodd, Mead, 1987.

Leff, Leonard J. *The Dame in the Kimono: Hollywood, Censorship, and the Production Code from the 1920s to the 1960s*. Doubleday, 1990.

Miller, Frank. *Censored Hollywood: Sex, Sin, and Violence on Screen*. Turner Publications, 1994.

Movie Censorship and American Culture. Smithsonian Institution Press, 1996.

Walsh, Frank. *Sin and Censorship: The Catholic Church and the Motion Picture Industry*. Yale University Press, 1996.

CHANEY, LON

Blake, Michael F. *The Films of Lon Chaney*. Vestal Press, 1998.

———. *A Thousand Faces: Lon Chaney's Unique Artistry in Motion Pictures.* Vestal Press, 1995.

———. *Lon Chaney: The Man Behind the Thousand Faces.* Vestal Press, 1993.

CHAPLIN, CHARLIE

Chaplin, Charlie. *Charles Chaplin: My Autobiography.* Plume, 1993.

Hale, Georgia. *Charlie Chaplin: Intimate Close-ups.* Scarecrow Press, 1995.

Lynn, Kenneth Schuyler. *Charlie Chaplin and His Times.* Simon & Schuster, 1997.

McDonald, Gerald D., et al. *The Complete Films of Charlie Chaplin.* Citadel Press, 1988.

Milton, Joyce. *Tramp: The Life of Charlie Chaplin.* Da Capo Press, 1998.

Robinson, David. *Chaplin: His Life and Art.* Da Capo Press, 1994.

CHINATOWN

(see also Jack Nicholson, Roman Polanski)

Biskind, Peter. "The low road to 'Chinatown.' " *Premiere,* June 1994.

CINEMA VERITÉ

Berliner, Todd. "Hollywood movie dialogue and the 'real realism' of John Cassavetes." *Film Quarterly,* Spring 1999.

Maslin, Janet. "The days of hand-held cameras and in-your-face films." *New York Times,* Nov. 13, 1997.

O'Connell, P. J. *Robert Drew and the Development of Cinema Verite in America.* Southern Illinois University Press, 1992.

CINEMATOGRAPHER

Boorstin, Jon. *The Hollywood Eye: What Makes Movies Work.* Harper & Row, 1990.

Darby, William. *Masters of Lens and Light: A Checklist of Major Cinematographers and Their Feature Films.* Scarecrow Press, 1991.

Krasilovsky, Alexis. *Women Behind the Camera.* Praeger, 1997.

Malkiewicz, J. Kris. *Cinematography.* Prentice Hall Press, 1989.

Maltin, Leonard. *The Art of the Cinematographer: A Survey and Interviews With Five Masters.* Dover Publications, 1978.

Rogers, Pauline B. *Contemporary Cinematographers on Their Art.* Focal Press, 1998.

CITIZEN KANE

(see also Orson Welles)

"Accepting for 'Citizen Kane'. . . ." *New York Times,* June 18, 1998 (editorial).

Carringer, Robert L. *The Making of Citizen Kane.* University of California Press, 1996.

The Citizen Kane Book. Limelight Editions, 1984.

Lebo, Harlan. *Citizen Kane: The Fiftieth Anniversary Album.* Doubleday, 1990.

Mulvey, Laura. *Citizen Kane.* British Film Institute, 1993.

CITY LIGHTS

(see Charlie Chaplin)

CLAY ANIMATION

Busby, Scott. "New techniques move cartoons." *Variety,* May 23, 1990.

"Claymation!" *National Geographic World,* December 1987.

Frierson, Michael. *Clay Animation: American Highlights 1908 to Present.* Twayne, 1994.

Goodman, Walter. "The festival of claymation." *New York Times,* April 17, 1987.

Clay Animation Home Page
http://www.intrepid.net/~hollyoak/clay.htm

CLOCKWORK ORANGE

(see also Stanley Kubrick)

Burgess, Anthony. *A Clockwork Orange.* Ballantine Books, 1988.

Nashawaty, Chris. " 'The old ultraviolence.' " *Entertainment Weekly,* December 15, 1995.

Rothstein, Edward. "Kubrick and Beethoven, a marriage made in hell." *New York Times,* March 15, 1999.

CLOSE ENCOUNTERS OF THE THIRD KIND

(see also Steven Spielberg)

DeWitt, Linda. "Steven Spielberg (When I Was a Kid)." *National Geographic World,* December 1997.

Spielberg, Steven. *Close Encounters of the Third Kind: A Novel.* Dell, 1980.

COMEDY

Bernheimer, Kathryn. *The 50 Funniest Movies of All Time: A Critic's Ranking.* Citadel Press, 1999.

Harvey, James. *Romantic Comedy in Hollywood, from Lubitsch to Sturges.* Da Capo Press, 1998.

Kerr, Walter. *The Silent Clowns.* Da Capo Press, 1990.

Langman, Larry, and Paul Gold, eds. *Comedy Quotes from the Movies.* McFarland, 1994.

Miller, Blair. *American Silent Film Comedies: An Illustrated Encyclopedia of Persons, Studios and Terminology.* McFarland, 1995.

Paul, William. *Laughing Screaming: Modern Hollywood Horror and Comedy.* Columbia University Press, 1994.

COMPOSITION

Blacker, Irwin R. *The Elements of Screenwriting: A Guide for Film and Television Writers.* Macmillan, 1996.

Cooper, Dona. *AFI Guide to Writing Great Screenplays for Film and TV.* Arco Publications, 1997.

CONNERY, SEAN

"Not fond of Bond." *Maclean's*, March 9, 1998.

Parker, John. *Sean Connery.* Contemporary Books, 1993.

Passingham, Kenneth. *Sean Connery, a Biography.* St. Martin's Press, 1983.

Pfeiffer, Lee. *The Films of Sean Connery.* Citadel Press, 1997.

Yule, Andrew. *Sean Connery: From 007 to Hollywood Icon.* D. I. Fine, 1992.

COOPER, GARY

Dickens, Homer. *The Complete Films of Gary Cooper.* Lyle Stuart, 1983.

"Gary Cooper." *Entertainment Weekly*, Fall 1996 (Special Collector's Issue).

"Gary Cooper." *Vanity Fair*, March 1991.

Janis, Maria Cooper. *Gary Cooper Off Camera: A Daughter Remembers.* Harry Abrams, 1999.

Meyers, Jeffrey. *Gary Cooper: An American Hero.* William Morrow, 1998.

COPPOLA, FRANCIS FORD

Bergan, Ronald. *Francis Ford Coppola: Close Up: The Making of His Movies.* Thunder's Mouth Press, 1998.

Coppola, Eleanor. *Notes/on the Making of Apocalypse Now.* Limelight Editions, 1991.

Cowie, Peter. *Coppola: A Biography.* Da Capo Press, 1994.

Lourdeaux, Lee. *Italian and Irish Filmmakers in America: Ford, Capra, Coppola, and Scorsese.* Temple University Press, 1990.

"So sue me." *Time*, July 20, 1998.

CORMAN, ROGER

Corman, Roger. *How I Made a Hundred Movies in Hollywood and Never Lost a Dime.* Da Capo Press, 1998.

Gubernick, Lisa. "Little shop of profits." *Forbes*, April 15, 1991.

McGee, Mark Thomas. *Roger Corman, the Best of the Cheap Acts.* McFarland, 1988.

Taylor, J. R. "Corman attractions: the king of frugal filmmaking splurges." *Entertainment Weekly*, May 19, 1995.

COSTUME FILM

Leese, Elizabeth. *Costume Design in the Movies: An Illustrated Guide to the Work of 157 Great Designers.* Dover Publications, 1991.

Men with Big Hair: The Costume Movie Site
http://www.costumes.org/subwebs/mwbh/mwbh.htm

CRITICISM

Ebert, Roger, ed. *Roger Ebert's Book of Film*. W. W. Norton, 1996.

Kael, Pauline. *5001 Nights at the Movies*. Henry Holt, 1991.

Maltin, Leonard, ed. *Leonard Maltin's Movie and Video Guide*. Plume, 1999 (annual).

Sillick, Ardis. *The Critics Were Wrong: The 501 Most Misguided Movie Reviews—And Film Criticism Gone Wrong*. Citadel Press, 1996.

CRUISE, TOM

"All eyes on them" and "Three of a kind." *Time*, July 5, 1999.

Clarkson, Wensley. *Tom Cruise: Unauthorized*. Hastings House, 1998.

Sellers, Robert. *Tom Cruise*. Robert Hale, 1997.

"Tom Cruise: The baby boom's biggest star stayed grounded, despite a broken home, dyslexia—and a pesky press." *People Weekly*, March 15, 1999.

CRUZE, JAMES

"James Cruze." *The Silents Majority*
http://www.mdle.com/ClassicFilms/ BTC/directb.htm

"James Cruze." *Thanhouser Company Film Preservation*
http://www.teleport.com/~tco/people/cruzej.htm

CUKOR, GEORGE

"Director George Cukor, 83, dies in L.A., 50-year career, many hits." *Variety*, January 26, 1983 (obituary).

Levy, Emanuel. *George Cukor: Master of Elegance*. Morrow, 1994.

McGilligan, Patrick. *George Cukor: A Double Life*. St. Martin's Press, 1991.

Phillips, Gene D. *George Cukor*. Twayne, 1982.

CULT FILM

Everman, Welch. *Cult Horror Films: From Attack of the 50 Foot Woman to Zombies of Mora Tau*. Citadel Press, 1993.

Everman, Welch. *Cult Science Fiction Films: From the Amazing Colossal Man to Yog: The Monster from Space*. Citadel Press, 1995.

Peary, Danny. *Cult Movies: The Classics, the Sleepers, the Weird, and the Wonderful*. Grammercy, 1998.

Roen, Paul. *High Camp; A Gay Guide to Camp and Cult Films*. Leyland Publications, 1997.

Schwartz, Carol A. *VideoHound's Complete Guide to Cult Flicks and Trash Pics*. Visible Ink Press, 1995.

CULTURAL CRITICISM

Marsden, Michael T. *Movies As Artifacts: Cultural Criticism of Popular Film*. Nelson-Hall, 1982.

Rollins, Peter C., ed. *Hollywood as Historian: American Film in a Cultural Context*. University Press of Kentucky, 1998.

Rosenstone, Robert A. *Visions of the Past: The Challenge of Film to Our Idea of History*. Belknap Press, 1996.

Russo, Vito. *The Celluloid Closet*. HarperCollins, 1987.

Toplin, Robert Brent. *History by Hollywood: The Use and Abuse of the American Past*. University of Illinois Press, 1996.

DAGUERREOTYPE

Barger, M. Susan, and William B. White. *The Daguerreotype: Nineteenth-century Technology and Modern Science*. Smithsonian Institution Press, 1991.

Forest, Merry A., and John Wood. *Secrets of the Dark Chamber: The Art of the American Daguerreotype*. Smithsonian Institution Press, 1995.

Richter, Stefan. *The Art of the Daguerreotype*. Viking, 1989.

DANCES WITH WOLVES

Blake, Michael. *Dances with Wolves*. Fawcett Books, 1990.

Caddies, Kelvin. *Kevin Costner: Prince of Hollywood*. Plexus, 1994.

Dances with Wolves: The Illustrated Screenplay and Story Behind the Film (abridged). Newmarket Press, 1991.

Rothstein, Mervyn. "For writer of 'Wolves,' rewards at last." *New York Times*, March 25, 1991.

Stevenson, Richard W. "7 Oscars for 'Wolves' lift a troubled studio." *New York Times*, March 27, 1991.

DAVIES, MARION

Davies, Marion. *The Times We Had: Life with William Randolph Hearst*. Ballantine Books, 1989.

Gordon, John Steele. "The mating game." *Forbes*, October 22, 1990.

Swanberg, W. A. *Citizen Hearst: A Biography of William Randolph Hearst*. Scribner, 1984.

"William Randolph Hearst and Marion Davies: The man who inspired 'Citizen Kane' found his equal in a fun-loving chorus girl." *People Weekly*, February 12, 1996.

DAVIS, BETTE

Considine, Shaun. *Bette and Joan: The Divine Feud*. Dutton, 1989.

Davis, Bette. *This 'n That*. ABC-CLIO, 1987.

Leaming, Barbara. *Bette Davis—a Biography*. Simon & Schuster, 1992.

Quirk, Lawrence J. *Fasten Your Seat Belts: The Passionate Life of Bette Davis*. William Morrow, 1990.

Ringgold, Gene. *Bette Davis, Her Films and Career*. Citadel Press, 1985.

Walker, Alexander. *Bette Davis: A Celebration*. Little, Brown, 1986.

DAY, DORIS

Day, Doris. *Doris Day: Her Own Story*. Morrow, 1976.

"Doris Day." *Entertainment Weekly*, Fall 1996 (Special Collector's Issue).
Gelb, Alan. *The Doris Day Scrapbook*. Grosset and Dunlap, 1977.
Young, Christopher. *The Films of Doris Day*. Citadel Press, 1977.

DEER HUNTER, THE
(see Robert De Niro, Martin Scorsese, Meryl Streep)

DEMILLE, CECIL B.
Brosnan, Peter. "Cecil B. DeMille's Ten Commandments set lay buried for 68 years, but a filmmmaker says he can dig it." *People Weekly*, April 1, 1991.
Higashi, Sumiko. *Cecil B. DeMille And American Culture: The Silent Era*. University of California Press, 1994.
Ringgold, Gene, and DeWitt Bodeen. *The Complete Films of Cecil B. DeMille*. Lyle Stuart, 1985.
Robb, David. "Directors fought hard, long for Guild." *Variety*, September 3, 1986.
"Cecil B. DeMille." *UCLA Film and Television Archive* http://www.cinema.ucla.edu/Content/filmtxt/demille.htm

DE NIRO, ROBERT
Bagli, Charles V. "De Niro and Miramax face problems in film studio plan." *New York Times*, May 4, 1999.
Brode, Douglas. *The Films of Robert De Niro*. Citadel Press, 1996.
Dougan, Andy. *Untouchable: A Biography of Robert De Niro*. Thunder's Mouth Press, 1996.
McKay, Keith. *Robert De Niro, the Hero Behind the Masks*. St. Martin's Press, 1986.
Powell, Elfreda. *Robert De Niro*. Chelsea House, 1997.
Weinraub, Bernard. "De Niro! Pacino! Together again for first time." *New York Times*, July 27, 1995.

DETECTIVE FILM
(see also Mystery-thriller)
Hardy, Phil, ed. *The BFI Companion to Crime*. University of California Press, 1997.
Langman, Larry. *A Guide to American Crime Films of the Forties and Fifties*. Greenwood Press, 1995.
Langman, Larry. *A Guide to American Silent Crime Films*. Greenwood Press, 1994.
Pitts, Michael R. *Famous Movie Detectives*. Scarecrow Press, 1979.
———. *Famous Movie Detectives II*. Scarecrow Press, 1991.
Tuska, Jon. *In Manors and Alleys*. Greenwood Press, 1988.

DIRECTOR

Gallagher, John Andrew. *Film Directors on Directing*. Greenwood Press, 1989.

Hollywood Directors, 1914–1940. Oxford University Press, 1976.

Hollywood Directors, 1941–1976. Oxford University Press, 1977.

Sarris, Andrew. *The American Cinema: Directors and Directions 1929–1968*. Da Capo Press, 1996.

———. *The St. James Film Directors Encyclopedia*. Visible Ink Press, 1997.

DISASTER FILM

Coupland, Douglas. "The abiding urge to watch things go ka-boom!" *New York Times*, February 9, 1997.

Rabinowitz, Howard. "The end is near! Why disaster movies make sense (and dollars) in the '90s." *Washington Monthly*, April 1997.

Rayner, Jay. "The Big Bang theory: Why we love watching our neighborhood bite the dust." *New Statesman*, August 9, 1996.

Svetkey, Benjamin. "Flirting with disasters: Run for your lives! Doom and destruction are on their way!" *Entertainment Weekly*, May 17, 1996.

DOCTOR STRANGELOVE

(see also Stanley Kubrick)

Lefcowitz, Eric. "'Dr. Strangelove' turns 30. Can it still be trusted?" *New York Times*, January 30, 1994.

Rabe, David. "Admiring the unpredictable Mr. Kubrick." *New York Times*, June 21, 1987.

DOCTOR ZHIVAGO

(see also David Lean)

Pasternak, Boris Leonidovich. *Doctor Zhivago*. Pantheon Books, 1997.

Ross, Alex. "Scoring for Oscar: the trills and chills of composing for Hollywood." *The New Yorker*, March 9, 1998.

Stanley, Alessandra. "Model for Dr. Zhivago's Lara betrayed Pasternak to K.G.B." *New York Times*, November 27, 1997.

DOCUMENTARY

Barnouw, Erik. *Documentary: A History of the Non-Fiction Film*. Oxford University Press, 1993.

Barsam, Richard M. *Nonfiction Film: A Critical History*. Indiana University Press, 1992.

Jacobs, Lewis. *The Documentary Tradition*. W. W. Norton, 1979.

Rothman, William. *Documentary Film Classics*. Cambridge University Press, 1997.

Webster, Nicholas. *How to Sleep on a Camel: Adventures of a Documentary Film Director*. McFarland, 1997.

DOUBLE INDEMNITY
(see also Billy Wilder)
Naremore, James. "Straight on down the line: making and remaking 'Double Indemnity.'" *Film Comment*, January-February 1996.
O'Toole, Lawrence. "Barbara Stanwyck." *Entertainment Weekly*, Mar. 1995 (Special Collector's Issue).

DRIVE-IN THEATER
McKeon, Elizabeth. *Cinema Under the Stars: America's Love Affair with the Drive-in Movie Theater*. Cumberland House, 1998.
Sanders, Don. *The American Drive-in Movie Theatre*. Motorbooks International, 1997.
Segrave, Kerry. *Drive-in Theaters: A History from Their Inception in 1933*. McFarland, 1992.

DUCK SOUP
Gehring, Wes D. *Leo McCarey and the Comic Anti-Hero Film*. Ayer, 1980.
———. *The Marx Brothers*. Greenwood Press, 1987.
Seaton, George, et al. *The Marx Brothers: Monkey Business, Duck Soup, and a Day at the Races (Classic Screenplays)*. Faber and Faber, 1993.
"Duck Soup (1933)." *AFI's 100 YEARS . . . 100 MOVIES (America's Greatest Movies)*
http://www.filmsite.org/duck.html

DUNAWAY, FAYE
Dunaway, Faye. *Looking for Gatsby: My Life*. Simon & Schuster, 1995.
"Faye Dunaway." *Entertainment Weekly*, Fall 1996 (Special Collector's Issue).
Hunter, Allan. *Faye Dunaway*. St. Martin's Press, 1986.
Malkin, Mark S. "Faye Dunaway." *Premiere*, October 1996 [interview].

E.T.: THE EXTRATERRESTRIAL
(see also Steven Spielberg)
Calio, Jim. "Director Steven Spielberg takes the wraps off E.T., revealing his secrets at last." *People Weekly*, August 23, 1982.
Kael, Pauline. "E.T. the extra-terrestrial." *The New Yorker*, June 14, 1982 (review).
Kakutani, Michiko. "The two faces of Spielberg—horror vs. hope." *New York Times*, May 30, 1982.
Sragow, Michael. "A conversation with Steven Spielberg." *Rolling Stone*, July 22, 1982.

EASTWOOD, CLINT
Gallafent, Edward. *Clint Eastwood: Filmmaker and Star*. Continuum, 1994.

Knapp, Laurence F. *Directed by Clint Eastwood: Eighteen Films Analyzed.* McFarland, 1996.

Maslin, Janet. "Getting in touch with his inner good guy." *New York Times*, March 19, 1999.

Schickel, Richard. *Clint Eastwood: A Biography*. Knopf, 1996.

Zmijewsky, Boris, and Lee Pfeiffer. *The Films of Clint Eastwood.* Citadel Press, 1993.

EASY RIDER

(see also Jack Nicholson)

Daly, Steve. "'Rider' in a storm." *Entertainment Weekly*, July 16, 1993.

Fonda, Peter, 1940. *Don't Tell Dad: A Memoir.* Hyperion, 1998.

Rodriguez, Elena. *Dennis Hopper, a Madness to His Method.* St. Martin's Press, 1988.

Singer, Mark. "Whose movie is this." *The New Yorker*, June 22, 1998.

"Uneasy rider." *Forbes*, January 22, 1996.

EBERT, ROGER

(see also Gene Siskel)

Ebert, Roger. *Roger Ebert's Movie Yearbook.* Andrews McMeel, 1999 (annual).

———. *Questions for the Movie Answer Man.* Andrews McMeel, 1997.

———, ed. *Ebert's Bigger Little Movie Glossary: A Greatly Expanded and Much Improved Compendium of Movie Cliches, Stereotypes, Obligatory Scenes [etc.].* Andrews McMeel, 1999.

———, ed. *Roger Ebert's Book of Film.* W. W. Norton, 1996.

———, and Gene Siskel. *The Future of the Movies.* Andrews McMeel, 1991.

Watson, Bret. "They still like to watch." *Entertainment Weekly*, May 17, 1996.

EDITOR

LoBrutto, Vincent. *Selected Takes: Film Editors on Editing.* Praeger, 1991.

Murch, Walter. *In the Blink of an Eye: A Perspective on Film Editing.* Silman-James Press, 1995.

Oldham, Gabriella. *First Cut: Conversations with Film Editors.* University of California Press, 1995.

Rosenblum, Ralph. *When the Shooting Stops, the Cutting Begins: A Film Editor's Story.* Da Capo Press, 1986.

EPIC

Fraser, George MacDonald. *The Hollywood History of the World.* Harvill Press, 1996.

McMurty, Larry. "Men swaggered, women warred, oil flowed." *New York Times*, September 29, 1996 (George Stevens's epic *Giant).*

Munn, Mike. *The Stories Behind the Scenes of the Great Film Epics*. Morgan and Morgan, 1983.

EXPANDED CINEMA
(see also Cinematographer, Experimental film)
Youngblood, Gene. *Expanded Cinema*. Dutton, 1970.

EXPERIMENTAL FILM
(see also Avant-garde)
Dixon, Wheeler W. *The Exploding Eye: A Re-visionary History of 1960s American Experimental Cinema*. State University of New York Press, 1997.
Ferguson, Russell, ed. *Art and Film Since 1945: Hall of Mirrors*. Monacelli Press, 1996.
Sterritt, David. *Mad to be Saved: The Beats, the '50s, and Film*. Southern Illinois University Press, 1998.
Suarez, Juan Antonio. *Bike Boys, Drag Queens, and Superstars: Avant-garde, Mass Culture, and Gay Identities in the 1960s Underground Cinema*. Indiana University Press, 1996.

EXPRESSIONISM
Hinrichs, Bruce. "A trip to the movies: 100 years of film as art." *The Humanist*, January-February 1996.
Jefferson, Margo. "Moonstruck magic by the grandfather of film fantasies (Georges Melies)." *New York Times*, November 15, 1997.

FAIRBANKS, DOUGLAS
Corliss, Richard. "The king of Hollywood." *Time*, June 17, 1996.
Herndon, Booton. *Mary Pickford and Douglas Fairbanks: The Most Popular Couple the World Has Ever Known*. W. W. Norton, 1977.
Hochman, David. "Douglas Fairbanks Sr.: the dashing daredevil." *Entertainment Weekly*, Fall 1996 (Special Collector's Issue).
"Douglas Fairbanks, Sr." *The Silents Majority*
http://www.mdle.com/ClassicFilms/FeaturedStar/star1.htm

FANTASIA
Bailey, Adrian. *Walt Disney's World of Fantasy*. Gallery Books, 1987.
Barron, James. "Stravinsky publisher sues Disney on 'Fantasia.' " *New York Times*, January 22, 1993.
Culhane, John. *Walt Disney's Fantasia*. Harry Abrams, 1987.
Finch, Christopher. *The Art of Walt Disney: From Mickey Mouse to the Magic Kingdoms*. Harry Abrams, 1995.
Olson, Eric J. "Mouse sees big picture with Imax 'Fantasia' deal." *Variety*, February 15, 1999.

FANTASY

Bailey, Adrian. *Walt Disney's World of Fantasy*. Gallery Books, 1987.

Clute, John, et al., eds. *The Encyclopedia of Fantasy*. St. Martin's Press, 1996.

Goldberg, Lee, ed. *The Dreamweavers: Interviews with Fantasy Filmmakers of the 1980s*. McFarland, 1995.

Stanley, John. *Creature Features: The Science Fiction, Fantasy, and Horror Movie Guide*. Berkley Publishing Group, 1997.

Weaver, Tom. *Science Fiction and Fantasy Film Flashbacks: Conversations With 24 Actors, Writers, Producers and Directors from the Golden Age*. McFarland, 1998.

Young, R. G., ed. *The Encyclopedia of the Fantastic Film: Ali Baba to Zombies*. Applause Theatre Books, 1999.

FARGO

Ascher-Walsh, Rebecca. "Queen Fargo." *Entertainment Weekly*, April 12, 1996.

Biskind, Peter. "Joel and Ethan Coen." *Premiere*, March 1996 (interview).

Roman, Monica. "New York Crix Circle takes trip to 'Fargo.'" *Variety*, December 16, 1996.

Weiner, Rex. "'Fargo' lauded with Indie Spirit." *Variety*, March 31, 1997.

FEATURE FILM

American Film Institute Catalogs: series covering feature films by various time periods and genres, including

Gevinson, Alan, ed. *American Film Institute Catalog: Within Our Gates: Ethnicity in American Feature Films, 1911–1960*. University of California Press, 1997.

Krasfur, Richard P., ed. *The American Film Institute Catalog: Feature Films, 1961–1970*. University of California Press, 1997.

Edera, Bruno. *Full Length Animated Feature Films*. Hastings House, 1984.

Short, K. R. M. *Feature Films as History*. University of Tennessee Press, 1981.

FIELD, SALLY

"Accepting a scary mission." *People Weekly*, May 11, 1998.

Bonderoff, Jason. *Sally Field*. St. Martin's Press, 1987.

Griffin, Nancy. "Table talk." *Premiere*, Winter 1993 (interview).

Schwarzbaum, Lisa. "Field days." *Entertainment Weekly*, February 17, 1995.

FILM NOIR

Hirsch, Foster. *The Dark Side of the Screen: Film Noir*. Da Capo Press, 1988.

Muller, Eddie. *Dark City: The Lost World of Film Noir*. St. Martin's Griffin, 1998.

Silver, Alain, and James Ursini, eds. *Film Noir Reader*. Limelight Editions, 1996.

———, and Elizabeth Ward, eds. *Film Noir: An Encyclopedic Reference to the American Style*. Overlook Press, 1992.

Stephens, Michael L. *Film Noir: A Comprehensive, Illustrated Reference to Movies, Terms and Persons*. McFarland, 1995.

FLYNN, ERROL

"Errol Flynn." *Entertainment Weekly*, Fall 1996 (Special Collector's Issue).

Flynn, Errol. *My Wicked, Wicked Ways*. Buccaneer Books, 1978.

Thomas, Tony. *Errol Flynn: The Spy Who Never Was*. Citadel Press, 1990.

Wiles, Buster. *My Days with Errol Flynn: The Autobiography of Stuntman Buster Wiles*. Roundtable Publishing, 1988.

FOLEY ARTIST

Harris, R. J. "The foley artists are a noisy bunch in moviemaking." *Wall Street Journal*, December 21, 1992.

Lobrutto, Vincent. *Sound-On-Film*. Praeger, 1994.

Weis, Elizabeth, and John Belton. *Film Sound: Theory and Practice*. Columbia University Press, 1985.

Movie Sound Effects: What Is a Foley Studio? http://interact.uoregon.edu/MediaLit/FA/MLCurriculum/LessonMovieSnd

FONDA, JANE

Andersen, Christopher P. *Citizen Jane: The Turbulent Life of Jane Fonda*. Holt, 1990.

Carlson, Margaret. "Back in the saddle again." *Time*, October 27, 1997.

Collier, Peter. *The Fondas: A Hollywood Dynasty*. Putnam, 1991.

Haddad-Garcia, George. *The Films of Jane Fonda*. Lyle Stuart, 1983.

Harrison, Barbara Grizzuti. "Self-fulfilling prophets: Oprah, Madonna, Jane Fonda . . . the entrepreneurial zealots who preach by example." *New York Times Magazine*, November 24, 1996.

FORD, HARRISON

"Harrison Ford: This strong, silent type reigns as the No. 1 movie star of our time." *People Weekly*, March 15, 1999.

Hochman, David. "Harrison Ford: Still a major force after 25 years, this unassuming hero is Indy Jones, the president, and a humble craftsman—all rolled into one." *Entertainment Weekly*, December 26, 1997.

Jenkins, Garry. *Harrison Ford: Imperfect Hero*. Carol Publishing Group, 1997.

Pfeiffer, Lee. *The Films of Harrison Ford*. Citadel Press, 1998.

Vare, Ethlie Ann. *Harrison Ford*. St. Martin's Press, 1987.

FORD, JOHN

Bogdanovich, Peter. *John Ford.* University of California Press, 1978.

Darby, William. *John Ford's Westerns.* McFarland, 1996.

Ford, Dan. *Pappy: The Life of John Ford.* Da Capo Press, 1998.

Gallagher, Tag. *John Ford: The Man and His Films.* University of California Press, 1988.

Lourdeaux, Lee. *Italian and Irish Filmmakers in America: Ford, Capra, Coppola, and Scorsese.* Temple University Press, 1990.

Tavernier, Bertrand. "Notes of a press attache: John Ford in Paris, 1966." *Film Comment,* July-August 1994.

FORREST GUMP

(see also Tom Hanks)

Groom, Winston. *Forrest Gump.* Doubleday, 1986.

Kakutani, Michiko. "Ready for his close-up: As Hollywood and Broadway remakes his classics, Billy Wilder, 90, holds forth on Proust, Zippos and 'Forrest Gump.' " *New York Times Magazine,* July 28, 1996.

Lippman, John. "Star and director of 'Gump' took risk, reaped millions." *Wall Street Journal,* March 7, 1995.

Weinraub, Bernard. " 'Gump' still isn't raking in huge profits? Hmm." *New York Times,* May 25, 1995.

FOSSE, BOB

Gottfried, Martin. *All His Jazz: The Life and Death of Bob Fosse.* Bantam Books, 1990.

Grubb, Kevin Boyd. *Razzle Dazzle: The Life and Work of Bob Fosse.* St. Martin's Press, 1989.

Henry, William A. "Melancholy end for a dancin' man; Robert Louis Fosse: 1927–1987." *Time,* October 5, 1987 (obituary).

Isherwood, Charles. "Fosse." *Variety,* January 18, 1999 (review).

FRANKENSTEIN

Bram, Christopher. "Whale's world." *Premiere,* December 1998.

Curtis, James. *James Whale: A New World of Gods and Monsters.* Faber and Faber, 1998.

Jones, Stephen, and Boris Karloff. *The Frankenstein Scrapbook: The Complete Movie Guide to the World's Most Famous Monster.* Citadel Press, 1995.

O'Connor, John J. "Biography: Boris Karloff: The Gentle Monster." *New York Times,* October 23, 1995.

Shelley, Mary Wollstonecraft. *Frankenstein, or, The Modern Prometheus.* Modern Library, 1999.

FRENCH CONNECTION, THE

Clagett, Thomas D. *William Friedkin: Films of Aberration, Obsession, and Reality.* McFarland, 1990.

Moore, Robin. *The French Connection: The World's Most Crucial Narcotics Investigation*. Bantam Books, 1970.

FROM HERE TO ETERNITY

Horton, Robert. "Day of the Craftsman: Fred Zinnemann." *Film Comment*, September–October 1997 (obituary).

Jones, James. *From Here to Eternity*. Dell, 1998.

Nolletti, Arthur, ed. *The Films of Fred Zinnemann*. State University of New York Press, 1999.

Sauter, Michael. "A Zinnemann toast." *Entertainment Weekly*, Mar. 28, 1997 (obituary).

Zinnemann, Fred. *A Life in the Movies: An Autobiography*. Scribner's, 1992.

FUTURISM

Humphreys, Richard. *Futurism*. Cambridge University Press, 1999.

Marinetti, F. T., et al. "The Futurist Cinema." *L'Italia Futurista*, November 15, 1916. Reproduced at http://www.unknown.nu/futurism/cinema. html

Tisdale, Caroline. *Futurism*. Thames and Hudson, 1985.

GABLE, CLARK

"Clark Gable." *Entertainment Weekly*, Fall 1996 (Special Collector's Issue).

Essoe, Gabe. *The Complete Films of Clark Gable*. Citadel Press, 1990.

Harris, Warren G. *Gable and Lombard*. Simon & Schuster, 1974.

Purtell, Tim. "Frankly, we gave a damn." *Entertainment Weekly*, November 13, 1992.

Wayne, Jane Ellen. *Clark Gable: Portrait of a Misfit*. St. Martin's Press, 1993.

GANGSTER FILM

Brode, Douglas. *Money, Women, and Guns: Crime Movies from Bonnie and Clyde to the Present*. Carol Publishing, 1995.

Hardy, Phil. *The BFI Companion to Crime*. University of California Press, 1997.

McCarty, John. *Hollywood Gangland: The Movies' Love Affair with the Mob*. St. Martin's Press, 1993.

Mottram, James. *Public Enemies: The Gangster Movie A-Z: From Cagney to Tarantino and Beyond*. Batsford, 1998.

Munby, Jonathan. *Public Enemies, Public Heroes: Screening the Gangster from Little Caesar to Touch of Evil*. University of Chicago Press, 1999.

GARBO, GRETA

Broman, Sven. *Conversations with Greta Garbo*. G.K. Hall, 1992.

"Greta Garbo." *Entertainment Weekly*, Fall 1996 (Special Collector's Issue).

"Greta Garbo and John Gilbert." *Vanity Fair*, February 1991.

Gronowicz, Antoni. *Garbo*. Simon & Schuster, 1990.

Paris, Barry. *Garbo: A Biography*. Knopf, 1995.
Rossellini, Isabella. "Greta Garbo: The sphinx." *New York Times Magazine*, November 24, 1996.

GARLAND, JUDY
Coleman, Emily R. *The Complete Judy Garland: The Ultimate Guide to Her Career in Films, Records, Concerts, Radio, and Television, 1935–1969*. Harper & Row, 1990.
Frank, Gerrold. *Judy*. Da Capo Press, 1999.
Morella, Joe. *Judy: The Complete Films and Career of Judy Garland*. Citadel Press, 1986.
Shipman, David. *Judy Garland: The Secret Life of an American Legend*. Hyperion, 1993.
Vare, E. A., ed. *Rainbow: A Star-Studded Tribute to Judy Garland*. Boulevard, 1998.

GENRE
Altman, Rick. *Film Genre*. Indiana University Press, 1999.
Basinger, Jeanine. *American Cinema: One-hundred Years of Filmmaking*. Rizzoli, 1994.
Gehring, Wes D., ed. *Handbook of American Film Genres*. Greenwood Press, 1994.
Jameson, Richard T., ed. *They Went Thataway: Redefining Film Genres*. Mercury House, 1994.
Lopez, Daniel. *Films by Genre: 775 Categories, Styles, Trends, and Movements Defined, with a Filmography for Each*. MacFarland, 1993.

GIANT
(see also Elizabeth Taylor)
Blau, Eleanor. "Film making father." *New York Times*, August 18, 1988.
Fein, Esther B. "In 'George Stevens,' son honors a film maker." *New York Times*, May 6, 1985.
Ferber, Edna. *Giant*. Buccaneer Books, 1996.
McMurty, Larry. "Men swaggered, women warred, oil flowed." *New York Times*, September 29, 1996.
Spoto, Donald. *Rebel: The Life and Legend of James Dean*. HarperCollins, 1996.

GILBERT, JOHN
Fountain, Leatrice Gilbert. *Dark Star*. St. Martin's Press, 1985.
"Greta Garbo and John Gilbert." *Vanity Fair*, February 1991.

GISH, LILLIAN
Gish, Lillian. *An Actor's Life for Me*. Viking Press, 1992.

———. *Lillian Gish: The Movies, Mr. Griffith, and Me*. Prentice-Hall, 1969.
Klady, Leonard. "Lillian Gish." *Variety*, March 8, 1993 (obituary).
"Lillian Gish: the first lady of film." *Entertainment Weekly*, Fall 1996 (Special Collector's Issue).

GODFATHER, THE, AND GODFATHER II, THE
(see also Marlon Brando, Francis Ford Coppola, Robert De Niro, Diane Keaton, Al Pacino)
Brown, Nick, ed. *Francis Ford Coppola's Godfather Trilogy*. Cambridge University Press, 1999.
Lebo, Harlan. *The Godfather Legacy*. Fireside, 1997.
Puzo, Mario. *The Godfather*. G.K. Hall, 1985.
Rothstein, Edward. "Chilling balance of love and evil." *New York Times*, March 23, 1997.

GOLD RUSH, THE
(see Charlie Chaplin)

GONE WITH THE WIND
(see also Clark Gable, Vivien Leigh)
Bridges, Herb. *The Filming of Gone with the Wind*. Mercer University Press, 1998.
Bridges, Herb. *Gone with the Wind: The Definitive Illustrated History of the Book, the Movie, and the Legend*. Simon & Schuster, 1989.
Cameron, Judy, and Paul J. Christman. *The Art of Gone with the Wind: The Making of a Legend*. Prentice-Hall, 1989.
Harwell, Richard, ed. *Gone with the Wind as Book and Film*. Paragon House, 1987.
Mitchell, Margaret. *Gone with the Wind*. 60th Anniversary ed. Scribner, 1996.
Molt, Cynthia Marylee. *Gone with the Wind on Film: A Complete Reference*. McFarland, 1990.

GOODFELLAS
(see also Martin Scorsese)
Cohn, Lawrence. "National critics group favors 'GoodFellas.' " *Variety*, January 14, 1991.
Corliss, Richard. "Married to the mob; in some spiffy new films, Hollywood hooks up with gangsters." *Time*, September 24, 1990.
"Critics group votes 'GoodFellas' best film." *New York Times*, January 8, 1991.
Linfield, Susan. 'GoodFellas' looks at the banality of mob life." *New York Times*, September 16, 1990.

GRADUATE, THE

(see also Dustin Hoffman, Mike Nichols)

Koltnow, Barry. "Dustin Hoffman reflects on the media, 'The Graduate' and new 'Mad City.' " *Knight-Ridder/Tribune News Service*, November 5, 1997.

Smith, Gavin. "Mike Nichols." *Film Comment*, May 1999 (interview).

Travers, Peter. "The 30 greatest movies of the Rolling Stone era." *Rolling Stone*, April 3, 1997.

GRAPES OF WRATH, THE

(see also John Ford)

Mico, Ted, et al., eds. *Past Imperfect: History According to the Movies*. Henry Holt, 1995.

Steinbeck, John. *The Grapes of Wrath*. Knopf, 1993.

GRIFFITH, D. W.

"D. W. Griffith: the first cinema magician directed the rest." *Life*, Fall 1990.

Graham, Cooper, ed. *D. W. Griffith and the Biograph Company*. Scarecrow Press, 1985.

Parshall, Gerald. "The first prince of Babylon." *U.S. News & World Report*, June 1, 1998.

Schickel, Richard. *D. W. Griffith: An American Life*. Limelight Editions, 1996.

Simmon, Scott. *The Films of D. W. Griffith*. Cambridge University Press, 1993.

GUESS WHO'S COMING TO DINNER

(see also Katharine Hepburn, Spencer Tracy)

Kramer, Stanley. *A Mad, Mad, Mad, Mad World: A Life in Hollywood*. Harcourt Brace, 1997.

Spoto, Donald. *Stanley Kramer, Film Maker*. Samuel French, 1990.

GUINNESS, ALEC

Guinness, Alec. *A Positively Final Appearance: A Journal 1996-98*. Viking Press, 1999.

———. *My Name Escapes Me: The Diary of a Retiring Actor*. Penguin USA, 1998.

Kakutani, Michiko. "My Name Escapes Me: The Diary of a Retiring Actor." *New York Times*, August 22, 1997 (review).

Robertson, Nan. "Colleagues pay tribute to Sir Alec Guinness." *New York Times*, April 28, 1987.

Tanitch, Robert. *Guinness*. Applause Theatre Books, 1991.

HACKMAN, GENE

Burr, Ty. "All about eaves." *Entertainment Weekly*, June 18, 1999.

Carvajal, Doreen. "The celebrity author who sat and wrote." *New York Times*, March 15, 1999.

Davidson, Casey. "Mincing words." *Entertainment Weekly*, October 11, 1996.

Hunter, Allan. *Gene Hackman*. St. Martin's Press, 1987.

HAIRSPRAY

Jay, Bernard. *Not Simply Divine : Beneath the Make-up, Above the Heels, and Behind the Scenes with a Cult Superstar*. Simon & Schuster, 1993.

Geist, William. "John Waters; the sick man of cinema cleans up his act, sort of, and splashes into the mainstream with Hairspray." *People Weekly*, March 14, 1988.

Ives, John G. *John Waters*. Thunder's Mouth Press, 1992.

Mandelbaum, Paul. "Kink meister: Film maker John Waters is living proof that nothing exceeds like excess." *New York Times Magazine*, April 7, 1991.

Meyers, Kate. "High Waters marks." *Entertainment Weekly*, April 29, 1994.

HANKS, TOM

Corliss, Richard, and Cathy Booth. "The film of the year. A perky new comedy. These are high times for our most versatile star." *Time*, December 21, 1998.

Gordinier, Jeff. "Tom Hanks: With his understated hero in 'Ryan,' will he steal a march on Oscar immortality?" *Entertainment Weekly*, March 1, 1999.

Jacobs, A. J. "Tom Hanks (Entertainer of the Year)" *Entertainment Weekly*, December 29, 1995.

Pfeiffer, Lee. *The Films of Tom Hanks*. Carol Publishing Group, 1996.

Quinlan, David. *Tom Hanks: A Career in Orbit*. B. T. Batsford, 1998.

HAROLD AND MAUDE

Bart, Peter. "A cult classic remembered." *Variety*, December 23, 1996.

Collins, Glenn. "Hal Ashby, 59, an Oscar winner whose films included 'Shampoo.' " *New York Times*, December 28, 1988 (obituary).

Lyall, Sarah. "Colin Higgins, writer, dies at 47; 'Harold and Maude' among films." *New York Times*, August 6, 1988.

HAWKS, HOWARD

Grimes, William. "Mystery of 'The Big Sleep' is solved." *New York Times*, January 9, 1997.

Haskell, Molly. "Screwball existentialist, male bonder." *New York Times*, July 10, 1994.

Hawks, Howard. *Hawks on Hawks*. University of California Press, 1982.

Hillier, Jim, ed. *Howard Hawks, American Artist*. Indiana University Press, 1997.

McCarthy, Todd. *Howard Hawks: The Grey Fox of Hollywood*. Grove Press, 1997.

HEPBURN, AUDREY

Harris, Warren G. *Audrey Hepburn: A Biography*. Simon & Schuster, 1994.
Krenz, Carol. *Audrey Hepburn: A Life in Pictures*. Metro Books, 1997.
Maychick, Diana. *Audrey Hepburn: An Intimate Portrait*. Carol Publishing Group, 1993.
Morley, Sheridan. *Audrey Hepburn, a Celebration*. Pavilion, 1993.
Paris, Barry. *Audrey Hepburn*. Putnam, 1996.

HEPBURN, KATHARINE

Andersen, Christopher P. *An Affair to Remember: The Remarkable Love Story of Katharine Hepburn and Spencer Tracy*. William Morrow, 1997.
Dickens, Homer. *The Films of Katharine Hepburn*. Citadel Press, 1990.
Edwards, Anne. *A Remarkable Woman: A Biography of Katharine Hepburn*. Morrow, 1985.
Hepburn, Katharine. *Me: Stories of My Life*. Knopf, 1991.
———. *The Making of The African Queen, or, How I Went to Africa with Bogart, Bacall, and Huston and Almost Lost My Mind*. Knopf, 1987.
Leaming, Barbara. *Katharine Hepburn*. Crown, 1995.

HESTON, CHARLTON

Heston, Charlton. *Charlton Heston's Hollywood: 50 Years in American Film*. Good Times Publishing, 1998.
Heston, Charlton. *In the Arena: An Autobiography*. Simon & Schuster, 1995.
Janofsky, Michael. "N.R.A. tries to improve image, with Charlton Heston in lead." *New York Times*, June 8, 1988.
Williams, John. *The Films of Charlton Heston*. Greenhaven Press, 1977.

HIGH NOON

(see also Gary Cooper)
Horton, Robert. "Day of the Craftsman: Fred Zinnemann." *Film Comment*, September-October 1997 (obituary).
Nolletti, Arthur, ed. *The Films of Fred Zinnemann*. State University of New York Press, 1999.
Sauter, Michael. "A Zinnemann toast." *Entertainment Weekly*, March 28, 1997 (obituary).
Zinnemann, Fred. *A Life in the Movies: An Autobiography*. Scribner's, 1992.

HILL, GEORGE ROY

Horton, Andrew. *The Films of George Roy Hill*. Columbia University Press, 1984.
"George Roy Hill." *E! Online* http://www.eonline.com/Facts/People/ 0,12,40501,00.html

HITCHCOCK, ALFRED

Auiler, Dan. *Hitchcock's Notebooks: An Authorized and Illustrated Look Inside the Creative Mind of Alfred Hitchcock*. Spike, 1999.

Kapsis, Robert E. *Hitchcock: The Making of a Reputation*. University of Chicago Press, 1992.

Spoto, Donald. *The Art of Alfred Hitchcock: Fifty Years of His Motion Pictures*. Doubleday, 1992.

Sterritt, David. *The Films of Alfred Hitchcock*. Cambridge University Press, 1993.

Wood, Robin. *Hitchcock's Films Revisited*. Columbia University Press, 1989.

HOFFMAN, DUSTIN

Brode, Douglas. *The Films of Dustin Hoffman*. Citadel Press, 1988.

Dworkin, Susan. *Making Tootsie: A Film Study with Dustin Hoffman and Sydney Pollack*. NewMarket Press, 1983.

Lenburg, Jeff. *Dustin Hoffman, Hollywood's Anti-hero*. St. Martin's Press, 1983.

Weinraub, Bernard. "Graduating to producer." *New York Times*, March 26, 1999.

Weinraub, Bernard. "Hoffman: A fresh face even as age catches up." *New York Times*, February 17, 1998.

HOPKINS, ANTHONY

Callan, Michael Feeney. *Anthony Hopkins: The Unauthorized Biography*. Scribner, 1994.

Falk, Quentin. *Anthony Hopkins: The Authorized Biography*. Interlink, 1994.

"Maybe Joe Black stole his soul." *Time*, December 28, 1998.

Sterritt, David. "Anthony Hopkins takes on a new role: that of director." *Christian Science Monitor*, April 19, 1996.

Van Gelder, Lawrence. "He's such an animal, but not a lamb." *New York Times*, June 4, 1999.

HORROR FILM

Brunas, Michael. *Universal Horrors: The Studio's Classic Films, 1931–1946*. McFarland, 1990.

Everman, Welch. *Cult Horror Films: From Attack of the 50 Foot Woman to Zombies of Mora Tau*. Citadel Press, 1993.

Mayo, Mike. *VideoHound's Horror Show: 999 Hair-Raising, Hellish and Humorous Movies*. Visible Ink Press, 1998.

Paul, William. *Laughing Screaming: Modern Hollywood Horror and Comedy*. Columbia University Press, 1994.

Stanley, John. *Creature Features: The Science Fiction, Fantasy, and Horror Movie Guide*. Berkley Publishing Group, 1997.

Sternfield, Jonathan. *The Look of Horror: Scary Moments from Scary Movies*. Courage Books, 1990.

HUNT, HELEN

"Actors' acting awards to 'As Good as It Gets.'" *New York Times*, March 10, 1998.

"Helen Hunt." *Entertainment Weekly*, October 30, 1998.

Kizis, Deanna. "Hunt." *Harper's Bazaar*, May 1999.

Sharkey, Betsy. "Getting the chance to make Hollywood lengthen its A-list." *New York Times*, November 9, 1997.

Tynan, Kenneth. "Helen Hunt." *Time*, August 3, 1998.

HUNTER, HOLLY

Foster, Jodie. "Holly Hunter." *Interview*, November 1995.

Lidz, Franz. "Holly Hunter." *Entertainment Weekly*, March 1994 (Special Issue).

Maslin, Janet. "Living Out Loud." *New York Times*, October 30, 1998 (review).

Spingarn, Jed. "Holly Hunter: Fiercely silent, her Ada speaks volumes." *Entertainment Weekly*, March 1994 (Special issue).

HUSTON, JOHN

Brill, Lesley. *John Huston's Filmmaking*. Cambridge University Press, 1997.

Hepburn, Katharine. *The Making of The African Queen, or, How I Went to Africa with Bogart, Bacall, and Huston and Almost Lost My Mind*. Knopf, 1987.

Huston, John. *An Open Book*. Da Capo Press, 1994.

Studlar, Gaylyn, ed. *Reflections in a Male Eye; John Huston and the American Experience*. Smithsonian Institution Press, 1993.

INCE, THOMAS M.

Hearst, Patricia. *Murder at San Simeon*. Scribner, 1996 (fiction).

"A Hearst 'Murder' legend." *Patty Hearst Online* http://www.pattyhearst. com/articles/usabookreview.htm

INDEPENDENT FILMMAKER/FILM

MacDonald, Scott. *A Critical Cinema: Interviews with Independent Filmmakers*. University of California Press, 1988.

Pierson, John. *Spike, Mike, Slackers and Dykes: A Guided Tour Across a Decade of American Independent Cinema*. Miramax Books/Hyperion, 1996.

Redding, Judith M. *Film Fatales: Independent Women Directors*. Seal Press, 1997.

Sullivan, Monica. *Videohound's Independent Film Guide*. Visible Ink Press, 1998.

INGRAM, REX

(see also Rudolph Valentino)

Goodman, Walter. "The Thief of Baghdad." *New York Times*, August 9, 1987 (video review).

O'Leary, Liam. *Rex Ingram: Master of the Silent Cinema* (1981?; out of print).

"Rex Ingram." *Internet Movie Database*
http://us.imdb.com/M/person-exact?Ingram%2C%20Rex%20%28II%29
"Rex Ingram." *The Silents Majority*
http://www.mdle.com/ClassicFilms/BTC/direct6.htm

IT HAPPENED ONE NIGHT

(see also Frank Capra, Clark Gable)

Cohen, Meg. "It happened one night." *Harper's Bazaar*, January 1994 (reminiscences of actress Claudette Colbert).

IT'S A WONDERFUL LIFE

(see also Frank Capra and James Stewart)

Alter, Jonathan. "It's a wonderful legacy: two of Stewart's classic characters helped change how we view our politics—and ourselves." *Newsweek*, July 14, 1997.
Barry, Dan. "50 years later, still a happy ending." *New York Times*, December 5, 1996.
Basinger, Janine. *The "It's a Wonderful Life" Book*. Knopf, 1986.
Burr, Ty. "It's a Wonderful Life." *Entertainment Weekly*, June 13, 1997.

JAWS

(see also Steven Spielberg)

Benchley, Peter. *Jaws*. Crest, 1991.
Griffin, Nancy. "In the grip of 'Jaws.'" *Premiere*, October 1995.

JAZZ SINGER, THE

(see also Sound, Vitaphone)

Fisher, James. *Al Jolson*. Greenwood Press, 1994.
"The Jazz Singer (1927)." *E! Online*
http://aol.eonline.com/Facts/Movies/ 0,60,8937,00.html
"The Jazz Singer: 70th anniversary celebration." *Turner Classic Movies*
http://tcm.turner.com/MONTH_SPOTS/9710/jazz_singer/jazz1.htm

JURASSIC PARK

(see also Steven Spielberg)

"Believe in magic: the birth of a digital dinosaur" and "Here come the DNAsaurs." *Newsweek*, June 14, 1993.
Browne, Malcolm W. "Visiting 'Jurassic Park' for real." *New York Times*, June 6, 1993.
Crichton, Michael. *Jurassic Park*. Knopf, 1990.

KAEL, PAULINE

Kael, Pauline. *Conversations with Pauline Kael*. University Press of Mississippi, 1996.

———. *I Lost It at the Movies: Film Writings, 1954–1965.* M. Boyars, 1994.

———. *5001 Nights at the Movies.* Henry Holt, 1991.

———. *Movie Love.* Dutton, 1991.

Slattery, William J., et al. *The Kael Index: A Guide to a Movie Critic's Work, 1954–1991.* Libraries Unlimited, 1993.

KAZAN, ELIA

Billingsley, Kenneth Lloyd. "Elia Kazan: Feted but not forgiven." *Christian Science Monitor*, March 10, 1999.

Dowd, Maureen. "Streetcar named betrayal; blacklist black tie at the Oscars." *New York Times*, February 24, 1999.

Kazan, Elia. *Kazan: The Master Director Discusses His Films.* NewMarket Press, 1999.

Kazan, Elia. *Elia Kazan: A Life.* Da Capo Press, 1997.

Maslin, Janet. "From 'Eden' to 'Streetcar.' " *New York Times*, November 22, 1996.

Weinraub, Bernard. "Time frees the Hollywood one." *New York Times*, January 24, 1999.

KEATON, BUSTER

Keaton, Buster. *My Wonderful World of Slapstick.* Da Capo Press, 1988.

Kline, Jim. *The Complete Films of Buster Keaton.* Citadel Press, 1993.

Meade, Marion. *Buster Keaton: Cut to the Chase.* Da Capo Press, 1997.

Oldham, Gabriella. *Keaton's Silent Shorts: Beyond the Laughter.* Southern Illinois University Press, 1996.

Rapf, Joanna E. *Buster Keaton.* Greenwood Press, 1995.

KEATON, DIANE

Appelo, Tim. "Unstrung heroine." *Entertainment Weekly*, August 22, 1997.

Collins, Nancy. "Annie Hall doesn't live here anymore." *Vanity Fair*, November 1995 (interview).

Dowd, Maureen. "Diane and Woody: still a fun couple." *New York Times*, August 15, 1993.

Greenberg, James. "Not at all unstrung, and calling the shots." *New York Times*, September 3, 1995.

KELLY, GRACE

Conant, Howell. *Grace.* Random House, 1992.

Englund, Steven. *Grace of Monaco: An Interpretive Biography.* Doubleday, 1984.

Lacey, Robert. *Grace.* Berkley Publishing Group, 1997.

Spada, James. *Grace: The Secret Lives of a Princess.* Doubleday, 1987.

KING KONG

Erb, Cynthia. *Tracking King Kong: A Hollywood Icon in World Culture.* Wayne State University Press, 1998.

Goldner, Orville. *The Making of King Kong: The Story Behind a Film Classic.* A. S. Barnes, 1975.

"'King Kong' poster is sold for $244,500." *New York Times*, April 17, 1999.

Wray, Fay. "The gorilla I left behind." *Premiere*, Winter 1994.

KUBRICK, STANLEY

"All eyes on them" and "Three of a kind." *Time*, July 5, 1999.

Baxter, John. *Stanley Kubrick: A Biography*. Carroll and Graf, 1997.

Jenkins, Greg. *Stanley Kubrick and the Art of Adaptation: Three Novels, Three Films*. McFarland, 1997.

LoBrutto, Vincent. *Stanley Kubrick: A Biography*. Da Capo Press, 1999.

Magid, Ron. "Stanley Kubrick's lost movie." *Entertainment Weekly*, June 18, 1999.

Walker, Alexander. *Stanley Kubrick Directs*. Norton, 1999.

LANGE, JESSICA

Ascher-Walsh, Rebecca, et al. "The 25 Greatest Actresses of the '90s." *Entertainment Weekly*, November 27, 1998.

Jeffries, J. T. *Jessica Lange: A Biography*. St. Martin's Press, 1987.

"Jessica's language." *Entertainment Weekly*, April 14, 1995.

Martin, James A. "When actresses enter that ghoulish stage." *Entertainment Weekly*, October 16, 1998.

LAWRENCE OF ARABIA

(see also David Lean)

Corliss, Richard. "A masterpiece restored to the screen: Lawrence of Arabia shows how ravishing films used to be." *Time*, February 6, 1989.

Kauffmann, Stanley. "Lawrence of Arabia." *New Republic*, October 6, 1997.

LEAN, DAVID

Brownlow, Kevin. *David Lean: A Biography*. St. Martin's Press, 1997.

Silver, Alain. *David Lean and His Films*. Silman-James Press, 1992.

Silverman, Stephen M. *David Lean*. Abrams, 1989.

Young, Pamela. "Master of spectacle: David Lean leaves a legacy of movie epics." *Maclean's*, April 29, 1991.

LEIGH, VIVIEN

Edwards, Anne. *Vivien Leigh: A Biography*. Simon & Schuster, 1977.

Molt, Cynthia Marylee. *Vivien Leigh*. Greenwood Press, 1992.

Vickers, Hugo. *Vivien Leigh*. Little, Brown, 1988.

Walker, Alexander. *Vivien: The Life of Vivien Leigh*. Grove Press, 1989.

LIGHTING

Darby, William. *Masters of Lens and Light: A Checklist of Major Cinematographers and Their Feature Films*. Scarecrow Press, 1991.

Goldman, Louis. *Lights, Camera, Action!: Behind the Scenes, Making Movies*. Abrams, 1986.

Schaefer, Dennis, and Larry Salvato. *Masters of Light: Conversations With Contemporary Cinematographers*. University of California Press, 1986.

Concert, Stage, and Film Lighting
http://www.a-ten.com/a_z/stage_lighting.html

LLOYD, HAROLD

Brownlow, Kevin. "Preserved in amber." *Film Comment*, March–April 1993.

D'Agostino, Annette M. *Harold Lloyd*. Greenwood Press, 1994.

Dardis, Tom. *Harold Lloyd: The Man on the Clock*. Penguin Books, 1984.

McCaffrey, Donald W. *Three Classic Silent Screen Comedies Starring Harold Lloyd*. Associated Universities Press, 1976.

LOCATION SHOOTING

Cross, Robin. *Movie Magic*. Sterling, 1995.

Hollywood on Location
http://www.hollywoodonlocation.com/

LOSEY, JOSEPH

Hirsch, Foster. *Joseph Losey*. Twayne, 1980.

"Joseph Losey." *Newsweek*, July 2, 1984 (obituary).

McCarthy, Todd. "Helmer Joseph Losey dies at 75, worked in Europe after blacklist." *Variety*, June 27, 1984 (obituary).

Palmer, James, and Michael Riley. *The Films of Joseph Losey*. Cambridge University Press, 1993.

Richards, Peter. "'Real ice, man': Joseph Losey's 'Modesty Blaise.'" *Film Comment*, July–August 1995.

LUBITSCH, ERNST

Burr, Ty. "'Shop' Keeper: Hanks or the memories? Does You've Got Mail improve upon 1940's The Shop Around the Corner?" *Entertainment Weekly*, May 7, 1999.

Crowe, Cameron. "Leave 'em laughing." *Newsweek*, Summer 1998 (special issue).

Eyman, Scott. *Ernst Lubitsch: Laughter in Paradise*. Simon & Schuster, 1993.

Hake, Sabine. *Passions and Deceptions: The Early Films of Ernst Lubitsch*. Princeton University Press, 1992.

Harvey, James. *Romantic Comedy in Hollywood from Lubitsch to Sturges*. Da Capo Press, 1998.

LUCAS, GEORGE

Bart, Peter. "George Lucas: The Double Feature." *Variety*, April 12, 1999.

Carrau, Bob. *Monsters and Aliens from George Lucas*. Abradale Press, 1996.

Champlin, Charles. *George Lucas: The Creative Impulse: Lucasfilm's First Twenty Years*. Abrams, 1997.

Pollock, Dale. *Skywalking: The Life and Films of George Lucas*. Da Capo Press, 1999.

Thompson, Anne. "George Lucas." *Premiere*, May 1999.

LUMET, SIDNEY

Boyer, Jay. *Sidney Lumet*. Maxwell Macmillan International, 1993.

Callahan, Maureen. "A streetwise legend sticks to his guns." *New York*, May 26, 1997.

Cunningham, Frank R. *Sidney Lumet: Film and Literary Vision*. University Press of Kentucky, 1992.

Lopate, Phillip. "Sidney Lumet, or the necessity for compromise." *Film Comment*, July–August 1997.

LUPINO, IDA

Donati, William. *Ida Lupino: A Biography*. University Press of Kentucky, 1996.

"Ida Lupino." *Variety*, August 14, 1995 (obituary).

"Ida Lupino, 77, actress and director." *People Weekly*, December 25, 1995.

Kuhn, Annette, ed. *Queen of the 'B's*. Greenwood Press, 1995.

Scorsese, Martin. "Behind the camera, a feminist." *New York Times Magazine*, December 31, 1995.

LYNCH, DAVID

Kaleta, Kenneth C. *David Lynch*. Twayne Publishers, 1992.

Lynch, David. *Lynch on Lynch*. Faber and Faber, 1997.

———. *Images*. Hyperion, 1994.

Nochimson, Martha P. *The Passion of David Lynch: Wild at Heart in Hollywood*. University of Texas Press, 1997.

*M*A*S*H**

(see also Robert Altman)

Goldstein, Patrick. "Rebel's return." *Vogue*, May 1992.

Hooker, Richard. *MASH*. Morrow, 1997.

MACGUFFIN

Taylor, David. "MacGuffin inflation." *Forbes*, November 21, 1994.

"What's a MacGuffin?" *MacGuffin Guide to Detective Fiction* http://www.macguffin.net/General/macguf_def.htm

MAGIC LANTERN

Bohn, Thomas W. *Light and Shadows: A History of Motion Pictures.* Mayfield, 1987.

Hepworth, Thomas Craddock. *The Book of the Lantern.* Ayer, 1978.

Quigley, Martin. *Magic Shadows; the Story of the Origin of Motion Pictures.* Biblo and Tannen, 1969.

MALTESE FALCON, THE

(see also John Huston)

Hammett, Dashiell. *The Maltese Falcon.* Vintage Books, 1992.

Harmetz, Aljean. "John Huston protests 'Maltese Falcon' coloring." *New York Times*, November 14, 1986.

Luhr, William, ed. *The Maltese Falcon: John Huston, Director.* Rutgers University Press, 1995.

MALTIN, LEONARD

Maltin, Leonard, ed. *Leonard Maltin's Movie and Video Guide.* Plume, 1999 (annual).

Maltin, Leonard. *Leonard Maltin's Movie Encyclopedia.* Penguin Books, 1995.

Matzer, Marla. "The moviegoer." *Forbes*, September 11, 1995.

MANCHURIAN CANDIDATE, THE

Condon, Richard. *Manchurian Candidate.* Jove Publications, 1988.

Corliss, Richard. "From failure to cult." *Time*, March 21, 1988.

Harmetz, Aljean. "'Manchurian Candidate,' failure in '62, now a hit." *New York Times*, February 24, 1988.

Pratley, Gerald. *The Films of Frankenheimer: Forty Years in Film.* Lehigh University Press, 1998.

MANKIEWICZ, JOSEPH

Canby, Vincent. "40 years of film magic." *New York Times*, November 20, 1992.

Dick, Bernard F. *Joseph L. Mankiewicz.* Twayne, 1983.

Geist, Kenneth L. *Pictures Will Talk: The Life and Films of Joseph L. Mankiewicz.* Scribner, 1978.

Gussow, Mel. "The man who made 'All About Eve' recalls his sometimes bumpy ride." *New York Times*, November 24, 1992.

O'Toole, Lawrence. "'All About Eve': fasten your seat belts for a backstage peek at a classic Broadway tale." *Entertainment Weekly*, March 1995.

MANN, ANTHONY

Basinger, Jeanine. *Anthony Mann.* Twayne Publishers, 1979.

Horton, Robert. "Mann and Stewart: two rode together." *Film Comment*, March–April 1990.

Jameson, Richard T. "Anthony Mann: a director of razor-sharp images and moral rigor." *American Film*, Jan. 1990.
Kemp, Phillip. "'The story of all wars': Anthony Mann's Men in War." *Film Comment*, July–August 1996.

MATHIS, JUNE
(see Rudolph Valentino)

MELODRAMA
Byars, Jackie. *All That Hollywood Allows: Re-Reading Gender in 1950s Melodrama*. University of North Carolina Press, 1991.
Cavell, Stanley. *Contesting Tears: The Hollywood Melodrama of the Unknown Woman*. University of Chicago Press, 1996.
Landy, Marcia, ed. *Imitations of Life: A Reader of Film and Television Melodrama*. Wayne State University Press, 1991.

METHOD ACTOR
Cole, Toby. *Acting: A Handbook of the Stanislavski Method*. Crown, 1995.
Hirsch, Foster. *A Method to Their Madness: The History of the Actors Studio*. Da Capo Press, 1986.
Stanislavski, Constantine. *An Actor Prepares*. Theatre Arts Books, 1989.
Strasberg, Lee. *A Dream of Passion: The Development of the Method*. New American Library, 1988.

METONYMY
Altman, Rick, ed. *Sound Theory, Sound Practice*. Routledge, 1992.
De Lauretis, Teresa. *Alice Doesn't: Feminism, Semiotics, Cinema*. Indiana University Press, 1984.
Metz, Christian. *Film Language: A Semiotics of the Cinema*. University of Chicago Press, 1991.
Chandler, Daniel. "Semiotics for Beginners: Metaphor and Metonymy." Reproduced at http://www.georgetown.edu/grad/CCT/505/semiotic.html

MIDNIGHT COWBOY
(see also Dustin Hoffman)
Brooker-Bowers, Nancy. *John Schlesinger: A Guide to References and Resources*. G.K. Hall, 1978.
Daly, Steve. "Midnight Cowboy: everybody's still talkin' about it." *Entertainment Weekly*, March 1995 (Special Collector's Issue).
Herlihy, James Leo. *Midnight Cowboy, a Novel*. Simon & Schuster, 1965.
Schlesinger, John. "John Schlesinger, Joe Buck and Ratso." *The New Yorker*, February 28, 1994.
Kilday, Greg. "Tales of Hoffman." *Entertainment Weekly*, March 4, 1994.

MILESTONE, LEWIS

Eksteins, Modris. "All Quiet on the Western Front." *History Today*, November 1995.

"Lewis Milestone." *Newsweek*, October 6, 1980 (obituary).

Millichap, Joseph R. *Lewis Milestone* (out of print).

MISTER SMITH GOES TO WASHINGTON

(see also Frank Capra, James Stewart)

Alter, Jonathan. "It's a wonderful legacy: two of Stewart's classic characters helped change how we view our politics—and ourselves." *Newsweek*, July 14, 1997.

Hertzberg, Hendrik. "Upset victory: 'Primary Colors' triumphs over the old politics of Hollywood." *The New Yorker*, March 23, 1998.

MIX, TOM

Mix, Paul E. *Tom Mix: A Heavily Illustrated Biography of the Western Star, With a Filmography*. McFarland, 1995.

Norris, Merle G. *Tom Mix Book*. World of Yesterday, 1989.

Woytowich, Andy. *Tom Mix Highlights*. Empire Publishing, 1989.

"Ye varmints! Tom's horse is gone again!" *New York Times*, August 12, 1989.

MODERN TIMES

(see Charlie Chaplin)

MONROE, MARILYN

Arnold, Eve. *Marilyn Monroe—an Appreciation*. Knopf, 1987.

Conway, Michael, et al. *The Complete Films of Marilyn Monroe*. Citadel Press, 1991.

Mailer, Norman. *Marilyn, a Biography*. Perigee Books, 1987.

Spoto, Donald. *Marilyn Monroe: The Biography*. HarperCollins, 1993.

Steinem, Gloria. *Marilyn*. Fine Communications, 1997.

MONTAGE

Devereaux, Leslie, and Roger Hillman, eds. *Fields of Vision: Essays in Film Studies, Visual Anthropology, and Photography*. University of California Press, 1995.

MURNAU, F. W.

"Resurrected Murnau classics headed for Telluride Festival." *Variety*, August 26, 1981.

Shepherd, Jim. *Nosferatu: A Novel*. Knopf, 1998 (fictionalized biography).

Ursini, James. *The Vampire Film: From Nosferatu to Bram Stoker's Dracula*. Limelight Editions, 1993.

"The Devil and Mr. Murnau." *The Silents Majority* http://www.mdle.com/ ClassicFilms/SCSC/murnau.htm

MUSIC

Hischak, Thomas S. *The American Musical Film Song Encyclopedia*. Greenwood Press, 1999.

Karlin, Fred. *Listening to Movies: The Film Lover's Guide to Film Music*. Maxwell Macmillan, 1994.

Marks, Martin Miller. *Music and the Silent Film: Contexts and Case Studies, 1895–1924*. Oxford University Press, 1997.

Prendergast, Roy M. *Film Music*. W. W. Norton, 1992.

Thomas, Tony. *Music for the Movies*. Silman-James Press, 1997.

MUSICAL FILM

Altman, Rick. *The American Film Musical*. Indiana University Press, 1987.

Aylesworth, Thomas G. *Broadway to Hollywood: Musicals from Stage to Screen*. Gallery Books, 1985.

Fordin, Hugh. *M-G-M's Greatest Musicals: The Arthur Freed Unit*. Da Capo Press, 1996.

Green, Stanley. *Hollywood Musicals Year by Year*. Hal Leonard Publishing, 1990.

Hemming, Roy. *The Melody Lingers On: The Great Songwriters and Their Movie Musicals*. NewMarket Press, 1986.

MUTINY ON THE BOUNTY

(see also Clark Gable)

"Mutiny on the Bounty (1935)." *E! Online* http://www.eonline.com/Facts/ Movies/0,60,11886,00.html

Nordhoff, Charles. *Mutiny on the Bounty*. Little, Brown, 1989.

"Silent witness to a mutiny is pulled from Bounty Bay." *New York Times*, January 12, 1999.

"The Best Picture 1935: Mutiny on the Bounty." *TheOscar.com* http:// www.theoscar.com/pics/pic35.htm

MY FAIR LADY

(see also George Cukor, Audrey Hepburn)

Grimes, William. "In 'My Fair Lady,' Audrey Hepburn is singing at last." *New York Times*, August 15, 1994.

Gussow, Mel. "Not just an ordinary man; he'll always be Henry Higgins, but Rex Harrison was also an interpretive artist of the first rank." *New York Times*, June 10, 1990 (obituary).

MY OWN PRIVATE IDAHO

Ansen, David. "Prince Hal in Portland: the risk-taking director of 'Drugstore Cowboy' makes a bold new movie on his hometown streets." *Newsweek*, April 15, 1991.

Handelman, David. "Gus Van Sant's northwest passage." *Rolling Stone*, October 31, 1991.

Meyer, Thomas J. “Dropping in on the down and out.” *New York Times Magazine*, September 15, 1991.

Sante, Luc. “The rise of the baroque directors.” *Vogue*, September 1992.

MYSTERY-THRILLER

(see also Detective film)

Cocchiarelli, Joseph J. *Screen Sleuths: A Filmography*. Garland, 1992.

Melvin, David Skene. *Crime, Detective, Espionage, Mystery, and Thriller Fiction and Film*. Greenwood Press, 1981.

McCarty, John. *The Fearmakers*. St. Martin's Press, 1994.

———. *Thrillers: Seven Decades of Classic Film Suspense*. Citadel Press, 1992.

Rubin, Martin. *Thrillers*. Cambridge University Press, 1999.

NEGRI, POLA

“Femme fatale silent film star Pola Negri succumbs in Texas.” *Variety*, August 5, 1987 (obituary).

Krebs, Albin. “Pola Negri, a vamp of the silent screen, dies at 88.” *New York Times*, August 3, 1987 (obituary).

Negri, Pola. *Memoirs of a Star*. Doubleday, 1970.

“Pola Negri.” *Vanity Fair*, May 1992.

NEOREALISM

(see also Experimental film)

White, Armond. “Sticking to the soul.” *Film Comment*, January–February 1997.

NETWORK

(see Sidney Lumet)

NEW AMERICAN CINEMA

(see also Experimental film)

Lewis, Jon, ed. *The New American Cinema*. Duke University Press, 1998.

NEWSREEL

Fielding, Raymond. *The American Newsreel, 1911–1967*. University of Oklahoma Press, 1972.

Headline Stories of the Century: A Newsreel Library of America in the News (videorecording). Questar Video, 1992.

The Reel World of News (videorecording). PBS Video, 1988.

NICHOLS, MIKE

Applebome, Peter. “Always asking, what is this really about?” *New York Times*, April 25, 1999.

Bart, Peter. "Gotham's guiding light." *Variety*, May 10, 1999.
Lemon, Brendan. "Nichols and timing." *Interview*, April 1998.
Schuth, H. Wayne. *Mike Nichols*. Twayne Publishers, 1978.
Smith, Gavin. "Mike Nichols." *Film Comment*, May 1999.

NICHOLSON, JACK
"Actors' acting awards to 'As Good as It Gets.' " *New York Times*, March 10, 1998.
Brode, Douglas. *The Films of Jack Nicholson*. Citadel Press, 1996.
McGilligan, Patrick. *Jack's Life: A Biography of Jack Nicholson*. W. W. Norton, 1994.
Shepherd, Donald. *Jack Nicholson: An Unauthorized Biography*. St. Martin's Press, 1991.
Thompson, Peter. *Jack Nicholson: The Life and Times of an Actor on the Edge*. Birch Lane Press, 1997.

NICKELODEON
Before the Nickelodeon: The Early Cinema of Edwin S. Porter (videorecording). Kino on Video, 1998.
Bowers, Q. David. *Nickelodeon Theatres and Their Music*. Scarecrow Press, 1997.
Musser, Charles. *Before the Nickelodeon: Edwin S. Porter and the Edison Manufacturing Company*. University of California Press, 1991.

NORTH BY NORTHWEST
(see also Alfred Hitchcock)
Chase, Donald. "My favorite year: 1959." *Film Comment*, September–October 1994.
Naremore, James, ed. *North by Northwest: Alfred Hitchcock, Director*. Rutgers University Press, 1993.

OLIVIER, LAURENCE
Hall, Peter. "Olivier: Exit the Emperor." *New York Times*, July 23, 1989 (obituary).
Hopkins, Anthony. "The Lightning of Olivier." *New York Times*, July 16, 1989.
Lewis, Roger. *The Real Life of Laurence Olivier*. Applause Theatre Books, 1997.
Olivier, Laurence. *On Acting*. Simon & Schuster, 1986.
———. *Confessions of an Actor: An Autobiography*. Penguin Books, 1984.
Spoto, Donald. *Laurence Olivier: A Biography*. HarperCollins, 1992.

ON THE WATERFRONT
(see also Marlon Brando, Elia Kazan)
Neve, Brian. "On the Waterfront." *History Today*, June 1995.

Schulberg, Budd. "The inside story of 'Waterfront.' " *New York Times Magazine*, January 6, 1980.

ONE FLEW OVER THE CUCKOO'S NEST
(see also Jack Nicholson)
Buckley, Tom. "The Forman formula." *New York Times*, March 1, 1981.
Forman, Milos, and Jan Novak. *Turnaround: A Memoir*. Villard Books, 1994.
Kesey, Ken. *One Flew Over the Cuckoo's Nest*. New American Library, 1989.
Slater, Thomas J. *Milos Forman*. Greenwood Press, 1987.
Weinraub, Bernard, and Andrea Higbie. "Oscar's glory is fleeting. Ask one who knows." *New York Times*, March 27, 1995.

PACINO, AL
Dullea, Georgia. "Al Pacino confronts a gala, kudos, fame and his own shyness." *New York Times*, February 22, 1993.
Schoell, William. *The Films of Al Pacino*. Carol Publishing Group, 1995.
Yule, Andrew. *Life on the Wire: The Life and Art of Al Pacino*. D. I. Fine, 1991.
Weber, Bruce. "Al Pacino, slouching (again) toward Shakespeare." *New York Times*, October 6, 1996.
Weinraub, Bernard. "De Niro! Pacino! Together again for first time." *New York Times*, July 27, 1995.

PATTON
Kim, Erwin. *Franklin J. Schaffner*. Scarecrow Press, 1985.
Morgan, Thomas. "Franklin J. Schaffner at 69; an Oscar-winning film director." *New York Times*, July 3, 1989 (obituary).
Purtell, Tim. "Oscar grouch." *Entertainment Weekly*, April 16, 1993.

PECKINPAH, SAM
Fine, Marshall. *Bloody Sam*. D. I. Fine, 1991.
Prince, Stephen. *Savage Cinema: Sam Peckinpah and the Rise of Ultraviolent Movies*. University of Texas Press, 1998.
Seydor, Paul. *Peckinpah, the Western Films: A Reconsideration*. University of Illinois Press, 1997.
Simmons, Garner. *Peckinpah: A Portrait in Montage*. Limelight Editions, 1998.
Weddle, David. *If They Move—Kill 'Em: The Life and Times of Sam Peckinpah*. Grove Press, 1994.

PHILADELPHIA STORY, THE
(see George Cukor, Katharine Hepburn, James Stewart)

PICKFORD, MARY

Brownlow, Kevin. *Mary Pickford Rediscovered: Rare Pictures of a Hollywood Legend*. Abrams, 1999.

Corliss, Richard. "The First Movie Star: A Pickford revival in books and videos proves there's still something about Mary." *Time*, June 28, 1999.

Eyman, Scott. *Mary Pickford, America's Sweetheart*. D. I. Fine, 1989.

"Mary Pickford: Little miss mogul." *Entertainment Weekly*, Fall 1996 (Special Collector's Issue).

Whitfield, Eileen. *Pickford: The Woman Who Made Hollywood*. University Press of Kentucky, 1997.

PLACE IN THE SUN, A

(see also Elizabeth Taylor)

Blau, Eleanor. "Film making father." *New York Times*, August 18, 1988.

Bosworth, Patricia. *Montgomery Clift: A Biography*. Limelight Editions, 1990.

Fein, Esther B. "In 'George Stevens,' son honors a film maker." *New York Times*, May 6, 1985.

Purtell, Tim. "No place in the sun." *Entertainment Weekly*, July 23, 1993.

PLATOON

(see also Oliver Stone)

"Oliver Stone's platoon buddies recall the war 20 years later." *People Weekly*, May 11, 1987.

Richman, Alan. "For his look back in anger at Vietnam, Platoon's Oliver Stone is bombarded with Oscar nominations." *People Weekly*, March 2, 1987.

Stone, Oliver. "A filmmaker's credo: some thoughts on politics, history, and the movies." *Humanist*, September–October 1996.

POITIER, SIDNEY

Bergman, Carol, and Nathan I. Huggins. *Sidney Poitier*. Chelsea House, 1989.

"From sir, with love." *Time*, April 28, 1997.

O'Connor, John J. "American Film Institute Salute to Sidney Poitier." *New York Times*, April 3, 1992.

Poitier, Sidney. *This Life*. Knopf, 1980.

"Sidney Poitier." *Entertainment Weekly*, Fall 1996 (Special Collector's issue).

POLANSKI, ROMAN

Leaming, Barbara. *Polanski, the Filmmaker as Voyeur: A Biography*. Simon & Schuster, 1981.

Polanski, Roman. *Roman*. Morrow, 1984.

Robinson, Jill. "Polanski's inferno." *Vanity Fair*, April 1997.

Wexman, Virginia Wright. *Roman Polanski*. Twayne Publishers, 1985.

POLLACK, SYDNEY

Dworkin, Susan. *Making Tootsie: A Film Study with Dustin Hoffman and Sydney Pollack*. NewMarket Press, 1983.

Hindes, Andrew, and Anita M. Busch. "Pollack packs a full bag." *Variety*, December 11, 1995.

"An Interview by Jonathan Mostow with Sydney Pollack." *Variety*, November 17, 1997.

Meyer, Janet L. *Sydney Pollack: A Critical Filmography*. McFarland, 1998.

Weinraub, Bernard. "Wounded by a flop, director tries again." *New York Times*, June 28, 1993.

POSTMODERNISM

Degli-Esposti, ed. *Postmodernism in the Cinema*. Berghahn Books, 1998.

Friedberg, Anne. *Window Shopping: Cinema and the Postmodern*. University of California Press, 1993.

Jencks, Charles. *What is Post-modernism?* St. Martin's Press, 1986.

Sharrett, Christopher. *Crisis Cinema: The Apocalyptic Idea in Postmodern Narrative Film*. Maisonneuve Press, 1992.

PREQUEL

Ackley, Laura A. "ILM harnesses the force for 'Star Wars' prequel." *Variety*, July 20, 1998.

"Get Ready for the Prequel Sequel." *Time*, May 24, 1999.

PRODUCER

Kanin, Garson. *Hollywood; Stars and Starlets, Tycoons and Flesh-peddlers, Moviemakers and Moneymakers, Frauds and Geniuses, Hopefuls and Has-beens, Great Lovers and Sex Symbols*. Viking Press, 1974.

Lazarus, Paul N. *The Film Producer*. St. Martin's Press, 1992.

Obst, Lynda Rosen. *Hello, He Lied: And Other Truths from the Hollywood Trenches*. Broadway Books, 1997.

PSYCHO

(see also Alfred Hitchcock)

Ansen, David. "'Psycho' Analysis: Director Gus Van Sant defends his controversial decision to remake Hitchcock's classic shocker." *Newsweek*, December 7, 1998.

Rebello, Stephen. *Alfred Hitchcock and the Making of Psycho*. W. W. Norton, 1990.

Sterritt, David. "Hitchcock's 'Psycho' still influences movies." *Christian Science Monitor*, July 31, 1990.

PSYCHOANALYSIS AND FILM

Art and Film Since 1945: Hall of Mirrors. Monacelli Press, 1996.

Bergstrom, Janet, ed. *Cinema and Psychoanalysis: Parallel Histories*. University of California Press, 1999.

Charney, Maurice, and Joseph Reppen, eds. *Psychoanalytic Approaches to Literature and Film*. Fairleigh Dickinson University Press, 1987.

Trosman, Harry. *Contemporary Psychoanalysis and Masterworks of Art and Film*. New York University Press, 1996.

Walker, Janet. *Couching Resistance: Women, Film, and Psychoanalytic Psychiatry*. University of Minnesota Press, 1993.

PSYCHODRAMA

Emunah, Renee, and Adam Blatner. *Acting for Real: Drama Therapy Process, Technique, and Performance*. Brunner/Mazel, 1994.

Karp, Marcia, et al., eds. *The Handbook of Psychodrama*. Routledge, 1998.

PULP FICTION

Ansen, David. "A tough guy takes Cannes." *Newsweek*, June 6, 1994.

Bernard, Jami. *Quentin Tarantino: The Man and His Movies*. HarperPerennial, 1995.

Clarkson, Wensley. *Quentin Tarantino: Shooting from the Hip*. Overlook Press, 1995.

Dawson, Jeff. *Quentin Tarantino: The Cinema of Cool*. Applause Theatre Books, 1995.

Tarantino, Quentin. *Quentin Tarantino: Interviews*. University Press of Mississippi, 1998.

Woods, Paul A. *King Pulp: The Wild World of Quentin Tarantino*. Plexus, 1998.

RAGING BULL

(see also Robert De Niro, Martin Scorsese)

Kael, Pauline. "Raging Bull." *The New Yorker*, December 8, 1980 (review).

La Motta, Jake. *Raging Bull*. Bantam, 1980.

RAIDERS OF THE LOST ARK

(see also Harrison Ford, Steven Spielberg)

Kael, Pauline. "Raiders of the Lost Ark." *New Yorker*, June 15, 1981 (review).

Schickel, Richard. "Slam! Bang! A movie movie." *Time*, June 15, 1981 (review).

RATING SYSTEM

"Film makers protest rating system." *New York Times*, July 23, 1990.

Harris, Mark. "Abridged too far?" *Entertainment Weekly*, January 15, 1993.

Mason, M. S. "Revamped film rating system: Why it changed, how it works." *Christian Science Monitor*, October 3, 1990.

MPAA (Motion Picture Association of America) Movie Ratings http://www. mpaa.org/movieratings/

RAY, NICHOLAS

Kennedy, Harlan. "The melodramatists." *American Film*, January–February 1992.

Ray, Nicholas. *I Was Interrupted: Nicholas Ray on Making Movies*. University of California Press, 1993.

Rosenbaum, Jonathan. "Looking for Nicholas Ray." *American Film*, December 1981.

REALIST CINEMA

Corkin, Stanley. *Realism and the Birth of the Modern United States: Cinema, Literature, and Culture*. University of Georgia Press, 1996.

Hillier, Jim, ed. *Cahiers Du Cinema: The 1950's Neo-Realism, Hollywood, New Wave*. Harvard University Press, 1986.

REAR WINDOW

(see also Grace Kelly, Alfred Hitchcock, James Stewart)

Greenhouse, Linda. "Final twist in 'Rear Window' case." *New York Times*, April 25, 1990.

Sharff, Stefan. *The Art of Looking in Hitchcock's Rear Window*. Limelight Editions, 1997.

Wharton, Dennis. "Studios' profits from released pix could go out the 'Rear Window.' " *Variety*, January 17, 1990.

REBEL WITHOUT A CAUSE

(see also Nicholas Ray, Natalie Wood)

Brush, Stephanie. "Alienation isn't what it used to be." *New York Times*, April 3, 1994.

Burr, Ty. "The first rebel yell." *Entertainment Weekly*, October 29, 1993.

Spoto, Donald. *Rebel: The Life and Legend of James Dean*. HarperCollins, 1996.

REDFORD, ROBERT

Gehring, Wes D. "The Populist Films of Robert Redford." *USA Today (Magazine)*, May 1999.

Kirn, Walter. "Robert Redford has a problem: the godfather of independent cinema continues to work in the studio system he abhors." *New York Times Magazine*, November 16, 1997.

McCarthy, Todd. "Robert Redford." *Premiere*, June 1998.

Rayner, Richard. "Existential cowboy." *The New Yorker*, May 18, 1998.

"Robert Redford." *Entertainment Weekly*, Fall 1996 (Special Collector's Issue).

Spada, James. *The Films of Robert Redford*. Lyle Stuart, 1984.

REID, WALLACE

Farrar, Geraldine. *Such Sweet Compulsion; the Autobiography of Geraldine Farrar*. Books for Libraries Press, 1970.

Myers, Eric. "Bizet-Riesenfeld: Carmen." *Opera News*, November 1997 (rerelease of 1915 film).

"Wallace Reid." *The Silents Majority* http://www.mdle.com/ClassicFilms/ FeaturedStar/perfor49.htm

REMAKE

Druxman, Michael B. *Make It Again, Sam: A Survey of Movie Remakes*. A. S. Barnes, 1975.

Horton, Andrew, and Stuart Y. McDougal, eds. *Play It Again, Sam: Retakes on Remakes*. University of California Press, 1998.

Limbacher, James L. *Haven't I Seen You Somewhere Before? Remakes, Sequels, and Series in Motion Pictures, Videos, and Television, 1896–1990*. Pierian Press, 1992.

Milberg, Doris. *Repeat Performances: A Guide to Hollywood Movie Remakes*. Broadway Press, 1990.

Nowlan, Robert A., and Gwendolyn Nolan. *Cinema Sequels and Remakes, 1903–1987*. McFarland, 1989.

ROAD PICTURE

(see also Easy Rider)

Broeske, Pat H. "On the road (again)." *Entertainment Weekly*, April 10, 1992.

James, Caryn. "On the road again: Uneasy riders." *New York Times*, February 26, 1989.

James, Caryn. "Today's Yellow Brick Road leads straight to hell." *New York Times*, August 19, 1990.

"Warren and Dustin, the road movies updated." *Life*, May 1986.

ROBERTS, JULIA

Churchill, Bonnie. "Just a normal girl-next-door superstar." *Christian Science Monitor*, May 28, 1999.

Joyce, Aileen. *Julia: The Untold Story of America's Pretty Woman*. Windsor, 1993.

"Julia Roberts." *Entertainment Weekly*, October 30, 1998.

Wallner, Rosemary. *Julia Roberts*. Abdo, 1991.

Young, Josh. "When Julia Roberts says no, other actresses cry, thanks!" *New York Times*, October 1, 1995.

ROCKY

Daly, Marsha. *Sylvester Stallone: An Illustrated Life*. St. Martin's Press, 1984.

"Sly's own Rocky." *Life*, February 1983.

Smith, Laura C. "Sly hits the Rocky road." *Entertainment Weekly*, November 17, 1995.

Stallone, Sylvester. "Knockout Punch." *Newsweek*, June 28, 1999.

ROCKY HORROR PICTURE SHOW, THE

(see also Susan Sarandon)

Gliatto, Tom. "Two decades of madness." *People Weekly*, November 6, 1995.

"In a Time Warp." *Newsweek*, January 18, 1999.

Smith, Laura C. "Chiming in at midnight: Two decades ago, 'The Rocky Horror Picture Show' made talking at the movies a craze." *Entertainment Weekly*, September 22, 1995.

Willens, Michele. "Give Tim Curry a role and he'll provide the relish." *New York Times*, November 7, 1993.

ROEG, NICOLAS

Feineman, Neil. *Nicolas Roeg*. Twayne, 1978.

Izod, John. *The Films of Nicolas Roeg: Myth and Mind*. St. Martin's Press, 1992.

Rayner, Jay, and Boyd Tonkin. "Nicolas Roeg talks to Jay Rayner about his new film 'Two Deaths.' " *New Statesman*, June 14, 1996.

Salwolke, Scott. *Nicolas Roeg Film by Film*. McFarland, 1993.

ROGERS, GINGER

Brubach, Holly. "Better than sex." *New York Times Magazine*, December 31, 1995 (obituary).

Croce, Arlene. "Ginger Rogers." *The New Yorker*, May 8, 1995.

———. *The Fred Astaire and Ginger Rogers Book*. Vintage Books, 1977.

Morley, Sheridan. *Shall We Dance: The Life of Ginger Rogers*. St. Martin's Press, 1995.

Rogers, Ginger. *Ginger: My Story*. HarperCollins, 1991.

RUDOLPH, ALAN

Carpenter, Teresa. "Back to the round table with Dorothy Parker and pals. . . ." *New York Times*, August 29, 1993.

Natale, Richard. ". . . And their reunion host." *New York Times*, August 29, 1993.

Ness, Richard. *Alan Rudolph: Romance and a Crazed World*. Twayne, 1996.

Smith, Gavin. "Alan Rudolph: 'I don't have a career, I have a careen.' " *Film Comment*, May–June 1993.

RYAN, MEG

Churchill, Bonnie. "Comic actress Meg Ryan forays into producing." *Christian Science Monitor*, May 23, 1995.

Dougherty, Margot. "Megastar." *Los Angeles Magazine*, January 1999.

MacSweeney, Eve. "Meg's dilemma." *Harper's Bazaar*, December 1998.

"Meg Ryan." *Entertainment Weekly*, October 30, 1998.

SARANDON, SUSAN

Ascher-Walsh, Rebecca. "Labor of love: with 'Dead Man Walking,' Susan Sarandon and Tim Robbins go from Oscar outlaws to golden couple." *Entertainment Weekly*, March 22, 1996.

Fuller, Graham. "Susan Sarandon: the bigger-picture revolution." *Interview*, October 1994.

Jacobs, Gloria. "Susan Sarandon (Woman of the Year)." *Ms. Magazine*, January–February 1996.

"The many faces of 'Thelma and Louise.' " *Film Quarterly*, Winter 1991.

"Susan Sarandon." *Entertainment Weekly*, Fall 1996 (Special Collector's Issue).

SAVING PRIVATE RYAN

(see also Tom Hanks, Steven Spielberg)

Canby, Vincent. "Saving a nation's pride of being; the horror and honor of a good war." *New York Times*, August 10, 1998.

Cochran, Jason. "Steven's War: World War II has long been Steven Spielberg's theater of operation." *Entertainment Weekly*, May 28, 1999.

Jameson, Richard T. "History's eyes: 'Saving Private Ryan.' " *Film Comment*, September–October 1998.

Maslin, Janet. "Critics give 'Private Ryan' their top award." *New York Times*, December 17, 1998.

Spielberg, Steven, ed. *Saving Private Ryan: The Men, the Mission, the Movie*. NewMarket Press, 1998.

SCARFACE

(see Howard Hawks)

SCHINDLER'S LIST

(see also Steven Spielberg)

Fensch, Thomas, ed. *Oskar Schindler and His List: The Man, the Book, the Film, the Holocaust and Its Survivors*. Paul S. Eriksson, 1995.

Grimes, William. "Spielberg wins at last with 7 Oscars for 'Schindler's List.' " *New York Times*, March 22, 1994.

Keneally, Thomas. *Schindler's List*. Simon & Schuster, 1993.

Klady, Leonard. "Sweet success for Spielberg's 'Schindler.' " *Variety*, March 28, 1994.

Palowski, Franciszek. *The Making of Schindler's List: Behind the Scenes of an Epic Film*. Birch Lane Press, 1998.

SCIENCE-FICTION FILM

Everman, Welch. *Cult Science Fiction Films: From the Amazing Colossal Man to Yog: The Monster from Space*. Citadel Press, 1995.

Schwartz, Carol A. *VideoHound's Sci-Fi Experience; Your Quantum Guide to the Video Universe*. Visible Ink Press, 1996.

Stanley, John. *Creature Features: The Science Fiction, Fantasy, and Horror Movie Guide*. Berkley Publishing Group, 1997.

Staskowski, Andrea. *Science Fiction Movies*. Lerner Publications, 1992.

Weaver, Tom. *Science Fiction and Fantasy Film Flashbacks: Conversations With 24 Actors, Writers, Producers and Directors from the Golden Age*. McFarland, 1998.

SCORSESE, MARTIN

Bliss, Michael. *Martin Scorsese and Michael Cimino*. Scarecrow Press, 1985.

Ehrenstein, David. *The Scorsese Picture: The Art and Life of Martin Scorsese*. Carol Publishing Group, 1992.

Friedman, Lawrence S. *The Cinema of Martin Scorsese*. Continuum, 1997.

Keyser, Lester J. *Martin Scorsese*. Maxwell Macmillan International, 1992.

Lourdeaux, Lee. *Italian and Irish Filmmakers in America: Ford, Capra, Coppola, and Scorsese*. Temple University Press, 1990.

SCREEN ACTORS GUILD

Moldea, Dan E. *Dark Victory: Ronald Reagan, MCA, and the Mob*. Viking, 1986.

Prindle, David F. *The Politics of Glamour: Ideology and Democracy in the Screen Actors Guild*. University of Wisconsin Press, 1988.

http://www.sag.com/

SCREWBALL COMEDY

Gehring, Wes D. *Screwball Comedy: A Genre of Madcap Romance*. Greenwood Press, 1986.

Sennett, Ted. *Lunatics and Lovers: A Tribute to the Giddy and Glittering Era of the Screen's "Screwball" and Romantic Comedies*. Limelight Editions, 1985.

Sikov, Ed. *Screwball: Hollywood's Madcap Romantic Comedies*. Crown Publishers, 1989.

SEARCHERS, THE

(see also John Ford, John Wayne)

O'Brien, Geoffrey. "The movie of the century: It looks both backward to everything Hollywood had learned about Westerns and forward to things films hadn't dared do." *American Heritage*, November 1998.

Thomson, David. "Open and shut: A fresh look at 'The Searchers.'" *Film Comment*, July–August 1997.

SENNETT, MACK

Sherk, Warren M. *The Films of Mack Sennett*. Scarecrow Press, 1998.

"Mack Sennett." *E! Online* http://aol.eonline.com/Facts/People/0,12, 18312,00.html

"Mack Sennett: The King Behind the Kops." *The Silents Majority* http:// www.mdle.com/ClassicFilms/FeaturedStar/keystone.htm#mack

SEQUEL

Druxman, Michael B. *One Good Film Deserves Another*. A. S. Barnes, 1977.

Limbacher, James L. *Haven't I Seen You Somewhere Before? Remakes, Sequels, and Series in Motion Pictures, Videos, and Television, 1896–1990*. Pierian Press, 1992.

Nowlan, Robert A., and Gwendolyn Nolan. *Cinema Sequels and Remakes, 1903–1987*. McFarland, 1989.

SERIAL

Cline, William C. *In the Nick of Time: Motion Picture Sound Serials*. McFarland, 1984.

Hayes, R. M. *The Republic Chapterplays: A Complete Filmography of the Serials Released by Republic Pictures Corporation, 1934–1955*. McFarland, 1992.

Limbacher, James L. *Haven't I Seen You Somewhere Before? Remakes, Sequels, and Series in Motion Pictures, Videos, and Television, 1896–1990*. Pierian Press, 1992.

Rainey, Buck. *Those Fabulous Serial Heroines: Their Lives and Films*. Scarecrow Press, 1990.

Schutz, Wayne. *The Motion Picture Serial: An Annotated Bibliography*. Scarecrow Press, 1992.

SHANE

Blau, Eleanor. "Film making father." *New York Times*, August 18, 1988.

Fein, Esther B. "In 'George Stevens,' son honors a film maker." *New York Times*, May 6, 1985.

Nichols, Peter M. "Restoring what time, and editors, took away; renovated film classics find their way back onto big screens and video, often in versions never seen before." *New York Times*, May 17, 1998.

Schaefer, Jack. *Shane*. Bantam Books, 1983.

SHORTS

Lahue, Kalton C. *World of Laughter; The Motion Picture Comedy Short, 1910–1930*. University of Oklahoma Press, 1966.

The Lumiere Brothers' First Films (videorecording). Kino on Video, 1997.

Maltin, Leonard. *The Great Movie Shorts*. Crown Publishers, 1972.

McCall, Douglas L. *Film Cartoons: A Guide to 20th Century American Animated Features and Shorts*. McFarland, 1998.

Okuda, Ted. *The Columbia Comedy Shorts: Two-reel Hollywood Film Comedies, 1933–1958*. McFarland, 1986.

Schrank, Jeffrey. *Guide to Short Films*. Hayden Book Co., 1979.

SILENCE OF THE LAMBS, THE

(see also Anthony Hopkins)

Bliss, Michael. *What Goes Around Comes Around: The Films of Jonathan Demme*. Southern Illinois University Press, 1996.

"Directors honor 'Silence of the Lambs.'" *New York Times*, March 16, 1992.

Grimes, William. "'Silence of the Lambs' dominates Oscars, winning 5 awards." *New York Times*, March 31, 1992.

Harris, Thomas. *The Silence of the Lambs*. St. Martin's Press, 1989.

SINGIN' IN THE RAIN

Churchill, Bonnie. "Gene Kelly: Soaked shoes and umbrella forever." *Christian Science Monitor*, February 6, 1996.

Hirschhorn, Clive. *Gene Kelly: A Biography*. St. Martin's Press, 1984.

Krebs, Albin. "Gene Kelly, dancer of vigor and grace, dies." *New York Times*, February 3, 1996 (obituary).

Morley, Sheridan. *Gene Kelly: A Celebration*. Trafalgar Square, 1998.

O'Toole, Lawrence. "The happy hoofer." *Entertainment Weekly*, February 16, 1996 (obituary of Gene Kelly).

SISKEL, GENE

(see also Roger Ebert)

Ebert, Roger, and Gene Siskel. *The Future of the Movies*. Andrews McMeel, 1991.

Peach, Kindra. "Gene Siskel." *Premiere*, May 1999 (obituary).

Svetkey, Benjamin. "Lights Down: As one half of the influential Siskel and Ebert, Gene Siskel brought movie criticism to the masses." *Entertainment Weekly*, March 5, 1999 (obituary).

Watson, Bret. "They still like to watch." *Entertainment Weekly*, May 17, 1996.

SLAPSTICK

In the Beginning: Film Comedy Pioneers (videorecording). Kino on Video, 1998.

Keaton, Buster. *My Wonderful World of Slapstick*. Da Capo Press, 1988.

Kerr, Walter. *The Silent Clowns*. Da Capo Press, 1990.

SNOW WHITE AND THE SEVEN DWARFS

Bailey, Adrian. *Walt Disney's World of Fantasy*. Gallery Books, 1987.

Finch, Christopher. *The Art of Walt Disney: From Mickey Mouse to the Magic Kingdoms*. Abrams, 1995.

Grant, John. *The Encyclopedia of Walt Disney's Animated Characters*. Hyperion, 1998.

Holliss, Richard. *Walt Disney's Snow White and the Seven Dwarfs and the Making of the Classic Film*. Hyperion, 1994.

Krause, Martin F. *Walt Disney's Snow White and the Seven Dwarfs: An Art in Its Making*. Hyperion, 1995.

SOME LIKE IT HOT

(see also Marilyn Monroe, Billy Wilder)

Chase, Donald. "My favorite year: 1959." *Film Comment*, September–October 1994.

Everitt, David. "The tart taste of Lemmon; from seaman to salesman, the actor shares some acidic flashbacks." *Entertainment Weekly*, January 17, 1997.

Phelps, Donald. "Golden boy: the life, times, and comedic genius of Joe E. Brown." *Film Comment*, November-December 1994.

SOUND

(see also Vitaphone)

Crafton, Donald. *The Talkies: American Cinema's Transition to Sound, 1926–1931*. University of California Press, 1999.

Eyman, Scott. *The Speed of Sound: Hollywood and the Talkie Revolution 1926–1930.* Simon & Schuster, 1997.

Kerner, Marvin M. *The Art of the Sound Effects Editor*. Focal Press, 1989.

Sarris, Andrew. *You Ain't Heard Nothin' Yet! The American Talking Film: History and Memory, 1927–1949.* Oxford University Press, 1998.

Weis, Elisabeth, and John Belton, eds. *Film Sound.* Columbia University Press, 1985.

SOUND OF MUSIC, THE

Hirsch, Julia Antopol. *The Sound of Music: The Making of America's Favorite Movie.* NTC/Contemporary Publishing.

Leemann, Sergio. *Robert Wise on His Films: From Editing Room to Director's Chair*. Silman-James Press, 1995.

Thompson, Frank. *Robert Wise*. Greenwood Press, 1995.

Windeler, Robert. *Julie Andrews: A Life on Stage and Screen.* Thorndike Press, 1998.

SPECIAL EFFECTS

The Art of Illusion: One Hundred Years of Hollywood Special Effects (videorecording). Smithsonian Video, 1995.

Hamilton, Jake. *Special Effects*. DK Publishing, 1998.

McCarthy, Robert E. *Secrets of Hollywood Special Effects*. Focal Press, 1992.

Scott, Elaine. *Movie Magic: Behind the Scenes With Special Effects*. William Morrow, 1995.

Smith, Thomas, and George Lucas. *Industrial Light and Magic: The Art of Special Effects*. Del Rey, 1991.

Vaz, Mark Cotta. *Industrial Light and Magic: Into the Digital Realm*. Del Rey, 1996.

SPECTACLE

"Comedy, spectacle, and new horizons." *The Movies Begin*, vol. 5 (videorecording). Kino on Video, 1994.

Rubin, Martin. *Showstoppers: Busby Berkeley and the Tradition of Spectacle*. Columbia University Press, 1993.

Zonn, Leo E., ed. *Place, Power, Situation, and Spectacle: A Geography of Film*. Rowman and Littlefield, 1994.

SPIELBERG, STEVEN

Baxter, John. *Steven Spielberg: The Unauthorized Biography*. HarperCollins, 1997.

Brode, Douglas. *The Films of Steven Spielberg*. Citadel Press, 1999.

Conklin, Thomas. *Meet Steven Spielberg*. Random House, 1994.

McBride, Joseph. *Steven Spielberg: A Biography*. Simon & Schuster, 1997.

Sanello, Frank. *Spielberg: The Man, the Movies, the Myth*. Taylor Publishing, 1996.

STAGECOACH

(see also John Ford, John Wayne)

Anobile, Richard J., ed. *John Ford's Stagecoach, Starring John Wayne*. Avon, 1975.

Besas, Peter. "Lineup nearly complete for San Sebastian; Ford's 'Stagecoach' to get 50th-anniversary tribute." *Variety*, August 23, 1989.

STAR SYSTEM

American Cinema. FoxVideo (New York Center for Visual History in coproduction with KCET and the BBC), 1995.

Kanin, Garson. *Hollywood; Stars and Starlets, Tycoons and Flesh-peddlers, Moviemakers and Moneymakers, Frauds and Geniuses, Hopefuls and Has-beens, Great Lovers and Sex Symbols*. Viking Press, 1974.

Marx, Kenneth S. *Star Stats: Who's Whose in Hollywood*. Price Stern, 1979.

Sennett, Robert S. *Hollywood Hoopla: Creating Stars and Selling Movies in the Golden Age of Hollywood*. Billboard Books, 1998.

Twentieth Century Fox: The First 50 Years (videorecording). 20th Century Fox Home Entertainment, 1997.

"Hollywood's Golden Age: R.K.O., Paramount, and 20th Century-Fox." *The Palace (Classic Films)* http://moderntimes.com/palace/golden.htm

STAR WARS

Daly, Steve. "A Monster Movie: George Lucas strikes back with Star Wars: Episode I—The Phantom Menace." *Entertainment Weekly*, March 26, 1999.

Kamp, David. "The Force is back." *Vanity Fair*, February 1999.

Lane, Anthony. "Star Bores." *The New Yorker*, May 24, 1999 (review).

McQuarrie, Ralph. *The Illustrated Star Wars Universe*. Bantam Books, 1995.

"Of Myth and Men: A conversation between Bill Moyers and George Lucas on the meaning of the Force and the true theology of Star Wars." *Time*, April 26, 1999.

Slavicsek, Bill. *A Guide to the Star Wars Universe*. Ballantine Books, 1994.

STEREOSCOPIC VIEWER

Darrah, William C. *The World of Stereographs*. Land Yacht Press, 1998.

Earle, Edward W. *Points of View, the Stereograph in America: A Cultural History*. Visual Studies Workshop, 1979.

Hayes, R. M. *3-D Movies: A History and Filmography of Stereoscopic Cinema*. McFarland, 1989.

National Stereoscopic Association http://nsa-3d.org/

STEWART, JAMES

Ansen, James. "The all-American hero." *Newsweek*, July 14, 1997 (obituary).

Dewey, Donald. *James Stewart: A Biography*. Regnery Publishing, 1996.

Fishgall, Gary. *Pieces of Time: The Life of James Stewart*. Scribner, 1997.

Quirk, Lawrence J. *James Stewart: Behind the Scenes of a Wonderful Life*. Applause Theatre Books, 1997.

Thomas, Tony. *A Wonderful Life: The Films and Career of James Stewart*. Citadel Press, 1997.

STONE, OLIVER

Beaver, Frank Eugene. *Oliver Stone: Wakeup Cinema*. Maxwell Macmillan International, 1994.

Kagan, Norman. *The Cinema of Oliver Stone*. Continuum, 1995.

Kunz, Don, ed. *The Films of Oliver Stone*. Scarecrow Press, 1997.

Salewicz, Chris. *Oliver Stone*. Thunder's Mouth Press, 1998.

STREEP, MERYL

Maychick, Diana. *Meryl Streep: The Reluctant Superstar*. St. Martin's Press, 1984.

McPherson, Conor. "24 hours with Meryl Streep." *Harper's Bazaar*, January 1999.

Patterson, Troy. "Meryl Streep: By taking mothering to new heights, she earned an 11th nomination—and maybe a golden statuette." *Entertainment Weekly*, March 1, 1999.

Pfaff, Eugene E. *Meryl Streep: A Critical Biography*. McFarland, 1987.

Weinraub, Bernard. "Finally, enough actresses to nominate for Oscars." *New York Times*, December 12, 1995.

STREETCAR NAMED DESIRE, A

(see also Marlon Brando, Elia Kazan, Vivien Leigh)

Maslin, Janet. "From 'Eden' to 'Streetcar.' " *New York Times*, November 22, 1996.

Schickel, Richard. "A Streetcar Named Desire." *Time*, November 1, 1993.

Williams, Tennessee, 1911–1983. *A Streetcar Named Desire*. New American Library, 1980.

STRUCTURALISM

Henderson, Brian. *A Critique of Film Theory*. Dutton, 1980.

Metz, Christian. *Film Language: A Semiotics of the Cinema*. University of Chicago Press, 1991.

Stam, Robert, et al. *New Vocabularies in Film Semiotics:*

Structuralism, Poststructuralism and Beyond. Routledge, 1992.

Chandler, Daniel. "Semiotics for Beginners." Reproduced at http://www.georgetown.edu/grad/CCT/505/semiotic.html

STUDIO PICTURE

Harmetz, Aljean. *The Making of the Wizard of Oz: Movie Magic and Studio Power in the Prime of MGM*. Hyperion, 1998.

Hay, Peter. *MGM—When the Lion Roars*. Turner Publishing, 1991.

Jewell, Richard B. *The RKO Story*. Arlington House, 1982.

Sperling, Cass Werner. *Hollywood Be Thy Name: The Warner Brothers Story*. University Press of Kentucky, 1998.

SUNSET BOULEVARD

(see also Billy Wilder)

Brode, Douglas. *The Films of the Fifties: Sunset Boulevard to On the Beach*. Carol Publishing Group, 1990.

Perry, George C. *Sunset Boulevard: From Movie to Musical*. Henry Holt, 1993.

Sikov, Ed. *On Sunset Boulevard: The Life and Times of Billy Wilder*. Hyperion, 1998.

SURREALISM

Gale, Matthew. *Dada and Surrealism*. Phaidon, 1997.

Hedges, Inez. *Languages of Revolt: Dada and Surrealist Literature and Film*. Duke University Press, 1983.

Kuenzli, Rudolf E., ed. *Dada and Surrealist Film*. The MIT Press, 1996.

SWANSON, GLORIA

"Gloria Swanson." *Time*, April 18, 1983 (obituary)

Madsen, Axel. *Gloria and Joe*. Berkley Books, 1989.

McCarthy, Todd. "Gloria Swanson, 84, star of motion pictures, dies in N.Y." *Variety*, April 6, 1983.

Swanson, Gloria. *Swanson on Swanson*. Random House, 1980.

TALMADGE, NORMA

Loos, Anita. *The Talmadge Girls: A Memoir*. Viking Press, 1978.

"Norma Talmadge." *Internet Movie Database* http://us.imdb.com/M/person-exact?Talmadge%2C%20Norma

"Norma Talmadge." *The Silents Majority* http://www.mdle.com/ClassicFilms/FeaturedStar/perfor52.htm

TAXI DRIVER

(see also Robert De Niro, Martin Scorsese)

Gates, Anita. "These stalkers are really just people who love too much." *New York Times*, August 11, 1996.

Patterson, Patricia, and Manny Farber. "The power and the gory." *Film Comment*, May–June 1998.

Schrader, Paul. "Paul Schrader on Martin Scorsese." *The New Yorker*, March 21, 1994.

Wolcott, James. "New York noir." *Vanity Fair*, July 1997.

TAYLOR, ELIZABETH

"Elizabeth Taylor: Weathering enough tragedies—and marriages—to sink the Titanic, Hollywood's leading lady transformed herself into a businesswoman and humanitarian." *People Weekly*, March 15, 1999.

Morley, Sheridan. *Elizabeth Taylor: A Celebration*. Pavilion Books, 1989.

Singer, Linda-Marie. *Elizabeth Taylor*. Chelsea House, 1998.

Spoto, Donald. *A Passion for Life: The Biography of Elizabeth Taylor*. HarperCollins, 1995.

Vermilye, Jerry. *The Films of Elizabeth Taylor*. Citadel Press, 1989.

TECHNICOLOR

Basten, Fred E. *Glorious Technicolor: The Movies' Magic Rainbow*. A. S. Barnes, 1980.

Haines, Richard W. *Technicolor Movies: The History of Dye Transfer Printing*. McFarland, 1993.

Limbacher, James L. *Four Aspects of the Film*. Ayer, 1978.

THALBERG, IRVING

Flamini, Roland. *Thalberg: The Last Tycoon and the World of MGM.* Crown Publishers, 1993.

Hay, Peter. *MGM—When the Lion Roars.* Turner Publishing, 1991.

Steichen, Edward. "Norma Shearer and Irving Thalberg." *Vanity Fair*, March 1992.

Thomson, David. "Appraising the lords." *Film Comment*, July-August 1982.

THIRD MAN, THE

(see also Orson Welles)

Greene, Graham. *The Third Man and The Fallen Idol.* Penguin, 1981.

Sragow, Michael. "Truer to the main men of the 'The Third Man.'" *New York Times*, May 9, 1999.

"'The Third Man.'" *Premiere*, June 1997.

THREE-DIMENSIONAL FILM

(see Stereoscopic viewer)

TITANIC

Ansen, David. "The court of King Jim." *Newsweek*, April 13, 1998.

Cameron, James. *Titanic: James Cameron's Illustrated Screenplay.* HarperCollins, 1998.

Gray, Timothy M. "Ship's Oscars come in." *Variety*, March 30, 1998.

Kirkland, Douglas, et al. *James Cameron's Titanic.* HarperCollins, 1997.

Parisi, Paula. *Titanic and the Making of James Cameron: The Inside Story of the Three-Year Adventure That Rewrote Motion Picture History.* NewMarket Press, 1998.

TO KILL A MOCKINGBIRD

Everitt, David. "A bushel of Peck: the star of 'To Kill a Mockingbird' marks its 35th anniversary edition by revisiting his career peaks." *Entertainment Weekly*, March 20, 1998.

Griggs, John. *The Films of Gregory Peck.* Citadel Press, 1984.

Lee, Harper. *To Kill a Mockingbird.* 35th anniversary ed. HarperCollins, 1995.

TOOTSIE

(see also Dustin Hoffman, Jessica Lange, Sidney Pollack)

Dworkin, Susan. *Making Tootsie: A Film Study with Dustin Hoffman and Sydney Pollack.* NewMarket Press, 1983.

Farber, Stephen. "How conflict gave shape to 'Tootsie.'" *New York Times*, December 19, 1982.

Gelbart, Larry. *Laughing Matters: On Writing Mash, Tootsie, Oh, God!, and a Few Other Funny Things.* Random House, 1998.

TOURNEUR, MAURICE

"Maurice Tourneur." *Internet Movie Database*
http://us.imdb.com/M/person-exact?Tourneur%2C%20Maurice

"Maurice Tourneur." *The Silents Majority*
http://www.mdle.com/ClassicFilms/BTC/direct9.htm

TRACY, SPENCER

Andersen, Christopher P. *An Affair to Remember: The Remarkable Love Story of Katharine Hepburn and Spencer Tracy*. William Morrow, 1997.

Deschner, Donald. *The Complete Films of Spencer Tracy*. Citadel Press, 1993.

Fisher, James. *Spencer Tracy*. Greenwood Press, 1994.

"Spencer Tracy." *Entertainment Weekly*, Fall 1996 (Special Collector's Issue).

TRADE PAPERS

The Hollywood Reporter
http://www.hollywoodreporter.com/

Variety Extra
http://www.variety.com/

TRAINSPOTTING

Alexander, Bryan. "The script doctor is in." *People Weekly*, November 10, 1997.

Dwyer, Michael. "No lack of roles for a chameleon from Scotland: not since Daniel Day-Lewis and Gary Oldman has Britain produced an actor as versatile as Ewan McGregor." *New York Times*, June 1, 1997.

Maslin, Janet. "Trainspotting." *New York Times*, July 19, 1996 (review).

Welsh, Irvine. *Trainspotting*. W. W. Norton, 1996.

TREASURE OF THE SIERRA MADRE, THE

(see also John Huston)

"Humphrey Bogart." *Entertainment Weekly*, Fall 1996 (Special Collector's Issue).

McCarty, Clifford, and Lauren Bacall. *The Complete Films of Humphrey Bogart*. Citadel Press, 1994.

Traven, B. *The Treasure of the Sierra Madre*. Thorndike Press, 1994.

2001: A SPACE ODYSSEY

(see also Stanley Kubrick)

Bizony, Piers. "2001 at 25." *Omni*, May 1993.

Clarke, Arthur C. *2001: A Space Odyssey*. New American Library, 1968.

Lyons, Patrick J. "'I have the greatest enthusiasm for the mission'; on HAL's birthday, measuring '2001' against reality. *New York Times*, January 13, 1997.

UNDERGROUND FILM

(see also Experimental film)

James, David E. *Allegories of Cinema: American Film in the Sixties*. Princeton University Press, 1989.

Renan, Sheldon. *An Introduction to the American Underground Film*. Dutton, 1967.

Tyler, Parker. *Underground Film: A Critical History*. Da Capo Press, 1995.

UNFORGIVEN

(see also Clint Eastwood)

Biskind, Peter. "Back in the saddle: Eastwood returns with a western in the revisionist tradition of 'The Wild Bunch.' " *Premiere*, August 1992.

Grimes, William. "Eastwood western takes top 2 prizes in 65th Oscar show." *New York Times*, March 30, 1993.

VALENTINO, RUDOLPH

James, Caryn. "A sex icon once, an oddity now." *New York Times*, November 8, 1991.

Miller, Lisa. "The evolution of America's leading men: from Rudolph Valentino to David Caruso." *Wall Street Journal*, January 7, 1994.

"Rudolph Valentino: the sultan of swoon." *Entertainment Weekly*, Fall 1996 (Special Collector's Issue).

Walker, Alexander. *Rudolph Valentino*. Stein and Day, 1976.

"Rudolph Valentino." *Silents Majority* http://www.mdle.com/ClassicFilms/FeaturedStar/star50.htm

VERTIGO

(see also Alfred Hitchcock, James Stewart)

Auiler, Dan. *Vertigo: The Making of a Hitchcock Classic*. St. Martin's Press, 1998.

Lyons, Donald. "Notes while falling." *Film Comment*, November–December 1996.

Raubicheck, Walter. *Hitchcock's Rereleased Films: From Rope to Vertigo*. Wayne State University Press, 1991.

VIDOR, KING

Kirkpatrick, Sidney. *A Cast of Killers*. G.K. Hall, 1987.

McCarthy, Todd. "King Vidor, 88, film pioneer, dies at his California ranch." *Variety*, November 3, 1982 (obituary).

Sayre, Nora. "Silents and talkies by King Vidor for the centennial of his birth." *New York Times*, February 11, 1994.

Vidor, King. *King Vidor*. Scarecrow Press, 1988 (interviews).

Vidor, King. *A Tree Is a Tree*. Samuel French, 1990.

VITAPHONE

Kreuger, Miles. *The Movie Musical from Vitaphone to 42nd Street.* Dover Publications, 1975.

"1926: sound motion pictures." *AT&T R&D Milestones* http://www. research.att.com/history/26talkie.html

"Talking pictures: the dawn of sound." *Association of Science-Technology Centers Web Site* http://www.astc.org/info/exhibits/dtalk.htm

VON STERNBERG, JOSEF

Bach, Steven. *Marlene Dietrich: Life and Legend.* Morrow, 1992.

DelGaudio, Sybil. *Dressing the Part: Sternberg, Dietrich and Costume.* Associated University Presses, 1993.

Hogue, Peter. "True Blue." *Film Comment*, March–April 1994.

Zucker, Carole. *The Idea of the Image: Josef Von Sternberg's Dietrich Films.* Farleigh Dickinson University Press, 1988.

VON STROHEIM, ERICH

(see also Sunset Boulevard)

Koszarski, Richard. "A film that almost got away; after nearly sixty years, Queen Kelly, Erich von Stroheim and Gloria Swanson's aborted epic, finally comes to the screen." *American Film*, March 1985.

Lennig, Arthur. *Stroheim.* University Press of Kentucky, 1999.

Noble, Peter. *Hollywood Scapegoat: The Biography of Erich von Stroheim.* Ayer, 1972.

Sorel, Nancy Caldwell. "Jean Renoir and Erich von Stroheim." *The Atlantic*, September 1987.

WAR FILM

DeBauche, Leslie Midkiff. *Reel Patriotism: The Movies and World War I.* University of Wisconsin Press, 1997.

Dittmar, Linda, ed. *From Hanoi to Hollywood: The Vietnam War in American Film.* Rutgers University Press, 1991.

Guttmacher, Peter. *Legendary War Movies.* Metro Books, 1996.

Kinnard, Roy. *The Blue and the Gray on the Silver Screen: More Than Eighty Years of Civil War Movies.* Citadel Press, 1996.

Quirk, Lawrence J. *The Great War Films.* Carol Publishing Group, 1994.

Wetta, Frank Joseph, and Stephen J. Curley. *Celluloid Wars.* Greenwood Press, 1992.

WAYNE, JOHN

Davis, Ronald L. *Duke: The Life and Image of John Wayne.* University of Oklahoma Press, 1998.

Kieskalt, Charles John. *The Official John Wayne Reference Book*. Citadel Press, 1993.

Pfeiffer, Lee. *True Grits: Recipes Inspired by the Movies of John Wayne*. Birch Lane Press, 1998.

Ricci, Mark, et al. *The Complete Films of John Wayne*. Lyle Stuart, 1985.

Wagner, Rob Leicester. *The Duke: A Life in Pictures*. Metro Books, 1997.

WEBER, LOIS

Acker, Ally. "Lois Weber." *Ms. Magazine*, February 1988.

Acker, Ally. *Reel Women: Pioneers of the Cinema, 1896 to the Present*. Continuum, 1991.

The Library of Congress and Smithsonian Video Present America's First Women Filmmakers (videorecording). Library of Congress, 1993.

Slide, Anthony. *Lois Weber*. Greenwood Press, 1996.

"Lois Weber." *Reel Women* http://www.reelwomen.com/weberbio.html

WELLES, ORSON

Brady, Frank. *Citizen Welles: A Biography of Orson Welles*. Scribner, 1989.

Callow, Simon. *Orson Welles: The Road to Xanadu*. Penguin USA, 1997.

Higham, Charles. *Orson Welles, the Rise and Fall of an American Genius*. St. Martin's Press, 1985.

Howard, James. *The Complete Films of Orson Welles*. Citadel Press, 1991.

Leaming, Barbara. *Orson Welles: A Biography*. Limelight Editions, 1995.

Taylor, John Russell. *Orson Welles: A Celebration*. Little, Brown, 1986.

WEST SIDE STORY

(see also Natalie Wood)

Garebian, Keith. *The Making of West Side Story* (out of print).

Gussow, Mel. "'West Side Story': the beginnings of something great." *New York Times*, October 21, 1990 (interview with Leonard Bernstein).

Holden, Stephen. "The songs of West Side Story." *New York Times*, February 25, 1996.

Leemann, Sergio. *Robert Wise on His Films: From Editing Room to Director's Chair*. Silman-James Press, 1995.

McDermott, Alice. "Teen-age films: love, death and the prom." *New York Times*, August 16, 1987.

Thompson, Frank. *Robert Wise*. Greenwood Press, 1995.

WESTERN FILM

Cameron, Ian Alexander, ed. *The Book of Westerns*. Continuum, 1996.

Cary, Diana Serra. *The Hollywood Posse: The Story of a Gallant Band of Horsemen Who Made Movie History*. University of Oklahoma Press, 1996.

Everson, William K. *The Hollywood Western*. Carol Publishing Group, 1992.

Key, Donald R., ed. *The Round-Up: A Pictorial History of Western Movie and Television Stars Through the Years*. Empire Publishing, 1995.

Kitses, Jim, and Gregg Rickman, eds. *The Western Reader*. Limelight Editions, 1998.

Yoggy, Gary A., ed. *Back in the Saddle: Essays on Western Film and Television Actors*. McFarland, 1998.

WHITE, PEARL

The Perils of Pauline (videorecording). Collectors ed. Madacy Entertainment Group, 1996.

Weltmann, Manuel. *Pearl White: The Peerless Fearless Girl.* A. S. Barnes, 1969.

"Pearl White." *Internet Movie Database*
http://us.imdb.com/M/person-exact?White%2C%20Pearl

"Pearl White." *The Silents Majority*
http://www.mdle.com/ClassicFilms/FeaturedStar/perfor36.htm

WILD BUNCH, THE

(see also Sam Peckinpah)

Bliss, Michael, ed. *Doing It Right: The Best Criticism on Sam Peckinpah's "The Wild Bunch."* Southern Illinois University Press, 1994.

WILDER, BILLY

Bart, Peter. "H'wood's Wilder moments." *Variety*, April 22, 1996.

Kakutani, Michiko. "Ready for his close-up: As Hollywood and Broadway remakes his classics, Billy Wilder, 90, holds forth on Proust, Zippos and 'Forrest Gump.' " *New York Times Magazine*, July 28, 1996.

Lally, Kevin. *Wilder Times: The Life of Billy Wilder*. H. Holt, 1996.

Sarris, Andrew. "From the Kaiser to the Oscar: in 90 years, Billy Wilder has survived both the Austro-Hungarian Empire and the Hollywood studio system." *New York Times Book Review*, December 27, 1998.

Sikov, Ed. *On Sunset Boulevard: The Life and Times of Billy Wilder.* Hyperion, 1998.

Zolotow, Maurice. *Billy Wilder in Hollywood.* Limelight Editions, 1988.

WIZARD OF OZ, THE

(see also Judy Garland)

Cox, Stephen. *The Munchkins Remember: The Wizard of Oz and Beyond.* Dutton, 1989.

Fricke, John. *The Wizard of Oz: The Official 50th Anniversary Pictorial History*. Warner Books, 1989.

Harmetz, Aljean. *The Making of the Wizard of Oz: Movie Magic and Studio Power in the Prime of MGM.* Hyperion, 1998.

Langley, Noel. *The Wizard of Oz: The Screenplay*. Delta, 1989.

Morella, Joe. *Judy: The Complete Films and Career of Judy Garland*. Citadel Press, 1986.

WOOD, NATALIE

Harmetz, Aljean. "How M-G-M protected Miss Wood's film." *New York Times*, December 2, 1981.

"Natalie Wood." *Entertainment Weekly*, Fall 1996 (Special Collector's Issue).

O'Connor, John J. "Starring Natalie Wood." *New York Times*, July 8, 1988.

"An unfinished life." *Newsweek*, December 14, 1981 (obituary).

Wood, Lana. *Natalie: A Memoir by Her Sister*. Putnam's, 1984.

WRITER

Bernstein, Walter. *Inside Out: A Memoir of the Blacklist*. Knopf, 1996.

Dardis, Tom. *Some Time in the Sun*. Limelight Editions, 1988.

Hamilton, Ian. *Writers in Hollywood, 1915–1951*. Harper & Row, 1990.

Lumme, Helena, and Mika Manninen, eds. *Screenwriters: America's Storytellers in Portrait*. Angel City Press, 1999.

Schanzer, Karl. *American Screenwriters: The Insider's Look at the Art, the Craft, and the Business of Writing Movies*. Avon Books, 1993.

WUTHERING HEIGHTS

(see also Laurence Olivier, William Wyler)

Berg, A. Scott. "Wuthering Heights." *New York Times Magazine*, February 19, 1989.

Bronte, Emily. *Wuthering Heights*. Modern Library, 1991.

Daly, Steve. "Jumping conclusions." *Entertainment Weekly*, March 6, 1992.

James, Caryn. "Wuthering Heights." *New York Times*, April 9, 1989.

Sterritt, David. "Goldwyn's masterpiece: Fresh look shows 'Wuthering Heights' timid, compared with Bronte novel." *Christian Science Monitor*, May 19, 1989.

WYLER, WILLIAM

Herman, Jan. *A Talent for Trouble: The Life of Hollywood's Most Acclaimed Director, William Wyler*. Da Capo Press, 1997.

"William Wyler is dead at 79." *Variety*, July 29, 1981 (obituary).

YANKEE DOODLE DANDY

(see also James Cagney)

Robertson, James C. *The Casablanca Man: The Cinema of Michael Curtiz*. Routledge, 1993.

Sayre, Nora. "Curtiz: a man for all genres . . . ." *New York Times*, November 29, 1992.

ZOËTROPE

Kukes, Roger. *Zoëtrope Book*. Klassroom Kinetics, 1983.

Hayes, Ruth. *Zoëtrope Animation* http://www.halcyon.com/rhayes/html/zoe.html

Index

A

B

C

D

E

F

G

H

I

J

K

L

M

N

O

P

Q

R

T

U

V

W

Y

Z